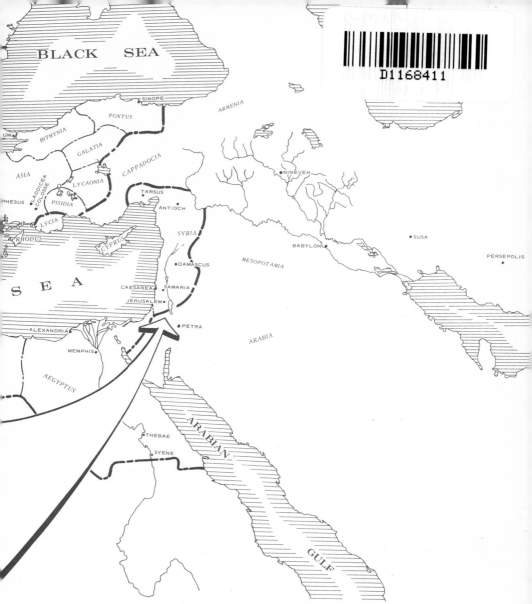

THE ROMAN WORLD
IN THE TIME OF JESUS

Introduction to the

NEW TESTAMENT

Introduction to the

NEW TESTAMENT

by

Everett F. Harrison

SENIOR PROFESSOR OF NEW TESTAMENT
FULLER THEOLOGICAL SEMINARY

WM. B. EERDMANS PUBLISHING COMPANY
GRAND RAPIDS, MICHIGAN

Copyright © 1964, 1971, Wm. B. Eerdmans Publishing Co.
All rights reserved.
Library of Congress Catalog Card Number 64-16589.
ISBN 0-8028-3106-0
Printed in the United States of America.

First Printing, August 1964
Second Printing, October 1965
Third Printing, October 1968
Fourth Printing, January 1971
Revised Edition, First Printing, August 1971
Revised Edition, Second Printing, November 1974
Revised Edition, Third Printing, July 1977

Reprinted, December 1982

Reprinted, July 1985

PREFACE

After having taught New Testament Introduction for twenty-five years, I was led to prepare this book primarily for the sake of my students, who were growing weary of taking notes diligently from day to day in the classroom. Perhaps other students will also find it useful as a means of becoming acquainted with the various lines of investigation that are germane to the approach to the New Testament. An effort has been made to bring the survey up to date in terms of current books and periodicals, but no claim is made to completeness, for the area to be covered is too vast. The brief bibliographies at the end of the chapters will aid the student who wishes to go more deeply into the various subjects.

Some topics have been put aside, not because they lack intrinsic importance, but because it did not seem possible or expedient to include them. For example, there is no section on the inspiration of the New Testament, for the reason that this belongs more properly to the prolegomena of systematic theology. A survey of the historical criticism of the New Testament would have been useful, but it would have made the present work unduly long. Some of this material is included incidentally in the discussion of various New Testament books.

Special thanks are due my colleague, Professor George Eldon Ladd, for the helpful suggestions he made in the course of reading the greater part of the manuscript.

EVERETT F. HARRISON

CONTENTS

Contents

Contents

Contents

LIST OF ABBREVIATIONS

BA — *Biblical Archaeologist*
BJRL — *Bulletin of the John Rylands Library*
BS — *Bibliotheca Sacra*
CGTC — *Cambridge Greek Testament Commentary*
DSS — Dead Sea Scrolls
EB — *Encyclopaedia Biblica*
EQ — *Evangelical Quarterly*
ET — *Expository Times*
HDB — *Hastings' Dictionary of the Bible*
HE — *The Ecclesiastical History of Eusebius*
HNTC — *Harper's New Testament Commentaries*
HTS — *Harvard Theological Studies*
HZNT — *Handbuch zum Neuen Testament*
IB — *Interpreter's Bible*
ICC — *International Critical Commentary*
IDB — *Interpreter's Dictionary of the Bible*
ISBE — *International Standard Bible Encyclopaedia*
JBL — *Journal of Biblical Literature*
JR — *Journal of Religion*
JTS — *Journal of Theological Studies*
KJV — King James Version
LCL — *Loeb Classical Library*
LXX — Septuagint, Greek translation of the Old Testament
MNTC — *Moffatt New Testament Commentary*
NBD — *New Bible Dictionary*
NIC — *New International Commentary*
NTD — *Das Neue Testament Deutsch*
NTS — *New Testament Studies*
RSV — Revised Standard Version
ST — *Studia Theologica*
TBC — *Tyndale Bible Commentaries*
TCERK — *Twentieth Century Encyclopaedia of Religious
            Knowledge*
THZNT — *Theologischer Handkommentar zum Neuen Testament*
WC — *Westminster Commentaries*
WTJ — *Westminster Theological Journal*
ZNTW — *Zeitschrift für die neuentestamentliche Wissenschaft*
ZTK — *Zeitschrift für Theologie und Kirche*

PART I

THE BACKGROUND

Chapter One

THE BACKGROUND

IN ASSESSING THE PROPER LIMITS WITHIN WHICH THE STUDENT
of the New Testament should move in his investigations, it
goes without saying that the books that constitute the New
Testament must be central. But no appraisal of these documents can be adequate that ignores their setting. Consequently,
one must reach back into the period between the Testaments,
at least to the Maccabean age, better still to the restoration
from Babylonian captivity, in order to understand the situation
presupposed in the Gospels and the Book of Acts. The Old
Testament closes with Israel under Persian rule; the New Testament opens with the nation under the sway of Rome. We
read of chief priests, synagogues, doctors of the Law, Pharisees,
Sadducees, and Herodians, the Council or Sanhedrin, and a
widespread dispersion of the Jews. All these need explanation
to one who is familiar only with Old Testament history.

Similarly, one cannot ignore the patristic period of the early
church, for its leaders made reference from time to time to

the text of the New Testament, often quoting it. Their allusions to various books of the New Testament are helpful in the study of the canon, which carries us to around A.D. 400. If the New Testament is not to be examined in isolation, a span of several hundred years before and after its composition must be included.

It is convenient to consider the background material from the standpoint of the history, institutions, and literature of the Jewish people. All three are closely interrelated, especially the first two, but there is advantage in studying them separately.

THE HISTORY

I. *The Persian Period.* During the Babylonian captivity Judah experienced a change of masters, owing to the Medo-Persian conquest of Babylon. The restoration to Palestine was made possible by the co-operation of Cyrus and was inspired by the leadership of three men: Zerubbabel in the rebuilding of the temple, Ezra in the establishing of the Law of Moses as the constitution of the renewed community, and Nehemiah in the rebuilding of the walls of Jerusalem and the reviving of the economic and spiritual life of the people.[1] Only a relatively small proportion of the nation returned to the land of their fathers, although they may confidently be thought of as the more godly element. They had learned the folly of idolatry and were resolved not to succumb henceforth to this sin lest they suffer as their fathers had done.

Yet the building of a community with strong religious bulwarks did not prove easy. Despite the covenant to serve the Lord and obey the Law of Moses (Ezra 10), the people drifted into neglect of worship and the payment of tithes. The sanctity of the Sabbath was ignored as well as the prohibition of mixed marriages (Neh. 13). At the time of Malachi the priests were deserving of severe rebuke for their corruption and independence. A partial cause of the decline lay in the resentment of the non-Israelitish and mixed population of Palestine at the attempt to reconstitute the nation Israel along purist lines. They did their best to hinder the effort. The Jews' unwillingness to permit the Samaritans to participate in the rebuilding of the temple (Ezra 4:1-2) produced a deep antagonism, reflected in the New Testament, and it led to the setting up of the schismatic worship at Mt. Gerizim referred to in John 4.

---

[1] Some scholars think that Nehemiah preceded Ezra.

4

Since the Persians would not tolerate the restoration of the Davidic kingship after experimenting with Zerubbabel, the highest official was the high priest, who was responsible in a general way to the Persian governor. The net effect of this arrangement was to introduce a secular and political strain into an office that had been historically only sacerdotal in character.

II. *The Alexandrian Period* (332-301 B.C.). After the battle of Issus and the withdrawal of Darius to the east, Alexander moved to secure the submission of Syria, Palestine, and Egypt before confronting his Persian adversary again on the field of battle. The whole Levant was profoundly affected by this man and his achievements. Following in the footsteps of his father, Philip of Macedon, as a man of war, and in the counsel of his principal teacher, the philosopher Aristotle, Alexander surpassed both in the sense that he proved to be a greater military genius than his father and in some of his ideas went beyond the vision of his teacher. His immediate military goal was to avenge the Persian invasion of Greece under Xerxes, but his far-reaching purpose was cultural, to hellenize the Orient. Philosophers and scientists accompanied him on his campaigns. Colonists of Greek origin followed in the wake of his armies. Alexander made an earnest effort to bridge the gap beween East and West, between Greek and barbarian, an effort symbolized by the elevation of conquered Persians to high administrative posts and by his own marriages to Oriental women.

The coming of Alexander to Palestine meant that this strategic land began to be exposed to the process of hellenization which did much to break down the distinctiveness of the Jews and seriously divide the nation in later years. But his control over Palestine brought no religious crisis, for he made no demand for personal worship such as was accorded to him in some places.

Death claimed the conqueror in 323, when only in his early thirties, worn out by the strenuous life he had lived. This event touched off a long struggle between his generals for the control of the empire. Four of them united in crushing the opposition at the battle of Ipsus (301 B.C.) though Ptolemy did not actually appear with his three allies. Of these, only Seleucus, who controlled Syria and a large territory to the east, and Ptolemy, who held Egypt, affected the destinies of the Jews. Ptolemy, who had held Palestine intermittently, now controlled it for a century. But Syria was not willing to let the claim go unchallenged indefinitely. Hence

5

Palestine became the battleground between these two kingdoms.

III. *The Egyptian Period* (301-198 B.C.). It should be kept clearly in mind that the rulers of Egypt in this time were Greeks. Ptolemy astutely chose for himself a corner of the empire where food was plentiful and where invasion was unlikely. His principal city, Alexandria, had been laid out by Alexander and his architect, and grew rapidly into one of the leading hellenistic centers, noted for its commerce and its culture. The first Ptolemy (Soter) founded the great library there, which continued for nearly a thousand years.[2] It was doubtless extended by Ptolemy Philadelphus (285-247 B.C.).

Up to this time there had been little contact between Jew and Greek, partly because the Jews were not a seafaring people, and also because of their aloofness from uncircumcised neighbors. But now Jews in great numbers moved into Egypt, where they acquired a knowledge of the Greek tongue and some appreciation of Greek literature. Josephus states that the Jews were accorded equal civic rights with the Macedonians.[3] It was during the reign of Philadelphus that the Jewish Law (Pentateuch) was translated into Greek. The other books of the Old Testament were done subsequently.

In this period Palestine experienced a process of peaceful hellenization, being exposed to the appeal of the Greek way of life — its language and art and the gaiety of its festivals and games. People frequented the amphitheaters and the public baths. As long as there was no attempt to interfere with the worship of the nation, this cultural influence continued to operate without violent opposition. In the following era such an attempt was made, with consequences which rocked Palestinian Jewry to its very foundations.

IV. *The Syrian Period* (198-167 B.C.). Efforts of the Syrians to undermine Egyptian control over the land were finally successful. At the battle of Paneas (198) Antiochus the Great defeated Scopas and his army. Shortly thereafter Antiochus himself tasted defeat at the hands of the Romans and was obliged to pay tribute. We learn of an attempt during his successor's reign to plunder the treasury of the temple at Jerusalem to relieve the fiscal distress. A crisis in Syrian-Jewish relations came during the regime of Antiochus IV (Epiphanes), who was ambitious to rule a

---

[2] See the discussion in *The Alexandrian Library*, by E. A. Parsons.
[3] *Antiquities* XII. i. 8.

strong state, thoroughly hellenized, even to the point of regulating the religious life of the people. He advertized his divinity on his coins, which bore the inscription, "of King Antiochus, God Manifest, Victory-bearer."

The conflict over hellenization in Judea had not been between the Syrians on the one hand and Jews on the other, but between the pro-hellenic party of the Jews and the party of resistance, also Jewish. Now the pro-hellenic group felt that they could be more aggressive because of the backing of Antiochus. The pressure was heavy on those who sought to resist the innovations of the Greek way of life. How far the process might have gone if it had continued along peaceful lines is debatable. But the action of the monarch to compel hellenization crystallized the spirit of resistance and led to open revolt. The opposition group were known as the Hasidim (pious ones). They were men who were committed to the defense of Jewish custom and religion in an attempt to stem the tide of apostasy. Their high purpose stood in contrast to the selfish adventurousness of their countrymen who were lightly treating their heritage in Judaism in order to get a place in the sun for Jerusalem among the Greek settlements of Syria and Palestine and a position of wealth and leadership for themselves.

The situation came to a head when Antiochus was in Egypt. Two local men were contending for the high priesthood in Jerusalem and violence broke out in the city between their followers. Learning of the disturbance, the king hurried back to his domains under the impression that Judea was in revolt against him[4] and ordered his soldiers to attack the populace, with a resultant heavy loss of life. Shortly after this, when he was once more in Egypt and was checked in his ambitions there by the Romans, he returned through Palestine in a bad frame of mind and determined to bring complete hellenization to the Jews by royal decree. The practice of Judaism was banned. Those who resisted were killed or sent into slavery. Such distinctives as Sabbath observance, circumcision, and the temple worship were prohibited. The Scriptures were destroyed. Finally, in December of the year 168 Antiochus confiscated the holy vessels and the treasury of the temple and built upon the brazen altar an altar for pagan sacrifice, offering swine upon it as a deliberate insult to the Jews.[5]

Doubtless this shocked many who were themselves Greeks

[4] II Maccabees 5:11.
[5] *Antiquities* XII. v. 4.

7

and in favor of the peaceful extension of their way of life among other peoples, for it meant that the Jews were being compelled to turn their back on their native religion, something sacred to the Greek mind as well as to the Hebrew.[6]

Some who had stood firm before now denied the faith, but many resisted and experienced martyrdom.[7] The light of Judaism seemed to be burning low, when suddenly it flamed forth with fierce vigor. A priest by the name of Mattathias, who had left Jerusalem and settled at Modin, found that he could not escape the issue even there. When the Greek commissioner came to the place and ordered Mattathias as a priest to take the lead in pagan worship, the old man had to make a decision. He refused to comply, and when another Jew came forward in his place, he cut him down and killed the Greek commissioner also. Then taking his sons with him he fled into the hill country. This incident was the spark which touched off rebellion throughout the land.

V. *The Maccabean Period* (167-63 B.C.). Others joined the revolt and aided in guerilla warfare against the authorities. At first the loyal Jews were grievously handicapped because their enemies cunningly chose the Sabbath for military encounters, when religious scruple kept the faithful from fighting. Mattathias and his sons, however, encouraged their followers to meet force with force. It was better to break a few Sabbaths now and have some to keep in the future than to die helplessly at the hands of the enemy. Mattathias was soon called by death, but his son Judas the Maccabee (Hammerer) assumed command and proved to be an excellent leader, skillful and daring. Gradually the Jews were strong enough to emerge from guerilla fighting into open battle with fair sized forces, and were able to gain control of Jerusalem except for the citadel, which was held by a Syrian garrison. The sanctuary was cleansed and rededicated, an event still memorialized in New Testament times (John 10: 22-23).

Rivalries within Syria weakened the effort against the Jews, so that General Lysias felt it expedient to grant religious freedom and withdraw his forces rather than try to fight on two fronts. This was the goal for which the Hasidim had been striving. They saw no point in continuing the struggle, being willing to accept political overlordship provided they could worship

---

[6] Max Radin, *The Jews Among the Greeks and Romans,* p. 142.
[7] I Macc. 1:63; II Macc. 6:18-7:42.

and maintain the customs of Judaism as their fathers had done. But the Maccabean leaders had aspirations for complete independence, so the struggle continued without the active help of the Hasidim. Judas appealed to Rome for aid, and a pact was concluded binding each party to mutual aid in time of war, but so loosely worded that Rome was not committed in this conflict. Nevertheless the Romans issued orders for Syria to leave Judea alone, but the communication came too late to save Judas and many Jews who perished with him at Elasa.

This reverse was not fatal to the Jewish cause for the reason that the Syrians were not able to follow it up. In addition to Rome's threat, internal weakness and problems of succession to the throne kept the resources of Syria so taxed that there was no possibility of a campaign that would crush Jewish resistance. Jonathan followed his brother Judas as leader of the independence movement. He was actually able to use military force outside Judea as well as suppress the pro-hellenic group within the country. Under his brother Simon, who succeeded to the leadership, the Jews achieved their political independence. This was granted about the year 143, and the new era was destined to continue for some 80 years, until the Romans in turn secured a firm grip on the country. For the present Rome acknowledged the independent state of the Jews and did not interfere in its affairs. Meanwhile Simon was declared in lawful assembly of the people to be high priest, military leader and civil governor "for ever, until there should arise a faithful prophet."[8] This language is interesting in that it demonstrates the consciousness that this arrangement was provisional due to the absence of a representative of the Lord. The voice of prophetic testimony had ceased.

It is not necessary for our purpose to consider the reigns of the. various Hasmonean[9] rulers beyond noting certain weaknesses which marred this period. The alliance with Rome was hardly in keeping with Old Testament teaching about the sufficiency of God as the refuge and strength of his people. No real effort was made to win over the pro-hellenic element which persisted in the country. Instead, these people were dealt with severely and were permanently alienated from the cause of the victors. There was a strange inconsistency in the policy of forcible imposition of Judaism on those outside Judea, such as was carried

8 I Macc. 14:41.
9 The name is derived from Hasmoneus, the great-grandfather of Mattathias (Josephus, *Antiquities* XII, vi, 1).

through in Idumea, especially as coming from a people who had themselves experienced the bitterness of religious persecution not so long before. Military strength was maintained by the use of mercenary troops, which occasionally were used against the Jews themselves. So this era was something less than a golden age, despite the freedom enjoyed from outside domination.

VI. *The Roman Period* (63 B.C. on). Rome had been active for some time in Egypt and Asia Minor, and more recently, in Syria. Participation in Jewish affairs came about when two brothers, Aristobulus and Hyrcanus, who were contending for the kingship, submitted their respective claims to Pompey at Damascus, only to be embarrassed by the fact that the people also sent a deputation rejecting both and favoring priestly rule.[10] Pompey promised to render a decision in due time. When he came to Jerusalem the people were divided in sentiment and not happy over the sight of a Roman army outside the gates. Meeting resistance to his entry to the temple area from the Aristobulus faction, Pompey took it by force. Thousands were killed during and after the assault, with the result that Roman occupation began on a note of bitterness. A heavy tribute was imposed on Judea, and many cities which had been captured by the Hasmonean rulers were freed and placed under the control of the province of Syria. Ten of the hellenistic cities (Decapolis), mostly to the southeast of the sea of Galilee, formed an anti-Semitic league for mutual protection and trade advantage.

As long as the Jews could look to men with royal blood as champions against the power of Rome, the danger of revolt was present. So while Aristobulus and his two sons were alive, the spirit of independence simmered, ready to burst into flame. Confusion in Roman politics whetted the hopes of the Jews for a return of home rule. The republic had fallen upon difficult days, with the senate unable to exercise effective leadership and various individuals seeking power through military means and bidding for popular support. Pompey, Caesar, and Crassus formed the First Triumvirate in 60 B.C. When dissension set in Caesar emerged victorious with the role of dictator.

In Palestine he made certain important changes. Hyrcanus, who had been high priest, was made ethnarch also, regaining thereby political status. On the grounds of the loyalty and peaceful intentions of the people under Hyrcanus, Caesar and other Roman officials made concessions to the Jews, including re-

---

[10] *Antiquities* XII. iii. 2.

duction in taxes, the restoration of certain territories, and exemption from military service on account of their Sabbath law. Jews in Asia Minor were to be undisturbed in the observance of their religious customs, including the support of the temple at Jerusalem. Such arrangements were quite in line with the Roman policy of non-interference in the religious life of conquered peoples, and they were honored almost without exception by subsequent rulers.

Caesar's settlement of Judean affairs had another aspect which was not so pleasing to the Jews, but which was nevertheless characteristic of Roman administrative genius. Instead of placing Hyrcanus under a Roman official, Caesar designated Antipater, the Idumean ruler who had supported Hyrcanus against his brother Aristobulus, as procurator of the entire country, including Judea, Samaria, and Galilee. For Rome this had a double advantage, since the Idumeans understood the Jews better than they did and could handle them more successfully, and furthermore could be counted on to remain loyal to Rome rather than throw in their lot with the Jews and turn against their overlords.

On the Jewish side, however, it rankled to have an Idumean in control of their land. As time went on, many leading Jews became disturbed by the fact that their own ruler, Hyrcanus, was hardly more than a figurehead, while the real power was being wielded by Antipater and his sons. One of these, Herod, was made responsible for Galilee when he was still in his teens, and showed such administrative ability as to win the praise even of Roman officials.

Following the assassination of Caesar, the Second Triumvirate was formed between Antony, Octavian, who was Caesar's nephew, and Lepidus. Antony took Asia as his sphere of influence. The Jewish nobles sought his ear in order to secure the riddance of Herod and his brother Phasael, who was administrative head of Jerusalem. Failing in this attempt, the Jewish leaders threw their support behind Antigonus, the only living son of Aristobulus, and called to their aid the Parthians from the East, who came as far as Jerusalem and demanded that the sons of Antipater as well as Hyrcanus meet with them. Sensing a trap, Herod fled the country and headed for Rome, not returning until he had the specific support of Antony, Octavian and the Roman senate. The latter body had made him king of Judea, but so far he had only the title.

Before leaving Judea Herod had made a move to strengthen his position with the Jews. He secured his betrothal to Mariamme, who belonged to the Hasmonean house. Five years were to

11

elapse before Herod could gain sufficient security to proceed with the marriage.

Little by little, against considerable odds, Herod forged his way. Roman generals, bribed by Antigonus, were unco-operative, but finally, when their legions had driven the Parthians out, they were ordered by Antony to aid Herod, who was able to confine Antigonus to Jerusalem and ultimately to capture him and put him to death. With the death of this man perished the Jewish hopes of a revival of Hasmonean power.

Even as Antigonus had enjoyed the support of the Sadducees, Herod turned to the Pharisees, who were the backbone of the national life. This he did out of expediency rather than piety. He knew the keen dislike in which this group held the Hasmoneans. On the other hand, from start to finish his policy was one of unwavering loyalty to Rome, that he might have its support, for he was clear-sighted in realizing that he could only maintain himself with the help of this world power. He had to be very careful at home lest he offend the Jews in some point which touched their religious convictions or prejudices. These were the lines within which he had to operate. A man of lesser ability could easily have lost out in one direction or the other.

When Octavian and Antony clashed, Herod was placed in a difficult position. Though he and Antony had been fast friends, his patience was strained almost beyond endurance when Antony, under the spell of Cleopatra, granted her request for territory after territory that had been under Herod's jurisdiction. This was bad enough, but when Antony fell in with Cleopatra's ambitions to set up a rival state in the East in opposition to Rome, it amounted to a declaration of war. Even then Herod, out of loyalty to Antony, would have gone to war at his side, but Cleopatra vetoed it. Herod contented himself with giving what aid he could to Antony in men and supplies. When Octavian emerged from the conflict victorious, Herod was caught on the wrong side for once, but played a dangerous game and won. On meeting Octavian he candidly confessed his attachment to Antony and left the impression that he could be just as loyal to Octavian, who forthwith forgave him and proceeded in a short time to enlarge his domains.

On the home front Herod was having a hard time domestically. He had married Mariamme shortly before capturing Jerusalem and overwhelming Antigonus. Apparently he loved her deeply, even though she was cold toward him. Her aloofness was prompted by her mother, who despised Herod. This marriage has been called the one political mistake of Herod's entire career.[11] Through false reports of her unfaithfulness, which he came to believe, Herod finally put his queen to death. Shaken by what he had done, the king became withdrawn and moody, and began to fail physically. He seemed to be headed for an untimely death. Though he rallied and lived out his threescore years and ten, he was not the same man. Having taken the path of suspicion and murder, he could not escape the nemesis the rest of his days, which were stained with violence and bloodshed. The multiplication of wives only added to the web of jealousy and intrigue in which his life was caught and rendered miserable.

Herod sought relief from his own troubles by throwing his energies into an ambitious program of public works. The founding of the empire (27 B.C.) under Octavian, who assumed the title of Augustus, was roughly coincidental with the great Roman peace that brought relief to the world after many decades of war in the provinces and struggle for power at Rome. The conditions were favorable, then, for restoration of destroyed communities in Palestine and for new endeavors that would be a fitting monument to the celebrated king of the Jews. Cessation of hostilities was favorable also to increased trade, which meant additional revenue for the royal coffers. Jerusalem itself and environs was decked out with a theater, amphitheater, and hippodrome, and the castle of Antonia to the north of the temple area, named in honor of Herod's friend Antony. Of special magnificence was Herod's palace, its two wings being named in honor of Augustus and Agrippa, the emperor's minister. The temple was restored and enlarged and speedily became famous far and wide for its beauty. Samaria was made over on a grand scale and renamed Sebaste, the Greek equivalent of Augustus. At Jericho Herod laid out a new city as a health resort and retreat from the court life at Jerusalem. A seaport was created at Caesarea after many years of hard labor. Though it was a time of peace, the wary king erected a series of strong fortresses in the land to discourage attack, and kept a respectable standing army.

Even beyond the borders of Palestine Herod made lavish gifts for construction work, including temples. The reason for this generosity may well be that he sought a satisfaction in the gratitude of others that his own subjects, in their suspicion and dislike, withheld from him.[12]

[11] Stewart Perowne, *The Life and Times of Herod the Great*, p. 70.
[12] *Ibid.*, p. 127.

13

But fortune did not smile on Herod indefinitely. His terrible domestic situation (he had ten wives altogether) and bodily affliction combined to weaken him and make him morose. He fell out of Augustus' favor for a time and also increasingly lost the support of the Pharisees. His enemies sensed that his strength was waning and they grew ever bolder in their defiance. A sample of this is contained in Josephus' story of a band of young men who were persuaded to cut down the golden eagle that Herod had placed over the great door of the temple, which in the eyes of the Jews was a pagan desecration.[13] But in Herod's eyes the act of the Jewish youths was no less than sacrilege and he ordered the conspirators to be burned alive. This was in the year of Herod's death, and it explains the barbarity of the order to slay the infants of Bethlehem. In his last days the king was a virtual madman, his body wracked with discomfort and his mind tortured by disappointment and bitterness toward his subjects.

Whatever blemishes Herod had, and they were many, he had succeeded in keeping the country from internal strife such as had marred the rule of the later Hasmoneans, and had been an effective go-between in Jewish relations with the Romans, so that no unwise act on either side was allowed to develop to a point of friction from which there could be no return.

After his death it was discovered that his final will named three sons to succeed him in the division of his kingdom: Archelaus to rule Judea and Samaria, Antipas to have Galilee and Perea, and Philip to administer the districts to the north and east of Galilee. Unfortunately for Archelaus, rioting broke out in Jerusalem and three thousand people were killed when the garrison was turned loose on the unruly Passover throng. Antipas and Archelaus, each hoping to be king of the country, presented rival claims before the emperor, who took some time in coming to a decision but finally honored the will of Herod much as it stood. Archelaus, however, was given the title of ethnarch rather than king, with the possibility of earning the latter title by proving himself. The effort of a delegation of Jews from Palestine to have Herodian rule abolished was unsuccessful, even though it was seconded by thousands of Jews at Rome. This element pressed for direct Roman rule as less of an evil than further experience with their Idumean masters.

Archelaus failed to make good on his probation. In a few years his misrule had so outraged his subjects that they loudly de-

13 *Antiquities* XVII. vi. 2-4.

manded his removal, to which Augustus acceded (A.D. 6). Judea became a Roman province ruled by a procurator who was responsible to Caesar and in a secondary sense to the governor of Syria. He had his headquarters at Caesarea rather than Jerusalem. This arrangement was set aside only once, during a brief interval of three years (41-44) when Herod Agrippa I was allowed to reign as king of the Jews. Consequently, when the Jewish leaders turned against Jesus of Nazareth, they brought him before the procurator, who at that time was Pontius Pilate, for the disposition of the case.

Since several Herods appear in the New Testament, it is necessary to differentiate them. In addition to Herod the Great, others so named are Antipas, who dealt with John the Baptist, and Herod Agrippa I, who beheaded James the son of Zebedee (Acts 12:1-2). Herod Agrippa II is called simply Agrippa in Luke's account (Acts 25:12). Another Herodian, called Philip in the New Testament (Mark 6:17) but apparently differentiated from Philip the tetrarch, is usually designated as Herod-Philip. The recurrence of the name Herod testifies to the impact of their progenitor Herod the Great.

Six decades elapsed between the deposition of Archelaus and the outbreak of the Jewish war of rebellion against Rome. The New Testament bears witness to the growing tension between the Jews and their Roman overlords. Christ taught submission to the state in temporal matters (Matt. 22:21), and this was the attitude also of some rabbis, but the nation as a whole found its situation increasingly distasteful and difficult. No small share of the responsibility belongs to the Roman administration, which declined after Augustus. Pilate's arrival in Judea was almost coincidental with the semi-retirement of Tiberius (A.D. 26), who tried to govern the empire from the island of Capri. His successor, Caligula (A.D. 37-41), roused the Jews to indignant protest by ordering the rearing of a statue of himself in the temple at Jerusalem. A people who acknowledged one God preferred to die rather than submit to such blasphemy. At this juncture Agrippa (later Herod Agrippa I), who had ingratiated himself with Caligula, prevailed on him to countermand the order, to the great relief of the Jews. At the death of Caligula, Agrippa assisted in the negotiations that brought his friend Claudius to the throne (A.D. 41-54); and was in turn rewarded by being made king of Judea (A.D. 41-44), with a territory approximating that of Herod the Great. His subjects treated him as one of themselves, and were exultant to have someone over them who really seemed to care for their interests. But his reign was brief, and with his death direct Roman administration was restored. Claudius was succeeded by the infamous Nero (A.D. 54-68), in whose reign Jewish-Roman relations reached the breaking point.

Not only did the emperors decline in quality, but also the procurators who were sent to preside over Jewish affairs. Pilate was bad enough, but later officials, with the exception of Festus, added to a lordly indifference to the welfare of the nation an ill-concealed tendency to defraud the people and enrich themselves in every possible way. The Roman philosophy of government was to the effect that the provinces existed to support the Roman establishment — the imperial court and all the appurtenances of administration, including the expenses of the far-flung legions that guarded the frontiers. As long as adequate funds were forthcoming, the private enrichment of its officials could be winked at, provided it did not become too scandalous. The Jews resented the financial burden imposed on them, not simply because of its oppressiveness in terms of money drained from the country but more particularly because of the implication contained in the annual tribute that they were not free. After all, they were the people of God, and should not be in bondage to any man.

This was precisely the position taken by the Zealots, who followed the lead of a certain Judas of Galilee. This man counselled the people to resist the efforts of the Romans to make a census of the Jews after Archelaus was removed.[14] Josephus fastens the blame for the war with Rome upon this group, which grew increasingly powerful and unscrupulous during the following decades. He makes them out to be brigands who found it to their advantage to stir up the nation to revolt, since they were then able on the plea of patriotism to kill the pacifists and plunder their possessions.

It is no doubt possible to make out a better case for the Zealots, as W. R. Farmer has attempted to do.[15] He finds links between them and the Maccabees, and believes that the revolt in both cases was fundamentally motivated by religious zeal. Certainly the picture that Josephus himself gives of the Zealots in the mopping-up operations after the fall of Jerusalem calls forth our intense admiration for their fortitude. They preferred death rather than to acknowledge the lordship of Caesar, which would contradict their monotheistic faith. A fair conclusion

---

14 Josephus, *Jewish War* II. viii. 1.

15 *Maccabees, Zealots, and Josephus;* cf. S. G. F. Brandon, *Jesus and the Zealots*, pp. 26-64.

is that the revolt against Rome was religiously based, the Jews being confident that God was with them, making them invincible against overwhelming odds. That some Jews yielded to baser motives of a personal sort is quite understandable. It would not be the first or last time that religion has been called on to justify outrageous conduct.

One of the victims of Jewish zeal in the period immediately preceding the war was James, the brother of our Lord and head of the Jerusalem church, who was condemned to death at the instigation of Ananus the high priest. Festus' successor had not yet arrived to assume his office, so the act went un-rebuked for the moment. It was doubtless prompted in part by the acquiescence of James in the admission of Gentiles to the Christian church without the imposition of circumcision and submission to the distinctives of the Law. This amounted to treason to Judaism (cf. p. 364).

The fall of Jerusalem in A.D. 70 did not deal to the church the same staggering blow it inflicted on Judaism, for the reason that the real strength of the Christian movement had by this time shifted to gentile areas.

BIBLIOGRAPHY

Abel, F. M., *Histoire de la Palestine,* 2 vols. Paris: J. Gabalda, 1952.

Bevan, Edwyn, *Jerusalem Under the High Priests.* London: Edward Arnold & Co., 1904.

Farmer, W. R., *Maccabees, Zealots, and Josephus.* New York: Columbia Univ. Press, 1956.

Josephus, *Bellum Judaicum,* 2 vols. Loeb Classical Library, Cambridge: Harvard Univ. Press, 1956.

——————, *Antiquitates Judaicae,* 2 vols. *LCL,* 1957.

Perowne, Stewart, *The Life and Times of Herod the Great.* London: Hodder & Stoughton, 1956.

——————, *The Later Herods.* New York: Abingdon Press, 1958.

Schürer, Emil, *A History of the Jewish People in the Time of Jesus Christ,* Div. I, 2 vols. Edinburgh: T. & T. Clark, 1896.

Tarn, W. W., *Alexander the Great,* Part I. Cambridge Univ. Press, 1951.

THE INSTITUTIONS

The strength of the Jewish nation lay in the fact that it succeeded in permeating life with religion to the point where the spiritual and the cultural elements were hardly divisible. So strong were the ties of Judaism that when some of the people found their lot cast in countries outside Palestine, they did not as a rule drift into conformity with the paganism around them, but maintained a solidarity of faith and cultus with their brethren in the homeland. Among the factors aiding in the maintenance of the distinctiveness of the Jewish nation were certain institutions and practices that are deserving of notice.

THE SYNAGOGUE

Although Jewish tradition teaches that the synagogue had a Mosaic origin, seeking thereby to have as venerable an authority as possible for its establishment, the most likely time for its origin is the Babylonian captivity. Here were combined the various factors necessary for its emergence — a chastened national conscience, capable teachers, whether prophets or priests, and a natural desire to come together for prayer and the worship of God.

When the temple was rebuilt, there was still a place for the synagogue, partly because it provided a rallying point for the local Jewish community on a weekly and even daily basis, partly because it had a different function, emphasizing instruction in the Law of God above all else. Although there were synagogues in the time of Jesus, the number greatly increased after the Romans destroyed the temple. People journeyed to the temple for sacrifice and the celebration of the national festivals, but they frequented the synagogue to be spiritually literate. Ten male members were required as a minimum for its establishment, and there could be more than one in a city.

Where they were available, scribes were accorded an honored place as teachers. Originally they were copyists and students of the Scriptures, but gradually moved into a place of greater contact with the people through the synagogue and made their learning accessible to them in the interpretation of the Word. This process was accelerated by the secularizing of the priests, many of whom yielded to the hellenizing influences of the time. Consequently, the proverbial function of the priests as teachers of the nation had all but disappeared in New Testament times.

Next in rank to the scribes were the elders, who served as rulers of the synagogue. To them was committed the oversight

18

of the services, the assignment of participation, and the maintenance of order (Luke 13:14). An indispensable figure was the attendant, who had charge of the rolls of Scripture and frequently doubled as teacher of the synagogue school.

Jewish sources for the worship in the synagogue are somewhat later than the New Testament, but they give a reasonably clear picture of what it must have been at the earlier period. The elements of the service included the *Shema,* or Israel's confession of faith (Deut. 6:4-9; 11:13-21; Num. 15:37-41), prayers, the reading of the Law and the Prophets, together with the necessary interpretation into Aramaic for Palestinian Jews (in the Dispersion, where the Greek translation was used, no such help was needed), an exposition or homily by some qualified person (Luke 4:16-21; Acts 13:15ff.), often based on the portion read in the service, then the blessing by which the congregation was dismissed.

The influence of the synagogue on Christian worship was considerable. A gathering of believers could be called a synagogue (James 2:2; cf. Heb. 10:25). Patristic writers sometimes use the word of Christian assemblies (*The Epistle of Ignatius to Polycarp* 4:2). It is clear from Justin Martyr's testimony (*Apology* 67) that the main ingredients of Christian worship in the second century were reading of the Scriptures, exposition, and prayer, as in the synagogue.

In the Dispersion the synagogue became a powerful instrument of propaganda. Although the Jews were thoroughly disliked by their Greek and Roman neighbors for their exclusivism in belief (the doctrine of one true and living God) and in custom (dietary and purification laws), they were nevertheless able to win a respectable number of converts to their faith. This process was no doubt aided by the spiritual restlessness and widespread search for satisfaction in forms of religion more personal than those afforded by city-state or empire, and also by the relatively high moral attainment of the Jew in contrast to the pagan.

The roots of proselytism are embedded in the early history of the Jews. Exodus 12:48 contains the provision that aliens who were resident in Israel and desired to partake of the Passover must receive circumcision. Henceforth such persons were numbered among the congregation and treated much as native Jews. It is clear, however, that the situation in the Dispersion of the first Christian century was quite different, for the Jews were in the minority, little islands of monotheism in a sea of pagan idolatry. It was much harder under such circumstances to win a Gentile and persuade him to become a Jew. The offense of circumcision was a strong barrier.

Proof of this is found in the presence of large numbers of Gentiles in the synagogue who had not taken this step, but who were content to accept the enlightenment of the teaching without full committal to Judaism. Whereas the proselyte must submit to circumcision and the yoke of the Law and undergo a complete body bath of purification, the God-fearer, as he is called in the New Testament, was under no particular obligation to Judaism. In the case of Cornelius we see a man who devoted himself to prayer and almsgiving, but who had not taken the decisive step that would have made him a proselyte. He was still uncircumcised (Acts 10:28; 11:3). The reluctance of Roman authorities to countenance mass additions to Judaism from among the Gentiles no doubt was a factor in limiting the number of proselytes.

It was among these God-fearing Gentiles that the Christian missionaries found their most fertile field for evangelism, and for this very reason incurred resentment. The Jews had hoped to influence these Gentiles to become full converts, but as it turned out they had simply prepared them for Christian propaganda instead. From the Christian standpoint it was a wonderful providence that these accessions to the gospel were already schooled in the Scriptures. Because of this the apostle Paul, in writing to gentile churches, was able to presuppose a fairly extensive acquaintance with the Old Testament and could build upon it in his own instruction.

THE TEMPLE

As we have seen, one of Herod's grandest achievements was the erection of a magnificent house of the Lord in Jerusalem. Built on the same site as the previous structures of Solomon and Zerubbabel, it was greatly extended in its ground plan. The Jews were averse to calling it Herod's temple, since the Idumean was not regarded as one of themselves, but they nevertheless took pride in it.

Inside the outer wall, which was pierced by eight gates placed at intervals, a double colonnade provided porticoes on all four sides, the one on the south side, known as the Royal Porch, being wider because of an extra row of pillars. Solomon's Porch (John 10:23) was on the eastern side. These porches looked out on a large court that completely surrounded the raised area containing the inner courts and the temple proper. Into this first court Gentiles could come, but a stone barrier, shoulder high, reminded them that they could go no further. The prohibition was reinforced by warnings inscribed on the gates that opened to the inner sections, to the effect that any one who transgressed the barrier was liable to death. Josephus quotes Titus as saying to the Jews that even a Roman was subject to this ban and its consequences.[16] The apostle Paul seems to have had this restriction of Judaism in mind when he states that Christ had made Jew and Gentile one in the church by breaking down the middle wall of partition (Eph. 2:14). This outer court is the most likely place for the assembling of the great throng that heard Peter speak on the Day of Pentecost. Here, too, the traffic in sacrificial animals and the changing of money went on. In this vast area, capable of holding scores of thousands of persons, the crowd mobbed Paul until he was rescued by Roman soldiers sent from the castle of Antonia, which stood at the northwest corner (Acts 21).

Moving up the terrace to the higher ground beyond, as one traveled from east to west he would encounter the court of the women, so named not because it was for their use exclusively but because they were permitted access to it. Here was located the treasury, where people deposited their contributions in the several receptacles provided for the purpose (Luke 21:1-4). Jesus seems to have resorted to this spot on occasion for his ministry of teaching (John 8:20).

By an ascent of several steps one would be brought to the great door (the Beautiful Gate of Acts 3:2) that opened the way to another court, a narrow strip called the court of Israel, and then to the court of the priests that surrounded the *naos* or temple proper. In this court stood the large altar of sacrifice, with the laver nearby, and looming up behind was the broad, tall front of the holy place, standing on an eminence and exposing wings jutting out on either side. Over the door a golden vine spread itself gracefully, the occasion, some think, for Jesus' remarks about the vine in John 15. The temple, like the tabernacle before, was divided into holy place and holy of holies, a heavy veil separating the two. At the crucifixion this was supernaturally torn asunder from top to bottom; the way into the holiest of all had been cleared by the death of the Lamb of God.

Pilgrims found their hearts beating faster as they neared the holy city and beheld the flashing gold of the shrine crowning the glistening white stones of the temple. This was the focal point of their national life. Jews throughout the world took pride in contributing to its upkeep in addition to paying the annual

---

[16] *Jewish War* VI. ii. 4.

half-shekel tax imposed on every male Israelite. This tax represented two days' work, on an average. The total amount collected must have been a large sum. Out of it were paid the necessary expenses of the daily morning and evening sacrifices, also salaries and repairs. In addition the treasury was enriched by votive gifts (recall the custom of Corban — Matt. 15: 5).

The temple would have been meaningless without an order of priests to maintain the cultus. At the head of this great company was the high priest, whose office had fallen into some disrepute by Herodian times, since Herod and his successors removed and installed incumbents to suit their purpose. Even so, the office could still wield considerable influence, especially when occupied by a man of personal strength. The priests, descendants of Aaron, were divided into twenty-four groups or courses. However, since only four courses returned from captivity (Ezra 2:36-39), it was arranged that each of these families should draw lots, five in number, so as to form once more the total of twenty-four divisions. Each course served for a week and was replaced on the Sabbath. During the week, when there was not sufficient demand for the presence of the entire course, the functions were rotated among the personnel, but on the Sabbath the entire course reported for service. Assisting the many thousands of priests was a large company of Levites who kept the temple in good order and provided leadership in the musical aspect of the worship.

On the economic side, the temple was a huge commercial establishment; on the spiritual side, it symbolized the presence of God among his people and also the uniqueness of the covenant nation. As such, it helped to seal the unity of Jews everywhere. It was the crown jewel of the holy city. In the war against Rome its defenders showed fanatical endurance and bravery, but when the temple was set on fire, their spirit was broken, and the fall of the city was only a matter of time.[17] After this catastrophe the sacrificial system was in abeyance. In its place the rabbis put the sacrifice of obedience to the Torah, with great emphasis upon almsgiving. They could more readily effect this transference because of the central place that the Law had acquired in the synagogue.

THE SANHEDRIN

It has always been noted that the ruling figure in the Jewish commonwealth after the captivity was the high priest. In the

17 Farmer, *op. cit.*, pp. 111-14.

Greek period notices begin to appear of a *gerousia* (senate) as the governing body of the nation[18] and operating under the leadership of the high priest.[19] This body may fairly be assumed to have been the predecessor of the Sanhedrin with which readers of the New Testament are familiar. The logic of history dictates that the judicial function of the elders, amply attested in the Old Testament and continuing throughout the intertestamental period, would apply also when the term *synedrion* (Sanhedrin) begins to be used as the name of this council. So the Sanhedrin was a court of justice along with other functions of a legislative and executive nature.

The term *synedrion* makes its appearance in the sources at the time of Gabinius, who administered the affairs of the province of Syria under Pompey's direction. In order to decentralize authority in the country and weaken Jerusalem, he divided Judea into five districts, each with its own council.[20] This was all undone by Caesar, so that the Jews once again had their own centralized supreme body. Under Herod the Great the council was almost eclipsed because of his dominance of the state and his murder of many of its members in retribution for supporting Antigonus. During the ministry of Jesus the Sanhedrin was again active and powerful, allowed to administer Jewish affairs without interference except in matters that would involve Roman policy and jurisdiction. The imposition of the death penalty required Roman confirmation.

Headed by the high priest, the council had seventy members drawn from the aristocratic, priestly ranks where Sadducean influence was strong, from the elders of the people and from the scribes. Because of its prestige its decisions were honored beyond the confines of Palestine.

THE PARTIES IN JUDAISM

Our chief source for the history of the Jews, Josephus, names four parties, which he calls sects.[21] He is careful to say, however, that the Zealots have nothing in common with the other three, which are presented from the standpoint of philosophical coteries. Josephus himself had been exposed to the influence of Sadducees, Pharisees, and Essenes, and was filled with admiration for the latter group, but ultimately identified himself with the Pharisees.

---

[18] I Macc. 12:6.
[19] Judith 4:8.
[20] *Antiquities* XIV. v. 4.
[21] *Jewish War* II. viii. 1-4; *Antiquities* XIII. v. 9.

Beyond question, the Pharisees left by far the deepest impression on Judaism. When the other groups faded, following the calamity of the fall of Jerusalem, this one maintained itself and became the driving force in rallying the nation around its religious heritage. In distinction from the priests, the Pharisees were laymen who banded themselves into brotherhoods committed to the faithful observance of the Law and the traditions of the elders. Their predecessors, it is thought, were the Hasidim of the Syrian and Maccabean periods. The name Pharisee means "separatist," but the nature of the separation remains to be determined. A possibility is separation from the politically minded Hasmoneans, but it seems more probable that the group's resolution to avoid all manner of sin and defilement lies back of the name. Aided by the scribes, who interpreted the Law and helped them apply it to the changing conditions of life, the Pharisees showed a remarkable zeal for their traditions. They regarded themselves as the true Israel of God, and as their influence increased they showed their dislike and contempt for the 'am ha-aretz, the common people who were ignorant and rather neglectful of the Law (cf. John 7:45-49). No group had such a hold on the rank and file of the population as the Pharisees, for they were looked up to as holy men, the custodians of the faith of the fathers. Unfortunately their zeal for the traditions of the elders resulted in the undermining of the authority of Scripture (Mark 7:13).

A discernible change came over the Pharisees in one respect during the first half of the first century A.D. From an earlier policy of relative indifference to the political fortunes of their country so long as they were permitted to devote themselves to piety, they gradually veered to a position of greater concern over the continued domination of the people of God by alien powers. In the end, many of their numbers were swept up into the nationalist wave sponsored by the Zealots.

Whereas the Pharisees were most influential in the synagogue and in the routine of daily life, the Sadducees entrenched themselves in the temple and in the Sanhedrin. The latter body included some Pharisees in its number, but the control was in the hands of the aristocratic priests. These were the product of a long history wherein the high priest had become drawn into the vortex of secular life and governmental administration, carrying others with him. Much less is known of the Sadducees than of the other parties. No one of their number left behind a history or description of them that has survived, and with the fall of Jerusalem their importance waned until they were entirely eclipsed by those of Pharisaic leaning. Their doctrinal beliefs are known from the New Testament, but beyond this was the cleavage between themselves and the Pharisees over the validity of tradition. They rejected the corpus of oral law, insisting that the Scripture alone is authoritative. Their great weakness was their lack of moral earnestness, their resort to expediency to insure the continuance of their worldly type of life. They seemed to be more anxious to please the Romans than to please God.

Of the Essenes Josephus gives a longer account than of the others. A few additional items of information come from Philo, Pliny, and some early Christian writers. At the beginning of the Christian era these people were found living a monastic type of life in communities west of the Dead Sea. Recruits were on probation for a year and were banned from the meetings of the society during this period. Only after two years more, when they were tested for strength of character, were they admitted to membership, taking vows to follow justice, honor, submission to rulers, truthfulness, and the keeping of the secrets of the society. Gainful pursuits had no place. Adherents surrendered all private property to the society, in which a community of goods prevailed. Seniority assigned members to four grades or classes.

The daily routine called for early rising and a period of devotion before a time of manual labor. After several hours of work the first meal of the day was taken, but only after bathing in cold water (ritual ablutions figured prominently in the life of the sect). Another period of labor followed; then came the second meal of the day. Not all the work was physical, for the group was interested in study and writing.

Testimony is somewhat conflicting about marriage. It seems that for the most part the Essenes repudiated it, perpetuating themselves by the flow of prospects into their ranks and by the taking over of other men's children for rearing. But there were some with Essenic tendencies and sympathies who practiced marriage. Another point of difficulty is the location. Josephus represents them as scattered in many cities.[22] These two items — marriage and location — may be related to one another. Some of the group chose to live in the ascetic communal fellowship near the Dead Sea. Others, following a less strict rule of life, were married and lived elsewhere.

Other features of the society were the absence of slavery and the abhorrence of war. These people may well have been the more devout and detached segment of the Hasidim who adopted

[22] *Jewish War* II. viii. 4.

the extreme measure of separating themselves from their fellow Jews.

Since 1947 the world has been made aware of a collection of writings, known as the Dead Sea Scrolls, that emanated from the Qumran community, which was located only a few miles south of Jericho, overlooking the Dead Sea. The headquarters of the group has been excavated and the writings studied with a view to determining, if possible, the relation of the community to the Judaism of the time. Evidence points to occupation of the site for a century or more before Christ down to the war with Rome, except for the period of Herod the Great. Was the community made up of Essenes? Opinion has been divided on this, but it is safe to conclude that the similarities between this group and the Essenes as they are pictured in the sources are sufficiently marked to indicate the essentially Essenic character of the settlement. A monastic life under strict disciplinary regulation, close study of the Scriptures and other sacred literature, the striving for a high type of morality, coupled with dissatisfaction over the condition of contemporary Judaism — these features characterize both. The location in the same general area is more readily explained on grounds of similarity than of dissent.

It is possible that elements of difference will tend to diminish with further study. For example, the warlike tendency of the Qumran group, as indicated by the Battle Scroll, may reflect the early history of those covenanters in Maccabean times, in distinction from the later developments that were known and described by Philo and Josephus.[23] Again, the alleged difference in the matter of animal sacrifice may well be dissipated with more careful exegesis, which seems to indicate that the Essenes did have such sacrifices, though they were not permitted to offer them where others did.[24]

The discovery of the Dead Sea Scrolls has reopened the question of possible Essene influence upon early Christianity.[25] Certainly the Qumran community was flourishing during the days of Christ and the period of the Jerusalem church and it was situated not far away. John the Baptist may well have had some contact with this group while he was in the wilderness. He used the same text of Scripture (Isa. 40:3) to justify his mission that

[23] Charles T. Fritsch, *The Qumran Community*, p. 109.
[24] John Strugnell, "Flavius Josephus and the Essenes: *Antiquities* XVIII. 18-22," *JBL*, 77 (1958), pp. 113-15.
[25] See the bibliography at the end of this section.

the New Covenanters of Qumran used to justify their withdrawal into the wilderness for the study of the Law, viewing themselves as the true Israel preparing the way for the golden age that was to come. But if John had such contact in his earlier days, he must have broken with the group in order to appeal to the nation as a whole along the lines of repentance.

In the case of Jesus of Nazareth, no solid basis has been found for any relationship with the Teacher of Righteousness, the founder and leader of the sect for some years. As far as the documents reveal, no messianic function was associated with this figure of the Qumran community. His death was not regarded as having redemptive significance.

Several parallels have been detected, however, between the Qumran group's organization and discipline and those of the early church, such as the breaking of bread, the community of goods, and the leadership of the Twelve (Qumran had a body of twelve laymen and three priests). But the priestly leadership of the sect fails of analogy in early Christianity, and some of the parallels likely depend on a common source (the twelve tribes of Israel, e.g., provide a sufficient background for rule by twelve men).

A bond between the two movements has been posited by some scholars because of alleged hostility toward the temple worship. It is granted that this bond does not include all the Jerusalem church or its leaders, but rather the Hellenists, with Stephen as their spokesman (Acts 7). But it is not at all clear that the hostility was similarly grounded. The Hellenists were chiefly motivated in their opposition by the entrenched stubbornness that refused to see in Jesus Christ one greater than the temple, rather than by the corruption of the priesthood, which so disturbed the Qumran group.

Some striking parallels have been adduced between the Qumran literature and the Fourth Gospel, particularly in the area of the dualistic structure of the thought; especially is this true of the contrast between light and darkness, truth and error. But whereas Qumran sees the resolution of the struggle only in the future, John pictures it in terms of realized eschatology. The darkness has been invaded and overcome by the person and work of Christ, so that the light is even now shining victoriously.

In Qumran we observe certain parallels, then, to early Christianity, a natural circumstance in view of the Judaic background of both. But at the core the two were radically different, for the one centered everything in the study of the Law, whereas the other made the incarnate Christ and his grace the focal point of its life. The one had a narrowly exclusive and localized fellowship, whereas the other moved out into a world mission with its gospel.

It is unfortunate that zeal to establish possible connection between Qumran and Christianity has shifted the center of study from the relation of this group to the Judaism of the day, for after all that is where the emphasis properly belongs. We can see more clearly than before that Judaism could take many forms within its unifying feature of loyalty to the Torah.

THE DISPERSION

Jewry was a widely diffused phenomenon at the beginning of the Christian era. A large settlement continued to exist in Babylonia, the descendants of those who for one reason or another did not return to Palestine after the Captivity. In the latter days of Jeremiah a company of Jews fled to Egypt, the precursors of many more in the hellenistic period. The Alexandrian era was marked by shifting of populations on a large scale, and the Jews were not slow to participate in it, for the outside world offered greater commercial opportunities than the limited resources of Palestine. Some were forced out by internal strife during the period of the later Hasmoneans. Others were removed as captives of war and were ultimately set free, with the result that most of them remained where they were and formed Jewish communities. But even more went abroad of their own volition. Heavy concentrations of Jews formed at Alexandria in Egypt, in Cyrenaica, in the major cities of Asia Minor and at Rome. Greece and Macedonia had their share also. Jews were more numerous outside Palestine than within the country, their numbers running into several millions. Indeed, it could be said that there was not a people in the world that did not contain a portion of this nation.[26]

Yet the ties with the homeland were maintained with considerable success. Jerusalem was the capital not only of Palestine but of world Jewry. Religiously it was to the Jews what Rome was to the world politically. To it the faithful resorted as pilgrims at festival time. Many returned to the land to spend their last days on its sacred soil and to be buried there (cf. Acts 2:5-11). To the attraction of the temple must be added the unifying power of the Torah. While it is true that the Law and other portions of the Scriptures had been, rendered

[26] Josephus, *Jewish War* II. xvi. 4.

into Greek (Septuagint) and could therefore be studied outside the land by those Jews who had made Greek their adopted language, still there was a natural inclination to look to the rabbis of Palestine for guidance in all matters of interpretation.

It is customary to speak of hellenistic Judaism as the development that occurred outside the land, with Josephus and Philo as leading representatives, the former having chief interest in expounding the history of his people for the benefit of the Romans, the latter being intent on philosophy, seeking to commend his faith to cultivated pagans. Josephus as a man of letters resided in Rome, and Philo made his home at Alexandria. This division into Palestinian and hellenistic Judaism, however, seems somewhat arbitrary, because the homeland of the Jews had for a long time been exposed to hellenizing influence. Any product of Judaism that shows marked effects of its hellenistic environment deserves to be called hellenistic, irrespective of geography.

Under the Ptolemies Alexandria had become a leading cultural center. Here, about the time of Christ, Philo wrote a number of treatises that reflect his debt to Greek thought. Rejecting Greek religion as polytheistic and degrading, he nevertheless adopted Greek philosophy to a generous degree and proposed to make use of it in commending his own ancestral faith to the pagan world. Superficially, the effort to awaken interest in the Jewish Law might seem futile, but Philo managed it by the way in which he handled the Scriptures, making use of the allegorical approach. The plain meaning was in most cases set aside to make room for the claim that Moses was talking about the very things that had engrossed the Greek philosophers, only doing it with greater insight because he had the benefit of special revelation. The highest wisdom was to be found in the Law of God. For example the trees that God caused to grow in the Garden indicate the virtues that God plants in the soul.

Philo made generous use of the Platonic theory of ideas, and he could do this the more readily since Judaism seemed to have something of the sort itself, such as the doctrine of the divine image in man at creation and the tabernacle as the reflection of a heavenly model. Yet the ideas were held by Philo in strict subordination to God, who alone *is* in the absolute sense. To Philo the ideas were not static patterns but dynamic causative factors, which he identified with the powers (Hebrew *hosts*) that surround and minister to the Almighty. Another term that served his thought well was *Logos*. This he tended to make equivalent to the ideas and the powers, but with various nuances

29

of meaning. As with later Judaism in general, in distinction from the Judaism of the biblical period, Philo felt the necessity of keeping God aloof from any direct contact with the world, so mediation in the philosophical sense had a central place in his thinking. An incarnation of Logos such as is posited in the Fourth Gospel would be impossible on Philo's presuppositions.

The influence of this philosopher on Judaism was checked by the spread and monopolizing force of Pharisaism. His influence on Christianity was felt in two areas. As the gospel came into contact with the pagan world, it was obliged to some extent to talk the language of religious philosophy. Traces of this are to be found in Paul and in the Fourth Gospel. Both writers were probably acquainted with Philo's work. Philo's influence was even stronger on the Alexandrian Fathers of the church, who thought of themselves as Christian Gnostics applying to the Scriptures the allegorical method of exegesis.

BIBLIOGRAPHY

Bruce, F. F., *Second Thoughts on the Dead Sea Scrolls.* Grand Rapids: Eerdmans, 1956, pp. 123-137.

Burrows, Millar, *The Dead Sea Scrolls.* New York: Viking Press, 1955, pp. 326-345.

——————, *More Light on the Dead Sea Scrolls.* New York: Viking Press, 1958, pp. 39-132.

Cross, F. M., Jr., *The Ancient Library of Qumran.* London: Duckworth, 1958.

Derwachter, F. M., *Preparing the Way for Paul.* New York: Macmillan, 1930.

Edersheim, Alfred, *The Temple.* London: The Religious Tract Society, 1908.

Gaster, T. H., *The Dead Sea Scriptures.* New York: Doubleday, 1956.

Guignebert, Charles, *The Jewish World in the Time of Jesus.* London: Routledge & Kegan Paul, 1939.

Juster, Jean, *Les Juifs dans l'empire romain.* Paris: Librairie Paul Geuthner, 1914.

Oesterley and Box, *The Religion and Worship of the Synagogue.* Bath: Pitman and Sons, 1907.

Moore, G. F., *Judaism,* 2 vols. Cambridge: Harvard Univ. Press, 1946.

Rowley, H. H., *The Dead Sea Scrolls and the New Testament.* London: S.P.C.K., 1960.

Schürer, E., "Diaspora," *HDB,* Extra Volume, pp. 91-109.

Stendahl, Krister (ed.), *The Scrolls and the New Testament.* New York: Harper & Brothers, 1957.

Wolfson, H. A., *Philo,* 2 vols. Cambridge: Harvard Univ. Press, 1948.

THE LITERATURE

In the intertestamental period there was an awareness that the prophetic office was in abeyance (I Macc. 4:46; 9:27; 14:41), but history moved on and needed recording. Men did not cease to think and to set down their thoughts in writing. So an extensive body of literature came into being that was utilized both by Jews and Christians.

It has been customary to group these writings into two classifications known as Apocrypha and Pseudepigrapha. The former includes books that came to be joined with Old Testament writings in various manuscripts of the Septuagint.[27] When the Greek Scriptures were rendered into Latin, these additional books were retained, although not without some controversy. Ultimately most of them were declared a part of Scripture by the Council of Trent (1546). In Protestant circles they have been used by some for purposes of edification but have not been considered Scripture in the canonical sense. The list includes: *I Esdras, II Esdras, Judith, Additions to Esther, The Wisdom of Solomon, Ecclesiasticus, Baruch, The Epistle of Jeremiah, The Song of the Three Holy Children, The History of Susanna, Bel and the Dragon, The Prayer of Manasseh, I Maccabees, II Maccabees.* In its original signification the term "apocrypha" meant things hidden, secret or esoteric, but for practical purposes the word may be regarded today as the equivalent of non-canonical. Roman Catholics prefer the term deutero-canonical, which is taken to mean recognition as canonical at a later time than the canon, but possessing an equal authority.

The term Pseudepigrapha properly denotes pseudonymous writings, bearing the names of Enoch, Baruch, Moses, *et al.,* whereas the real authors are unknown. Appearing at a time when prophetic testimony had ceased, these writings presumably gained in popularity by being adorned with the names of notable men of biblical times. However, not all the works classed among the Pseudepigrapha are pseudonymous, whereas among the Apocrypha pseudonymous works are included (e.g., *Wisdom of Solomon*). Many of this second group are apocalyptic in character, but this is not true of all. Such a feature can hardly be used to distinguish these writings from the Apocrypha, since *II Esdras,* which belongs to the Apocrypha, is definitely

---

[27] For a good statement on the process that most likely accounts for this mingling see H.B. Swete, *Introduction to the Old Testament in Greek,* p. 225.

apocalyptic. In view of this mixed situation, C. C. Torrey proposed the abandonment of the dual terminology in favor of one term for all, namely, apocryphal literature.[28] This is a sensible suggestion and will be followed here.

The literature in question came into being in the second and first centuries B.C. and in the first century A.D., written for the most part in Hebrew or Aramaic. For various reasons, official Judaism discountenanced it by the end of the first century A.D. After all, it was too late to be inspired. Furthermore, the Jewish leaders could more consistently call for the rejection of Christian writings if they also repudiated Jewish writings that originated after the cessation of the Spirit's activity in the literary field. The historical situation seemed to them to demand a conserving of the past, a concentration of attention upon the expounding of the Scriptures and the scribal traditions. So it remained for Christians to perpetuate these "outside" works in Greek translation and in other languages. Some documents contain Christian interpolation. It is of interest to note that the Dead Sea Scrolls include, along with writings authoritative for the Qumran community, many others in fragmentary form — *Tobit, The Wisdom of Solomon, Ecclesiasticus, The Epistle of Jeremiah, Jubilees, Enoch, The Book of Noah, The Testament of Levi, The Testament of Naphtali, The Sayings of Moses, The Scroll of the Patriarchs, Psalms of Joshua, A Vision of Amram, The Prayer of Nabonidus.*[29] Some of these were unknown previously. A few may have originated at Qumran. The presence of all these in the caves indicates that a few decades prior to the banning of such books by Jewish authorities they were in use in the wilderness communities.

ANALYSIS AND DESCRIPTION

1. *Historical.* (i) *I Esdras* (Greek for Ezra). This book is the one that stands in closest relation to the Old Testament. It bears the name of a biblical figure and carries over most of its content from the later historical books. It follows fairly closely, in many places word for word, the biblical narrative from II Chronicles 35 (the passover of Josiah) through Ezra and Nehemiah, concluding with Ezra's reading of the Law. A section peculiar to the book (3:1 - 5:6) was apparently introduced to explain how the building of the temple, which was interrupted by Samaritan opposition, was resumed under Darius.

---

28 *The Apocryphal Literature,* pp. 10-11.
29 W. S. LaSor, *Amazing Dead Sea Scrolls,* rev. ed., 1957, pp. 45-47.

Three bodyguards of the king were keeping watch after a feast, and to while away the time they decided to write down the thing that in their estimation was the strongest and to put their opinions under the king's pillow. Later the king called his court together to have the theses expounded and defended. One acclaimed wine, another the king, and the third pronounced for women, with the proviso that truth was stronger still. This last was proclaimed the winner (it is no surprise that his name is Zerubbabel) and when asked to state his reward called upon the king to make good his vow to rebuild Jerusalem and the temple and to restore the holy vessels. It is probable that the book originated about the middle of the second century B.C., in Egypt.

(ii) *I Maccabees.* This book describes the trials of the Jews at the hands of Antiochus Epiphanes and the events that grew out of his persecution of Israel. It covers a period of forty years, from the accession of Antiochus in 175 to the death of Simon Maccabeus in 135, and is a primary source for the history of the Maccabean struggle. Written in the early years of the first century B.C., in Palestine, the book bears evident marks of having been penned by a devout patriot.

(iii) *II Maccabees.* Covering a shorter period, from 176 to 171, *II Maccabees* recounts the sufferings of the Jews in the days of Antiochus. It contains some material not found in *I Maccabees.* The story is told with less detachment, for the preoccupation of the writer is with religion more than history. He magnifies the miraculous and is jealous for the name of the Lord, especially as enshrined in the temple. Because of emphasis on resurrection in connection with the martyrdoms, it has been conjectured that the writer was a Pharisee. His work was done probably a little later than *I Maccabees.* Instead of building on *I Maccabees,* the author confesses his dependence upon a five-volume work by a certain Jason of Cyrene, whose narrative he seeks to compress (2:23).

2. *Fictional.* *Tobit* and *Judith* belong here. They were written not so much to give pleasure as to convey the truth that God watches over his people and blesses them in accordance with their faithfulness.

(i) *Tobit.* Tobit was a pious Hebrew who lived in Nineveh in the days of Shalmaneser. Becoming ceremonially unclean by burying the body of a slain Israelite, he slept out of doors, only to be blinded by sparrow dung. On the same day a young woman named Sarah, living at Ecbatana in Media, was blamed by a maidservant for the death of Sarah's seven husbands, each of whom died on the night of the wedding. The reader is informed that the real culprit was Asmodaeus, an evil spirit who was enamored of Sarah and resentful of her marriages. Both Sarah and Tobit, in their respective places, were crying to God, dispirited and ready to die. God heard their prayers and made their paths to cross in a remarkable way.

Recalling that he had left some money in a Median town, Tobit sent his son Tobias to fetch it, accompanied by Azarias. who is actually the angel Raphael. At the edge of the river Tigris, in the act of washing himself, Tobias is attacked by a large fish, which is finally overcome and lugged ashore. He is urged by his companion to save the heart, liver and gall, and is later told that the two former items, when burned, make a smoke that will drive away an evil spirit, whereas the gall is efficacious when used to anoint the eyes of the blind.

The travelers lodge at the home of Raguel, father of Sarah. Along the way, Azarias has sung the praises of the maiden to young Tobit, who proposes marriage. Recalling the words about the fish entrails, the bridegroom prepares incense from these, which serves to drive away the evil spirit. During the course of the wedding festivities, Azarias proceeds to the place where the money was deposited and brings it back. He then accompanies bride and groom to Nineveh, where Tobit and his wife are grief-stricken, thinking that their son must have perished along the way. Sorrow is turned to joy at the reunion, especially when Tobias applies the gall to his father's eyes, resulting in restoration of sight.

His work completed, Azarias reveals his true identity, takes credit for bringing the prayers of the needy parties before God, then ascends. The story closes with a beautiful prayer by Tobit.

The writer's historical standpoint is disclosed by his reference (cast in a prophetic mold) to the Restoration and the rebuilding of the temple, "but not like to the former house" (14:5). A date early in the second century B.C. is most likely.

(ii) *Judith*. This book contains a warning at the very beginning against being taken as history, for Nebuchadnezzar is pictured as king of the Assyrians. The monarch is snubbed by certain kingdoms of the west, and in retaliation sends his general Holofernes to deal with them. In fear, the Jews prepare for invasion. The city of Bethulia stands in the invader's path and is put under siege. Supplies are low and the elders of the city are contemplating surrender when Judith, a beautiful widow, puts them to shame for such a thought, and proceeds to take matters into her own hands. Putting on her finery and taking food for herself and maid, she approaches the enemy lines and asks to be conducted to Holofernes, who is captivated by her beauty. She leads him to think that Israel's God will shortly intervene, but she does not say how or on whose behalf. Nightly she and her maid are passed through the sentry lines that she might have a time of devotion. Then one night, after a feast with Holofernes that leaves him in a drunken stupor, she decapitates him and puts his head in her bag, then slips out for her nightly trip beyond the lines, only to go at once to Bethulia and declare what God has done through her. Nerved for battle, the men of Israel are able to rout the host of the enemy, which is now in confusion without its commander. Throughout the nation there is rejoicing, giving of thanks to God and praise of Judith.

This product of orthodox Judaism is probably to be dated some time in the latter half of the second century B.C., though it may be later.

3. *Sapiential.* The typically Hebrew approach to wisdom was not speculative, differing in this respect from the Greek. Wisdom must work itself out in conduct rather than in vagaries of thought. Hebrew wisdom confessed its dependence upon God rather than human discovery. It is true that one can find passages, even in the canonical Scriptures, where wisdom seems to be based merely on observation of nature and human life, but doubtless the intention was to make this subordinate to divine illumination.

(i) *Ecclesiasticus,* or *The Wisdom of Jesus ben Sirach.* The former title is due to the use of the book for instructional purposes in the early church. The other is more commonly employed today. Sometimes it is called simply *Sirach.* From a time notice given in the prologue it is possible to date the work at about 180 B.C. A Palestinian Jew is indicated as the author (50:27), one who had gained considerable experience through travel.

Wisdom is assigned a divine origin in the very first verse, and within the confines of the first chapter is extolled in a beautiful trilogy: to fear the Lord is the beginning of wisdom (1:14); to fear the Lord is the fullness of wisdom (1:16); and the fear of the Lord is the crown of wisdom (1:18). Wisdom has its seat in the Law of Moses in a special sense (24:23ff.). It is personified at several points.

There is considerable similarity to the Book of Proverbs. Practically all the relationships of life are passed in review and the prudent thing to do is set forth for multifarious situations — friendship, home life, business (borrowing and lending), diligence, thrift, etc. Samples of the writer's skill in the art of gnomic expression are these:

As the going up a sandy way is to the feet of the aged,
So is a wife full of words to a quiet man (25:21).

He that teacheth a fool is as one that glueth a
potsherd together (22:7).

In this book wisdom covers social convention as well as ethical and moral matters. So the reader has a handbook on manners, among other things. A somewhat condescending air toward the common man mars the writing, approaching in this respect the Pharisaic attitude toward the *'am ha-aretz.*

(ii) *The Wisdom of Solomon.* Of a quite different sort, this book is the "Gem of the Apocrypha." The name is due to the fact that the writer assumes the standpoint of Solomon (9:8-9). This, however, cannot be taken seriously in view of the affinities with Greek modes of thought. We have here a product of Alexandrian Judaism that has been variously dated from before 100 B.C. to A.D. 40. The contents divide naturally into two main parts. In chapters 1-9 wisdom receives unbounded praise; in chapter 10-19 a historical review of some leading figures in Israel's early history, followed by a narration of the fortunes of the nation in Egypt and then in the wilderness, is intended to demonstrate at once the folly of idolatry and the blessedness of those who adhere to the Lord. There is a growing tendency among scholars to assign the two parts to different authors, but the case for diversity of authorship is not overwhelming.[30] The purpose of the book may well have been twofold: to renew the faith of Jews in their God and their way of life, and to win pagans to their faith.

(iii) *Pirke Aboth,* or the *Sayings of the Fathers.* Here are collected the wise utterances of many rabbis ranging from pre-Christian times down through the second century A.D. and even later.

4. *Apocalyptical.* This type of literature cannot be understood apart from an appreciation of the historic position and outlook of the writers. It flourished because of the strain placed upon the Jewish people by reason of their long experience of subjection to various foreign powers — from the Persian on down to the Roman occupation. Had God forgotten his people? According to the apocalyptists he had not, but would vindicate both himself and his covenant nation by future de-

---

[30] W. O. E. Oesterley, *An Introduction to the Books of the Apocrypha,* pp. 205-206.

liverance, when all opposition, whether human or angelic, would be swept away.

No doubt the writers of these messages of hope received their inspiration in part from the Hebrew prophets, but their own work differed in certain particulars. Whereas prophecy addressed itself mainly to the needs of its own generation, the apocalypse manifested an almost exclusive interest in the future. H. H. Rowley draws this contrast: "Speaking generally, the prophets foretold the future that should arise out of the present, while the apocalyptists foretold the future that should break into the present."[31] Unlike the prophets, these writers withheld their names, taking instead names made familiar by Israelitish history. Their work could be called deterministic in the sense that they picture the world as having a certain course to run, with a fixed goal. Understandably there is a greater harshness displayed toward the enemies of Israel than in the prophets. The individual comes into prominence to a greater extent, too, especially in connection with resurrection and the rewards of the future life. The apocalypses are totally lacking in ethical teaching. Instead of calling the nation to repentance they stress the distinctive position of Israel as the people of God and the certainty of their future vindication. This type of writing possesses an esoteric character not found in the prophets, as a rule. Coupled with the revelations given by visions concerning the unseen world and the future is an emphasis on sealing and secrecy. These things are withheld from the rank and file of men.

Whether prophecy waned from exhaustion or was terminated by divine decree or was eclipsed by the rise of legalism with its concentration on the Law, its decline undoubtedly paved the way for the rise of apocalyptic.

One should not insist, however, upon a total dissimilarity between prophecy and apocalyptic. At least it appears valid to say that Jesus made use of the forms of apocalyptic and yet spoke in terms that are truly prophetic of the breaking in of God's kingdom upon the order of history with transforming power. Because he linked this teaching with the present manifestation of God's purpose in his own person and work, he was speaking prophetically.[32]

(i) *The Book of Enoch.* This stands foremost among the apocalypses. It is also called *Ethiopic Enoch* to distinguish it from the *Slavonic Enoch* or the *Secrets of Enoch.* This book of over one hundred chapters belongs to the pre-Christian period,

---

[31] *The Relevance of Apocalyptic,* 2nd ed., 1947, p. 35.
[32] See the discussion by G. E. Ladd, "Why Not Prophetic-Apocalyptic?" *JBL,* 76 (1957), pp. 192-200.

probably in its entirety. The name of Enoch is attached to it with considerable propriety, in view of his translation to heaven. Presumably he would be well fitted to set forth the mysteries of the heavenly bodies that bulk rather large in this work. The work, which consists of five books plus introduction and conclusion, opens with visions of future judgment, passes on to an account of the angels who sinned (Gen. 6), narrates the heavenly excursions of Enoch, lays bare the mysteries of heaven and hell and the coming and glory of the Messiah, and outlines the history of the world in the so-called apocalypse of weeks. The most important section is the book of similitudes (chaps. 37-71), in which the Son of man passages occur. So far this portion has not been found among the other fragments of *Enoch* in the Qumran materials.

(ii) *The Apocalypse of Baruch* (not to be confused with the *Book of Baruch*). This is concerned with the fate of Jerusalem at the time of the Babylonian captivity, but also looks forward to the coming of Messiah, holding out the prospect of comfort and blessing in connection with his appearing. This work, divided into seven parts, with the fasts of Baruch coming in between, belongs to the first century A.D. or even later. Some think that the destruction of the temple furnished inspiration for its writing. Many passages show resemblance to the Apocalypse of Ezra.

(iii) *The Assumption of Moses*. This work contains the revelations given through Israel's venerable leader to Joshua prior to his departure. Israel's future is unfolded down into Roman times, with a prediction of the establishment of the messianic kingdom 250 times (1750 years) after Moses' death. Extant copies do not record the actual assumption, indicating that this part has been lost. Judging from the testimony of Origen, the book contained an account of the contest between Michael and Satan over the body of Moses (cf. Jude 9). The work breathes a strong nationalistic spirit and comes from the early part of the first century A.D.

(iv) *Apocalypse of Ezra* (chaps. 3-14 of the apocryphal *II Esdras;* chaps. 1-2, 15-16 are later Christian additions). This writing is of capital importance for the doctrinal development in Judaism. It appears to have been written late in the first century A.D., and reflects the depleted condition of Israel after the destruction of Jerusalem. A note of sorrow and perplexity pervades the writing. Sin, the paucity of the saved, and the justification of the ways of God are major concerns. The writer might well be called the Paulinist of this epoch of Judaism. Eschatology gets its share of attention, including the portrayal of extraordinary signs of the end-time, the reign of Messiah, and final judgment. There are a few Christian interpolations.

5. *General.* Some other writings in the nature of apocalypses and testaments belong here, but they are of minor importance and can be passed by for our purpose. However, several works that are generally classified with the Pseudepigrapha but are not to any great extent apocalyptic deserve to be mentioned.

(i) *Jubilees.* This consists of material supposedly revealed to Moses, covering the interval from the creation to the Exodus in a series of jubilees or forty-nine-year periods. Its other name, the *Little Genesis,* marks it off as acknowledged to be inferior to the canonical history. Jewish theory insisted that God revealed not only the Law to Moses in written form, but an unwritten tradition also, thus affording opportunity to read back later developments into the early history of Israel. So the patriarchs are pictured as devotees of the Law. Great stress is laid on the proper observance of the festivals of the Jewish year as well as the Sabbath. The writer presents his case for a solar calendar in place of the lunar type that was prevalent in Israel. Eschatology is not developed to any great extent except in angelology, but what there is seems to favor the idea that the messianic kingdom was being realized to the extent that the Law was being faithfully kept. Widely divergent dates have been given to this work, from exilic times to the last few decades before the Christian era. It is perhaps best located in the Maccabean period.

(ii) *The Sibylline Oracles.* These differ from other writings in that they belong to a distinct type of literature. In the Graeco-Roman world various women called sibylls gained a reputation for speaking oracles, which were much sought after by nations and individuals. Though the official Roman oracles perished, others were produced in answer to popular demand. Both Jews and Christians saw an opportunity for propaganda by injecting their tenets into writings of this character. Twelve out of the fifteen comprising the collection are now extant. The Jewish elements are chiefly found in Book III and consist in a resumé of history, Israel's included, a portrayal of the dire conditions that will prevail prior to the end, a prophecy of the overthrow of the wicked and the turning of the world to the worship of Jehovah, with accompaniments of peace and prosperity. A figure answering to Messiah is introduced in Book V, lines 414ff.

(iii) *Psalms of Solomon.* Coming from shortly after the middle of the first century B.C., the *Psalms of Solomon* reflect disillusionment with the Hasmonean dynasty and set forth a coming son of David as the Messiah of Israel (Psalm 17 and 18). A typically nationalistic picture of Israel's future glory features these Psalms.

(iv) *Testaments of the Twelve Patriarchs.* These documents consist of the reputed sayings of each of the sons of Jacob to his children shortly before his death, on the analogy of Jacob himself in Genesis 49. Each testament contains a biographical sketch of the patriarch, usually setting forth both his virtues and his vices, then a section of exhortation, and finally predictions concerning his descendants. This production is difficult to classify. In a few cases visions are introduced which may warrant inclusion among the Apocalypses, but the work as a whole is moralistic and prophetic rather than apocalyptic.

There is little agreement as to origin and date. Discovery of fragments of the Testament of Levi as well as of a Testament of Napthtali at Qumran has introduced a new factor into the problem, but these fragments are too inadequate a basis for insisting on Qumran provenance for the Testaments as a whole. R. H. Charles posited a Jewish origin for this literature and accounted for Christian elements on the theory of interpolation. More recently a trend has set in to make the Testaments of Christian origin on the ground that "the Christian elements are so interwoven with the texture of the whole work that they form an integral part of it" (M. de Jonge, who makes the Testaments Christian but regards them as taking over considerable Jewish material and possibly not emerging until late in the second century).[33] F. M. Cross, Jr. asserts, "Those views are correct which insist that the received editions of 1 Enoch and the Testaments of the Twelve Patriarchs came from Jewish-Christian hands which supplemented and reworked (rather than merely interpolated) Essene editions.[34]

6. *Philosophical.* Here no doubt belongs *IV Maccabees,* a treatise dealing with the devout reason and maintaining that human virtues (following here the Stoical analysis) are best developed with the aid of divine revelation as found in the Mosaic Law. The passions of men are intended by God to be controlled. For illustration the writer turns to the material of *II Maccabees,* contrasting the madman Antiochus Epiphanes

[33] "The Testaments of the Twelve Patriarchs and the New Testament" in *Studia Evangelica,* 1959, p. 548.

[34] *The Ancient Library of Qumran,* p. 149.

with the brave endurance of the martyrs. The work belongs somewhere in the first century B.C. Its general outlook concerning wisdom is somewhat similar to the treatises of Philo.

7. *Apologetical.* Though the *Letter of Aristeas* and *III Maccabees* could be classified otherwise, they have in common an evident purpose to exalt Judaism. The former purports to be the work of a Gentile who was a member of the embassy sent by Ptolemy II to Jerusalem to obtain translators of the Hebrew Scriptures into Greek for the royal library. He writes to his brother Philocrates about his trip and eulogizes everything Jewish, including the Septuagint translation, to which he devotes the closing portion of his letter. The *Letter of Aristeas* can no longer be regarded as authentic, since it bears tokens of having been composed at a later time. On the other hand it undoubtedly contains some valuable tradition concerning the origin of the LXX, especially the tacit admission that the real background for the making of the translation was the need of Egyptian Jews for such a work rather than court patronage motivated by literary interest, though this is placed in the foreground. In *III Maccabees* the reader is treated to an account of the attempt of Ptolemy IV to enter the temple at Jerusalem, only to be divinely repulsed and stricken down. After his recovery, the king determined to vent his displeasure on the Jews in his kingdom. After harassing them in various ways, he finally planned their mass extermination under the feet of hundreds of intoxicated elephants. A vision of angels turned the elephants against the king's troops instead, causing him to recognize his error and rescind his order. Reversing his stand completely, he began to favor the Jews, whose position was now secure.

8. *Miscellaneous.* Here may be put for the sake of convenience the remaining books of the Apocrypha, which are brief and of minor importance. The *Book of Baruch* purports to have been written in Babylon by the secretary of Jeremiah. After being read to the exiles there, it was forwarded to Jerusalem. Though quite diverse in its materials and varied in its literary forms, the book deals mainly with the reasons for the captivity and holds out hope for restoration.

The unknown author of the *Epistle of Jeremiah* writes to those who were about to go into Babylonian captivity, warning them that the time will be long and urging them to stand fast against the temptation to idolatry.

One of the additions to Daniel, inserted after 3:23, is the *Prayer of Azariah* (Abednego) and the *Song of the Three Holy*

41

Children. The prayer receives answer in the coming of the angel of the Lord into the fiery furnace, who secures the three against the effects of the flames. The three then mingle their voices in praise. The *History of Susanna* relates the experience of Daniel in rescuing a Jewish woman who was threatened by two lascivious elders. When repulsed by her, they accuse her publicly of infidelity to her husband. Daniel then comes forward to save the woman from death by convicting the two elders of fraudulent testimony. *Bel and the Dragon* deals with Daniel's exposure of idolatry. In the first tale Daniel and king Cyrus are in disagreement over the worship of the god Bel, the king pointing to the god's consumption of offerings as proof of his reality. Daniel convinces him by sprinkling powdery material on the floor of the temple, revealing thereby the footprints of the priests and their families who came by night through a secret entrance to make away with the offerings. Furious over this revelation, the king orders the demolition of the idol and the death of the priestly establishment. In the second story Daniel's debate with the king concerns a dragon that was venerated as a god. Daniel claims that he is able to kill the dragon, thus destroying the myth of his deity. This he accomplishes by preparing a pitchy substance and throwing it into his jaws, whereupon the dragon bursts asunder. These two assaults on the popular worship lead to a demand for vengeance on Daniel, so he is thrown into the den of lions, where he is miraculously fed and also preserved for days from the ferocity of these beasts, leading to the royal admission of Daniel's God as incomparable.

The additions to the Book of Esther, six in number, seem to have served the double purpose of satisfying curiosity by giving details where the canonical text is merely summary in nature, and also by providing a more definitely religious tone to the book by naming God explicitly.

In the *Prayer of Manasseh,* purporting to be a penitent plea for help on the part of the erstwhile king of Judah, a prisoner in Babylon, the last of the Apocrypha is accounted for.

Many works from the intertestamental period have not been included here (the list keeps growing with fresh discoveries), but enough have been described to give a cross-section of the literature as a whole.

INFLUENCE ON THE NEW TESTAMENT

The intertestamental era has been called "a period unrivalled for religious wavering and confusion." We should not expect, then, that the literature that emanated from it can provide a bridge in all respects between the teaching of the Old Testament and that of the New. In the case of the writings produced under hellenic influence, the nature and destiny of man are viewed quite differently than in the Hebrew Scriptures. The body is depreciated and no place is found for a physical resurrection. In Palestine the course of political events left its mark on the literature, particularly in the area of the messianic hope. When confidence in human leaders waned and foreign oppression became grievous, the tendency was to look for a transcendent breaking into history such as predominates in the apocalypses. Foreign influences tending to the secularizing of life had their effect, too, in the stiffening of resistance through applying the Law more rigorously. This brought on an era of legalism that is attested in the Gospels and that had some effect also on the early church in connection with the Judaizing controversy. The merit of almsgiving, which formed a substantial element of Pharisaic righteousness, was enunciated as early as *Tobit.* "Alms doth deliver from death, and it shall purge away all sin" (12: 9). *Judith* reflects the importance of ceremonial correctness and ritual purity, with emphasis on fasting and prayers, such as one encounters in the Pharisaism of the Gospels.

Formal acknowledgment of their debt to the intertestamental literature by New Testament writers is rare. Jude 14-15 is an example of quotation from a non-canonical source (*Enoch* 1:9). Since the New Testament contains a few instances of quotations from pagan writings (Acts 17:28; I Cor. 15:33; Titus 1:12), it is not surprising that a book like *Enoch,* which had attained a semi-sacred status in Christian circles, should be utilized in this fashion. There is, however, no proof that the writer considered *Enoch* on a par with Scripture. Jude 9 may depend on *The Assumption of Moses,* though the document as we have it, being fragmentary, does not contain the episode referred to.

The writer of the Epistle to the Hebrews appears to have drawn upon extra-biblical material in his recital of the exploits of men and women of faith. Some of his allusions in 11:34-35 tally with reports in *II Maccabees* 6:18-7:42 concerning the martyr death of Eleazar the aged scribe and that of the mother and her seven sons. The tradition of the death of the prophet Isaiah, sawn asunder at the order of Manasseh (*Martyrdom of Isaiah* 5:1), may well be in mind at verse 37. Jannes and Jambres (II Tim. 3:8) do not appear by name in the Old

43

Testament but were probably well-known from other ancient writings (cf. *Damascus Document* 7:19).

One of the clearest instances of dependence is Paul's use of material from the *Wisdom of Solomon* 12-14 for his argument in the first chapter of Romans. The witness to God in the creation, and the sin of idolatry and its consequences in the moral life of men are spelled out in much the same language. The apostle's words in Romans 1:32 seem reminiscent of the statement in the *Testament of Asher* 6:2. In the *Testament of Judah* we read that the drunkard is led to glory in his shame (14:8), recalling Philippians 3:19. Several verbal parallels may be detected between *Sirach* (*Wisdom* also) and the Epistle of James, and to a lesser extent between *Sirach* and the Petrine Epistles. These are largely gnomic in character. It was only natural that the cultural and religious heritage of early Christian writers should show itself in their works.[35] Perhaps the greatest influence along this line is in the language employed in the apocalyptic portions of the New Testament. For example, the description of a voice as the voice of many waters occurs in the *Apocalypse of Ezra* 6:17 and Revelation 1:15, 14:2. The bride appearing as a city is mentioned in the *Apocalypse of Ezra* 7:26 and in Revelation 22:1. These instances are by no means solitary.

It should be added that verbal coincidences do not necessarily prove literary dependence. The possibility always exists that some things had become so much a part of common religious terminology that the writer was not thinking of any particular source as he made use of a certain term or phrase. Furthermore, items that appear in the Old Testament, in the Apocryphal literature, and in the New Testament may owe their appearance in the New Testament to their use in the Old rather than to the intermediate source. So, for example, the messianic figure is designated in the book of *Enoch* under such titles as the Anointed, the Elect One, the Righteous One, and the Son of Man. But all of these are derived ultimately from the Old Testament.

In certain respects the New Testament reflects the developments of the intertestamental period in a rather positive way. The general world view is sharply dualistic, and this in a twofold sense. In addition to the contrast between the powers of light and darkness, or God and the devil, is the antithesis between the

[35] W. Fairweather, "Development of Doctrine in the Apocryphal Period," *HDB*, Extra Volume, p. 295.

present age and the age to come. The latter, which is a staple element of the teaching of Jesus and Paul, is not found in the Old Testament, although the seeds of it may be detected in the prophetic outlook.

Not a great deal is said in the intertestamental literature about sin, yet the doctrine is advanced in two respects. In the *Apocalypse of Ezra* there is a grappling with the problem of original sin. The effect of Adam's trangression is seen as humanity-wide (3:21; 7:118). One senses a kinship with Pauline teaching in Romans 5:12-21. The work is late enough to reflect Christian teaching, but it is doubtful that a Jewish writer would make conscious use of Christian positions. In several places a description of the working of sin in human life is treated under the doctrine of the good and evil impulse.[36] Paul's description in Romans 7 has a close affinity to this typical Jewish analysis.

Salvation is generally associated with fidelity to the Law, but the writer of the *Apocalypse of Ezra* is pessimistic about the power of the Law to save, although he holds it in the highest honor (9:36-37). It must be granted that in the realm of redemption the New Testament does not depend on the Apocrypha but builds solidly on the Old Testament.

In the Apocryphal literature the proliferation in angelology is a marked feature. Seven archangels surround the throne of God (*Tobit* 12:15). Six of them are indicated by name in various places, but the New Testament names only one. The organization of angels and their association with the forces of nature are features of New Testament teaching, but on a much more restrained basis than in the literature we are considering. Even more noticeable is the absence of vagaries about the heavenly bodies and other natural phenomena that clutter the apocalypses.

The final judgment is a standard item in the apocalyptic writings, but there is considerable wavering as to the exact place that it occupies in the scheme of the future, whether before or after the messianic kingdom. The kingdom itself does not have uniform treatment. With the growth of the transcendental emphasis there came a shifting of expectation away from an earthly kingdom to one which is heavenly. The latter became the more common presentation. This left the problem of the earthly, nationalistic promises to Israel to be resolved. It is quite possible that the most finished form of apocalyptic teach-

---

[36] *Testament of Asher* 1:3-9 is the earliest passage.

ing represents something of an amalgam — an earthly messianic kingdom of a temporary character, to be followed by the eternal state.[37] This is the pattern in the Apocalypse of John.

It would be wholly unnatural for the writers of the New Testament to do their work in a vacuum, ignoring the religious ideas that had been taking shape among their own people. Yet the practical absence of direct quotation from the inter-testamental literature and the exclusion of apocalyptic fantasies reveal a selectivity that is impressive and may safely be viewed as providential. The contribution of the later literature is there as a factor, but it is distinctly subordinate to the Old Testament influence.

BIBLIOGRAPHY

Charles, R. H., (ed.), *The Apocrypha and Pseudepigrapha of the Old Testament,* 2 vols. Oxford: Clarendon Press, 1913.

Fairweather, W., "Development of Doctrine in the Apocryphal Period," *HDB,* Extra Volume. Edinburgh: T. & T. Clark, 1904, pp. 272-308.

Metzger, B. M., *An Introduction to the Apocrypha.* New York: Oxford University Press, 1957.

Pfeiffer, R. H., *History of New Testament Times.* New York: Harper & Brothers, 1949.

Rowley, H. H., *The Relevance of Apocalyptic.* London: Lutterworth Press, 1944.

Russell, D. S., *The Method and Message of Jewish Apocalyptic.* Philadelphia: The Westminster Press, 1964.

Stanton, V. H., *The Jewish and the Christian Messiah.* Edinburgh: T. & T. Clark, 1886.

Torrey, C. C., *The Apocryphal Literature.* New Haven: Yale Press, 1945.

[37] See Enoch 91:12-17.

PART II

THE LANGUAGE
OF THE NEW TESTAMENT

Chapter Two

THE LANGUAGE OF THE NEW TESTAMENT

FAR FROM BEING A MERE COLLECTION OF BOOKS, THE BIBLE
possesses a unity that makes it possible for the reader to move
with comparative ease from Malachi to Matthew. This is
true despite the outward difference occasioned by the altered
historical situation and the changed form that revelation takes,
perhaps best expressed by the sweeping contrasts enunciated in
the opening words of the Epistle to the Hebrews.

Both divine and human factors enter into this spiritual unity,
the fact that God is revealing himself and that he is acting
through his covenant people throughout. Salvation is of the
Jews. Of all the writers of the New Testament Luke alone was
a Gentile. This very circumstance, however, poses a problem,
for the Jews had largely ceased to use their native Hebrew
tongue during the period of the Exile, turning instead to the
widely current Aramaic, a language closely related to the He-

brew. A New Testament produced in Aramaic was a possibility linguistically, but even so Aramaic was not ideally equipped for the conveyance of the message of the completed revelation of God, which called for niceties of distinction hardly necessary for the oracular flow of the prophet or the writing of a history, but requisite for the closely knit argumentation of an apostle. An Aramaic New Testament would have comparatively few readers outside the nation Israel. On the other hand, if the message of the Christian faith could be sent forth in the Greek tongue, which had become the truly international language of the day, the Word could penetrate almost anywhere in the Graeco-Roman world.

Two facts, then, are clear. God evidently purposed to use his own people Israel as the instruments for communicating Christianity to the world, yet their own language was not a suitable medium for the task. He could not afford to lose the Hebraic medium, representing as it did all the background and spiritual experience of centuries of cultivation. In his providential overruling he gave to the devout Hebrew heart a Greek tongue in order to make itself intelligible to the world. It is necessary to outline the historical development that made this achievement possible.

THE RISE OF THE KOINE

Greek was in use hundreds of years before the time of Christ and has continued down to our own day as a living language. The beginnings of literature may be placed roughly about 800 B.C. or somewhat earlier in the works of Homer and Hesiod. By the time the classical period proper had set in, two factors had played a leading part in molding the language. One was the periodic incursion onto Greek soil of Indo-European people, whose coming brought modifications in the native speech of the various localities. Due to the broken character of the terrain of the Grecian peninsula, once these linguistic alterations became established, they tended to perpetuate themselves. In this way the various dialects came into being. While a literature grew up in only three or four of these, the spoken dialects were many.[1] Of the literary dialects, namely, Doric, Aeolic, and Ionic, the latter achieved prominence beyond the others. Attic, a branch of the Ionic, was the language of Athens, the city-state that fostered a brilliant galaxy of writers in various fields. Consequently, to speak of classical Greek is virtually to speak

---

[1] C.D. Buck, *The Greek Dialects,* pp. 3-9.

of Attic. This type of Greek was not confined to Athens or Attica but spread with the colonizing activity of the Athenians across the Aegean and beyond. It is the largest single element behind the Greek of the New Testament.[2] Some distinctively Ionic words appear there too, as well as Doric forms.[3] Aeolic influence is minimal.

In the fourth century B.C. the Grecian city-states were conquered by Philip of Macedon. When his son Alexander the Great ventured beyond Hellas for his wide-ranging conquest of the Orient, he recruited men for his army from all parts of Greece. Their close association in the ranks played a vital role in the emergence of a new type of Greek, which had already begun to take shape because of increasing contact between the various city-states. Those elements of speech that were most widely current already and those that were most readily adapted from the various dialects tended to survive, whereas the less useful were dropped. In a remarkably short time a new Greek medium was forged out, known today as *koine* (its full description is ἡ κοινὴ διάλεκτος). The word means "common." This Greek was indeed the language of the common people and the common means of communication in the hellenistic age (ca. 300 B.C. to ca. A.D. 500).

Wherever the army of Alexander went, this language went. Since the conquered peoples of Asia represented diverse national and linguistic units, there was a definite need for a common medium of communication, which helped the spread of Greek in the Levant. The colonists made the hold of Greek permanent. Only after the passage of several centuries, in the sixth century A.D., did the *koine* give way to its successor, the Greek of the Byzantine period, which in turn yielded to the advent of modern Greek in the fifteenth century.

It must not be assumed, however, that everything written in Greek during the hellenistic period was composed in *koine*. Some authors looked upon the current language as a sad deterioration from the product of the golden age of letters, and made a conscious effort to imitate classical models in their own work. For this reason a portion of the literature in the *koine* period is not properly *koine*. Even among those who avoided this anachronism there were writers who inclined more to the Attic style than to

---

[2] The noting of this influence is one of the major objectives of the Blass-Debrunner Grammar.

[3] Arndt and Gingrich, *A Greek-English Lexicon of the New Testament*, pp. xi-xxv.

the vernacular of their own time. Their work is called literary *koine*.

The common Greek speech fell somewhat short of becoming universal in the Graeco-Roman world, though it had a wide dissemination. In the West it had to compete with Latin, and did remarkably well, invading the cultural life of Rome and holding its place throughout the west until about A.D. 200. Then Christian literature in Latin began to appear. But in the first century Paul found Greek his natural medium in writing to the church at Rome. We have testimony from the Book of Acts (14:11) that native languages maintained their sway in the highland regions of the hinterland of Asia Minor.

Palestine was multilingual in the time of Christ. Aramaic was doubtless the language of the common people. That Jesus spoke it is beyond all doubt from the Gospel records. Hebrew persisted in some circles, particularly under rabbinic influence. From Jesus' reading of the Scriptures in the synagogue it appears that he was familiar with this tongue also. Several references to Hebrew occur in the New Testament (John 5:2; 20:16; Acts 22:2, etc.). A persistent tradition in the early church insists that Matthew was written in Hebrew. Scholars have inclined to the view that these are really references to Aramaic, on the ground that the retention of the more honorable term was a matter of national pride or else that a loose use of terms was permissible where there was no special point in distinguishing Aramaic from Hebrew but only the necessity of indicating what was Semitic as opposed to Greek. A strong case can be made for the position that these allusions to Hebrew were intended literally,[4] in which case the prevalence of Hebrew alongside Aramaic must be assumed.

Greek influence was strong in Galilee, where contact with the hellenic world was closer than was the case in Judea. That Christ and the apostles were able to speak Greek is a practical certainty. Even in Jerusalem Greek-speaking Jews gravitated to a synagogue of their own (Acts 6:9). The superscription on the cross included Greek.

Latin was the language of the Roman occupation forces in Palestine, but few Jews presumably were versed in it. Since many Romans knew Greek, communication could be achieved under ordinary circumstances by this means.

---

[4] J. M. Grintz, "Hebrew as the Spoken and Written Language in the Last Days of the Second Temple," *JBL*, 79 (1960), pp. 32-47.

SOURCES FOR THE KOINE

One of the first pagan writers was Polybius (second century B.C.). Others, such as Epictetus and Plutarch, belong to the first two centuries A.D. Of the Jewish writers Philo and Josephus are of special importance (first century A.D.). Since these men made use of the literary *koine,* their writings do not accurately reflect the language of everyday life.

Biblical writings, broadly considered, include the Septuagint, the New Testament, and the Greek Fathers of the early Christian centuries.

The nonliterary papyri began to be seriously noticed toward the close of the nineteenth century. These documents had nothing to do with literature in the technical sense, but were in the nature of business or personal notes, some of them written with evident difficulty by people of limited education. Here was the Greek of the home and the market place, brought to light in the modern era after lying unnoticed for nearly two thousand years in the preserving dryness of the Egyptian sands. Adolph Deissmann won the honor of first drawing attention to the similarity between the vocabulary of these nonliterary papyri and that of the New Testament.[5] Others prominent in this research were Grenfell and Hunt and George Milligan. J. H. Moulton combined with Milligan to produce *The Vocabulary of the Greek Testament,* illustrating many New Testament terms from the papyri and other nonliterary sources.

From these papyri has come the demonstration that the New Testament was written in the popular language of the day. Formerly it had been difficult to classify, for it did not conform closely to the Greek that was written in the same general period, viz., the literary Greek of the hellenistic era. Its Semitized character was explained by the Hebraic heritage of the writers and their familiarity with the Septuagint, and the net result was labelled biblical or Holy Ghost Greek. Those who argued from the side of classical Greek tried to bring the New Testament into line with this earlier stage of the language, but of course had little success. The puzzle was solved with the discovery that the gospel had been enshrined in the humble terminology of daily life, in large part, affording a parallel to the condescension in-

---

[5] See his *Bible Studies* (1901) and his *Light from the Ancient East* (1910). The former work deals with lexicography; the latter is wider in its scope. Both make use of the testimony of ostraca and inscriptions as well as papyri.

volved in the incarnation. The Scriptures have become more human without ceasing to be divine.

Indicative of the great change involved in the new outlook is the fact that whereas Thayer's lexicon contained a list of 767 New Testament words that he isolated as biblical Greek, Deissmann was able to reduce the list to 50 by finding the others in the papyri. This figure has since been further reduced. Presumably this classification will not vanish entirely, because the New Testament contains a few terms that seem to have been coined by the writers.

In spite of the demonstration that the New Testament was written in *koine,* one ought not to assume that there is no essential difference between it and the language of the nonliterary papyri. The New Testament, by and large, has superior Greek, occasioned in part by the ability of its writers to produce a more polished result, in part by the more elevated nature of the themes that engrossed them, and in part by their religious and cultural heritage. Arthur Darby Nock has said, "Any man who knows his classical Greek authors and reads the New Testament and then looks into the papyri is astonished at the similarities which he finds. Any man who knows the papyri first and then turns to Paul is astonished at the differences. There has been much exaggeration of the *koine* element in the New Testament."[6] There are indeed a considerable number of words for which parallels are lacking in the papyri but which are present in Greek authors.[7]

The value of the nonliterary papyri for New Testament study is limited because of the virtual absence of theological terminology. Yet the help in other respects must be gratefully acknowledged. The New Testament emerges as a document which could speak to the ordinary man in contemporary terms, but terms which required help from the Old Testament and from the Christ-event to make it fully intelligible.

An important factor setting the Greek of the New Testament somewhat apart from the popular language is the Semitic element in it. A Semitism is any item of syntax, vocabulary or linguistic influence of a more subtle sort in the Greek text that can be traced to Hebrew or Aramaic origin.[8] For example,

[6] *JBL,* 52 (1933), p. 138.

[7] See examples cited by E. K. Simpson, *Words Worth Weighing in the Greek New Testament,* pp. 13-15. The same author concludes that "a large proportion of the New Testament vocabulary may be classed as the *common property* of literary Hellenistic and popular parlance" (p. 15).

[8] See W. F. Howard's discussion in J. H. Moulton's *Grammar of New Testament Greek,* Vol. II (Appendix), pp. 412-485; also C.F.D. Moule, *An Idiom Book of New Testament Greek,* pp. 171-91.

the Hebrew style of writing was predominantly paratactic, a series of independent clauses strung together by co-ordinating conjunctions. Normal Greek style is hypotactic, the main clause having one or more dependent clauses suspended on it, which often make use of the participial construction. Occasionally Semitic words are transliterated into Greek, as in the case of Abba and Hosanna. A more delicate instance of Semitic influence is seen in Paul's expression, "weight of glory" (II Cor. 4:17), which reflects the circumstance that in Hebrew the common word for glory comes from a root meaning "to be heavy."

Some items that appear to be Semitisms may nevertheless have become standard Greek usage because Egypt, the source of the nonliterary papyri, was also the home of the Septuagint. It is possible that some Semitic expressions had become absorbed into the Greek of this area and were no longer consciously treated as foreign elements, just as certain Latin, French, and German expressions have been absorbed into English (e.g. ex officio, elite, ersatz).

Latinisms are more sparsely represented in the New Testament writings — about 30 in all. Examples are denarius, centurion, colony, legion. In addition there is a sprinkling of words from other sources (e.g., Paradise, from the Persian).

SOME CHARACTERISTICS OF THE KOINE

The student of historical Greek grammar is able to detect certain changes in the structure of the language that mark the hellenistic period as compared with the classical era. The dual number is gone, so that only singular and plural numbers remain. Adjectives in the superlative form are not numerous, comparative forms being substituted, understood in a superlative sense. Use of the optative is sharply curtailed (the NT has only a few dozen examples). Some changes in spelling appear. There is a noticeable fondness for piling up prepositions in compound forms in the effort to increase the effectiveness of words. Diminutives are more common. The periphrastic construction of the verb is more widely employed, as is the conjunction ἵνα, which is no longer confined to the indication of purpose. The door is opened to more new words from various sources, and vernacular terms attain a higher status than they formerly enjoyed. Old words get new meanings. Most striking of all is the breaking down of the Attic precision in sentence structure, opening the way to greater variety and simplicity.[9]

---

[9] For a more complete account, see Nigel Turner's discussion in Moulton's *Grammar of New Testament Greek*, Vol. III, pp. 2-4.

THE NEW TESTAMENT WRITERS

Only a few observations will be attempted at this point. Though all employ the *koine,* the New Testament writers do not stand on an equal plane in the quality of their Greek. Luke, the writer of the Epistle to the Hebrews, and Paul (at times) show distinct leanings toward a more literary standard than their fellows. Peter (in his First Epistle) and James exhibit considerable elegance. The rest vary from good idiomatic expression down to somewhat rough style and irregular constructions, some of which, at least, may be intentional (e.g., the use of ἀπό in Rev. 1:4; cf. 1:5).

THE INFLUENCE OF THE SEPTUAGINT

Semitic influence on the New Testament, as noted above, occurs in the area of syntax, where it is readily detectable in such constructions as "And it came to pass" (Luke 2:1, 15) and "They feared a great fear" (Mark 4:41). Equally important is the influence of the LXX, often doubtless unrealized by the writers themselves, on their thought patterns and phraseology. Even more important is the impact of the LXX in stamping Hebraic concepts on Greek terms so that the theological vocabulary is frequently enriched. New Testament writers inherited this legacy.

One example occurs in connection with the word *truth.* In classical Greek the term basically connotes what is evident, what is real. The Hebrew term lays emphasis on what is not only substantial but also dependable. In the ultimate sense the guarantee of truth lies in God who is faithful. In both traditions truth occurs quite naturally as the opposite of falsehood or error. But in John 14:6 and Ephesians 4:21, for example, the thought passes beyond reality and even genuineness to the concept of a quality upon which one can build his life for time and eternity. The proper understanding of truth in such passages must look to the Hebraic conception for the key.

Glory (δόξα) is another case in point. Its two most prevalent meanings in classical Greek are "opinion" and "reputation." In the LXX the former meaning drops away, whereas the second is retained. Since the dominant Hebrew term for reputation, honor, etc. was also used for the glory of God in terms of his luminous theophanies, δόξα, when employed by the translators in such instances, acquired a sense it did not possess in classical Greek. The influence of this new development is discernible in the New Testament, where glory in the sense of light-manifestation is the foil for the revelation of the uniqueness and perfection of Jesus Christ (Luke 9:32; II Cor. 4:6; John 1:14).

56

Again, ὁμολογέω in classical usage means basically "to agree to" or "to agree with." In the LXX it took on new meanings such as "to confess" and "to give thanks," "to praise." These latter, as well as the classical Greek meaning, are carried over into the New Testament.

The tracing of the usage of Greek words with theological significance from their classical setting through the LXX into the New Testament (not neglecting secular sources of the hellenistic period) is the method pursued in the multi-volume *Theologisches Wörterbuch zum Neuen Testament,* edited successively by Gerhard Kittel and Gerhard Friedrich.[10] Almost universally the value of this work has been cordially recognized. To be sure, it has had its critics, notably James Barr, who finds too much dependence on etymology, some unwarranted intermingling of philosophical-theological judgments with those which are linguistic, too much emphasis on words in isolation rather than consideration of the demands of context, as well as too great a readiness to move from word to concept and to put Hebrew and Greek concepts in contrast to one another.[11] These and other objections point out dangers for those who work in the biblical languages as the basis for exegesis and biblical theology, but it is doubtful that Barr's strictures can be said to invalidate the Kittel method or render nugatory the solid results achieved by its use.

QUOTATIONS FROM THE OLD TESTAMENT IN THE NEW

Here the influence of the LXX is readily discernible also, since the wording of the Greek text is usually followed more or less closely by the New Testament writers. Even Matthew and Paul, who turn to the Hebrew when it suits their purpose, usually are content to draw on the Greek text.

Comparison of the quotations in their New Testament form with the Hebrew and Greek texts as found in the Old Testament discloses rather frequent variations from these texts as we now have them. This should not be regarded as strange in view of the following considerations. (1) The text of the LXX was in a somewhat fluid state in New Testament times. Likewise, the Hebrew text had not yet been officially established, a development which occurred in the following century (Massoretic text). Early Rabbinic quotations sometimes disclose variation from the stand-

[10] Eng. tr., *Theological Dictionary of the New Testament,* by G. W. Bromiley.
[11] *The Semantics of Biblical Language.*

ardized text which has come down to us. (2) Some writers, especially Matthew and Paul, may have been influenced by the methodology underlying the Aramaic Targums. For the most part these translations of the Hebrew Old Testament have a tendency to paraphrase and interpret rather than to render literally. (3) Verbatim quotation was not expected in antiquity, a situation which was altered by the invention of printing. Writers often depended on memory. The important thing was faithful reproduction of the sense. (4) The dawn of the age of fulfilment brought in by Christ understandably affected the form in which some Old Testament passages were cited. A passage inevitably meant something more, something different, when seen in the light of Christ and the gospel. An example is Paul's use of Habakkuk 2:4 in Romans 1:17.

As to the use made of quotations, they are adduced in connection with the fulfilment of prophecy (Matt. 2:6), in confirmation of theological propositions (Gal. 3:10-11), or more loosely as illustrative parallels (Matt. 12:40). Sometimes the link between two passages seems rather slender (I Cor. 14:21). This very fact reveals an eagerness to cite Scripture whenever possible and testifies to the veneration in which it was held.

Barnabas Lindars (*New Testament Apologetic,* 1961) advances the theory that in the main quotations were originally used for apologetic purposes, especially to meet the objections of unbelieving Jews, and that with changing situations the same text was sometimes given a new application. This is a helpful approach, but it requires careful handling.[12]

BIBLIOGRAPHY

Arndt and Gingrich, *A Greek-English Lexicon of the New Testament and Other Early Christian Literature.* Chicago: The University of Chicago Press, 1957, pp. ix-xxv.

Blass-Debrunner, *A Greek Grammar of the New Testament and Other Early Christian Literature.* Chicago: The University of Chicago Press, 1961.

Clines, David J. A., "The Language of the New Testament" in *A New Testament Commentary,* edited by G. C. D. Howley, F. F. Bruce, and H. L. Ellison. Grand Rapids: Zondervan Publishing House, 1969, pp. 30-36.

Dodd, C. H., *The Bible and the Greeks.* London: Hodder & Stoughton, 1935.

---

[12] R. H. Gundry, *The Use of the Old Testament in Matthew's Gospel,* pp. 159-163.

Johnston, George, "The Language of the New Testament" in *A Companion to the Bible,* edited by H. H. Rowley. Edinburgh: T. & T. Clark, 1963, pp. 19-26.

Kennedy, H. A. A., *Sources of New Testament Greek.* Edinburgh: T. & T. Clark, 1895.

Lieberman, Saul, *Greek in Jewish Palestine.* New York: The Jewish Theological Seminary of America, 1942.

Metzger, B. M., "The Language of the New Testament," *The Interpreter's Bible.* New York: Abingdon-Cokesbury Press, 1951, Vol. 7, pp. 43-59.

Moulton, J. H., *Grammar of New Testament Greek.* Edinburgh: T. & T. Clark, 1906, esp. chaps. I and II.

Robertson, A. T., *A Grammar of the Greek New Testament in the Light of Historical Research.* 4th ed., New York: Doran, 1923, pp. 3-139.

Sevenster, J. N., *Do You Know Greek?* Leiden: E. J. Brill, 1968.

Simpson, E. K., *Words Worth Weighing.* London: The Tyndale Press, 1946.

Turner, Nigel, in Moulton's *Grammar of New Testament Greek,* Vol. III, Edinburgh: T. & T. Clark, 1963, pp. 1-9.

——————————, "The Language of the New Testament" in *Peake's Commentary on the Bible,* ed. by Matthew Black and H. H. Rowley. London: Thomas Nelson and Sons, 1962, pp. 659-662.

——————————, *Grammatical Insights into the New Testament.* Edinburgh: T. & T. Clark, 1965.

PART III

THE TEXTUAL CRITICISM
OF THE NEW TESTAMENT

Chapter Three

THE TEXTUAL CRITICISM OF THE NEW TESTAMENT

IN ORDER TO EXEGETE THE TEXT, IT IS NECESSARY TO KNOW something about the science of textual criticism, for frequently a choice must be made between competing readings before the task of exegesis can be undertaken.

Textual Criticism has sometimes been known as Lower Criticism to distinguish it from Higher Criticism, which attempts a critical evaluation of the text in terms of authorship, date, purpose, etc., of the various books that compose the New Testament. If the term Lower Criticism is employed, it should be understood to be not a designation of something inferior but rather of something basic to the other approach.

The ultimate purpose of this discipline is to discover what the writers of the New Testament actually wrote.

THE MATERIALS

The text of the New Testament exists in three forms, so far as the ancient period is concerned: Greek manuscripts recording a part or the whole of the New Testament; versions, or translations of the Greek text into other languages (when this is done directly from the Greek the result is called an immediate version; when the translation is made from a source that is itself a translation from the Greek the result is called a mediate version); patristic citations, or quotations of portions of the New Testament text by the early Fathers of the church as preserved in their writings. These are in Greek or Latin for the most part.

Editors of the Greek New Testament in modern times often include with the text a *critical apparatus,* which is designed to place before the student the more important variant readings that occur in ancient sources. The evidence bearing on these variants is listed in the order given above: manuscripts, versions, patristic citations.

The Greek manuscripts, whether of a portion or of the whole of the New Testament, total nearly 5300. Of these, 267 or more are called uncial manuscripts. These are written in capital letters. In addition, there are more than 2768 minuscule manuscripts, written in small letters more or less joined together in the flowing style of ordinary handwriting. Over 2146 Greek lectionaries are in existence also. These contain groupings of portions of the New Testament for appropriate Scripture lessons for church worship. They are being given more consideration for textual study than they were a few years ago. Finally, there are more than 81 papyri containing portions of the New Testament text. This fact calls for a brief discussion of the materials used for writing in ancient times.

Writing materials. In New Testament times, and for many years before, papyrus was employed throughout the Mediterranean world. It was made by taking the pith of the papyrus plant, which grew abundantly in the lower waters of the Nile, cutting it into strips, laying these horizontally and vertically, and fusing them by glue and pressure into a sheet that approximated our typewriter paper in size. These sheets were then glued together to make a roll. In literary productions the writing was in two, three or four columns. The writing was done on the side where the fibers ran horizontally (known as the *recto).* Occasionally the writing was continued on the back side (*verso;* see Revelation 5:1).

Although some papyrus rolls have been found that are longer, the standard size for convenience was no greater than about 35 feet in length. The longer books of the New Testament approximated this limit, in all likelihood.

At about the close of the apostolic age, the practice began of quiring sheets of papyrus, making in effect a book. This is known as the *codex.*

In New Testament times other materials besides papyrus were sometimes employed in writing. Leather was used for the Qumran Scrolls. Paul mentions certain parchments 'of which he had need (II Tim. 4:12). By the fourth century parchment or vellum had begun to supplant papyrus. Made from the skins of animals, it was prepared by washing and scraping, rubbing and dressing, until a smooth surface was achieved. This substance was more durable than papyrus. The leading manuscripts of the New Testament are of vellum.

These ancient manuscripts were hard to read, as they had no break between words. Everything was run together. Accents were seldom employed. Where these occur they are usually observed to have been inserted by later hands. Little was done, then, to serve the convenience of the reader. Space was precious.

Method of enumeration of MSS. Uncial MSS are designated by Roman letters, such as B; Greek letters, such as Ψ; Hebrew letters, such as א; or by arabic numbers with a zero prefixed, such as 0128.

Arabic numbers designate minuscule MSS, such as 63. Lectionaries are indicated by arabic numbers, followed by Evl in a superior position in the case of a lectionary of the Gospels, or by Apost in a superior position to indicate a lectionary composed of materials from the rest of the New Testament, or by the letter "l" followed by an arabic number. Papyri are indicated by arabic numbers preceded by a capital P, with the figure in a superior position.

One should not confuse MSS designated by the same letter; for example, D is a MS of the Gospels, but D of the Pauline Epistles is a different document, usually designated as D_2.

LEADING MSS OF THE GREEK NEW TESTAMENT

1. *Codex Vaticanus* (B). Generally conceded to be the most important of all, this document is in the Vatican Library at Rome. It dates from the fourth century. This was a crucial period, for several reasons: persecution had ceased and copies of the Scripture were now being multiplied. Constantine ordered 50 copies for the churches in Constantinople alone. Vellum was now in more common use than papyrus for such purposes (B is a vellum MS). The use of the codex was now standard.

MS B is not complete. Hebrews is lacking from 9:14 to

65

the end. Other omissions are the Pastoral Epistles, Philemon, and the Apocalypse. This document contains the Old Testament in Greek as well as the New Testament.

The writing is in three columns. The MS bears evidence of the work of the usual proofreader in addition to the copyist himself, and there is one more corrector of a later date, whose handwriting differs from that of the others.

2. *Codex Sinaiticus* (א). This document gets its name from the place of its discovery, Mount Sinai, in the monastery of St. Catherine. Tischendorf made contact with this MS on his second trip to this spot, in 1844. In 1859 he had a chance to inspect the whole MS, but was prevented from taking it with him for further study. Permission was finally granted for him to borrow the document, however, and with help it was copied at Cairo. For a consideration the Russian government procured the MS, which was in turn acquired by the British government and is now in the British Museum. Tischendorf dated the MS at A.D. 331. Several scribes, in addition to the corrector, have left their mark on the document.

Aleph has the so-called Eusebian Canons. These were tables devised by Eusebius, who depended on the work of Ammonius before him, and they were designed to assist the reader in locating parallel passages. Since B lacks these, it has been judged to be a bit earlier than Aleph. Some have theorized that both these MSS were among the 50 prepared by order of Constantine.

3. *Codex Alexandrinus* (A). This is lodged in the British Museum. It belongs to the fifth century and is fairly complete. It is especially helpful in the Apocalypse, where good MS witnesses are rather scanty.

4. *Codex Ephraemi Rescriptus* (C). This belongs to the fifth century and is now located in Paris. It is a palimpsest, the original text of Scripture having been erased to make room for the sermons of Ephraem the Syrian. Chemicals have been used to bring out the underlying writing, but it is not always legible. A new edition of the MS is being prepared by R. W. Lyon.

5. *Codex Bezae* (D). This belongs either to the fifth or sixth century. Its present home is Cambridge, England. Covering the Gospels and Acts, it is a bilingual MS with the Greek on the left and the Latin on the right.

6. *Washington Codex* (W). This gets its name from its location in Washington, D.C. It is sometimes called the Freer MS

after the man who purchased it in Egypt. A photographic facsimile was made by H. A. Sanders and published in 1912. The MS dates from the fourth or fifth century. It contains the Gospels, and is of special interest because of an addition to the text of Mark 16:14 (consult the Moffatt translation for this material).

7. *The Chester Beatty Papyri.* These were secured by Mr. Beatty in Egypt in 1931. The New Testament portions are known as P45 (Gospels), P46 (Epistles), and P47 (Revelation). Their special importance lies in the fact that they belong to the third century, whereas the leading uncials come from the following century. They are in codex form rather than in rolls.

8. *Other papyri discoveries.* P52 is a fragment of the Fourth Gospel (18:31-33; 37-38), dealing with Christ before Pilate. It belongs to the first half of the second century. Note the importance in relation to the traditional dating of John. Egerton Papyrus 2 contains three leaves of material dated either at the end of the first or early in the second century. Some of the material relates to matters covered in the Synoptic Gospels, though stated in somewhat different language here. The most important part contains a portion of John's Gospel, chapter 5, beginning with the words, "Search the Scriptures." This material was published by Bell and Skeat under the title, *Fragments of an Unknown Gospel* (1935). Recently published is P66, Papyrus Bodmer II. This covers John's Gospel and is dated around A.D. 200. It is of considerable value because of its early date and the relative completeness of the text in contrast to P45. Even more important is P75, which may go back to a period somewhat earlier than 200. It contains chapters 1-5 and 8-9 almost intact, also portions of chapters 6-7 and 10-15, and most of Luke as well (3-24).

Manuscripts are made available to students in three ways: (1) photograph, (2) printed edition, (3) collation. A collation assumes a standard Greek text and simply notes the deviations from that text that are present in a given MS, indicating them by chapter and verse.

Versions

These are translations of the text into other languages, made necessary by the demand for the New Testament in the tongues of those who did not speak Greek. The utility of these for textual study is partly their early date (in some cases 150 years or so earlier than our leading Greek MSS) and their fixed geographical position, testifying to the type of text used in a particular locality. As the versions are translated back, the text from which they were taken can be fixed within close limits.

Certain disadvantages inhere in the use of the versions. MSS containing the versions have been liable to the same processes and influences that have produced variants in the Greek MSS. These influences will be discussed later as we look into the tendencies of scribes. One special danger here is conformation. For example, a monk engaged in copying a Latin MS might alter the text as he copies in order to make it conform to Greek texts that he values highly. Another difficulty is that allowance must be made for possible error in translating from the Greek, owing partly to differences in the two languages. For example, Latin has no definite article and Coptic lacks the passive voice. In any event, however, the extent of the Greek text receives attestation from the copy.

Versions are important only as they give testimony concerning Greek texts that are no longer in our possession. The three principal versions are the Syriac, the Latin, and the Coptic.

1. *Syriac.* The gospel spread early from Syria into Mesopotamia, to such centers as Damascus, Aleppo, and Edessa, where Syriac was used. This is a Semitic language having an alphabet similar to that of Hebrew and Aramaic. About A.D. 150 efforts began to be made to translate the New Testament into Syriac.

(i) *The Diatessaron of Tatian.* This work weaves the materials of the four Gospels into one continuous narrative. It has been preserved through the Arabic and some other translations. In 1920 at Dura on the Euphrates, the so-called Dura Fragment was discovered, namely, fourteen imperfect lines of the Diatessaron in Greek. On the basis of this bit of text, Kenyon observes, "Tatian handled his materials with freedom . . . . if we had the original *Diatessaron* intact, great caution would have to be used to determine the Gospel texts on which he worked."[1]

(ii) *The Old Syriac.* This belongs to about A.D. 200 and is attested by the Sinaitic Syriac and the Curetonian Syriac. The former is a palimpsest of the Gospels, fragmentary in character, discovered in 1892 by Mrs. Lewis and her sister Mrs. Gibson at the Monastery of St. Catherine on Mt. Sinai. The Curetonian came from Egypt and was published by Cureton of the British Museum in 1848. It contains the Gospels, but not in complete form.

[1] F. G. Kenyon, *The Text of the Greek Bible,* p. 116.

(iii) *The Peshitta,* or common Syriac version. This comes from the fifth century, but is dependent on the earlier or old Syriac, being a revision of it. A few books were not included in the Peshitta, namely II Peter, III John, Jude, and Revelation, thus reflecting the uncertainty about the canonical position of these books in that area of the church.

(iv) *The Philoxenian-Harklean Syriac.* The former was the work of Philoxenus, bishop of what was known as Hierapolis in New Testament times, done in 508. Extant copies of his work contain only the books omitted from the Peshitta. The Harklean was done by Thomas of Harkel, being a revision of the Philoxenian, but containing more of the New Testament. Its value lies in its slavish rendering of the Greek, with the result that its exemplar can be the more easily established.

(v) *The Palestinian Syriac.* This is probably a fifth-century work, independently done, so not affected by the previous Syriac versions. It was confined to Palestine and its text is found largely in lectionaries.

2. *Latin.* About A.D. 200 Latin began to figure seriously in the Western Church, where Greek had predominated. It is possible that even before this time some translation had been done into Latin. North Africa, Italy, and southern Gaul were the areas needing a Latin version (Spain also later on). It is customary to divide the *Old Latin Version* into African and European. They are symbolized by small letters: a, b, k, etc. By about 400 repeated copying had so badly corrupted the manuscripts of the version that Damasus, bishop of Rome, commissioned Jerome with the task of putting out a standard text (both Old Testament and New Testament) of the Latin Bible. For the New Testament Jerome depended considerably on the Old Latin. It would be very helpful if we could be sure what kind of Greek MSS Jerome used for correcting the Old Latin. The result of his work is the Latin Vulgate, which became the text of the Western church in the Middle Ages and was made official at the Council of Trent. The Old Latin continued in use for a time, but was gradually supplanted.

3. *Coptic.* The Christian Copts of Egypt needed the New Testament in their language. The Sahidic Version belongs to Upper Egypt (200?); the Bohairic was done, somewhat later, for lower Egypt. Being more literary, it became the official version of the Coptic church.

Other versions of lesser importance include the Armenian, the Georgian (based on the Armenian), the Ethiopic, the Gothic, and the Arabic.

THE FATHERS

As noted above, this is the third source for materials attesting the text of the New Testament. The advantages that they possess for textual study are the early date of many of these quotations and their fixed character both as to time and place (it is known when and where these men lived, hence their quotations are evidence for the text used in those areas at the time). Disadvantages are encountered too: sometimes the works of these early Fathers are lost and have been preserved fragmentarily in the writings of others at a later time, especially in Eusebius' *Ecclesiastical History;* the Fathers had a tendency to quote from memory, leaving a margin for error in the quotation; it is possible that even when a text is consulted rather than memory, the Father will use more than one text, resorting now to one, now to another. However, when these men give themselves to a discussion of textual matters *per se* and therefore quote with care, their material is of great value. Cyprian is an example of consistent quotation — from the Old Latin. It is apparent that the testimony of the versions and that of the Fathers tend to correlate. For example, if three men in the western area of the church give a type of text in their quotations that agrees with the text in our MSS of the Old Latin Version, we are reasonably safe in concluding that they all made use of said version.

THE HISTORY OF THE STUDY OF THE TEXT OF THE NEW TESTAMENT

We do not consider the ancient period here, nor the medieval, when Western Europe was using the Latin Vulgate almost exclusively and few men were in position to consult the original.

The history of the study of the text from Erasmus on may be divided for convenience into three periods: (1) The vogue of the Textus Receptus (1516 to about 1750); (2) The period of struggle and transition to a better text (1750-1830); (3) The vogue of the improved text (1830 to the present).

THE VOGUE OF THE TEXTUS RECEPTUS (1516 TO ABOUT 1750)

The Renaissance brought a quickened interest in Greek, and this factor, coupled with the invention of printing, brought on the age of the printed Greek Testament. Early in the sixteenth century, a race to publish the first printed Greek New Testament developed between Cardinal Ximenes of Spain and Erasmus. The former published the Complutensian Polyglot. Though much of the work was done before that of Erasmus, it was not published until 1522. Erasmus managed to get his out in 1516, spurred on by Froben, a printer at Basel. He also had some papal encouragement. It is difficult for us to conceive what a revolution was stirred up by his New Testament. Men were ignorant of the Bible, knowing only such portions of it as were used in the liturgy of the services. Erasmus furnished a Greek text plus a Latin translation and accompanying notes. He also furnished a preface to each Gospel and Epistle. The notes, which were enlarged in succeeding editions, were often pointed and not complimentary to the clergy. On I Corinthians 14:19 he wrote: "St. Paul says he would rather speak five words with a reasonable meaning in them than ten thousand in an unknown tongue. They chant nowadays in our churches in what is an unknown tongue and nothing else, while you will not hear a sermon once in six months telling people to amend their lives." Erasmus published five editions, and the book became immensely popular despite much clerical opposition. As a critical work the first edition was of little value, but Erasmus improved it, making use of the Complutensian Polyglot after it appeared. The third edition (1522) became famous because of its inclusion of I John 5:7. Erasmus had promised to put it in if it could be found in any Greek MS. When it was found in a single MS 61 (16th century), he had to abide by his promise, even though, as he suspected, this was translated back into Greek from the Latin. It got into the Latin by mistaking one of Cyprian's comments as part of the text of Scripture. It continues to stand in the King James Version as a reminder that diligence is needed in order to free the text from additions to the original.

The limited textual resources of Erasmus are strikingly illustrated by the fact that he was obliged to translate from the Latin into the Greek for five of the last six verses in the Apocalypse in order to complete his Greek Testament. Yet for all its limitations it continued to hold a place of usefulness for about three hundred years.

Erasmus' third edition was followed by Stephanus in *his* third edition, which included readings from other sources also. This is deserving of mention because this edition became the standard for Great Britain (the following year, 1551, he published an edition that for the first time included the verse divisions to which we are so accustomed).

The Elzevir brothers set up an establishment in Leyden from

which they issued several editions of the Greek New Testament. Their second edition (1633) is important in that it became the standard for the continent of Europe even as the third edition of Stephanus became the standard for Britain. These two differed in approximately two hundred readings. This edition of Elzevir has another claim to fame. In the preface the assertion was made that this text is now received by all. The Latin term here used (Textus Receptus) has continued in use to denote the general type of text employed in this and other editions of the time, all more or less dependent on the work of Erasmus. This type of text rests on manuscripts that are late in origin. It is the text that underlies the King James Version.

Though the Textus Receptus is far from being the most accurate text now available, it is well not to magnify unduly the degree of difference from the improved text now in common use. Hort commented as follows: "The proportion of words virtually accepted on all hands as raised above doubt is very great; not less, on a rough computation, than seven-eighths of the whole. The remaining eighth, therefore, formed in great part by changes of order and other comparative trivialities, constitutes the whole area of criticism." He goes on to narrow the area of difference: "The words in our opinion still subject to doubt only make up about one-sixtieth of the whole New Testament." Again: "Substantial variation is but a small fraction of the whole residuary variation, and can hardly form more than a thousandth part of the entire text."[2] This amount of crucial variation may seem to some to be so insignificant as to render unnecessary the work of textual criticism. But since we are dealing with the Word of God, no labor is too great to perform the service of establishing the text as it should be in every detail, so far as that is possible.

Fortunately the study of the text was not atrophied following the appearance of the King James Version in 1611, though this translation came to possess a kind of definitive character in the popular mind. Scholars continued to labor to get an improved text, but for some time accepted the Textus Receptus as their starting point, contenting themselves with adding variants from manuscripts that had not been known to their predecessors.

John Mill (1707) displayed great industry in the collection of textual materials. He noted 30,000 variations in the MSS

[2] F. J. A. Hort, *The New Testament in the Original Greek,* Introduction, p. 2.

at his disposal, and made considerable use of patristic citations. A start was made in weighing the worth of individual documents rather than treating them more or less alike in value. No significant departure was ventured, however, from the basic Textus Receptus.

Richard Bentley, a Cambridge professor, issued certain proposals for arriving at a better Greek Testament (1720). He suggested a greater use of the ancient versions and more thorough collation of the known Greek MSS. With the aid of helpers he did considerable collating himself, but did not live to produce a Greek text. However, his suggestion about the greater value of ancient as opposed to later authorities was bound to bear fruit.

J. A. Bengel did his work under the shadow of the Textus Receptus, though he was not satisfied with it. He published a text in 1734, and was the first to stress the genealogical method, namely, the classification of MSS into families on the basis of obvious kinship. That is, MSS are related to one another by copying. It is often possible to trace them to a common source. Bengel perceived that the number of MSS behind a reading is less important than the consideration of their relationship. For instance, if it is discovered that nine out of ten MSS with which one is dealing have a common original, these nine should count as one rather than nine and should not necessarily have greater weight than the one that lies outside their circle. Bengel is also noteworthy for the introduction of the famous maxim, "The harder reading is to be preferred to the easier." This is due to the tendency of scribes to smooth over difficulties in the text.

J. J. Wettstein of Basel put out a Greek text in 1751-1752, based on the study and collation of more than 100 MSS. He is famous for his collection of parallel passages from rabbinical and classical sources to illustrate passages of the New Testament. Later study is indebted to him for his system of notation. He denoted uncials by capital letters and the cursives by arabic numbers. By reason of an uncontrolled temper he lived a tempestuous life filled with conflicts.

THE PERIOD OF STRUGGLE AND TRANSITION TO A BETTER TEXT (1750-1830)

The second period opens with the influential figure of J. J. Griesbach (1745-1813). His text was issued in 1775-1777. He did not really break with the Textus Receptus, but developed still further the family treatment of MSS. As Vincent puts it, "The task which lay before Griesbach was to vindicate the authority of the older codices, to classify authorities, and to use them critically and consistently for the restoration of the text."[3]

Griesbach made a start in recognizing the course of events in the early centuries respecting the transmission of the text, preparing the way for the more thorough analysis of Westcott and Hort at a later period. He detected a type of text that he called Western, characterized by scribal glosses and therefore needing correction. He detected also the Alexandrian type, which he felt was an attempt on the part of ancient scribes to improve the Western. A third type, which resulted from the use of the two named above, he called the Constantinopolitan. He also developed a maxim that has come to rank alongside that of Bengel, namely, that the shorter reading is to be preferred to the longer. Griesbach's real failure lay in not taking the logical step of striking for an improved text rather than clinging to the Textus Receptus. The struggle continued for some decades, with advocates for both positions.

THE VOGUE OF THE IMPROVED TEXT (1830 TO THE PRESENT)

The beginning of the third period is associated with the name of Lachmann, who in 1831 published a Greek text that abandoned the Textus Receptus and went back to the old MSS for its basis. He had a limited objective — to restore the text of the fourth century. It seems strange that he did not aspire to get back to the original text of the New Testament as his goal.

Tischendorf, already noted in connection with ℵ, was an ardent collector of MSS and a prolific editor. He put out 24 editions of the Greek New Testament. His greatest effort was in connection with his Eighth Edition, which has been the standard for many years because of the vast quantity of MS material cited. It is no longer adequate, however.

Tregelles, who published his Greek Testament in several parts over the years 1857 to 1879, felt that it was necessary to work for the best text obtainable. He appreciated the fact that documents were not to be evaluated in terms of their age (that is, the date of their origin) but by the age of the text that they contain. He realized that documents late in origin sometimes preserve an

---

[3] M. R. Vincent, *A History of the Textual Criticism of the New Testament*, p. 101.

ancient type of text. Souter notes that Tregelles did for the English-speaking world what Lachmann had done for the continent, namely, to point the path of progress away from the Textus Receptus.

Henry Alford began his work with attachment to the Textus Receptus (1849), but as he revised his work he gradually parted company with it and declared for the improved text.

Westcott and Hort are monumental in the field of textual criticism. Their work is enshrined in two volumes, one presenting their text of the New Testament, but without a critical apparatus, the other an introduction written by Hort, explaining the principles upon which their text was constructed. These volumes were the fruit of nearly thirty years of work. Their purpose was nothing short of restoring the original text in so far as that was possible. Their textual theory followed somewhat the lines laid out by Griesbach, but their work was more searching and more comprehensive.

THE THEORY OF WESTCOTT AND HORT

All the documents may be classified on the basis of genealogical relationship into four groups. One group is labeled *Syrian*. This is latest in point of time, and is attested by the vast majority of the MSS. The name Syrian derives from the conclusion that in Syria (probably at Antioch) a textual revision took place during the first half of the fourth century, made necessary by the corrupt state of the text at that time. Uniformity was needed so that appeal could be made to a text acceptable throughout the church. Since this text, once arrived at, became the standard, naturally most of the great host of MSS made in subsequent years reflected this type of text. In the making of the revision, it was apparently hard to reject anything that had been passing as Scripture, so the tendency was to combine readings, a process known as *conflation*. For example, in Luke 24:53 one textual tradition, attested by several MSS, declares that the disciples were blessing God in the temple, while another tradition attests the reading that they were praising God. The great bulk of MSS, however, have a reading that states that they were praising and blessing God. It seems inescapable that the two older types of text were combined and this fuller form of the text continued to be copied in the centuries that followed.

In addition to the Syrian type of text, Westcott and Hort posited the existence of three pre-Syrian types. The *Western* was characterized by a tendency to include legendary material and scribal glosses. Westcott and Hort were not too happy with the term Western, though they used it. C. R. Gregory calls it the Re-Wrought Text. He describes it as follows: "This text had in the second century a certain fascination for the Christian gaze. It retains some of that power today. Alongside of the Original Text it was more juicy, more popular, and more full. It left almost nothing out. It added almost all it could lay hands upon."[4] The second pre-Syrian type was the *Alexandrian*. It was more a text tendency than a text type. Some MSS reveal a trend in the direction of correcting readings in the interest of grammatical accuracy and polish. This type had its home in Egypt, hence the term Alexandrian. The third pre-Syrian type is known as the *Neutral*, because it did not deviate in either of the directions taken by the other two. Again and again as Westcott and Hort tested the distinctive readings of this type, they found that these readings commended themselves as superior and original.

The pre-Syrian types found their attestation in these sources: Western: D, the Old Latin, Old Syriac, such Fathers as Cyprian, Irenaeus, Tertullian. Alexandrian: C, L, Origen, and occasionally some others. Neutral: Aleph, B, 33, the Coptic, Origen in part.

A complicating factor is mixture. For example, Aleph has some admixture of Western readings in the Gospels, especially in Luke, whereas B has a similar situation here and there in Paul's Epistles.

Some of the more important conclusions from the theory of Westcott and Hort are as follows:

(1) A reading not found in Western, Alexandrian or Neutral witnesses must be Syrian; it should therefore be rejected as late and unreliable.

(2) A reading found in Western or Alexandrian types cannot be allowed without support from the Neutral.

(3) A reading found in the Neutral type but absent from the Western must be suspected. This situation is called by Westcott and Hort a Western non-interpolation.

These men emphasized repeatedly that the number of witnesses behind a particular reading means nothing. It is the quality of those witnesses that counts. Others who have followed in their general pattern of thought are Gregory, Souter, Warfield, A. T. Robertson. Their theory continues to hold an

---

4 *Canon and Text of the New Testament*, p. 490.

important place, even though somewhat modified by various factors.

Westcott and Hort were attacked by adherents of the superiority of the Textus Receptus, notably by Burgon and Miller.[5] The objections of these men were in part *a priori* and theologically colored, to the effect that God would not permit his church to have a defective text for hundreds of years, with the better text confined to a few documents. When it is realized that the text of many of the Greek and Latin classics rests on a handful of manuscripts, the force of this objection is greatly diminished. Another objection was the paucity of examples of conflation. Hort cited only eight, but he could have given others. Burgon and Miller challenged Hort to show evidence that the Syrian Recension occurred as a historic event. As a matter of fact, Hort did not insist on a single event, but supposed that there were at least two stages in the process of revision. His opponents theorized that the great bulk of MSS, which are late, could have stemmed from lost originals that were earlier than Aleph, and B. Robertson gives the answer to this plea: ". . . no purely Syrian readings have been found that are supported by early Patristic evidence. The Syrian readings which have such support are also either Western or Neutral."[6] This point has been called the cornerstone of Hort's theory.

More recently the Westcott and Hort theory has had a resolute foe in the person of H. C. Hoskier. He insisted that "B does not exhibit a 'neutral' text, but is found to be tinged, as are most other documents, with Coptic, Latin and Syriac colours, and its testimony therefore is not of the paramount importance presupposed and claimed by Hort and by his followers."[7] He goes on to assert that the Textus Receptus served in large measure as the base that B tampered with and changed.

Various other issues have been raised from time to time in addition to the complaint that in this theory too much reliance was placed on a single manuscript (B). Actually, considerable confidence was placed in Aleph also. It is undoubtedly true that Westcott and Hort tended to shield their pet manuscripts from blame. This is seen in the terminology used to

[5] *The Traditional Text of the Holy Gospels,* 1896, and *The Causes of the Corruption of the Traditional Text of the Holy Gospels,* 1896.
[6] *An Introduction to the Textual Criticism of the New Testament,* p. 191.
[7] *Codex B and its Allies,* Part I, p. 465.

mark instances of Neutral interpolations, which were called by Westcott and Hort Western non-interpolations.

The genealogical method has been attacked on the ground that it is set forth in terms of theoretical rather than actual documents. While the method has been employed successfully to demolish the supremacy of the Textus Receptus, it has not been successful in demonstrating that the Neutral text can be equated with the originals. It does not supply criteria for decision between two lines of descent both of which are ancient, as in the case of the Western and Neutral types.

It had been objected that a text type limited to one geographical area (Egypt) can hardly be regarded as truly representative of what the church universal had at the beginning. But this objection has lost some of its validity with the discovery of several fragmentary portions of the New Testament in southeastern Palestine having close affinity with the Neutral type.[8]

No doubt the Western text should be rated somewhat higher than Westcott and Hort were disposed to do. Black argues that Codex Bezae has preserved more of the primitive 'Aramaized' Greek text that belonged to the earliest period of circulation than is the case with Aleph and B.[9]

A frequently expressed judgment is to the effect that the so-called Neutral text was the result of considerable revision, which Westcott and Hort underestimated. This opinion, despite its currency, is now being called in question, and the change has come because of the fact that the vast majority of the papyrus fragments of the New Testament, most of them earlier than Aleph and B, reflect in general the same type of text found in these leading manuscripts. Especially is this true of P[75]. A comparison of this document with Codex Vaticanus leads Calvin L. Porter to say, "There is now available evidence which suggests that the text type of which P[75] and Codex Vaticanus are witnesses was established by the year 200."[10] The text type in question, then, deserves to be regarded as a transmitted rather than a revised text. So in large part the position of Westcott and Hort has been remarkably substantiated by the progress of the science of textual criticism in the last few years.

8 B. M. Metzger, "Recently Published Fragments of the Greek New Testament," *ET*, 63 (1952), p. 311.
9 Matthew Black, *An Aramaic Approach to the Gospels and Acts,* 2nd ed., 1954, pp. 214-15.
10 *JBL,* 81 (1962), p. 375.

FURTHER DEVELOPMENTS

Other workers since Westcott and Hort will be noted briefly. One is Von Soden, whose work was completed by 1913.[11] His text is not materially different from that of Westcott and Hort, but he developed his own system of notation. In part this has been adopted for use in the Nestle text. He divided the MSS into three groups denoted by K, H, and I. The K stands for *Koine,* and means what Westcott and Hort meant by Syrian. The H stands for Hesychian, and denotes the Egyptian textual tradition, amounting to a combination of the Neutral and the Alexandrian. The I symbol means much the same as Westcott and Hort meant by the term Western. The trouble with Von Soden's work lies in its complexity, for his K group is subdivided into 17, so that the student is bewildered. The I (Jerusalem) group is likewise found to have 14 subdivisions. The whole analysis is unwieldy.

Alexander Souter published not only his *Text and Canon of the New Testament* (1912), but shortly before this put out his text of the New Testament, wherein one has before him the text used by the Revisers in their work of rendering the 1881 English Revision. Its special utility is the indication of the more important separate documents that support the various readings listed in the apparatus.

The Nestle text has gained wide acceptance, attested by a total of 26 editions. This is due to the fact that it is kept abreast of the discovery of new materials and reflects current critical judgment as to what should stand in the text and what should be relegated to the apparatus. The grouping of witnesses in accordance with the Von Soden scheme is somewhat puzzling to students, as is the failure to list competing readings in all cases. But it is a pocket edition with emphasis on the essentials. It has an eclectic text built upon the consensus or majority of the Westcott and Hort, Weiss, and Tischendorf readings. In recent editions the changes in the text have been comparatively few.

Other Greek Testaments, by Vogels (1920), Merck (1933) and Bover (1943), have not proved as useful as Nestle's.[12]

The *Caesarean* text type is a modern discovery. As early as 1868 Ferrar of Trinity College, Dublin, found affinities in

---

[11] *Die Schriften des Neuen Testaments in ihren ältesten erreichbaren Textgestalt,* I, 1902-1910; II, 1913.

[12] For an account and evaluation of these, see J. Harold Greenlee, *An Introduction to New Testament Textual Criticism.*

four minuscules (13, 69, 124 and 346). Research added several others to this group as time went on. In 1902 Kirsopp Lake presented his conclusion that minuscules 1, 118, 131 and 209 belonged together. It was discovered that in Mark, especially, this group was closely related to that isolated by Ferrar. A few years later came the discovery that Codex Theta (containing the Koridethi Gospels) was related to the other two. It became the fashion to speak of the Theta family. Then it was pointed out that in his later works Origen, instead of using the Neutral type of text, made use of one that was strikingly akin to that of the Theta family. Since his later work was done at Caesarea (the earlier was done at Alexandria), scholars began to speak of a Caesarean text. Then came the discovery of the Chester Beatty Papyri, which revealed kinship with the above-mentioned documents, especially in Mark. But since these Papyri emanated from Egypt, the Caesarean text could hardly be confined to Palestine. Some felt it necessary to posit a pre-Caesarean text and locate it in Egypt. Others doubted that all these witnesses had sufficient homogeneity to warrant the isolation of a distinct text type.

B. H. Streeter, who had a leading part in the identifying of the Caesarean type of text, is known also for his theory of "local texts." (See *The Four Gospels* [1925], pp. 27-76.) He set forth the view that somewhat divergent types of text grew up around the various leading centers of the Christian faith during the second century and later. He identified five of these. In Alexandria the text attested by B and secondarily by Aleph, L, the Sahidic and Bohairic was at home. He proposed the term Alexandrian instead of the Westcott and Hort Neutral. The second center was Antioch, where the Sinaitic Syriac was specially influential, also the Curetonian. Third was Caesarea, its type attested by Theta and 565 in Mark, also by family 1, family 13, etc. Fourth, Italy and Gaul can be linked together, with D in a primary position of influence, with b and a as auxiliary. Finally, Carthage was partial to k, especially in the first two Gospels, with e an influence also, and to some extent W. By ascertaining the text that is common to all of these areas it should be possible to come reasonably close to the original documents of the New Testament.

Streeter characterized the Caesarean text as roughly midway between the Neutral and the Western as to the type of text represented. It sometimes adds material (in keeping with the Old Syriac, D, and the Old Latin), but also on occasion has omissions that put it in the same class with B and its allies as against the Western witnesses.

Streeter emphasized the unsatisfactory situation created by speaking simply of a Western type of text (Westcott and Hort had admitted this state of affairs also). He insisted that the Western ought to be divided into what was truly Western (see his fourth classification) and what was Eastern, which in fact had two branches, the one predominant at Caesarea, the other at Antioch.[13] While all three have some resemblances, their differences are sufficient to warrant separate classification.

The textual situation in Egypt in the latter part of the second century is somewhat complicated, with increasing evidence for the early existence of the type found later in Aleph and B, but with the undoubted presence of the Western text also, at least in the case of Clement of Alexandria, and later on the Caesarean, which represents an intermediate type. Perhaps it is possible to hold that the first type was at home here from the beginnings of Christianity in this region, and that the Western text was an importation. Streeter advances the reminder that Clement came to Alexandria from Italy and could easily have been influenced by what he had known and used in those earlier days.[14]

As noted somewhat in passing, the nomenclature of Westcott and Hort has experienced some alteration by later scholars. Now we hear of Koine and Byzantine instead of Syrian. Instead of Neutral we hear of Alexandrian or, less appropriately, Hesychian. This is confusing to the student, and requires him to ascertain the viewpoint of the writer who uses these terms. So, for example, he must discover whether a writer means by Alexandrian what Westcott and Hort meant or whether it is being used in the later sense of the virtual equivalent of Neutral.

Kenyon has proposed a fresh grouping of text types, as follows: (α) the Received Text; (β) the text designated as Neutral by Westcott and Hort; (γ) the Caesarean text; (δ) the Western text; (ϵ) the Syrian text, including the testimony of the Syriac, Armenian and Georgian versions; (ζ) the remainder.[15]

G. Zuntz in *The Text of the Epistles* (1953) has stressed the importance of P^{46} for establishing the text of Paul's letters. The concurrence of this document with one or more Western witnesses may be strong enough evidence, in his opinion, to outweigh the rest of the testimony. This makes specialized use of the observation made by Westcott and Hort that when the Neutral and Western witnesses were found to be in agreement,

[13] The Caesarean attested by Θ and 565, the Antiochian by sy^s sy^c.
[14] *The Four Gospels*, p. 57.
[15] *The Text of the Greek Bible*, p. 197.

one could be reasonably sure that he had the true text, for these two divergent lines of testimony could only agree in the original.

It should be noted here that some modern scholars have become rather pessimistic about the advisability of following one text type in order to arrive at a decision on the true reading in a given instance, preferring to give weight to all the factors in the situation. They have thus become eclectic in their methodology. On this approach the relegation of the external evidence to a secondary role is almost inevitable.

A significant development has taken place in the evaluation of the Byzantine or Koine type of text, which Westcott and Hort dismissed as of no real value in the process of textual criticism. Occasionally this text-type may have preserved the true text. Metzger gives an example of a reading preserved only in the Byzantine manuscripts which nevertheless commends itself as original.[16] It is especially because of the fairly large number of Byzantine readings found in the papyri that a re-evaluation of this text-type is needed. On this matter G. Zuntz gives the following testimony: "A number of Byzantine readings, most of them genuine, which previously were discarded as 'late,' are anticipated by P[46]. Our inquiry has confirmed what was anyhow probable enough: the Byzantines did not hit upon these readings by conjecture or independent error. They reproduced an older tradition."[17] The findings of E. C. Colwell are equally relevant. "The Bodmer John (P[66]) is also a witness to the early existence of many of the readings found in the Alpha text-type (Hort's 'Syrian'). Strangely enough (according to our previous ideas), the contemporary corrections in that papyrus frequently change an Alpha-type of reading to a Beta-type of reading (Hort's 'Neutral'). This indicates that at this early period readings of both kinds were known, and the Beta-type were supplanting the Alpha-type — at least as far as this witness is concerned."[18] It was formerly customary to dismiss Byzantine readings in Fathers prior to Chrysostom as due to scribal activity which assimilated what was written to the (now) standard Byzantine text. But it is no longer necessary to resort to this explanation. This elevation of the Byzantine text to a higher status does not mean, however, a return to the position of Burgon. It only means that Byzantine readings should be taken into account instead of being dismissed out of hand.

[16] B. M. Metzger, *The Text of the New Testament*, pp. 238-239.
[17] *The Text of the Epistles*, p. 55.
[18] *Studies in Methodology in Textual Criticism of the New Testament*, pp. 47-48.

A conviction is growing among textual scholars that although variant readings are found all along the line of transmission of the text from the beginning, the preponderance of them go back to the second century. As greater care was taken in copying and as the process of editing developed, the problem of variation became less serious. The period of extreme divergence antedated the rise of the various text-types.

Colwell has pointed out the necessity of recognizing that text-types did not emerge full-blown but experienced a process of growth, so that later witnesses to a given type have a more definitive text than earlier witnesses.[19]

Certain major textual projects deserve mention. In 1935 the work of S. C. E. Legg began to appear. One volume on Mark and one on Matthew were published by the Oxford Press before the project was discontinued. This effort has been merged into a larger undertaking located at Oxford and Chicago. The American office of *The International Project to Establish a Critical Edition of the Greek New Testament* is now located at Claremont, California, where the enterprise is being speeded up by the discovery by two staff members, Wisse and McReynolds, of a new profile method of grouping and evaluating minuscule manuscripts.[20] The immediate goal is the preparation of a critical apparatus for Luke.

In 1958 the British and Foreign Bible Society published a Greek New Testament edited by G. D. Kilpatrick, using the Nestle text that it employed in its edition of 1904, with some changes. The apparatus includes the latest available evidence by individual documents rather than by the use of symbols (except for the TR — Textus Receptus) for text-types or groups of manuscripts.

In 1966, edited by Kurt Aland, Matthew Black, Bruce M. Metzger, and Allen Wikgren, and under the sponsorship of The United Bible Societies (five) *The Greek New Testament* appeared. Variant readings listed with manuscript evidence are restricted to those regarded as possessing importance for the interpretation of the text, with the needs of the Bible translator primarily in view. A third edition is in preparation.

The Nestle text continues to be issued, now under the direction of Kurt Aland. Despite its small size, it lists several times the number of variant readings included in Bible Society New Testament. Aland and associates at Münster are working hard to produce a Greek Testament that will have a full critical apparatus, a modern Tischendorf. When this is realized there will still be a place for the modest manual edition for ready reference.

[19] *Ibid.,* pp. 15-20.
[20] *JBL,* 87 (June 1968), pp. 192-197.

THE PRACTICE OF TEXTUAL CRITICISM

PRINCIPLES AND PROCEDURES FOR THE ANALYSIS AND INTERPRETATION OF THE EVIDENCE

Here it is necessary to become familiar with the work of Westcott and Hort in greater detail. These are the steps employed:

1. *Internal Evidence of Readings*

"The most rudimentary form of criticism consists in dealing with each variation independently, and adopting at once in each case out of two or more variants that which looks most probable."[21] Two procedures are employed here. The one is the appeal to *intrinsic probability,* which looks at the problem in hand from the standpoint of the author of the text (Paul, John, *et al.*). It means that we should ask ourselves the question, Which of these competing readings is most likely to have been written by the author? Clearly, in order to give an intelligent response here, it is necessary to know something about the thought patterns and vocabulary of the writer. It is necessary also to examine the course of thought both in the broad and narrow context of the disputed passage to see which reading is most in accord with the progress of thought.

The second procedure involved here is the appeal to *transcriptional probability.* This asks the question, Which of these competing readings looks as though it is the work of a scribe (in contrast to the author)? In order to apply this canon of criticism to good advantage, it is necessary to know something about the habits of scribes. Their errors are accidental or intentional.

Accidental errors.

(1) Faulty division of words (due to no separation between words in the texts copied). An example is in I Timothy 3:16, where some MSS divide the second word in the verse into two words — "we confess how" instead of "confessedly."

(2) Mistaking of one letter for another. For example, see Romans 12:11 (where *season* appears in some MSS instead of *Lord*).

(3) The use of abbreviations in MSS. This sometimes led to confusion and misreading.

21 Hort, *op. cit.,* p. 19.

84

(4) Homoeoteleuton. Omission of words is sometimes due to the fact that words with similar endings lie adjacent to one another. As the eye returns to the text for copying, it may fall on the wrong word. Sometimes whole lines have been dropped out for the same reason.

(5) Dittography. This is the unintentional writing of the same word a second time, where it occurs only once in the exemplar.

(6) Haplography. This is the writing once of something that should be repeated.

(7) Errors of the ear. As one scribe took dictation from another, one word closely resembling another was often substituted for the one actually spoken. A common variation of this type involves the Greek words for "you" (pl.) and "we." Another example is the confusion between short and long o when the sound was pronounced rapidly.

(8) Errors of memory. Being human, a scribe might permit his mind to wander momentarily and write something different from what stood in his exemplar.

(9) Errors of judgment. The principal danger here was of inserting into the text what was merely a marginal comment in the exemplar.

Intentional changes.

(1) Orthography. Some scribes had peculiar spelling habits, which are reflected in their work.

(2) Grammatical corrections in the interest of a more literary product. These were a special feature of the Alexandrian text type (Westcott and Hort).

(3) Changes to remove historical difficulties. So, for example, Origen confesses to have altered Bethany in John 1:28 to Bethabara because he could find no evidence for a Bethany in the Jordan valley.

(4) Harmonistic corruptions. Scribal zeal to bring the wording of a passage into agreement with the wording in a parallel passage in another Gospel accounts for some variants.

(5) Doctrinal alterations. There is considerable divergence of opinion on this matter. Are there places where the text has been changed in the interest of doctrinal viewpoint? E. C. Colwell goes so far as to say, "The majority of the variant readings in the New Testament were created for theological or dogmatic reasons."[22] He surely cannot mean by this the

[22] *What Is the Best New Testament?*, p. 53.

actual majority, for the vast majority are devoid of all theological significance, being matters of orthography, synonyms, easily confused words, etc. A recent work by C. S. C. Williams, *Alterations to the Text of the Synoptic Gospels and Acts* (1951), deals with this problem. Even if all his contentions are admitted, the amount of such alteration is not great.

Three maxims have come to be rather widely employed in evaluating transcriptional probability. First, the shorter reading is to be preferred over the longer. Scribes had a natural tendency to add rather than subtract. Second, the harder reading is to be preferred over the easier. Scribes had a tendency to smooth out a construction that to them seemed awkward. Third, that reading is to be preferred which will most readily explain the origin of the other reading or readings. These maxims are not infallible, but they are useful when applied with discretion.

The application of intrinsic probability and of transcriptional probability usually brings the student out to the same point. In other words, these two methods are complementary and combine to establish the proper reading. Of the two, intrinsic probability is the more difficult to apply with objectivity. Too often the preference of the student is imputed to the author. If intrinsic probability will not always enable us to decide what the author wrote, it should at least operate to enable us to decide what the author did not write.

Internal evidence of readings as a process must wait upon the ascertaining of the external evidence, that is, the actual readings of the MSS. Then transcriptional probability should be applied, followed by the appeal to intrinsic probability. In this way one is less liable to the settling of a reading on the basis of what appeals to him.

2. *Internal Evidence of Documents*

We have been considering the approach to individual readings. The same approach may be made to whole documents. That is to say, where a given manuscript has distinctive readings that mark it off as different from the Textus Receptus, it is possible to take each distinctive reading and apply to it both transcriptional and intrinsic probability. If these distinctive readings are found to commend themselves repeatedly by this process, the document that contains them will be pronounced a good MS. With this excellence established, the student will then feel obliged to reconsider the few instances in which he decided against the readings of this MS. Further study of those variants may convince him that at least some of them are worthy of acceptance. Thereafter, when he finds that this particular document supports a certain reading, he will have such a high opinion of the document that only the most serious considerations will lead him to reject its testimony. It is in this way that such MSS as Aleph and B have gained a position of acknowledged eminence.

3. *Genealogical Evidence*

This step, as Hort puts it, "consists in ceasing to treat documents independently of each other, and examining them connectedly as parts of a single whole, in virtue of their historical relationships."[23] (Review what was said above under Bengel.) Manuscripts are grouped in families, since one is copied from another. Several MSS may go back to a single exemplar. The establishing of genealogical connection is predicated on the principle that "identity of reading implies identity of origin." In the use of genealogical evidence the great foe is mixture. This is not the same thing as conflation, which is combining of readings to make a longer one. Mixture is the result of following a different exemplar now and then, so that the copied product does not reproduce throughout a single exemplar. To untangle this mixture is a delicate and sometimes impossible task.

4. *Internal Evidence of Groups*

Based on genealogical relationship, it is possible to treat a group of documents as a single unit. For example, Aleph and B form a binary unit, in which case one does not consider Aleph plus B, but rather Aleph B. What one is really dealing with in this case is the common ancestor of Aleph and B. They cannot be considered in this fashion throughout their entire compass, because, as noted above, there is some Western admixture in them at different points. Even a good MS can be found in error now and then. Its readings must be checked by transcriptional and intrinsic evidence. Robertson points out that Aleph B C L, an otherwise good group, goes astray at Matthew 27:49 (end of the verse). "Intrinsic evidence of single readings will not allow it. Transcriptional evidence of single readings explains its origin as a clumsy addition from John 19:34."[24]

[23] *Op. cit.*, p. 39.
[24] *Op. cit.*, p. 182.

5. *Evidence of Classes*

This was the crowning achievement of Westcott and Hort. We have already covered it in stating their theory of the early history of the text of the New Testament. Later research has added the Caesarean type and has seen the advisability of breaking up the Western, which is too unwieldy and lacking in homogeneity to be considered as a unit.

6. *Conjectural Emendation*

Because of the wealth of MS testimony to the New Testament, there is scarcely any place where the text is to be regarded as hopeless and subject to reconstruction by the ingenuity of the critic. Now and then the student will observe "cj" in the apparatus, coupled with the name of some textual critic, indicating his surmise as to what the text should be at this point.

Westcott and Hort granted that there may be several dozen *primitive errors* in our leading MSS. Even when the originals were copied, the possibility of errors in the first copying must be acknowledged. Transcriptional and intrinsic probability will assist, as a rule, in the clearing up of these. See, for example, Romans 8:2, where the leading MSS have "thee" after the verb "freed." From the standpoint both of author and scribe the logical reading is "me."

EXAMPLES

Knowledge of the principles and procedures in textual criticism is one thing; actually to engage in the work of the science is quite another. The student will gain in confidence as his experience increases. A few examples are given here, preceded by a listing of the various classes and the documents that illustrate them. These examples should be worked through by the student with the help of the Nestle Greek New Testament. If aids are available that list the manuscript testimony in greater detail, these may be profitably employed in addition.

Byzantine (Hort's Syrian): Late uncials such as E, F, G, H, K, M, S, U, V, Y, Ω; A (in the Gospels); at times C and W; nearly all the minuscules; the late versions; the late Fathers (Chrysostom and after). In the Nestle apparatus look for the German K (Koine) as the symbol for this type of text.

Hesychian (Hort's Neutral): B, ℵ, L, R, T, Z, Ξ (in the Gospels); Δ (in Mark); P. Q; Ψ (in Mark); P⁴⁶ frequently; 33; the Bohairic and Sahidic; sometimes the Latin Vulgate; Origen, especially in his earlier works.

Caesarean: So far this text type has been isolated in a definite way only for the Gospel of Mark. The leading witnesses are P⁴⁵, W, Θ; the MSS grouped under families 1 and 13; Origen in his later works.

Western: D; The African portion of the Old Latin (k, e, and Cyprian); to a lesser degree the European Latin, with a and b as leading representatives.

Syrian: Chief witnesses are the Old Syriac, the Armenian and Georgian versions.

Kenyon notes that there is a residue left over that does not fit into any category.

(1) Luke 2:14. The nominative form εὐδοκία is backed by Byzantine testimony (summarized by the Koine symbol); Caesarean (Θ); and has the support of the Syriac and the Bohairic, Origen (in part of his quotations), and Eusebius. The competing reading, the genitive εὐδοκίας, which stands in the Nestle text, gets support from the Hesychian (B and א, the asterisks indicating the reading in the manuscript proper as distinct from the reading inserted by later hands). A and W join the more characteristically Hesychian witnesses here. The Western type of text stands here also, represented by D, the combined Latin versions, and many of the Latin Fathers.

It should be noted that the combination of Hesychian and Western witnesses strongly points to εὐδοκίας as the true reading. Transcriptional probability favors it, since, on the presumption that εὐδοκίας stood in the text, a change to the nominative could easily have been made on the ground that the latter was smoother, better Greek, making the word parallel to εἰρήνη. Intrinsic probability is quite in accord also, especially if the sense be, "among men of (God's) good pleasure." Parallels have been found in the Qumran literature.[25] The exegete is now free to explain the verse as meaning that through the birth of Jesus peace may be realized in the case of men who are the objects of God's good pleasure.

(2) John 1:18. The debate here concerns the words μονογενὴς θεός. Examination of the apparatus reveals that the student must choose between four alternatives. In support of ὁ μονογενὴς υἱός (prefixed by a symbol indicating that in the estimation of many this reading has a good claim to be regarded as the original, in contrast to the reading adopted for the text) are the following: the Koine symbol; Θ; the con-

[25] Ernest Vogt in *The Scrolls and the New Testament* (ed. by Krister Stendahl), pp. 114-17.

sensus of the Latin versions; the Curetonian Syriac. This means that the reading in question has Byzantine support. Other elements are less sharply defined. D is defective here, so cannot be cited. The second option is ὁ μονογενὴς θεός, which is supported by P[75]; a corrector of ℵ; 33; Clement. The third is Burney's conjecture — μονογενὴς θεοῦ. Finally, the reading of the text has the following witnesses: P[66]; Hesychian testimony represented especially by B and ℵ; the Palestinian Syriac; Irenaeus; Origen. It is rather unusual to find Irenaeus deserting the Western camp, as he does in this instance.

The decision in this case lies between the first and fourth alternatives. On the side of transcriptional probability, the fourth is the harder reading. It is more likely, then, to have been the original, since the temptation would have been present to alter the reading to the more ordinary ὁ μονογενὴς υἱός. Intrinsic probability is not decisive, for either reading is agreeable to the Johannine presentation of the person of Christ (cf. 1:1; 3:16).

(3) John 7:53 — 8:11. For the inclusion of this section in the text of the Gospel at this place we note the testimony of the Koine group; D and most of the remaining witnesses, several of them bearing asterisks or obelisks calling attention to some doubt about the passage; several manuscripts of the Old Latin; the Latin Vulgate; the Palestinian Syriac. There are also witnesses for the placing of this pericope in three other positions in the Gospel.

For the omission of this portion the following witnesses are cited: P[66]; P[75]; the Hesychian witnesses, which in this case are principally B and ℵ; the uncials N and W; Θ; others not listed here; several codices of the Old Latin; Syriac; several early Fathers both in East and West.

In support of the passage, then, we find the Byzantine class, backed by Western witnesses, though the Old Latin is divided. Westcott passes the observation that this section is omitted by the oldest representatives of every kind of evidence (MSS, Versions, Fathers).[26] The case for omission gets powerful support from the Hesychian class, aided by the important Papyrus Bodmer II and many Western witnesses. From the standpoint of transcriptional probability, the varying position of the passage in the MSS points to uneasiness as to its rightful place at this point in the Gospel, which in turn casts doubt on its originality. Intrinsic probability casts its vote in the same direction. West-

26 *The Gospel According to John* (Greek Text), Vol. II, p. 379.

cott notes a number of peculiarities that indicate John was not the author of this section.[27] As to the possible origin of the passage, Eusebius states that Papias "has expounded another story about a woman who was accused before the Lord of many sins, which the Gospel according to the Hebrews contains."[28]

(4) The ending of Mark's Gospel. Here there are three possibilities: the abrupt ending, which closes the Gospel at 16:8 with the words ἐφοβοῦντο γάρ; the short ending, placed by Nestle at the very end of the Gospel text; the long ending, consisting of verses 9-20.

It is expedient to discuss the second possibility first. This ending is usually found between the other two in the manuscripts, but sometimes stands in place of the long ending. Such evidence as it has indicates that it was an early reading, but it can lay no real claim to originality, for several reasons. First, as Hort points out, the vagueness and generality of the last sentence finds no parallel in the Gospel narratives.[29] Second, it is evident that the reading in question would not have been originated by anyone who had the long reading before him. Third, it is clear that the reason for the origin of the short ending is the abruptness of the ending at 16:8, which some scribe or editor sought to smooth out into something more finished. What should be borne in mind above all else here is the fact that this ending bears witness to the abrupt ending, not to the long ending. Its origin is explained by the abrupt ending, not by the long ending. To anticipate our judgment on the long ending, it should further be stated that the geographical distribution of the evidence for the short ending shows that in widely separated areas of the church, at an early time, the long ending was not known. What was known was the abrupt ending patched up with the help of the short ending.

Turning to the evidence for the long ending, we find that it is great in bulk. The Koine testimony is here, plus W, Θ, much of the Latin, part of the Syriac, etc. On the other hand, B and ℵ omit, as does k, the Sinaitic Syriac, some Armenian codices, Clement, Origen and Eusebius. The latter says that the most accurate copies known to him and almost all the copies available ended with the words, "they were afraid."[30] Transcriptional probability favors the abrupt ending. If the long ending were

27 *Ibid.*, p. 381.
28 *HE* III. xxxix. 17.
29 *Notes on Select Readings* (Appendix to his Introduction), p. 44a.
30 See Hort, *op. cit.*, pp. 30-31.

original, it is difficult to account for the loss of these verses in our leading MSS. On the other hand, given the abrupt ending as the original, it is easy to see that there was a felt need for supplementation.

Intrinsic probability points in the same direction, for the material in the long ending is not agreeable to the style of Mark and does not fit well the preceding verses of the chapter. The word for "week" in verse 9 is not the same as in verse 2. Mary Magdalene's background, given in verse 9, is hardly natural here after her appearance in the story at verse 1 without any such description. The reader looks for something to be said in these closing verses that will fittingly fulfill what is stated about Peter in verse 7, but all he finds is a series of generalities. Finally, although the material in verse 18 might conceivably be congruent with the place that the miraculous element holds in the Gospel, it is perhaps more accurate to see a thaumaturgical motif here such as one finds in the apocryphal Gospels.

Whether Mark's hand was stayed by death or whether the original ending was lost in some way, or whether the abrupt ending represents Mark's deliberate intention to close his record in a fashion agreeable to the style of his narrative, we have no means of knowing. Either of the former alternatives would seem to be more likely than the third.

BIBLIOGRAPHY

Clark, K. W., "The Textual Criticism of the New Testament" in *Peake's Commentary on the Bible.* London: Nelson and Sons, 1962, pp. 663-670.

Colwell, E. C., *Studies in Methodology in Textual Criticism of the New Testament.* Grand Rapids: Eerdmans, 1969.

Greenlee, J. H., *Introduction to New Testament Criticism.* Grand Rapids: Eerdmans, 1964.

Gregory, C. R., *Canon and Text of the New Testament.* New York: Chas. Scribner's Sons, 1907.

Hort, F. J. A., *The New Testament in the Original Greek.* Introduction and Appendix. London: Macmillan, 1881.

Kenyon, F. G., *The Text of the Greek Bible.* London: Duckworth, 1937.

Lake, K., *The Text of the New Testament.* 4th ed., New York: Edwin S. Gorham, 1908.

Metzger, B. M., *The Text of the New Testament.* New York and London: Oxford University Press, 2nd ed., 1968.

Robertson, A.T., *An Introduction to the Textual Criticism of the New Testament.* 2nd ed., New York: Doubleday, Doran, 1928.

Taylor, Vincent, *The Text of the New Testament.* London: Macmillan, 1961.

Vaganay, Leo, *An Introduction to the Textual Criticism of the New Testament.* London: Sands, 1937.

Warfield, B. B., *An Introduction to the Textual Criticism of the New Testament.* New York: Thomas Whittaker, 1889.

Zuntz, G., *The Text of the Epistles.* London: The British Academy, 1953.

PART IV

THE CANON

Chapter Four

THE CANON

THE TERM CANON HAS COME TO BE APPLIED TO THE WRITINGS
that make up the New Testament because they constitute the
norm for Christian faith in documentary form. *Canon* is a
Greek word denoting a straight rod; it came to be used for a bar
or ruler and was variously applied to special objects. Certain
metaphorical applications developed out of the literal meaning,
such as standard and model. Patristic writers apply it to the
rule of faith or the standard of apostolic teaching handed down
in the church. That teaching, when put in creedal form, was
known as the canon of truth. By a natural development, the apostolic writings were designated as canonical to indicate their authoritative character and to distinguish them from other Christian literature. Ultimately the noun was employed for the corpus
of writings that had gained general recognition in the church
as Holy Scripture.[1] The examples of the use of the word in

[1] For a more complete account of the history of the word, see
Souter, *The Text and Canon of the New Testament,* pp. 154-56.

the New Testament do not exhibit this technical sense, but are more general: "rule" is a good translation in Galatians 6:16, whereas in II Corinthians 10:13-16 a carefully delimited sphere is the idea.

HISTORY OF THE CANON

Before one can adopt a position on the theology of the canon, i.e., give an explanation for the acceptance of certain books as Scripture by the church, he must trace the use of these books in the early church and note the occasional testimonies of the Fathers to them.

THE NEW TESTAMENT

It is hardly reasonable to expect to find here any definite information on the canon, at any rate on the limits of it. But at least two things are worth noting. Exhortations are given from time to time concerning the public reading of apostolic writings (I Thess. 5:27; Col. 4:16; I Tim. 4:13; Rev. 1:3; 2:7, 11, 17, 29; 3:6, 13, 22). Of these; Colossians 4:16 has special interest in that it involves an additional feature, namely, the circulating of an epistle to at least one other church, and the admonition to obtain a second epistle from the other church (Laodicea) that it might be read in the church at Colossae. It is a reasonable inference that neither the writer nor the readers looked upon such documents as having only momentary value. A need for them might well arise elsewhere, warranting their preservation.

Further, the New Testament bears witness to something approaching a collection of books. In II Peter 3:15, 16 attention is called to the writings of Paul ("in all his epistles") and the observation is made that the unlearned and unstable wrest these epistles, as they do *the other Scriptures*, to their own destruction. Since II Peter is written to a rather general audience, at least not to a single church, a widespread knowledge of Paul's writings is implied. It is impossible to know how many epistles of Paul the writer had in mind, but several are in view, and they are placed on a par with the Old Testament writings. The value of this testimony depends upon the estimate of the date of II Peter, which some put as late as the middle of the second century, thus eliminating it as a witness for the apostolic age. But there are serious difficulties involved in denying its authenticity, as later discussion of this book will attempt to show.

In I Timothy 5:18 a statement quoted from Deuteronomy 25:4, "You shall not muzzle a threshing ox," is coupled with another, "The laborer is worthy of his hire" (Luke 10:7), and the term Scripture is applied to both. The most natural inference is that Luke is given the status of Scripture here and put on a level with the Old Testament. To be sure, the Pastoral Epistles have been challenged as to their Pauline authorship and as to a date within Paul's lifetime. But even if they are relegated to the following generation, this testimony to the standing of a Gospel as Scripture is extremely valuable.

THE POST-APOSTOLIC AGE

This is the period of the Apostolic Fathers and the Apologists. For our purpose it carries us up to the last quarter of the second century, to the emergence of the Old Catholic Church and the testimonies of such men as Irenaeus, Clement of Alexandria, and Tertullian.

1. Clement of Rome. Writing to the Corinthian church (ca. 95), Clement makes copious use of the Old Testament, which he cites as Scripture, the work of the Holy Spirit. He makes explicit mention of Paul's First Epistle to the Corinthians (chap. 47) and shows familiarity with the teaching of Christ. The Epistle to the Hebrews is known, likewise several others. Clement is acquainted with "the words of the Lord Jesus" (chaps. 13 and 46), but the use of written Gospels at these points is debatable. Lightfoot affirms and Sanday rejects (with caution) such a hypothesis.[2] This much is clear, that Clement, when referring to material emanating from Christ or the apostles, nowhere uses the term Scripture. His introduction of Christ's sayings by "The Lord spake," etc., may be called, with Lightfoot, an archaic form of citation in contrast to the habit of later writers who did not hesitate to label such utterances as Scripture.

2. *The Epistle of Barnabas.* Though it bears the name of a New Testament figure, this writing belongs to the early part of the second century. Generous use is made of the Old Testament in order to show how it points to Christ. Several times reference is made to the teaching of Jesus. Though the term Scripture is not used of these materials, the words "many [are] called but few chosen" (Matt. 22:14) appear, introduced by a formula that is common for the quotation of Old Testament Scripture — "as it stands written" (4:14).

---

[2] J. B. Lightfoot, *Apostolic Fathers*, Part I. S. Clement of Rome, II, 52, 141; W. Sanday, *The Gospels in the Second Century*, pp. 63-68.

3. Ignatius. Bishop of Antioch, Ignatius was martyred at Rome during the reign of Trajan (98-117). As he journeyed through Asia Minor, a captive of the empire, he wrote seven epistles to various churches. In one of these he refers to some who say, "If I do not find it in the archives, I do not believe in the gospel" (*Philadelphians* 8:2). Though the archives could conceivably be taken to refer to Gospel records, they are more likely the Old Testament Scriptures of which the gospel is the fulfillment. While Ignatius is acquainted with Gospel materials, he nowhere alludes to such materials as Scripture or quotes an individual Gospel by name. He is aware that Paul wrote letters and is familiar with several of them (*Ephesians* 12:2), and carefully distinguishes his own position from that of the apostles (*Romans* 4:3).

4. Polycarp's *Epistle to the Philippians* (ca. 115). This work abounds with language drawn from the New Testament.[3] More than once statements are attributed to Jesus, introduced by the words, "The Lord said." In citing Paul, Polycarp several times uses the introductory phrase, "knowing that," which Lightfoot takes to be a formula of citation (see 1:15; 5:1). Most striking is the quoting of Psalm 4:5, "Be angry and sin not," followed immediately by Ephesians 4:26, "Let not the sun go down upon your wrath," and the prefacing of the combined statements with the words, "as it is said in these Scriptures" (12:1).

5. The *Didache,* or *Teaching of the Twelve Apostles.* Some have assigned this to the close of the first century, but a date somewhere in the first quarter of the second century is a safer conclusion. Numerous citations from Matthew are used, but without naming the source. Twice the writer uses the expression, "As you have [it] in the gospel" (15:3, 4), which may well imply the use of written records, but the appeal is to the message, not to a particular Gospel. The word Scripture is not used in connection with these allusions.

6. The *Shepherd of Hermas.* From the same general period, this writing shows acquaintance with the teaching of the Gospels and with several of the Epistles, but there is no citation of any of this material as Scripture.

7. The *Martyrdom of Polycarp* and the *Epistle to Diognetus.* These later works classified with the Apostolic Fathers have nothing substantial to contribute.

---

[3] E. J. Goodspeed, *A History of Early Christian Literature,* p. 24, notes that "Polycarp knows the Pauline letters, Acts, Hebrews, and I Peter."

8. Papias, Bishop of Hierapolis (130-140?). From the title of his work, *Exposition of the Oracles of the Lord,* it is evident that the documents involved were considered Scripture (see the use of "oracles" in Rom. 3:2). Fragments of this work preserved in Eusebius mention Matthew and Mark by name,[4] thus confirming the assumption that the canonical Gospels were used as the basis of this exposition. Incidentally, this is the first specific mention by name of any Gospel.

The attempt to maintain that the work of Papias was simply a narrative account of Jesus' discourses based on tradition has not been successful. His own statement, "but I will not scruple also to give a place along with my interpretations to all that I learned carefully and remembered carefully in time past from the elders," clearly implies a distinction, in view of the word *also,* between the material to be interpreted and the oral traditions that are looked upon as something additional.[5]

From Eusebius' silence about any testimony of Papias to Luke and John it is precarious to assume that Papias had not included them with the others as the basis of his own exposition. Any failure to include them would likely have evoked comment from Eusebius.

It has sometimes been held that Papias disparaged books in favor of oral tradition and therefore cannot be a valid witness to canonical development in the church. This opinion is grounded on a misunderstanding of his meaning when he says, "I did not suppose that information from books would help me as much as the word of a living and surviving voice."[6] In view of his high regard for Mark it seems clear that the books referred to are accounts of traditional material that Papias considered less helpful than immediate contact with the "elders." The books in question here, then, are not to be identified with our written Gospels, which Papias used in his *Exposition.*

9. *The Gospel of Truth.* This recently discovered work with observable Gnostic tendencies is probably attributable to Valentinus around A.D. 140. It has an important contribution to make to the study of the New Testament canon, since its use of the canonical writings is so comprehensive as to warrant the conclusion that in Rome at this period a New Testament was in existence that corresponded very closely with what we have today. Further-

---

[4] *HE* III. xxxix. 14-16.
[5] See Lightfoot, *Essays on the Work Entitled Supernatural Religion,* p. 157.
[6] *HE* III. xxxix. 4.

more, what is utilized, whether from the Gospels, the Acts, the letters of Paul, Hebrews, or the Revelation, is regarded as authoritative.

10. Justin Martyr. An early apologist, Justin Martyr wrote around the middle of the second century two apologies and his *Dialogue with Trypho the Jew*. His *First Apology*, chapter 67, contains a famous passage descriptive of Christian worship. "On the day called Sunday, all Christians gather together to one place and the memoirs of the apostles or the writings of the prophets are read as long as time permits, and when the reader has ceased, the president verbally instructs and exhorts to the imitation of these good things. Then we all rise together and pray, and as we said before, when our prayer is ended, bread and wine and water are brought, and the president in like manner offers prayers and thanksgivings, according to his ability, and the people assent, saying 'Amen.' " Here Justin speaks of the memoirs of the apostles, which he explicitly says in the preceding chapter are also called Gospels.

The question is, Can these be identified with our canonical Gospels? This is rendered probable by the consideration that there is substantial agreement between Justin's allusions to items in the life of Christ and the corresponding material in our Gospels. Furthermore, when Justin refers to traditions not found in our Gospels, he does not cite Gospel authority for them.[7] Six times he uses the formula "it is written" in connection with the Gospels, but not in connection with items derived from other sources.

It must be granted that there is often a lack of verbal agreement between Justin's quotations and our present text of the Gospels, but this disparity is relieved by the following observations: (1) like the early Fathers in general, he may be presumed to have quoted largely from memory, and (2) his quotations from pagan Greek writers and from the LXX show no less striking differences from those texts than his citations from the Gospels.

Justin's failure to refer to the Epistles as Scripture may well have been due to the apologetic character of his work. Jews and pagans would be less impressed by the testimony of such writ-

---

[7] George T. Purves, *The Testimony of Justin Martyr to Early Christianity*, p. 188, notes that the only exception is Justin's allusion to the bloody sweat in Gethsemane, mentioned in Luke 22:44 but bracketed by many editors as lacking sufficient manuscript evidence.

ings than by the Old Testament allusions and the utterances of Jesus of Nazareth.

Regarding the Apocalypse, Justin bears testimony that it was the work of "a certain man among us whose name was John, one of the apostles of Christ" (*Dial.* 81). It can hardly be doubted that he knew John's Gospel also, though the use he made of it was for doctrinal rather than historical data.

11. Tatian. In describing the innovations of a heretical group know as Encratites, Eusebius mentions Tatian as their leader and goes on to state that "he composed in some way a combination and collection of the Gospels, and gave this the name of *The Diatessaron,* and this is still extant in some places."[8] The presence of the four Gospels in this work is explicitly affirmed by Epiphanius (315-404). In the fifth century Theodoret reports having found over 200 such books in the churches of Syria, which he ordered replaced by the Gospels of the Four Evangelists. Tatian's *Harmony* places the Gospel materials in a continuous narrative, beginning with John 1:1, omitting parallel passages. So it is not a Harmony in the modern sense of the word. Diatessaron means "through four," and assures us that shortly after the middle of the second century (170), in Syria at any rate, the four Gospels were accepted as canonical.

12. The Muratorian Canon (170 or somewhat later). Of unknown authorship, the document gets its name from Muratori, who discovered an eighth-century Latin manuscript of it in a library at Milan, which was published in 1740. Unfortunately the manuscript is mutilated at the beginning and probably also at the end, but it is nevertheless of immense value as giving what is likely a fair consensus of the view of the canon held by the church in the West toward the end of the second century. It is reasonably certain that the list of New Testament books contained herein was drawn up in conscious opposition to the canon of the heretic Marcion, whose theological views were unacceptable to the church at Rome. Marcion's heresy is referred to by name, and the description of the Gospels as a whole — "all things in all (of them) are declared by the one sovereign Spirit" — suggests a side-glance at Marcion with his deliberate choice of Luke to the exclusion of the other three, and recalls Tertullian's outburst, "What Pontic mouse ever had such gnawing powers as he who has gnawed the Gospels to pieces?"[9] Marcion published his own recension

---

8 *HE* IV. xxix. 6.
9 *Against Marcion* Bk. I. Chap. 1.

of Luke and ten epistles of Paul, not including the Pastorals in his list. These constituted his New Testament.

In the Muratorian Canon the opening words apparently have to do with Mark (the portion dealing with Matthew is lost). Then Luke and John are mentioned, followed by the Acts, then the thirteen epistles of Paul, beginning with I Corinthians and concluding with the two to Timothy. Pseudo-Pauline letters to the Laodiceans and to the Alexandrians are mentioned, but not as accepted. The list is rounded out by the Epistle of Jude, two of John, also his Apocalypse, with the indication that some accept that of Peter but others will not have it read in the church. Some scholars have felt that the text is corrupt here and originally indicated one epistle (rather than Apocalypse) of Peter as accepted, with doubt cast on the second epistle. If this critical emendation be accepted, only Hebrews, James, and one epistle of John are absent.[10] As Westcott notes, the Muratorian Canon is not an individualistic document, the statement of a personal opinion or the expression of a novel theory, but a deliberate exposition of the views of the church universal so far as the writer is acquainted with its outlook and practice.[11]

Before continuing our historical survey, it may be well to note here that during the patristic period the earlier witnesses speak of Gospel and Apostle rather than of individual Gospels or Epistles. This terminology attests a consciousness that special importance was to be attached to those documents that dealt with the historical unfolding of the gospel in the ministry of Jesus and to those in which Paul expounded that message in terms of the needs of the churches. The twofold division of Marcion's canon, however truncated, reflects this fundamental outlook. In addition, especially after the time of Marcion, the church recognized the Book of Acts as the needed "bridge" between the Gospels and the Epistles.

LATER PATRISTIC WRITERS

Toward the close of the second century Christian literature becomes more extensive, with prominent voices in various geo-

---

10 The Latin original is given in *Some Early Lists of the Books of the New Testament*, edited by F. W. Grosheide. An English translation is available in Henry Bettenson's *Documents of the Christian Church*. Daniel J. Theron, *Evidence of Tradition*, includes both the original and a translation.

11 *A General Survey of the History of the Canon of the New Testament*, 4th ed., p. 217.

graphical areas speaking out in behalf of their local congregations, but also out of a conscious oneness with believers in the church universal. Such men are Irenaeus of Lyons in Gaul, Clement of Alexandria, and Tertullian of North Africa. If it is ascertained that the testimony of these leaders with respect to the canon is in agreement, it will follow that their verdict is the consensus of the widely separated sections of the church that they may be said to represent.

1. Irenaeus. For more than one reason Irenaeus is of special importance. He came originally from Asia Minor, where he sat at the feet of Polycarp, who was privileged to have personal contact with several "eyewitnesses of the Word of life."[12] Later, as presbyter at Lyons, he had constant intercourse with his bishop, Pothinus, who likewise had been associated with Christians of apostolic days. Having spent some time at Rome, Irenaeus was in position to reflect the knowledge and judgment of this prominent center of the faith where leading apostles had ministered. Consequently his associations were both ancient and widely diffused. Furthermore, as Lightfoot points out, he is "the first extant writer in whom, from the nature of his work, we have a right to expect explicit information on the subject of the Canon."[13] He was the first theologian of the Old Catholic Church.

In his Epistle to Florinus he mentions the instruction he had received as a boy from Polycarp and states that this venerable figure "reported all things in agreement with the Scripture."[14] He is familiar with the names of the Gospel writers and the traditions surrounding their work. "The Word," he says, ". . . gave to us the Gospel in a fourfold shape, but held together by one Spirit."[15] In the same passage Irenaeus gives several reasons why there are four Gospels. But these reasons, however fanciful and mystical — such as the existence of four directions and four winds — are not the actual grounds upon which he receives four Gospels and no more, but a justification for the existence of these only as given by God. In addition to the Gospels, Irenaeus makes reference to the Book of Acts, First Peter, First John, all the Epistles of Paul except Philemon, and the Revelation. Lack of mention of a few books does not constitute proof of their non-canonical standing in the eyes of

---

[12] *HE* V. xx. 6.
[13] *Essays on Supernatural Religion*, p. 271.
[14] *HE* V. xx. 6.
[15] *Against Heresies* III. xi. 8.

Irenaeus, since he does not furnish a formal list of New Testament writings.

2. Clement of Alexandria. We have the testimony of Eusebius that this Father wrote explanations of all the canonical Scriptures, including the disputed writings (which will be treated later), and even commented on the Epistle of Barnabas and the Apocalypse of Peter.[16] He was clear, however, in his understanding of the line between canonical and apocryphal in respect to the Gospels. After quoting a saying of an apocryphal nature, he says, "we do not find this saying in the four Gospels that have been handed down to us, but in that according to the Egyptians.[17]

3. Tertullian refuses to use any other Gospels than those that the church acknowledges as inspired and authoritative.[18] In a single passage he mentions Corinthians, Galatians, Philippians, Thessalonians, Ephesians, and Romans as samples of apostolic writings.[19] Concerning some of the Catholic Epistles he is silent.

The consentient testimony of these three witnesses from a period close to the end of the second century is sufficient to establish that there was a body of authoritative writings revered by the church as a whole. The only question that remains unsettled is the extent of the canon, which involves a discussion of the disputed books. Before turning to this, we should glance at a great leader of the following generation.

Origen of Alexandria. Speaking of the four Gospels "which alone are uncontroverted in the church of God spread under heaven," Origen then proceeds to name them.[20] In his commentary on Joshua, translated into Latin probably by Rufinus, he takes occasion to say that Paul thundered with the fourteen "trumpets" of his epistles. C. R. Gregory thinks it doubtful whether Origen himself wrote "fourteen," thus assigning Hebrews to Paul, or whether the figure was changed from thirteen to fourteen by the translator.[21] This Father indicates some doubt in the church of his time about II Peter and II and III John. Little, if anything, of the complete New Testament is lacking in Origen and therefore in the Egyptian church of his time.

---

16 Westcott notes (*op. cit.*, p. 354) that when other patristic testimony is considered, no evidence can be adduced for Clement's attitude on James, II Peter, and III John. But silence is not equal to rejection.

17 *Miscellanies* III. xiii.

18 William Sanday, *op. cit.*, p. 318.

19 *Against Marcion* IV. 5.

20 *HE* VI. xxv. 4.

21 *The Canon and Text of the New Testament*, p. 225.

DISPUTED BOOKS

Either because of omission from patristic testimony in some quarters or because of being named with a degree of question, the following lacked universal endorsement in the early centuries: Hebrews, James, II Peter, II and III John, Jude, and the Revelation. Hebrews, questioned in the West because of uncertainty as to apostolic authorship, gained acceptance in the East under the plea of the Alexandrians that it was Pauline in some sense, and in due time it was classified as one of Paul's letters. In the case of James, several factors may have operated: uncertainty as to the identity of the James in question, the problem as to the meaning of the Twelve Tribes scattered abroad, and the scarcity of distinctive Christian teaching on the doctrinal side. Doubt arose respecting II Peter because it differs so greatly in vocabulary and somewhat in style from the First Epistle. It seems to have had limited circulation also. Failure to include II and III John is understandable in view of their brevity, personal nature, and the relative unimportance of their contents. Jude was plagued with uncertainty as to the apostolic standing of the writer, who seems to set himself apart from the apostles (v. 17). John's Apocalypse had a solid place in the canon in the earlier patristic period, being questioned only by the sect known as the Alogi, but generally received throughout the church. The failure of writers in the East during the fourth century to include it in the New Testament may be assigned to the influence of the criticism of Dionysius of Alexandria, who argued the great differences between the Revelation and the Fourth Gospel as ground for concluding that another John must have written the Apocalypse. Influenced by Dionysius, Eusebius felt that it was wise to put the book not only among the acknowledged writings (Homologoumena) but also with the non-genuine, saying that some reject it.[22]

THE TESTIMONY OF THE VERSIONS

In Syria the church was Syriac-speaking, and during the second century had the Gospels in this tongue, as attested by the Diatessaron and the *Old Syriac*. Manuscript evidence for the rest of the New Testament at this early period is lacking, but there is no reasonable ground for doubt that most of the books were translated. Kenyon finds support for this position in the

[22] *HE* III. xxv. 2-4.

fact that "Armenian translations of commentaries by St. Ephraim on the Acts and Pauline Epistles are extant, which imply the use of a Syriac text earlier than the Peshitta."[23] The Peshitta, the common version or official Bible of the Syriac Church, was rendered in the fifth century. It reflected the reluctance of the East to receive certain books, since II Peter, II and III John, Jude and Revelation were lacking. In the following century these deficiencies were made up in the Philoxenian Syriac.

Toward the end of the second century the Christians of Egypt had the New Testament in the native Coptic tongue, at least in the Sahidic, and a few decades later in the Bohairic. However, since the manuscripts that attest the text come from varying periods, especially for the Sahidic,[24] it is precarious to insist on a complete New Testament from the beginning.

With respect to the Latin, it is well-known that Jerome prepared the Vulgate shortly before 400 because the Old Latin stood in dire need of revision. The inclusion of the complete New Testament in the Vulgate may be regarded as presumptive evidence of its presence in the Old Latin. As early as 180 there is indication of a collection of Paul's letters in North Africa, and if this be true, the Gospels must surely have been in use also.[25]

Concerning other versions it is unnecessary to make inquiry, since they pertain to more remote areas of the church and belong to somewhat later times.

THE FOURTH CENTURY

In this period the church comes more and more to a position of unanimity regarding the canon. Eusebius (260-340) lists only James, Jude, II Peter, II and III John as disputed books (Antilegomena). Cyril, Bishop of Jerusalem (315-386), accepts all but the Revelation. Athanasius, Bishop of Alexandria, in his 39th Festal Epistle (367), is the first to cite all 27 books.

During this era the church was free to engage in discussion at various councils, now that the threat of official Roman persecution was past. That it had been able to hold some gatherings, at least on a local scale, prior to this time, is indicated by Tertullian's broadside levelled at the *Shepherd of Hermas*. In his treatise on modesty (chap. 10) he states that this writing had been "habitually judged by every council of churches . . . among

23 *The Text of the Greek Bible*, p. 122.
24 Arthur Vööbus, *Early Versions of the New Testament*, p. 217.
25 *Ibid.*, p. 37.

apocryphal and false [writings]." This suggests that discussions on the canon may have been fairly common in some areas, but this is only an inference. At the Council of Laodicea (363) the books of the Bible seem at first sight to have been made the subject of special study. This was a local gathering attended by only a few delegates. The 59th canon records the decision of the council regarding the contents of Scripture. With reference to the New Testament, all the books are present except the Revelation. However, since not all the sources have this final canon of the council, it is probable that the list of books was added at a later time.[26] Firmer ground is reached with the Third Council of Carthage (397), which declared that these 27 books and these only were to be received as canonical.

It has sometimes been asserted that the canon derives both its form and authority from church councils, as though the church had no recognized Scripture prior to their action. Such is not the case. What the councils did was to certify the canon that was already widely acknowledged in the church. Conciliar action did not provide for the first time a rule of faith and practice, but rather gave public and united testimony to that which the church had long known and used and cherished as its authoritative guide. This is readily apparent from the testimonies of the Fathers that we have already noted, which are representative but by no means complete. Only in the case of disputed books could conciliar action be construed as legislative in any sense, and only as speaking in behalf of the majority who already received these books as Scripture.

If the church did not derive its notion of the uniqueness of these books from the action of councils, what then was the basis upon which it revered them above other Christian writings and carefully distinguished them as alone normative for the faith? This is the next subject for investigation.

PRINCIPLES GOVERNING CANONICITY

THE TESTIMONY OF THE ANCIENTS

This subject is seldom discussed by the early Fathers in a formal way, but enough information is available to enable us to know how they justified the reception of the New Testament books as authoritative to the exclusion of others.

---

[26] Gregory, *op. cit.*, pp. 266-67.

First, these books had *apostolic origin.* It was clear from
the New Testament that Jesus had chosen certain men and
had conferred on them the dignity of apostles in order that they
might be responsible and informed witnesses to himself and
authoritative guides of the infant church. The teaching of
these men was accepted by the church as possessing the authority
of Christ. Consequently, when they wrote, their testimony had
a unique place in the esteem of believers. Their writings were
read in the churches. Even so early a figure as Clement of Rome
recognized that Paul wrote to the Corinthians "with true inspiration," whereas he himself can claim neither apostolic rank
nor inspiration.[27] Ignatius sharply distinguished between himself
(a bishop of the church) and the apostles Peter and Paul, though
he was headed for martyrdom such as they had endured.[28]

Even in the New Testament period apostles received communication from Christian groups (e. g., I Cor. 7:1), but such
letters were not preserved and included with those of the apostles.
This easily overlooked fact underscores the uniqueness of the
writings of those who were qualified to declare Christian truth and
its implications for the church because of designation by Christ
himself.

The importance of apostolicity in the eyes of the early church
may be seen by recalling the history of the Epistle to the Hebrews and the Apocalypse of John. The former was more widely
received in the East than in the West for the reason that the
name of Paul had become attached to it by the Alexandrians.
In the West, Tertullian, because he ascribed the book to Barnabas,
was not willing to receive it as Scripture in the full sense. As
to the Apocalypse, Dionysius of Alexandria weakened its position
in the East by the force of his literary criticism, pointing out
certain differences between it and the Gospel of John and thereby bringing into question its apostolic origin. The reason for
its ultimate reception in the East was the insistence upon its
apostolic authorship by various leaders of the church, despite
the contrary opinion of Dionysius.

Again, the readiness of some church Fathers to give canonical rank to such works as the *Didache,* the *Epistle of Clement,*
and the *Shepherd of Hermas,* is explicable when it is perceived
that the authors might be confused with genuinely apostolic figures.
The full name of the *Didache* is the *Teaching of the Twelve
Apostles.* Clement of Alexandria probably endorsed the *Epistle*

27 *I Clement,* Chap. 47.
28 *Romans,* Chap. 4.

of Clement (of Rome) on the same ground as his successor, Origen, who identified this writer with the person mentioned by Paul in Philippians 4:3. This would not make Clement an apostle in the narrower sense such as pertained to the Twelve and to Paul, but he might be regarded as an apostle in the somewhat looser sense in which the term is occasionally employed in the New Testament. The acceptance in some quarters of the *Shepherd of Hermas* as canonical is to be traced to the belief that the author was the one mentioned in Romans 16:14.

Apostolicity in the strict sense will not account for all the books of the New Testament, however. Some theory had to be devised to accredit Mark and Luke. Here the church fell back upon the consideration that these men wrote under the direction of Peter and Paul respectively, so that their work possessed the authority of these apostolic men.[29] We may feel the need of caution in regarding this explanation as entirely valid, but again it reveals the strength of the hold that the test of apostolicity had on the church. Actually, when to Mark and Luke we add the writer to the Hebrews and Jude, the list of those who stand outside the apostolic circle is rather imposing. But all these men were close to the source of the stream of Christian tradition and the Spirit was free to use them as well as the more official representatives of the church.

Second, the Fathers stressed the *reception* of the New Testament writings by the original churches and the continued knowledge and use of these documents by later generations.[30] This is a natural corollary to apostolicity. Readers of the New Testament have noted the care that Paul displayed on occasion to make certain his writings were accepted as genuine (writing his signature with his own hand and committing the documents to trustworthy messengers, II Thess. 3:17; cf. 2:2). Each local church would be able to vouch for any such communication that another group might wish to copy and use. The practice of reading should be noted in this connection. To make use of a writing in connection with Christian worship was not absolute evidence of its canonical standing (e. g., I Clement was read in the Corinthian church alongside Scripture late in the second century), but it was tantamount to this. For the most part such reading was confined to canonical books.

Third, *consistency of doctrine* with the standard already pos-

[29] Tertullian, *Against Marcion* IV. 5.
[30] *Ibid.* See also Origen's testimony in *HE* VI. xxv. 3-4; Irenaeus, *Against Heresies* III. i. 1.

sessed in the Old Testament and in the teaching of the apostles was a useful requirement, enabling the church to expose and repudiate heretical writings, such as those of the Gnostics, and also many of the Apocrypha.

H. E. W. Turner notes that a measure of conflict might arise in the application of these criteria. A book might be widely received and appreciated and yet turn out to be unapostolic. Such was the case with the *Shepherd of Hermas,* which had to be excluded from use in public worship, but which was countenanced for purposes of private edification.[31] This helps to explain the origin of a class of early Christian literature known as ecclesiastical, distinguished alike from canonical and from spurious writings, containing such works as the *Epistle of Clement* and the *Epistle of Barnabas,* as well as the *Shepherd of Hermas.*

THE ROMAN CATHOLIC POSITION

Scripture is independent of the church so far as its inspiration is concerned. This is of God only, so that when Scripture is viewed in isolation, it possesses its own canonical authority. Practically, however, as Scripture comes into contact with human lives, it requires the voice of the church to authenticate it as well as to interpret it.[32] Another feature is the recognition of the validity of unwritten tradition alongside that of Scripture. The Council of Trent, at its fourth session, April 8, 1546, committed the church to honor along with Scripture "the unwritten traditions which, received by the Apostles from the mouth of Christ himself, or from the Apostles themselves, the Holy Ghost dictating, have come down even unto us, transmitted as it were from hand to hand." In its extent, the Roman Catholic New Testament is identical with that agreed upon at the Third Council of Carthage.

THE REFORMERS

Luther, with typical independence, singled out certain books as basic on the ground that they exhibit Christ. On the other hand, he relegated four books to a secondary position, putting Hebrews, James, Jude, and the Revelation at the end of his New Testament in a detached position. He did not deny to other Christians the right to consider these books on a par with the rest, but for himself found them inferior for various reasons.

---

31 *The Pattern of Christian Truth,* p. 250.
32 John E. Steinmueller, *A Companion to Scripture Studies,* I, 48.

Calvin commented on the New Testament in a comprehensive way, but he passed by II and III John and the Revelation. This does not mean he refused to honor them as Scripture, though he seems to have had reservations about them. Knowing the doubts of the ancients on other Antilegomena, he nevertheless was not particularly disturbed about these books, and received them.

Calvin's contribution to the doctrine of Scripture emerged in connection with his teaching on the believer's assurance concerning the word of God. This assurance is provided by the testimony of the Holy Spirit working with the word read or heard in preaching.[33] Quite obviously this work of the Spirit is chiefly concerned with the central issue of the gospel message and cannot be relied upon to settle the limits of the canon. But it provides a measure of certification of the canon on the subjective side to supplement the objective factors centering in the reception of the New Testament documents by the early church. Logically the external testimony comes first, for internal testimony, owing to the fact that some material in the sacred record pertains to mundane matters of fact as distinct from spiritual instruction, is limited in its power to give confirmation. It is difficult to conceive of the Spirit as attesting one name in a genealogical list as opposed to a possible alternative. Furthermore, if internal testimony were sufficient for establishing the word of God, it should be possible on this basis to settle every disputed text of the New Testament, thus eliminating the necessity for textual criticism. No one conversant with the problems will affirm that the testimony of the Spirit can properly be appealed to in this realm.

MODERN STUDY

For the English-speaking world the work of B. F. Westcott has proved of abiding worth. He emphasized the importance of a superintending providence guiding the church from the beginning to an appreciation of the books that time and use confirmed. He writes regarding the canon: "Its limits were fixed in the earliest times by use rather than by criticism; and this use itself was based on immediate knowledge."[34] Again, he affirms that it was under the influence of the Spirit that the church

[33] Bernard Ramm's *The Witness of the Spirit* gives a helpful exposition of Calvin's position.
[34] *History of the Canon,* 4th ed., p. 496.

113

recognized in the New Testament the law of its constitution.[35] The formation of the canon was an act of the intuition of the church.[36]

The German scholar Harnack, with a keen interest in Christian origins, included the canon in the scope of his studies. According to Harnack, the canon came into being rather suddenly, at about the beginning of the last quarter of the second century, as the conscious and deliberate creation of the Old Catholic Church, in order to meet the challenge of Gnosticism and Montanism. At first the church had only the Old Testament as Scripture in the strict sense of the word. Its need of instruction on an immediate basis was provided by the ministry of prophets, whose utterances were viewed as the word of God. This situation was changed by the emergence of the two movements mentioned above. The Gnostics (and for the immediate purpose Marcion may be classed with them) rejected the Old Testament and appealed to certain writings that the church had been using, notably the Epistles of Paul, in the case of Marcion. This obliged the church to declare itself. Marcion forced the hand of the church when he set up his canon.

Harnack undoubtedly overestimated the influence of Marcion on canonical developments within the church, primarily because he did not distinguish sufficiently between the principle of canonicity and the drawing up of a formal list of books. As Westcott states, "The canon of Marcion may have been the first which was publicly proposed, but the general consent of earlier Catholic writers proves that within the Church there had been no need for pronouncing a judgment on a point which had not been brought into dispute."[37] Our survey of the history of the canon has shown us that before Marcion's time there is reasonably clear evidence of the Gospel canon and a collection of Paul's writings.[38] It is hazardous to conclude that Marcion must be credited with the idea of a canon embracing Gospel and Apostle.[39] He was a competitor but not an innovator in the strictest sense of the word. Tertullian and other Fathers charge Marcion with rejecting books. This in itself presupposes in the minds of these men the acknowledged position of such books in

[35] *Ibid.,* p. 498.
[36] *Ibid.,* p. 56.
[37] *Ibid.,* p. 326.
[38] See especially the use of the word "Scripture" and the formulas by which Scripture was commonly introduced, e.g., *Barnabas* 4:14; II *Clement* 2:4; Polycarp, *Philippians,* Chap. 12.
[39] E. C. Blackman, *Marcion and His Influence,* pp. 29-31.

114

what was in fact a canon, even though it had not been published as such. W. C. van Unnik makes the point that the generous use of the New Testament books in the *Gospel of Truth* implies the authoritative position of these books at Rome *before the condemnation of Marcion* (italics ours).[40]

Montanism began to be a menace to the church's life shortly after the time of Marcion. Montanus insisted that the prophetic gift was permanently granted to the church and that he himself was an authoritative prophet of the Lord. Harnack claimed that whereas the church up to this time had accepted the prophetic as the norm of authoritative divine utterance, it was now obliged by the pressure of Montanism with its vagaries to call upon the principle of apostolicity, which of course made revelation beyond the apostolic age impossible. But Harnack tended to exaggerate the importance of the prophetic element in the early church. Evidence points to the fact that even in the apostolic age it was necessary to examine critically the utterances of those who professed to have the gift (I Cor. 12:10; 14:29).[41] It is not clear that prophecy can be identified with revelation in the fullest sense. Certainly the case of Agabus points to a very limited and specific function (Acts 11:28; 21:10). There can be no doubt that the church from the beginning looked to apostles rather than prophets for its primary guidance. In Ephesians 4:11, for example, prophets are subordinated to apostles.

Goodspeed seems to share with Harnack the feeling that the dominance of the Spirit in the life of the church logically makes a written canon unnecessary. "That the early church should have made itself an authoritative scripture and placed it side by side with the Old Testament is from some points of view strange." Then he goes on to explain that the church "possessed an inner guide, the Spirit of God, the mind of Christ, far superior to written rules and records."[42] Yet it is certainly right to say that there is no conscious antinomy in the Scripture or in the early church, so far as can be detected, between a written rule and the guidance of the Spirit. One of the classic statements of inspiration, II Peter 1:20-21, makes this apparent. Christianity is the religion of a book as well as of the Spirit. A written rule, while subject to the vicissitudes of copying and also of interpretation, had great advantage over occasional prophetic utterances that needed to be tried.

[40] *The Jung Codex*, F. L. Cross, ed., p. 125.
[41] Cf. Floyd V. Filson, *Which Books Belong in the Bible?*, p. 107.
[42] *Interpreter's Bible*, I, 63a.

Goodspeed approaches the study of the canon largely from the standpoint of the historian, and his chief contribution is the emphasis upon the formation of collections that together make up the New Testament, especially the Epistles of Paul and then the Gospels.[43] He tends to put the collection of Paul's letters later than necessary, however. In seeking to show that these had fallen into disuse shortly after being penned by pointing to the failure of the Synoptic Gospels and Acts to make use of them, he dubiously employs the precarious argument from silence. How can it be shown that the writers of the Gospels or of Acts felt under obligation to use epistolary material? The fact that they did not do so simply shows their fidelity to the task to which they had set themselves.

Zahn, who was a contemporary of Harnack, had considerable dispute with him over this subject of the canon. He maintained that a canon existed before the time of Marcion, and pointed to the lack of conciliar action in the latter part of the second century relative to this important matter. He insisted that the canon was not created by the church in the sense that bishops or councils formulated it. In his judgment the important factor in canonical development was the cultus, the use of the New Testament writings in the worship of the church. It was the suitability of the writings for this purpose that gave them a place in the canon. Zahn's view has a measure of truth, surely, but it would be hard to substantiate in the case of all the books of the New Testament, some of which are obviously less suited than others for ecclesiastical use because of their brevity and in some cases their rather private character.

Karl Barth, in his view of the canon, moves along traditional lines. "In no sense of the concept could or can the Church give the Canon to itself. The Church cannot 'form' it, as historians have occasionally said without being aware of the theological implications. The Church can only confirm or establish it as something which has already been formed and given."[44] Again, "For the obvious core of the history of the Canon is this, that within the various churches, and with all kinds of vacillations, particular parts of the oldest tradition have gradually been distinguished and set apart from others in the appreciation and acceptance of Christendom, a process which proper and formal canonization by synodic resolutions and the like could only sub-

---

43 See his *Formation of the New Testament*.
44 *Church Dogmatics*, I/2, p. 473.

sequently confirm. At some time and in some measure (with all the chance features which this appreciation and acceptance may have strengthened) these very writings, by the very fact that they were canonical, saw to it that they in particular were later recognized and proclaimed to be canonical."[45]

W. G. Kümmel doubts the validity of apostolic authorship as a valid criterion for canonicity. In its place he proposes a chronological criterion. Writings composed after the first quarter of the second century cannot be regarded as original witnesses and hence must be excluded, since the canon means basically a testimony to the early Christian history. Any book lying outside the chronological limits of the apostolic kerygma can and ought to be excluded.[46] Diem points out that the chronological test runs into some difficulty with *First Clement,* which clearly meets the demands of the time test but does not have canonical rank. To say that it was excluded because of contents is hardly a sufficient answer, since it is not heretical.[47]

Cullmann develops his view of the canon from within the framework of *Heilsgeschichte* (history of salvation, or saving history) and the importance of the apostolate as the authenticated medium of Christ for the teaching of the church. He holds that *"the infant Church itself distinguished between apostolic tradition and ecclesiastical tradition,* clearly subordinating the latter to the former, in other words, subordinating itself to the apostolic tradition."[48] Again, "The fixing of the Christian canon of scripture means that *the Church itself,* at a given time, traced a clear and definite line of demarcation between the period of the apostles and that of the Church, between the time of foundation and that of construction, between the apostolic community and the Church of the bishops, in other words, between apostolic tradition and ecclesiastical tradition. Otherwise the formation of the canon would be meaningless."[49] It is not the difference between oral and written tradition that is of major importance, but that the tradition was fixed by the apostles. "By establishing the *principle* of a canon the Church recognized that *from that time* the tradition was no longer a criterion of

---

[45] *Ibid.,* p. 474.
[46] "Notwendigkeit und Grenze des Neutestamentlichen Kanons," *ZTK,* 1950, pp. 385ff.
[47] *Dogmatics,* p. 208.
[48] *The Early Church,* p. 87.
[49] *Ibid.,* p. 89.

truth."[50] Its unreliability was already beginning to be apparent in the proliferation of apocryphal writings.

Seeking to meet the Roman Catholic objection that Scripture by itself is a dead thing, requiring the vital life of God flowing through the church to support and implement it, Cullmann insists on the truth that Scripture is not rightly used if it is not apprehended as the means of the risen Lord's continuing ministry in the church even as that ministry was manifest in the witness of the apostles during their lifetime.

A weakness in Cullmann's position is that it requires a degree of self-consciousness on the part of the early church in this matter of canonical development that the sources of the middle of the second century do not indicate. This is the perennial problem in dealing with the canon. The historical materials are too limited to satisfy the historian, so he must call upon theological theory to bridge the gap.

CONCLUSION

The principle of canonicity cannot be divorced from the idea of authority, in this case a divine authority, in spite of the obvious fact that the Scriptures were written by men. Back of the written word lies the oral tradition concerning Christ and his work, and back of the oral tradition lies the preaching of the apostles as authoritative spokesmen for Christ (cf. II Cor. 13:3), and back of this apostolic testimony lies Christ himself as the one whom the Father sent to accomplish redemption for the world. Christ both authenticated the Old Testament Scriptures and promised the activity of the Spirit of truth as making possible what became in fact the New Testament. So in the ultimate sense Christ is the key to canonicity.

The very character of New Testament revelation was bound to make the written record that enshrined it authoritative. If the church was conscious of the fulfillment of Old Testament prophecy in the life and mission of Christ and in its own beginnings, it was inevitable that the church should regard the record of these fulfillments as partaking of the same authoritative character as the Old Testament, which now for the first time spoke to men's hearts with fullness of meaning as seen in the light of the new and completed revelation.

Some people are disturbed because there was not complete agreement in the early church as to which books should stand

---

[50] *Ibid.*, p. 90.

in the New Testament canon. Some measure of discussion was no doubt necessary in order to satisfy as many minds as possible and lead to a consensus. The important fact to remember here, however, is this, that the very fact of discussion about the right of books to stand in the canon presupposes the idea of a canon, the idea of a body of writings sacred and authoritative in a unique sense. Passing disagreement on a few books should not be allowed to overshadow in importance the vastly greater measure of agreement on the majority of the books. Furthermore, basic agreement on the canon by various sections of the church on a voluntary basis (apart from and prior to action by church councils) is a noteworthy fact that should be given its full weight.

It is unrealistic to expect that the church at the end of the first century would be aware that it had a complete canon in its possession and would give united expression to that fact so as to close the issue of New Testament Scripture once for all. The church was extending itself territorially, with limited contact between its various segments, and had no pressure either from without or from within to make a definitive statement on the subject of the canon. To quote G. W. H. Lampe, "The early church did not possess the critical or historical equipment to define the canon quickly, uniformly, or exactly; but it gradually succeeded in isolating such early works, in addition to the gospels and the recognized apostolic epistles, as it believed to embody the general doctrinal position of the apostles. That there were loose ends here and there — an epistle or two not universally accepted which came to be acknowledged, and a sub-apostolic book or two which were very nearly accepted but which came to be rejected, did not seem to the early Church to be a matter of any great moment. Under the guidance of the Spirit in the Church at large the apostolic tradition handed down in the Churches came to take the form of defined Scriptures."[51]

The church's uncertainty regarding a few books may be a matter of some concern to us, but we see that on the whole it was irenically handled, and became dissolved as the books in question became more and more widely known and used. On the other hand, the violence of the church's reaction to the effort of Marcion to set up a restricted canon is a testimony to the fact that the church was aware of its larger riches, which it refused to deny to itself.

It is of some interest to observe that the books that raised most

[51] *Scripture and Tradition,* ed. by F. W. Dillistone, p. 43.

questions in the early church are grouped last in the order of our English Bible, from Hebrews to Revelation, although two which stand near the end, I Peter and I John, were rarely held in any doubt.

The indefiniteness of address common to the so-called Catholic Epistles may have ministered to their tardiness in gaining general acceptance, for there was no one church, in such cases, which received the letter and vouched for it to others. This may have counterbalanced the consideration that the very indefiniteness of destination presupposes a fairly wide original reception.

As to this problem of tardiness in acceptance of a few books and the related problem of a few non-canonical books being treated as canonical by a few men, J. Norval Geldenhuys advances the explanation that these conditions were largely due to the expansion of the church. This state of affairs did not exist at first nor did it last indefinitely, for the church gradually came to agreement.[52]

Doubtless some questions remain unanswered. Because the term "Scripture" is applied to New Testament writings only occasionally in the sub-apostolic age, the student may conclude that the apostolic writers were themselves not aware of composing Scripture. This is quite possible, for to them Scripture meant the Old Testament. What is essential, however, is to approach the matter from the divine standpoint, from the standpoint of God's purpose to provide the finished revelation. Even from the human standpoint there was awareness on the part of the apostles that God was speaking and commanding through them. So the lack of awareness of composing Scripture is no more damaging to the cause of canonical authority than is a similar situation among Old Testament writers.

Another question pertains to the role of the church in relation to the canon. Is the canon dependent on the church or does it occupy a position apart from and above the church, in some fashion approximating the relation of Christ to the church? Much depends on how the matter is stated. In so far as men were needed to write the documents and secure their transmission and make known their contents, the canon is indeed dependent on the church. On the other hand, to maintain that the church "created" Scripture is a contradiction of what the church has always understood when it has described these writings as the word of God. As Barth has again reminded us, the canon is something given to the church.

[52] *Supreme Authority*, pp. 117-18.

A final question is a favorite with theologial students. What about apostolic writings that have not survived (e.g., the letter alluded to in I Cor. 5:9)? If one of these should be recovered today, would it rightfully have a place in the canon? It is wise to fall back on the providence of God which has permitted the recovery of many ancient documents but nothing apostolic. If the New Testament has been sufficient, under God, for the life of the church throughout all these centuries, it hardly needs supplementation at this late date. The question is hypothetical.

NEW TESTAMENT APOCRYPHA

Etymologically the word Apocrypha denotes hidden or secret things, thus suggesting esoteric writings. But when such writings are suspect as to the reliability of their contents, the word tends to acquire an unfavorable connotation. In the ordinary speech of our time that which is apocryphal is untrue. It is well, however, to avoid any prejudgment suggested by the term and to be content to use it simply in contrast to canonical. Actually it is employed also in contrast to that class of books already referred to as ecclesiastical, which stood on a much higher footing in the early church than the apocryphal.

The apocryphal writings are later than those that make up the New Testament. Some of them appeared as early as the second century, and they continued to emerge for several hundred years. Their use of the New Testament materials varies from close dependence in matter and spirit to great liberty and considerable departure from the norm of the gospel message. As to form, all the literary types found in the New Testament — Gospels, Acts, Epistles, and Apocalypses — have their representatives in this literature.

Two factors were largely responsible for the creation of these writings. One was the desire for further information about the life of Jesus and the careers of the apostles. Scripture has little to say about our Lord prior to the opening of his ministry. This gap was an invitation and even a challenge to supply the deficiency by calling upon the resources of the imagination. In the case of the apostles, the labors of most of them are passed by in the canonical Acts. Curiosity was aroused about the place and nature of their ministries, and the apocryphal Acts were intended to meet the demand for just such information. Epistles and Apocalypses were not produced in the same profusion as Gospels and Acts.

A second factor was the desire of those with heretical tendencies to foist their ideas on the church with the alleged endorsement of Christ or the apostles. By far the most common of these tendencies was the Gnostic. Even some of the Fathers of the church were to a degree affected by Gnostic notions, so that the provenance of some of the writings involved, as to whether they came from the bosom of the church or from definitely heretical sources, is a nice question.[53] It was rather easy to claim the authority of Jesus for teaching that went beyond that of the New Testament, since he himself had hinted that he had much to say that he was unable to impart to his disciples at the time (John 16:12). This was an open door for Gnostic propaganda, especially as it was put in the lips of the resurrected Saviour.

Extra-canonical Gospels and Acts are ordinarily characterized by a multiplication of the miraculous and a forsaking of the sobriety of the biblical works of power for that which is merely thaumaturgic. The importance of the gospel message for the effecting of conversion is often eclipsed by the sheer force of the marvels performed by emissaries of the cross.

We are assured that the leaders of the church were quite aware of the harmful effects of this literature. Origen commented, "The church receives only four gospels; heretics have many, such as the gospel of the Egyptians, the gospel of Thomas, etc. These we read, that we may not seem to be ignorant to those who think they know something extraordinary, if they are acquainted with those things which are recorded in these books."[54] Ambrose is credited with saying, "We read these that they may not be read by others; we read them that we may not seem ignorant; we read them, not that we receive them, but that we may reject them; and may know what those things are, of which they make such a boast."[55]

A knowledge of the apocryphal writings has a twofold value. First, the student is able to compare this literature with the acknowledged books of the New Testament. If he has misgivings about the formation of the canon, feeling that perhaps the endorsement of the books was somewhat arbitrary, it is morally certain that he will be won to a position of complete

[53] An excellent statement of the Gnostic position is given by A. F. Findlay, *Byways in Early Christian Literature*, pp. 118-21.

[54] First Homily on Luke, commenting on 1:1.

[55] Quoted by Archibald Alexander, *The Canon of the Old and New Testaments*, 1851, p. 276.

confidence in the superiority of the New Testament books on the basis of comparison. Second, since this literature is bound to reflect the beliefs and practices of those who wrote, a window is opened upon the nature of Christianity in the post-apostolic age. Such things as the loss of the fine edge of the teaching of grace, the emergence of the conception of Christianity as a new law, the undue exaltation of the sacramental element of the faith, and the growing veneration of Mary are some of the impressions received. Actually, the influence of the apocrypha goes far beyond the early history of the church; it extends well into the medieval period. "The reliefs of ancient sarcophagi, the mosaics of Christian basilicas, the miniatures of illuminated manuscripts, the stained glass windows of the cathedrals, the mystery plays — all owe their inspiration to the New Testament Apocrypha."[56]

Most of these writings exist in fragmentary form. Knowledge of their contents derives in part from the occasional comments of the early Fathers about them. The standard work has been *The Apocryphal New Testament,* by M. R. James, but now Edgar Hennecke's *New Testament Apocrypha* adds new material.

APOCRYPHAL GOSPELS

These relate mainly to the nativity of Jesus or to his childhood or to his death and resurrection.

1. *The Protevangelium of James.* This title was first given to the work in the sixteenth century. Origen refers to it simply as the Book of James, for this second-century document purports to come from James the brother of our Lord. The reader becomes acquainted with the names of Mary's parents, Joachim and Anna, and learns of the angelic visitation to Anna and the promise of a child to be born in her old age. When only three, Mary is placed in the temple in the care of the priests. At twelve, since the priests refuse to keep her any longer, she is awarded to one of several widowers, namely, Joseph, who is already an old man with several children. After this comes the story of the annunciation, then the enrollment for taxing, the account of the birth (in a cave), etc., much of it in close agreement with the Scripture narratives. One interesting detail is to the effect that Mary's pregnancy was brought to the attention of the temple authorities, who gave to her and to Joseph the water of jealousy to test their innocency. Both survived the ordeal. This

---

[56] Johannes Quasten, *TCERK,* pp. 52-53.

item seems designed to expose the baselessness of the calumnies of the Jews against the purity of Mary. The book supports her perpetual virginity, which became such a marked feature of Catholicism.

2. *Pseudo-Matthew.* This fifth-century account depends upon the *Protevangelium* for the first part of its narrative and the *Gospel of Thomas* for the latter part. The central portion is distinctive in that it deals with the flight to Egypt. On the way lions and leopards, instead of harming the party, bow before Jesus and show the way through the desert. Entering Egypt, the holy family lodges in a temple housing numerous idols. As the child enters, the idols fall. These and other events are cited as fulfilling the Old Testament Scriptures.

3. *The Gospel of Thomas.* This famous writing, known at least as early as the time of Origen, presents the boy Jesus in the light of a wonder worker. It does not seem to matter that he works harm as well as good by his miraculous power. Here the thaumaturgic element has outrun any ethical norm. Jesus molds clay pigeons on the Sabbath. When objection is raised, he claps his hands, whereupon the pigeons take to the air and fly away. When a child running through the village bumps him on the shoulder, he cries, "Thou shalt not finish thy course," and forthwith the child drops dead. When the parents come to expostulate with Joseph, they are smitten with blindness. A certain teacher, desiring to have Jesus as a pupil, soon regrets the arrangement, for when he is asked by the child to explain the letter Alpha and is unable to do so, Jesus elaborates its meaning and makes fun of his teacher, to the great discomfort of the latter. This incident reflects an esoteric interest and may be a Gnostic touch in the childhood tradition.

Boyhood miracles are excluded by the canonical Gospels, both on the ground that the turning of water into wine at Cana was the beginning of miracles (John 2:11) and because those among whom he had been brought up at Nazareth were astonished at his works of power, indicating that they did not associate such deeds with his early years (Mark 6:2-3).

4. *The Gospel According to the Hebrews.* This enjoyed a high reputation among the Fathers, so it is judged that the contents were largely unobjectionable, being closely related to the text of Matthew. A few of its distinctive sayings will be treated later under *Agrapha.* The exact relation between this document and the *Gospel of the Egyptians* is not clear. Some connection must be assumed also with the *Gospel of the Ebionites,*

124

which Epiphanius described as a falsified and mutilated version of Matthew.

5. *The Gospel of Peter.* Emanating from the second century, this account is notable for its docetic tendency. On the cross Jesus is silent, as one who feels no pain. He cries out, "My power, my power, thou hast forsaken me." This writing presumably owes its origin to the group who taught that the divine Christ came upon the man Jesus at the baptism and departed from him on the cross. It was regarded as impossible for the heavenly Christ to be involved in actual suffering. A strong anti-Semitic bias is discernible also. Blame for the crucifixion is fastened on Herod rather than Pilate and the prayer of Jesus for forgiveness is omitted. An attempt is made to describe the resurrection. As the soldiers and elders watch, three figures emerge from the tomb, two of them supporting the third, whose head reaches into the heavens. Behind them comes the cross. A voice from heaven asks, "Hast thou preached to them that sleep?" To this question an affirmative answer is given from the cross. In this way the document reveals an interest, widespread in the early church, in Christ's preaching to the dead between death and resurrection.

6. *The Gospel of Nicodemus* or *Acts of Pilate.* Nicodemus is represented as the writer of this work, which probably is to be dated in the fourth century. The trial of Jesus before Pilate is amplified to include testimony of those who are favorable to Jesus, including the impotent man of John 5 and the blind man of John 9. Details of the crucifixion include the names of the two malefactors, Dysmas and Gestas, and the name of the soldier who wielded the spear, Longinus. Special prominence is given to Nicodemus and Joseph of Arimathea, the latter reporting an appearance of the Lord to him before the dawning of the first day of the week. Others than disciples are represented as seeing and hearing Jesus and reporting to the Sanhedrin. Part II of this document, which did not belong to it originally, is known as "The Descent into Hell." Christ's coming into the realm of the dead is vividly described, resulting in the binding of Satan and the freeing of the saints — Adam, Isaiah, John the Baptist and others.

These are some of the more prominent of the Apocryphal Gospels. The full texts, so far as these are available, may be consulted in James' volume. That the craving for this sort of literature is not dead finds demonstration in sporadic modern attempts to satisfy it. See E. J. Goodspeed, *Strange New Gospels,* 1931.

APOCRYPHAL ACTS

These writings are as far as possible based on the Book of Acts, which shows an acknowledgment of its canonical position. But the motivation is different, resulting in quite a different atmosphere. Whereas Luke was content to magnify the progress of the gospel, subordinating the personal element in the lives of the apostles and also their miraculous deeds to this objective, the apocryphal Acts idolize the apostles and exaggerate the miraculous, portraying it for its own sake. In view of this freedom, one cannot expect to find much of historical value in these records.

A Gnostic tinge is observable in most of them, resulting in a false view of the humanity of our Lord, and also an Encratite strain in the demand for an ascetic type of life that bans marriage, the eating of meat and the drinking of wine. After noting a tendency to modalism in handling the relation between the Father and the Son, Findlay comments, "When the divinity of Jesus is stressed in such a way that no distinction between the Father and the Son is recognized, the inevitable consequence is that His humanity fades into the background and becomes shadowy and unreal."[57]

Five of these works, the *Acts of Peter, John, Andrew, Thomas,* and *Paul,* came to be known as the *Leucian Acts* because of the tradition that a certain Leucius had gathered them into a corpus. When heretical groups, especially the Manichaeans, sought to elevate these writings to apostolic rank, the church repudiated them, even though the *Acts of Paul* had been highly regarded by many churchmen as markedly superior to the others. Now all of them were branded as heretical (by the fifth century). Although the leaders of the church spoke against such writings, their protests could not break the hold of their popularity with the rank and file. As a compromise, they attempted to rewrite them so as to eliminate the most objectionable features. But they felt obliged to retain the miraculous element that catered to people's fancy and captivated their imagination.

1. *The Acts of Paul.* The most entertaining portion of this book is called the *Acts of Paul and Thecla.* This maiden listened to Paul preach in Iconium and became greatly interested, so much so that under the influence of his preaching she dedicated herself to a life of perpetual virginity and would have nothing more to do with the young man to whom she was engaged to be married. Paul was put in prison for influencing

[57] *Op. cit.,* p. 204.

126

the girl and before long both were brought to trial. Paul was driven from the city and she was condemned to death by burning, but the fire was miraculously quenched. Rejoining Paul, she went with him to Antioch, where her great beauty caught the eye of an official named Alexander, who sought to embrace her in public. Resisting him, she tore the wreath from his head and damaged his attire. For this she was brought before the governor and was sentenced to death. Wild beasts were loosed against her, but a lioness acted as her guardian from the others. When the lioness was killed, Thecla jumped into a tank containing some seals, exclaiming, "I am baptized in the name of Jesus Christ on the (or my) last day." A strange fire appeared that formed a wall of protection for her and also accomplished the death of the seals. Further measures were attempted, but when the queen fainted, the whole effort was called off and Thecla was released. Her last days were spent at Seleucia, where she continued to teach the word of God.

Something is learned about this work from Tertullian, who referred to it in trying to cope with those who insisted on the right of women to take official leadership in the church. "But if the writings which wrongly go under Paul's name, claim Thecla's example as a license for women's teaching and baptizing, let them know that, in Asia, the presbyter who composed that writing, as if he were augmenting Paul's fame from his own store, after being convicted, and confessing that he had done it from love of Paul, was removed from his office."[58]

2. *The Acts of John.* A second century product, it is famous for its recital of the incident in which, because of the prayer of John, the temple of Artemis at Ephesus collapsed, resulting in the conversion of many people. Great stress is laid upon the unreality of Christ's humanity. Detachment from the world and the disavowal of marriage are held up constantly as the ideal for the Christian.

3. *The Acts of Andrew.* After preaching and performing a wide assortment of miracles at various places around the Aegean basin, this apostle concludes his labors in Achaia, where his death is occasioned by the refusal of a noblewoman to return to her husband after her conversion. It is said that Andrew hung on the cross for three days, preaching to the people as his life gradually ebbed away.

4. *The Acts of Peter.* Around the close of the second century a work was written that has for its major theme the account of

[58] *On Baptism*, Chap. xvii (Thelwall's translation).

competition between Simon Magus, who is now located in Rome, and the apostle Peter, divinely directed to go there to thwart the deception of this Satan-filled man. After various episodes, the two men come face to face in the presence of Roman senators and many others for a test of strength. Peter raises a dead man to life. Simon appears to duplicate the feat, but his work is revealed as fraudulent. Finally, to regain his prestige, Simon mounts up over the city on an alleged ascent to God. Peter's prayers avail to bring him down, with the result that Simon's leg is broken in three places. From this accident he is unable to recover, so that death ensues shortly thereafter.

5. *The Acts of Thomas.* A third century work emanating from the Syrian branch of the church, this popular narrative relates that Thomas received India as his sphere of service. Rebellious at this assignment, he refuses to go, whereupon the Lord arranges that he should be sold as a slave to a merchant from India who happens to be in Jerusalem at the time representing his king Gundaphorus. Thomas is known as a carpenter. On arrival in India, he receives a command to build a palace for the sovereign, and is provided with funds for this purpose. But he gives away the money in alms to the poor. When the king inquires about the palace, he is informed by Thomas that it is built, but that he cannot see it until he departs this life. Enraged, the king puts Thomas in prison and prepares tortures designed to end the apostle's life in misery. Meanwhile the king's brother dies and his soul is taken to heaven. Desiring to dwell in a splendid abode that he sees there, he is informed that he cannot, for it has been built for his brother. Forthwith the soul is permitted to return to the body and the restored man reports his findings to the king, who proceeds to release Thomas from prison.

Further deeds of Thomas follow, many of them concerned with the conversion of wives who thereupon refuse to cohabit with their husbands. Finally, when king Misdaeus finds that both his wife and son have embraced the new faith, he orders the execution of the apostle. So the story is brought to a close with an account of Thomas' martyrdom. It can hardly be doubted that the first part of the narrative was influential in spreading the notion that one could accumulate merit through giving alms to the needy.

EPISTLES

These are few in number and comparatively unimportant, so a brief account of some of them is sufficient.

1. *The Epistle of the Apostles.* Emanating from about the

128

middle of the second century, this is an orthodox work purporting to be the united testimony of the apostles directed against heretical tendencies, naming specifically Simon (Magus) and Cerinthus. Special features are the opening confession of faith that emphasizes the reality of the incarnation, and the disclosures of the Lord after his bodily resurrection in response to numerous questions from the apostles, including teaching on eschatology. Of some interest is a section containing a prediction of the conversion of Saul of Tarsus.

2. *The Epistle to the Laodiceans.* First mention of this work occurs in the Canon of Muratori. Unquestionably the inspiration for it was furnished by Paul's allusion to an epistle from Laodicea in Colossians 4:16. The writer has taken a few excerpts from Paul's letters, especially Philippians, and has strung them together without any particular organization.

3. *The Corinthian Correspondence of Paul.* Also known as the "Third Epistle to the Corinthians," it is imbedded in the *Acts of Paul.* It consists of a reply to a letter sent to Paul at Philippi from the Corinthians who were disturbed by the views of certain Gnosticizing teachers that seemed novel to these believers. Paul's reply stresses the reality of the bodily life of the Lord and the future bodily resurrection of the saints.

4. *Letters of Christ and Abgar.* The latter was king of a small Mesopotamian country to which the Christian faith came around A.D. 200. Presumably this correspondence is designed to make it appear that the gospel reached this area early in the apostolic age. The king writes to Jesus, requesting him to come and heal him. In his reply Jesus says he is unable to come but promises to send one of his followers when he himself has returned to the Father.

5. *The Correspondence of Paul and Seneca.* Since these figures were contemporary, someone could not resist the temptation to bring them together in this fashion. Consisting of fourteen brief letters, probably deriving from the fourth century, this collection is quite valueless.

APOCALYPSES

The most famous are the *Apocalypse of Peter* (2nd century) and the *Apocalypse of Paul* (4th century). The former consists of three parts: an eschatological discourse spoken by Christ in the presence of Peter and others, modeled after the material in Matthew 24; a section portraying Paradise; a longer section setting forth the sufferings of the wicked in hell, the punishments varying according to the offense, but almost invariably involving fire. The second work is longer and is built on the passage in II Corinthians 12 dealing with the taking up of Paul into Paradise. He learns that whatever is wrought among men, both of good and evil, is reported to God by the angels. He watches as souls leave the earth. The righteous are claimed by the good angels, the wicked by the evil angels. Visions of heaven and hell follow. In Paradise he meets with the saints of former days. In hell he witnesses lurid scenes of punishment as the wicked are visited for their sins. The descriptions are similar to those in the *Apocalypse of Peter.*

AGRAPHA

Related to the study of the canon is the consideration of sayings attributed to Jesus that are not found in the authenticated text of the Gospels. The term "Agrapha," meaning literally "unwritten things," is the technical term for such sayings. Certain hints in the New Testament point to their existence: (1) In the prologue of his Gospel, Luke states that many had undertaken to write an account of the things that had been accomplished (in connection with the ministry of Jesus). Some genuine sayings of the Master that are not reported by the Evangelists may well have been included in these writings. (2) At the close of the Gospel according to John it is noted that Jesus did many signs in addition to those that are included in this account (21:25). Since the signs utilized in the Fourth Gospel are nearly always accompanied by words of explanation and application, a presumption is created that these other signs involved sayings of Jesus. (3) The fact that the Lord was active in a teaching ministry of approximately three years' duration is agreeable to the supposition that his spoken message was far bulkier than what is contained in our Gospels. Doubtless the Palestinian church had much of this material in its possession in oral form. Some of it may have perished because of the fortunes of history that brought about the gradual eclipse of the Hebrew branch of the church, but a part of it must have found its way meanwhile into other areas of the church where it was preserved.

SOURCES

Sources for the Agrapha are four in number.

1. *The New Testament.* Paul attributes to Jesus the saying, "It is more blessed to give than to receive" (Acts 20:35), which is lacking in the canonical Gospels. Another example pertains to

the words of institution of the Lord's Supper (I Cor. 11:25). One could also include the pericope concerning the woman taken in adultery (John 7:53-8:11) and possibly the words about the Lord's return in I Thessalonians 4:16-17a.

2. *The Textual Evidence of Early Manuscripts of the New Testament.* Especially to be noted here is the so-called "Western" type of text. One of the most famous of sayings of this sort involving Jesus runs as follows: "On the same day he beheld a certain man working on the Sabbath, and said to him, 'Man, if indeed thou knowest what thou art doing, thou art blessed; but if thou knowest not, thou art accursed and a transgressor of the law'" (Luke 6:5). This could well be a genuine saying, fitting in with our Lord's known attitude toward the Sabbath.

3. *The Literature of the Early Church.* It will be found almost invariably that the Fathers who cite Agrapha depend upon non-canonical Gospels for their information.[59] From the *Gospel according to the Hebrews,* according to Jerome, comes this account (following upon the resurrection of the Savior). "But when the Lord had given the linen cloth (shroud) to the priest's servant, he went to James and appeared to him. For James had taken an oath that he would not eat bread from that hour in which he had drunk the cup of the Lord, until he should see him rising from them that sleep." Farther on the Lord is represented as saying, "Bring me a table and bread." Following this, the text runs, "He took the bread and blessed, and broke, and gave to James the Just, and said to him, 'My brother, eat thy bread, inasmuch as the Son of Man hath risen from them that sleep.'" This is clearly a later addition to the Gospel tradition, designed to amplify I Corinthians 15:7 and to make it appear that James was a believer prior to the resurrection.

The most commonly reported saying of all, "Be ye approved money changers" (or, "Show yourselves approved bankers") was understood by the Fathers to mean, "Cultivate spiritual discernment" or "Prove all things; cling to the genuine." This has the ring of an authentic utterance, and is not an isolated phenomenon, since Jesus several times illumined the calling of a disciple by comparison with various earthly occupations.[60]

4. *Modern Papyri Discoveries.* Near the close of the last century, at the site of ancient Oxyrhynchus in Egypt, fragments were unearthed that contained several sayings attributed to Jesus, some

---

[59] J. Jeremias, *Unknown Sayings of Jesus,* p. 21.
[60] *Ibid.,* p. 90.

of them incomplete because of damage to the text. Probably the most famous of these reads as follows: "Jesus saith, 'Wheresoever there are two, they are not without God, and where there is one alone, I say I am with him. Lift up the stone, and there thou shalt find me: cleave the wood, and there am I.'" This has been endorsed by several scholars as a likely word from the Carpenter to lonely toilers. But the form of the saying seems to lay stress upon the ubiquity of Christ in a fashion agreeable to Gnostic notions. This judgment is confirmed by the occurrence of the saying about the wood in the recently discovered *Gospel according to Thomas*. Perhaps a true saying of our Lord has been garbled to give a desired effect.

The Gospel according to Thomas (not to be confused with the childhood Gospel) contains not only the Oxyrhynchus sayings, but many (40 or more) unknown before. In 1945 or 1946 peasants at Nag-Hamadi (known as Chenoboskion in ancient times) dug up more than 40 manuscripts in the Coptic tongue, the library of a Gnostic group, and thus added substantially to the store of documentation for Gnosticism. Our interest centers in the aforementioned writing, which contains approximately 114 sayings of Jesus.[61] It is not a Gospel in the accepted sense, since it does not contain a narrative framework. The opening lines deserve to be quoted, since they set the tone for the work as a whole. "These are the secret words which the living Jesus spoke and Didymos Judas Thomas wrote. And He said, 'Whoever finds the explanation of these words will not taste death.'" In typical Gnostic fashion Christ is magnified as the Revealer whose words have a deeper meaning than the ordinary person is apt to find in them.

Approximately half the sayings are akin to those in the canonical Gospels, but generally in somewhat different words. Like most of the Agrapha they reflect the Synoptic tradition much more closely than the material in the Fourth Gospel.

GENUINENESS

With the increase of extra-canonical sayings, the question of genuineness becomes all the more pressing. Those that are clearly

[61] For the text and translation prepared by a group of scholars, see *The Gospel according to Thomas*, New York: Harper, 1959; for a judicious appraisal of the Gospel, see Otto A. Piper, "The Gospel of Thomas," *The Princeton Seminary Bulletin*, Oct. 1959, pp. 18-24; for a more elaborate treatment, see *The Theology of the Gospel according to Thomas* by Bertil Gärtner, New York: Harper, 1961.

modifications or extensions of acknowledged sayings of our Lord sometimes disclose the motivation behind the alteration or addition. Some are clearly inventions designed to promote special points of view by claiming the authority of Christ. The safest norm for judgment is the corpus of sayings attributed to our Lord in the canonical Gospels. If the new sayings agree in outlook and spirit and if they are true to the Palestinian setting and the period of the ministry, they present a reasonable basis for at least tentative acceptance as genuine utterances of our Lord.

BIBLIOGRAPHY

Aland, Kurt, *The Problem of the New Testament Canon.* London: A. R. Mowbray and Co., 1962.

Beare, F. W., "Canon of the NT," *IDB.* New York: Abingdon Press, 1962.

Blackman, E. C., *Marcion and His Influence.* London: SPCK, 1948.

Bruce, F. F., *The Books and the Parchments.* London: Pickering and Inglis, 1950, pp. 102-111.

Diem, Hermann, *Dogmatics.* Edinburgh: Oliver and Boyd, 1959, pp. 194-223.

Filson, Floyd V., *Which Books Belong in the Bible?* Philadelphia: Westminster Press, 1957, pp. 101-164.

Findlay, A. F., *Byways in Early Christian Literature.* Edinburgh: T. & T. Clark, 1923.

Goodspeed, E. J., *The Formation of the New Testament.* Chicago: Univ. of Chicago Press, 1926.

Grant, R. M., *The Formation of the New Testament.* New York: Harper and Row, 1965.

Gregory, C. R., *The Canon and Text of the New Testament.* New York: Charles Scribner's Sons, 1907, pp. 7-295.

Von Harnack, Adolf, *The Origin of the New Testament.* London: Williams and Norgate, 1925.

Harris, R. Laird, *Inspiration and Canonicity of the Bible.* Grand Rapids: Zondervan Publishing House, 1957, pp. 199-282.

James, M. R., *The Apocryphal New Testament.* Oxford: Clarendon Press, 1924.

Jeremias, J., *Unknown Sayings of Jesus.* London: SPCK, 1958.

McNeile, A. H., *An Introduction to the Study of the New Testament.* Second Edition Revised by C. S. C. Williams. Oxford: Clarendon Press, 1953, pp. 310-372.

Ridderbos, Herman, "The Canon of the New Testament," in *Revelation and the Bible,* ed. by Carl F. H. Henry. Grand Rapids: Baker Book House, 1958, pp. 189-201.

Ridderbos, H. N., *The Authority of the New Testament Scriptures*. Grand Rapids: Baker Book House, 1963.

Sanday W., *The Gospels in the Second Century*. London: Macmillan, 1876.

Souter, A., *The Text and Canon of the New Testament*. New York: Charles Scribner's Sons, 1913, pp. 149·248.

Westcott, B. F., *A General Survey of the History of the Canon of the New Testament*. 4th ed., London: Macmillan, 1875.

Zahn, Theodor, *Geschichte des Neutestamentlichen Kanons*, 2 vols. Erlangen: 1888-1892.

————————, *Grundriss der Geschichte des Neutestamentlichen Kanons*. Leipzig: 1901.

PART V

THE LITERATURE OF THE NEW TESTAMENT

Chapter Five

THE GOSPELS

THOUGH THE GOSPELS WERE NOT THE FIRST DOCUMENTS PER-
taining to the Christian movement, they fittingly occupy a place
at the forefront of the New Testament, since they record what
happened at the "beginning," the events that were later recognized
to have central significance for the faith of the church and its
message to the world.

Since one of the terms for this message is *gospel,* the use of
the same word as a designation for the records of Jesus' activity
must be understood as a deliberate effort to indicate the nature
of these records. To say they are biographies or histories is to
ignore the testimony of the caption. Granted that biographical
and historical material is found here, yet this material must be
viewed as part of a spiritual message.

In modern times there is danger of losing sight of this. "The
Gospel according to Matthew" is often viewed simply as a
convenient tag. "Matthew's Gospel" will do just as well. But
this manner of speaking magnifies the distinctiveness of each

writing and the importance of the human author. In the eyes of the early church these documents were virtually one. Together they embraced the gospel, which was set forth by Matthew, Mark, Luke, and John. The Christ-event was responsible for creating a new type of literature.

THE WORD "GOSPEL"

In the LXX the exact form εὐαγγέλιον does not occur, though there is a handful of references in the plural and a few involving a related word εὐαγγελία. All these occurrences reflect one Hebrew word meaning "tidings," which are generally good, but not invariably, as would appear from the fact that the adjective "good" is added in II Samuel 18:27. Sometimes the word means reward for bringing good tidings, as in II Samuel 18:22. This latter idea is absent from the use of the word in the New Testament. What is more important, the plural form disappears, as though to emphasize by the uniform use of the singular that the one item of good news surpassing all others is now being proclaimed, for God has visited his people with salvation.

THE MULTIPLICATION OF GOSPELS

One must ask himself why it is that the church was not content to create and endorse a single account that would be definitive and would be universally used throughout the Christian community. Perhaps this would have been the case had the church deliberately set out to make a record pertaining to the life and labors of Jesus at the beginning of its own existence. But the apostles were engrossed in the task of bearing their witness to Jesus and shepherding new converts. As long as Christianity was a local phenomenon, confined to a Palestinian setting, nothing written was needed, seeing that the apostles could supply all necessary information by word of mouth.

With the spreading abroad of the church, conditions were changed. No longer could the apostles meet the demand for information by their personal presence and testimony. The very physical situation of the Christian groups in their widely scattered condition called for the emergence of Gospel accounts. It is not surprising that, according to tradition, our four Gospels appeared in different areas of the church. Once these records became known and used, even on a somewhat local basis, a strong attachment to them would naturally be felt in these areas. Any effort to withdraw a Gospel from circulation would meet with vigorous protests. So the church did not find it expedient to eliminate all but one.

Another factor must be reckoned with in the effort to explain the plurality of Gospels in the early church. It was the sheer fascination of the subject. Men found the story of Jesus of Nazareth so alluring and so inexhaustible that many, as Luke tells us in his Prologue, were challenged to undertake the task of writing it.

As movements of doubtful orthodoxy began to spring up in the second century, they tended to favor whichever of the Gospels was most congenial to their point of view. So Matthew became associated with the Ebionites, Luke with the followers of Marcion, and John with most of the Gnostic groups. This appropriation of orthodox Gospels for unorthodox purposes must have been annoying to the Fathers, but they could not very well disown a Gospel because of its use by heretics.

An attempt at uniformity was made by Tatian toward the end of the second century in the creation of his *Diatessaron.* But this proved unacceptable, both from the standpoint of orthodoxy, since Tatian was Encratite in his sympathies, and from the standpoint of expediency, since the four Gospels were too strongly entrenched to be dislodged.

The church may well have felt that any embarrassment occasioned by the presence of more than one account of our Lord's ministry, each with its own peculiarities, was more than compensated for by the added weight that these diverse Gospels contributed to the oral testimony of the church concerning the basic facts of the *kerygma,* culminating in the glorious resurrection of the Lord. The very fact of variety only served to throw into sharper relief the truthfulness of the central facts of the ministry so clearly attested in all the accounts.

THE VALUE OF THE GOSPEL RECORDS

Since these documents did not appear until a generation after the events that they record, their reliability might seem to be seriously imperiled by this long interval. Such would indeed be the case if the interval were a void. But all this time the church was preaching and teaching the message that is enshrined in the Gospels, guided by the testimony of the apostles and others who were close to our Lord in the days of his flesh. Repetition of an ordinary story may well bring addition and substantial alterations, but this was no ordinary story. It was epochal in its spiritual significance. The church was jealous for its faithful preservation. When the written Gospels began to appear, they could only be received and continue to hold a place of esteem in the life of the church if they perpetuated the message that had been current in oral form.[1] It is inconceivable that the Gospels were introduced as a corrective to the oral tradition.

This does not mean entire uniformity between the two. As the oral tradition spread from place to place, minor differences must inevitably have arisen in it as opposed to the oral tradition found in other places, if only from the fact that there were many witnesses who could tell the same incidents from somewhat different standpoints, out of personal knowledge and observation. When the written records began to circulate in such areas, no doubt slight variations were detected between the new written form and the form the people had been accustomed to in their local oral tradition. This may have led to some textual variants such as are embodied in our manuscripts. Divergences occur in the reporting of the same event. We find that such events are sometimes differently placed in the various accounts. There can be little doubt that this is often due to the desire of the writer to group his material for a certain effect rather than to an effort to record precise history or to contradict the received tradition. Scholars have detected difficulties in the reporting of Jesus' parabolic teaching and have concluded that at times the setting of the parable may have been altered and the conclusion varied.[2] Their conclusions are not necessarily valid, but these and other detailed problems are matters for careful critical research. They cannot be lightly dismissed. However, in dealing with the broad issue of reliability, certain phenomena of a positive nature are infinitely more important.

Three items of this sort that engender confidence in the Gospel records must suffice for our purpose. One concerns the use of the title Son of Man. If this title had been ascribed to Jesus by the early church, there would be no reason, one would think, for refraining from referring to Jesus in this way. Yet the Gospels scrupulously confine the use of this title to Jesus' testimony to himself, and the same is true of the Acts, with a single exception (7:56). This fact points to a concern to reproduce Jesus' self-testimony with fidelity.

---

[1] For an elaboration of this point, see E. F. Scott, *The Validity of the Gospel Record.*

[2] See J. Jeremias, *The Parables of Jesus,* 1954; C. H. Dodd, *The Parables of the Kingdom,* p. 29. A forthcoming book, *Royal Theology,* by Ronald A. Ward, will consider this problem (see chap. VII).

A second item concerns the death of Christ. From the prominence given to the Passion narrative in the Gospels, it is evident that this feature of our Lord's career loomed large in the thought and proclamation of the church. Before the Gospels were published, teaching was current that believers had been crucified with Christ and should therefore regard themselves as dead to sin. In writing to the congregation at Rome, Paul assumes that his readers know something of this and he seeks to reinforce it. This means that prior to the writing of Mark an experiential theology had developed around the death of Christ. What would be more natural for this author (Mark), writing from Rome, than to inject this element into his presentation of the cross? Yet we look in vain for it. The nearest thing to it is the teaching on discipleship, which is grounded in the historical situation of our Lord's ministry and is no afterthought.

Thirdly, we note the place given to Gentiles in the Gospel accounts. By the time they were written, Christianity had its great strength outside of Palestine and among Gentiles. If the Gospel writers had yielded to the temptation to justify this state of affairs, they could have injected considerable contact between Jesus and Gentiles into the gospel story. Yet Jesus is presented as sent unto the lost sheep of the house of Israel. It is the unfaithfulness of the covenant nation that opens the door to Gentiles *en masse*. There are hints that the message will go out to the Gentiles, but the historical priority of the Jew is preserved.

THE GOSPEL PATTERN

A sense of the inner unity in the Gospel is obtained by noting a striking similarity in the way the story of Jesus is developed. The gospel begins, so we are informed by Mark, with the work of John the Baptist as intimately related to that of Jesus. Even the Fourth Gospel, with all its diversity from the Synoptics, gives prominence to the ministry of the Baptist. Then follows the main body of material devoted to the activity of Jesus in performing various acts of power and in ministering by the spoken word — the latter being addressed mainly to the multitudes but sometimes to his more intimate followers. Finally, the story reaches its close and climax in the death and resurrection.

When the material is examined in a little more detail, it is seen to reveal certain emphases that appear more or less in all the accounts. Among these are the two geographical foci of the ministry, Galilee and Jerusalem, the division created by Jesus in the nation resulting in disciples on the one hand and official opposition on the other, and the relating of Jesus' ministry to Old Testament prophecy.

All this bears strong witness to the impact of a person and a ministry upon the thinking of the early church. It was impossible to portray Jesus and his mission without following these general lines. The kernel of it all was the impact made by Jesus as the promised Christ. A Gospel could not be written that did not reflect this pre-eminent position. Since this is the burden of apostolic preaching as it is reported in the Book of Acts, one naturally concludes that this element more than any other shaped the framework of the Gospels. The Gospels, at their core, are the deposit of the preaching of the church.[3]

THE ORDER OF THE GOSPELS

The order of the Gospels will be handled in connection with the treatment of the individual documents, but it is of interest that the early church did not have a uniform tradition in this matter. The Eastern order is that of our present arrangement in the English Bible, but the Western order put the Gospels in the following sequence: Matthew, John, Luke, Mark. It is likely that this order takes account of the apostolic rank of the first two writers.

THE SYNOPTIC PROBLEM

From the early days of the church the phenomena of the first three Gospels created discussion. Here were documents covering much the same ground, viewing the ministry of the Lord in much the same light, having certain striking verbal agreements and also striking differences. As a rule, Matthew was regarded as the first writer, the other two being derived from him in some way and to some degree. Augustine thought that Mark abbreviated Matthew. Chrysostom explained the brevity of Mark on the ground that he wrote in connection with Peter, who was a man of few words!

In the eighteenth century a change came in the approach to the problem. Whereas the church up to this time had been concerned chiefly to explain the differences in the three accounts, now attention became directed more particularly to the agreements. How were these to be explained?

The use of the term "synoptic" dates from Griesbach (1745-

---

[3] For a more complete treatment of this subject, see Otto Piper, "The Origin of the Gospel Pattern," *JBL,* 78 (June 1959), pp. 115-24.

1812). This Greek word means "a seeing together," and it is aptly applied to the first three Gospels in view of the fact that their records have so much in common. The Synoptic problem, then, has to do with the mutual relations of these accounts. It takes no notice of the Fourth Gospel. As someone has said, "It is a problem of domestic relations and not of foreign relations."

Westcott's tabulation of the materials in all the Gospels on a percentage basis is useful in giving a bird's-eye view of the situation.[4]

	Peculiarities	Coincidences
St. Mark	7	93
St. Matthew	42	58
St. Luke	59	41
[St. John	92	8]

This does not mean that the coincidences are in exact verbal agreement, but it does mean that they represent so close an affinity as to make probable, if not certain, some mutuality of relationship in the origin of the Synoptic material.

It will be noted that Mark has little that is peculiar to his own account. In fact, when the questionable ending of the Gospel (16:9-20) is excluded, scarcely 30 verses remain that are truly unique. These will be found in 1:1; 2:27; 3:20-21; 4:26-29; 7:2-4; 3:2-37; 8:22-26; 9:29, 48-49; 14:51-52. In addition, Mark has some material in the story of the epileptic boy not found in Matthew and Luke (chap. 9). The same is true of the discussion over the great commandment (12:32-34). At the close of the eschatological discourse, the language varies considerably from the other accounts (chap. 13). Mark's narratives tend to be somewhat longer than the parallels in the other Synoptics. An exception is the description of the temptation of Jesus.

Over half of the content of Matthew is the same or closely similar to that of Mark. Only about 40 verses of the Markan material fail to appear in Matthew. Nearly one-third of his Gospel is peculiar to himself. About 200 verses are shared with Luke and not found in Mark.

Luke, it will be observed, has a smaller percentage of common material than Matthew. One factor in this is the absence of a section that in Mark covers 6:45-8:26, and which is paralleled

[4] *An Introduction to the Study of the Gospels,* 5th ed., p. 191.

143

in Matthew for the most part. But there are many other briefer passages of Mark also omitted by Luke. Then he has a rather lengthy nativity section that is quite different from Matthew's shorter account, and he includes 16 parables that are not found elsewhere. His Passion narrative shows considerable independence. It has been reasonably conjectured that Luke's omission of so much material common to Mark and Matthew was due to the necessity of keeping the length of his Gospel within limits feasible for a papyrus roll. In order to use his special contributions he was obliged to sacrifice some items that found a place in Mark and Matthew.

Such, in broad outline, is the situation with regard to the first three Gospels. Several attempts have been made to explain the relationship between them, and these will be set forth here in brief.

1. *Oral Tradition.* This hypothesis was championed by B. F. Westcott and Arthur Wright. They held that the preaching and teaching of the leaders of the early church naturally tended to give a certain fixed form to the traditions regarding Jesus and his ministry as the stories were told and retold. This in itself goes far to account for the similarities in the Synoptics, for the written accounts built upon the oral testimony of the apostles. Differences were accounted for largely on two grounds: first, special contributions were made by individuals supplementing the more general information that could be furnished by the apostolic group as a whole; second, the particular aim of each writer had something to do with the choice of materials. Peter is regarded as the one who influenced the tradition the most in its central stream, and Mark's Gospel is the reproduction of this tradition in its essence.

Certain objections have been lodged against this theory. (i) One difficulty is the problem of control over the tradition as it spread beyond the Jerusalem area into many other regions prior to the era of written Gospels. It is hard to see how the tradition could have remained thoroughly fixed. Stanton comments, "On the oral hypothesis, it is necessary to assume that the common outline of the Gospel narrative could be carried to and preserved in places widely removed from one another, with but little change in the order of a long series of sections, and to a large extent in the same words."[5] (ii) Whereas Mark, on this theory, is made the very substance of the gospel tradition, it then becomes difficult to explain the absence from Mark of materials common to

[5] *The Gospels as Historical Documents,* II, 22.

Matthew and Luke. Surely such material would have been as much a part of the original oral gospel as that which is present in Mark. It is found to be largely a record of our Lord's teaching, and therefore of such high interest and authority, one would think, as to give it a firm place in the original gospel tradition. The admission of Wright that the two types of tradition existed side by side in the early church in a state of friendly rivalry is hardly satisfactory. Why were they not combined? (iii) It is damaging to the theory that at important junctures in the life of Jesus where one would expect verbal agreement among the Synoptists if they drew from a common pool of information, considerable divergence is manifest, even in brief statements. Such is the case with respect to the reports of what Jesus said in instituting his Supper in the Upper Room. One would expect also a greater degree of agreement in reporting the wording of the super-scription on the cross. Conversely, where relatively unimportant details are involved, there is often verbal agreement, a circum-stance that seems to argue in favor of written sources. There is one place, at least, in which all three accounts preserve a side statement or parenthetical expression (Mark 2:10 and parallels).

Though it is not an adequate and conclusive solution, the oral tradition theory should not be ruled out completely, for the oral stage of transmission must have powerfully affected the choice of written materials. It has been influential in the rise of Form Criticism, to be discussed later.

2. *Immediate Dependence.* That is, the Synoptists made use of each other's accounts. On such a theory, six combinations are pos-sible, and each has been found endorsement. Naturally such a large measure of disagreement among scholars has not tended to credit the method. It succeeded far better in accounting for the material common to the Synoptics than in explaining the presence of ele-ments peculiar to the individual writings. Then, too, there seems to be no conclusive evidence that Matthew and Luke saw each other's work.

3. *Mediate Dependence.* This is sometimes called the *Urevan-gelium* theory, since it presupposes the existence of one primitive Gospel from which all three Synoptists drew their material. Once again the differences between the documents are hard to explain on such a basis. There is also the problem of the disappearance of a Gospel so valuable as to be a source for so many writers.

4. *The Fragmentary Theory.* This view is connected with the name of Schleiermacher, who labored early in the nineteenth cen-tury. According to it, in the beginning the sayings and deeds of Jesus were preserved in separate, detached form. From these the

Gospel writers drew their material. In so far as they used the same fragments, their accounts agree; wherein they used different portions, their records necessarily diverge. On such a view it is strange that there could be any structural unity between the various accounts. We could not expect any such agreement in order of events as the Gospels present. This view also has experienced something of a revival in connection with Form Criticism.

5. *Two-Document Hypothesis.* Sometimes hailed as the greatest advance in the history of Synoptic criticism, this theory makes Mark the basic document on which Matthew and Luke drew for some of their material and posits a source designated as "Q" (the initial letter of the German word for "source") in order to account for the non-Markan material shared by these two Gospels. The latter source is considered to be basically a report of the teaching of Jesus. Between these two sources the great bulk of the Synoptics is accounted for.

Justification for the priority of Mark is based on a comparative study of the first three Gospels which takes note of their contents, language, and sequence of narrative.

When one considers that Jesus had an almost continuous public ministry extending over approximately three years, that he wrought many mighty works and discoursed frequently to the people, the total data must have been extensive, most of it lodged in the memories of his disciples. In view of the large amount of material available, it is quite astonishing that the Synoptics should cover so much of the same ground. We have already seen what a large area they have in common. Some sort of literary relationship is probable. One must still inquire as to which of the three had priority, but a hint of the results of such an inquiry is already contained in the fact that it is easier to understand how Matthew and Luke depended on Mark than to explain how Mark, with Matthew and Luke before him, omitted so much that they contain.

The second investigation pertains to the language in which the content is expressed. It was the contention of Streeter that in the actual words used by the three Synoptists where their material coincides, there is striking agreement. Sometimes even the construction of the sentence is the same. The most notable example is Mark 2:10 and parallels, where all three accounts preserve the break occasioned by the sudden shift from direct statements by Jesus to the evangelists' observation that he turned to the paralytic: "But that you may know that the Son of man has authority on earth to forgive sins" — he said to the paralytic — "I say to

146

you, rise, take up your pallet, and go home." Another example is found in Mark 2:20 and parallels. "But days will come when the bridegroom will be taken away from them, and then they will fast in that day." While there is minor variation here to the extent that Matthew has "in that day" and Luke "in those days," the remarkable thing is that all three accounts have the identical form for "taken away," a word that occurs only here in all the New Testament. Literary dependence seems to be demanded by both examples.

But the insistent question as to which account came first has still to be answered. As a general rule, the same order in the narratives is observed by all three. The truly significant thing is that when Matthew and Luke fail to agree in sequence with Mark, they also fail to agree with each other. This is strong evidence that where they agree with Mark as to order it is because they are following Mark. It is all the more impressive when one recalls that the Synoptists rarely are concerned to provide the reader with precise indications of time and place for the events they record. This makes their agreement in order the more significant and points to literary dependence as the most reasonable explanation.

A clinching item is the character of Mark's writing, well described by Streeter. "Mark reads like a shorthand account of a story by an impromptu speaker — with all the repetitions, redundancies, and digressions which are characteristic of living speech."[6] Coupled with this is the circumstance that Matthew and Luke differ from Mark in such a way as to suggest that they have altered the Markan text with a view to improving it. For example, in describing the Spirit's action in leading Jesus into the wilderness to be tempted, Mark, as he often does, uses the historic present, whereas Matthew has the aorist and Luke the imperfect tense (Mk. 1:12; Matt. 4:1; Lk. 4:1). Again, Matthew and Luke change Mark's designation of Herod Antipas as "king" to the more accurate "tetrarch" (Mk. 6:14; Matt. 14:1; Lk. 9:7).

Indeed, it is easy to understand how Matthew and Luke would make use of Mark and add to it, but it is far from easy to understand why Mark would have been written at all if it came after the others, seeing that virtually its entire content is contained in the other two.

As noted previously, Matthew and Luke have considerable material in common that is not derived from Mark. Examination shows that this is largely discourse ascribed to Jesus. It is difficult

[6] *The Four Gospels,* p. 163.

147

to account for the presence of this material in these two Gospels apart from the assumption that they have drawn upon a common source (Q). Students are by no means agreed upon the exact contents of this hypothetical document,[7] and some have questioned its very existence. Q persists, however, as a symbol, even for those who think of it as applying to an oral rather than to a written source. The identification of Q with the Logia or oracles of Matthew, of which Papias speaks, has been made by many, but it is by no means certain. A. M. Farrer launched a vigorous attack on the Q hypothesis, arguing that Luke was acquainted with Matthew and if this be true, the necessity for postulating a common source disappears. It is easier to assume the use of a known source than one which is unknown.[8] He makes the further point that when it is admitted that narrative material is included in Q, involving some of the most strategic events of the early part of our Lord's ministry, it is inconceivable that such a document would not go on to include the Passion, which, in fact, Q does not. Farrer is not particularly distressed over the fact that Luke places a good deal of the Q material in a different order from Matthew, arguing that Luke followed his own plan, which is discernible in other areas of his Gospel also. Yet he seems subject to criticism in this respect, as noted by R. H. Fuller: "Matthew has tidily collected the Q material into great blocks. Luke, we must then suppose, has broken up this tidy arrangement and scattered the Q material without rhyme or reason all over his gospel."[9] Advocates of Matthew's priority tend to dismiss Q as unnecessary, as Farrer has done, including Butler[10] and Farmer.[11] But it remains the most probable solution, despite its hypothetical character.

With reference to the position that Matthew preceded Mark, it should be observed that in that case Mark's failure to use the material contained in the Sermon on the Mount becomes a vexing problem. It will not do to say that Mark was interested in Jesus'

---

[7] Attempted reconstruction of Q may be found, e.g., in Harnack, *The Sayings of Jesus,* 1908, and A. M. Hunter, *The Work and Words of Jesus,* 1950. Moffatt, *Introduction to the Literature of the New Testament,* pp. 197-202, cites 16 different arrangements.

[8] "On Dispensing with Q," in *Studies in the Gospels,* ed. by D. E. Nineham, 1955, pp. 55-86.

[9] *The New Testament in Current Study,* p. 74.

[10] B. C. Butler, *The Originality of Matthew;* see a critique by G. M. Styler in C. F. D. Moule's *The Birth of the New Testament,* pp. 223-232.

[11] W. R. Farmer, *The Synoptic Problem;* see review by F. W. Beare in *JBL,* 84 (Sept. 1965), 295-297.

actions rather than in his teaching, since some teaching is incorporated (chap. 4 especially).

There is no enthusiasm for the position that Matthew depended on Luke. Judging by the great dissimilarity between their accounts of the nativity and of the resurrection, one naturally concludes that they did not make use of each other's work.

This brief survey of the Two-Document Hypothesis must suffice except for noting the investigation of A. M. Honore.[12] Only his conclusions are given here, which are as follows: (1) Mark is the main link between Matthew and Luke; (2) both Matthew and Luke used Mark; (3) Matthew did not use Luke; (4) Luke did not use Matthew; (5) Matthew and Luke used sources other than Mark (i.e. Q); (6) Q was not a single document. The author states, "All the conclusions, with the exception of 6, are confirmed by two independent studies. It is therefore safe to accept them. To me they are the more convincing because during most of the investigations I was inclined to believe that the received critical opinion was wrong. It seems, instead, that the received critical opinion is right, though one must have reservations about the exact *character* of Q. This does not mean that one must necessarily accept the received opinions so far as the dating of the gospels is concerned, or as regards the earlier history of the documents. In particular, I should like to say that the variations in editorial policy which these studies have revealed in Matthew may indicate that the Matthew we have is not the first edition of that work. The prehistory of the gospels is a subject calling for delicate analytical tools" (p. 135).

6. *Four-Document Hypothesis.* This further development in source criticism beyond the Two-Document theory came with the work of B. H. Streeter. This involved the use of his Proto-Luke theory, that Luke made a first draft of his Gospel, which he later incorporated into his finished work. Streeter noted five sections where Luke seemed to be independent of Mark (3:1-4:30; 6:12-8:3; 9:51-18:14; 19:1-27; 22:14-24:53). Furthermore, Luke 3:1ff. gives the appearance of the beginning of a book, whereas the last section ends with the passion and resurrection narratives, the closing events of the life of Jesus. So it is reasonable to conclude that these sections together formed a separate Gospel account, one which is almost as long as Mark. Streeter held that later on Luke added material from Q to form Proto-Luke, then at a later time inserted borrowings from Mark and added the nativity materials to form the present Gospel according to Luke.

---

[12] "A Statistical Study of the Synoptic Problem," *Novum Testamentum,* 10 (Apr.-July 1968), 95-135.

In working out his Four-Document theory, Streeter was impressed with the probability that several prominent centers of Christianity made a contribution toward Gospel origins. He agreed that Mark emânated from Rome, perhaps as early as 60, and held that Q probably came from Antioch, around the year 50. He went on to posit an additional source, M (the private source of Matthew), as emanating from Jerusalem about the year 65. It was a sayings source, the existence of which was assumed on the basis of considerable difference between the discourse material in Matthew and that in Luke. Streeter noted a strong Judaistic tendency in much of this material.[13] The fourth document was L (the private source of Luke), assigned to Caesarea about the year 60. L, it should be noted, consists of five sections mentioned in the preceding paragraph. The final stages in the making of our present Matthew and Luke are regarded as occurring at Antioch about 85, for the former, and at Corinth (?) about 80 for the latter. The final Matthew included some Antiochene material of a narrative nature not otherwise accounted for.[14]

Though the Proto-Luke element in Streeter's view has not been widely adopted, his theory as a whole has commended itself. It provides a broader base for the gospel tradition than the Two-Document Hypothesis afforded. Non-Markan material has thereby gained in status and is not so readily discarded as unreliable.

7. *Recent Study.* For approximately a generation after World War I interest in literary (source) criticism of the Gospels waned because of the rise of Form Criticism. But something of a revival has occurred in recent years. Articles on the subject have appeared from time to time in the periodicals, and several books have been published. W. L. Knox, starting with a suggestion made by Eduard Meyer in 1921 that in Mark there is evidence of earlier sources, undertook to isolate those sources. He judged them to be nine in all.[15] There is bound to be difference of opinion as to the success of an undertaking of this kind. It gains a certain plausibility from the fact that the Prologue of Luke's Gospel makes reference to attempts to draw up an account of Jesus' activities. There is no antecedent improbability in supposing that such may have existed when Mark wrote his Gospel and that he made use of some of the material. Knox wrote a similar volume on Luke and Matthew, which appeared in 1957.

---

13 *The Four Gospels,* pp. 254-59.
14 See Streeter's chart on p. 150.
15 *The Sources of the Synoptic Gospels.* Vol. I, St. Mark, 1953. See summary on p. 150.

In 1954 the Roman Catholic scholar Leo Vaganay published his *Le problème synoptique,* introducing criticism of the Two-Document Hypothesis as inadequate and emphasizing that the problem is far too complicated to be solved in such simple terms. This had already been recognized by advocates of the Four-Document Hypothesis, but Vaganay proceeds along different lines. He posits a source that he calls Mg, which he takes to be a Greek translation of an original Aramaic Gospel (relying here on the Papias tradition on Matthew). He supposes that, like Mark, it began with the ministry of John the Baptist and ended with the Passion narrative. The document contained at its heart five books, gathered around the five discourses of Jesus. He believes that Matthew has quite faithfully carried out the pattern of this earlier Gospel. Mark and Luke used it also.

The second source predicated by Vaganay, which he calls Sg, is a Greek translation of an original Aramaic sayings-collection. He thinks Matthew used it as it was, but that Luke made substantial alterations in it. Thus he would account for the variations between them where they seem to be covering the same ground. It is held that Matthew depended on Mg as his primary source and upon Sg as a secondary source.

Mark is accepted as the first of our present Gospels, in line with most scholarly opinion. It is viewed as a combination of Mark's verbal memory of Mg, which represents the early Jerusalem catechetical teaching, largely influenced by Peter, and Peter's preaching at Rome, about which we learn from patristic writers. So Mark is not a strictly literary production, dependent altogether upon sources, as Matthew and Luke are. He did not know S (the Sayings Source).

The foundation of Vaganay's thesis is that Mg, his theoretical document, and not Mark, is the primary source of the Synoptic tradition. Among other things, he seeks to prove that there is no literary dependence between Matthew and Luke. Luke made use of Mark and of Mg, and also of Sg (for the central part of his Gospel).

This theory, in addition to being complicated, hardly does justice to Mark, which is reduced to "a literary enigma."[16]

Many Roman Catholic scholars accept a modified two-document hypothesis that is similar to the position of Streeter. It may be diagrammed as follows:

[16] For other objections, see A. Wikenhauser, *New Testament Introduction,* pp. 238-39.

151

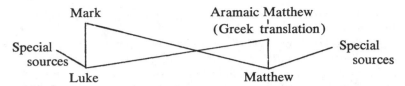

The special sources may be roughly equated with Streeter's M and L. For many these symbols are useful as denoting the added material found in Matthew and Luke rather than as documents in the strict sense.

A new departure has been made in Synoptic critical study by Pierson Parker.[17] He seeks to show that the legalistic controversy in the early church has left its mark upon the Gospels no less than upon some other parts of the New Testament. The most distinctive feature of his theory is the positing of a Jewish Christian Gospel written before Mark. It was of special interest to Christian Jews in Palestine. Mark used it, but eliminated anything that could be construed as anti-Gentile in character. Matthew used this early source also, but at a time when the controversy had subsided, so that excision of materials was not necessary. Q is retained as another source for Matthew. Luke is derived from Mark and Q. The existence of M is challenged. "M is simply those parts of the Jewish Christian Gospel which Mark left out." The theory is ingenious, but labors under the disadvantage of assuming an additional source for which objective evidence is lacking.

Our review of the Synoptic problem has been far from exhaustive. Enough ground has been covered to show something of the wide variety of opinion, and this in turn reflects the difficulty of the subject. Some students despair of any ultimate solution and would perhaps echo the words of J. A. Froude, written many years ago, "It might almost seem as if the explanation was laid purposely beyond our reach."[18] However, the labor has not been entirely wasted. As Vincent Taylor has said, "Scholars who have failed to establish a hypothesis are our benefactors; they stand at the end of lanes we might otherwise be tempted to explore and tell us that these are by-paths."[19]

One reason for reluctance on the part of some students to follow the trend of critical Synoptic research is their concern to honor the guidance of the early church, which gives Matthew priority over Mark. But much of this tradition may be simply the echo of prior opinion, instead of being founded on inde-

17 *The Gospel Before Mark,* 1953.
18 *Short Studies on Great Subjects,* 1893, I, 276.
19 *The Formation of the Gospel Tradition,* 1933, p. 3.

pendent research. Internal criticism must be allowed its voice in such matters.

More serious is the feeling that literary dependence of one writer upon another is difficult to square with any respectable view of inspiration. Men ask, "Would God permit the Gospel records to be framed on the basis of copying one from another?" This objection sounds weighty, but it is not as serious as it seems to be, for the copying, if we may call it such, is not of the slavish variety. Rather, there are factors of omission, addition, and also considerable freedom of expression where the material is basically the same. Furthermore, the analogy of the Old Testament Scriptures must not be forgotten. Nearly one-fifth of the Old Testament consists of deuterographs or repetitions of identical or very similar material. The most prominent example is the relation of Kings and Chronicles. Yet among the Jews there was no bar to the acceptance of both as Scripture, and our Lord apparently acquiesced, for he accepted the Jewish canon. The church did the same. Therefore, if we are compelled on the basis of the evidence to accept a theory of literary dependence, it should not be felt that this impugns the doctrine of inspiration. Originality is not a necessary qualification for Scripture.

It may well be that Synoptic Criticism has too readily relegated Matthew and Luke to the position of editors who are at times quite unimaginatively dull in their following of sources, at other times quite perverse in their attempted originality. They ought rather to be thought of as men who had a keen interest in the material that passed through their hands and a full knowledge of the extent of the tradition, from which they were drawing what served their purpose to best advantage.[20]

In conclusion, it is well to recall that Jesus gave to his followers the double charge to preach and to teach. As we study the epistles, we find the terms *kerygma* and *didache,* answering to this twofold command. The former embraces the gospel message for the unsaved, whereas the latter is chiefly concerned with unfolding the implications of the gospel for Christian living. In the Book of Acts there is preaching and also *didache,* though the latter is not drawn out in sufficient detail to enable us to trace its outline. In Mark we apparently have a record that specializes in *kerygma,* though not to the total neglect of teaching, to be sure. Matthew and Luke, it seems, drew upon a common store of teaching materials relating to the ministry of Jesus, whether oral or written. There is some additional material in

---

[20] See N. B. Stonehouse, *Paul Before the Areopagus,* pp. 126-27.

Matthew and Luke not accounted for by any such analysis. As noted, Streeter posited the special sources M and L to cover these elements.

Literary criticism involves a measure of conjecture that must be frankly recognized. Conclusions must therefore be regarded as tentative and always subject to review. And whatever analysis is adopted, one will still make use of the Gospels in their present form.

FORM CRITICISM

Another approach to the problem of Gospel origins arose in Germany following the close of World War I. It is known as *Formgeschichte* ("form history"), and bears in English the title of Form Criticism. It emerged at a time when many scholars had concluded that source criticism had spent itself. A new procedure was in order. Change was in the air. As W. K. L. Clarke observed, "It is annoying to be obliged to reconsider the two-document hypothesis just when it has got into the textbooks, but Canon Streeter from one side, the post-war Germans from another, have shaken it seriously."[21]

Certain individuals had an important part either in preparing the way for this new development or in initiating it. At the beginning of the century Wilhelm Wrede in his *Das Messiasgeheimnis in den Evangelien* had disturbed the current views of Mark as a reliable picture of the historical Jesus by maintaining that it was permeated with a theologizing tendency in its portrayal of the Messiahship of Jesus. In the same general period J. Wellhausen wrote a series of commentaries on the Gospels in which he emphasized a principle of criticism that was to play a vital role in *Formgeschichte*. It is this, that "a literary work or a fragment of tradition is a primary source for the historical tradition out of which it arose, and is only a secondary source for the historical details concerning which it gives information."[22] The bearing of this on the Gospels will appear directly. It was reserved for K. L. Schmidt to open the door for the new methodology by his book on the framework of the Synoptic tradition (*Der Rahmen der Geschichte Jesu,* 1919), in which he sought to show that the greater part of Mark consisted of separate episodes or anecdotes strung to-

21 *New Testament Problems,* 1929, p. 24.
22 So stated by Bultmann in "The New Approach to the Synoptic Problem," *JR,* 6 (July 1929), p. 341.

gether artificially by an editor who leaned heavily on such devices as the word "immediately" to make a transition from one incident to another.

The work of Schmidt was particularly important in that it detached the various bits of tradition from any historical framework imposed, as he thought, by the Evangelists, and left the critic free to study these bits of tradition for their own sake.

Most influential among the scholars developing the new point of view were Martin Dibelius, especially in his book *Die Formgeschichte des Evangeliums* (1919),[23] and Rudolf Bultmann in his *Die Geschichte der synoptischen Tradition* (1921).[24]

Form criticism places great weight upon the oral period lying between the ministry of Jesus and the rise of the written Gospels, during which time the traditions about Jesus were taking shape. The theory operates on certain rather well-defined principles. First, the Synoptic Gospels belong to a type of literature that should be designated as folk literature, tales and sagas that enshrine stories of interest or value to certain peoples. Form criticism thus allies itself with the method of Comparative Religion. Second, the Gospels are fundamentally, for the historian, a reflection of the faith and life of the early church. They should not be viewed as objective accounts of the historical Jesus. It has often been noted how greatly this principle has affected the whole outlook of Bultmann, so that in his *Theology of the New Testament* (two volumes) he devotes only about sixty pages to the subject of Jesus and almost apologizes for giving that much space. To him any great consideration of this subject is unnecessary, because we cannot know the historical Jesus. All we have is the church's interpretation of him, which presents basically a mythical figure, that is, one who transcends the category of the human. The implication is that this picture may have been substantially altered. Just how much of the tradition goes back to Jesus himself is a moot question on which Bultmann prefers to be noncommittal. Third, following Schmidt, the units of tradition, usually quite small in themselves, are regarded as artificially put together by the evangelists according to their ideas or fancies. The units do not always appear in the same place in the Synoptics, so it is quite open to the critic to give them a setting of his own, based on his knowledge of the early church. Fourth, the units are characterized by a certain form,

[23] The English translation, *From Tradition to Gospel*, appeared in 1935.

[24] English Translation: *The History of the Synoptic Tradition*, 1963.

155

of which there are several types. Fifth, the Gospels are community productions having back of them a definite social situation,
a life situation (*Sitz im Leben*), which is to be sought in the
early church and not in the history of Jesus.

The objective behind all this is stated by Bultmann as follows:
"On the basis of this study (of the forms) it becomes possible
to discover the nature of the editorial redaction in the Gospels
and to distinguish those portions of the tradition which are
original from the secondary elements supplied by the Gospel
writers. By comparing the literary styles in the Gospels with
parallel literary expressions of hellenistic and rabbinical literature,
light is thrown on the question as to whether a given utterance
originated on Palestinian or on Hellenistic soil."[25]

It is necessary to set forth the nature of the forms from which
this type of criticism gets its name. These cover both the deeds
and words of Jesus.

(1) Pronouncement stories (Vincent Taylor's term) or *apoph-
thegmata* (Bultmann) or Paradigms (Dibelius, in recognition
of their use in Christian preaching). These involve incidents,
quite brief as a rule, ending in an aphorism or famous saying
that drives home the lesson. An example is the passage regarding the tribute money, ending in Jesus' notable pronouncement about rendering to Caesar and to God (Mark 12:17).

(2) Miracle stories. Bultmann finds the same stylistic characteristics for the general run of Jesus' miracles as are common
to those reported in the hellenistic world: a statement of the
malady, with special stress on its dire character so as to magnify
the cure; the account of the healing; a statement of the effect on
those who are present. Due to the correspondences, Bultmann
concludes that these belong to the hellenistic phase of the ex-
panding church rather than to its Palestinian phase. Dibelius
distinguishes miracles that are closely connected with the proclamation of the kingdom, which he therefore subsumes under
Paradigms, and others that are stories complete in themselves
and abounding in detail. These he calls "tales," and thinks that
in them Jesus is simply pictured as a wonder-worker having
exceptional potency.

(3) Stories about Jesus. These have considerable variety and
therefore are not easy to classify. It is readily admitted by the
form critics that there are mythological elements in the portrayal
of Jesus, for example, in the transfiguration. The tendency is regarded as full-blown in the Fourth Gospel. The category of

25 *Op. cit.,* p. 337.

myth is applied to those elements of the Gospel exposition of Jesus that present him in a guise transcending the human and the natural.

(4) Sayings of Jesus. These are of several types. One is *wisdom words*. Since Judaism was rich in gnomic literature, this element in Jesus' teaching is to be expected. Yet there must be a suspicion, according to Bultmann, that at least some of the sayings of this type attributed to Jesus have been put in his mouth by the Evangelists. A second type may be called *prophetic sayings*. These include the Beatitudes and the utterances of a more apocalyptic nature, such as the prediction of the destruction of the temple. Again, there are statements that may be called *legislative,* in which Jesus gives teachings about prayer, fasting, divorce, forgiveness, and a variety of other topics. Sometimes these are classified as church words. Then there are certain "I" sayings in which the person of Jesus is made prominent in some way. Finally, there is a well-defined group of sayings known as *parables,* Jesus' favorite device for expounding the kingdom of God.

(5) The Passion story. While complete agreement is lacking among the form critics, some seeing it as a sustained, well-knit narrative, in contrast to the fragmentary nature of the other Gospel materials, others seeing it as a piecing together of short fragments later embellished, it is nevertheless regarded as one of the forms.

Undoubtedly the form critics have performed a service in emphasizing the existence of forms in the gospel tradition. But the use made of the forms is at least open to debate. The idea that the primitive traditions are relatively few and that much of the Gospel record has to be attributed to accretion, that is, the creation of the Christian community, is contrary to probability. Bultmann seems to suggest that the process that produces many imaginative details in the apocryphal Gospels, such as the supplying of names to people who are anonymous in Scripture, was already working among the Evangelists. He gives some examples, such as the supplying of the names of Peter and John (Luke 22: 8) in contrast to the simple mention of two disciples in Mark 14:13. Granted that the problem of accretion is not easily handled, yet it is only fair to say that the trend is not always to greater specificity or amplification in Matthew and Luke as opposed to Mark. Two examples must suffice. It is Mark who identifies the blind beggar at Jericho as Bartimaeus, the son of Timaeus, where the other accounts leave him nameless. At the beginning of the eschatological discourse, those who query

157

Jesus about the sign are vaguely described as "they" in Luke, are identified as "the disciples" in Matthew, but in Mark they are specified by name — Peter, James, John, and Andrew. Mark 5:42 represents another example in point. The primary Gospel is rather often the most definite and detailed.

In writing their accounts, the Evangelists must have been sorely pressed to limit themselves, for it is certain that Jesus maintained a more or less continuous activity during the years of his ministry and must have spoken hundreds of times. The real utility of the forms is not to enable us to distinguish between primitive and late tradition but to enable us to recognize in them helpful means for the perpetuation of the teaching of Christ. Far from being artificial literary devices, they represent in many cases the most natural means for recording an event. This is particularly true of the pronouncement stories.

E. Fascher, the historian and critic of the movement (*Die formgeschichtliche Methode,* 1924), not only pointed out that form critics differ rather widely among themselves as to the forms, but advanced a much more serious objection, namely, that the materials of the Gospels are vastly different from the substance of folk literature. The laws governing popular tradition are not applicable to a situation in which matter is far more important than the form.

Form criticism either forgets or minimizes the regulating influence of the apostles and other witnesses of the life of Jesus. In their desire to honor the Lord, these leaders would not be a party to the habit of ascribing to Jesus what in fact did not originate with him at all. The presence of hundreds of people in the early church who had known and followed our Lord in the days of his flesh must have had a powerful effect in keeping the tradition true to the facts.

The notion that much of the material in the Gospels is the result of random selection of isolated bits of tradition does not satisfy. It ignores the existence of the Gospel pattern with its common outline running through all the accounts. T. W. Manson observes that on form critical principles, "we need some explanation why it was possible for the details of the story to be remembered and the general outline forgotten."[26]

Indeed, the very idea that there was no biographical interest on the part of the early church in Jesus of Nazareth is incredible.

[26] "Present-day Research in the Life of Jesus," in *The Background of the New Testament and its Eschatology,* ed. by W. D. Davies and D. Daube, 1956, p. 213.

It is utterly fanciful to see in the choice of materials for our Gospels simply those things that had an existential interest for Christians. Jesus himself was the greatest interest they had, as the Acts and the Epistles abundantly attest.

The theory of form criticism is not substantiated by the Prologue of Luke. This theory makes the community the creator, custodian, and transmitter of the tradition. Individual authorship and influence upon the tradition are reduced almost to the vanishing point as factors to be considered. But in Luke's opening words we find that there was a certain group, much smaller than the church as a whole, that preserved the tradition and made it available to those who wrote. Incidentally, the Prologue also attests that not Luke alone, but those who preceded him in writing about Jesus, were not setting out to write on the ideas and practices of the early church but on the things that had been fulfilled among his followers. It is well to remember that the picture of the church as a creative entity is in need of proof. "The documents of the NT confirm the findings of sociology and anthropology according to which collectivities are receptive rather than creative entities."[27] Even in the case of folk literature, it is faulty reasoning to conclude from the fact that groups preserve and pass literature on that this literature arises from groups rather than from individuals.

F. G. Kenyon has maintained that the time element required for the hypothesis of form criticism is not available. He writes: "There is simply not time for the elaborate processes required for Dibelius' *Formgeschichte,* which has won rather surprising popularity, but which presupposes, first the dissemination of stories of the life and teachings of Jesus, then their collection and classification into groups according to their character, and then the formation of continuous narratives in which they were utilized."[28] No doubt he intends to include the thought that time is lacking for the injection of mythological elements.

F. F. Bruce points out that early Christians "made a clear distinction between actual pronouncements of Jesus and their own judgments on disputed points (cf. I Cor. 7:10, 12, 25)."[29] This militates against the *Gemeindetheologie* approach, which makes the Gospels chiefly valuable for the insights they give us into the faith and life of the early church. It must be granted that one can hardly write without some reference, however veiled, to

[27] Otto Piper, "The Origin of the Gospel Pattern," *JBL,* 78 (June 1959), p. 123.

[28] *The Bible and Modern Scholarship,* 1948, p. 52.

[29] Baker's *Dictionary of Theology,* p. 228a.

his own situation. It must be granted, also, that the needs of the church may well have had something to do with the preservation and use of some traditions over others. But nevertheless it is a perversion to regard the Gospel materials as shaped by the church rather than by the influence of Jesus. Floyd V. Filson notes how the parables become a test case in this matter. "All attempts to make the apostolic age responsible for the creation of any considerable amount of the gospel material shatter upon the evidence of the parables. This is the characteristic teaching form in the Synoptic Gospels. It is noticeably absent from the rest of the New Testament and from other early Christian literature. If the apostolic age had created these masterly mediums of teaching, other writings of that time would naturally have reflected the same method. But they do not. The primitive Church preserved a sense of the difference between Jesus' teaching method and their own ideas and methods."[30]

Revolting against the extremes of form criticism, Harald Riesenfeld has lashed out against it as "one of those scientific dogmas or myths which have their day and then must gradually be set aside if they are not to impede the further development of investigation."[31] In his attempt to find the *Sitz im Leben* of the Gospel tradition, he rejects both preaching and catechetical instruction, and feels that the words of Jesus had a holy character in the estimation of the early Christian community and were probably for this reason not quoted in the missionary preaching. He traces the beginning of the Gospel tradition back to Jesus himself. He suggests, on the analogy of the Jewish rabbinical method, that Jesus had his disciples commit his instruction to memory.[32] This position appears extreme on the other side, since it does not fit in with the variations in the reports of that teaching in the Gospels.

R. O. P. Taylor has attacked the form-critical assumption that the oral tradition floated about in fragmentary form at first. In his *Groundwork of the Gospels* (1946) he roots the origin of the Gospel tradition in the need that the early church had for such material in its worship. He believes that the church enjoyed from the beginning an integrated story of Jesus' ministry provided by the apostles, and that this was recited in the public services. Mark based his Gospel on this, as did the others, since it was the only authorized version, if we could use the term, of the tradition.

30 *Origin of the Gospels,* 1938, p. 109.
31 *The Gospel Tradition and its Beginnings,* 1957, p. 7.
32 *Ibid.,* p. 24.

160

Thus it appears that with the passage of time the case for form criticism has been weakened. In the hands of moderates it may still have limited utility. But in the hands of Bultmann it has been allied with considerable skepticism. "It appears that the outline of the life of Jesus, as it is given by Mark and taken over by Matthew and Luke, is an editorial creation, and that as a consequence our actual knowledge of the course of Jesus' life is restricted to what little can be discovered in the individual scenes constituting the older tradition."[33] Over against this may be put the statement of C. S. C. Williams, "Form-Criticism is a literary, not an historical instrument, and cannot be used for a final verdict on any section of the New Testament."[34] The time has come to shake off the inhibitions that form criticism has imposed on the study of the life and ministry of Jesus and to begin again to view it as a whole and as influenced primarily by Jesus himself rather than by the early church.

REDACTION CRITICISM

During the vogue of Form criticism attention was focused on the separate units which the evangelists had utilized and arranged according to individual preference. Little attention was paid to the writer and to the possibility that he was more than an assembler of units of tradition. This limitation of the Form critical method has gradually been recognized, with the result that the study of the Gospels today is proceeding more and more along the lines of investigating the contribution of the writers, who are no longer viewed as editors in a pedestrian sense, whose work can be set aside as somewhat mechanical and even a hindrance to our understanding, but as men who had a definite theological interest and purpose which shaped their choice and arrangement of materials. This means that the Synoptics are now being examined as totalities in an effort to grasp the thrust of the evangelist in each case.

It should be clear that the term "editor" or "redactor" is ambiguous. For example, Form critics could speak of Mark as a redactor, but this meant largely that he had supplied verbal connections between the units of tradition in order to make a continuous narrative. His work was set aside in order to get at the units themselves. He was scarcely more than a hack. But editorial work can be creative, as we are aware in modern journalism. It is in this sense that the Gospel writers should be evaluated. Instead

[33] *JR* 6 (July 1929), p. 343.
[34] *ET,* 67 (1956), p. 345.

of concentrating on the common tradition underlying the Synoptics, as Form criticism does, Redaction criticism directs its attention to that which is peculiar to the individual writers.

As a matter of fact, both types of editorial work can be detected in the Gospel records. When Matthew smooths out a Markan construction or substitutes a more dignified term for a colloquialism, and when Luke removes a Markan Semitism or Latinism, editorial work of the ordinary type is involved. But the shaping of the material by the use of special titles for the Savior or by the underscoring of certain developments in the course of Jesus' ministry belongs to the higher order of editorial work and provides the means for discerning the purpose of the writer. It does not follow that the writer is giving an individualistic interpretation of the ministry of our Lord, one which is peculiar to himself, in the hope of winning converts to his point of view. The uniqueness may lie in the emphasis given to a certain aspect of the ministry, such as the relation of Jesus to the Jewish nation or his attitude toward the Gentiles or his training of the disciples or his handling of the future in terms of the divine purpose. Close attention needs to be given to the triple tradition to see what each evangelist has done with his sources by omission, addition, or alteration to suggest his theological as distinct from his literary concern. Even the choice of a single word may be significant, as in the diverse terms used by the evangelists at the beginning of their accounts to serve as a caption for the whole ("gospel" in Mark; "book" in Matthew; "narrative" in Luke).

This new approach to the Synoptics has been well summarized by Robert H. Stein. "Redaktionsgeschichte seeks to discover the qualitative and quantitative uniqueness that distinguishes the evangelists from their sources, and, having ascertained these, it then seeks to ascertain the *Sitz im Leben* out of which each evangelist wrote and the particular purpose for which he wrote his gospel."[35]

Looking back over the history of investigation of the Synoptics, it is of interest to note the shift of emphasis which has occurred. Early in the century the Gospels were studied with a view to focusing on Jesus' ministry to discern the historical situation in which he moved. Then came Form criticism and the utilization of the same records to provide an understanding of the early church. Now attention is being drawn to the contribution made to the tradition by the individual Gospel writers.

When Redaktionsgeschichte is applied to the study of the text,

---

[35] *JBL,* 88 (March 1969), 54.

certain effects upon the exegetical process naturally follow.[36] For one thing, the student should not be too intent on trying to harmonize two similar accounts, for he may thereby erase or disguise something the writer intended to bring out in accordance with his purpose. Also, one should bring the tentative results of his exegetical findings in a given section of the Gospel to the test of compatibility with the overall thrust of the document as a whole. The tendency to assign a Gospel to a school rather than to an individual may be expected to diminish.

Several German works embodying the use of the new method have now been translated and are available for more detailed study, including the following: Willi Marxsen, *Mark the Evangelist,* 1969, Abingdon; Marxsen, *Introduction to the New Testament,* 1968, Fortress Press; G. Bornkamm, G. Barth, and H. J. Held, *Tradition and Interpretation in Matthew,* 1963, Westminster Press; Hans Conzelmann, *The Theology of St. Luke,* 1960, Harper and Brothers.

ARAMAIC ORIGINS

Since Jesus spoke Aramaic as his mother tongue, a fact attested by occasional retention of an Aramaic word or phrase by the Evangelists, the question arises whether our Gospels may have existed originally in Aramaic and were then translated into Greek. One of the earliest researchers in this field, G. Dalman, whose chief contribution was to survey the words of Jesus for the Aramaic flavor in them and to investigate the background for Jesus' utterances,[37] refrained from undertaking the task of translating his sayings back into Aramaic.[38] He held that written Aramaic sources for Jesus' words could not be established. Much may still be learned from Dalman's work, even though his assumption that the Aramaic spoken by our Lord could be best understood by comparison with the Targums of Onkelos and Jonathan has now been demonstrated to be incorrect.[39] The Palestinian Aramaic of Jesus' time was not the same as the more bookish Aramaic of the Targums of a later period.

Scholars have been able to come closer to the language spoken by Jesus through discovery of fragments of the Palestinian

---

[36] William L. Lane, "Redaktionsgeschichte and the De-historicizing of the New Testament Gospel," in *Bulletin of the Evangelical Theological Society,* 11 (Winter 1968), 32.

[37] *The Words of Jesus,* 1909; *Jesus-Jeshua,* 1929.

[38] *Jesus-Jeshua,* p. xi.

[39] P. Kahle, *The Cairo Geniza,* p. 130.

Pentateuch Targum by P. Kahle in the Cairo *Geniza.* One highly interesting fact deserves to be noticed in this connection. Jesus was addressed, as we know, not only as Rabbi but as Rabboni (Mark 10:51; John 20:16). The Targum mentioned above has the same word, fully pointed, in exact agreement with its Greek transliteration in the passage cited.[40] In 1957 Matthew Black was able to report the discovery of the complete Jerusalem Targum, in distinction from fragments uncovered by Kahle, made by Professor Macho of Barcelona.[41]

The claim that written Aramaic Gospels existed, from which our Greek Gospels were made, was put forward most forcibly by C. C. Torrey. He held that apart from the first two chapters of Luke, the last chapter of John and the quotations from the Old Testament, all the materials of the four Gospels were rendered into Greek from Aramaic.[42] On this basis he felt justified in contending that the Gospels appeared in their original form by the middle of the first century. Torrey professed to find some 250 mistranslations, which he thought he could remove by postulating an Áramaic original that in each case had been misunderstood or misconstrued. His general position was shared by A. T. Olmstead, J. A. Montgomery, and Millar Burrows, but vigorously opposed by the Hellenists Goodspeed, Riddle, and Colwell.

Certain objections have been raised against the Aramaic theory. (1) There is no objective evidence for the existence of such documents. Furthermore, as Albright has stated, "There is absolutely no trace so far of a continuous Aramaic literary tradition spanning the interval between the Achaemenian and earliest Hellenistic period on the one hand, and the second century A.D. on the other.[43] It is true that some Aramaic fragments were brought to light among the Dead Sea Scroll finds, and also the Genesis "Apocryphon," much of which was in too poor condition to decipher, but Albright's statement remains true in its broad sweep. It might be maintained that Aramaic originals for the Gospels once existed and then were lost or destroyed, but this is only an inference from the position demanded by the Aramaic approach.

(2) The theory is considerably weakened by the necessity of ranging far and wide into other Semitic languages to build up a

[40] *Ibid.*, p. 129.

[41] *NTS,* 3 (July 1957), pp. 306-309.

[42] See his works, *The Four Gospels,* 1933; *Our Translated Gospels,* 1936.

[43] *The Background of the New Testament and its Eschatology,* ed. by Davies and Daube, p. 155.

linguistic background for supposed mistranslations. Such evidence can only be valid if it can be shown that the feature in question is common to Aramaic and the languages to which appeal is made.

(3) Disagreement among advocates of the general position as to specific cases of mistranslation weakens the theory.[44]

(4) Even if the possibility of such mistranslations be conceded, it remains difficult to suppose that they could have passed undetected and uncorrected into the Greek Gospel tradition.

(5) Many of the proposed alterations are not necessarily an improvement over the Greek. Because the Greek is rough in places, it need not therefore be suspected. Smoothness is not an infallible criterion for authenticating a text.

(6) The early church had Greek speaking believers in it from the very beginning. These people would need access to Greek rather than Aramaic records of the gospel.

It is significant that important modern translations of the New Testament, such as the Revised Standard Version and the New English Bible, have been largely unaffected by the claim of mistranslations and have nearly always rendered the Greek text as it stands.

T. W. Manson, while regarding Aramaic originals for our present Gospels as conjectural, was prepared to accept the position that there was an Aramaic document behind the source Q.[45] This view has been shared by a number of other men.

Considerable illumination of vocabulary and syntax has been achieved by Matthew Black through his studies in Aramaic. He refuses to endorse Torrey's position, and states his own view in much more cautious terms. He says, ". . . we have to do with a translation-tradition, sometimes literal, mostly, however, literary and interpretative, but generally bearing the stamp upon it, in one feature or another, of its Aramaic origin. Whether that source was written or oral, it is not possible from the evidence to decide."[46]

BIBLIOGRAPHY

Black, Matthew, *An Aramaic Approach to the Gospels and Acts.* 2nd ed., Oxford: Clarendon Press, 1954.

[44] D. W. Riddle, "The Logic of the Theory of Translation Greek," *JBL*, 51:18-19.
[45] *ET*, 47:7-11.
[46] *An Aramaic Approach to the Gospels and Acts*, 2nd ed., p. 206.

Bea, Augustin Cardinal, *The Study of the Synoptic Gospels.* New York: Harper and Row, 1965.

Bultmann, Rudolf, *The History of the Synoptic Tradition.* 3rd ed., New York: Harper & Row, 1963.

Bultmann, Rudolf and Kundsin, Karl, *Form Criticism.* New York: Harper and Row, 1962.

Dibelius, Martin, *From Tradition to Gospel.* New York: Charles Scribner's Sons, 1935.

Dodd, C. H., *The Apostolic Preaching and its Developments.* London: Hodder & Stoughton, 1936.

Filson, Floyd V., *Origins of the Gospels.* New York: The Abingdon Press, 1938.

Goodspeed, E. J., *New Chapters in New Testament Study.* New York: Macmillan, 1937, Chap. 6.

Hawkins, J. C., *Horae Synopticae.* Oxford: Clarendon Press, 1909.

Hoskyns, E. and Davey, N., *The Riddle of the New Testament.* London: Faber and Faber, 1931.

Koch, Klaus, *The Growth of the Biblical Tradition.* New York: Charles Scribner's Sons, 1969.

Lightfoot, R. H., *History and Interpretation in the Gospels.* London: Hodder & Stoughton, 1935, pp. 1-56.

McGinley, L. J., *Form-Criticism of The Synoptic Healing Narratives.* Woodstock: Woodstock College Press, 1944.

Richardson, Alan, *The Miracle-Stories of the Gospels.* London: SCM Press, 1941.

Scott, E. F., *The Validity of the Gospel Record.* New York: Charles Scribner's Sons, 1938.

Stanton, V. H., *The Gospels as Historical Documents.* Cambridge: University Press, 1930, Part II.

Streeter, B. H., *The Four Gospels.* New York: Macmillan, 1925.

Taylor, R. P. O., *The Groundwork of The Gospels.* Oxford: Alden Press, 1946.

Taylor, Vincent, *The Formation of The Gospel Tradition.* London: Macmillan, 1933.

Torrey, C. C., *The Four Gospels.* New York: Harper & Bros., 1933.

Westcott, B. F., *An Introduction to the Study of the Gospels.* 5th ed., London: Macmillan, 1875.

166

Chapter Six

THE GOSPEL ACCORDING TO MATTHEW

ONE WHO HAS FAMILIARIZED HIMSELF WITH THE OLD TESTA-
ment finds the transition to the New Testament made fairly
smooth for him by the fact that this particular Gospel stands
first in the literary expression of the new covenant, breathing as
it does to a notable degree the atmosphere of the Old Testament Scriptures. Agreeable to its Semitic flavor is the early
church report that its original form was Hebrew (or Aramaic).
This is one of the pressing problems that challenge the student of
Matthew.

ORIGINAL FORM

Eusebius ascribes to Papias the following tradition. "Matthew
collected [a variant reading has 'wrote'] the oracles in the
Hebrew language, and each interpreted them as best he could."[1]
Unfortunately Eusebius makes no comment on this quotation,

---

[1] *HE* III. xxxix. 16.

and opinions have varied as to its meaning. It is usually assumed that Hebrew here means Aramaic. From Eusebius also comes the report that when Pantaenus, the head of the catechetical school at Alexandria, went to India, he found that Matthew's Gospel had preceded him, having been brought there by Bartholomew, written in Hebrew letters.[2] Irenaeus probably depends on Papias in affirming that Matthew issued a written Gospel among the Hebrews in their own dialect.[3] Origen has substantially the same thing to say, declaring that Matthew published it "for those who from Judaism came to believe, composed in Hebrew letters."[4] Jerome's statement is that "Matthew, also called Levi, an apostle after being a publican, first in Judea, on account of those who believed from the circumcision, wrote a Gospel of Christ in Hebrew letters and words; but who afterwards translated it into Greek is not certainly known."[5] From other statements by Jerome it appears that he wrongly identified the Gospel according to the Hebrews with the Gospel according to Matthew, the two resembling each other quite closely. Jerome later admitted this confusion.

Despite this tradition of a Semitic original, the Fathers have no information on the translation of it into Greek. What they knew and used for themselves was a Greek Gospel.

The attempt to get at the meaning of Papias centers in the discussion of the two words "oracles" (*logia*) and "interpreted" (*hērmēneusen*). Regarding the former, two views are worth considering. The word has been understood to refer to a group of the sayings of Jesus, which have in turn been identified with the Q source. Ground for this identification has been sought in the observation that certain differences between Matthew and Luke in their use of Q are most easily explained as variant renderings of a Semitic original.[6] The other view considers that the *logia* should not be confined to discourse material, since in Eusebius' account, just a few lines above his reference to Matthew, in a section dealing with Mark, *logia* embraces both things said and done by Jesus. This circumstance is thought to be favorable to the conclusion that Papias had the entire Gospel of Matthew in view, not simply discourse material, though evidence for the use of *logia* as a description of a single biblical book

---

2 *Ibid.,* V. x. 3.
3 *Against Heresies* III. i. 1.
4 *HE* VI. xxv. 4.
5 *De Viris Illustribus* iii.
6 T. W. Manson, *The Teaching of Jesus,* p. 27.

seems to be lacking. In the New Testament and the Fathers *logia* is a synonym for Scripture.[7]

As to the word "interpreted," several possibilities emerge. (1) It has been understood in connection with public reading. People not familiar with Aramaic required a translation into Greek. (2) Private readers did the best they could to make out the sense, not being well versed in the Aramaic. (3) If the oracles could be thought of as *testimonia,* that is, collections of Old Testament prophecies fulfilled in Jesus Christ, then the sense would be that each person sought to set forth the fulfillment from his knowledge of the facts of gospel history. (4) The word "interpreted" is understood in terms of translation, not as in (1), but as referring to various attempts to render into Greek for permanent use. This understanding of "interpreted" brings it into line with the New Testament use of the word (as in John 1:41). Was our Greek Matthew then simply one of these attempts?

If *hērmēneusen* is construed in terms of interpretation rather than translation, which is possible linguistically, then the passage may reflect the feeling of the church in Asia Minor that the gospel story was not easily understood, being in fact a kind of mystery.[8]

The whole question is fraught with great uncertainty. It may even be that Papias, like Jerome, confused the *Gospel according to the Hebrews* or something like it with an Aramaic Matthew. The crux of the difficulty is that the Greek Matthew bears the marks of having been done as an original work rather than a translation of an Aramaic original. The evidence that our Matthew is not a translation of a Semitic original but a Greek composition is sufficient to be convincing. (1) The use of the Greek Mark accounts for a considerable portion of the book. (2) For the quotations from the Old Testament which are common to Matthew, Mark, and Luke, the LXX is verified as the source. Further, in the quotations which Matthew alone uses (apart from those introduced by the fulfilment formula), he generally follows the LXX. (3) In the Q material used by Matthew there are some 20 examples of the $μέν$-$δέ$ construction, a feature which rarely occurs in translation Greek. (4) The genitive absolute occurs approximately once in every 20 verses in Matthew, which is a much higher percentage than would be expected in translation Greek (the Pentateuch, for example, has one occurrence in approximately 140 verses).

[7] J. B. Lightfoot, *Essays on Supernatural Religion,* pp. 172-76.
[8] Otto Piper in *The Princeton Seminary Bulletin,* Oct. 1959, pp. 19-20.

CONTENTS

I. The Preparation (1:1 — 4:11) includes the infancy narratives, the work of John, and Jesus' baptism and temptation.

II. The Ministry in Galilee (4:12 — 18:35) embraces the use of Capernaum as headquarters, the Sermon on the Mount, some representative miracles, a collection of parables, opposition from Pharisees, family, and fellow-townsmen, withdrawals to Phoenicia and to Caesarea Philippi, where prediction by Jesus of his messianic death sets the tone for much of the remaining narrative.

III. The Ministry in Judea and Jerusalem (19:1 — 28:15). This section includes the discourse on the future and the closing events associated with Jesus' rejection, followed by resurrection.

IV. The Program for the Future (28:16-20).

CHARACTERISTICS

In addition to the recital of the basic facts of Jesus' ministry common to the Synoptic tradition, Matthew's Gospel reveals certain individual characteristics.

(1) Eschatology has a large place, especially in the parables and in the discourse on the last things (24-25; cf. 28:20).

(2) Jesus speaks repeatedly of God as Father.

(3) Teaching on the kingdom is dominant and the terminology used is the kingdom of heaven.

(4) The royal majesty and authority of Jesus the Christ is set forth (25:31-46; 28:18-20) and his pre-eminence over Israel's prized institutions: the Law (5:21-22, 27-28), the sabbath (12:8), the prophet (12:41), the temple (12:6), and the king (12:42).

(5) To an unusual degree interest is manifested in fulfilled prophecy. Whereas all the Evangelists give some attention to this, Matthew goes out of his way to provide an Old Testament setting for significant events in Jesus' life, especially in its early stages: his birth (1:23), his birthplace (2:6), the return from the Egyptian sojourn (2:15), the killing of the babes of Bethlehem (2:18), residence in Nazareth (2:23), the work of the forerunner (3:3), the location of his principal labors (4:15-16), his healing ministry (8:17), his demeanor as God's servant (12:18-21), the parabolic cast of his teaching (13:35), the offer of himself to Israel (21:5), and his arrest (26:56). With the exception of the reference in 2:6, which is attributed to the scribes, each one of these is prefaced with a formula indicating the fulfillment of Scripture. These quotations are not in any substantial agreement with the LXX, but appear to be

independent citations relying more on the Hebrew than on the Greek text. In his remaining citations Matthew follows the LXX closely, in agreement with the other Synoptists. It should be noticed that Matthew is not content to treat this subject as Luke usually does, by simply observing that Jesus fulfilled what was written of the Christ in the prophetic Scriptures (Luke 24:27, 44), but gives precise and detailed data to illustrate this phenomenon.

Sometimes Matthew has been accused of finding prophecies and inventing fulfilments to match. Such a procedure would weaken his whole presentation for those who were informed on the events of Jesus' life. Furthermore, it is demonstrable that Matthew did not follow such a course. R. H. Fuller writes, "Matthew did not invent the tradition of the virginal conception to square with Isaiah 7:14 or the birth at Bethlehem to square with Micah 5:1. For both these traditions are found independently in Matthew and Luke, which proves that they are prior to both evangelists."[9]

(6) This Gospel has a strong Judaic background. The persistent emphasis on God's kingdom and Christ as his chosen king roots itself in the Old Testament, as does the concept of righteousness, which six times appears on the lips of Jesus and is not once attributed to him by Mark or Luke. The contrast between the wise and the foolish, so common to the sapiential literature of the Old Testament, shows itself here, being peculiar to Matthew alone. There is a nicely balanced appreciation of the authority and relevance of the Old Testament as in 5:17, and the presentation of the necessity of a new age introduced by John the Baptist but only arriving in full force with the work of Jesus the Messiah (11:13).

This Gospel is sensitive also to the phenomena of current Judaism: its emphasis upon external acts of piety, the love of recognition found in its leaders, the proselyting activity of the Jews, the practice of binding and loosing in relation to authority, and even a hint as to the dispute between the two schools of thought on divorce (19:3). These are only samples of the local color that shines through.

In the *Pirke Aboth* or *Sayings of the Jewish Fathers* there is a eulogy of the man who takes upon himself the yoke of the Torah (3:6). Such a sentiment may lie back of the statement attributed to Jesus, "Take my yoke upon you and learn of me"

[9] *A Critical Introduction to the New Testament*, p. 117.

(11:29). In the very next verse of the *Aboth* one of the sayings of the rabbis is quoted as follows, "When ten men sit together and are occupied with the Torah, the Shekinah is among them" (3:7), to which the words of Jesus in Matthew 18:20 may well have been directed, "For where two or three are gathered together in my name, there am I in the midst of them."

(7) A notable concern is manifested for Gentiles. This would not be so striking were it not for the strong emphasis on Jesus' exclusive mission to his own nation Israel (15:24). Only in Matthew's account are the Twelve warned against going among the Gentiles and the Samaritans, and are charged to go simply to the lost sheep of the house of Israel (10:5-6). Yet the introduction of the Magi at the beginning of the Gospel seems to be a pointer looking to a large share in the Christ by other peoples than Israel, and this becomes explicit at the close of the Gospel in the wording of the Great Commission (28:19). The way is prepared for this by the teaching of Jesus during the last week before the Passion, when he underscored the rejection of Israel because of the nation's rejection of him. Peculiar to Matthew is Jesus' declaration that the kingdom will be taken from Israel and given to a nation producing the fruits of it (21:43). The entering of the nations into the inheritance of Israel is part of Jesus' eschatological teaching (8:11-12).[10]

(8) Matthew is the one Gospel that mentions the church (16:18; 18:17). A basis in the Old Testament is to be discerned here (cf. Acts 7:38), for Jesus' hearers were familiar with the idea of the assembly or congregation of the Lord. The element of newness was the distinctiveness of this predicted entity as belonging to Jesus.

(9) The teaching of our Lord has special prominence. Matthew shows considerable skill in preserving the general historical framework of Mark and inserting into it the extra teaching material that Mark does not have. He has arranged five discourses of Jesus placed at intervals through the book, each ending similarly, "When Jesus had finished. . . ." These are as follows: The Sermon on the Mount (5:3-7:27); the instruction of the disciples for their mission (10:5-42); parables of the kingdom (13:3-52); the obligations of discipleship (18:3-35); the eschatological discourse (24:4-25:46). Some would add the condemnation of the scribes and Pharisees in chapter 23, though it is not teaching in the same sense as the others. Sometimes the insistence upon five discourses is related to the idea

10 For a full discussion of this subject, see J. Jeremias, *Jesus' Promise to the Nations.*

172

The Gospel According to Matthew

that Matthew is deliberately pitting Jesus' new law over against the five books of Moses. This can hardly be established, since the Jews generally regarded the books of Moses as one — the Law. The completeness of Matthew, with this special attention to the teaching of Jesus, no doubt accounts in large measure for the popularity of this Gospel in the early church.

(10) The two broad divisions of the ministry are more clearly recognized than in the other Gospels, blocked off by means of the phrase, "from that time," the first relating to the opening of the public ministry (4:17), the second to Jesus' concentration upon the instruction of the Twelve as to the culmination of his mission in death and resurrection (16:21).

PURPOSE

Unlike the Fourth Gospel, Matthew has no precise statement giving the reason for the drawing up of this account, but it clearly has the same general purpose as the others, to set forth such a knowledge of Jesus Christ and his work as to make possible an intelligent decision for him and the gospel. But in an exceptional way, this Gospel seems intended to serve as a teaching manual for the church. This is made patent by the accent upon teaching in connection with the Great Commission.

It is impossible to overlook the apologetic element also in Matthew. At the very beginning Jesus' pedigree is given in such a way as to connect him with the Davidic and Abrahamic covenants. Far more than in any other Gospel he bears the title Son of David. His legislative authority is underscored in his teaching. His miracles bear him witness. Yet the leaders of the Jews repudiate him. These leaders have shown themselves unworthy to shepherd the people; their opposition to Jesus reflects on them, not on him (chap. 23). The people, spurred on by their leaders, accept bloodguiltiness for themselves and their children in demanding the crucifixion of the Nazarene (only in Matthew). The tension between believing and unbelieving Jews is clearly reflected in the story of the virgin birth, which is so told as to silence Jewish accusations that Jesus was illegitimately born. The same is true of the handling of the resurrection story, where the Jewish explanation of the empty tomb is noted (28:11-15). Jesus had all the necessary credentials as God's anointed, yet the nation rejected him. Like Moses, he taught the people, only to have them murmur and revolt. Like Joshua, he offered them rest, not in the land, however, but in himself (11:28), and found only a few who were ready to respond. It is not strange that he envisioned better things among the Gentiles.

BACKGROUND

A Palestinian origin for the gathering of the materials of the Gospel seems a necessity, irrespective of the actual place of composition. One touches Judaism at its center here. Comparison of the Gospel with the writings of the Qumran community reveals certain links with that group also. For example, the puzzling statement about hating one's enemies (5:43), not found in the Old Testament, is paralleled in the *Manual of Discipline* i, 4, 10. Schubert suggests that Jesus' reference to the "poor in spirit" in the first beatitude means that he had in mind "those to whom worldly goods were nothing" and that in so speaking "he aligned himself with one of the basic tenets of the Essenes."[11]

Yet in view of the breadth of outlook found in Matthew, one is obliged to concur in the statement that "the setting of this Gospel was not in some exclusive and narrow group of Jewish Christians, but rather in some place and group which had contacts with the wider Church."[12]

The actual place of origination for the Gospel cannot be positively fixed. Patristic testimony favors Judea, though this may be only an inference from its Semitic atmosphere. Modern study has tended to fix upon Antioch, where a large Jewish population existed from early hellenistic times. Since the other Gospels are associated with prominent centers, it is probable that Matthew should be also. Favorable to Antioch is the fact that the writings of Ignatius indicate knowledge of the Gospel early in the second century. A few examples must suffice. In a single passage he refers to the virgin birth of Jesus (uncommon in the Fathers) and says that Jesus was baptized by John that "all righteousness might be fulfilled by him."[13] In writing to Polycarp he appears to quote Matthew 10:16, saying, "Be prudent as the serpent in all things and pure as the dove for ever."[14]

More recently S. G. F. Brandon has sought to make a case for the origin of the Gospel in Egypt, presumably at Alexandria.[15]

---

11 "The Sermon on the Mount and the Qumran Texts," in *The Scrolls and the New Testament,* ed. by Krister Stendahl, p. 122.

12 Floyd V. Filson, *A Commentary on the Gospel according to Matthew,* p. 14.

13 *Smyrnaeans* 1:1.

14 *Polycarp* 2:2.

15 *The Fall of Jerusalem and the Christian Church,* pp. 177-78, 217-48.

DATE

There is some testimony for a very early date, Theophylact (11th cent.) putting it in the eighth year after the ascension and Nicephorus (9th cent.) in the fifteenth year. But these are isolated claims not supported by earlier and better known Fathers. The Gospel itself suggests that a considerable interval had elapsed between the events of the ministry and the time of writing (27:7-8; 28:15). A reasonable period must be allowed for the circulation of Mark and its use in the composition of Matthew. Are there factors that call for a fairly extensive interval? Some have thought so, based on such considerations as the following.

First, the trinitarian baptismal formula (28:19) is said to be of late origin, nowhere reflected in the Book of Acts, which takes note of the baptism of a large number of persons. In the Acts baptism is in the name of Christ. It should be remembered, however, that we do not have a step-by-step report of a baptismal service in the Acts, but only statements of a summary nature. It is quite possible that the Matthean formula was used but that Luke simply gives the significance of baptism in his account. This is supported by the circumstance that in the *Didache* the two are treated as synonymous. In chapter 7 reference is made to baptism and instruction is given as follows: "Baptize ye in the name of the Father, and of the Son, and of the Holy Spirit." In chapter 9 those who have been baptized are referred to as having been baptized in the name of the Lord.

Second, Matthew's report of the eschatological discourse of Jesus is thought to have been influenced by the actual event of the fall of Jerusalem in A.D. 70. The language of 22:7 is specially pertinent. Harnack, who put the date of Matthew around 75, says, "The catastrophe of Jerusalem vibrates in this Gospel as in no other."[16] This viewpoint seems suspicious of the possibility of genuine prophecy. It is possible to hold that the Gospel preserves our Lord's prophetic utterances even though the date of writing was after the event in question.

Third, appeal is made to the general impression created by the materials of the Gospel that at the time of its composition the church had a well formulated organization, worship, and ethical code, all of which presupposes a more advanced stage of ecclesiastical development than is apparent in the other Synoptics. One will be impressed by this line of argument to the degree that he is ready to apply the *Sitz im Leben* principle.

[16] *Chronologie*, I, 654.

We are perhaps on safer ground in the use of this principle if we emphasize the tension between believing and non-believing Judaism, which seems to have left its mark on the Gospel, especially in the infancy narrative and in the woes on the Pharisees. This tension was growing in the 60s, attested by the murder of James the Just. Jewish Christians must have been regarded by their fellow countrymen as guilty of treason because of their flight from Jerusalem to Pella prior to the destruction of Jerusalem.[17] The gap rapidly widened till Christians could find no toleration in the fold of Judaism. Action taken by Gamaliel II, around 80, to pronounce anathema on the Christians may well reflect the influence of Matthew's Gospel. It made unpleasant reading to Jews who were determined in their opposition to Jesus as the Messiah. A date for Matthew sometime between 70 and 80 seems to fit the circumstances to best advantage. It may be of interest that Eusebius held that Matthew had been written after Mark and Luke.[18]

AUTHORSHIP

We have touched on authorship to some extent in dealing with the original language. The voice of antiquity speaks in behalf of Matthew the publican, though some of the testimonies may be echoes of their predecessors rather than independent judgments based on knowledge or research. The Gospel itself makes no claim regarding authorship. There may. be a bit of confirmation of the popular verdict in the fact that Matthew's list of apostles reads, "Matthew the tax-gatherer" (10:3), whereas the other lists in Mark, Luke, and Acts simply call this man Matthew. It is possible that Matthew inserted the information about his previous employment in order to emphasize his unworthiness to take this place assigned to him by Christ. All the Synoptists report the call and also the feast that followed in Matthew's house, Luke calling it a great feast. But in Matthew's account nothing is said about its magnitude, nor is it even indicated that the feast was held in his house (the text reads, "in the house"). Elsewhere the Gospels are silent about this man, except for recording his name among the Twelve.

The objection to Matthean authorship is twofold. First, the vivid, lifelike touches that one would expect in a record written by an eyewitness are absent here. It is often just these touches

17 *HE* III. v. 3.
18 *HE* III. xxiv. 6-7.

that are removed in the author's use of Markan material. Perhaps the writer felt that these were not essential to the kernel of the story, and since he had to abbreviate in order to add other material, these lively details could be eliminated. The second objection is counted even more serious. How can it be supposed that Matthew the apostle could bring himself to incorporate almost *in toto* the work of Mark, a man who lacked apostolic dignity? A possible answer here is that Matthew was not deferring to Mark so much as to Peter, the acknowledged leader of the apostles, whom tradition makes responsible for the material in Mark.

Goodspeed has come to the defense of Matthean authorship.[19] He is impressed by the numerical interest of the writer of the Gospel as displayed in the genealogy and in the parables that involve monetary items, and feels that the training and experience of the tax collector show themselves at these points. He thinks that Jesus, sensing the opposition to him, deliberately chose Matthew with a view to having him make a record of his work that would survive him. He argues that Matthew's name is associated with the Gospel because he was the one who gave it its Greek dress. The Greeks were not interested in Aramaic (barbarian) origins, but they were bound to be interested in knowing and preserving the name of the man who wrote in Greek.

This last consideration loses some of its point if the Gospel was put out for the benefit of a Jewish-Christian public, as seems to be the case from the nature of the materials in it. A cautious judgment on authorship grants that there is a nucleus of the Gospel deriving from Matthew, in accordance with the statement of Papias. Whether the whole of the Gospel can be attributed to him is less certain. As Sanday says, "It would . . . be easy to understand how the name that belonged to a special and important part of the first Gospel gradually came to be extended over the whole."[20] Yet it may be that Matthew himself was responsible for the final form of the Gospel in its Greek dress as well as for the earlier Aramaic form, on the analogy of Josephus' *Jewish War,* which appeared in original draft in Aramaic before being published in Greek. The evidence on authorship is hardly decisive enough to warrant a confident decision.

---

[19] *Matthew, Apostle and Evangelist.*
[20] *The Gospels in the Second Century,* p. 156.

RECENT STUDY

B. W. Bacon, building on suggestions made before his time, asserted that Matthew is a compilation of materials furnished largely by Mark and another source, which he thought to be somewhat more extensive than Q. Aside from the preamble in chapters 1-2 and the epilogue in chapters 26-28, the Gospel is regarded as falling into a fivefold structure, with narrative material preceding the discourses in each case. Bacon also noted a targumizing tendency in Matthew.[21]

G. D. Kilpatrick, while recognizing that the Gospel could have more than one utility, including the catechetical, is not satisfied with this as the main thrust. Some things in Matthew would be of little value to those coming into the church, but of great interest and concern to those already in the church, especially its leaders. Having challenged the catechetical theory, he goes on to suggest that the Gospel was framed for liturgical use, to aid the worship of the church.[22] The analogy of the synagogue service might be said to create a presumption in favor of the liturgical use of New Testament Scriptures, but it is possible that a rather long period elapsed before this actually occurred. Cullmann has argued cogently against the idea that early believers had a service of ministry of the word as distinct from the observance of the Lord's Supper.[23] Worship was a far more fluid and spontaneous thing in the apostolic age than at the time of Justin, when the reading of the Gospels had become a definite part of the service. At the beginning worship centered in the remembrance of Christ in his death. Apart from catechetical instruction of new converts, the ministry of the word seems to have been confined to the preaching of the gospel to non-Christian audiences.

Dom Butler has attempted to set aside the widely accepted dictum of Mark's priority in favor of Matthew.[24] In his argumentation, however, he has not succeeded in breaking through the barrier of the Markan order as determinative for Matthew.[25]

Krister Stendahl not only provides a review of previous tendencies in the study of Matthew, but goes on to set forth his own view that the Gospel is the product of a school that operated along lines somewhat paralleling those of the Qumran group, with particular concern for interpretation of the Old

21 *Studies in Matthew,* 1930.
22 *The Origins of the Gospel according to St. Matthew.*
23 Oscar Cullmann, *Early Christian Worship,* pp. 26-36.
24 B. C. Butler, *The Originality of St. Matthew.*
25 See a critique by H. G. Wood in *ET,* 65 (Oct. 1953), pp. 17-19.

Testament in such a way as to lend support to the Christian movement.[26] Special attention is paid to the ten instances in which the quotation of the Old Testament is introduced by the formula, "that it might be fulfilled," where divergence from the text of the LXX is apparent. This rather free handling of the textual data invites comparison with the *Habakkuk Commentary* of the Dead Sea Scrolls in which the text of the prophet is likewise handled in rather free fashion with the intent of showing how the Teacher of Righteousness, a leading figure in the Qumran sect, fulfilled the terms of the ancient prophecy. Stendahl concludes that Matthew is the product of a school with Christological interest and with concern for the duties of church leaders, for discipline, etc.

Some problems respecting this view present themselves. If this method of interpretation, which Stendahl calls *Midrash pesher*, was in use at the time of Christian origins and even before, there does not seem to be any valid objection to the possibility that an individual could have utilized the method.[27] A feature of Stendahl's reconstruction is the very late dating of the Gospel, near the end of the first century. That the Hebrew-Christian element in the church would have to wait so long a time for a Gospel is unlikely.

Gärtner finds additional difficulties with Stendahl's thesis.[28] He questions the suitability of the term *pesher* for the material in Matthew, since in the Qumran sect's use of the term what is involved is either an interpretation of a consecutive text such as *Habakkuk* or different fixed passages of text as in the *Damascus Document*. Gärtner also suggests that whatever may be said for the catechetical *Sitz im Leben* of Matthew, one must not overlook the evidence from the New Testament itself (as in Acts 4:8ff.) that the use of Old Testament passages introduced by the fulfillment formula has its most natural origin in the missionary preaching to the Jews.

BIBLIOGRAPHY

Bacon, B. W., *Studies in Matthew*. New York: Henry Holt, 1930.

Broadus, John A., *Commentary on the Gospel of Matthew*. Philadelphia: American Baptist Publication Society, 1887.

Farrer, Austin, *St. Matthew and St. Mark*. Westminster: Dacre Press, 1954.

[26] *The School of St. Matthew.*

[27] E. Earle Ellis, *Paul's Use of the Old Testament*, p. 147.

[28] "The Habakkuk Commentary (DSH) and the Gospel of Matthew," *ST*, 8 (1955), pp. 1-24.

Filson, Floyd V., *Commentary on the Gospel according to St. Matthew*. New York: Harper & Bros., 1960.

Kilpatrick, G. D., *The Origins of the Gospel according to St. Matthew*. Oxford: Clarendon Press, 1946.

Knox, W. L., *The Sources of the Synoptic Gospels*, Vol. II (St. Luke and St. Matthew). Cambridge University Press, 1957.

Lagrange, M. J., *Evangile selon Saint Matthieu*. 9th ed., Paris: J. Gabalda, 1948.

McNeile, A. H., *The Gospel according to St. Matthew*. London: Macmillan, 1938.

Plummer, Alfred, *An Exegetical Commentary on the Gospel according to St. Matthew*. London: Robert Scott, 1909.

Schlatter, A., *Der Evangelist Matthäus*. Stuttgart: Calwer, 1929.

Schniewind, Julius, *Das Evangelium nach Matthäus*, Vol. 2 of *Das Neue Testament Deutsch*. 6th ed., Göttingen: Vandenhoeck & Ruprecht, 1953.

Stendahl, Krister, *The School of St. Matthew*, Vol. XX of *Acta Seminarii Neotestamentici Upsaliensis*. Uppsala, 1954.

Stonehouse, N. B., *The Witness of Matthew and Mark to Christ*. Philadelphia: The Presbyterian Guardian, 1944.

Tasker, R. V. G., *The Gospel according to St. Matthew*, Tyndale NT Commentaries. Grand Rapids: Eerdmans, 1961.

Williams, A. Lukyn, *The Hebrew-Christian Messiah*. London: SPCK, 1916.

Zahn, Theodor, *Das Evangelium des Matthäus*. 3rd ed., Leipzig: A. Deichert, 1910.

Chapter Seven

THE GOSPEL ACCORDING TO MARK

IN THE ANCIENT CHURCH THIS BOOK DID NOT COMMAND THE attention given to Matthew and even to Luke, but in the modern period it has forged ahead of its companions and now occupies the place of chief consideration among the Synoptics.

RECOGNITION BY THE EARLY CHURCH

Most primitive is the account of Papias contained in Eusebius. "And the Presbyter used to say this, 'Mark became Peter's interpreter and wrote accurately all that he remembered, not, indeed, in order, of the things said or done by the Lord. He had not heard the Lord, nor had he followed him, but later on, as I said, followed Peter, who used to give teaching as necessity demanded but not making, as it were, an arrangement of the Lord's oracles, so that Mark did nothing wrong in thus writing down single points as he remembered them' "[1] (Lake's translation).

[1] *HE* III. xxxix. 15.

In view of the words, "as I said," it may be held with some confidence that in this sentence Papias is speaking, so that the words of John the Presbyter are confined to the first sentence. Judging from Papias' usage, *interpreter* means translator, in which case Peter's discourses that are in view here were likely delivered to Aramaic-speaking audiences.[2] Zahn dissents from this, preferring to understand that the word is used in a more general sense of the service of one who makes the work of another known.[3]

The Presbyter seems bent on defending Mark against detractors. This is probably the case in his use of the word *accurately* and is certainly reflected in his comment that Mark did not write *in order*. Presumably there were Gospel accounts in existence when Mark's work was published (Luke speaks of "many" in his Prologue), and they may well have given a different order than is found in Mark. Papias seeks to explain that Mark's order is due to the fact that he was not a follower of the Lord but was dependent upon the public testimony of Peter, which was of occasional character.

A second witness is Irenaeus. "After the death of these (Peter and Paul) Mark also, the disciple and interpreter of Peter, himself handed down to us in writing the things which were preached by Peter."[4] In addition to confirming the relation of Mark to Peter, this statement gives information both as to the place of publication (for the context fixes the death of Peter and Paul in Rome) and the time, namely, after the decease of the two apostles.

The opening words of the Muratorian Fragment apparently give the final portion of the writer's statement about Mark's Gospel. "But at some he was present, and so he set them down." By *some* it is possible to understand occasions at which Peter spoke.

Clement of Alexandria's description of the origin of the Gospel differs from previous accounts in respect to the time and circumstances of its creation. "When Peter had preached the word publicly in Rome and announced the gospel by the Spirit, those present, of whom there were many, besought Mark, since for a long time he had followed him and remembered what had been said, to record his words. Mark did this and communicated the

2 On this point see J. H. Moulton, *Grammar of New Testament Greek*, II, 31.
3 *Introduction to the New Testament*, II, 441-44; 454-56.
4 *Against Heresies* III. i. 2.

Gospel to those who made request of him. When Peter knew of it, he neither actively prevented nor encouraged the undertaking."[5] Some have seen here a tendency to bring the origin of the Gospel into the lifetime of Peter in order to have the advantage of his concurrence in the project. This may well reflect the growing esteem in which Peter was being held by the church. Another account by Clement carries the process still further, indicating that Peter ratified the work for reading in the churches.[6]

Jerome's statement adds nothing beyond the claim that Mark was the first bishop of Alexandria.[7] Since the Alexandrian Fathers are silent on this matter, little confidence can be placed in this observation.

Certain things should be noted by way of summary concerning the information cited above. (1) It points to a Roman origin for the Gospel. This is confirmed by Mark 15:21, where it is stated that the Roman soldiers who conducted Jesus from Pilate's judgment hall to Calvary compelled Simon of Cyrene, the father of Alexander and Rufus, to go along with them and bear the cross of Jesus. Here the writer is adding a touch of human interest to his account, intended especially for Roman readers, since it is known from Romans 16:13 that Rufus and his mother lived at Rome. The Roman origin of Mark is confirmed to some extent by the presence of Latinisms, that is, Latin terms transliterated into Greek. Since the use of Latin followed Roman officialdom and administration, Latin terms could have been used in almost any quarter of the empire, but the larger proportion of Latinisms in Mark over the other Gospels may be significant. The list includes: δηνάριον, κοδράντης, κεντυρίων, κῆνσος, κράβαττος, λεγιών, μόδιος, ξέστης, πραιτώριον, σπεκουλάτωρ, φραγελλοῦν and a few phrases. Especially crucial is the fact that occasionally the writer uses a Latin term to explain a Greek word (12:42; 15:16).[8]

(2) Mark is identified as the interpreter of Peter. On the linguistic side, as noted above, this may well mean that the Aramaic flavor of the Gospel is a faithful reflection of Peter's spoken word. Certainly Mark is "the most Aramaic of the Gospels."[9] From the standpoint of content, it is helpful to note that the general outline of the material in Mark coincides well

[5] *HE* VI. xiv. 6-7.
[6] *HE* II. xv. 2.
[7] *Preface to Matthew.*
[8] A. Wikenhauser, *New Testament Introduction,* p. 166.
[9] W. F. Howard in Moulton's *Grammar of New Testament Greek,* II, 481.

with the report of Peter's preaching in the house of Cornelius (Acts 10). The brief account of the apostle's sermon contains the following ingredients: the beginning of Jesus' mission in Galilee following John's baptismal activity; the anointing of Jesus by God with the Holy Spirit and power (an evident allusion to his baptism); his beneficent ministry characterized especially by many healings; his death and resurrection. When this outline is stretched over the Gospel of Mark it will be seen to agree faithfully with what the Evangelist has incorporated into his work. Mark may be regarded as a catechetical expansion of the *kerygma*.[10] The writer may have drawn on other sources than Peter's discourses.

Although the mention of Peter by name in this Gospel cannot be said to be disproportionately great, the allusion to him in 16:7, "Go, tell his disciples and Peter. . ." is best explained as a personal reminiscence. The other Evangelists do not record it.

(3) If Peter's connection with Mark's Gospel is what the ancients represent it to have been, then we have in this work, in the ultimate sense, the testimony of an apostle and eyewitness. This is made probable by the Gospel itself, for again and again the narrative has a fullness, a freshness, and a liveliness that set it apart from the other Synoptics. One may take the account of the healing of the epileptic boy as an example out of many in order to certify this impression. Swete is justified in saying, "Where the three Synoptists are on common ground, St. Mark is usually distinguished by signs of the minuter knowledge which comes from personal observation or from personal contact with an eyewitness."[11]

AUTHORSHIP

On the identity of Mark, the traditional writer of this Gospel, with the John Mark of Acts 12:12, there is general agreement.[12] This young man left his home in Jerusalem to accompany Barnabas and Paul as a helper on the first missionary journey (Acts 13:5), but parted from them at Perga and returned to Jerusalem (Acts 13:13). At the start of the second journey, Barnabas proposed that Mark go along, but Paul dissented (Acts 15:37), bringing on a cleavage between himself and Barnabas. Of

---

10 H. E. W. Turner in *ET*, 71 (June 1960), p. 261.
11 *The Gospel according to St. Mark*, p. lxxv.
12 For a discussion of the misgivings of J. Weiss, see Vincent Taylor, *The Gospel according to St. Mark*, pp. 26-27.

184

Mark's association with Barnabas following this, Luke has left no record. The loyalty of Barnabas to young Mark is explained, at least in part, by blood relationship. From Colossians 4:10 we learn that Mark was a cousin of Barnabas. The same passage discloses the fact that Mark was with Paul at the time of writing, which implies a restoration of their friendship and collaboration in the work of the Lord (cf. Philemon 24). At this juncture Mark was on the point of making a trip to Asia Minor. Later Paul coveted his presence and help during his last days of imprisonment at Rome (II Tim. 4:11). Mark's association with Peter is attested in I Peter 5:13, where the affectionate term "my son" may indicate Peter's expectation that Mark would carry on his work in some measure even as Paul expected that Timothy would do in his own case.

Mark has not intruded himself upon the pages of the Gospel story unless it be at one point where he refers to a young man who followed along with Jesus after his arrest, when the disciples had fled. Capture by the soldiers was averted by slipping out of his garment as they clutched at it and by fleeing into the night (Mark 14:51-52). The introduction of such an isolated incident points more logically to the writer than to any other. Stauffer observes, "It may well be that Mark wished to introduce his own portrait into a 'dark corner' of this nocturnal scene, as artists loved to do even in antiquity."[13]

From certain allusions in the Fathers it has been thought that Mark, known as the "stump-fingered," had disfigured himself to avoid priestly service, but the earliest source of information explains the epithet as due to the fact that he had small fingers in proportion to his frame as a whole.[14]

As one who ministered to Barnabas and Paul and also to Peter, Mark was a suitable figure to relate the ministry of Jesus in such a way as to emphasize his mission in terms of humble service (Mark 10:45).

PURPOSE

It is somewhat awkward that this, the earliest of the Gospels, should not declare its design in explicit statement, as is done in connection with the Fourth Gospel. However, this lack can be reasonably supplied by careful attention to the materials which are utilized. It is evident from the caption that Mark is concerned to present the story of Jesus Christ as "gospel." Yet the

---

[13] *Jesus and His Story,* p. 121.
[14] *The Anti-Marcionite Prologue to Mark.*

title is ambiguous, for it might mean the gospel that Jesus Christ preached or the gospel about Jesus Christ. In this very obscurity lies the key to what Mark is trying to say. Jesus did indeed preach the good news of God associated with the inbreaking of the kingdom of God and man's need of repentance (1:14), but the person and work of our Lord are linked with the gospel in the closest manner (10:29; 13:9, 10). This sets the pattern for the church, which must continue to preach the gospel and must make it center in the mission of the Son of God. The strong emphasis on preaching may help to account for the relatively slight attention to the teaching of Jesus.

To the emphasis on Jesus as the Son of God Mark adds Jesus' self-interpretation of his mission in terms of the Servant-concept, including both the activity of the ministry and its culmination in his vicarious death (10:45).

An apologetic strain may be present also, designed to explain how this divine Son of God could have been rejected by his own people among whom he ministered. Hardness of heart led to a lack of appreciation of his ministry (3:5) and culminated in official repudiation by the Sanhedrin (14:61-64). Even the disciples had some hardness of heart, but this concerned failure to grasp his teaching (6:52; 8:17). They were not wholly deficient in faith and loyalty.

Mark may have had in mind that the publication of his Gospel would encourage the Roman church, which about this time was feeling the effects of persecution at the hands of Nero. He mentions persecution as the lot of the disciple at a point where the other Synoptists lack it (10:30).

DATE

It is generally assumed that the time of writing must have been between A.D. 65 and 70. Nero fired Rome in the summer of 64 and this led to open persecution of the Christians, who were blamed for the catastrophe. During the next few years both Peter and Paul lost their lives. It is possible that the general tradition about Mark's relation to Peter may be correct and yet that the insistence on the publication of the Gospel after his death may be in error. The question is complex, involving the relation of Mark to the other Synoptics and the time of publication of the Book of Acts. That is to say, Acts follows Luke (Acts 1:1), and if it was written near the end of Paul's first imprisonment, it would require a date in the early 60s, which would in turn require a somewhat earlier date for Luke and a still earlier date for Mark.

Harnack's dating for Mark (50-60) is not widely held today, though C. C. Torrey, largely because of his theory of Aramaic originals, was prepared to accept a date around the middle of the century. T. W. Manson has endorsed the interval from 58 to 65. It must be confessed that we do not possess the data for a precise dating of the Gospel. See the discussion on the date of Acts.

CONTENTS

Certain broad divisions stand out. (1) Preparation (1:1-13), including John's ministry, Jesus' baptism and temptation. (2) Proclamation (1:14—8:26), headed by Jesus' announcement that the kingdom was at hand (1:14-15), followed by representative samples of his activity in Galilee: the call of disciples, several healings and exorcisms and numerous confrontations with the scribes and Pharisees. Action centers largely in the region of the sea of Galilee. There are several allusions to teaching, but not much of the content is stated. (3) Prediction (8:27—10:52). The crucial meeting at Caesarea Philippi sets the stage for the transfiguration and the departure for Jerusalem marked by further teaching to the disciples on the Master's forthcoming death and resurrection. (4) Passion (11:1—16:8). The triumphal entry leads to the temple cleansing and this in turn to debates with Jewish leaders, culminating in arrest, trial, death and the empty tomb.

CHARACTERISTICS

(1) Great prominence is given to the gospel. The word stands as a caption for the entire book (1:1), unlike the other Synoptics. Jesus is represented as giving it a central place in his preaching (1:14-15). This divine message is worthy of the sacrifice of life itself by the disciple (8:35; 10:29). It must be proclaimed to all nations (13:10; 14:9). Mark is thoroughly kerygmatic in its emphasis.

(2) Mark lays great stress on the element of secrecy imposed by Jesus in connection with his healings (1:44; 5:43; 7:36; 8:26) and exorcisms (1:25, 34; 3:12). A similar ban is laid on the disciples concerning his Messiahship (8:30) and the disclosure at the transfiguration (9:9). The prohibition in 9:30-31 is designed to avoid crowds that he might give time to the disciples. The demand for secrecy and silence is understandable on the

basis of Jesus' recognition that only the consummation of his ministry could banish the misconception of his mission held by the disciples. As for the public, excessive preoccupation with his mighty works could easily foster a false idea of his purpose and excite revolutionary hopes. Outside of Galilee (5:19; 9:27) and during the closing days in the Jerusalem area (10:52) no such restriction was needed. The ban on the public belongs to the early days of the ministry and on the disciples it applies from Caesarea Philippi. For Wrede's view of these phenomena, see p. 190.

(3) Repeatedly Mark notes that as Jesus taught or moved about, great throngs of people gathered around him (1:33, 45; 2:2, 13, 15; 3:7, 9, 20; 4:1, 36; 5:21, 24, 31; 6:34; 8:1; 9:15, 25; 10:1, 46). The increase in the crowds entailed a corresponding concern on the part of the scribes and Pharisees, who frequently confronted and challenged him. These features, especially the former, diminish in the Jerusalem area.

(4) A curious feature of the narrative is the enclosing of one episode within another (5:25-35a; 6:17-29).

(5) Some of the linguistic features such as the detailed, vivid character of the narrative and the presence of Latinisms have been already noted. But there are others. One is the roughness of the writer's Greek, revealed by such things as broken sentence structure (2:10; 11:32), abundant use of the historical present intermingled with past tenses, parenthetical remarks (3:30; 7:19), and colloquialisms such as would be expected in popular speech. These are quite understandable if Mark was intent on reproducing Peter's style of speaking. The preponderance of parataxis is also natural under these circumstances. Semitisms are frequent, also the historic present and use of diminutives.

(6) Mark is the Gospel of action. This is seen not alone in the writer's omission of the birth narrative and in his concern to report the deeds of Jesus more fully than his words, but also in the repeated use of the adverb εὐθύς ("immediately"), which occurs more than forty times. It should be observed, however, that even though Mark does not give an extensive report of Jesus' teaching, he often remarks on the fact that Jesus taught, without indicating what was said (2:13; 4:23; 6:2, 6, 34; 10:1; 12:35).

(7) In this Gospel the emotions of Jesus are given a prominent place: his compassion (1:41; 6:34; 8:2), his indignation (3:5; 8:2; 10:14), his distress and sorrow (14:33, 34). Twice it is reported that he sighed (7:34; 8:12).

(8) Gentiles have some prominence, as seen particularly in the account of the temple cleansing (11:17) and in connection with the future preaching of the gospel (13:10; 14:9).

(9) Special attention is given to Jesus' cultivating of the dis-

ciples in order to prepare them for their future ministry. At times the disciples appear in a poorer light here than in the other Synoptics, when, for example, they make bold to criticize Jesus for stating that someone touched him in the throng (5:31), which Matthew omits and Luke puts more mildly. Another instance is the perplexity of the three disciples on the Mount of Transfiguration over what Jesus' reference to rising from the dead could mean (9:10), an item which is absent from the other Synoptics. Again, Jesus' indignation at the disciples for rebuking those who brought little ones to him (10:13-14) fails to appear in the accounts of Matthew and Luke. This feature of Mark ought not to be unduly pressed, however, since Mark does not include the observation that the disciples begged Jesus to send away the Syro-Phoenician woman who was bothering them (Matt. 15:23). The same is true of the Master's rebuke of Peter for using his sword in the garden (Matt. 26:52; Luke 22:51). So the allegation that Mark has no love for the disciples is an exaggeration.

(10) Mark is pre-eminently the Gospel of the passion of Christ. More than two-fifths of this account deals with the journey to Jerusalem and the events that transpired there (10:32ff.).

(11) The high Christology of this Gospel is literally thrust upon the reader in the very first verse, where Jesus Christ is designated as the Son of God. This status is attested by the Father (1:11; 9:7), by demons (3:11; 5:7), by Jesus himself (13:32; 14:61), and by the centurion at the cross (15:39).

(12) As noted in the discussion of textual criticism, the so-called abrupt ending of this Gospel undoubtedly represents the conclusion of Mark's own words. In the last few years a number of voices have been raised in favor of the idea that this ending was the actual close of the Gospel as Mark intended it. Examples of sentences ending in γάρ have been cited from Greek literature, and even an occasional paragraph. The German scholar Lohmeyer supported the abrupt ending by giving a specialized interpretation to verse 7, where the angelic message to the women directs them to go into Galilee, whither the Lord will precede them, promising to see them there. So, for practical purposes, the Gospel ends with the promise of the eschatological coming, according to Lohmeyer, not simply with a resurrection appearance. This makes it, he judges, a fitting close to the Gospel, and helps to explain its termination in a way that would otherwise be abrupt indeed. But the language, to the effect that Jesus is going before the disciples into Galilee, is fitting for an appearance but is not so naturally taken to be parousia language.

189

RECENT STUDY

In 1835 Lachmann advocated the priority of Mark among the Synoptics, a position that has become widely accepted and has sometimes been cited as the one solid achievement of the literary criticism of the Synoptic Gospels.

Increasingly throughout the rest of the nineteenth century Mark was the Gospel that invited attention, in contrast to its status in the early church, where it was quite neglected. It became customary to contrast Mark with John. The latter was late in time and heavily theological, whereas Mark was free from theologizing tendencies and could be counted on to give a rather faithful picture of the historical Jesus as he was. For this reason Mark became the favorite of the liberal school. Then, at the turn of the century, came Wrede and Wellhausen, with their insistence that Mark, instead of containing merely a historical presentation, was shot through with dogmatic elements. Wrede's work[15] theorized that the early church held to Jesus' Messiahship only in an eschatological framework, but that gradually the view gained ground that there must have been evidences during his ministry that pointed toward this ultimate Messiahship status. Mark sought to read this messianic element back into the ministry of Jesus by the literary device of the secret. The disciples and others, even the demons, are charged by Jesus not to make him known, so that his Messianic status, revealed by his miracles, is kept from public proclamation. The upshot is that Mark is declared to be entirely unreliable by reason of this intrusion of a Christological element artificially injected.

Wellhausen emphasized the fragmentary character of the gospel traditions and the somewhat artificial way in which they were connected by Mark. These conclusions were carried forward by K. L. Schmidt,[16] who saw in Mark much editorial redaction in the joining together of the separate bits of tradition. This conception of the origin of Mark has been criticized by T. W. Manson on the ground that people wanted something more than disconnected stories. He writes, "They wanted the story of the Ministry as a whole; and Mark is the first to meet that demand. But if an outline of the Ministry had then to be created out of nothing for this purpose, it can only be that for the thirty years between the end of the Ministry and the composition of Mark, Christians in general were not interested in the story of the

---

15 *Das Messiasgeheimnis in den Evangelien.*
16 *Der Rahmen der Geschichte Jesu.*

Ministry and allowed it to be forgotten."[17]   Clearly such a state of affairs is most improbable.

R. H. Lightfoot has injected into the study of Mark the importance of geography by contending that in the mind of its author Galilee was "the land divinely chosen as the sphere of revelation."[18] Judea, on the other hand, is the land of darkness and sin and death, where Jesus does little but move on to his passion. The contrast is reinforced by the way in which Galilee comes into prominence again as the place of revelation of the risen Lord rather than Jerusalem (16:7). The view in question seems to read more into this geographical antithesis than is intended by Mark.[19] Surely Jesus revealed himself in Tyre and Sidon and the Decapolis and Caesarea Philippi, areas that lay outside Galilee proper. It must not be thought that he was passive and relatively inactive when he left Galilee, for he taught extensively in Judea as well as in Jerusalem (10:1).

A special approach to Mark has been made by Philip Carrington, archbishop of Quebec, in his book, *The Primitive Christian Calendar,* wherein he sets forth the so-called calendrical theory of the origin of this Gospel. His thesis concerns the first ten chapters of Mark, the portion exclusive of the passion narrative, and maintains that this material is arranged for use in connection with the high points of the church year, with enough additional material for use on the intervening Sundays.

Carrington emphasizes that early Christianity grew out of Judaism and undoubtedly took over its festal observances. The Book of Acts and the Epistles testify to the importance of Passover, Pentecost, and Firstfruits. In the author's judgment they are so crucial as to have affected Gospel writing. This novel interpretation of the origin of Mark turns it into a lectionary. But the view is difficult to maintain, for the few glimpses we have into early Christian gatherings suggest far more informality than would be possible with a prescribed course of reading. Paul's allusions to worship in I Corinthians 11-14 make no mention of reading, whether of Old Testament or New Testament Scripture. It is damaging to the view also that the first adequate picture of Christian worship to come down from the ancient church (in Justin Martyr) contains the observation that the

---

[17] "Present-day Research in the Life of Jesus," in *The Background of the New Testament and Its Eschatology,* ed. by Davies and Daube, p. 213.

[18] *Locality and Doctrine in the Gospels,* pp. 49-50, 106-26.

[19] For fuller discussion, see N. B. Stonehouse, *The Witness of Matthew and Mark to Christ,* pp. 38-49.

writings of the prophets or the memories of the apostles were read *as long as time permits*. This does not look like a prescribed ritual of reading for the day.[20]

Austin Farrer, convinced that the materials of Mark do not present a plausible historical connection, turns to theological and symbolical patterns, aided by numerics, as the key to the understanding of the book.[21] The order in Mark is not historically sequential but cyclic. For example, the healing narratives reveal a pattern in which "the evangelist's purpose is to exhibit Christ's many healing works as types and anticipations of the one great healing work performed on the cross and in the Easter sepulchre."[22] This interpretation has suggestive features, but it is probably too subtle and involved to be foisted on the writer of the Gospel. Furthermore, the notion that the readers of the Gospel would have discerned the patterns as Farrer has done is rather dubious.

James M. Robinson has sketched the various approaches to this problem of history in Mark through the critical literature of the modern period, and has provided an interpretation of the Markan materials. "The history which Mark selects to record is presented in its unity as the eschatological action of God, prepared by John the Baptist, inaugurated at the baptism and temptation, carried on through the struggles with various forms of evil, until in his death Jesus has experienced the ultimate of historical involvement and of diabolical antagonism. In the resurrection the force of evil is conclusively broken and the power of God's reign is established in history."[23] Again, "Mark's understanding of the Church is rooted in a new understanding of history as the interplay of blessedness and suffering."[24]

Willi Marxsen (in *Mark the Evangelist*) holds that Mark started with the passion narrative, which was basically traditional material, and worked backward in constructing his account, which deserves to be called the Galilean Gospel. It is this emphasis on Galilee that discloses the element of redaction most clearly. We must read Mark from the standpoint of the evangelist's own time and the Christian circle to which he belonged, centered in Galilee during the sixties, earnestly awaiting the Parousia, which failed to materialize. The viewpoint adopted is a

20 See further, W. D. Davies' contribution to *The Background of the New Testament and its Eschatology*, pp. 124-52.
21 *A Study in Mark; St. Matthew and St. Mark.*
22 *A Study in Mark*, p. 52.
23 *The Problem of History in Mark*, p. 53.
24 *Ibid.*, p. 56.

192

carry-over of much of the Form criticism approach, in that the crucial data are thought to reflect Mark's own period rather than the time of Jesus, an arbitrary assumption. A further difficulty is that the claim of Galilean origin for the Gospel necessarily discounts both the ancient testimony to a Roman origin and the several items in the Gospel itself which tend to corroborate this tradition.

BIBLIOGRAPHY

Carrington, Philip, *The Primitive Christian Calendar.* Cambridge University Press, 1952.

——————, *According to Mark,* Cambridge University Press, 1960.

Cole, R. A., *The Gospel according to St. Mark, TBC.* Grand Rapids: Eerdmans, 1961.

Cranfield, C. E. B., *The Gospel according to St. Mark.* Cambridge University Press, 1959.

Grant, F. C., *The Earliest Gospel.* New York: Abingdon-Cokesbury, 1943.

Guy, Harold A., *The Origin of the Gospel of Mark.* London: Hodder & Stoughton, 1954.

Lightfoot, R. H., *The Gospel Message of St. Mark.* Oxford: Clarendon Press, 1950.

Lohmeyer, Ernst, *Das Evangelium des Markus.* 11th ed., Göttingen: Vandenhoeck & Ruprecht, 1951.

Manson, T. W., *Studies in the Gospels and Epistles.* Manchester University Press, 1962, pp. 28-45.

Marxsen, Willi, *Der Evangelist Markus.* 2nd ed., Göttingen: Vandenhoeck & Ruprecht, 1959. Eng. trans., Abingdon, 1969.

Menzies, Allan, *The Earliest Gospel.* London: Macmillan, 1901.

Nineham, D. E., *Saint Mark.* New York: Seabury Press, 1968.

Rawlinson, A. E. J., *St. Mark, WC.* 7th ed., London: Methuen, 1949.

Robinson, James M., *The Problem of History in Mark, Studies in Biblical Theology* No. 21. Naperville: Alec R. Allenson, 1957.

Swete, H. B., *The Gospel according to St. Mark.* 3rd ed., London: Macmillan, 1927.

Taylor, Vincent, *The Gospel according to St. Mark.* London: Macmillan, 1952.

Chapter Eight

THE GOSPEL ACCORDING TO LUKE

ALTHOUGH THIS ACCOUNT HAS MUCH IN COMMON WITH THE
other Synoptic Gospels, it has this distinguishing feature, that its
writer composed the Book of Acts also, with the result that his
combined literary product makes Luke the largest contributor
to the New Testament from the standpoint of bulk. Unity of
authorship is indicated by the circumstance that both documents
are dedicated to the same person, a certain Theophilus, and the
second writing refers back to the former as having proceeded from
the same author (Acts 1:1).

Examination of the close of Luke's Gospel and the opening of
the Acts shows how the writer has fitted his materials together.
This is especially noteworthy in the treatment of the ascension,
which is only hinted at in the Gospel (24:51)[1] but is the subject of formal statement and description in Acts 1:2, 9. From
the standpoint of gospel history the resurrection was more decisive than the ascension, but from the standpoint of apostolic
history the ascension had a definitive place as the basis for the
exaltation of Christ and the outpouring of the Spirit. The concept of witness is another element binding the two books together
(Luke 24:48; Acts 1:8).

---

[1] Bodmer Papyrus XIV (P[75]), however, must now be added to
the witnesses for the longer reading that specifically mentions the ascension.

Luke alone of the Gospel writers set before himself the task of giving an exposition of the beginnings of the Christian movement. In so doing, he chose not to limit himself to the account of the rise and progress of the Church, thus leaving it to the individual reader to fill in the background of Christ's ministry in whatever way he could, but elected to draw up his own record of the ministry so as to furnish a continuous narrative. Luke is the first Christian historian. What he doubtless intended as volumes one and two of his work have become sundered because of the desire of the early church to include his Gospel with the other three. Modern writers have sought to recapture the author's original intent by speaking of Luke-Acts. It is clear from the opening of the Acts that a previous work had been produced and that a close connection is intended between the two. But comparison with the practice of Josephus, the first-century Jewish historian, makes it reasonably certain that Luke conceived of his two books as parts of a single whole. At the beginning of Book II of his work *Against Apion,* Josephus refers to Book I as the former book or first volume of his work. Luke was aware of the habit of historians of the hellenistic period and adapted his own writing to this model.

AUTHORSHIP

The ancients declare that Luke the physician, the companion of Paul, wrote the Gospel. Among the early testimonies is that of the Canon of Muratori with its difficult text. Suggested emendations affect details, but do not bring into question Luke's authorship.

From the same general period comes the affirmation of Irenaeus that Luke, the follower of Paul, recorded the gospel that was preached by him (Paul).[2] The idea that when Paul referred to "my gospel" (Rom. 2:16) he had in mind the Gospel account drawn up by Luke, was widely current among the Fathers. This notion will not stand examination in the light of the Prologue, where the testimony of eyewitness is made the basis of the materials used. Paul does not qualify as an eyewitness.

The *Anti-Marcionite Prologue to the Gospel,* composed at a time (ca. 175) when the church was contending strongly against this heretic who had mutilated Luke's account and included it in his own canon, makes Luke a native of Antioch in Syria. In addition, this document places the death of Luke in Boeotia at

[2] *Against Heresies* III. i. 1.

the advanced age of eighty-four. A variation is found in the so-called *Monarchian Prologue to Luke,* dated around 200 but regarded as fourth century by many scholars. Here Luke's death is placed in Bithynia at the age of seventy-four. Other details are substantially in agreement with previous notices.

Origen links the third Gospel with Paul's statement about a certain brother "whose praise is in the gospel throughout all the churches" (II Cor. 8:18), making it appear that Paul was referring to praise of Luke's account. Jerome did the same, despite the fact that the passage affords no proper basis for such an interpretation (see the RSV translation of this verse).

The Lukan writings themselves contain no explicit statement of authorship, yet they are not completely anonymous, for the writer refers to himself in the Prologue ("it seemed good to me also") and at the beginning of the Acts ("in the former treatise I made"). It goes without saying that he must have been known by name to the recipient of the combined work, Theophilus, and therefore to others as well. This conclusion is strengthened by the circumstance that the patristic writers make much of apostolicity as the criterion for the reception of books. In view of this tendency, the very fact that the third Gospel bears the name of Luke rather than some apostolic figure in the stricter sense speaks eloquently in favor of the tradition.

Because of the intimate relationship between Luke and Acts, it is natural that any data derived from the Acts bearing on authorship should be applied also to the Gospel. At several points in the narrative "we" sections occur (Acts 16:10-17; 20:5-21:18; and 27:1-28:16), indicating, it seems, the presence of the writer in the company of Paul and others. The first passage describes the journey from Troas to Philippi, the second narrates Paul's last journey up to Jerusalem, and the third traces the events of the journey from Caesarea to Rome, when Paul was a prisoner. These sections may be described as excerpts from a travel diary. By a process of elimination one can arrive at the identity of the man who made these notes. It is well to start with the observation that this individual went to Rome with Paul. If the Prison Epistles were written from Rome, which we assume to be the case, they may be taken as yielding information about the friends of Paul who were with him during part or all of his detention there. They are the following: Epaphras, Epaphroditus, Timothy, Tychicus, Aristarchus, Mark, Jesus called Justus, Demas and Luke. Of these, Epaphras and Epaphroditus did not arrive in the company of Paul, hence could not have described the sea voyage. Tychicus, Aristarchus, Timothy and Mark are ruled out because they are all mentioned at some point in the Book of Acts in the third person. Demas later deserted the apostle, making the identification dubious. Further, there is no tradition in his favor as author. Two remain, Jesus called Justus and Luke. Since there is no indication that the former was with Paul during the events reported in the "we" sections, and since patristic testimony to his authorship is lacking, Luke only is left, and he is supported by the tradition, as noted above. His presence with Paul during his imprisonment is stated in Colossians 4:14 and Philemon 24. In addition there is a reference to him in II Timothy 4:11, which seems to belong to a later period.

Cadbury is disposed to discount the decisiveness of this approach to authorship on the ground that this very process of elimination is likely the ground on which the church of the second century arrived at the conclusion that Luke was the writer, without any independent knowledge of his identity.[3] But this process of elimination is only a secondary means of approach. The name of the author would not be a secret when the name of the one to whom the work was dedicated was explicitly stated. As Dibelius says, "Both writings . . . were offered to the literary reading public from the very beginning under the name of Luke as author."[4] Streeter points out also that if Luke-Acts was published at Rome, which he thinks was the case, there would be a necessity from the first to distinguish its author from the writer of Mark, which had already been published in the same city.[5]

An attempt has been made to minimize the bearing of the "we" sections upon authorship from another standpoint, namely, by assuming that Luke's travel diary was utilized by the final editor of the Acts, who permitted the first person plural to remain instead of altering to "they." Such a procedure, if it actually occurred, is very strange. Why did not the final editor conform these sections to his own practice elsewhere in the book where source material is utilized? Cadbury writes, "That in the 'we' passages he should have chosen to retain the 'we' is admittedly peculiar."[6] F. F. Bruce asks, if the first person is a literary device to suggest greater authority for the reliability of the material, why the author has not utilized the device more pervasively through the book.[7] There is no reasonable ground

[3] *Beginnings of Christianity*, II, 260-62.
[4] *Studies in the Acts of the Apostles*, p. 89.
[5] *The Four Gospels*, p. 560.
[6] *The Making of Luke-Acts*, p. 358.
[7] *The Book of Acts*, p. 328, fn. 22.

for hesitation here, it would seem. Luke has left his trade mark on these sections. The style and language, as Harnack has painstakingly shown, identify the writer with the one who composed the rest of the book. "Everywhere, where the subject-matter in the least allows of it, we hear the voice, we see the hand, and we trace the style of the author of the whole work."[8]

That the writer of Luke-Acts was a Gentile seems sufficiently indicated by a number of things. For one, as Cadbury notes,[9] he mentions that the field of blood in Jerusalem was called in *their* language (the language of the Jews) rather than in his own, Akeldama (Acts 1:19). Again, his fondness for the city points in the same direction, since this was the geographical unit of significance among the Greeks but not among the Hebrews, except for the special importance of Jerusalem. Further, he has a feeling for the sea, which comes out in the descriptions of travel by water, particularly in Acts 27. The Jews did not find the sea congenial, at least not in the Roman period. These observations about the writer of Luke-Acts accord well with Paul's testimony concerning Luke, for although he does not affirm in so many words that Luke was a Gentile, he mentions him in Colossians 4:14 after he has concluded the list of his fellow workers who belonged to the circumcision (v. 11).

Luke's background and position in the hellenic world seem reasonably established by a comparison of the earlier and later portions of Acts. The early part is narrated in such a fragmentary way as to strike the reader as peculiar if it emanated from one who belonged to the Palestinian Christian community, whereas the second half of the book has much more detail, even though the narrative has moved away from the original center of the faith and away from the labors of the original apostles.

It remains to note Paul's remark in Colossians 4:14 that Luke was a physician. This observation has driven students to a close examination of the vocabulary of Luke-Acts to ascertain whether or not it bears evidence of having come from the hand of a medical man. In 1882 W. K. Hobart published a work entitled *The Medical Language of St. Luke,* in which he compared the vocabulary of the Lukan writings with the works of four physicians of the ancient world, including Hippocrates and Galen. His conclusion was that the biblical writer employs medical language when narrating miracles of healing and that in

---

[8] *Luke the Physician,* p. 66. The whole of chap. II is devoted to this subject.
[9] *The Book of Acts in History,* p. 35.

his general narrative portions he inclines to the use of medical language, in contrast to other New Testament writers. Hobart also sought to show that in sections where no comparison with other New Testament writers was possible, the author of Luke-Acts made use of phraseology "which from habit and training a physician would be likely to employ."[10]

Harnack also was impressed by the medical terminology of Luke-Acts[11] but was content to argue from a narrower vocabulary than that which Hobart put forward.

Cadbury has made Hobart's conclusions less convincing by pointing out a defect in his method. "While he shows most diligently that the words he catalogues are employed by the medical writers, he does *not* show that they are *not* employed by other writers with no professional training."[12] Cadbury examined the works of certain hellenistic writers and found that of the 400 words catalogued by Hobart, 300 are found in both the Septuagint and Josephus. Two profane authors were examined also, with this result, that over ninety percent of Hobart's list was found either in Plutarch or Lucian or both.

The net result of the various investigations is that the language of Luke-Acts is thoroughly compatible with the authorship of a medical man, but does not prove that he must have been a physician. There are touches here and there that suggest a professional interest, such as the description of the woman with the issue of blood. Whereas Mark says that she had suffered much from many physicians and had spent all her resources and was not improved but rather grew worse (Mark 5:26), Luke rises to the defense of his profession by noting that her trouble was incurable. This woman was a hopeless case (Luke 8:43).[13] Harnack draws attention to the narrative in Acts 28:8-10, which seems to point to Luke's share in the gifts bestowed by the inhabitants of Malta as an indication of Luke's participation in the work of healing.[14] This report does not demand the use of human medical skill but suggests it.

In summary, the evidence for Lukan authorship is sufficiently clear to make the early church tradition reasonable and acceptable, even though some elements of the evidence are not as decisive as they were once thought to be. Lucius of Cyrene (Acts 13:1)

---

[10] *The Medical Language of Saint Luke*, p. xxx.
[11] *Luke the Physician*, pp. 15-17, 175-98.
[12] "The Style and Literary Method of Luke," *HTS*, VI, 41.
[13] For other examples, see A. T. Robertson, *Luke the Historian in the Light of Research*, pp. 92-95.
[14] *Luke the Physician*, pp. 15-16.

and the Lucius mentioned in Romans 16:21, thought by some to be references to Luke, have nothing substantial to connect them with Luke-Acts.

Eusebius and others state that Luke was a native of Antioch in Syria. Codex Bezae has a "we" passage in Acts 11:28, indicating support for the idea that Luke was in the city at the time the gospel began to be preached there, but this may well be an intrusion into the text based on tradition. The fact that Luke remained in Philippi (there is no "we" section in the description of the ministry of Paul as he moved on to Thessalonica, Athens, and Corinth) may point to some personal connection with that community. Luke probably remained there until Paul's last journey to Jerusalem.

THE PROLOGUE

This section (Luke 1:1-4) was presumably intended to introduce not only the Gospel but the Acts as well. That it was written after the body of the Gospel was completed may be inferred from the fact that the following verse (v. 5) lacks a connecting particle, which seems to show that Luke began his writing at this point rather than with the Prologue.

Beyond the interest that these introductory verses have for appreciation of Luke's literary ability is their value as a testimony to Gospel writing in general and to Luke's work in particular. Those who wrote, Luke tells us, were occupied with "the things fulfilled among us." A synonym would be the Christ-event. The phrase (the verb used here is $\pi\lambda\eta\rho\circ\phi\circ\rho\epsilon\hat{\iota}\nu$) ought not to be interpreted in the narrow sense of the fulfillment of specific prophetic passages, which is conveyed by the related term $\pi\lambda\eta\rho\circ\hat{\upsilon}\nu$ (Luke 4:21; Acts 1:16), but rather of what has come to realization in the sense of *Heilsgeschichte* (cf. II Tim. 4:17, where the word is used in a different setting).

Those who conveyed this information to Gospel writers are described as eyewitnesses and ministers of the word. Doubtless these were chiefly the apostles, though a larger circle could well be intended. To be able to qualify, however, they must have been with the Lord *from the beginning* (v. 2). A comparison of Mark 1:1, which is followed immediately by a statement of the ministry of John the Baptist, and Acts 1:21-22 makes it evident that the reference in Luke is to the inception of the public ministry of Jesus. The period of the ministry was largely a time of observation and learning for these men, though there was limited service. With the rise of the church came opportunity to be ministers of the word in a more meaningful sense. They *delivered* what they knew to those who wrote. This highly important term, which has for its noun form the word "tradition," emphasizes the fidelity and care with which the data were handled and transmitted (cf. I Cor. 11:23; 15:3).

This, then, is the pattern for previous Gospel writing. Luke does not appear to be critical of his predecessors (note the word *also* in v. 3), yet feels that he has something to contribute. In addition to the eyewitness reports and the writings to which he refers, he made such investigation on his own account as he deemed helpful (v. 3). The word παρηκολουθηκότι means literally to follow alongside or to follow closely. Cadbury understands it differently, taking it to be Luke's way of affirming his personal adhesion to the Christian movement.[15] This additional activity on Luke's part was conducted "from the first," which is not the same thing as the phrase "from the beginning" already noted at verse 2. By this quick stroke of the pen Luke gives justification and advance notice of his inclusion of the nativity narratives (Luke 1-2). Ramsay argued cogently that Mary the mother of Jesus was the historian's authority for this portion of the Gospel.[16]

Further, Luke stresses his purpose to write accurately and in order. The latter adverb may glance back at the work of the many who have preceded him. It is quite possible that for the most part they were brief and lacking any systematic arrangement. Luke occasionally disregards chronological order, so the present statement should probably be understood in a somewhat broader sense of a well conceived, artistically structured narrative.

Finally, the historian's purpose is to convey certitude concerning the things that were current as elements in the catechetical instruction of the early church (v. 4) in line with the practice of the early church as cited by Luke in Acts 2:42. The content must have been the apostolic tradition which later, in its written form, approximated the content of the Gospels. However, Luke's term here may mean simply "informed."

READERS

Only one is mentioned, a certain prominent individual named Theophilus. The epithet κράτιστε is used also of the Roman governors Felix (Acts 24:3) and Festus (Acts 26:25), and

---

[15] *The Making of Luke-Acts,* pp. 345-47.
[16] *Was Christ Born at Bethlehem?* pp. 75-36.

serves to rule out the notion that Theophilus is merely a generic term for all believers as beloved of God, for it indicates a person of station (contrast I Cor. 1:26ff.). But this address to Theophilus is really a dedication. A parallel may be noted in the dedication of Josephus' work *Against Apion* to the most excellent Epaphroditus. It may well be that Theophilus was expected to assist in the publication of Luke's work. At any rate one may safely conclude that Gentile readers are in view. Ramsay notes that Luke's care to inform his readers about points on the geography of Palestine, even the simplest, is in sharp contrast to his assumption of geographical knowledge on their part for the Greco-Roman world.[17] He deliberately avoids items that would be puzzling to Gentile readers such as the word "rabbi" that occurs four times in Mark and the same in Matthew. Another example is the avoidance of the Semitic "hosanna" in connection with the triumphal entry of Jesus into Jerusalem.

DATE AND PLACE OF WRITING

There is little to guide the student regarding the time of composition beyond the conclusion that use of Mark makes Luke later than the earliest Gospel. Streeter argues for a date after A.D. 70 on the ground that Luke has radically changed the eschatological picture of Mark with its exposition of the coming of the abomination of desolation and attendant miseries into a description of the fall of Jerusalem, substituting something known for something that had failed to materialize.[18] This would involve a radical handling of the sources by Luke, which his own declarations and the general character of his work belie. The language of Luke 21:20 is too general to necessitate a description of an achieved fact (cf. I Thess. 2:16).

It has often been noted that the two-year period during which Paul was kept a prisoner in Caesarea would have afforded Luke an opportunity to carry on such investigation as would fit him to write his Gospel. This does not mean that Luke must have put his Gospel together in final form at that time. Luke could have gained access to Mark's Gospel during his sojourn at Rome with Paul at the time of Paul's second imprisonment, in the early 60s. See the discussion on the date of Acts.

The *Monarchian Prologue to Luke* states that he wrote his Gospel in the regions of Achaia, but the reliability of this

---

[17] *Op. cit.,* pp. 55-57.
[18] *The Four Gospels,* p. 540.

tradition is uncertain. Nothing can be positively affirmed about the place.

ACCURACY OF THE RECORD

This is more of an issue in connection with the Acts than in the case of the Gospel, but here also the question comes into focus if for no other reason than that Luke has professed to give particular pains to providing a reliable account.

The chief point of tension has been the account of the enrollment made by order of Augustus, at which time Jesus was born in Bethlehem (Luke 2:1ff.). No contemporary sources have been available to certify this enrollment. However, it should be recognized that Luke would have brought suspicion on his work as a whole if he had gone astray in a matter that was commonly known if it occurred at all. Further, early critics of Christianity, who were presumably at home in the history of the New Testament period, failed to seize on this item and make use of it. The presumption is, therefore, that they found no fault with it.[19]

Modern research has gone far to vindicate Luke, although we cannot speak of proof in this matter of the enrollment. The probability of the presence of Quirinius in Syria at the requisite time stems from two sources. First is the testimony of the Tibur inscription that the Roman official therein described (acknowledged to be Quirinius by competent historians — the inscription is broken and the name lost) was imperial legate in Syria and took the position of legate a second time. Second is the discovery by Ramsay of two inscriptions, one in Pisidian Antioch and one near the city, honoring a certain prefect who served under Quirinius in this region during his campaign against the tribe of Homonadenses. Ramsay himself was convinced that the time was agreeable to the period demanded by Luke's account.[20] It is possible, then, to picture Quirinius as a special representative of the emperor in this region rather than governor in the technical sense.[21]

The problem of squaring Luke's account with that of Josephus (*Antiquities* XVIII. i. 1), who mentions only the taxing in A.D. 6, may be solved, according to Stauffer, by recognizing that where taxation had not been entrenched, it was a long, drawn-out process.

---

[19] Ramsay, *op. cit.*, pp. 70-71.
[20] *The Bearing of Recent Discovery on the Trustworthiness of the New Testament*, pp. 289-90.
[21] Ramsay, *op. cit.*, p. 239.

He understands Luke's account to refer to the first stage, the *apographa,* a systematic listing of all taxable persons and property, for which purpose all had to appear personally. Later came the *apotimēsis,* the concluding phase, which was the official assessment of taxes. It is this that Josephus describes. In Stauffer's reckoning, Quirinius went to the East in 12 B.C., commenced the census (*apographa*) in 7 B.C. and did not complete it until A.D. 7. The completion of this arduous task in fourteen years may be regarded as an achievement demonstrating the energy of Quirinius. In Gaul, where there was great resistance, it required more than forty years.[22]

Stauffer's solution is preferable to the view that Luke is associating the birth of Jesus with the census under Quirinius in A.D. 6. This would bring Luke into conflict with his own setting for the nativity as being in the days of Herod, king of Judea (1:5), since Herod died in 4 B.C. It would also mean that Jesus began his ministry at approximately A.D. 36 (cf. Lk. 3:23), too late to fit into the chronology of the apostolic age.

CONTENTS

The material may be grouped as follows: (1) Prologue (1:1-4); (2) Nativity narratives (1:5—2:52); (3) Preparation for Jesus' ministry (3:1—4:13); (4) Ministry in Galilee (4:14—9:50); (5) Ministry on the way to Jerusalem (9:51—19:27); (6) Ministry in Jerusalem (19:28—24:53).

CHARACTERISTICS

(1) In agreement with the large place given to the Holy Spirit in the Book of Acts, Luke's Gospel magnifies the role of the Spirit in the life and ministry of Jesus. The Spirit imbues the forerunner (1:15), is active in the conception of the Son of God (1:35), comes upon him at the baptism in an unusual manifestation (3:22), fills him for his ministry (4:1) as the prophetic word had announced (4:18), gives enablement for the temptation (4:1-2), endues him for his work when he has vanquished the evil one (4:14) and imparts joy in the midst of his labors (10:21).

(2) The temple is frequently mentioned, not only in connection with passion week but uniquely in the nativity narratives (1:8, 21-22; 2:27, 37), including the boyhood visit (2:41-51). At the very close the disciples are pictured there (24:53), thus preparing the reader for the central significance of the temple in the life of the early church (Acts 2:46; 3:1).

22 E. Stauffer, *Jesus and His Story,* pp. 21-32.

(3) Frequent references to angels (over 20 times) serve to enhance the awareness of the heavenly and revelatory character of the Christ event (1:11, 26; 2:9, 13).

(4) Certain distinctives stand out in Luke's passion narrative. The charges advanced by the Sanhedrin against Jesus are detailed in Pilate's presence (23:2). Answering to these three allegations is the thrice-given declaration of the governor that he can detect no crime in the accused (23:4, 15, 22). The inclusion of the appearance of the prisoner before Herod attests Luke's historical interest and concern to provide as complete an account as possible.

(5) The use of a specific passage from Isaiah 53 in 22:37, supported by numerous instances of the influence of the verbiage of Isaiah 40—66, suggests, when taken with 24:27, 44, 46, that Luke seeks to emphasize the redemptive mission of the Lord. In keeping with this perspective is his generous use of δεῖ to indicate Jesus' awareness of that mission as his appointed task (4:43; 13:33; 22:37; 24:44).

(6) Attention is often centered on Jerusalem, both in the early chapters and in the narrative from 9:51 on. The sending ahead of messengers, including the seventy, gives an impressive and almost royal aura to this journey. Such an entourage may help to explain the great crowds that surged about Jesus when he reached Judea, despite an apparent decrease in popularity during the previous months.

(7) Luke alone of the Evangelists binds the sacred narrative to secular history (2:1-2; 3:1).

(8) Unique to Luke are certain items in the birth and infancy stories. These are: the birth of John the Baptist, the annunciation, the adoration of the shepherds, the circumcision of Jesus, his presentation in the temple, and the visit to Jerusalem at the age of twelve. There is a strong Semitic flavor in these two chapters, both in vocabulary and sentence structure, which contrasts markedly with the Prologue. On this subject Matthew Black writes, "The choice appears to lie between a theory of Hebrew or Aramaic sources translated or found in Greek translations by Luke, or of simple Lucan composition in Semitic Greek, owing much, if not everything, to the LXX."[24] Black has also advanced the suggestion that since Luke was at home in Antioch and since Syriac was well known there, our author may well have become familiar with this language.[25] Since this tongue is closely allied to Aramaic, the

[24] "The Problem of the Aramaic Element in the Gospels," *ET*, 59 (April 1948), 173.

[25] *An Aramaic Approach to the Gospels and Acts*, 2nd ed., p. 15.

Semitic cast of the early part of Luke and also of the first few chapters of Acts becomes more understandable.

(9) Luke has a special section (9:51—18:14) that raises a few difficulties, not the least of which is the geographical setting of the material. At the outset Jesus is pictured as determinedly setting out for Jerusalem, and this destination is stated again in 13:22 and 17:11. The itinerary begins through Samaria, and before long Jesus is pictured in Bethany, on the outskirts of Jerusalem (10:38-42), but the rest of the material does not have Jerusalem for its setting. Notices of time and place are rather vague (e. g., 11:1; 12:1). It seems that this section is dominated more by ideology than by geography. It begins under the impulse of the transfiguration motif, and this is regarded as shaping the course of the remainder of the ministry in a notable way. Jerusalem is the goal and the ascension is the crown (9:51). Others view this section of the Gospel as a collection of materials for which Luke had no definite position in the story of the ministry.

(10) It is impossible to know to what extent Luke was dependent upon the "many" to whom he refers in his Prologue. But the use of Mark is sufficiently demonstrated. In this use, Luke interlards his own material, inserting it into the Markan outline. This is true of the long section just noted, often called the Travel Narrative, and also of a shorter section, 6:20-8:3.

(11) Luke's writing has a literary character. After a study of his diction, Cadbury was able to affirm, "The vocabulary of Luke, while it has its natural affiliations with the Greek of the Bible, is not so far removed from the literary style of the Atticists as to be beyond comparison with them."[26]

(12) Luke frequently records the popular response to Jesus' ministry. He is fond of stating that Jesus was surrounded and followed by great crowds that were filled with amazement at his works (5:26; 7:16-17; 11:14; 13:17; 14:25). Yet he does not speak of Jesus' compassion on the multitude. This is reserved for individuals.

(13) Prominence is given to certain groups. Luke mentions the poor as often as Matthew and Mark combined. Correspondingly large place is given to the subject of the rich and their wealth, often by way of warning. The word "woman" occurs with great frequency, and many individual women are mentioned by name. Jesus appears as the champion of outcasts and sinners.

(14) Prominence is given to certain concepts. Among these are prayer (both in Jesus' teaching and practice), praise, joy, peace,

[26] *The Style and Literary Method of Luke,* p. 38.

forgiveness, weeping, love and friendship, wisdom and understanding, glory, authority, and spirit (both the Holy Spirit and the human spirit). Notices of time and place are more frequent than in the other Synoptics.

(15) It is notable that Luke has a more pronounced biographical interest than other Gospel writers. Information is supplied about Jesus' ancestors, his kinsfolk and parents, the place and circumstances of his birth, his boyhood development, the freedom with which he mingled among men in his social relationships, his exposure to temptation (not only at the inception of the ministry, but throughout, according to Luke 22:28), his frequent resort to prayer, etc. This is the Gospel of the **manhood** of the Master.

(16) Jesus is shown as the healer of the bodies of men and also as their deliverer from sin. Luke alone among the Synoptists gives him the title of Savior. It may seem strange, in the light of this fact, that he fails to record the saying of Jesus in Mark 10:45, paralleled in Matthew 20:28, the famous ransom passage. Possibly Luke is less concerned with the philosophy of the cross than with the mission of Christ as a whole, as the outworking of the saving purpose of God. Only in his account of the transfiguration do we read of Jesus' departure to be accomplished at Jerusalem.

(17) Luke rivals Matthew in laying emphasis on Jesus as king and on the kingdom of God. It is noteworthy that in two places (4:43 and 9:2) he mentions the heralding of the kingdom where the other Gospels are silent.

(18) Whereas Matthew interested himself in the detailed and somewhat haggadic fulfillment of the Old Testament in Jesus of Nazareth, Luke is more concerned to establish the broad connection between Jesus' work and the prophetic pattern (see especially Luke 4:16ff.; 24:25, 44-47). Luke is the chief exponent among the Evangelists of *Heilsgeschichte,* which has been admirably defined by C. K. Barrett as "a continuous historical process which was the vehicle of God's saving purpose."[27]

(19) Luke's is a versatile history. A. M. Farrer has given classic expression to this: "What strikes us about St. Luke is not his hellenism but his versatility. His history unfolds in the bosom of Jewish piety and works its way out into the hellenistic agora."[28]

RECENT STUDY

Interest in the Lukan writings is currently experiencing some-

[27] *Luke the Historian in Recent Study,* p. 64.
[28] "On Dispensing with Q" in *Studies in the Gospels,* D. E. Nineham, ed., p. 69.

207

thing of a revival. In this connection a shift is noticeable from the historical and archeological interest of Ramsay and the literary analysis approach of Harnack to a concern for the message of Luke, his theological interest.

Of greatest importance here is the work of Hans Conzelmann. The title of his book in the English translation (*The Theology of St. Luke,* 1960) is less suggestive of the contents than the title of the German original, *Die Mitte der Zeit.* This midpoint of time, as Luke conceives of it, is the ministry of Jesus, which stands between the old order of the Law and the Prophets (Luke 16:16) and the period of the church, which will be concluded by the Parousia. As Jesus is the end of the old, so is he the beginning of the new order.

Luke's reconstruction is conceived as a solution to a vexing problem, the delay of the Parousia and the consequent necessity that the church somehow adjust itself to continuing in the midst of the world order for an indefinite time, though not without a hope of ultimate consummation. The evangelist gives a central place to the kingdom of God, but by dropping insistence on repentance he removes the element of imminence (p. 114). "As the End is still far away, the adjustment to a short time of waiting is replaced by a 'Christian life' of long duration, which requires ethical regulation and is no longer dependent upon a definite termination" (p. 132). The Holy Spirit is pictured as resting only on Jesus for the period of his ministry but becoming available to his church from Pentecost on.

Conzelmann has provided many helpful insights, but his conclusions are vulnerable, especially at two points. He contends that the 'today' of Jesus' ministry (Lk. 4:21), the time of fulfilment, of salvation, "does not extend into the present in which the author lives, but is thought of as a time in the past" (p. 195). However, it is this same Luke who sees the church age as a period in which Jesus continues to be active (Acts 1:1). As far as the delay of the Parousia is concerned, this theme is overworked. If Luke's outlook had been as powerfully affected by this conception as Conzelmann supposes, it is strange that he has put into his record the speech of Peter in Acts 3 in which the return of the ascended Lord is presented as conditioned simply on repentance by the nation which crucified him.

Helmut Flender complains that Conzelmann "lacks a clear grasp of the real presuppositions of Luke's thought."[29] His own research has led him to discern in Luke a dialectical parallelism.

---

29 *St. Luke: Theologian of Redemptive History,* p. 6.

For example, "In place of the shift of aeons which according to Paul was inaugurated with the resurrection of Jesus, the transition for Luke is from this world into the celestial world which exists concurrently" (p. 19). A threefold pattern is claimed for the materials brought under review: (1) the level of human ambiguity is contrasted with (2) the level of heavenly consummation; (3) in living faith in Jesus as the Son of God the heavenly reality is present on earth (p. 46).

The central section of Luke (9:51—18:14), so difficult to label and to fit into the totality of Luke's work, is attracting attention. C. F. Evans thinks a clue can be found by comparing 9:51-52 with Deuteronomy 1:21-25. Luke's travel narrative is then found to have many parallels with Deuteronomy.[30] Bo Reicke's approach to this section is to note the complete absence of place names and to conclude that Luke, desiring to preserve some important instructional matter of Jesus, some of it Q material, some of it derived from traditions available to him, inserted it here, giving it "a superficial relation to the biographical framework by inserting a few remarks on the Lord's going up to Jerusalem."[31]

BIBLIOGRAPHY

Cadbury, H. J., *The Making of Luke-Acts.* New York: Macmillan, 1927.

Conzelmann, Hans, *The Theology of St. Luke.* New York: Harper and Row, 1960.

Creed, J. M., *The Gospel according to St. Luke.* London: Macmillan, 1950.

Ellis, E. Earle, *The Gospel of Luke,* The Century Bible. London: Thomas Nelson and Sons, 1966.

Flender, Helmut, *St. Luke, Theologian of Redemptive History.* Philadelphia: Fortress Press, 1967.

Geldenhuys, Norval, *Commentary on the Gospel of Luke, NIC.* Grand Rapids: Eerdmans, 1951.

Godet, F., *A Commentary on the Gospel of Luke,* 2 vols. 5th ed., Edinburgh: T. & T. Clark, 1893.

Harnack, A., *Luke the Physician.* New York: G. P. Putnam's Sons, 1908.

Lagrange, M. J., *Evangile selon Saint Luc.* 8th ed., Paris: J. Gabalda 1948.

Leaney, A. R. C., *The Gospel according to St. Luke.* New York: Harper & Bros., 1958.

[30] "The Central Section of Luke's Gospel," in *Studies in the Gospels,* D. E. Nineham, ed., pp. 37-53.
[31] *The Gospels Reconsidered,* p. 109.

Manson, William, *The Gospel of Luke.* New York: Harper & Bros., 1930.

Plummer, Alfred, *A Critical and Exegetical Commentary on the Gospel according to St. Luke, ICC.* New York: Charles Scribner's Sons, 1910.

Ramsay, W. M., *Luke the Physician.* London: Hodder & Stoughton, 1908.

Robertson, A. T., *Luke the Physician in the Light of Research.* Edinburgh: T. & T. Clark, 1920.

Stonehouse, N. B., *The Witness of Luke to Christ.* Grand Rapids: Eerdmans, 1951.

Taylor, Vincent, *Behind the Third Gospel.* Oxford: Clarendon Press, 1926.

Chapter Nine

THE GOSPEL ACCORDING TO JOHN

FAR MORE ATTENTION HAS BEEN DEVOTED TO THE STUDY OF
this Gospel than to any of the others, both because of its de-
votional quality and the difficulties that it presents on the side
of critical investigation.

CONTENTS

211

    4. The prayer (17:1-26).
    5. The betrayal, arrest and trial (18:1-19:16).
    6. The crucifixion and burial (19:17-42).
    7. The resurrection appearances (21:1-29).
    8. The purpose of the Gospel (20:30-31).
  XI. The Epilogue (21:1-25).

CHARACTERISTICS

(1) The style is simple. One has only to compare the opening lines with the Lukan Prologue to sense how different are the two compositions. Most of the terms used are common words, and the structure is largely paratactic, with considerable repetition. According to some evaluations, these features make the writing tedious, turgid, and tiresome (so E. F. Scott). But many, on the contrary, have recognized the marvel of the literary achievement involved, that in spite of the limitations of style, the effect upon the reader is so compelling. No doubt the greatness of the theme has much to do with this, but the skill of the writer must be reckoned with also.

(2) The thought is profound. Probably no book of the New Testament has invited and provoked more perusal and reflection. The reader is encouraged to hope that by letting his gaze linger on the simply worded text he may be able to penetrate to the tantalizing depths of meaning that he senses are lying there. Hoskyns has declared, "The theme of the Fourth Gospel is the non-historical that makes sense of history, the infinite that makes sense of time, God who makes sense of men and is therefore their Saviour."[1]

(3) In seeking to isolate the outstanding elements of language, it is well to divide them into three groups.

a. Non-theological terms that relate to style. Here one notes exceptionally frequent occurrences of $\tilde{\iota}\nu\alpha$, $o\tilde{\upsilon}\nu$, $\pi\acute{\alpha}\lambda\iota\nu$, $\dot{\alpha}\mu\acute{\eta}\nu$, also words meaning to see and to speak.

b. Terms that bear more definitely on the message but are used almost as frequently in one or more of the Synoptic Gospels. Here belong flesh, sin, law, judge, word ($\lambda\acute{o}\gamma os$), sign, water, Scripture, work, glory and glorify, hour, die, Jesus, Christ, father (mostly of the Heavenly Father), send, eternal and age.

c. Terms bearing on the teaching of the book whose use so far exceeds that in the other Gospels as to be outstanding. Notable here are the words for witness (verb and noun), believe (the noun "faith" is lacking), live and life, love (verb and noun),

---

[1] *The Fourth Gospel,* pp. 129-30.

212

abide or remain, truth and true, Jew, world, feast, and possibly light (darkness does not occur as often). Certain of the words require special care on the part of the interpreter, as they are not always used with the same connotation, e.g., flesh, believe, world.

(4) Flanked by the Prologue (1:1-18) and the Epilogue (chap. 21), the body of the work features the words and works of Jesus, culminating in the events of the Passion. The miracles are called signs. Seven of them are singled out, in addition to Jesus' own resurrection, as follows: water turned to wine (2:1-11); the healing of the nobleman's son (4:46-54); the healing of the invalid man (5:2-9); the feeding of the five thousand (6:1-14); Jesus' walking on the sea (6:16-21); the healing of the man born blind (9:1-7), and the raising of Lazarus from the dead (11:1-44). Other signs are noted but not described in detail (2:33; 6:2; 20:30). The words of Jesus, in many cases, are occasioned by the signs, as interpretations or applications of them, such as the discourse on the bread of life following the feeding of the multitude. At other times the didactic material is in the nature of discussion or controversy occasioned by a miracle, as in chapter five. The discourses are revelatory of the person of Christ and feature the "I Am" sayings. One of them, delivered in the upper room to the Twelve alone, is especially relevant to the life and service of the church, inasmuch as it is a projection into the future and a statement of the divine provision for the needs of Christ's people.

(5) This Gospel places large emphasis on the national feasts or festivals of the Jews and Jesus' attendance upon them. Three passovers are mentioned (2:23; 6:4; 13:1), also the feast of tabernacles (7:2) and dedication (10:22). In addition there is an unnamed festival (5:1). If this were passover, it would mean the adding of another year to the length of the ministry of our Lord. There is little agreement among scholars on the identification.

(6) In line with the prominence given to these festivals is the placing of a considerable part of the activity of Jesus in the area of Judea rather than Galilee. But while John is the principal source of our information about the Judean ministry, the Synoptics give hints of Jesus' presence in this region from time to time, despite the fact that it is only in connection with the passion narrative that these documents place him in Jerusalem for any extended ministry. These allusions include the reference to Martha and Mary (Luke 10:38-42), the intimation of previously established friendships with the owner of the colt (Mark 11:1-6)

213

and the owner of the house with the upper room (Luke 22:7-13), also the lament of the Savior over the holy city — "how often would I have gathered thy children together. . .and you would not" (Luke 13:34).

Scott Holland has shown that the Judean ministry as sketched in John is quite essential to the right understanding of the Synoptics, for the latter present Jesus' visit to Jerusalem, culminating in the events of the Passion, as involving a foregone conclusion. Jerusalem is hostile and the issue is already determined. The Messiah will die there. John alone has shown how this result has been achieved through the repeated presentation of himself to the nation at the center of its life, only to be repudiated each time. The city had had its time of visitation. Now it is too late. Only desolation is now in prospect.[2]

(7) In John's Gospel our Lord is not often pictured addressing great throngs of people, as in the Synoptics. Rather, it is the personal side of his ministry that is unfolded in conversations with various individuals. Of these, the contacts with Nicodemus and the woman of Samaria are the most extended. Furthermore, certain key figures in the drama of Jesus' mission are presented with greater fullness and with special consideration of the divine purpose with reference to them. Such is the case with John the Baptist and Judas.

(8) The deity of the Son is given great prominence. This does not mean that the presentation is basically different from that in the Synoptics. Any sense of cleavage is due to an unfortunate tendency in the history of criticism to rate too low the Christology of the Synoptics. The same leading titles — Messiah, Son of God, Son of man — are found in both traditions. Granted that the claim to deity in John is set forth in bolder and balder language, and is kept to the fore with great persistence, yet it is not apotheosis. It is coupled with and balanced by repeated confessions on the part of Jesus that he is dependent on the Father.

Because of special emphasis on the deity, the humanity of Jesus gets correspondingly less attention. But to claim that the Fourth Gospel presents a docetic Christ is to forget the clear teaching of the incarnation (1:14) and to assume a disjunction between this teaching and the materials of the book as a whole.

Two items in the Christological pattern of John do not appear in the Synoptics, at least in any clearly defined fashion. One is the pre-existence of the Son (1:1, 14; 8:58; 17:5). The other is his designation as the Logos (1:1, 14), which in the thought

[2] H. Scott Holland, *The Fourth Gospel*, pp. 34-37.

of the writer probably found its source in the Old Testament doctrine of the Word, and so served to establish a connection with previous revelation just as the Synoptics, especially Mark and Matthew, had done at the very beginning of their accounts (the reference to the "word" in Luke 1:2 is almost certainly not personal). At the same time the term Logos could be appreciated by readers of the Gospel who had a philosophical background, and would give promise to them that some of their problems regarding history and life, God and man, time and eternity, would find answer in what followed.

(9) Pivotal to the understanding of this Gospel is the place Jesus occupies in relation to Judaism, fulfilling its legitimate hopes and opposing its aberrations. He is greater than the Torah (1:17), than the temple (2:19-21), than its shekinah glory (1:14), than the significance and satisfaction of the feasts (7:37-39). He accepts worship as his rightful due (9:38; 20:28).

(10) In mentioning John's relation to the Synoptics we here simply raise the question as to the intention of the writer. Did he work in complete independence of the Synoptic tradition, or did he hope to supplant it; or did he seek to supplement it, especially in regard to the Judean ministry? Hardly to supplant, for the prevalence of the Synoptic pattern is sufficiently attested by the fact that three accounts of this general nature gained acceptance in the church. It would be rash to assume that an account laid out on different lines would take the place of the others. Supplementation is a possible motive. Certainly this element is present. But perhaps even more important is the purpose of delineating the person and work of Jesus in such a way as to interpret their deeper significance. The problem may still remain of the great disparity between the material of this Gospel and the Synoptics, but it is possible that still other accounts could have been penned presenting yet different aspects of the Savior and his work, so rich and varied were the facets of his self-revelation. John seems to strike out along his own lines for the most part.

DATE

The previous discussion has assumed the priority of the Synoptics over John. Doubt has been cast over this position by P. Gardner-Smith in his book, *St. John and the Synoptic Gospels* (1938). He seeks to show that instances of alleged dependence of the Fourth Gospel upon the Synoptics do not require the use of documents but only of oral tradition. So John could have been written first if other factors warrant. Some evidence of a

215

gradual acceptance of this position must be acknowledged, although there is still a considerable body of scholars who judge that John knew one or more of the Synoptics,[3] making an early date for the Fourth Gospel questionable.

It can probably be assumed that the apostolic preaching in the early days of the church would be reflected to a considerable degree in the tradition when it took written form. With this as a clue, we note that such a summary as Peter gives of the ministry of Jesus in Acts 10:37-39 agrees far more closely with the material in the Synoptic Gospels than with the contents of John. Surely it is more natural that the church should have first of all in its possession records that emphasize the factual side of the ministry of our Lord rather than one that is to a much larger extent interpretative. The interest that the Fourth Gospel shows in the Logos and in the pre-existence of Christ can best be understood in connection with a later stage than that which meets us in the Synoptics.

From the Prologue of Luke, furthermore, it appears that up to the time at which Luke wrote, no apostle had composed a Gospel. So far apostles had simply been the media of information for those who had written. This puts John later than Luke.

The dating of the Gospel cannot be precise, but some limits can be set. F. C. Baur of Tübingen placed it well down into the second century, about 170, on the ground that it failed to reflect the legalistic controversy that so greatly agitated the early church, a controversy that must have passed away by the time the Gospel was written. It has been necessary to abandon this view. Archaeological evidence requires that the book be dated no later than about the end of the first century. The Roberts Fragment, discovered in Egypt and published in 1935 by the Rylands Library, contains a few verses from chapter 18. Paleographers have assigned it to the first half of the second century. Some years must be allowed between the time of writing of this papyrus and the original work, especially if the Gospel itself was composed at Ephesus, the traditional site. Further testimony of a similar sort is furnished by the discovery in Egypt of a portion of chapter 5, contained in Egerton Papyrus 2, which belongs to the early part of the second century. This was published by Bell and Skeat in 1935 in a volume entitled *Fragments of an Unknown Gospel.*

At the opposite pole from Baur's view is the position of E. R.

---

[3] W. G. Kümmel, *Introduction to the New Testament,* pp. 143-145.

Goodenough, that John is the earliest of the Gospels.[4] The Evangelist gives us little of what is found in the Synoptics for the reason that he knew little of it. So Goodenough would account for the failure of the writer to include the virgin birth and the institution of the Lord's Supper. But the evidence looks the other way. The people who appear on the pages of the Fourth Gospel are assumed to be familiar to the reader when they occur also in the Synoptics. Nicodemus, on the other hand, requires identification (3:1). It is inconceivable that anyone who was at all in close touch with developments in the early church could fail to mention the Lord's Supper because of ignorance.

Archaeological evidence (to be mentioned later) points to the fact that the writer must have ascertained the topographical details of his account of Jesus' ministry before the holocaust of A.D. 70, which covered or altered many sites in the area of Jerusalem. But this does not require the writing of the Gospel, as distinct from the gathering of materials, before that date.[5]

The Fourth Gospel (the very terminology contains an assumption of relative date) can safely be assigned to the period of the last two decades of the first century.

PLACE OF WRITING

Patristic testimony points to Ephesus. Irenaeus is explicit on this point.[6] Others, such as Polycarp, testify to John's residence there, and Polycrates mentions Ephesus as his place of burial. In the Apocalypse, which was widely attributed to John in the early church, the central place of Ephesus among the churches of Asia is apparent (Rev. 1:11; 2:1). The care with which the author of the Gospel states the subordination of John the Baptist to Jesus becomes understandable in the light of the presence of the disciples of John in Ephesus (Acts 19:1-3).

Alexandria is favored by some, for various reasons. One is the use of the Gospel by Egyptian Gnostics, another the discovery of the papyrus fragments already mentioned. Then there is the alleged influence of Philo upon the Logos concept in the Prologue and the supposed affinity between the Gospel and the Hermetic writings.[7] A disadvantage in this position is lack of

[4] *JBL*, 64 (June 1945), pp. 145-82.
[5] See W. F. Albright's statement in the Dodd Festschrift volume, *The Background of the New Testament and its Eschatology*, p. 170.
[6] *Against Heresies* III. i. 1.
[7] For a more complete statement see J. N. Sanders, *The Fourth Gospel in the Early Church*, pp. 40-42.

support from the Fathers, as well as grave doubt that John depends on Philo and the Hermetists.

Antioch also has had its protagonists, because the epistles of Ignatius seem to reflect the thought and the terminology of this Gospel. Further, in the Armenian version of Ephraem's commentary on the Diatessaron of Tatian there is an appended note in Syriac stating that John wrote in Antioch. But it is not known upon what the tradition is based, and the testimony itself is rather late.

AUTHORSHIP

The question of authorship should be approached both from the standpoint of what the ancients have to say and from the impression that the book itself conveys. The external testimony begins, oddly enough, with a statement found at the close of the Gospel itself (21:24), where an unidentified group ("we know") certify that the disciple whom Jesus loved (v. 20) is the one who wrote the things that make up this record and that the testimony contained therein is true. It is generally assumed that this group must have been leaders of the church in the province of Asia, possibly elders of the Ephesian church. The beloved disciple is left unnamed. Some have concluded that he might be Lazarus (cf. 11:3, 5), but the further mark of identification as the one who leaned on Jesus' bosom (v. 20) points back to the meeting in the Upper Room, where only apostles were present.

The post-apostolic age did not produce a large Christian literature, and those who wrote were not especially concerned about questions of authorship, at least of the Gospels. Ignatius and Justin show knowledge of the Fourth Gospel, but have nothing to say about the writer. Among the earliest witnesses to Johannine authorship are the *Anti-Marcionite Prologue to John* and the Muratorian Canon, both in the second half of the second century. Irenaeus, Tertullian, and Clement of Alexandria from approximately the same period, agree on John the Apostle. The testimony of Irenaeus is of crucial importance. Between himself and the beloved apostle stood only one generation of Christians. Of the men of that period Polycarp of Smyrna in the East and Pothinus of Lyons in the West, both of them pupils of John, were leaders of the church, and Irenaeus had close contact with them both. In his *Epistle to Florinus*[8] he recalls his early days when he used to sit in Polycarp's house and listen to him discourse about his intercourse with John and others who had

[8] *HE* V. xx. 6.

218

seen the Lord. Consequently, when Irenaeus declares categorically that after the publication of the other Gospels John also wrote his, while he was dwelling in Ephesus,[9] it is to be assumed that he is giving no other view of the authorship of the Fourth Gospel than that which he inherited from a disciple of John himself.

Critical opinion has not been uniformly cordial to the testimony of Irenaeus. After all, he was scarcely more than a boy when he left for Gaul, and he may well have been mistaken about the identity of the John who wrote the Gospel. In the West he would not be likely to meet with any who could correct his misapprehension. However, the words of H. P. V. Nunn deserve to be pondered. "If the rest of the people in Asia knew perfectly well that John the Evangelist was not the Apostle and could have corrected the childish mistake of Irenaeus, had an opportunity been given them to do so, how was it that when Irenaeus, in his later life, promulgated his quite unfounded statement that the Apostle wrote the Gospel everyone believed him both in the East and in the West?"[10]

The external testimony to Johannine authorship has been challenged along other lines as well. For one thing, it is pointed out that when Ignatius in the first decade of the second century wrote his letter to the Ephesians (chap. 12) he had something to say about Paul and his relation to the Ephesians, but nothing about John. This objection is not weighty, because a man bound for martyrdom would naturally be more interested in Paul the martyr than in one who died a natural death. The silence of Ignatius cannot reasonably be construed as an argument against the Ephesian residence of John and his relation to the Fourth Gospel.

Another approach has been made by advancing the claim that John the Apostle suffered martyrdom at an early period. The De Boor Fragment (7th or 8th century) contains a statement attributed to Philip of Side, as follows: "Papias in the second book says that John the theologian and James his brother were killed by Jews." Substantially the same account is given by a later figure, George the Sinner (9th century). How unreliable this statement is may be gathered from its inaccuracies. John was not known as the theologian as early as the time of Papias. James was not killed by the Jews but by order of Herod Agrippa I. It is not difficult to understand how a tradition of this sort could arise, seeing that Jesus had predicted that James and John

---

[9] *Against Heresies* III. i. 1.
[10] *The Authorship of the Fourth Gospel*, p. 36.

would drink his cup. Martyrdom seemed more honorable for the apostles than natural death. But according to Galatians 2:9 John was active in the affairs of the Jerusalem church several years after the death of James.

Again, some have preferred to place reliance in a divergent tradition to the effect that there was another John at Ephesus, called the Elder, with whom John the Apostle may have become confused. Support for the existence of John the Presbyter has been found in the words of Papias: "If ever anyone came who had followed the presbyters, I inquired into the words of the presbyters, what Andrew or Peter or Philip or Thomas or James or John or Matthew, or any other of the Lord's disciples, had said, and what Aristion and the presbyter John, the Lord's disciples, were saying. For I did not suppose that information from books would help me so much as the word of a living and surviving voice."[11] This statement is far from clear. It could be argued, of course, that the change of tense in the verb "say" points to the decease of the men referred to in the first group, so that the second reference to John must indicate a different person. Yet it is possible that the same person is intended in both places, only that he is seen under two conditions, first as associated with other apostles and presumably laboring in Palestine, then as accessible to Papias, along with Aristion, at a time when the other apostles had passed away. No barrier to this view is presented by the fact that in the second instance John is called the presbyter, seeing that the apostles have been called presbyters earlier in the sentence (cf. the opening words of II and III John). It should be observed that the expression, "the Lord's disciples," is used in connection with both groups.

Eusebius accepted the reports about two Johns in Ephesus and found in the statement of Papias sufficient ground to distinguish the two and to proceed to the suggestion that it was John the Presbyter who had penned the Apocalypse and John the Apostle the Gospel. Before the time of Eusebius a noted church leader and biblical critic, Dionysius of Alexandria, had suggested a difference of authorship for the two books. Eusebius followed by assigning the Apocalypse to John the Presbyter, although Dionysius, for all his acuteness, had not detected two Johns in the Papias statement. Modern negative criticism has clung to the two Johns but has tended to diverge from Eusebius by tending to retain John the Apostle as author of the Apocalypse and assigning the Gospel to John the Presbyter. It would appear

---

[11] *HE* III. xxxix. 4.

that too much has been made of a shadowy figure who may never have existed at all.

Still another ground for rejection of the testimony of Johannine authorship has been found in the position of an Asia Minor sect that emerged about A.D. 170 and denied John's authorship both of the Gospel and the Apocalypse. The name of this sect — Alogi — seems to have been fabricated by Epiphanius, a clever stroke on his part since it pointed at once to their rejection of the Logos teaching and also to their lack of reason. Earlier Irenaeus had spoken of a group that rejected the Gospel and the prophetic Spirit therein promised.[12] Their reaction was likely produced by Montanist excesses. It is not certain that the group referred to by Irenaeus is the same as that which was dubbed Alogi by Epiphanius, though they are usually identified. It would be grasping at a straw to reject John's authorship because of this single and uncertain voice lifted against the unanimity of the church.

In summary, the external testimony is strong. Some are troubled that it does not begin at an earlier point, but this would be damaging only if earlier testimony existed that pointed to another than John. It is possible that the use of the Gospel by the Gnostics may have made for reticence about it on the part of orthodox men in the early part of the second century.

Today it is customary to concede the strength of the traditional position in so far as it depends on ancient testimony, but to hold that this is more than counterbalanced by what the Gospel itself has to tell us about the writer. Here the critic comes down heavily on the sharp differences between the Johannine picture of Jesus and his work and that found in the Synoptics. Some of these differences are noted here.

(1) Parables in the proper sense of the word are lacking in John, yet they constitute the staple of Jesus' teaching according to the Synoptics. But Jesus did not always teach by means of parables. The Sermon on the Mount is devoid of them apart from the conclusion. In John much of the teaching comes out in debates with opponents or in intimate contact with the disciples. In the Synoptics the crowds are mixed, so the parable serves well to veil the truth from the disinterested and to excite the desire for clearer understanding on the part of the earnest.

(2) Certain events in which John the Apostle figured personally, such as the transfiguration and the Gethsemane episode, are not mentioned in the Fourth Gospel. It is true that the

---

[12] *Against Heresies* III. xi. 9.

transfiguration fails to appear as an event, but it appears nevertheless, transmuted into something more than physical, something that showed itself to the eye of faith throughout the ministry (1:14). In similar fashion the writer has failed to narrate the institution of the Lord's Supper, yet in the opinion of many he has deliberately preserved its essential teaching in the discourse on the bread of life, which may be said to show knowledge of that institution. As for Gethsemane, the writer places Jesus and the disciples in the garden (18:1) and he knows what transpired there (18:11). The omission of the agony may be due to a statement of something akin to it at an earlier point (12:27) as well as to the difficulty of introducing it in chapter 18 immediately after the prayer of chapter 17 with its confidence and serenity. The contrast might be too jarring.

(3) Additions are fully as disconcerting as omissions, and in no case more disconcerting than in the report of the raising of Lazarus. In the Fourth Gospel it is presented as a crucial element in the final rejection of Jesus, yet the Synoptics are silent about it. To make matters worse, the writer may even have plundered the Synoptic tradition to obtain the name of Lazarus and the setting of death, with an added hint of resurrection (Luke 16:20, 22, 31). Can it be seriously thought that an author would risk the credit of his whole work by an invention that could readily be exposed? He lays himself open to investigation by locating the residence of Lazarus and citing the names of his sisters. The miracle serves to illustrate the power that Jesus claimed in John 5:21ff. and also to point prophetically to his own resurrection. From our limited knowledge we can only hazard reasons for the presence of an item in one account and its absence from another. The Synoptists do not cite miracles in their reports of the closing week except for the cursing of the fig tree and the healing of the ear of the slave of the high priest. It was left for John as the reporter and interpreter of the Judean ministry to give an account that belonged to his special province of testimony.

(4) The discourses of the Fourth Gospel have been widely discounted in critical circles. A. T. Olmstead, for example, though willing to accept the historical framework of John and even to build his book, *Jesus in the Light of History,* around it, nevertheless rejected the discourses. A stumbling block here is the fact that the style of the discourses closely resembles that of the narrative portions. Must one not conclude, therefore, that the writer has put words in Jesus' mouth? The objection is serious only if it can be shown that he has misrepresented the

teaching of our Lord, and here the problem is to account for the material, with all its grandeur, as the work of a disciple. If these words are not a faithful mirroring of Jesus' thought, though not necessarily his *ipsissima verba,* then we must suppose that among the early Christians there was a religious genius rivalling Jesus himself. It is significant that students of rabbinic literature have a high view of the Johannine discourses. Israel Abrahams writes, "Most remarkable of all has been the cumulative strength of the arguments adduced by Jewish writers favourable to the authenticity of the discourses in the Fourth Gospel, especially in relation to the circumstances under which they are reported to have been spoken."[13]

(5) The manner in which the Messiahship of Jesus is treated is so different from the handling of the same theme in the Synoptics as to suggest an unhistorical idealization. Whereas the Messiahship is unfolded only gradually in the Synoptics, in John it is boldly announced almost from the beginning (1:41; cf. 4:26). The Johannine situation can doubtless be explained from the side of John the Baptist. Though he did not publicly proclaim Jesus as the Christ, he evidently considered him in this light (3:28-30). It is natural to suppose that he shared this conviction with his disciples, which accounts for their readiness to follow Jesus at the cost of leaving John. It is not necessarily true that Peter's confession of Jesus as the Christ at Caesarea-Philippi was a conviction arrived at on the spot. It may well have been a judgment of long standing, which had been maturing and now came to open acknowledgment.

Regarding this whole area of alleged tension between John and the Synoptics, W. F. Albright offers some wise counsel. "One of the strangest assumptions of critical New Testament scholars and theologians is that the mind of Jesus was so limited that any apparent contrast between John and the Synoptics must be due to differences between early Christian theologians. Every great thinker and personality is going to be interpreted differently by different friends and hearers, who will select what seems most congenial or useful out of what they have seen and heard. From Socrates to the most recent men of eminence there are innumerable examples. The Christian might *a fortiori* suppose the same to be true of his Master."[14]

It is ironical indeed that John's Gospel, with its earnest periodic

---

[13] *Cambridge Biblical Essays,* p. 181.
[14] *The Background of the New Testament and its Eschatology,* p. 171, n. 1.

reminder to the reader that the writer is bearing a *witness* growing out of competence and opportunity and devotion to the Lord, should be judged historically inferior to the Synoptics, where this element of witness is absent. And to go only half-way by accepting the narrative portions but ruling out the discourses is to introduce an artificial disjunction between the two elements that is highly unsatisfactory, as Albright notes in the contribution referred to above.

Present-day students are usually quite willing to grant that Westcott's analysis of the internal evidence as requiring that the author must have been a Jew and a Palestinian, an eyewitness, a disciple of Jesus, and the apostle John himself is sound right up to the final item. There they tend to balk.[15] This is so despite the recognition of the fact that the beloved disciple was a close companion of Peter and that the Book of Acts and Galatians testify that John and Peter were constant companions. Acts 4:13 is counted unfavorable to John, for the description of Peter and John is said to involve two technical terms designating those who were ignorant of Torah.[16] The force of this may be granted, but not necessarily the conclusion that is drawn from it. The surprised reaction of the Sanhedrin to the fishermen disciples in itself shows that a stage had been reached in the development of John that could eventually make him competent to write on matters germane to Judaism and Christianity. Again, the writer's use of "beloved disciple" has exposed him to criticism as being excessively egotistical for one of the original apostles. But the epithet would be even more objectionable coming from some imaginary writer who did not belong to that circle. If it was a true description of John, why should he not use it, especially since it did not imply lack of love by the Master for the others? A difficulty of a different kind is found in the writer's covert allusion, apparently to himself, though this is not certain, as "another disciple" who, as well as Peter, followed Jesus after his arrest, and is said to have been known to the high priest (18:15). Then a little later it is stated that the beloved disciple appeared at the cross and subsequently took Mary to his own home (19: 27). Both these items seem somewhat incongruous for a Galilean fisherman. About the former, in the absence of information, it is useless to speculate. The passage may serve to recall the testimony of Polycrates that John "was a priest wearing the *petalon*,"[17] a

15 *IB*, VIII, 440b.
16 C. H. Dodd, *The Interpretation of the Fourth Gospel*, p. 82, n. 1.
17 *HE* III. xxxi. 3.

word which has proven mysterious to interpreters. The reference in 18:15 has been influential in causing some scholars to assign the book to an unknown, identified only as John of Jerusalem. But an apostolic figure seems clearly intended here. As for the other passage, the word "home" used by some translators is misleading. The idea would be more faithfully set forth by saying that the disciple took her to his own quarters, which may well have been temporary lodgings. On the other hand, if John had private means (Mark 1:20), he may have acquired a residence in Jerusalem, which would help to explain his connection with the high priest and his presence in Judea during the Baptist's ministry. The fishing business need not have engrossed him throughout the year. Finally, it is hard to identify the beloved disciple with the hot-headed, intolerant, ambitious son of Zebedee whom we meet in the Synoptics. But this is largely because we have allowed ourselves to be affected by Christian art, which has given to John a special aura of saintliness. To be the object of Jesus' love is not necessarily the same thing as being specially lovable in character.

Among scholars of moderately conservative views, particularly in Britain, it is usual to find the opinion that the substratum of the Gospel is the testimony of John the Apostle, but that the actual composition is due to another, presumably some disciple or person close to him. It is doubtful, however, that the facts in the case demand even this measure of concession. There seems to be no decisive reason for rejecting John in favor of another.

The latest suggestion regarding authorship gives the nod to John Mark, for which an ingenious case has been made out by Pierson Parker.[18] His theory answers certain problems but raises others in their place. Can we really suppose, for example, that John Mark was present in the Upper Room? And who then wrote the Gospel according to Mark? Confidence in tradition would be seriously shaken on this new hypothesis.

PURPOSE AND READERS

These can be conveniently considered together. A more precise statement of purpose is given than in connection with the other Gospels (20:31). These things have been written in order to induce faith in Jesus as the Christ, the Son of God. That the writer is using the former title with the full recognition of

[18] *JBL,* 70 (June 1960), pp. 97-110. See also his vigorous rejection of Johannine authorship in *JBL,* 81 (March 1962), pp. 35-43.

225

its Hebraic background and force as the Anointed is apparent
from the fact that on two occasions he makes use of the Hebrew
term "Messiah" (1:41; 4:25). W. C. van Unnik notes that the
objective of Paul's preaching in the synagogues of the Dispersion
is the same, to present Jesus as the Christ.[19] This suggests that
the Fourth Gospel was primarily directed toward the Jews
of the Dispersion, and indeed it manifests a strong interest in
those outside the land (7:35; 10:16; 11:52). Others share this
view. John's "overmastering concern is that 'the great refusal'
made by his countrymen at home should not be repeated by
those other sheep of God's flock among whom he has now found
refuge."[20] This judgment represents a shift from the view of
B. W. Bacon and E. F. Scott that the Gospel is an adaptation
of the Christian message for Greek readers. Dodd inclines to the
idea that intelligent Greeks are in view. No doubt Jews of the
Dispersion are included among the intended readers, but the
universal tone of the Gospel (3:16; 10:16; 12:32) is a warning against restricting the circle of recipients too narrowly.

Competing readings in 20:31 render somewhat uncertain the
avowed purpose of the writing, whether to constrain the unsaved
to believe or to deepen faith among believers. Both designs have
been fulfilled in the use of the Gospel.

A subsidiary purpose is to make clear Jesus' superiority to
John the Baptist. The presence of Baptist adherents at Ephesus
(Acts 19:1-7) suggests the need for such an emphasis. Certain
passages lend themselves readily to this objective (1:7-9, 30;
3:30) and the same motif may underlie 1:35-42.

Another minor purpose is to counter docetic views of the person of the Lord Jesus. This is fairly obvious in 1:14 and in
passages where "flesh" is used of him (6:51, 53-56; cf. I John
1:1, also John 19:34-35).

PRINCIPAL CONCEPTS

(1) Of primary importance is the Father-Son relationship
that pervades the book, given out mainly in terms of the self-
revelation of the Son. The Synoptic tradition has much less
along this line, but the presence of Matthew 11:27 is significant.
It has been called "a preliminary stage in the development of
Johannine thought."[21] The Son is sent of the Father to reveal
him and to give life to the world.

(2) A corollary of this is the necessity for faith in the Son

[19] *Studia Evangelica*, pp. 395ff.
[20] J. A. T. Robinson, *NTS*, 6 (January 1960), pp. 130-31.
[21] J. Jeremias, *Unknown Sayings of Jesus*, p. 68.

as well as in the Father. Faith is intimately connected with knowledge (8:32; 10:38) and the issue is eternal life (3:15; 17:3). Correspondingly, unbelief issues in condemnation (3:18).

(3) It is central to the Johannine presentation that believers are made partakers of the divine life, made one with the Father and the Son and with one another. This new life is best expressed in terms of love, for this is the nature of God.

(4) Eschatology is presented both in a futuristic pattern and as realized. As for the former, there is a last day (6:39-40). Resurrection will lead to life or judgment (5:29). Christ will return to receive his own (14:3; 21:22) and to judge (5:27; 12:48). Eternal life has a futuristic emphasis at times (12:25). On the other hand, an even stronger emphasis falls on the possession of life now (5:24) or of judgment (3:18; 16:11).

(5) Not only is there a foreshortening of the eschatological perspective, but also a paradoxical handling of the motif of glory. While glory is still presented in its post-resurrection context (12:16; 17:24), it is also attached to the death of the Saviour (12:23; 13:31). The Son's obedience unto death, fulfilling the Father's will, is triumph, not tragedy (cf. 21:19). In line with this, the substance of the teaching keeps the death of Christ before the reader more consistently and climactically than in the Synoptics.

(6) The ecclesiastical element in John, at least in so far as it relates to the sacraments, has been a hotly debated issue. The church nowhere appears in name, yet it seems to be present under various symbols, such as the sheep in relation to the shepherd (chap. 10) and the branches in relation to the vine (chap. 15). Scholars have found allusions to baptism in chapter 3 and to the Lord's Supper in chapter 6. Granting that these sacraments were well established in the church a considerable time before John wrote, it would not be necessary to repeat the commands of Christ respecting these observances. The way would be open to treat them from the standpoint of their significance. Barrett writes, "The truth (in John's view) seems to be that they hang not upon one particular moment or command, but upon the whole fact of Christ in his life, death, and exaltation, and that they convey nothing less than this whole fact."[22]

(7) The foil for the unfolding of the blessings to be found through believing in Jesus of Nazareth is the stubbornness and blindness of the nation that refuses to acknowledge him (1:12-13). Usually the term "the Jews," used by the writer dozens of

[22] *The Gospel according to St. John*, p. 71.

times, refers to the leaders of the people. John has been accused of anti-Semitism, but the label is misleading, for he has no lack of respect and appreciation for Israel's past. He writes under the shadow of the awful tragedy that a nation so richly blessed of God could so grossly misunderstand his dealings with them in the sending of his Son as to spurn him and seal their own doom. But there is no abandonment of the nation in favor of the Gentiles.

SPECIAL STUDY

(1) Aramaic background. Is the Gospel a translation of an Aramaic original? Burney, Torrey and others have so argued, but the case for this position has not been proved. E. C. Colwell has demonstrated that many of the syntactical features of the Gospel that had been relied on to demonstrate an Aramaic original, such as parataxis and asyndeton, were common also to hellenistic Greek writings where there could be no conceivable possibility of Aramaic influence.[23] Yet the impression of an Aramaic background for the Gospel lingers. Black notes that the Aramaic *z^eqaph,* which in the passive means "to be lifted up," has also a special meaning, "to be crucified."[24] This may account for the way John uses ὑψωθῆναι in 3:14; 12:32, 34. Barrett concludes, "Perhaps it is safest to say that in language as in thought John treads, perhaps not unconsciously, the boundary between the Hellenic and the Semitic."[25]

(2) Topography. Discoveries over the last several years have shown that the writer was fully familiar with the land in which Jesus moved, and has accurately described the various spots involved in his narrative. In concluding an article on this subject, R. D. Potter states, "Time and again, it will be found that those who have lived long in Palestine are struck by the impression that our author did so."[26] We must be content here to deal with only one item. In John 19:13 it is stated that during the trial of Jesus, Pilate had his seat of judgment set up in a place called Λιθόστρωτον, meaning "paved with stones." John notes that the Semitic equivalent is *Gabbatha.* Many scholars have ventured the opinion that Pilate had established his *praetorium* at the Herodian palace to the west of the temple area. But no pavement has come to light there. Now, however, the excavations of Père

---

23 *The Greek of the Fourth Gospel.*
24 *An Aramaic Approach to the Gospels and Acts,* 2nd ed., p. 103.
25 *The Gospel according to John,* p. 11.
26 *Studia Evangelica,* p. 335.

Vincent have uncovered a large pavement at the Castle of Antonia located at the northwest corner of the temple precincts. And here the justification for the name Gabbatha ("ridge" or "high ground") appears, since that is a true description of it with respect to the surrounding terrain.[27]

(3) John and Qumran. Professor Kuhn of Heidelberg has traced the dualism of the Qumran group, a strongly ethical dualism expressed often in the symbolism of light and darkness, to Iranian influence, and has noted that it must be distinguished from the dualism of Greek Gnosticism, which is physical in nature. The frequent use of light and darkness as well as Spirit of truth and spirit of error in John suggests affinity with Qumran rather than with Gnosticism in the ordinary sense, so that the efforts of Bultmann to find a strong Gnostic strain in the Fourth Gospel that would place it in a hellenic orbit are now seen to be misguided. But Johannine thought goes beyond that of Qumran, for the two principles that in the Qumran literature remain locked in conflict are not on a more or less equal plane in John. Christ the Light of the world has come and the darkness is now passing. It is no longer necessary merely to look wistfully for the victory, seeing that it has come through the Son of God.[28]

A further use of the Qumran data has been made by Cullmann, who points out that John has been an enigma because it does not fit into the pattern of the Jewish Christianity of the Jerusalem church or the hellenistic Christianity of the mission churches whose founding is described in the Acts. Just as the scrolls have shown that the old distinction, Palestinian Judaism versus hellenistic Judaism, is too simple, for Judaism had many divergent points of view, so early Christianity may be expected to yield similar diversity. The term "Hellenist" becomes crucial. Cullmann thinks the term denoted those with non-conformist tendencies. Certain of these men seem to have been in the early church from its inception. That they derived something from Qumran is likely from their attitude toward the temple, which is reflected in Stephen's address in Acts 7 and has something in common with the Qumran attitude of hostility toward the temple and its priesthood. The Fourth Gospel fits into the pattern in the sense that the temple is transcended and the person

---

[27] W. F. Albright, *The Archeology of Palestine* (1949), p. 245. See also A. M. Hunter's article, "Recent Trends in Johannine Studies" in *ET*, 71 (March 1960), pp. 164-67.

[28] See the discussion by R. E. Brown in *The Scrolls and the New Testament*, ed. by Krister Stendahl, pp. 183-207.

of Christ is put in its place.[29] Certain elements of the argumentation are open to question, but this new approach to the Gospel helps very much to vindicate it as the expression of a special type of early Christianity that is perceptibly different from that reflected in the Synoptics, yet fundamentally one with it.

(4) Dislocations of text. This has long been a subject of discussion, with various suggestions for improvement of the order, but nothing has commanded anything like universal or even general assent.[30] Against the idea are the lack of manuscript witnesses for such dislocations and the difficulty of demonstrating that the misplacing of papyrus sheets would create the disorders at the places where dislocations are claimed.

(5) Use of the Old Testament. Some would find here the most important key to the understanding of the Gospel.[31] Actual quotations are not abundant, and are drawn both from the Hebrew and the LXX. Their purpose is essentially to fortify the Christological thrust of the book.[32] Beyond this, however, it must be recognized that the Old Testament in its broader scope is the ever-present foil for the presentation, beginning with John 1:1. Frequent allusion is made to Old Testament figures and events.

(6) The Problem of Chapter 21. Was this closing portion written by the Evangelist or by another? Good arguments can be advanced in support of both positions. The statement of purpose in 20:30-31 makes a natural conclusion for the book. Furthermore, since 21:24 is not the composition of the author, and verse 25 raises problems, it is easy to maintain that the chapter as a whole is an addition. If so, the person or persons involved must have been close to the author, since many of his literary characteristics are reproduced here.

(7) The Use of Tradition. A significant contribution to this subject has been made by C. H. Dodd.[33] In connection with his abandonment of the view that John was dependent on the Synoptics, he was led by his research to conclude that "behind the Fourth Gospel lies an ancient tradition independent of the other

[29] Oscar Cullmann, "A New Approach to the Interpretation of the Fourth Gospel," *ET,* 71 (Oct. and Nov. 1959) pp. 8-12, 39-43.

[30] See the arrangement of Moffatt's translation of John, also F. R. Hoare, *The Original Order and Chapters of St. John's Gospel* and the discussion in Barrett's commentary, pp. 18-21.

[31] Stephen Neill, *The Interpretation of the New Testament 1861-1961,* p. 320.

[32] See Edwin D. Freed, *Old Testament Quotations in the Gospel of John.* Leiden: E. J. Brill, 1965.

[33] *Historical Tradition in the Fourth Gospel.* Cambridge: 1963.

gospels, and meriting serious consideration as a contribution to our knowledge of the historical facts concerning Jesus Christ."[34] Another feature of Dodd's work is his discovery of several brief parables in John, which tends to bridge somewhat the gap between it and the Synoptics, though the difference remains great in this area.

(8) The Jewish background. A contribution to Johannine studies has been made by Aileen Guilding in her research into the influence of the triennial lectionary of the Palestinian synagogues upon the structure and terminology of the Fourth Gospel, built as it is so largely around the Jewish feasts.[35] The major difficulty here is that John has not included the whole cycle of Jewish festivals, since Pentecost is lacking. So doubt is cast on the legitimacy of this schematization.[36]

(9) The Wider Milieu. Dependence on Philo, claimed by some, is dubious, for in the very section where the interests of the two writers seem most clearly to coincide, namely, the Prologue, they are seen to be divergent in their concepts, since Philo has no place for an incarnate, personal Logos in whom one must put his trust for salvation.[37]

Dodd has instanced a number of parallels between John and the Hermetic writings of Egypt which could suggest a somewhat similar background of thought, such as the concepts of light, life, and knowledge of God, but he discounts the idea of any "substantial borrowing."[38] One may question any dependence here, since the *Hermetica* belong to a somewhat later period than John.

Several scholars, Bultmann among them, see the influence of Oriental Gnosticism on the Fourth Gospel, especially in terms of a mythological figure who comes from the world of light to reveal and redeem, that those imprisoned in the darkness of the material world may find release. However, there does not appear to be evidence for a redeemer in gnostic thought prior to New Testament times.[39] That John's language has something in common with Gnosticism is reasonably clear, but this is not evidence of agreement. Barrett writes, "Only gradually did the main body

---

[34] *Ibid.*, p. 423.

[35] *The Fourth Gospel and Jewish Worship* (1960).

[36] See Leon Morris, *The New Testament and the Jewish Lectionaries.* Tyndale Press: 1964.

[37] C. H. Dodd, *The Interpretation of the Fourth Gospel*, p. 73.

[38] *Ibid.*, p. 53.

[39] R. H. Fuller, *The New Testament in Recent Study*, pp. 119-122; cf. Rudolf Schnackenburg, *The Gospel according to St. John*, Vol. I, pp. 543-557; R. E. Brown, *The Gospel according to John*, Vol. I, pp. LIV-LVI.

of the Church come to perceive that, while John used (at times) the language of gnosticism, his work was in fact the strongest reply to the gnostic challenge; that he had beaten the gnostics with their own weapons, and vindicated the permanent validity of the primitive Gospel."[40]

(10) Literary criticism. Once more the name of Bultmann comes to the fore, since in his commentary he has made a notable attempt to isolate several sources. Of these, the two which receive special treatment are a signs source detectable in the narrative portions of chapters 1-12, and a revelation source discernible in the discourses of Jesus. The latter is judged to have been originally gnostic in nature, but adapted by the Evangelist. The task of the critic is to separate the contributions of the Evangelist from source material, a task which Bultmann concedes to be difficult because the Evangelist often molds his style to that of the source. This concession indicates the subjective nature of this kind of criticism.[41] There is also ground for doubt that a signs source would circulate separately from discourse material, seeing that they are so closely integrated in John. Yet Schnackenburg is prepared to give cautious endorsement to a signs source[42] and Fortna has given his support after a detailed investigation.[43]

(11) The setting for the Gospel. In *History and Theology in the Fourth Gospel,* J. Louis Martyn sets forth his case for viewing the book as a "two-level drama" in which the writer superimposes on the historical material other data reflecting his own time. The latter, which deals mainly with the hostility of the synagogue toward Jews who have become Christians, needs to be sorted out by critical methods. Martyn's reconstruction is ingenious, but it assumes that Jesus' warning of excommunication and of death (16:2) cannot be genuinely prophetic and must therefore be understood as a description of the situation when the Gospel was composed.

BIBLIOGRAPHY

Bacon, B. W., *The Fourth Gospel in Research and Debate.* New York: Moffat, Yard and Co., 1910.

[40] C. K. Barrett, *The Gospel according to St. John,* p. 113.

[41] For a careful and extended treatment of Bultmann's work on John, see Dwight Moody Smith, Jr., *The Composition and Order of the Fourth Gospel,* Yale University Press, 1965.

[42] Rudolf Schnackenburg, *The Gospel according to St. John,* Vol. I, pp. 66-68.

[43] Robert T. Fortna, *The Gospel of Signs.* Cambridge University Press, 1970.

Barrett, C. K., *The Gospel according to St. John*. London: SPCK, 1955.

Bauer, Walter, *Das Johannesevangelium, HZNT*. Tübingen: Mohr, 3rd ed., 1933.

Boice, J. M., *Witness and Revelation in the Gospel of John*. Grand Rapids: Zondervan, 1970.

Braun, F. M., *Jean le theologien et son évangile dans l'église ancienne*. Paris: J. Gabalda, 1959.

Brown, R. E., *The Gospel according to John*. Garden City, N.Y.: Doubleday, 2 vols., 1966-1970.

Bultmann, R., *Das Evangelium des Johannes*, Meyer series. Göttingen: Vanderhoeck & Ruprecht, 12th ed., 1952.

Burney, C. F., *The Aramaic Origin of the Fourth Gospel*. Oxford: Clarendon Press, 1922.

Corell, Alf, *Consummatum Est*. London: SPCK, 1958.

Dodd, C. H., *Historical Tradition in the Fourth Gospel*. Cambridge University Press, 1963.

——————————, *The Interpretation of the Fourth Gospel*. Cambridge University Press, 1953.

Drummond, James, *An Inquiry into the Character and Authorship of the Fourth Gospel*. London: Williams and Norgate, 1903.

Freed, E. D., *Old Testament Quotations in the Gospel of John*. Leiden: E. J. Brill, 1965.

Garner-Smith, P., *Saint John and the Synoptic Gospels*. Cambridge University Press, 1938.

Godet, F., *Commentary on the Gospel of St. John*. Edinburgh: T. & T. Clark, 3rd ed., 3 vols., 1895.

Holland, H. Scott., *The Fourth Gospel*. London: J. Murray, 1923.

Hoskyns, E. C., *The Fourth Gospel*. London: Faber & Faber, Ltd., 1940.

Howard, W. F., *The Fourth Gospel in Recent Criticism and Interpretation*. London: Epworth Press, 4th ed., 1955.

——————————, *Christianity According to St. John*. London: Duckworth, 1943.

Käsemann, Ernst, *The Testament of Jesus*. Philadelphia: Fortress Press, 1968.

Lagrange, M. J., *Evangile selon Saint Jean*. Paris: J. Gabalda, 3rd ed., 1927.

Lee, E. K., *The Religious Thought of St. John*. London: SPCK, 1950.

Lightfoot, R. H., *St. John's Gospel*. Oxford: Clarendon Press, 1956.

Macgregor, G. H. C., *The Gospel of John, MNTC*. New York: Harper and Brothers, 1929.

Manson, William, *The Incarnate Glory*. London: James Clarke and Co., Ltd., 1923.

Martyn, J. L., *History and Theology in the Fourth Gospel*. New York: Harper and Row, 1968.

Morris, Leon, *Studies in the Fourth Gospel*. Grand Rapids: Eerdmans, 1969.

Nunn, H. P. V., *The Authorship of the Fourth Gospel*. Windsor, 1952.

Odeberg, Hugo, *The Fourth Gospel*. Amsterdam: B. R. Grüner, 1968 (reprinted from the Uppsala 1929 edition).

Rigg, W. H., *The Fourth Gospel and its Message for Today*. London: Lutterworth Press, 1952.

Robinson, J. Armitage, *The Historical Character of St. John's Gospel*. London: Longmans, Green and Co., 2nd ed., 1929.

Robinson, J. A. T., *Twelve New Testament Studies, Studies in Biblical Theology* No. 34. Naperville: Alec R. Allenson, Inc., 1962, chaps. VII and VIII.

Sanday, William, *The Authorship and Historical Character of the Fourth Gospel*. London: Macmillan, 1872.

——————, *The Criticism of the Fourth Gospel*. Oxford: Clarendon Press, 1905.

Sanders, J. N., *A Commentary on the Gospel according to St. John, HNTC*. New York: Harper and Row, 1968.

——————, *The Fourth Gospel in the Early Church*. Cambridge Univ. Press, 1943.

Schlatter, A., *Der Evangelist Johannes*. Stuttgart: Calwer, 1948.

Schnackenburg, Rudolf, *The Gospel according to St. John*. New York: Herder and Herder, Vol. I, 1968.

Scott, E. F., *The Fourth Gospel*. Edinburgh: T. & T. Clark, 1906.

Smith, D. M., Jr., *The Composition and Order of the Fourth Gospel*. New Haven: Yale University Press, 1965.

Tasker, R. V. G., *The Gospel according to St. John*. Grand Rapids: Eerdmans, 1960.

Temple, William, *Readings in St. John's Gospel*. London: Macmillan, 1945.

Tenney, Merrill C., *John: The Gospel of Belief*. Grand Rapids: Eerdmans, 1948.

Wead, D. W., *The Literary Devices in John's Gospel*. Basel: Friedrich Reinhardt, 1970.

Westcott, B. F., *The Gospel according to St. John* (on the AV). London: John Murray, 1882; (on the Greek text), 2 vols., 1908.

Wiles, Maurice F., *The Spiritual Gospel*. Cambridge Univ. Press, 1960.

Chapter Ten

THE BOOK OF ACTS

IN OUR STUDY OF THE CANON IT WAS NOTED THAT THE PATRISTIC references to the New Testament books, particularly in the second century, divided them into Gospel and Apostle, answering to our terminology Gospels and Epistles. These stood out as natural groupings. But they could scarcely furnish all the light the church needed on its own origins. In fact, the Gospels did little more than to anticipate the church, whereas the Epistles presuppose it. A work was needed to describe the rise and development of this great spiritual entity that would at the same time be a binding element between Gospels and Epistles. The Book of Acts fills exactly that need. It is no wonder that Harnack pronounced it the pivotal book of the New Testament. The Acts is the bridge between Gospels and Epistles.

CONTENTS

I. The Ministry of the Risen Christ to the disciples, terminating in the Ascension (1:1-11).
II. The Witness of the Disciples in Jerusalem (1:12-7:60).
III. The Witness in Judea and Samaria (8:1-40).
IV. The Witness to Jews and Gentiles in the Land of Palestine and in the Regions Beyond (9:1-28:31).

1. The conversion and call of the apostle to the Gentiles (9:1-31).
2. The labors of Peter at Lydda, Joppa and Caesarea (2:32-11:18).
3. The communication of the gospel to the Hellenes by the Hellenists (11:19-30).
4. Persecution of the Jerusalem church (12:1-23).
5. The first missionary journey (12:24-14:28).
6. The apostolic council (15:1-35).
7. The second missionary journey (15:36-18:22).
8. The third missionary journey (18:23-20:2).
9. Paul's journey to Jerusalem (20:3-21:25).
10. The arrest of Paul and his witness as a prisoner (21:26-26:32).
11. The journey to Rome (27:1-28:16).
12. Paul's witness in Rome (28:17-31).

AUTHORSHIP

The problem of authorship has been considered in connection with the Gospel according to Luke. Some attention should be paid here, however, to the negative approach to authorship so far as it bears on the Book of Acts. One such approach was made by A. C. Clark, *The Acts of the Apostles* (1933). He made a statistical study of the vocabulary of Luke and Acts, placing special emphasis upon the smaller parts of speech such as particles, conjunctions, and prepositions, and he found sufficient disparity to cause him to question the widely accepted verdict that the two books had the same author. W. L. Knox, *The Acts of the Apostles* (1948), went over the data and came out with a different answer, pointing out that Clark's methodology was faulty because it did not take account of Luke's sources as distinct from his own style of writing, and did not consider the effect of the LXX upon his work.

Another approach has been made by comparing the Acts with the Epistles of Paul. If Luke was the companion of Paul and the author of Acts, how does it come about that so many of the activities of the apostle that are noted by Paul himself in his epistles fail to appear in the Book of Acts? An example is the catalogue of his sufferings in II Corinthians 11:23-27, and some of his dealings with the church at Corinth. These crop up in the letters to that church but are absent from the Acts. And why is there so much about the external activities of Paul and so little about the inner side of his work, his problems and his reflections? And why do the author of Acts and Paul differ so much, as in the representation of the Apostolic Council at

236

Jerusalem? It is claimed that this disparity between the Acts and the Epistles of Paul can only be explained on the basis of ignorance or willful suppression of information by the author of Acts.

Looking first at the former alternative, it must be granted that if the writer of the Acts is demonstrated to be ignorant of Paul's activities to any appreciable degree, this would seem to require the elimination of Lukan authorship from serious consideration. But it should be recognized that in a history it is just such an emphasis upon external events that one expects to find. In the more intimate atmosphere of the epistles some things appear that would not be expected at all in a historical narration. Furthermore, many of the personal touches in the letters of Paul were drawn out of him, so to speak, by the accusations of others, to which he felt obliged to make reply. This is especially true of his sufferings, which he would hardly have recounted had it not been necessary to shut the mouths of those who boasted of their achievements and depreciated the apostle. In the Acts, Luke contents himself with reporting the founding of Paul's churches and occasional return visits for the sake of pastoral oversight. We naturally have to look to the epistles for an insight into the problems that developed in those churches.

The failure of the Acts to reflect a knowledge of the epistles of Paul is doubtless to be understood in a similar way. Before this can be regarded as a serious obstacle in the way of receiving the Acts as a product of Luke's pen, it must be demonstrated that the scope of his work required the use of these epistles if he had known of them. It is not at all certain that he had access to them, since he was in Philippi most of the time during which the pre-captivity letters were composed.

The other alternative is willful suppression, or its corollary, the coloring of facts. Windisch maintains this, for example, in regard to the account of the Apostolic Council (Acts 15). He finds certain unhistorical features in this account, and concludes from this that Luke could not have written it, since he must have known the actual state of affairs in the church.[1] Luke represents the legalistic controversy as settled at the Council, whereas Paul's letters give the distinct impression that it continued to plague his churches for some time. A reasonable conclusion, however, is that Luke and Paul describe the Jerusalem meeting from somewhat different points of view, since

[1] *The Beginnings of Christianity*, Jackson and Lake, edd., II, 298-348.

237

Paul in Galatians was interested only in the theological aspect, the bearing on the gospel message, whereas Luke was interested in the ecclesiastical implications, the averting of a break between the Jewish and Gentile elements in the church. For this reason the decree (Acts 15:29) was important for Luke but not for Paul, who fails to mention it. With reference to the decisiveness of the action taken at Jerusalem, it is true that the church settled the issue, but it is equally true that the Judaizing element was not willing to abide by the decision, but continued to make trouble in the Pauline congregations.

Much that seems incompatible in the Acts and the Pauline Epistles ceases to be a vexing problem once the simple fact is recognized that general spiritual agreement between two persons does not dictate that their interests must entirely coincide. Paul makes a good deal in his letters of the collection for the poor saints at Jerusalem, but Luke fails to give it a place in his record beyond its inclusion in Paul's statement before Felix (Acts 24:17). Again, although Luke shows considerable interest in Paul's plan to go to Rome (Acts 19:21; 23:11), doubtless because it related so directly to the design of his history, he says nothing about the apostle's plan to go on to Spain, which we know from Romans 15 to have been exercising the mind of Paul when he wrote that letter.

PURPOSE

As noted already, Luke's objective in his twofold work was to provide a co-ordinated account of Christian origins. This conclusion is not dependent upon the wording of Acts 1:1, although the translation of the KJV gives verbal support to this conception, whereas the rendering of the NEB, "I wrote of all that Jesus did and taught from the beginning," removes that support. In the Acts Luke undertakes to trace the fulfillment of the earthly mission of Jesus in terms of the establishment of his church by men whom he had trained, and the spread of the movement under the impulsion of the Holy Spirit whom he had promised. The work is religious history, and as such was intended to be both informative and edifying, tracing the progress of the gospel from Jerusalem to Rome (cf. 19:21; 28:14).

A second purpose may be admitted, which is apologetic in nature. Jewish opposition to the gospel is pictured as not being confined to restrictive measures and persecution in the land of Palestine, but as voiced in the hearing of Roman authorities when Paul and others were accused of disturbing the peace and of fostering a spirit of disloyalty to Caesar (17: 7; 18:13). At every opportunity, it seems, Luke injects something into his story that vindicates the Christian witnesses against any suspicion of being a menace to the empire. Especially important is the decision of Gallio (18:14-15). The Jews enjoyed the right of religious propaganda under Roman protection and were naturally jealous of their privilege. It irked them to see the Christians, who at the first were all Jews, take advantage of this situation and presume on the same privilege for themselves. Luke seeks to show that the Roman government refused to be stampeded into repressive measures against the Christians. At Rome itself Paul had liberty to evangelize (28:30-31).

There is also, perhaps, in a subsidiary sense, a polemic thrust at the Jews. Again and again the historian pictures the gospel being presented to the Jews, only to be rejected by them. At the same time it is emphasized that Gentiles have an eagerness to accept the message. It is especially impressive that this twofold reaction to the gospel should be the note on which the whole account closes (28:23-28). Luke is presenting on the historical plane the problem to which Paul addresses himself on the theological plane (Romans 9-11).

DATE

A strong case can be made out for a date of composition shortly after the close of the two-year period noted at the end of the book, during which time Paul remained in captivity awaiting trial, or around A.D. 63, despite Moffatt's claim that this is preposterous.[2] In the year 64 Rome was burned and suspicion placed on the Christians, with resulting persecution. On the supposition that the book was written after this event, it is strange that the repercussions of it are not felt at all. Another crucial event occurred in A.D. 70, when Jerusalem fell. This had far-reaching effects on the church as well as on Judaism. But here, too, there is nothing in the book to suggest that such an event has taken place. Most important of all, the failure of the Acts to record the resolution of Paul's case, whether it turned out adversely for him or favorably, seems inexplicable except on the assumption that the book was written before the decision was reached. If Luke took pains to record the death of James the apostle and of Stephen, it is strange indeed that he should

[2] *The Historical New Testament*, p. 414.

cut off his narrative without telling of the fate of the man whose story he had been narrating in some detail through more than half of his account. Some scholars have favored the theory that Luke intended to write a third account in which the rest of Paul's career would be described. This conjecture is sometimes coupled with the view that the Acts was hurried into publication in order to aid Paul at his trial, since some items in the book would reflect Roman attitudes toward Paul and vice versa. But whether non-Christians could be expected in any numbers to consult a work that had so much that is extraneous to this problem remains doubtful.

A factor adverse to the early date for the book is its relation to Luke's Gospel and the relation in turn of that Gospel to Mark. Unless one sets aside the patristic testimony regarding the time of publication of Mark and puts it considerably earlier, there is no possibility of placing Luke and Acts in the early 60s. This difficulty can be met if one follows the suggestion of T. W. Manson that Peter was in Rome, and Mark with him, for the approximate period of A.D. 55 to 60. Mark's rough notes on Peter's preaching could then have been made available to Luke on his arrival at Rome with Paul.[3] Though Manson holds to an early date for Acts, he places it after the conflagration of the year 64.[4] On this position, the absence of information regarding Paul's fate is hard to explain. There is no certainty about the place, though if one holds the early date he naturally inclines to Rome.

A date in the last decade of the first century has been advocated by those who think that Luke shows dependence on the Jewish historian Josephus. But it is hardly logical to hold that Luke depends on Josephus and yet be obliged to admit that Luke shows wide divergence from him in relating events that are supposedly the same. An example is the Theudas incident mentioned in Acts 5:36.[5] It is no wonder that Lukan de-

[3] *Studies in the Gospels and Epistles*, p. 40.
[4] T. W. Manson writes, "I think that the most obvious occasion for such a public defence of Christianity comes with the savage attack on the Church made by Nero in A.D. 64 and the Jewish war of A.D. 66-70. The publication of Luke-Acts could be placed at any time in this period of crisis (64-70) or in the years immediately following" (*Studies in the Gospels and Epistles*, p. 56).
[5] See *Antiquities* XX. v. 1. It is not clear that the same person is in view in the two accounts, since Luke assigns him 400 followers and Josephus a very great multitude. Theudas in the Lukan account came on the scene before the time of Gamaliel's address, whereas in Josephus he is assigned to a later period, in the reign of Claudius.

pendence on Josephus is less and less insisted on by modern writers.

Another problem to be faced in dating the book late is the gap that exists between the primitive outlook of Acts in matters ecclesiastical and sacramental and the much more developed position observable in Clement of Rome and especially in Ignatius.

CHARACTERISTICS

(1) The Acts is distinctly a missionary document, with the Great Commission of 1:8 the key to its structure (cf. Luke 24:47). The gospel is preached and the church formed, first in Jerusalem, then in Judea, then in Samaria, then in the Gentile world.

(2) The account is necessarily fragmentary, for the complete story could not be told in the compass Luke allotted to himself. In our English versions the title is given as "The Acts of the Apostles," which raises expectations that are not fulfilled, since the apostles as a body appear only in the early part of the book and their labors are not traced on an individual basis except for Peter and later for Paul. Nothing is said about the planting of the faith in Egypt, where a strong church developed. A shorter title is common in the manuscripts, either simply "Acts" or "Acts of Apostles." Likely there was no title given to the work by the author. For him the Acts was Part Two of his two volume work. Some compensation for the fragmentary character of the account is achieved by the device of summaries placed at intervals throughout the book, which state in general terms the progress of the gospel as a result of the activity carried on in the preceding period (6:7; 9:31; 12:24; 16:5; 19:20; 28:31). A curious feature of the second summary is that churches are mentioned in Galilee despite the fact that the narrative does not recount the planting of churches there. This is but a further indication of the partial nature of the history. Even in the second half of the book, where Luke is concerned almost entirely with the labors of Paul, the narrative is uneven in the sense that at times it is highly condensed, tracing in a sentence movements that required weeks to accomplish (e.g., 18:22; 19:1), whereas at other times it is quite detailed, as in the account of the sea journey and shipwreck. Luke's presence or absence is an important factor in assessing these inequalities.

(3) Two leading centers, Jerusalem and Antioch, dominate the story, and parallel to these are the two leading apostles, Peter and Paul.

241

(4) Speeches are prominent in the Acts. Some of them could be called sermons. F. F. Bruce divides them into four categories, as follows:[6] evangelistic; deliberative (e.g., the addresses in chap. 15); apologetic (Stephen's address and Paul's various defenses); and hortatory (Paul's words to the Ephesian elders). Some observations on the criticism of these speeches will come before us later. Here it is sufficient to observe that the most common feature of the evangelistic messages is their concentration on the resurrection of Christ, without which there would have been no message and no church to proclaim it.

(5) Terms for speaking and preaching and bearing witness are common. The word (or the word of God or of the Lord) is of very frequent occurrence, and the same is true of Gentile. The word church is prominent, also apostle, believe, and baptize. These are some of the terms that help to convey the atmosphere of the book.

(6) The Holy Spirit is the key to the success of the Christian mission. He is the source of effective utterance (4:8), of miraculous power (13:9-11), of wisdom in the councils of the church (15:28), of administrative authority (5:3; 13:2), and of guidance (10:19; 16:6-10).

SOURCES

Luke's own presence is attested by the "we" sections (16:11-17; 20:5-21:18; 27 and 28), and for the movements of Paul that he did not personally witness he could have the first-hand report of the apostle, including information on his conversion and early relation to the Jerusalem church. Luke must have come into contact with Barnabas and Mark at Antioch, and of course he knew Silas also. Philip of Caesarea could have been of help to him, and many others also. Written sources for at least part of the early chapters are likely. Judging by the probabilities in the case, these were Aramaic, and this is corroborated at times by the awkward construction that is not readily attributable to Luke himself (3:16 is a prime example).

HISTORICAL VALUE OF THE BOOK

For one thing, the writer is thoroughly conversant with the proper terminology for various Roman officials. He knows when to designate a man as a proconsul (the term for the official in charge of a senatorial province) and when to use the term for

6 *The Speeches in the Acts of the Apostles.* The Tyndale New Testament Lectures for 1942.

governor, which was proper in the case of a ruler of an imperial province or a procurator. This may seem simple enough, but the classification of provinces sometimes changed, as in the case of Achaia, so that accuracy depended upon first-hand knowledge or careful investigation.[7] Luke is not found wanting. His term for the leading man on the island of Malta seems general, roughly the equivalent of our expression, "the head man" (28:7), but Malta inscriptions have shown that ὁ πρῶτος was a technical term for the governor of the place. Luke knows how to designate the town clerk at Ephesus (see the references in Bauer's lexicon bearing on Ephesus under γραμματεύς). His use of πολιτάρχαι for the rulers of Thessalonica brought him under critical fire until an inscription was discovered on the Vardar Gate of the city beginning with the words, "In the time of the Politarchs." The inscription is housed in the British Museum. In one case, at first sight, Luke seems to fail, for he calls the rulers of Philippi στρατηγοί, equivalent to *praetor*, whereas the technical term for those in charge of the Roman colony was *duumviri*, but Luke's term was popularly used, as inscriptions attest. Perhaps his fairly long residence in the city accustomed him to the popular term to the point where he used it almost instinctively.

It is necessary to evaluate the historian's work as a whole in addition to checking it in details. Our inability to check at every point because of lack of information will not greatly disturb us if we are persuaded of his ability and diligence and honesty. Sir William Ramsay puts the matter well: "We might ask whether it is a probable or possible view that the author can be unequal to himself, that in one place he can show very high qualities as an accurate historian, and that in another place, when dealing with events equally within the range of his opportunities for acquiring knowledge, he can prove himself incompetent to distinguish between good and bad, false and true. He that shows the historic faculty in part of his work has it as a permanent possession." [8] The only problem untouched here concerns Luke's handling of his sources, but one would expect him to use all due care in corroborating the information wherever this was possible.

Historical accuracy has an important bearing on the purpose of writing. The more the apologetic design of the work is stressed, the more imperative becomes the obligation laid upon Luke to present the facts. In so far as he had a Roman audience

---

[7] J. B. Lightfoot, *Essays on Supernatural Religion*, p. 292.
[8] *Bethlehem*, p. 40.

in view, he had to show himself fully familiar with matters that pertained to imperial jurisdiction. Although the Romans were not as well informed on Jewish affairs as they might have been, they could make investigation. In both areas, then, Luke could not afford to make mistakes and risk exposure, lest his story fail to carry weight and accomplish its purpose.

One might object that this leaves to one side the sphere of distinctly Christian matters, which would not be so readily ferreted out by investigators who might wish to check the record. Here, too, factors other than the strictly historical have to be reckoned with. But as Adolph Schlatter reminds us, "Our literary sources furnish us unparalleled help, for the disciples' intercourse with Jesus set them under the standard of truth. They spoke as they thought, acted as they were compelled to act, and showed themselves for what they were."[9] Luke could not have been appreciably removed from this influence.

RECENT STUDY

A few years prior to the middle of the nineteenth century F. C. Baur of Tübingen developed a point of view that has become known as tendency criticism. He sought to penetrate to the tendency or purpose behind the writing of a book in order to fit it into a grandiose scheme dictated by philosophical principles. Heavily influenced by Hegelianism, he sought to apply its formulas to the field of biblical study. Starting with a certain situation as thesis, he looked for opposing factors that could be denominated antithesis, then for the attempted reconciliation or synthesis. So thorough-going was the criticism that Baur attempted to assign all the New Testament books to some place in this pattern of things. He found a point of departure in the early chapters of First Corinthians, where the Peter party and the Paul party gave him his thesis and antithesis, for which further support was found in Galatians 2. Baur judged that the sharper the antagonism the earlier and more authentic is the document that records it. He concluded that Acts was a harmonistic work, probably written by a Paulinist who sought to show that Paul tried to minister among his own people the Jews, but was prevented by Jewish opposition. The writer also did all he could to minimize the legalistic controversy and gloss it over in the interests of harmony. Acts could safely be put well down in the second century and treated as of little value.

Baur made use of the Clementine literature, a series of docu-

9 *The Church in the New Testament Period,* p. 3.

ments emanating from the third century that may fairly be thought to embody second-century tradition. Peter is the hero in these writings, and his great antagonist is Simon Magus. But to Baur this was simply a thinly veiled reference to Paul. He concluded that if Paul had been so hated in the second century, he could well have been hated even more in the first. Passages, like Acts 15, that picture Peter and Paul as in accord must be dismissed as unreliable.

It is plain today that Baur erred in maintaining that Peter and Paul were in sharp disagreement in principle. They stood together in behalf of Gentile freedom to enter the church without circumcision. The true cleavage was between Paul and the original apostles on the one hand, and the Judaizers on the other. Baur was in error also in assuming that the legalistic controversy continued long after Paul was removed from the scene. For this no evidence is forthcoming.

Baur's position was attacked from the conservative side by Zahn and Lightfoot, whose researches into patristic literature showed knowledge of New Testament books at earlier times than Baur had posited for their composition. An equally devastating attack came from Ritschl, who had been a disciple of Baur. He viewed the Old Catholic Church as characterized by legalism, with Christianity understood as a new law. This was not the inheritance of Jewish Christianity of the Judaizing type, but was the result of the Old Testament, the teaching of Christ, and the failure of the church to understand the message of Paul in relation to the Mosaic law. Ritschl's view of Acts was much more favorable than that of Baur.

Toward the close of the last century, criticism moved farther and farther away from the extreme position of Baur and his school. In place of his tendency criticism, men like Pfleiderer, Holtzmann, and Jülicher put unconscious as opposed to conscious fiction. H. J. Holtzmann expressed the difference thus: "Where, according to the Tübingen criticism, the author of Acts *would* not see, according to the new interpretation, for the most part he *could* not see."[10] Yet a late date was retained as essential to this point of view. The book was written so long after the events it related that it could not be expected to give a faithful account.

The early part of the present century brought a change, largely through the labors of two men, Harnack in Germany and Sir William Ramsay in Great Britain. Harnack made his

[10] *Hand-Kommentar zum Neuen Testament,* p. 308.

contribution in philology and source-criticism, whereas Ramsay worked mainly in the fields of geographical, archaeological and historical research. Both started out heavily prejudiced against the Book of Acts as a reliable account of Christian beginnings. Both men came to an almost idolizing devotion to Luke. This was especially true of Ramsay. It is interesting to note that along with increasing respect for the historical value of Acts went a natural shift in the dating of the book. Harnack ended up with a date in the early 60s, Ramsay settling for a somewhat later period. The latter's statement of his change of view has abiding interest. "The present writer, starting with the confident assumption that the book was fabricated in the middle of the second century, and studying it to see what light it could throw on the state of society in Asia Minor, was gradually driven to the conclusion that it must have been written in the first century and with admirable knowledge. It plunges one into the atmosphere and the circumstances of the first century; it is out of harmony with the circumstances and spirit of the second century."[11]

More recent study on the Acts by those steeped in the critical tradition has often been less favorable in its attitude. Harnack's work has been regarded as hurried and ill-considered, and Ramsay's devotion to Luke stigmatized as partisan. Though the five volume work, *The Beginnings of Christianity,* is the result of contributions from several scholars, the general orientation observable there is that the Acts bears marks of carelessness, and that the discrepancies with Paul's acknowledged letters are too many and too serious to be passed over lightly.[12] The nod goes to the position that an unknown author wrote it near the end of the first century. A corollary of this general viewpoint advocates the giving up of the old procedure of attempted harmonization of the Acts and the epistles of Paul. The epistles alone ought to be taken as a sure guide. If the Acts corroborates these sources, fine, but if the epistles are silent on a matter, the information of the Acts should not be assumed to be necessarily trustworthy.[13] Thus the Book of

[11] *Pauline and Other Studies,* p. 199.

[12] Two writers who have been somewhat critical of this voluminous work and have taken a more favorable view of the Acts are F. C. Burkitt, *Christian Beginnings* (1924) and W. L. Knox, *The Acts of the Apostles* (1948).

[13] See D. W. Riddle in *The Study of the Bible Today and Tomorrow,* ed. by H. R. Willoughby, p. 322.

Acts is relegated to a distinctly lower position than Paul's letters.

Harmonization is often a difficult and thankless task. Just now it is distinctly out of favor, even though H. J. Cadbury has suggested a new Paley to replace the old *Horae Paulinae,* constructed in the light of certain new positions regarding the epistles of Paul.[14] But it should be kept in mind that on the central issue of Paul's relation to the apostles and the Jerusalem church Luke is careful to show even as Paul himself does, especially in Galatians, that Paul did his best to keep in touch with the mother church, visiting it on a number of occasions. That there are differences in the viewpoint from which these visits are described in the two sources is obvious.

One of the most distinctive contributions to the criticism of the Acts has been made by Martin Dibelius, especially in his *Aufsätze zur Apostelgeschichte,* a series of essays gathered together and published in 1951, which appeared in English dress in 1956 under the title *Studies in the Acts of the Apostles.* The viewpoint is essentially the same as that which the author enunciated in *A Fresh Approach to the New Testament and Early Christian Literature* (1936). Speaking broadly, the materials of the Acts can be divided into two parts, which Dibelius calls tradition and composition. The former consists of information to which Luke fell heir and which he handles as best he can, adding summaries to piece it together. The composition element, however, is Luke's own special contribution, and it is to be found mainly in the speeches. Right here the form criticism approach that Dibelius employed in the study of the Gospels comes into play with reference to the Acts. The speeches are not to be understood as reports of what was actually spoken by various people in the early days of the church, but are Luke's own creations, by which he manages to preach to the people of his own time toward the end of the first century. So Luke turns out to be more of a theologian and a preacher than a historian. The speeches are introduced not for the sake of the supposed audience at the time cited in the Acts, but for the sake of the readers of the book.

In this construction, Dibelius counts heavily on the supposed influence of Greek historiography on Luke the Greek. This tradition goes back to Thucydides, who confessed to the difficulty of reproducing speeches word for word and consequently allowed himself the liberty of making speakers say what in his

[14] *The Book of Acts in History* (1955), p. 123.

opinion they should have said on a given occasion, "adhering as closely as possible to the general sense of what they really said."[15] Dibelius assumes that Luke stood in this tradition and therefore composed the speeches in terms of what should have been said, though he grants that the missionary sermon had no counterpart among the Greeks. His position has been criticized by Bertil Gärtner in several respects.[16] The speeches in the Acts are brief and not stylistically elaborated as are the Greek models. Most important of all, there is reason to think that Luke has been more influenced by the pattern of history writing in the Old Testament than among the Greeks. In the Hebrew setting, "historiography becomes a divine interpretation of the course of events."[17] It is this religious view of history that is basic to the understanding of Luke's contribution. The speeches are homogeneous with divine revelation in Christ and the growing understanding of that revelation as reflected in the church's faith and evangelism. They are not artificial, nor can they be successfully sundered from their proper matrix in the first few decades of the church's life.

Gärtner devotes the greater•part of his book to a discussion of the Areopagus speech and finds himself obliged to differ radically from Dibelius, who sees its fabric made up of Stoic natural theology. Careful study of the speech reveals, on the contrary, that its ideas and terms are truly Pauline.[18]

Beyond question the speeches are decisive for forming a conclusion about the trustworthiness of the Acts. Any verdict on them ought to include the evidence both of similarity and diversity — similarity because of agreement on the *kerygma,* diversity because of the setting, whether Jewish or Gentile, and because of the individual approach of the speaker. It is instructive, for example, that Peter should include references to the earthly ministry of Jesus (10:38-41), whereas Paul is virtually silent about this, moving from Old Testament prophecy to fulfillment in the redemptive acts of Jesus (cf. chap. 13). The difference is attributable to the varying backgrounds of the two men. Again, it is no doubt significant that Paul should preach justification (13:39), in view of the prevalence of this theme in his epistles. It is hard to suppose that Luke injected this to give a Pauline

[15] *History of the Peloponnesian War.* I. xxvi. 1.
[16] *The Areopagus Speech and Natural Revelation* (1955).
[17] *Ibid.,* p. 9.
[18] Other helpful material on Paul's Athenian address is available in F. F. Bruce, *The Speeches in Acts,* pp. 13-18, and in N. B. Stonehouse, *Paul Before the Areopagus,* chap. I.

touch. If that were the case, one would expect to find it coming out in other connections as well.

H. J. Cadbury's work, *The Book of Acts in History,* aims to study "the relation of the Book of Acts to its wider contemporary environment," and "to illustrate the Book of Acts from contemporary history." The four strands that are investigated are the Greek, the Roman, the Jewish, and the Christian elements. It is shown that sometimes these components lie imbedded together in a passage. The author undertakes to place Luke's work in its historical and cultural milieu.

Although there has been a tendency to minimize the historical aspect of Luke's work in favor of emphasizing his theology, due mainly to the work of Dibelius and Conzelmann, the neglect of Luke the historian has not been total. Most notable is the contribution of A. N. Sherwin-White. His conclusions closely parallel those of Ramsay at an earlier period. Acts reflects the conditions of the first century rather than those of the second, and sometimes the author reveals a detailed knowledge that only contemporary information could readily provide. Especially informative are the chapters on Roman citizenship and on Paul's relations with Felix and Festus. Sherwin-White's general conclusion is strongly stated: "For Acts the confirmation of historicity is overwhelming. Yet Acts is, in simple terms and judged externally, no less of a propaganda narrative than the Gospels, liable to similar distortions. But any attempt to reject its basic historicity even in matters of detail must now appear absurd. Roman historians have long taken it for granted."[19]

Making use of Sherwin-White's researches and endorsing them, R. P. C. Hanson comments, "This accumulation of facts, then, suggests very strongly that in the author of Acts we are dealing with somebody who lived during the first century, and not the second; but more than this, that parts at least of his narrative correspond closely to a particular period of history, roughly from A.D. 41 to 70, which may even be limited to the end of Claudius' reign and the beginning of Nero's. It seems likely that he has some close connexion with that period, either of sources or of personal experience; we are driven by the facts of the case to this conclusion."[20]

A further observation comes from the pen of W. Den Boer. "St. Luke, who is rarely included among the historians, portrays

[19] *Roman Society and Roman Law in the New Testament,* p. 189.
[20] *The Acts (The New Clarendon Bible),* p. 11.

249

the life of the first Christians for us more as history than does Eusebius with the history of the first centuries."[21]

Turning to the thought of Luke, it will not be necessary to restate the view of Conzelmann, already considered under Luke's Gospel, but it should be noted that a few scholars are insisting that Luke's theology is not that of early Christianity but rather that of primitive Catholicism.[22] But there is much which looks the other way. Conzelmann writes, "The following, among other considerations, are definite marks of early Catholicism: the understanding of the church as an institution of salvation, an institutional definition of the ecclesiastical office (priesthood) and the sacraments, tying the Spirit to the institution and making the tradition secure through apostolic succession. All these features are lacking in Luke or can be found only in initial traces. Above all, the idea of succession is totally absent."[23]

In his book *The Theology of Acts in Its Historical Setting* (1961) J. C. O'Neill seeks to establish the thesis that "Luke and Justin Martyr held common theological positions without being dependent on each other." This means that he is prepared to date Acts between A.D. 115 and 130. Such a dating does not fit with the numerous data emphasized by Ramsay and Sherwin-White as pointing to a first-century locus, nor is it compatible with the absence of any reference in Acts that indicates a knowledge of Paul's letters which must have been current by the first quarter of the second century.

Charles H. Talbert sees in Luke-Acts a defense against Gnosticism.[24] Various data are adduced which can indeed fit an anti-Gnostic pattern, but if Luke was really concerned to combat this menace it is strange that he does not identify the heresy or make his target clear as is done, for example, in the Johannine writings. To condemn something by being careful to say nothing about it is strange procedure.

On the question of sources employed by Luke, Jacques Dupont is obliged to say, "Despite the most careful and detailed research, it has not been possible to define any of the sources used by the author of Acts in a way which will meet with widespread agreement . . . he is not satisfied with transcribing

21 "Some Remarks on the Beginnings of Christian Historiography," *Studia Patristica*, Vol. IV, p. 361.

22 H. Käsemann, *New Testament Questions of Today*, p. 22; P. Vielhauer, "On the 'Paulinism' of Acts," in *Studies in Luke-Acts*, ed. by Keck and Martyn, p. 49.

23 "Luke's Place in the Development of Early Christianity," in *Studies in Luke-Acts*, ed. by Keck and Martyn, p. 304.

24 *Luke and the Gnostics* (1966).

his sources, he rewrites the text by putting the imprint of his vocabulary and his style everywhere."[25]

One of the more fruitful avenues of study in the future will likely be in the area of patient and detailed comparison of the Gospel of Luke with Acts. An example of this type of research is supplied by Floyd W. Filson, who is able to show that the journey motif is a prominent feature of both phases of Luke's work.[26]

BIBLIOGRAPHY

Barrett, C. K., *Luke the Historian in Recent Study*. Philadelphia: Fortress Press, 1970.

Bruce, F. F., *The Acts of the Apostles*. Grand Rapids: Eerdmans, 1951.

——————, *Commentary on the Book of Acts*. Grand Rapids: Eerdmans, 1954.

Burkitt, F. C., *Christian Beginnings*. London: Univ. of London Press, 1924.

Cadbury, H. J., *The Book of Acts in History*. New York: Harper & Bros., 1955.

Clark, A. C., *The Acts of the Apostles*. Oxford: Clarendon Press, 1933.

Dibelius, Martin, *Studies in the Acts of the Apostles*. New York: Chas. Scribner's Sons, 1956.

Dodd, C. H., *The Apostolic Preaching and Its Developments*. London: Hodder & Stoughton, 1936.

Dupont, Jacques, *The Sources of the Acts*. New York: Herder and Herder, 1964.

Easton, B. S., *Early Christianity*. London: SPCK, 1955.

Gasque, W. Ward, and Martin, Ralph P. (edd.), *Apostolic History and the Gospel*. Grand Rapids: Eerdmans, 1970.

Goguel, Maurice, *The Birth of Christianity*. New York: Macmillan, 1954.

——————, *The Primitive Church*. London: Allen and Unwin, 1964.

Haenchen, Ernst, *Die Apostelgeschichte*. Göttingen: Vandenhoeck & Ruprecht, 1956.

Hanson, R. P. C., *The Acts, The New Clarendon Bible*. Oxford: The Clarendon Press, 1967.

Harnack, A., *The Acts of the Apostles*. London: Williams and Norgate, 1909.

——————, *The Date of the Acts and of the Synoptic Gospels*. London: Williams & Norgate, 1911.

[25] *The Sources of the Acts,* p. 166.
[26] "The Journey Motif in Luke-Acts," *Apostolic History and the Gospel,* ed. by Gasque and Martin, pp. 68-77.

Jackson, F. J. Foakes, and Lake, Kirsopp, (edd.), *The Beginnings of Christianity*. 5 vols. London: Macmillan, 1922-33.

Keck, Leander E., and Martyn, J. Louis, *Studies in Luke-Acts*. Nashville: Abingdon, 1966.

Knox, W. L., *The Acts of the Apostles*. Cambridge Univ. Press, 1948.

Meyer, Eduard, *Ursprung und Anfänge des Christentums*, 3 vols. Stuttgart and Berlin: J. G. Cotta, 1923.

Munck, Johannes, *The Acts of the Apostles, The Anchor Bible*. Garden City, N.Y.: Doubleday, 1967.

O'Neill, J. C., *The Theology of Acts in Its Historical Setting*. London: S.P.C.K., 1961.

Rackham, R. B., *The Acts of the Apostles, WC*. London: Methuen, 1901.

Ramsay, W. M., *St. Paul the Traveler and the Roman Citizen*. New York: G. P. Putnam's Sons, 1896.

Ropes, J. H., *The Apostolic Age*. New York: Chas. Scribner's Sons, 1906.

Schlatter, A., *The Church in the New Testament Period*. London: SPCK, 1955.

Sherwin-White, A. N., *Roman Society and Roman Law in the New Testament*. Oxford: The Clarendon Press, 1963.

Talbert, Charles H., *Luke and the Gnostics*. Nashville: Abingdon, 1966.

Weiss, Johannes, *Das Urchristentum*. Göttingen: Vandenhoeck & Ruprecht, 1917 (Eng. tr., *Earliest Christianity*, 2 vols. New York: Harper & Bros., 1959).

Williams, C. S. C., *A Commentary on the Acts of the Apostles*. New York: Harper & Bros., 1958.

Chapter Eleven

INTRODUCTION TO THE EPISTLES

OF THE 27 BOOKS THAT COMPRISE THE NEW TESTAMENT, 21 are epistles. Even the Book of Revelation, though in substance an apocalypse, has epistolary features, as may be seen from the address (1:4), followed by the letters to the seven churches, and from the conclusion (22:21).

By way of contrast, not a single epistle is found among the Old Testament canonical books. References to the writing of letters are plentiful enough. David, for example, wrote to Joab, giving him instructions concerning Uriah the Hittite (II Sam. 11:14). This situation reflects a setting common to all letters, for they are necessitated by the obstacle that distance places in the way of desired communication between two people or parties. Jeremiah wrote a letter to his countrymen in the Babylonian exile, a testimony to the divided condition of the nation (Jer. 29). It was this very document, no doubt, that inspired the so-called *Letter of Jeremiah* in the early part of the hellenistic age. A more famous writing is the *Letter of Aristeas* that purports to recount the circumstances surrounding the making of the Septuagint.

In the period of the early church it was the spread of the gospel to widely separated localities and the necessity of keeping

in touch with the congregations established there that called
forth epistles from the leaders of the church. Goodspeed remarks,
"The letter of Christian instruction was in fact almost as distinctive a Christian contribution to literary types as the written
gospel."[1]

Ordinarily four persons or parties were involved in the whole
process of communication by letter, namely, the author, the
secretary, the messenger, and the recipient. A letter written with
the author's hand was especially prized. A. Deissmann remarks
on this in connection with a letter written by a marine serving
with the Roman military to his father in Egypt. In it the son
expresses a desire to do obeisance to his father's hand, which
may well be an indirect request for a letter in the father's own
handwriting — an intimate touch from home.[2] It is likely that
the author of Third John wrote the letter himself, judging from
verse 13. Paul wrote Galatians 6:11 to the end in his own hand,
according to his testimony. Whether he wrote a complete epistle
in this fashion is difficult to say. It is likely that his habit was
to use a secretary, then append his own signature (cf. II Thess.
3:17; I Cor. 16:21; Col. 4:18).

Occasional examples of the first person plural in Paul's writings pose a problem. Are these to be treated as genuine plurals
pointing to the inclusion of others along with Paul, or are they
instances of the editorial plural? We can probably do no better
than conclude with Karl Dick that there is nothing that will
serve as an overall principle of guidance. Each case has to be
studied and decided on its own merits.[3]

Secretaries or notaries public were widely employed in the
hellenistic period for letter writing, partly because of fairly common illiteracy or very limited education, partly because of the
inconvenience that people experienced in keeping writing materials
at hand in good condition. Shorthand was in use among the
Romans at least from the time of their occupation of Palestine,
and among the Greeks it goes back to a considerably earlier
time. By this means a secretary could take a letter by dictation,
write it up, then submit it to the employer for approval and
transmission. Even with this help, dictation was a slow process,
and this tended to pave the way for dictation merely in terms of
the general sense that the author wished to convey, so that an experienced secretary was counted on to fill out the letter in ap-

---

1 *The Formation of the New Testament*, p. 25.
2 *Light from the Ancient East*, 4th ed., p. 181, n. 14.
3 *Der schriftstellerische Plural bei Paulus* (1900).

propriate language.[4] This raises an important question for the study of the New Testament epistles. Did the authors extend freedom of this sort to their helpers? One safeguard against abuse is the fact that the writers of the epistles were not dependent upon public secretaries who were pagans. Rather, they were able to call upon the services of believers, who no doubt counted it a privilege to assist in this fashion (Rom. 16:22). Another check is furnished by the examination of the style of the document in question. If it bears marks of a conversational background such as a writer would employ who kept his readers in mind and thought of them as he spoke, we reasonably conclude that the substance is faithfully reproduced. In Paul's case the very fact that such a thing as a Pauline style is discernible, despite the use of different secretaries, gives assurance that the use of these helpers has not placed a barrier between the writer and the reader.

Messengers are mentioned in connection with the dispatch of several of the New Testament epistles. Such people, like the amanuenses, were Christians with a personal knowledge of the recipients of the letter. An imperial postal service had been introduced by Augustus, as indicated by Suetonius in his *Lives of the Caesars,*[5] but this was for official business rather than general use. It is apparent from Acts 15:32 that the messenger could be expected to reinforce the message by his own word. Paul's habit was to commit certain personal items to the courier so as not to clutter up the letter with such matters (Eph. 6:21; Col. 4:7).

Recipients could be individuals (Timothy, Titus, Philemon) or a local church (Philippians) or a group of churches (Galatians) or Christians in a wider area (I Peter). Sometimes the communication is so general as to bear no address (I John). The situation in connection with Philemon is somewhat unique in that the address is both to the individual and to the church of which he is a part.

THE FORM OF THE LETTERS

One of the benefits that archaeology has conferred upon New Testament study is the unearthing of numerous papyrus letters, most of them from Egypt, some of them contemporaneous with the age of Christian beginnings. A comparison of these documents from everyday life, whether of a personal or business

[4] Otto Roller, *Das Formular der paulinischen Briefe,* p. 18.
[5] *Augustus,* xlix.

nature, with the letters of the New Testament shows certain similarities. The opening sentence has this pattern: A to B, greeting (χαίρειν), as in James 1:1. Then follows the main body of the letter in which the business in hand is stated. Toward the end greetings are in order, though they are not always included. Then comes a word of farewell (ἔρρωσο, cf. Acts 15: 29) or εὐτύχει, "be prosperous" (not found in the New Testament). The principal differences between the New Testament letters and those from daily life appear at the beginning and the end, where grace, peace, and occasionally other terms replace the secular type of greeting. It is a matter of interest that grace is from the same root as the secular word for greeting. Peace, of course, was the standard form used among the Hebrews (I Sam. 25:6). Paul's letters ordinarily contain a few words of thanksgiving for the readers, placed after the greeting.

EPISTLE OR LETTER?

One result of the study of the letters of the papyri has been the raising of the question as to the proper designation of the New Testament epistles. A. Deissmann has written vigorously and at some length on this issue.[6] His contention is that even though the letter and the epistle may be similar in form, they represent two distinct types of writing. Whereas the epistle is a conscious literary effort designed for publication, the letter is private in character, written for a specific occasion and certainly not designed for posterity. It matters not that a letter may be written to a whole church rather than an individual. If it has the marks of a letter, it is not properly an epistle. Deissmann is obliged to grant that Paul's letters are not uniform, Philemon and II Corinthians being the most personal, Romans the least so. Yet even Romans is not a treatise or essay. Most of the Catholic Epistles, on the other hand, are properly designated epistles rather than letters. James may be taken as an illustration. From its very address it is plain that it must have required multiplication in order to reach its intended readers.

Deissmann has made his point and made it well. At the same time he has shown himself reluctant to admit literary elements in the writings of Paul, and for this has been criticized by Sir William Ramsay.[7] The impression of Paul as an artisan who writes with difficulty, as set forth by Deissmann, is somewhat

---

[6] *Bible Studies*, pp. 1-59; *Paul*, pp. 1-26; "Epistolary Literature" in *EB*. v. i.; *Light from the Ancient East*, pp. 1-251.
[7] *The Teaching of Paul in Terms of the Present Day*, pp. 412-47.

less than convincing. In the judgment of J. Weiss, Paul's letters are not creations of the moment, dashed off in a hurry, but have behind them much careful thought. Time was required to compose them. They differ, therefore, from the improvisations that constitute an ordinary letter.[8] In a true sense they are the works of an artist. Who can fail to see that the apostle could have handled his business with Philemon over Onesimus in half the space if he had been content with mere statement of fact and formal request? But if he had chosen to write in this fashion, the charm of the letter, which consists in its delicacy and pathos, would be lacking.

In emphasizing the occasional character of the letters, Deissmann is technically correct in asserting that the apostle did not consciously write for later generations, but he does not seem to sense the importance of apostolic authority as making the letter normative for other times and places, nor does he do sufficient justice to the use of a letter in another congregation after it has served its purpose among the original circle of readers (Col. 4: 16). Furthermore, even though the writers thought only in terms of meeting the needs of Christians in their own time, in the providence of God they so wrote that their work has abiding value and authority for the church universal. Full justice should be done to both the human and divine factors. Paul's writings are timeless because they have Christ for their central theme. This lifts them immeasurably above the letters from everyday life.

In passing it is worth observing that a letter is less susceptible to forgery than an epistle. Whereas the latter has little or no circumstantial coloring reflecting a certain historical situation, the former abounds in it. The very things that create difficulties for the modern student of II Corinthians, for the reason that he cannot be sure at times what the writer is referring to, though obviously the original readers knew, are sure marks of genuineness. Another good example is in II Thessalonians 2:5-6.

Perhaps more than is usually supposed, Paul's letters were written in response to missives sent to him by various churches. It is recognized that much of the material in I Corinthians is in reply to a letter from his friends in Corinth (7:1ff.). The RSV has made an effort to set before the reader, by the device of quotation marks, the words and phrases that seem to be reproduced by the apostle from such a letter (cf. I Cor. 8:1-5). J.

---

[8] *Das Urchristentum,* pp. 309-10 (Eng. tr., *Earliest Christianity,* II, 408).

Rendel Harris has made out a plausible case for the view that I Thessalonians, Colossians, and Philippians have back of them written communications from these churches.[9]

THE NEW TESTAMENT LETTERS
AND THE CHRISTIAN DIDACHE

One of the most important aspects of the life of the early church was its instruction of converts, the setting forth of Christian duties for the members of the body of Christ. This is the chief burden of the letters, though the doctrinal foundation on which the teaching rests is not neglected. It is emphasized ever and again that believers are partakers of something new, that they have nothing to do with the old manner of life from which they have been redeemed. Theirs is a holy calling. Certain specific duties and responsibilities pertain to the saints by reason of their position in the home or society, and these are outlined in the *Haustafeln* passages (e.g., Eph. 5:21-6:9), so called because they deal with the various groups that constitute the household — husbands, wives, children, masters, servants. Other passages deal with mutual Christian relationships in the larger context of the church as a whole, stressing love and helpfulness. Then the believer is instructed how he should walk with respect to the outside world represented by society and the state. To crown it all, he is reminded that he is a pilgrim, that his real home is in heaven, and that he must be alertly watchful for the coming of the Lord.

The similarity in the wording of these injunctions as they appear in various epistolary writers suggests that there is a common source for the teaching in the oral instruction of the church. This is more probable than the theory of literary dependence. The homogeneity of the teaching may be explained partly from the Old Testament background where certain well-known requirements are laid down for Gentiles seeking admission to the congregation of Israel, partly from the teaching of Christ as treasured in the memory of the apostles, and partly from the authoritative guidance furnished to the church by the apostles themselves as they faced the problems of the Christian community in its growth and development.[10]

[9] *The Expositor*, 5th series, VIII (1898), 401-410.
[10] For a fuller discussion, see Philip Carrington, *The Primitive Christian Catechism*; E. G. Selwyn, *Commentary on First Peter* (Essay II and appended note); E. F. Harrison, "Some Patterns of the NT Didache," *BS* 119 (April 1962), 118-28.

CLASSIFICATION OF THE EPISTLES

Paul's writings constitute the largest group, and these divide chronologically into the Eschatological, which belong to the second missionary journey (I, II Thessalonians); the Soteriological, written during the third missionary journey (Galatians, I and II Corinthians, Romans); the Imprisonment or Ecclesiological emanating from the first Roman imprisonment (Ephesians, Colossians, Philemon, Philippians); and the Pastoral (I Timothy and Titus during a period of release, II Timothy from the second Roman imprisonment). This is the traditional position, which will have to be assessed in the light of critical revision. The Tübingen school was willing to concede only the *Hauptbriefe* to Paul, that is, the four leading doctrinal epistles — Galatians, I and II Corinthians, and Romans. Since the time of Baur a more sober criticism has restored others to Paul, so that the only group that is challenged is the Pastorals, although two or three other individual letters have failed to gain universal acceptance.

The second group is known as the General or Catholic Epistles. This designation is not entirely felicitous, especially in the case of Hebrews, II and III John, which have a localized destination. Hebrews and James have a definitely Jewish cast, which is shared to a lesser degree by I and II Peter and Jude.

BIBLIOGRAPHY

Bruce, F. F., "The Epistles of Paul" in *Peake's Commentary on the Bible*. London: Nelson, 1962, pp. 927-939.

Eschlimann, J. A., "La rédaction des Épîtres pauliniennes d'après une comparaison avec les lettres profanes de son temps," in *RB*, 53, 1946, 185-196.

Meecham, Henry G., *Light from Ancient Letters*. London: Allen and Unwin, 1923.

Rigaux, B., *Saint Paul et ses lettres*. Paris: Desclée de Brouwer, 1962, pp. 165-199.

Roller, Otto, *Das Formular der paulinischen Briefe*. Stuttgart: W. Kohlhammer, 1933.

Seitz, O. J. F., "Letter" in *IDB*. New York: Abingdon, 1962.

Wikenhauser, Alfred, *New Testament Introduction*. New York: Herder and Herder, 1958, pp. 346-351.

Chapter Twelve

THE THESSALONIAN EPISTLES

ESTABLISHMENT OF THE CHURCH

PAUL'S SECOND MISSIONARY JOURNEY TOOK HIM AND HIS COM-panions, Silas, Timothy, and Luke, onto European territory for the first time. After a limited stay at Philippi and the gathering of a few converts with whom Luke remained as shepherd, the missionaries pushed westward along the Egnatian Way, a famous Roman road that stretched across Macedonia between Philippi in the East and Dyrrhachium in the West on the Adriatic Sea. Amphipolis and then Apollonia made convenient overnight stopping places en route. But the real objective was Thessalonica, an important center at the head of the Thermaic Gulf. Named for the stepsister of Alexander the Great, this city may have had as many as 200,000 people in Paul's day. Its modern designation, Salonika, reflects the ancient name. When Macedonia was organized as a Roman province in 146 B.C., the city was made the seat of government and was fondly called "the mother of all Macedon." It looked like a strategic location for a church (I Thess. 1:8).

Well situated for trade, Thessalonica attracted a community of Jews, which Luke notices by his reference to the synagogue (Acts 17:1). Paul was given opportunity to speak on three

260

Sabbaths and followed his usual procedure with a Jewish audience, expounding the Old Testament prophetic announcements and their fulfillment in Jesus of Nazareth (Acts 17:2-3; cf. Acts 13). The result was typical also, in that Jewish believers were outnumbered by the God-fearing Greeks who had been attending the synagogue out of attachment to Judaism. Special mention is made also of prominent women converts. Resentment over the apostle's success in drawing away such a large company flared in the form of a riot inspired by the Jews. Unsuccessful in locating Paul at the home of a disciple named Jason, the mob dragged this man before the rulers of the city, blaming him for sheltering the missionaries but crying out much more vociferously against his guests who had eluded them. The complaint was that they were upsetting society wherever they went, and more specifically, were opposing the decrees of Caesar by alleging that there was another king, even Jesus. This was a charge of treason. It probably stemmed from Paul's synagogue preaching to the effect that Jesus was the Messiah, the Davidic king promised to the Jewish people. This was now being twisted into a claim of political competition. Jesus' kingship fits well with the truth of his return, which attains prominence in Paul's letters to this church.

The authorities took a pledge from Jason and other believers, which may have meant a commitment to send Paul and his companions away (which happened immediately), or a general guarantee that nothing would be done to incite further trouble in the city by preaching of the kind that had led to this violence. That Jason pledged the permanent absence of Paul from the city is not likely, in view of the apostle's attempt to return on more than one occasion (I Thess. 2:18).

It has seemed improbable to some students that Paul could have gathered so many converts after a period of only three Sabbaths in the synagogue, unless indeed he had a strong ministry during the week in the market place. About this Luke has nothing to report. J. B. Lightfoot surmised that a period of labor followed the three Sabbaths of synagogue testimony, and that it was a time of special ingathering among the Gentiles.[1] He concluded this from three elements in the situation: (1) the large number of Gentile converts reported by Luke and confirmed by the correspondence (I Thess. 1:9); (2) the fact that Paul engaged in manual labor during this period, as though he settled there for a time (II Thess. 3:8); (3) the notice in Philippians

---

[1] *Biblical Essays*, p. 259, n. 6.

4:16 that he received financial aid more than once from his Philippian friends while he was at Thessalonica. The third consideration is the most decisive in favor of a longer stay.

FIRST THESSALONIANS

BACKGROUND

On leaving the city, Paul had a brief ministry in Beroea and Athens, and was joined in the latter place by Silas and Timothy. But they did not remain long with him, for Paul sent them back into Macedonia on separate missions, Timothy to Thessalonica (I Thess. 3:2) and Silas probably to Philippi. Both men rejoined the apostle in Corinth (Acts 18:5). Timothy's report was favorable, it seems, for Paul comments in the First Epistle on the growth and zeal of his converts. Nevertheless they needed counsel on several points. First, persecution had broken out, for which Paul may have felt in a measure responsible, since its first outbreak came during his ministry in Thessalonica. At any rate, he undertook to bring encouragement to his readers, commending them for fidelity in their trials (2:14; 3:1-4). Second, there was a current of criticism against Paul, probably set in motion by Jewish opposition, which not only found fault with the conduct of his ministry in Thessalonica but also, it seems, ventured to call in question his motives. This elicited from Paul a defense of his conduct (2:1-12). Third, the Christian standard of holiness required reiteration for the benefit of those who had so recently come out of paganism, where moral ideals were low (4:1-8). Fourth, the death of certain members of the congregation created concern for their welfare by loved ones and raised questions concerning their participation in the final salvation to be attained at the coming of the Lord. Paul sought to give instruction and comfort suitable to this situation (4:13-18). Fifth, a tendency to restlessness and inattention to daily tasks, which may have been due to an unhealthy attitude toward the return of Christ, needed rebuke (4:11). Sixth, there was some failure to understand the place of spiritual gifts and even a tendency to repress them (5:19).

The possibility that First Thessalonians was in part a reply to a letter from the church to Paul was suggested by J. Rendel Harris, as noted above, and has been more fully explored by Chalmer E. Faw.[2] The latter points out that the formula that

2 "On the Writing of First Thessalonians," *JBL*, 71 (Dec. 1952), 217-25.

occurs in 4:9 and 5:1 (cf. 4:13) is confined elsewhere in Paul to replies made concerning inquiries directed to him by letter (several passages in I Corinthians). The possibility for such a background for First Thessalonians may be admitted, but the obvious difference between this letter and First Corinthians is the lack of any mention of a letter. It would be almost a discourtesy on Paul's part to fail to mention such a communication if he had received it. Also, can we be certain that these matters that Paul introduces by this formula were not broached to him orally by Timothy? One of them, brotherly love, is hardly a subject that a church would inquire about, it seems. This would leave only one clear-cut instance (5:1), since 4:13 is not decisive.[3]

AUTHENTICITY

The authenticity of the epistle was challenged by F. C. Baur and later by the Dutch School that denied the Pauline authorship of all the books traditionally ascribed to him. The chief ground of objection to this epistle was the lack of doctrinal emphasis. "No dogmatic idea whatever is brought into prominence."[4] One wonders on what ground Baur excludes the Parousia from this category. Dogmatic teaching varies from epistle to epistle. Philippians, for example, has very little, and in this respect could be compared to First Thessalonians. Baur also complains of "want of originality." To him the injunctions of the letter are almost platitudes. He also finds the outburst against the Jews in 2:14-16 quite unlike the apostle. In his view some things in the letter are not in keeping with a newly established church, such as the claim that the faith of these converts had become known everywhere (1:8) and that their love had reached out to include all the brethren in Macedonia (4:9-10). The teaching on eschatology is regarded as taken from First Corinthians 15 and expanded and shaped by a later writer. This objection is especially vulnerable. Would such a writer make Paul expect the return of the Lord in his lifetime (4:15) when as a matter of fact the apostle was now dead? Objections such as these could hardly be expected to carry sufficient weight to upset the accepted view of authorship. The personality of Paul is clearly etched here, and the teaching is fully consonant with what a newly formed group of Gentile believers would need.

[3] See the discussion in B. Rigaux, *Les épîtres aux Thessaloniciens*, p. 56.
[4] F. C. Baur, *Paul, His Life and Works*, II, 85.

OUTLINE OF CONTENTS

The salutation and thanksgiving for the conversion and zeal of the Thessalonians (1:1-10) leads into a review and defense of Paul's ministry among them (2:1-12) and the effect of that ministry on the believers (2:13-16). The apostle discloses at length his affection and concern for his flock (2:17-3:10), and then turns to prayer on their behalf (3:11-13). A section devoted to instruction takes up in turn the necessity for holiness (4:1-8), brotherly love (4:9-10), orderly conduct (4:11-12), the comfort to be derived from the hope of the Lord's return (4:13-18), and the need of watchfulness and sobriety in view of his coming (5:1-11). After a series of brief exhortations (5:12-22), the epistle concludes with a prayer (5:23-24), final requests (5:25-27), and the benediction (5:28).

DATE

The time of writing can be fixed approximately, in that Paul's stay at Corinth coincided at least partially with the incumbency of Gallio as proconsul of Achaia, an event noted on the Delphi Inscription.[5] This inscription reproduces a letter to the city of Delphi from the emperor Claudius in which Gallio and his proconsulship are mentioned. Claudius refers to himself as invested with tribunician power for the twelfth time and acclaimed Imperator twenty-six times. Since the last-named honor came to him twenty-seven times, this letter must be dated close to the end of his reign. Further, the twenty-seventh occurrence must also be dated in the twelfth year of his tribunician power, which corresponded to the year A.D. 52. This fixes the presence of Gallio in Achaia by that year, but does not determine the time of his arrival. However, it is known that these officials began their official duties in the summer,[6] and since Gallio had already referred to Rome the matter dealt with in the inscription (now fragmentary), it seems that he must have taken office in the summer of 51. From the Acts it appears that Paul was brought before him shortly after his arrival, and that this was fairly close to the end of Paul's stay in the city. Since the Corinthian ministry was of eighteen months' duration (Acts 18:11), it likely began in the year 50. First Thessalonians can probably be assigned to this year, though some prefer 51.

---

[5] The text may be consulted in J. Finegan, *Light from the Ancient Past*, p. 282.
[6] Deissmann, *Paul*, p. 280.

On this dating, First Thessalonians is almost certainly the first of Paul's letters. The only serious competitor is Galatians, which would be earlier if it could be dated prior to the Apostolic Council. This question will be discussed in connection with the Galatian letter, but the probabilities favor the allocation of this highly doctrinal epistle to a later time than the Thessalonian correspondence.

SECOND THESSALONIANS

AUTHENTICITY

This cannot be questioned on the ground of external evidence, for the Canon of Muratori contains it, as does Marcion's canon at a still earlier time. Irenaeus makes specific reference to it. Internal considerations, however, have been relied on to prove it un-Pauline. Some of the more weighty of these will be examined briefly.

First, it is thought unlikely that the apostle could have written two letters with such marked similarities and within a short time of each other. The objection loses much of its force when the observation is made that at most the parallels are not more than a third of the total contents of these epistles and that they often occur in different connections, which is hardly what one would expect if an unknown writer were at work in the second letter, using I Thessalonians as a model.[7] Paul was not averse to saying the same thing more than once if he felt the situation needed it. He was no dilettante.

Second, the representation of the Lord's Return is too different from that contained in the first epistle to be from the same author. Instead of being set forth as an imminent event, it is said to follow two other future events, namely, the apostasy and the revelation of the man of lawlessness. It is certainly true that the teaching has a different cast, but this appears to have been dictated by the needs of the church. False notions about the Return (2:1-2) necessitated an orderly statement of the prophetic program in broad outline. In his exposition of these things the apostle indicates that the teaching is not really new to his readers, so he can hardly be accused of novelty (2:5). Actually, the first epistle mentions times and seasons (5:1) and this is agreeable to the handling of the theme in II Thessalonians 2:1ff.

Third, since the eschatological teaching of the apostle does

[7] George Milligan, *St. Paul's Epistles to the Thessalonians*, p. lxxxiii.

not elsewhere include the figure of the man of lawlessness (2:3), it has been concluded that Paul is not the author here. This has been presented in its sharpest form by those who see dependence on the Nero legend, which maintained that this emperor was not really dead, but would reappear in the East and assert his old power.[8] Some pretenders are said to have arisen to seek popular support on the basis of this expectation. If this is the background of chapter 2, clearly Paul could not have written the epistle, for its composition would have to be put later than his time. But this attempted tie-up between Paul's man of lawlessness and the Nero Redivivus tale is purely gratuitous.

Fourth, it is alleged that the tone of the two epistles is too different to permit the supposition that they have the same author. The first epistle is bright, warm and commendatory, whereas the second is far less intimate, even cold and sharp. The difference is there, but this does not rule out the hand of Paul in either case, any more than the difference in tone between the Corinthian letters is so damaging as to be decisive. It is certainly open to us to suppose that Paul was in sufficiently close touch with the situation in Thessalonica to know the conditions in the church and what was needed to meet them. One may perhaps point to the apostle's double description of himself, first as a nurse, then as a father (I Thess. 2:7, 11). In the first epistle we see the nurse's tenderness and in the second the father's discipline.

BACKGROUND

Neither in the letter itself nor in Luke's account of Paul's ministry at Corinth is there any explicit statement of a fresh contact between Paul and the Thessalonian Christians that might account for this second communication. But the apostle has been hearing of certain unsatisfactory conditions among some of the members (3:11) and has apparently learned of an attempt to promote a line of teaching about the Lord's Return through the use of a letter assertedly from him (2:2).

The latter was probably the chief incentive for the writing of the second letter, since the contents bear principally on the subject of the Lord's further coming. But Paul was desirous, apart from the pressure of such special circumstances, of keeping in close contact with his converts, who were young in the faith and needing his counsel, so he welcomed the opportunity to write again.

[8] *Ibid.*, p. 172. See also K. Lake, *The Earlier Epistles of St. Paul*, pp. 78-79.

OUTLINE OF CONTENTS

Paul begins on a note of encouragement, being thankful to God for the increase in faith and love among his readers, noting that this development has occurred in the midst of persecutions (1:3-4). He assures his friends that the position of persecutor and persecuted will be radically altered at the return of Christ, who will give rest to his afflicted saints and heavy punishment to those who have troubled them (1:5-10). This prepares the way for the main section of the letter, which deals with the Day of the Lord. The premonitory signs of this Day are the apostasy and the revelation of the man of lawlessness (2:3). In the providence of God a restraining influence now keeps this figure from the achievement of supreme and godless rule, that he may appear only at the divinely appointed time, and then to meet swift retribution at the hands of the returning Savior (2:8). Mingled thanksgiving and admonition (chiefly the latter) mark the remainder of the letter. Idle and meddlesome and recalcitrant characters are a detriment to the cause and must be disciplined (3:6-15). While they wait for the Savior, believers must be sober and diligent.

RELATIONSHIP TO THE FIRST EPISTLE

One approach to their comparative study emphasizes that the terminology of the second epistle is so steeped in the Old Testament, in contrast to the first epistle, as to suggest a different group of readers. Harnack advanced the notion that there were two separate bodies of believers at Thessalonica, one Gentile and the other Jewish, and that the first epistle went to the former group, the second to the latter. A hint of this condition was thought to be discernible in I Thessalonians 5:27, in Paul's injunction that his letter be read to all the holy brethren, as though there were others besides the original recipients. But this is a strained explanation. Both letters have the same address. The Jewishness of II Thessalonians should not be overstated, since the use of the Old Testament is confined to phraseology and does not extend to formal quotation. It is really unthinkable that Paul would countenance the formation of two groups of believers in the same city, the one Gentile and the other Jewish, which would be a virtual denial of Christian unity. It would be especially out of place after the momentous decision of the Apostolic Council, which tended to break down barriers between the two elements.

Another problem pertains to the chronological order of the two letters. Certain reputable scholars have come out for the position that II Thessalonians was written first.[9] They are able to point to the fact that references to the persecutions endured by the Thessalonians are in the present tense in the second epistle (1:4-7), whereas they are uniformly in the past tense in the first epistle (1:6; 2:14-15; 3:2-4). This does not establish the conclusion that sufferings were past entirely when Paul wrote the first epistle. Persecution may be expected at any time (3:3). In these sections, as in several others, the apostle is in a reminiscent mood as he writes, hence the accent on the past.

A second observation is to the effect that in contrast to the simplicity and immediacy of the second epistle, as something dashed off to meet an emergency, I Thessalonians is "a more deliberate and carefully thought out letter."[10] This is not a strong argument. Surely we should expect that the apostle would recall at some length the circumstances of the founding of the church and its early development in his first communication with the congregation rather than in a later one, and this is exactly what we find in the first epistle.

Third is the claim that the reference to Paul's autograph in II Thessalonians 3:17 has point only in the first letter of a correspondence, as though setting a pattern for which the church should be watchful in the future. It should be noted, however, that Paul did not include such an item in all his letters, and the rather obvious fitness for it in this case is the warning at an earlier point in the letter against accepting communications purporting to be from his hand but which were not (2:2).

In reversing the order of the two epistles, Manson conjectures that Paul sent Timothy from Athens with II Thessalonians. This has a certain awkwardness, since Timothy is joined with Paul and Silas in the address. And on this assumption it is hard to understand how Paul could have any precise knowledge of conditions in the church as a basis for writing unless Timothy had returned to Thessalonica from Beroea before rejoining Paul at Athens. The Acts contains no hint of this (see 17:14). It was in fact that very uncertainty about conditions in the church that led Paul to send Timothy back from Athens (I Thess. 3:1-3).

DATE

On the basis of the priority of I Thessalonians, the second epistle can safely be allocated to a time only a few months later. Silas and Timothy are still with the apostle.

---

9 One of the most recent is T. W. Manson, *Studies in the Gospels and Epistles*, pp. 268-78.

10 *Ibid.*, p. 270.

BIBLIOGRAPHY

Denney, James, *The Epistles to the Thessalonians, Expositor's Bible.* New York: A. C. Armstrong and Son, 1902.

Dibelius, Martin, *An die Thessalonicher I, II, HZNT.* 3rd ed., Tübingen: Mohr, 1837.

Eadie, John, *A Commentary on the Greek Text of the Epistles of Paul to the Thessalonians.* London: Macmillan, 1877.

Ellicott, C. J., *St. Paul's Epistles to the Thessalonians.* 3rd ed., London: Longmans, Green, 1866.

Frame, J. E., *A Critical and Exegetical Commentary on the Epistles of St. Paul to the Thessalonians, ICC.* New York: Chas. Scribner's Sons, 1912.

Hendriksen, William, *Exposition of I and II Thessalonians.* Grand Rapids: Baker Book House, 1955.

Lightfoot, J. B., *Notes on the Epistles of St. Paul.* London: Macmillan, 1895, pp. 1-136.

Milligan, George, *St. Paul's Epistles to the Thessalonians.* London: Macmillan, 1908.

Morris, Leon, *The Epistle of Paul to the Thessalonians, TBC.* Grand Rapids: Eerdmans, 1957.

————————, *The First and Second Epistles to the Thessalonians, NIC.* Grand Rapids: Eerdmans, 1959.

Neil, William, *The Epistles of Paul to the Thessalonians, MNTC.* London: Hodder & Stoughton, 1950.

Plummer, Alfred, *A Commentary on St. Paul's First Epistle to the Thessalonians.* London: Robert Scott, 1918.

————————, *A Commentary on St. Paul's Second Epistle to the Thessalonians.* London: Robert Scott, 1918.

Rigaux, B., *Les épîtres aux Thessaloniciens.* Paris: J. Gabalda, 1956.

Von Dobschütz, Ernst, *Die Thessalonicherbriefe*, Meyer series. Göttingen: Vandenhoeck & Ruprecht, 1909.

Chapter Thirteen

THE EPISTLE TO THE GALATIANS

AUTHENTICITY

SINCE NO DOUBT REGARDING PAULINE AUTHORSHIP IS ENTERtained today, this position may be assumed. Marcion placed Galatians first in his list of Paul's letters. F. C. Baur found support in Marcion's list for his own attitude toward the epistles, for he noted that the Pastorals were absent entirely and that, of the remainder, Galatians, I and II Corinthians and Romans occurred at the beginning, apparently as a group by themselves, with the Thessalonian letters coming next and Philippians last. This seemed to Baur to suggest two units, both arranged in chronological order. Baur called the second group deutero-Pauline and found reasons to reject them as unauthentic, retaining only the first four *Hauptbriefe* as unquestionably the work of Paul.[1]

BACKGROUND

Paul's converts in Galatia were in danger of losing their grip on the gospel of grace that he had taught them, because of the activities of certain men who were troubling them (1:7) and upsetting them (5:12). One man seems to have been a ringleader

---

[1] *Paul, His Life and Works,* I, 255-59.

270

(5:10). It is customary to describe these agitators as Judaizers, whose aim was to convince Gentile Christians that in addition to putting faith in Jesus as the Christ they must follow the same procedure as converts to Judaism, namely, to accept circumcision and observe the Mosaic law and the customs. In order to attack the gospel that Paul had proclaimed among these people, it was expedient to attack the legitimacy of his position as an apostle and to make it appear that he was inferior to the original apostles. For this reason Paul found it necessary to defend his apostleship as well as his gospel, to show that he had an independent call directly from the risen Lord and that he had his gospel from the same unimpeachable source. Further, he was able to demonstrate that when he did confer with members of the apostolate, he was found to be in agreement with them concerning the gospel.

Some students have seen evidence in 6:13 that some of the Gentile Christians were accepting circumcision and were becoming at least as avid in their efforts to win over other Gentile believers to the Judaizing cause as were the Jewish Christians who started the propaganda.

It is usually assumed that the agitators came from outside Galatia (cf. Acts 15:1), although nothing in the letter demands this conclusion.

The doctrinal portion of the epistle is designed to show that one is not justified by works of law but only through faith in Christ (2:16), that the law was not given for this purpose anyway, but to prepare the way for Christ's redemptive work (3:19), and that the Spirit who is given to believers produces such fair fruit as no fleshly attempt to keep the law can rival (5:22).

According to J. H. Ropes, following Lütgert, Paul was actually fighting on two fronts in this epistle, for he had not only to silence the Judaizers but also to rebuke the spiritual perfectionists who had taken Paul's doctrine of freedom from the law and had carried it to dangerous lengths, after the fashion of a similar group in the church at Corinth.[2] One does not get the impression, however, that Paul's teaching on the Spirit in this epistle is set forth as a polemic against a libertine tendency. The only unquestionable adversary is the Judaizing position.[3]

[2] "The Singular Problem of the Epistle to the Galatians" in *HTS*, XIV (1929).

[3] The statement in 5:15 is too indefinite to be cited as support for the existence of two distinct parties.

DESTINATION

The letter is addressed to the churches of Galatia (1:2). Unfortunately, the term Galatia is ambiguous. The name itself is due to the Gauls, a people of Celtic origin. In the fourth century B.C. a considerable number of them left their homeland in Gaul and migrated southward and eastward. For a time they harried Italy, then turned to the Grecian peninsula. Repulsed at Delphi in 279 B.C., they moved on, some of them to Thrace, others to north central Asia Minor, where three tribes of them settled in and around the three centers of Ancyra (modern Ankara), Pessinus, and Tavium. They were useful to the Romans in local wars and were allowed to expand their territory, especially southward. Finally, on the death of their leader Amyntas, their entire holdings were constituted the Roman province of Galatia in 25 B.C. Thus, at the time Paul wrote, Galatia might mean North Galatia, the territory occupied originally by the Gauls, or it might indicate the whole province and consequently include the South Galatian cities of Pisidian Antioch, Iconium, Lystra and Derbe, which Paul evangelized on his first missionary journey and visited on his second.

While the address of the epistle does not restrict the readers to either section of the province, the reference to Paul's sickness in 4:13 effectively does this. This affliction, whatever it was, brought Paul to the vicinity of the readers of the letter, presumably for recovery. Ramsay conjectured that the apostle contracted fever in the lowlands of Pamphylia during his first missionary journey (Acts 13) and sought relief by proceeding to the higher ground around Pisidian Antioch.

The problem of destination arises not only from the general character of the address in the letter, but also from the circumstance that Luke, in his account of Paul's missionary activity, does not use the noun Galatia. Instead, he states that Paul and his companions passed through the region of Phrygia and Galatia after having been in Derbe and Lystra (Acts 16:6). Later, according to his account, Paul passed through the same territory, which is described in reverse order (18:23). In both cases Galatia is an adjectival form.

The older view, argued by Lightfoot and still held predominantly by German scholars, favors North Galatia as the destination of the letter. The South Galatia theory, championed by Ramsay and others, has gained in popularity over the last several decades.

Certain things have been urged in favor of the North Galatian

272

theory. (1) Luke seems to use territorial rather than official (i.e., provincial) language in describing Paul's work. Thus he mentions Pisidia (13:14) and Lycaonia (14:6). The presumption is, therefore, that the same must be true when he mentions the apostle's journeys through the Galatian region, which came after he had left these communities in the South. (2) The grammar of 16:6 can only mean that the missionaries came into the Galatian region after they had attempted to go into Asia, and this was clearly after the visit to the southern cities, at any rate Derbe and Lystra, had been completed. It is argued also that 18:23 implies a tour through North Galatia before the undertaking of the Ephesian campaign. (3) In reporting Paul's work in the southern cities Luke has nothing to record about a sickness such as the apostle cites in Galatians 4:13, and his account at this point is quite detailed. (4) Conversely, whereas Luke records severe persecution, especially the stoning at Lystra, Paul has nothing to say in his letter about such experiences. (5) It is not conceivable that the apostle would address the people in the South as "Galatians" (3:1), for they would not consider themselves such and would only be offended by such an identification. Residence in Galatia did not make them Galatians in the ethnic sense.

On the other side, advocates of the South Galatian view advance certain claims in support of their position. (1) The language of Acts 16:6 is quite in keeping with their view if Luke's statement is understood as referring to Galatic Phrygia, that is, the portion of Phrygia that had been included in the Roman province of Galatia. Likewise, what is said of Paul's movements in Acts 18:23 does not imply a trip into North Galatia, but in the same general region as the journey of Acts 16:6. (2) It is much more likely that Paul would be writing to churches of which Luke has given a report than to churches about which we lack any explicit testimony as to their establishment. (3) Whereas the Lukan account mentions the confirming of disciples (18:23), it says nothing about the founding of churches, either here or in Acts 16:6. (4) It is known that the Galatian churches shared in the collection for the poor of the Jerusalem church (I Cor. 16:1), yet in the list of men who accompanied Paul to Jerusalem with the fund there is no representative from North Galatia, whereas two men, Gaius of Derbe and Timothy, both of South Galatia, are named (Acts 20:4). Since, however, some other churches lacked representatives, this is not decisive. (5) South Galatia was more accessible to the Judaizing propagandists than was North Galatia, especially if

273

they came from the South. (6) Barnabas is mentioned in Galatians 2:13, and he was Paul's companion in South Galatia, but not beyond this area. While it may be granted that the mere mention of his name settles nothing, since he is referred to in I Corinthians 9:6 even though we have no record of his presence at Corinth, yet the language "even Barnabas" (Gal. 2:13) suggests a disappointment over him that the readers would be able to understand because of personal contact with him. (7) If the order in which the readers of First Peter are addressed is also the order of evangelism, this means that North Galatia was evangelized from the north, by someone who took ship to Pontus and then proceeded overland in a southerly direction.

Not all the considerations given in support of the two views have equal weight. Some depend on possibilities rather than facts that can be certified, as for example, the problem of "Galatians" in direct address. Here such a passage as II Corinthians 9:2, 4 has been used as analogous by proponents of the South Galatian theory, but the matter is still strenuously debated.

Why should the question of destination receive so much attention? Partly for its own sake, to tidy up a loose end in biblical study, but also because it has a bearing on one's conception of Paul's objectives and procedures as a missionary. Ramsay was strong in his emphasis on the fact that the apostle moved in areas where Roman control was effective, where Roman communications were available, and where Graeco-Roman culture was exerting strong influence.[4] These conditions obtained in South Galatia to a far greater degree than in the northern section. There is still another reason for pursuing this question of destination. It has a bearing on the time at which the Galatian epistle was written. To this we turn next.

DATE AND PLACE OF WRITING

The proper starting point here is Paul's reference to a preaching of the gospel among the Galatians on two occasions (4:13). Although it is quite possible for τὸ πρότερον to mean simply "originally" or "formerly" (cf. I Tim. 1:13), there does not seem to be any need for it here at all if Paul preached on one visit only.

On the North Galatian theory the writing of the letter would be possible after Paul had settled at Ephesus (Acts 19:1), or could be placed after his departure from the city, when he was

---

[4] *The Church in the Roman Empire*, p. 9.

in Macedonia or even in Corinth, and thus any time from about A.D. 53 to 56. Lightfoot favored putting it fairly close to the writing of Romans because of the marked affinity between the two epistles.

On the South Galatian theory the epistle could have been written any time after the close of the first missionary journey, perhaps at Antioch or on the way to Jerusalem to attend the Apostolic Council, in which case "the brethren who are with me" (1:2) would be Paul's traveling companions. The reason such an early date (48-49) has been thought feasible is that on the first missionary journey Paul and Barnabas doubled back from Derbe to Pisidian Antioch, thus visiting the churches twice on the one journey (with the exception of Derbe). But it is doubtful that Paul would look at such a visit, following so closely on the first, as distinctly different and capable of separate mention. If this is correct, the second visit would have to be identified with that mentioned in Acts 16:1ff., and Galatians must be placed sometime thereafter.

The solution of this problem depends upon another, namely, the identification of Paul's visits to Jerusalem as they are given in the Acts and in Galatians. It will be convenient to start with the testimony of Paul and then include the information found in the Acts. According to Galatians 1:18, Paul first went to Jerusalem following his conversion in order to see Peter. He was able to see James the Lord's brother also (1:19). There seems to be no reasonable room for doubt that this visit is the same as that to which Luke refers in Acts 9:26ff.

According to Galatians a second visit to Jerusalem occurred fourteen years after the first (2:1ff.). However, Acts records two visits in addition to that of 9:26ff. One is the so-called famine visit when Paul and Barnabas brought relief funds from the Antioch church (11:30), and the other is for the meeting of the Apostolic Council. So the problem is whether the visit in Galatians 2 is to be identified with the visit of Acts 11:30 or with the later one of Acts 15.

In favor of equating Galatians 2 with Acts 15, Lightfoot noted the following points: the geography is the same; the time is the same, or not inconsistent; the persons are the same, including the description of the agitators; the subject of dispute is the same; the character of the conference is in general the same; the result is the same.[5] The point of greatest difficulty with Light-

[5] *St. Paul's Epistle to the Galatians*, pp. 123-24.

foot's analysis is his assertion that the character of the conference in the two cases is in general the same, for the account
in the Acts pictures a general assembly in action, whereas
Paul's narrative deals with a private session between himself and
Barnabas on the one hand, and the Jerusalem leaders, James,
Cephas and John, on the other. Further, in the Acts account we
read of the formulation of the decrees to be sent to the Gentile
churches (Acts 15:29), of which nothing is said in Galatians 2.

To avoid these difficulties, the choice can be made in favor
of identifying Galatians 2 with Acts 11:30, the famine visit.
In this case we have a ready explanation for Paul's failure to
mention a general convocation. It had not yet taken place. In
the same way the failure to mention the decrees is accounted for.
Those who advocate this position frequently seek to support it
by pointing out that Paul committed himself to cite every contact with the Jerusalem church (Gal. 1:20). Therefore he could
not omit the famine visit. But it should be noted that contact with Jerusalem meant one thing only for Paul in the defense
of his apostleship. It meant contact with those who were
apostles before him (1:17). They were the accredited representatives of Christ, the men to whom, presumably, the Judaizers
appealed over against Paul. On the famine visit Paul probably
had no contact whatsoever with the apostles. Elders only are
mentioned (Acts 11:30). One may infer from what follows
immediately at the beginning of chapter 12 that it was not safe
for an apostle to be in Jerusalem. James the son of Zebedee
was killed and Peter was put in prison.

A possible point of contact between the two accounts is
the matter of relief for the poor, since Galatians 2:10 cites Paul's
agreement to remember them, at the insistence of the Jerusalem
apostles. In view of the use of the present tense in the verb
μνημονεύωμεν, it could be affirmed that the force of the sentence
is something like this: "You have manifested your concern for
our poor by your presence here with a gift, but do not go so
far away in your work among the Gentiles and become so pre-
occupied with them that you forget the needs of our people in
the future." This is a perfectly possible construction, but the
present tense may simply mean that Paul is to be ever mindful
of the needs of these people in the mother church, without
any side glance at the fact that he had just brought relief to
them. Olaf Moe thinks that it would have been a glaring example of poor taste for the Jerusalem leaders to bring such a

pointed reminder to Paul when he had just manifested his hearty interest by bringing a gift from Antioch.[6]

The effort to explain Paul's statement in Galatians 2:2 (that he went up to Jerusalem in accordance with revelation) as fitting in with the prophecy of Agabus (Acts 11:28) comes to nothing, for Paul would hardly use revelation for something communicated to him through another when throughout chapter 1 he has been using revelation only of that which came to him directly from the Lord (1:12, 15).

A real barrier to the identification of these visits is Paul's assertion that the Jerusalem apostles endorsed his call to minister among Gentiles and recognized his God-given success among them (Gal. 2:7-8). How could this have occurred on the famine visit, at a time when Paul had not yet commenced his missionary work?[7] It is doubtful that his brief teaching ministry at Antioch suffices to account for his words.

There is a chronological difficulty also. The opening words of Acts 12:1, "now about that time," serve to link the persecution under Herod and his death with the events of the previous chapter, and apparently with the famine visit in particular. The death of Herod is one of the few fixed dates of the apostolic age (A.D. 44). We know that the visit to which Paul refers in Galatians 2 came fourteen years after his first visit, which in turn was three years after his conversion. It is possible, but not likely, that the fourteen years are intended to refer back to the conversion. Subtracting 17 from 44, one gets the figure 27 as the date of Paul's conversion, which is too early. Even if one prefers the figure 14 the date of A.D. 30 is still too early. Granted that we have no way of knowing what the precise interval was between the famine visit and the death of Herod (possibly as much as two years), still the chronology throws its weight against the identification of Galatians 2 and Acts 11:30.

Furthermore, it is hard to see why there should be need for a second meeting and discussion of the problem of the reception of Gentiles into the church (Acts 15) if the matter had been settled at the top level on a previous visit (Acts 11; Gal. 2).

In view of the difficulties encountered in trying to fit the records of Paul and Luke into one another, it is not altogether surprising to find that some scholars hold that Acts 11 and Acts 15 are alike descriptions of the visit of Galatians 2 derived from different sources and therefore not the same in

[6] *The Apostle Paul*, I, 153.
[7] Donald Guthrie, *The Pauline Epistles*, p. 86.

their perspective.[8] But if this were true, grave doubt would be cast on Luke's ability as a historian.

T. W. Manson has advanced the opinion that the second visit in Galatians was followed by the first missionary journey, which brought Paul back to Antioch. Then and there occurred the episode related in Galatians 2:11-14, which in turn occasioned the Apostolic Council. He thinks that the issue of circumcision was not germane to that meeting, but that the question of table fellowship was, hence the formulation of the decrees. He thinks that the demand for circumcision of Gentile Christians, reported in Acts 15:1, 5, did not come until later, perhaps in connection with the visit noted in Acts 18:22.[9] This in itself is highly improbable. How could the issue have been so long delayed? Other features are unsatisfactory also.

Perhaps we should take a second look at the possibility of equating Galatians 2 and Acts 15. For one thing, it is well to note that the identification of the first visit (Acts 9; Gal. 1) is seldom if ever questioned, yet there are obvious differences in the accounts that the student may readily check for himself. This should prepare us to find difficulties at least equally as great in the more important subsequent visit mentioned by Paul. It may be possible to hold that Luke is interested in telling the story of the Apostolic Council as a landmark in the history of the church, playing up its public features, including the decrees, whereas Paul is solely concerned, in the very nature of his argument, with his apostolic office and his right to proclaim the gospel as it had been revealed to him. It may be that he does nevertheless pay his respects to the public gathering that took place in connection with that visit (the word "them" in Gal. 2:2) before going on to emphasize his private meeting with the leaders.

Based on the tentative identification of Galatians 2 and Acts 15 it is possible to hold that Paul wrote Galatians from Ephesus, where he spent the greater part of three years. A Macedonian situation might account better for a letter rather than a visit to Galatia, in view of the greater distance, but since the apostle was in the midst of an intensive campaign at Ephesus that was affecting the whole of the province of Asia, with daily meetings going on, he may have felt that he could not afford to leave this work and must content himself with a letter to the Galatian churches.

Little help can be gleaned as to the time from the word

8 See Kirsopp Lake in *Beginnings of Christianity,* V, 201.
9 *Studies in the Gospels and Epistles,* pp. 168-89.

278

"quickly" in 1:6. It may simply refer to the readiness with which the Galatians were succumbing to Judaizing propaganda. The point at which the propaganda commenced remains undetermined, hence the date should be left fluid. It may have been as early as 53, but a year or so later is possible.

OUTLINE OF CONTENTS

The introduction (1:1-9) anticipates the body of the epistle by stressing Paul's apostleship, his amazement at the apparent defection of the Galatians to a strange gospel, and his insistence that the message of the gospel must be preserved in its purity and preached in its simplicity.

Paul defends his apostleship (1:10-2:21) as based on God's sovereign and gracious intervention in his life (1:10-17) and as owing nothing to the teaching of the other apostles (1:18-24), but nevertheless freely acknowledged by them, as was his gospel (2:1-10). Paul even withstood Peter successfully when the latter erred in his conduct (2:11-21).

The main body of the epistle (3:1-4:31) is concerned with showing that the gospel is based on divine grace apart from works of the law. This was true in the initial experience of the Galatian believers (3:1-5), true also of Abraham (3:6-9). The law carries a curse (3:10-14) and cannot invalidate the earlier promise to Abraham and his seed (3:15-18). The law was given not in order to save but to let men know that they need a Savior (3:19-4:7). Therefore, why should believers put themselves under bondage to it (4:8-11)? A plea to return to the former cordial relations enjoyed by readers with the writer when he first preached the gospel to them (4:12-20) is followed by an allegorized account of Hagar and Sarah as representing the covenants of law and promise (4:21-31).

The final section (5:1-6:15) deals with the application of the gospel in terms of liberty (5:1-12), love (5:13-15), the fruit of the Spirit (5:16-26), helpful service (6:1-10) and separation from the world (6:11-15).

The conclusion (6:16-18) contains a prayer, a personal testimony, and a benediction.

CHARACTERISTICS

(1) The tone of the letter is noticeably sharp, especially in dealing with the Judaizers (e. g., 5:12), but also in rebuking the Galatians (4:20). (2) The absence of the usual thanksgiving at the beginning of the letter is closely connected with

this intensity of feeling and with the urgency to address the problem at hand and rescue the readers from the grip of error. (3) The apostle shows great versatility in his presentation, calling on Scripture, experience, logic, warning, exhortation and other devices to accomplish his end. (4) Next to Second Corinthians, this is the most autobiographical of Paul's letters. The reason for this is plain. In the first two chapters, where the personal element bulks largest, all the references to "the gospel" are also found. The apostle is citing his experience because of its bearing on the issues discussed in the letter as a whole. (5) The ending is unique. From 6:11 on the apostle writes with his own hand, using large letters, in order to impress the leading truths of the epistle the more firmly upon his readers in these closing lines. (6) This is the only epistle of Paul addressed to a group of churches.

No writing could better demonstrate how the creation of a certain moment can become a norm for all time. The issue that had to be decided was whether Christianity should be determined by Judaism or develop in terms of its own genius. More specifically, the question was the very continuance of the gospel in its simplicity and purity. Was more needed for admission to the church than faith in Christ and his finished work? This epistle answers eloquently, No!

It was this epistle that illumined the mind of Luther at the Reformation and enabled him to stand firmly on the principle of justification by faith alone.

We lack precise information about the effect of the epistle in meeting the Galatian crisis, but from I Corinthians 16:1 and possibly II Timothy 4:10 (where there is an alternative reading Gaul) it appears that the Judaizing error was rejected by the churches as a whole. The very preservation of the letter looks in the same direction.

BIBLIOGRAPHY

Buck, Charles H., Jr., "The Date of Galatians," *JBL*, LXX (June 1951), 113-122.

Burton, E. D., *A Critical and Exegetical Commentary on the Epistle to the Galatians, ICC*. New York: Chas. Scribner's Sons, 1920.

Duncan, G. S., *The Epistle of Paul to the Galatians, MNTC*. New York: Harper & Bros., 1938.

Eadie, John, *A Commentary on the Greek Text of the Epistle of Paul to the Galatians*. Edinburgh: T. & T. Clark, 1869.

Ellicott, C. J., *A Critical and Grammatical Commentary on St. Paul's Epistle to the Galatians.* 3rd. ed., London: Longmans, 1863.

Lagrange, M. J., *Epître aux Galates.* Paris: J. Gabalda, 1950.

Lake, K., *The Earlier Epistles of St. Paul.* London: Rivingtons, 1919, pp. 253-323.

Lietzmann, H., *An die Galater, HZNT,* 2nd ed., Tübingen: Mohr, 1923.

Lightfoot, J. B., *St Paul's Epistle to the Galatians.* London: Macmillan, 1896.

Munck, J., *Paul and the Salvation of Mankind.* Richmond: John Knox Press, 1959, pp. 87-134.

Oepke, A., *Der Brief des Paulus an die Galater, THZNT.* 2nd ed., Berlin: Evangelische Verlagsanstalt, 1957.

Ramsay, W. M., *A Historical Commentary on St. Paul's Epistle to the Galatians.* New York: G. P. Putnam's Sons, 1900.

Ridderbos, H. N., *The Epistle of Paul to the Churches of Galatia, NIC.* Grand Rapids: Eerdmans, 1953.

Ropes, J. H., *The Singular Problem of the Epistle to the Galatians.* Cambridge: Harvard Univ. Press, 1929.

Schlier, H., *Der Brief an die Galater,* Meyer series. 11th ed., Göttingen: Vandenhoeck & Ruprecht, 1951.

Zahn, T., *Der Brief des Paulus an die Galater.* 2nd ed., Leipzig: A. Deichert, 1907.

Chapter Fourteen

THE CORINTHIAN CORRESPONDENCE

THE CITY OF CORINTH

SITUATED ON A NARROW NECK OF LAND THAT CONNECTS THE Peloponnesus and northern Greece, this metropolitan center was the crossroads for travel and commerce both north and south and also east and west. With its two seaports, Cenchrea on the side of the Aegean and Lechaeum at the edge of the Gulf of Corinth to the west, it was so strategically located that after the Romans destroyed the city (146 B.C.) they found it necessary to re-build on the same location a century later. As a Roman colony, Corinth grew rapidly and had well over half a million people when Paul visited it in the course of his second missionary journey. It was the capital of Achaia at this time.

The city shared the common Greek love of philosophy and speculation, but in a derived rather than original sense. It could not boast of a single man of letters. Attention to commerce and the pleasures of life did not seem to mix well with intellectual pursuits. People came to Corinth for a good time. On the highest point in the city stood the temple of Aphrodite with its many hundreds of temple women who doubled as entertainers in the city's night life. Archaeologists have recovered some of their flutes. On the Isthmus stood the stadium where athletic contests were held every other year, second only in popularity to the Olympian Games (cf. I Cor. 9:24-27). Trade brought people of all kinds to Corinth. This mixed population, together with the prosperity of the place, fostered a licentious spirit that was notorious even in Greece. Here was "a city in which all the brutality of the west and all the sensuality of the east met and were rolled into one."[1]

FOUNDING OF THE CHURCH

It is understandable that Paul approached the challenge of such a city with some trepidation (I Cor. 2:3). Day by day he worked with his hands along with Aquila and Priscilla (Acts 18:3) and from Sabbath to Sabbath he presented the gospel in the synagogue. Silas and Timothy aided in the preaching after their arrival from the North (II Cor. 1:19). When opposition forced Paul to leave the synagogue he found a refuge nearby and continued to minister with considerable success among the Gentiles (Acts 18:8). Even so, the odds were heavily against him, and he seems to have needed divine encouragement, which was given in an unusual way (Acts 18:9). Ultimately the Jewish opposition brought him before Gallio the proconsul, where the apostle was vindicated, and was left free to continue his work for some time (Acts 18:18). Gallio's judgment seat has been excavated in recent years.[2]

The church probably represented a cross section of the local inhabitants. In the main they were not distinguished for learning or position (I Cor. 1:26ff.), although the very language of this passage suggests that there were exceptions such as Sosthenes (Acts 18:17; I Cor. 1:1) and Erastus (Rom. 16:23). A prominent man of this name is memorialized in stone.[3] He may well have been the Erastus of Scripture. Some of the converts had been deeply stained with sin (6:11).

PAUL'S RELATIONS WITH THE CHURCH

After a stay of eighteen months the apostle left for Ephesus, where he finally settled down for his longest ministry in one place (Acts 19). Little is known about his contacts with the Corinthian church during the greater part of this time. This was the period of Apollos' labor, and as long as matters went

[1] R. D. Shaw, *The Pauline Epistles,* 3rd ed., p. 130.
[2] *BA,* XIV (1951), 91-92.
[3] *Op. cit.,* p. 94. Oscar Broneer writes, "A re-used paving block preserves an inscription, stating that the pavement was laid at the expense of Erastus, who was *aedile* (Commissioner of Public Works)."

smoothly, there was no need for Paul's intervention. No doubt Apollos and Sosthenes kept him informed. But because of his position as founder of the church, Paul's help was sought in due time when problems arose. Those who belonged to Chloe reported a lack of harmony (I Cor. 1:11), and a letter was sent to Paul at Ephesus in which several questions were put to him by the church (I Cor. 7:1, 25; 8:1; 12:1; 16:1, 12). It may be that the three brethren mentioned in I Corinthians 16:17 brought the letter to him. These two contacts form the chief background for the writing of I Corinthians. In the epistle Paul promised a visit (4:19), which he hoped to make by way of Macedonia (16:5) but which he could not make until Pentecost (16:8).

A still earlier letter is alluded to in I Corinthians 5:9 in which he counselled the church not to fraternize with immoral persons. The congregation misunderstood him to mean immoral men of the community in general, an impression Paul corrects (vv. 10-11). It may be that the church deliberately misconstrued what Paul wrote, out of a spirit of indifference to moral considerations and a dislike for discipline.[4] Since Paul restated the matter clearly, there was no need to preserve this brief communication, which may have been destroyed. Because II Corinthians 6:14-7:1 seems related to this theme and intrudes itself rather awkwardly into the text of the second epistle, some have conjectured that this is the lost letter or part of it. What militates against this is the fact that the passage in II Corinthians warns against association with unbelievers rather than brethren who are guilty of wrong conduct.

Even as I Corinthians had a predecessor, so apparently did II Corinthians. It is often referred to as the "painful" letter. Paul describes it as written with many tears and anguish of heart (II Cor. 2:4) and so strong in its language that he regretted for a time that he had written it (II Cor. 7:8). The background for this letter is somewhat on the following order. When Paul wrote the first epistle, he berated the Corinthians in caustic language for their gross misinterpretation of what the Christian life demanded of them (I Cor. 4:8-13). He then promised to send Timothy and added a threat to come in person to deal with their lofty complacency. Doubtless the apostle sent Timothy with some misgiving as to his ability to handle the situation (I Cor. 16:10). Little came of this visit, and Timothy's report was far from encouraging. So Paul determined to leave

---

[4] *IB,* X, p. 6a.

his work at Ephesus and visit Corinth in person, since conditions were worsening. That he had a bitterly disappointing experience is plain from his statement in II Corinthians 2:1, "But I determined this with myself, that I would not come again to you in sorrow." It is evident that these words cannot apply to the visit during which Paul founded the church, so they must apply to a later one that preceded his last visit reported in Acts 20:2. There are other hints as well in II Corinthians pointing to this episode, since the final visit to the church is described in terms of coming a third time (12:14; 13:1-2).

It appears from II Corinthians 12:18 that Paul had entrusted the severe letter to Titus. Earlier in the book he recounts his stark anxiety at not finding Titus in Troas, from whom he expected a report on conditions at Corinth following the receipt of his communication. So pressed in spirit was the apostle that he found it impossible to carry on his work of evangelism, though the opportunity was there (2:12). Hurrying over to Macedonia he found Titus, and was greatly relieved to discover that a change had come over the congregation. The ringleader in the trouble had been dealt with, and the church was once more in rapport with the apostle and submissive to his authority (II Cor. 2:5ff.; 7:5-13).

Against this background Paul wrote II Corinthians, which reflects the trouble he has had with the church and also the joy of reconciliation. But some problems remain, so all is not rosy, as the closing chapters clearly intimate. Second Corinthians is designed to prepare the way for the final visit of Paul.

Of all the letters the apostle wrote to the Corinthians, the severe letter is the most obscure, since only its general character is indicated and nothing of its contents. A fairly common position in critical circles holds that this letter is not lost, but has been preserved in whole or in part in II Corinthians 10-13. The way has been prepared for this supposition by the observation that these closing chapters seem out of place in the sense that they are filled with criticism and invective, whereas the opening chapters are characterized by gratitude for restored relations and by affection for the Corinthians. This exchange of warmth for censure is regarded as a faulty approach psychologically, one which Paul would not have made, for by making it he would have risked destroying all the good will he had built up in the previous portion.[5]

[5] For a more complete statement see A. Plummer, *ICC,* on II Corinthians, p. XXX.

The most complete exposition of this point of view is found in J. H. Kennedy's work.[6] The high points are as follows. Neither II Corinthians 1-9 or 10-13 should be regarded as a complete letter. Rather, 1-9 is the beginning of one letter and 10-13 is the end of another. It is in 10-13 that we are to see the severe letter, though it is not fully preserved there.

This view is not free of objection. For one thing, to suppose such a state of affairs involves the charge of gross carelessness on the part of the Corinthians in thus mixing up the letters of the apostle or else of willful action that would accomplish nothing. One could understand the destruction of an uncomplimentary epistle much more readily than its preservation in wrong position. The manuscript tradition unanimously supports the integrity of II Corinthians. More serious, however, is the fact that chapters 10-13 are silent about the individual who had caused Paul so much embarrassment and grief, against whom he had demanded that disciplinary action be taken by the congregation. This individual is referred to in the early part of II Corinthians where the apostle is expressing gratitude for the compliance of the church and is asking a tempering of the punishment (2:5ff.; 7:11). Kennedy endeavored to meet this objection by supposing that the offender had been mentioned in the part of the severe letter that is not preserved in chapters 10-13. In the nature of the case this is only a possibility that cannot be verified.

Still greater doubt is cast on the theory when chapters 10-13 are carefully compared with Paul's brief observations about the nature of the severe letter, especially the word about its being composed with tears (II Cor. 2:4). As Allan Menzies notes with reference to chapters 10-13, "They are a fighting piece, in which stroke follows stroke too quickly to leave room for tears; they are full of the sense of power; whatever situation the Apostle imagines for himself, he is to come out of it with flying colours. It was certainly in no mood of humiliation or mental anguish — in no minor key — that he wrote these chapters."[7] Furthermore, the reader detects in these chapters what R. V. G. Tasker has aptly called a "playful strain" that hardly suits the atmosphere of a painful letter.[8]

One may still feel that there is considerable force in the plea of Plummer that the psychological approach is wrong if chapters

6 *The Second and Third Epistle of St. Paul to the Corinthians* (1900).
7 *The Second Epistle to the Corinthians*, p. XIX.
8 *The Second Epistle of Paul to the Corinthians*, TBC, p. 32.

10-13 are allowed to stand in their present position as an integral part of II Corinthians. However, this is eased somewhat when one notes that the epistle has three well-defined sections and that the mood in each reflects the perspectives of the apostle in the successive phases of his relations with the church. That is to say, chapters 1-7 look backward and reflect Paul's extreme anxiety and his relief through the good report of Titus; chapters 8-9 reflect the apostle's present position in Macedonia, with the satisfaction he feels in the generosity of the churches in that area and his renewed confidence in what the Corinthians will do to fulfill their obligations toward the fund for the Jerusalem church; chapters 10-13 reflect an aspect of Titus' report that is not dealt with in the first section, namely, that there is still some opposition at Corinth that the apostle must face on his arrival. Here he gives notice that he will deal with it in summary fashion. The nature of this opposition will be examined at a later point. It is unfortunate that discussions on chapters 10-13 often labor the sharpness of the language without keeping in focus the plaintive desire of the apostle to express his love toward the church (11:11; 12:14-15, 19). Both factors are present and should be given due weight. Not all is vitriolic abuse by any means.

As to what happened to the painful letter if it is not preserved in II Corinthians, the suggestion of Dibelius is as good as any, that after reconciliation between Paul and the church, this document may have been disposed of by mutual consent.[9]

FIRST CORINTHIANS

AUTHENTICITY

Attestation is earlier than for any other of Paul's letters. About A.D. 95 Clement of Rome wrote to the Corinthians in the name of the Roman church, and cited our epistle, for the reason that it had been occasioned by the existence of a factious spirit, a condition that still existed when Clement wrote and to which he makes reference. "Take up the epistle of the blessed Paul the Apostle. What did he first write to you at the beginning of his preaching? With true inspiration he charged you concerning himself and Cephas and Apollos, because even then you had made yourselves partisans" (Lake's translation).[10] The

---

[9] *A Fresh Approach to the New Testament and Early Christian Literature*, p. 154.
[10] *First Clement* xlvii.

language of Clement may help to explain the position accorded the epistle at the head of Paul's letters in the Canon of Muratori. No shadow of doubt rests on the reception of the letter by the ancient church, and this is practically the case with the modern church as well.

OUTLINE OF CONTENTS

Initial consideration is given to divisions that threaten the harmony of the church (1:10-4:21). In passing to matters of discipline (5:1-6:20) the apostle finds it necessary not only to give instruction but to rebuke the spirit of proud self-sufficiency that was rife. A case of incest occupies his attention first, followed by the problem of lawsuits among believers that were being brought to pagan magistrates, and then by teaching on the sanctity of the body. The latter prepares the way for more specific counsel on marriage and celibacy (7:1-40). The discussion of the pros and cons of eating food that had been offered to idols is enlivened and elevated by the introduction of far-reaching principles, illustrated from the practice of the apostle himself, including one's individual rights as a Christian, concern for one's brother, and the overarching consideration of the ultimate glory of God (8:1-11:1). Questions relating to public worship follow, including the decorum of women and the proper observance of the Lord's Supper (11:2-34), then a long section on spiritual gifts and their exercise, with the eulogy to love set as a gem in the very center (12-14). The epistle rises to its climax in the resurrection chapter (15), then tapers off in various admonitions, discussion of personal plans, and greetings (16).

Most if not all of these matters reflect the pagan Greek background of the Corinthians. Love of wisdom and human philosophy lay at the base of the factions and colored the outlook on resurrection. This attachment to human wisdom is shown to be inimical to the divine wisdom that centers in the cross. Again, the closely related love of speech, especially of the persuasive variety, comes out in connection with the factions and may be said to account in part for the prominence accorded the gift of tongues. The Greek spirit of levity and superficiality is reflected in the general attitude of the church toward morality and in the riotous observance of the love feast connected with the Lord's Supper. Individual liberty was being asserted with reference to the eating of meat offered to idols, with a tendency to disregard the effect of such indulgence on the tender consciences of those who were offended by the practice. This same insistence on freedom, with no sense of the line of separation between the church and the world, was expressed in the slogan "all things are lawful for me" (6:12; 10:23). It forced Paul to deal more largely with ethical matters than he was accustomed to do in his correspondence with churches.

THE DIVISIONS IN THE CHURCH

No special problem presents itself respecting Paul and Apollos, both of whom ministered in Corinth and attracted admirers. Paul brings in Apollos with himself in his exposition of what the Christian minister should be (3:5-6; 4:6). He could scarcely have ignored Peter in such a connection if the latter had ministered in the city. Probably others in the church, or those who came from the outside, introduced the name of Peter because of his prominence as well-known leader of the Palestinian church in the early days. The use of the Aramaic form Cephas (1:12) instead of Peter points in this direction. The Christ group occasions real difficulty, because there is nothing said of them that provides basis for positive identification. Baur, on account of his theory of conflict between the particularistic and universalistic elements in the early church, identified the Christ group with the Peter party and linked the Apollos group with those of Paul. Some scholars think of the Christ party as responsible for the emphasis on unrestricted freedom that Paul sought judiciously to combat without denying the true freedom believers have in Christ. Schlatter is of the opinion that the tenets of this group owed something to borrowings from Johannine teaching that were utilized without taking over other elements from John that would have made for restraint.[11]

Johannes Munck takes an unusual approach by denying that there were factions at all. He acutely observes that the threat of σχίσματα (1:10) belongs only to the future, and can be expected to develop only if the present troubles are deepened and intensified.[12] Meanwhile, it is strife, not division in the full sense, which is vexing the church (1:11). Munck also notes that the groups are not mentioned after the first four chapters, which is strange if they were decisive for the life of the local church and for early Christianity.

[11] *The Church in the New Testament Period*, pp. 186-87.
[12] *Paulus und die Heilsgeschichte*, pp. 127ff. (Eng. tr., *Paul and the Salvation of Mankind*, pp. 135ff.).

Paul's handling of the situation indicates rather that the real complaint against the groups is that they are a carry-over of a Greek love for wisdom, which is being applied to the gospel, and a love for philosophy, which is now being applied to Paul and others, who are being regarded as sophists seeking to gather a coterie of admirers around themselves. In boasting of their leaders with whom they identify, the Corinthians are really boasting of themselves. All this is contrary to the gospel and to the spirit of men like Paul and Apollos, who are merely servants.

This much seems to be clear, that the discussion in First Corinthians lends no color to the idea that Judaizing propaganda was being dispensed by the Cephas group or those who aligned themselves with Christ in a special sense. The word "law" occurs only 9 times (it is entirely absent from II Corinthians), as opposed to 32 in Galatians and 72 in Romans, and in no case in a setting that suggests a polemic against false teaching (15:56 is probably no exception). The verb "to circumcize" occurs only twice, and the noun once. All of these are found in a passage that deals with the principle of remaining in one's calling, so they are not pointedly theological but rather practical. We hear nothing of justification by faith versus works of the law.

CHARACTERISTICS

The greatest single overall emphasis seems to be on the unity of the local church as the body of Christ, which is brought out not only in connection with the discussion of the groups but also in relation to the Lord's Supper and to spiritual gifts. A corollary is the sanctity of the church as a part of Christ, and the application to the individual life as well.

Terms that stand out are words for know and judge or discern, spirit and spiritual, wisdom, world, church, authority, love, holy and sanctify.

Certain emphases carry over markedly from I to II Corinthians, such as the nature of the gospel and apostleship, Satanic opposition to the work of the Lord, and the need of discipline and judgment in bringing spiritual health to the body corporate.

Behind the discussion of every point is the tie of tender concern of the spiritual father for his children (4:14-15). They were problem children, and for that reason gave deep concern, but love never failed. Indicative of the direct, personal approach of the apostle is the fact that the pronoun "you" occurs 146 times.

DATE AND PLACE OF WRITING

It is apparent from the closing chapter that Paul is still at Ephesus in the midst of a strenuous work. The time can be fixed in the year 55 or possibly 56. No certain indication of the bearer is given. Some have identified him as Titus but the three brethren mentioned in 16:17 may have performed this service.

SECOND CORINTHIANS

AUTHENTICITY

Notices by early church writers are fewer than for I Corinthians. Rather strangely, Clement of Rome has nothing to say about a second letter, though some of its material would have been useful to him in his own epistle.[13] From this circumstance Goodspeed concludes that II Corinthians was not in the first collection of Paul's writings.[14] The Muratorian Canon states that Paul wrote twice to the Corinthians, and Irenaeus from the same period quotes the letter more than once and attributes it to Paul.

There can be no doubt concerning its authorship on the basis of comparison with I Corinthians, which has such excellent attestation, for clearly the very same apostle is dealing with the very same people who still require correction and encouragement to an unusual degree.

READERS

All the saints who are in Achaia are included with those in Corinth. This may be due to the fact that people outside the city would be expected to contribute to the fund that is discussed in chapters 8-9 (cf. 9:2; 11:10), or it may be explained on the basis of Paul's anxiety for the Christian cause in outlying areas that could be affected by the troubles in Corinth that he is seeking to settle by his epistle.

OUTLINE OF CONTENTS

The apostle begins by pouring out his gratitude for God's consolation. He had need of it, for added to his own peril and close call with death (probably at Ephesus) was his agony of spirit over conditions in Corinth. God delivered him from the first distress and brought relief from the other by the good tidings

---

[13] See J. H. Kennedy, *op. cit.*, pp. 143ff.
[14] *The Formation of the New Testament*, pp. 30-31.

that Titus brought him from Corinth when the two met in Macedonia. The leading offender against Paul had been punished. These items — the coming of Titus and the news about the offender — which lie close together in the first two chapters, recur in 7:5-15. The material in between is in the nature of a digression on the Christian ministry, notably that of Paul himself, which emphasizes at once the glory of the calling and the suffering it entails.

A part of the mission of Titus had been to stir up the Corinthians to greater efforts in bringing together a respectable contribution for the poor saints at Jerusalem (8:6). To spur this work on, the apostle penned chapters 8-9, in which he combines the human incentive of matching the generosity of the Macedonians with the supreme example of Christ (8:9).

In the closing portion one finds a strong contrast between the apostle's ministry, both in its spirit and accomplishments, and that of certain men who are branded false apostles (11:13). The identification of these men and their activities at Corinth has proved difficult. Some scholars have made them out to be Judaizing teachers of much the same stripe as those who infested Galatia. In one passage, indeed, Paul mentions the introduction of another Jesus and a different gospel (11:4), but in the absence of refutation on his part it is hardly conceivable that a strong doctrinal deviation is in view. Certainly in their character and ways they were misrepresenting the Lord Jesus and his message. If they could be called servants of Christ in a nominal sense (11:23), in a more exact sense they are emissaries of Satan (11:13-15). It may be that they actually were Judaizers, but were holding their fire until they had established themselves firmly in the church. The assault on Paul's apostleship recalls the tactics employed in Galatia. It is clear that these interlopers were Hebrews (11:22) and that they depreciated Paul in shameless fashion, poking fun at his bodily presence (10:10), casting doubt on his apostleship (11:5; 12:11-12), and using the very thing that accented his humble and sacrificial spirit — his refusal to accept financial support — as incontestable proof of his own awareness that he had no right to the office (11:7-11). It is fairly evident that these men had "taken over" at Corinth and were demanding support and putting on airs (11:20). There is no doubt that Paul felt the sting of this situation keenly, and made no attempt to hide his indignation, lashing out at these "super" apostles (12:11) for their tactics. But he had a point of real strength, which runs through his whole discussion of ministry, something that is sadly lacking in these newcomers, but which has been a mark of his own Christian service through the years — his suffering for Christ's sake. It is this that he throws into the lists as he brings himself to boast a little in order to shut the mouths of the pretenders (11:23ff.; 12:9-10). They cannot begin to match his record in something that should characterize all servants of Christ (cf. I Cor. 4:9-13).

It would be wrong, however, to think that the false apostles are Paul's main concern in the last four chapters. Munck is probably right in his contention that these visitors have only a minor part to play in the Corinthian drama, and that the apostle's major complaint is with the church for permitting these men to sweep them off their feet. Have his converts profited so little from his message and his example that they cannot detect a counterfeit ministry when it comes along?

If these outsiders arrived just as the church had been restored to right relations with Paul, the annoyance of the apostle is the more readily understood.[15] It is easier, on this supposition, to account for the concentration of Paul's blast against them at the close of the epistle, after he has taken account of the repentance and restoration of the church as a whole.

CHARACTERISTICS

(1) This is without question the most personal of Paul's letters. While his thought is often hard to follow through these pages, the revelation of his heart may be grasped without difficulty. Perhaps this is the greatest value of the epistle.[16] In a sense it is more pastoral than the letters that are usually so designated. The apostle can hardly restrain his impatience to move to regions beyond and preach the gospel (10:16), but he nobly refuses to leave until the crisis in Corinth is settled for good. Rome and the West will have to wait. He cannot shirk his pastoral responsibility.

(2) Weakness, grief, peril, tribulation, comfort, boasting, truth, ministry, glory — these are some of the terms that stand out and serve to carry the thread of the thought. They underscore the fact that the epistle is less doctrinal than Galatians and Romans and even than I Corinthians. The few doctrinal sections (e.g., chaps. 3 and 5) are introduced because of their connection with the task and privilege of ministry.

15 Munck, *op. cit.*, p. 185.
16 Tasker, *op. cit.*, p. 9.

DATE AND PLACE OF WRITING

There is every reason to believe that Paul wasted no time after his meeting with Titus before communicating with the church. The year 55 or possibly 56 is the approximate time, a few months after I Corinthians, and Macedonia (Philippi?) the place.

RECENT STUDY

The allusive character of the Corinthian correspondence, which often leaves the reader in some uncertainty as to the meaning of the apostle, though it furnishes first-rate evidence of the genuineness of the letters (seeing that a forger would not leave so many loose ends), has led to various theories about the composition of the letters and the nature of Paul's relations to the church at Corinth. Such investigations continue to be made.

Composition of the letters. While the integrity of I Corinthians is generally upheld, there are stumbling blocks such as the diverse attitudes of Paul expressed in chapters 8 and 10 regarding the eating of food offered to idols and the abrupt intrusion of a section in chapter 9 dealing with his apostleship. However, reasonable explanations can be offered for these and other phenomena. Paul is not always an orderly writer. After reviewing two attempts at reconstructing Paul's movements and letters, C. K. Barrett comments, "The fact that each reconstruction makes good sense is an argument against both, for they cannot both be right, and the sense that one makes, and quite possibly the sense that both make, must be due to the scholar making the reconstruction."[17] An elaborate refutation of partition theories concerning I Corinthians is provided by J. C. Hurd, Jr.[18]

The integrity of II Corinthians is generally acknowledged to be a more difficult problem, centering in Paul's severe language in chapters 10-13 after the satisfaction expressed over restored relations in the early portions of the letter. Günther Bornkamm has reaffirmed the view that these chapters are part of the painful letter written between I and II Corinthians, insisting that the difference in tone between these chapters and 2:14-7:4 is that the earlier chapters were written at a time prior to the success of the false apostles which constitutes the background for chapters 10-13. Still requiring explanation is the strange feature that an editor would allow the jarring inconsistency presented by placing 10-13 in the last position when as a matter of fact, on theory, this material was written earlier than 2:14-7:4. Born-

17 *The First Epistle to the Corinthians*, p. 14.
18 *The Origin of I Corinthians*, pp. 43-47, 114-142.

kamm seeks to justify this by the observation that it was the rule in the early church period to place warnings against false teachers at the end of a document (e.g. II Peter, the Pastorals, Acts 20:19ff.). Finally, the lack of patristic testimony to II Corinthians prior to Marcion suggests that the various fragments composing it had not yet been united during the apostolic age.[19]

Defenders of the integrity of II Corinthians are still to be found. Dissatisfied with the arguments for the sundering of chapters 10-13 from the rest of the letter, W. H. Bates finds testimony to considerable antagonism between Paul and the church in the preceding chapters, so the two sections are not totally dissimilar. He contends that as the last two chapters of Galatians reinforce the earlier chapters of that letter in stronger language, the closing portion of II Corinthians does the same thing.[20]

Likewise, A. M. G. Stephenson finds evidence in chapters 1-9 as well as in 10-13 of Paul's displeasure with the state of the church at Corinth (e.g. 2:17). He also points out the difficulty that in 12:18 Paul talks about a previous visit of Titus to Corinth. This means that chapters 10-13 cannot be the severe letter, since the first visit of Titus to the city was on the occasion of delivering that very letter.[21]

Paul's relationship to the Corinthian church. Here the concern is to arrive at an understanding of the state of the Christian community after Paul's departure from the city, particularly in terms of the influences within and from outside the church which called for reaction on the part of the apostle.

Of considerable importance is the existence of factions in the church. As already noted, Munck played this down, but T. W. Manson[22] came to feel that the influence of Peter was crucial to the growth of the anti-Paul sentiment in the church, not necessarily because Peter personally appeared there, but because representatives of the Jerusalem congregation called in question the work of the apostle to the Gentiles. He thinks that the unnamed person who tried to build on Paul's foundation (I Cor. 3:10-17) is Peter. He notes that in defending his apostleship Paul singles out Peter from the rest of the Jerusalem apostles for special mention as though to insist on equality with him (9:5). Perhaps Paul's extensive treatment of the eating of food offered to idols

---

[19] "The History of the Origin of the So-called Second Letter to the Corinthians," *NTS*, 8 (April 1962), 258-264.

[20] "The Integrity of II Corinthians," *NTS*, 12 (Oct. 1965), 56-69.

[21] "A Defence of the Integrity of 2 Corinthians," in *The Authorship and Integrity of the New Testament.* London: SPCK, p. 94.

[22] *Studies in the Gospels and Epistles,* pp. 190-224.

without any statement of what the Jerusalem council had determined on this issue is to be construed as a deliberate snub on his part in the face of agitators from Jerusalem who were telling the Corinthians what Jerusalem had already decided on this issue with the help of Peter's counsel (Acts 15). Manson thinks that the Corinthian correspondence reveals that Paul's troubles at Corinth were basically due to the ignoring by the leaders at Jerusalem of the agreement they had entered into which gave Paul a free hand in the Gentile mission (Gal. 2:9).

In essential agreement with Manson is Barrett's conclusion, "If there is a connection between the troubles of 2 Cor. x-xiii and those of I Corinthians, it is to be found, not, as is often supposed, in the Christ-group, but in the group of Cephas."[23]

Opinions vary as to whether or not Gnosticism was part of the Corinthian complex with which Paul had to deal. Walter Schmithals maintains that the apostle's adversaries in most of his churches were Gnostics.[24] But this involves reading too much into Paul's correspondence. The very term Gnosticism cannot easily be given a definite content at this early period. A moderate statement by Willi Marxsen is more acceptable than the extreme view of Schmithals. "It is a matter of argument whether we should call these opponents Gnostics or not. There is certainly no evidence here of the mythological or speculative soteriology that is a feature of many Gnostic systems, but on the other hand there are Gnostic phenomena to be noted. The self-glorying of the opponents indicates perfection. The man filled with the Spirit has an impressive appearance and can display powerful manifestations — features which are present among the opponents. We cannot call them pure Gnostics, but rather representatives of a syncretism in which Christian, Jewish and Gnostic elements are combined. Such syncretism — with other combinations as well — was nothing unusual at that time."[25]

A work by John Coolidge Hurd, Jr. is an effort to understand Paul's treatment of the various controversial topics in I Corinthians with the help of the "previous" letter (I Cor. 5:9-11).[26] He finds that in responding to questions broached by the church in written communication Paul is calm and orderly, relying on persuasion. In dealing with matters of which he has been informed orally he is not composed and relies on authoritative

[23] "Christianity at Corinth," *BJRL,* 46 (March 1964), 297.
[24] *Die Gnosis in Korinth.* Göttingen, 1956.
[25] *Introduction to the New Testament* (1968), pp. 87-88. See also R. McL. Wilson, *Gnosis and the New Testament,* pp. 53-55.
[26] *The Origin of I Corinthians* (1965).

pronouncements. It is in 1:11-6:11 that the latter type emerges. The author proposes to study the former type, however, in this investigation. He concludes that the questions of the church arose out of the "previous" letter, so that the communication sent by the congregation to the apostle should be understood as a point-by-point reply to what he had written. In essence Hurd's position is that the church found the apostle's counsel in this letter confusing, at odds with his teaching when he was in their midst. Has he changed his mind? Has he abandoned his strong stand on Christian liberty? Hurd thinks the situation becomes comprehensible if the "previous" letter did contain counsel of a rather different nature from his original teaching, dictated by the fact that in the interim he had come to an understanding with the Jerusalem church. This understanding required him to push the Apostolic Decree (Acts 15:20) with its injunctions about immorality and meats offered to idols in return for full recognition of his apostolic status and achievements among the Gentile churches. The decree was then cited in the "previous" letter. So I Corinthians is a kind of compromise in which Paul seeks to endorse his original teaching of which the church has reminded him in its letter and at the same time to throw in reservations in line with his "previous" letter.

This rather involved and ingenious theory is ably and carefully expounded, but is not without weaknesses. In the nature of the case it cannot be proved or disproved, since the "previous" letter is not available. Somehow the picture of Paul making a deal with the Jerusalem authorities to strengthen his own position is not wholly convincing. And as Barrett points out, there is some doubt that all these developments involving shifts on Paul's part could have taken place in the relatively short interval between his departure from Corinth and the writing of I Corinthians.[27]

BIBLIOGRAPHY

Barrett, C. K., *The First Epistle to the Corinthians, HNTC.* New York: Harper and Row, 1968.

———————, "Christianity at Corinth," *BJRL,* 46 (March 1964), 269-297

Ellicott, C. J., *A Critical and Grammatical Commentary on St. Paul's First Epistle to the Corinthians.* London: Longmans, 1887.

Godet, F., *Commentary on St. Paul's First Epistle to the Corinthians,* 2 vols. Edinburgh: T. & T. Clark, 1889.

Grosheide, F. W., *Commentary on the First Epistle to the Corinthians, NIC.* Grand Rapids: Eerdmans, 1953.

[27] *Op. cit.,* pp. 7-8.

Héring, Jean, *The First Epistle of Paul to the Corinthians*. London: Epworth Press, 1962.

——————————, *The Second Epistle of St. Paul to the Corinthians*. London: Epworth Press, 1962.

Hodge, Charles, *An Exposition of the First Epistle to the Corinthians*. New York: Robert Carter, 1857.

——————————, *An Exposition of the Second Epistle to the Corinthians*. New York: Robert Carter, 1859.

Hughes, P. E., *Paul's Second Epistle to the Corinthians, NIC*. Grand Rapids: Eerdmans, 1962.

Hurd, John Coolidge, Jr., *The Origin of I Corinthians*. New York: Seabury Press, 1965.

Lietzmann, H., *An die Korinther I & II, HZNT*. Tübingen: Mohr, 1949.

Manson, T. W., *Studies in the Gospels and Epistles*. Manchester Univ. Press, 1962, pp. 190-224.

McFadyen, J. E., *The Epistles to the Corinthians*. London: Hodder & Stoughton, 1911.

Menzies, Allan, *The Second Epistle of the Apostle Paul to the Corinthians*. London: Macmillan, 1912.

Morris, Leon, *The First Epistle of Paul to the Corinthians, TBC*. Grand Rapids: Eerdmans, 1958.

Munck, Johannes, *Paul and the Salvation of Mankind*. Richmond: John Knox Press, 1959, pp. 135-167.

Plummer, Alfred, *A Critical and Exegetical Commentary on the Second Epistle of St. Paul to the Corinthians, ICC*. New York: Scribner's, 1915.

Robertson, A. T., *The Glory of the Ministry*. New York: Fleming H. Revell, 1911.

Robertson, A., and Plummer, A., *A Critical and Exegetical Commentary on the First Epistle of St. Paul to the Corinthians, ICC*. 2nd ed., New York: Scribner's, 1911.

Schlatter, A., *Paulus der Bote Jesu*. Stuttgart: Calwer, 1934.

Tasker, R. V. G., *The Second Epistle of Paul to the Corinthians, TBC*. Grand Rapids: Eerdmans, 1958.

Weiss, J., *Der erste Korintherbrief*, Meyer series. Göttingen: Vandenhoeck & Ruprecht, 1910.

Windisch, H., *Der zweite Korintherbrief*, Meyer series. Göttingen: Vandenhoeck & Ruprecht, 1924.

Chapter Fifteen

THE EPISTLE TO THE ROMANS

THE CITY OF ROME

ACCORDING TO THE ANCIENTS, THIS FAMOUS METROPOLIS WAS founded in 753 B.C. In Paul's time it had a population of well over a million people (one inscription puts it over four million), the majority of whom were slaves. The success of the Caesars abroad brought fabulous wealth to this center of the empire, attested by numerous imposing buildings. People from many lands thronged its streets, and with them came their religions. Paul felt an obligation toward Greek and barbarian alike and had no doubt that the gospel he preached possessed a power to save men from sin that was sadly lacking in the current systems of human thought (Rom. 1:14, 16). He was willing to wait for a propitious time for challenging the great metropolis for Christ, namely, when he had proved the worth of his message in the eastern sector, but he could never pass it by. Acts 19:21 testifies to his fixed purpose to visit the city, which is supported by the apostle's own statement in Romans 15:23. He conceives of his missionary work thus far as pointing inescapably toward Rome. On a great circle he has moved from Jerusalem to Illyricum. The logic of the geography leads inevitably to the capital city.[1]

---

[1] Paul probably thought in terms of "up to Illyricum" rather than into it, which would have taken him in a northerly rather than westerly direction. See Sanday and Headlam on Rom. 15:19 (*ICC*).

FOUNDING OF THE CHURCH

Almost nothing is known of Christian beginnings in Rome, but there are hints and indications from various sources that favor the conclusion that the faith had been established and propagated there for some years before Paul wrote. The most natural construction to be put on his words is that the church has existed for a considerable time (1:13; 15:23). All Christendom has heard of the faith of the Roman saints (1:8). When the emperor Claudius expelled the Jews from Rome at the middle of the century, some of these people had in all probability become believers in Christ.

Suetonius states that the reason for the expulsion order was the tumult constantly being stirred up at the instigation of Chrestus (*impulsore Chresto*).[2] It is widely assumed, and probably correctly so, that Chrestus is to be understood as Christus (these vowels are confused elsewhere). Some have held that this may well be a reference to Christ, but not certainly to Jesus as the Christ.[3] But it is unlikely that abstract controversy over the Messiah would so agitate the Jewish population as to bring on a deportation order. It is more probable that it was the proclamation of Jesus as the Christ that inflamed the Jews there, just as it had done elsewhere. While it cannot be dogmatically asserted that Aquila and Priscilla were Christians when they came to Corinth, the silence of Luke about their conversion in the latter place favors the view that they were believers when they came (Acts 18:2, 3). If so, this argues for a community of Christians in Rome before the middle of the century.

It is common knowledge that Christians were sufficiently numerous by the time of Nero to be described by Tacitus as a great multitude (*multitudo ingens*), and his reference is only to those who were convicted and lost their lives.[4] This was A.D. 64, after the burning of Rome.

The source of the Christian witness at Rome is a puzzle. Believers at Pentecost constitute one possibility, since visitors from Rome were in attendance (Acts 2:10), but it is only a possibility. Whereas Luke describes the spread of the gospel to Antioch by a spontaneous movement led by laymen, he says nothing of such a movement from Jerusalem to Rome. In view of the constant communication between Antioch and Rome, the gospel may have gone west from this important trade center.

---

2 *Claudius* XXV.
3 See the discussion in K. Lake, *The Earlier Epistles of St. Paul,* p. 375.
4 *Annals* XV. 44.

That Peter had anything to do with the founding of the Roman church is highly improbable. The Book of Acts testifies to his presence in Palestine more or less continuously up to and including the time of the Apostolic Council (cf. Gal. 2:1-10), and Paul mentions a few years later that Peter is engaged in missionary work, presumably itinerating here and there in the East (I Cor. 9:5). Paul's failure to include a greeting to him in writing Romans shows that Peter was not there at the time, and nothing in the epistle indicates that he had anything to do with the establishment of the church. Paul could hardly have written to the Romans that his policy was not to build upon another's foundation (15:20) if Peter had founded this church. It may be concluded from I Peter 5:13 that Peter was in Rome in the 60s, but this is much too late to permit a share in the initial stage of the work.

The testimony of Clement of Rome mentions the martyr deaths of Peter and Paul[5] and apparently locates them in Rome ("among us").[6] Since the background for the discussion in Clement is the deleterious effect of envy and strife, it is quite possible, as Cullmann thinks, that the opposition noted by Paul in Philippians 1 grew more violent, and that when Peter arrived to try to pacify the Jewish Christian element, he was unsuccessful, so that in the end the two leaders died because they were virtually betrayed by alleged Christians who disagreed with their position.[7]

It will not do to rely on the testimony of Irenaeus, which couples the names of Peter and Paul in preaching the gospel and founding the Roman church.[8] He cannot mean the founding of the church in the strict sense, for it is obvious that Paul did not claim the Romans as his converts, so it is likely that Irenaeus is thinking of the ministry of Peter in Rome in much the same way as that of Paul, namely, as helping to establish more firmly a work that actually went back to an earlier time.

The testimony of Ambrosiaster (4th cent.) is the most helpful of the patristic references. "It is established that there were Jews living in Rome in the times of the apostles, and that those Jews who had believed [in Christ] passed on to the Romans the tradition that they ought to profess Christ but keep the law . . . . One ought not to condemn the Romans, but to praise their faith; because without seeing any signs or miracles and without seeing any of the apostles, they nevertheless accepted

[5] *First Clement*, V.
[6] *Ibid.*, VI.
[7] *Peter, Disciple — Apostle — Martyr*, p. 107.
[8] *Against Heresies* III. 1. 1.

faith in Christ, although according to a Jewish rite." While this testimony is not as ancient as some of the others, it seems to go back to a genuine tradition, for it does not attempt to capitalize on Peter or on the use of miracles. That a church did not require an apostolic foundation is evident from the case of Syrian Antioch.

THE COMPOSITION OF THE CHURCH

Ambrosiaster's statement bears witness to the belief that at the beginning Jews formed the nucleus, but that a considerable group of Gentiles, perhaps larger in number (it is they who are called the Romans), very soon became an important element in the church.

It may be questioned, on an a priori basis, that Paul would have written to a congregation that was mainly Jewish, in view of his distinctive sphere of labor among the Gentiles (Gal. 2:9). His reference to himself as an apostle to Gentiles (11:13) is most readily understood if his readers are non-Jews, at least in the main (cf. 1:5; 15:16, 18). Especially strong is the language of the introduction in which the readers are labelled Gentiles (1:5, 6, 13). In referring to Israel (9:3), the apostle calls them "my" brethren and "my" kinsmen (not *ours*).

A case for Jewish readers has been attempted on the basis of the large use of the Old Testament, but this is clearly indecisive in view of a similar situation in Galatians, which was written to Gentiles. On the same grounds, the large place given to the Mosaic law cannot be used to determine that the readers are Jewish. Abraham is called "our forefather" (4:1), but this is robbed of any great force by Paul's reference to Israel as "our fathers" in another Gentile epistle (I Cor. 10:1). It is true that chapters 9-11 are without a parallel in their completeness of treatment of the Jewish question, but it is precarious to reason from this that Jews alone were greatly concerned with such matters. One could argue that here Paul is bent on giving to Gentile readers a greater appreciation for the Jewish provenance of the gospel and the place that the nation holds in the purpose of God.[9] One could point in this connection to the line of

9 J. H. Ropes observes, after noting the decisive nature of the apostle's counterattack against the Judaizing menace in Galatia, "What Paul dreaded in the difficult situations which successively presented themselves at Thessalonica, at Corinth, and elsewhere, was not too *much* Judaism, but rather that the Christians would retain too *little* of the sound Jewish theology and morals on which Christianity rested" (*Studies in Early Christianity*, S. J. Case, ed., p. 365).

thought in 15:27, where Paul defends the fund for the Jerusalem church on the ground that it is only right that the Gentiles, having gained a share in the spiritual heritage of their Jewish brethren, should pass on to them some of their material blessings. Little notice has been taken of the fact that in 15:19 the apostle describes his missionary travels as having their inception at Jerusalem rather than Antioch. This must be regarded as a deliberate attempt to impress upon Gentile readers the importance of the mother church, which they could easily depreciate, if only from the standpoint of distance, to say nothing of the political insignificance of Jerusalem as compared to Rome.[10]

The edict of Claudius may have changed the balance of the church by forcing the temporary departure of the Jews. Even though this ban no longer existed when Paul wrote (Nero was now emperor), it is possible that some Jewish Christians had not returned to the city at the time. This could explain in part the dominance of Gentiles in the church.

Greetings in the closing chapter are addressed to at least three groups (16:5, 14, 15) in addition to a general salutation to the main body of believers (v. 16), but there is little to be learned from this circumstance about the Jewish/Gentile complexion of the church. The size of the city may have dictated the growth of local meeting places.

AUTHENTICITY

The book does not lack external support, including a place in the canon of Marcion and in the Muratorian fragment. Internal evidence is especially strong, for the language, theology and spirit are unmistakably Paul's. Certain undesigned coincidences between Romans and Acts are worthy of note also: (1) the collection for the poor saints, which Paul is on the point of taking to Jerusalem (15:25, 26; cf. Acts 24:17); (2) the apostle's announced purpose to visit Rome as a matter of long standing (1:13; 15:23, 24; cf. Acts 19:21); (3) his apprehension about the forthcoming visit to Jerusalem (15:30-31; cf. Acts 20:22, 23).

Although the Dutch School, toward the close of the last century, building largely on the negativism of Bruno Bauer, denied that

---

[10] Other arguments for a predominantly Jewish membership, such as the priority of the Jew (1:16; 2:9, 10), the care taken to combat antinomianism (6:1ff.) and the assumption that "all the churches of the Gentiles" implies a contrast to the Roman Church (16:4) are not sufficiently weighty to warrant special consideration.

this and all the other Paulines really belonged to Paul, their position has little more than antiquarian interest today.[11]

DATE AND PLACE OF WRITING

A key for the dating is found in Paul's observations about the collection for the poor saints (chap. 15). Whereas it is evident from I Corinthians 16:1-3 and II Corinthians 8-9 that the fund was then in the process of accumulation, by the time Romans is written the task has been completed. Paul is about ready to begin the journey to Jerusalem with the representatives of the contributing churches. So Romans was written after II Corinthians. From Acts 20:3 we learn that Paul spent only three months in Corinth before a plot of the Jews drove him off, necessitating a change of plans from a sea to a land journey by way of Macedonia. Consequently, Romans must have been written only a few months later than II Corinthians, probably in the year 57 (or late in 56), and presumably from Corinth, since Paul commends Phoebe, from the nearby city of Cenchraea, who is apparently ready to depart for Rome and presumably became the bearer of the letter. Since Gaius (16:23) is likely the same person as the Gaius of I Corinthians 1:14, this tends to strengthen the case for Corinth as the place of origin of the letter, as does the reference to Erastus the treasurer of the city (16:23), who is plausibly identified with the individual so named and his work described on a Corinthian inscription, as previously noted.[12]

PURPOSE

This can be conveniently treated by asking two questions. Why was this letter written at all? And why should his letter take the particular form and have the particular emphases that we find in it? The first question is the more readily answered, since the solution is found in the circumstances of the apostle. He has completed his work in the East, including the adjustment of differences with the Corinthian church. All that remains is to go to Jerusalem with the fund his churches have raised, and then he will be free to go West to Rome and beyond. In the opening up of a new field it will be of immense advantage to

---

[11] For refutation of this position, see R. D. Shaw, *The Pauline Epistles,* pp. 63-84, also R. J. Knowling, *The Witness of the Epistles,* pp. 133-243.
[12] For a statement of the position that Romans may have been written from Philippi, see T. M. Taylor, *JBL,* 67 (1948), pp. 281-95. He builds on the uncertainty that Romans 16 really had a Roman destination.

have the wholehearted co-operation of the important Roman church, which may become to him in the West what Antioch has been to him in the East. It may be said, of course, that since the time of departure was so near, little gain could be had in writing. Why not be content with a verbal presentation of the gospel when the apostle reached Rome? Or, why not send a brief note through Phoebe, with a promise of more elaborate communication on a personal basis? It may be that Paul's apprehension about trouble at Jerusalem or along the way was more strongly rooted than he allowed himself to express. In that event, this well-rounded statement of the message of the gospel as he knew it and proclaimed it would be a fitting memorial of his ministry and an adequate basis for missionary outreach by the Roman church.

The second question, which concerns itself with the form and substance of the letter, has been variously answered in accordance with one's opinion that the determining influence was the situation in the Roman church, with which Paul was at least moderately well acquainted through friends and fellow laborers, or in Paul's own experience as missionary and pastor. The difficulty one encounters in taking the former of these approaches is the dearth of material in the letter itself pointing to local conditions at Rome. One might argue that the teaching on the Christian's relation to the state has special relevance to Rome, but this is by no means certain. Peter could write in substantially the same vein to churches far removed from the capital. One could hardly expect the apostle to delve into any special problems at Rome, for he could not claim these believers as his own spiritual children. In line with this, the letter has an impersonal quality that suggests that the author does not have specific men and women with their peculiar needs before him as he writes.

So it is probably safer to conclude that Romans is a digest of the gospel message as Paul has been proclaiming it to numerous groups since his conversion, including the practical application of Christian truth to the various aspects of life in the church and in the world. Even so it is not quite a complete exposition of Paul's theology, as some have claimed, for it has no formal teaching on the church and very little on eschatology.

CHARACTERISTICS

(1) The lengthy introduction, unusual for Paul, is most easily explained on the ground that he is writing to a church that is not of his own planting. He is feeling his way, getting acquainted, as it were, in these opening lines.

(2) The conclusion of the letter is also peculiar in that it contains the names of a large number of people whom the apostle greets personally. This phenomenon calls for special consideration later on.

(3) Despite the introduction and conclusion, which entitle Romans to be called a letter, the body of the work has almost nothing of the occasional character common to Paul's letters. It is more of a treatise than a letter. In this respect it is in sharp contrast with I Corinthians, for example.

(4) Large use is made of the Old Testament, either by direct quotation or use of its terminology. In this way Paul fulfils the expectation he creates by his allusion to the holy writings in 1:2. More than half of the Pauline examples of γέγραπται are found in Romans. It was a valuable asset to be able to say, when dealing with doctrinal truth, *it stands written*. The practice of grouping together Scriptures that pertain to a certain theme is illustrated in 3:10ff. Undoubtedly the practice was older than Paul, so in this case he may have made use of an existing *florilegium*.

(5) The doctrinal discussion proceeds in the fashion of debate, as though the apostle had before him one who objected to some of his positions and interposed questions from time to time. The problem here is to know whether this use of question is merely a rhetorical device to enliven the discussion, or whether in the background lies the actual experience of the apostle in his preaching and teaching. It is tempting to adopt the latter position and see in Romans not the work of a day merely but of a decade or more of proclamation of the gospel, something forged out through heated debate and prolonged thought.[13]

(6) The irenic spirit of Romans stands in contrast to the polemic character of Galatians, with which it has considerable affinity. There has been a hard struggle, but now the battle is won, and Romans, with its placidity, reflects this fact. For example, both epistles deal with circumcision, but whereas the verb "to be circumcised" is used in Galatians several times, a testimony to the crisis in the Galatian churches, it is completely absent from Romans. In Galatians Paul warns of the curse that attends failure to keep the law, but there is nothing of this in Romans. Detachment from any Judaizing crisis permits a positive approach to the whole gamut of teaching on salvation.

(7) The vocabulary of Romans, as expected, is rich in theo-

[13] T. W. Manson, *Studies in the Gospels and Epistles*, p. 240.

logical terms — words for sin, wrath, death, law, righteousness and justify, reckon, faith and believe, life, hope, circumcision and uncircumcision, Israel and Jew, and the Gentiles.

OUTLINE OF CONTENTS

Starting with the theme of salvation as the revelation of God's righteousness (1:16-17), the apostle demonstrates that all men, Jew and Gentile alike, lack this righteousness (1:18-3:20) but God has graciously provided it through the redeeming death of his Son, so that one may be freely justified on the ground of faith in Christ (3:21-5:21). Next he unfolds the transforming power of God's righteousness as a vital force in Christian experience, despite the resistance of sin working through the flesh (6:1-8:39), then passes to a special aspect of the righteousness of God, namely, as seen in his dealings with the nation Israel (9:1-11:36). He concludes by pointing out that the justified man is responsible to bear a witness to God in the various spheres of life — political, societal, and fraternal (12:1-15:13).

INTEGRITY

Certain peculiar textual data call for examination.[14]   (1) A few witnesses omit the words "in Rome" (1:7, 15), namely, G, Origen, and Ambrosiaster. (2) The benediction in 16:20 has an unstable position, being located by some witnesses at verse 24 and by others at the very end of the chapter. (3) The doxology (16:25-27) finds its place at the end of the book in the leading MSS and in most of the Versions, but by some, mostly of the Koine type, it is placed after 14:23. Still others put it in both places. P[46] has it at the end of chapter 15. G omits it entirely, and this is the case with Marcion also. (4) There are indications of the existence of a short recension of the book that lacked chapters 15 and 16. For one thing, in Rufinus' translation of Origen's Commentary on the closing verses of Romans it is stated that Marcion removed the doxology and either cut away or separated the last two chapters from the rest of the epistle. Again, in his work against Marcion, Tertullian, in working his way through Romans, refuting Marcion as he goes, mentions the passage on the judgment seat of Christ (Rom. 14:10) as occurring at the end (*clausula*) of the epistle. Since

---

[14] For literature on this complicated subject, the student may consult the following: Hort's *Introduction,* pp. 111-113; K. Lake, *The Earlier Epistles of St. Paul,* pp. 324-70; Sanday and Headlam, *ICC.*

Tertullian is seeking to counter Marcion's position, it is probable that he is using Marcion's text. It is of interest that Tertullian himself makes no use of chapters 15 and 16 anywhere in his writings, which is true also of Irenaeus and Cyprian. Additional evidence of the lack of these chapters has been found in the Latin chapter headings in Codex Amiatinus of the Vulgate. The next to the last of these gives a title that deals with Romans 14:15-23, and the last relates to the doxology in 16:25-27. A similar situation exists in other Latin MSS. Lightfoot has shown that this system of headings in Amiatinus goes back to the Old Latin.[15] These items are probably sufficient to establish the existence of a short form of Romans dating from the second century, though they are not regarded as decisive by all textual experts.[16]

Various conjectures have been made to account for the short recension. Paul himself may have been responsible for it in order to use the main portion of the epistle as a circular letter to be sent to other churches, in which case the references to Rome in chapter 1 were naturally deleted along with the last two chapters. Another possibility is that the excision of the last two chapters may have been due to their lack of suitability for reading in church services. Both these views suffer from the difficulty that a break at 14:23 is unnatural, for it cuts right into the middle of Paul's discussion about the strong and the weak brother. More plausible is the notion that Marcion may have been responsible for the shortening, since he would find 15:8 especially inimical to his viewpoint (note v. 4 also). The placing of the doxology at the end of chapter 14 as attested by some MSS is understandable as a move to give the epistle a fitting close.

It has also been held that the shorter form of the epistle, whether ending with chapter 14 or 15, was original with Paul. The former alternative is very improbable, since the material in 15:1-13, which belongs so naturally to chapter 14, would then be introduced awkwardly, as though to suggest that Paul had not properly rounded out his original thinking on this subject. Some items in the introduction are quite unsuitable to a circular letter, whereas they fit Rome (see vv. 8 and 10). The latter alternative, that Paul closed with chapter 15, has more to commend it, and must be treated at greater length.

It has long been held by some scholars that the intended destination of chapter 16 was not Rome but Ephesus, despite the

---

15 *Biblical Essays,* p. 362.
16 See, e.g., the comments of Hort (*Intro.,* pp. 111-13).

lack of MS evidence for its separate existence. This view is grounded on several items. (1) The improbability that Paul had so many friends in a church he had not visited and the corresponding probability that he had many at Ephesus. (2) The reference to Priscilla and Aquila in vv. 3-4. At the time Paul wrote I Corinthians, they were with him in Ephesus (16:19). At the time II Timothy was written, they were likewise in the city (4:19). The conclusion is natural that they were there when the chapter that we are considering was written. (3) Epaenetus is called the first fruits of Asia unto Christ (v. 5). (4) It is strange that Paul knows not only the names but so much about the labors of the various individuals greeted here that he can distinguish between those who labored and those who labored much in the cause of the gospel. This is natural if they are located at Ephesus, but not so natural for Rome. (5) The warning against those who cause divisions and offenses (vv. 17-18) comes in awkwardly if written to a church over which Paul had no pastoral control, whereas it would be natural if directed to Ephesus, especially in the light of his prediction to the Ephesian elders in Acts 20:29-30.

In opposition to the Ephesian and in support of the Roman destination of the chapter several items have been put forward. (1) Travel was relatively easy at this period, so there is nothing strange in the removal of three people from Ephesus to Rome in the interval between the writing of I Corinthians and Romans. It is particularly understandable in the case of Priscilla and Aquila, who had been in Rome before going to Corinth.[17] (2) A letter consisting almost wholly of greetings is, as Lietzmann phrased it, a monstrosity. If this portion is but a fragment of a longer letter, then the rest is missing. (3) Since it was Paul's practice to avoid personal greetings in writing to churches where the congregation as a whole was known to him, lest he be guilty of partiality, it must be regarded as strange that he would single out these people if he were writing to Ephesus. The situation in Romans, however, is parallel to that in Colossians, written to a church Paul did not found, where he permits himself to extend greetings (4:15, 17). During years of labor in the East the apostle could have met many of these people who, by the time Romans was written, had gravitated to the capital. (4) The name of Rufus (v. 13) is connected with Rome by reason of the reference to him in Mark 15:21, since this Gospel emanated from Rome. (5) While the observation that many

---

[17] See Dodd's discussion in *MNTC*, pp. xx-xxi.

of the names in the chapter are Roman is not decisive, for they were current elsewhere also, more decisive is the fact that several names, with greater or less certainty, have been connected with early Christianity in Rome. These are the households of Narcissus (v. 11) and Aristobolus (v. 10), and two individuals, Nereus (v. 15) and Ampliatus (v. 8.).[18] (6) When the final chapter is separated from the rest of the epistle, this means that Paul closed his message to Rome with the words, "The God of peace be with you all. Amen." No analogy for such a close can be cited from any of Paul's letters. He always ends on the note of grace.

A somewhat different solution has been put forward by T. W. Manson.[19] Starting with the clue that P[46] puts the doxology at the close of chapter 15 (though it includes chapter 16), Manson finds in this circumstance evidence that a form of Romans was current at one time without chapter 16. He thinks P[46] attests the letter as Paul wrote it and sent it to Rome. Later on it lost chapter 15 by Marcionite influence. Concurrently with the writing of the letter to Rome, Paul sent a copy to Ephesus, with chapter 16 added, which is a covering letter introducing Phoebe and containing greetings. Ultimately the whole letter, minus any indication of Roman destination, found its way to Egypt, where mixture took place resulting in that form of the text of the epistle that is attested by our leading manuscripts (containing the references to Rome in chapter one and the doxology at the end of the book).

Manson sees in Paul's act of sending the letter to both East and West an indication of his consciousness that the contents provided a summary of the gospel message he had been preaching (chaps. 1-11) and also a summary of the practical problems he had dealt with in his eastern churches, especially Corinth. The view is very attractive, but one may still hold to the Roman destination of chapter 16 as at least equally probable.

Considerable discussion has centered in the doxology also (16:25-27). It has been viewed as Marcionite in character (the gospel a mystery kept secret through the ages but now revealed), although the reference to prophetic Scriptures would seem to be so un-Marcionite as to cancel the other item. Another approach, based on the fact that Romans sometimes stands last in the ancient lists of Paul's epistles, contends that the doxology was attached by someone as a fitting close to the

---

[18] Dodd, *op. cit.*, pp. xxii-xxiii.
[19] *Studies in the Gospels and Epistles*, pp. 225-41.

Pauline corpus. However, even though the doxology is ponderous in structure, its components so well fit the material of Romans as to make entirely probable its Pauline authorship.

THEOLOGICAL THOUGHT

It is certainly true, as Leon Morris points out, that from the standpoint of statistics, God is the chief subject.[20] There is reason for this. In some of the major sections the discussion is virtually limited to God and man (e.g. 1:18-3:20 and 9:1-11:36). However, Paul starts immediately with the gospel (1:1) and relates it to salvation, which he treats in terms of the *righteousness* of God (1:17). This righteousness is viewed first from the positive side, bringing acceptance for the one who believes, an acceptance that excludes all compromise with the justice of God. Then the divine righteousness is treated from the negative standpoint as demanding judgment for sinful humanity which has a sufficient knowledge of God to make failure to acknowledge and serve him inexcusable. Jew and Gentile share this judgment.

When the need of mankind is sufficiently expounded, exposed in terms of character and deed and supported by Scripture (3:10-18), the propitious moment has arrived for the introduction of the theme of divine *grace* manifested in the gift of Jesus Christ, who appropriately dominates the next section (3:21-5:21). His propitiatory work brings justification and redemption to the believing sinner. Once again the reminder is given that the righteousness of God is at work in all this (3:25-26). Grace rules out the acquisition of righteousness by human works. There cannot be two ways of salvation (4:3-5; cf. 11:6). In grace the believer continues to stand while he rejoices in the hope of sharing the *glory* of God (5:2). His acceptance does not exempt him from trial and suffering, but through it all he is sustained by the love of God (5:5). The grand climax comes in the truth that as sin reigned in death, grace will reign through righteousness to eternal life through Christ (5:21).

If God's gracious provision in Christ is received by faith, the righteous standing that results is eternally valid. But there is no promise of instant perfection. Rather, the Christian man must realize that there is a law of sin operating in his being in obedience to the old nature. How is the hold of sin to be broken? This is the theme of chapters 6-8. Here the death of Christ is reasserted, but not in isolation as the death of the just for the

[20] "The Theme of Romans," in *Apostolic History and the Gospel* (ed. by Gasque and Martin), pp. 249-263.

unjust, but pictured as involving the believer, who has been joined to Christ in that death, a truth expressed by baptism into Christ. Death to sin calls for resolute separation from sin, and resurrection with Christ means a new type of life in response to God. One must consciously refuse obedience to sin and serve the righteousness of God with all his redeemed powers. The Mosaic law might seem to help in this process, but not so in reality, for the law simply demonstrates the powerlessness of the flesh to please God. Paul pictures himself in a representative sense as knowing the demands of the law and wanting to fulfill them but being frustrated by sin working through the flesh. At this point the Spirit, seldom mentioned thus far, comes into his own (chap. 8). When the believer lives by the Spirit, he is able to fulfill the righteous demands of the law (8:4; cf. Gal. 5:23). He is led by the Spirit and assured of his relationship to God (8:16). His weakness in prayer is balanced by the Spirit's powerful intercession (8:26-27). And so the thought mounts up to the cry of triumph that bids defiance to every foe as the redeemed lives in anticipation of the glory that is yet to dawn. Meanwhile nothing can separate from the love of God in Christ.

The theme of salvation gives ample scope for the development of *Heilsgeschichte* (history of salvation, or the sweep of the divine purpose down through the ages as set forth in Scripture). Advance notice of this emphasis is hinted at early in the epistle (1:2). Creation was a necessary stage in the execution of the divine purpose (1:19-20). Adam is compared and contrasted with the man Christ Jesus, teaching that the ruin and condemnation brought upon the race by the first man are countered and removed by the obedience of Christ so that men may have acquittal and life (5:12-21). Abraham is presented as the model for justification by faith alone (chap. 4). The law is drawn into the discussion also as the agent to make man aware of his sin (3:20; 7:13). For a second time the creation is cited, not now as revealing God but as disclosing the effects of man's sin on his environment (8:20), yet awaiting its own deliverance when that of man is fully accomplished. The nation Israel is not forgotten. Its failure to welcome the Messiah is laid to its reliance on human righteousness rather than submission to God's (10:3). Yet all is not lost, for some Israelites are being saved (11:1, 5). And the best is yet to come, for all Israel will share this blessing (11:25-26). Meanwhile the sight of God's grace at work among the Gentiles is calculated to create jealousy in Israel and work toward their ultimate restoration. These magnificent truths constrain to praise of God (11:36).

BIBLIOGRAPHY

Bardenhewer, O., *Der Römerbrief des heiligen Paulus.* Freiburg: Herder, 1926.

Barrett, C. K., *A Commentary on the Epistle to the Romans, HNTC.* New York: Harper, 1957.

Barth, Karl, *Der Römerbrief* (1919). Eng. tr. by E. C. Hoskyns, Oxford University Press, 1933.

Calvin, John, *To the Romans.* Eng. tr. by John Owen; reprint, Grand Rapids: Eerdmans, 1947.

Gifford, E. H., *The Epistle of St. Paul to the Romans.* London: John Murray, 1886.

Godet, F., *Commentary on St. Paul's Epistle to the Romans,* 2 vols. Edinburgh: T. & T. Clark, 1883.

Haldane, Robert, *Exposition of the Epistle to the Romans.* New York: Robert Carter, 1860.

Hodge, Charles, *A Commentary on the Epistle to the Romans.* Reprint rev. ed. of 1864, Grand Rapids: Eerdmans, 1964.

Hort, F. J. A., *Prolegomena to Paul's Epistles to the Romans and the Ephesians.* London: Macmillan, 1895.

Lagrange, M. J., *Epître aux Romains.* Paris: J. Gabalda, 1950.

Leenhardt, F. J., *The Epistle to the Romans.* Eng. tr. 1961, London: Lutterworth.

Liddon, H. P., *The Epistle of Paul the Apostle to the Romans.* 2nd ed., London: Longmans, Green, 1893.

Lietzmann, H., *An die Römer, HZNT.* 4th ed., Tübingen: Mohr, 1933.

Michel, O., *Der Brief an die Römer,* Meyer series. Göttingen: Vandenhoeck & Ruprecht, 1955.

Moule, H. C. G., *The Epistle of St. Paul to the Romans.* 5th ed., New York: A. C. Armstrong and Son, 1902.

Murray, John, *The Epistle to the Romans,* 2 vols., *NIC.* Grand Rapids: Eerdmans, 1959, 1965.

Nygren, A., *Commentary on Romans.* Eng. tr. 1949, Philadelphia: Muhlenberg Press.

Sanday, W., and Headlam, A. C., *A Critical and Exegetical Commentary on the Epistle to the Romans, ICC.* 5th ed., New York: Scribner's, 1905.

Schlatter, A., *Gottes Gerechtigkeit.* 2nd ed., Stuttgart: Calwer, 1952.

Shedd, William G. T., *A Critical and Doctrinal Commentary upon the Epistle of St. Paul to the Romans.* New York: Scribner's, 1879.

Chapter Sixteen

THE PRISON EPISTLES

FOUR LETTERS OF PAUL ARE DESIGNATED AS THE PRISON EPISTLES
because the apostle was in bonds when he wrote them (Phm.
1 and 9; Col. 4:18; Eph. 3:1; 4:1; 6:20; Phil. 1:7, 13, 14).
Some prefer to describe them as Captivity Epistles, since Paul
was in detention but not necessarily in prison in the technical
sense.

Of these letters, three are so closely linked together that they
must be assigned to the same time and place. It is clear from
Colossians 4:7 and Ephesians 6:21 that Tychicus was the
bearer of these two epistles, and the great similarity between
them points to their composition at the same time. From
Colossians 4:9 we learn that Tychicus had as companion on this
journey a certain Onesimus. Since the letter to Philemon plainly
discloses that its bearer is Onesimus, this writing is thereby
brought into the same orbit with Ephesians and Colossians. This
is confirmed by the fact that Archippus is addressed by Paul
in Philemon and gets a message from him in Colossians (4:17).
These three epistles, then, emanated from the apostle at the
same time and must have originated at one place. The location,
however, has been and still is disputed. Some contend for
Caesarea, others for Rome, and still others for Ephesus. It re-

mains to examine these views and assess their strengths and weaknesses.

TIME AND PLACE

(1) *Caesarea.* The possibility that the slave Onesimus may have fled to this city may be granted, but this could be claimed with equal force for Ephesus and with perhaps greater force for Rome, on account of remoteness and the difficulty of detection among its masses.

Since Paul was at Caesarea for the same length of time as at Rome (two years) and under similar conditions, with friends having access to him (Acts 24:23), he could have written from this city as readily as from Rome. However, a certain difference in the apostle's situation should be noted. Whereas Paul's liberty to preach at Rome is clearly stated in Acts 28:30-31, there is no indication of any preaching at Caesarea beyond what occurred in the presence of Roman officials. The point has some importance in view of Paul's request in Ephesians 6:19-20 and in Colossians 4:3-4 for prayer that he may be able to measure up to the opportunity that he has for witness, even though he is in bonds.

It is held likely that Paul would seek to communicate with some of his churches during his detention at Caesarea. This may be admitted, but positive evidence for the letters we are considering is lacking.

The most damaging thing for the Caesarean theory is the statement in Philemon 22, "But withal prepare me also a lodging: for I trust that through your prayers I shall be given unto you." There is absolutely nothing in the Caesarean situation that points toward a promise of release. And once appeal had been made to Caesar, any trip to Asia Minor was out of the question.

Further, there is considerable doubt that a man in the position of Onesimus would have been able to gain access to Paul at Caesarea, whereas the more informal setting at Rome would not impose so great a barrier (Acts 28:30-31).

Finally, it is odd that Paul would omit from his list of those who were a comfort to him (Col. 4:10-11) the name of Philip, whose home was in Caesarea (Acts 21:8).

(2) *Rome.* This is the traditional position, favored by the certainty of Paul's imprisonment there (Acts 28) and by the circumstance that certain traveling companions on the trip to Rome appear by name in the Prison Epistles. Luke, whose presence on the journey is attested by the "we" section in Acts 27-28, is mentioned in Philemon 24 and Colossians 4:14 as being

with Paul. Aristarchus was another who apparently accompanied Paul to Rome (Acts 27:2), and he appears in Philemon 24 and Colossians 4:10.

Somewhat hostile to the Roman theory is the announced purpose of Paul to visit Philemon (v. 22). This seems strange in view of the apostle's plan to go beyond Rome to Spain (Rom. 15:28). It is possible that the Spanish mission was abandoned or postponed, and that a trip back to the East was felt necessary in view of the disturbed condition of the Colossian church and possibly other factors as well.

(3) *Ephesus.* This alternative has enjoyed increased popularity in recent years.[1] It is built mainly on certain statements in the Corinthian correspondence that have been thought to point to a detention of the apostle in this city: he has been in prisons more frequently than the pseudo-apostles at Corinth (II Cor. 11:23); he has fought with wild beasts at Ephesus (I Cor. 15:32); and has had a crisis experience, apparently at Ephesus, of which he says, "We had the sentence of death in ourselves" (II Cor. 1:8-10). In addition, some statements in Romans 16 may apply, provided this chapter be taken as directed to Ephesus. Priscilla and Aquila "risked their necks" to save Paul from some peril (v. 4), and two others, Andronicus and Junias, are described as Paul's fellow prisoners (v. 7).

It should be noted that the only statement here that specifically mentions imprisonment is not linked to Ephesus but is very general, including in its scope the whole background of the apostle's service and suffering. Nothing decisive can be made out of the allusion to wild beasts, which is likely figurative. The New English Bible renders as follows: "If, as the saying is, I 'fought with wild beasts' at Ephesus, what have I gained by it?" The marginal reading — "If, as men do, I had fought wild beasts at Ephesus, what good would it be to me?" — puts the experience quite beyond the realm of actuality. Paul was given to figurative language at times (cf. the "fierce wolves" in Acts 20:29). His Roman citizenship also rules out an actual encounter with wild beasts.

That the apostle had serious opposition at Ephesus and was greatly depressed is no doubt indicated, especially in II Corinthians 1, but that is as far as the evidence takes us. Luke's account of Paul's stay at Ephesus is rather lengthy, yet he says nothing about an imprisonment. Even though he was not

---

[1] For a full statement of it, see George S. Duncan, *St. Paul's Ephesian Ministry* (1930).

personally present (there is no "we" section for the Ephesian ministry), he would have learned of such an incident without fail. Further, even if Paul had been imprisoned for some reason, it would be expected that the error would be rectified quickly, as it was at Philippi, as soon as the apostle's Roman citizenship was asserted. The alternative of protective custody is not convincing, as this would be an admission by the authorities of their inability to furnish public protection to a Roman citizen. Even if an Ephesian imprisonment were established, this would only indicate the possibility, not the certainty, that the epistles under discussion emanated from this place.

The situation of Paul's companions may throw some light on the question, since he mentions several people as present with him in his imprisonment. If they can be placed at Ephesus, this could be construed as evidence favorable to the Ephesian provenance of these epistles. Aristarchus is one of these, and he is called Paul's fellow prisoner (Col. 4:10). It happens that he is mentioned in Acts 19:29 as one who was seized by the Ephesian mob during the uproar in the theater. But even if we assume what the text does not say, that he was thereupon imprisoned, nothing is said about Paul's having been seized along with him.

However, Aristarchus and Epaphras, both of them listed as Paul's fellow prisoners (the latter in Phm. 23) cannot be proved to have been imprisoned at Rome. But it should be noted that the word prisoner which is used for these men (συναιχμάλωτος) is not the same as that which Paul employs for himself (δέσμιος). Since there is no military background for the capture of either man, it is reasonable to conclude that the term is used figuratively to denote a voluntary sharing of Paul's imprisonment.[2] Another possibility is that close association with the apostle brought these men under suspicion and led to their confinement for a time. The matter is indecisive. Luke also was a companion of Paul at the time of writing (Col. 4:14), and there is no evidence for his presence at Ephesus, whereas he went with Paul to Rome. On the other hand, Timothy, who is mentioned in these letters as present with Paul (Col. 1:1; Phm. 1) does not appear by name in Luke's account of the trip to Rome. But it is hard to think of him as not present, in view of his long and close association with the apostle. He qualifies from the Ephesian standpoint, as Luke links him with the Ephesian residence of Paul (Acts 19:22; cf. I Cor. 16:10).

[2] See Lightfoot on Colossians 4:10.

The balance of probability seems to favor Rome over Ephesus, at least for the three epistles considered. A somewhat stronger case can be made out for the Ephesian provenance of Philippians. For one thing, the letter presupposes several journeys that must have been time consuming. News of Paul's plight had to reach the church, then Epaphroditus made his trip with a gift. Then tidings of the serious illness that befell Epaphroditus after delivering the gift had to be reported back to the church. On top of this, it seems that word of the distress caused by this report among the Philippians came back to Epaphroditus, giving him added concern (2:26). Then there was Epaphroditus' journey back to Philippi with the epistle (2:25) and the promise of a visit by Timothy, who would then report back to the apostle (2:19). These various trips present no problem if they occurred between Ephesus and Philippi, since a week would suffice for such a journey under ordinary conditions. On the other hand, a good month would be required to cover the distance between Rome and Philippi. Even so, the journeys could undoubtedly be fitted into the two-year period Paul was in Rome. The news that he was going to Rome may have been taken from Caesarea to Philippi, in which case Epaphroditus could arrive in Rome about the same time as the apostle, or before. Travel was fairly easy in the empire at this period.

Paul's references to the Praetorium (1:13) and to believers who belonged to Caesar's household (4:22), once regarded as strong evidence of Roman destination, can equally well be understood in terms of Ephesus, if Praetorium be understood in terms of the Praetorian Guard. A personal sense is natural in view of the following words, "and to all the rest." Inscriptional evidence points to the presence of members of this famous contingent at Ephesus and also to slaves of Augustus.[3] If taken in the sense of a building, it could mean "Government House," to use Manson's phrase,[4] which would be found at important centers throughout the empire, and in this case would refer to the Proconsular court. F. W. Beare, however, throws in a word of caution. "Asia . . . was a senatorial province; and it is not to be taken for granted that there would be either men of 'Caesar's household' or a permanent military headquarters there."[5]

On the Ephesian hypothesis, the sending of Timothy presents

[3] McNeile-Williams, *Introduction to the Study of the New Testament*, p. 182.
[4] *Studies in the Gospels and Epistles*, p. 159.
[5] *IB*, XI, 135a.

no problem, since Acts 19:22 reports a mission by him from Paul to Macedonia.

Paul's expressed purpose to come to Philippi himself as soon as he is released (2:24) is likewise easy to fit into his movements as reflected in Acts 20:1. It is pointed out, on the other hand, on the Roman theory, that this purpose to visit Philippi runs into the difficulty that when Paul left the East he expected to go through Rome to Spain. This is an important argument, and seems to be a strong feature of the case for Ephesus. However, if one may grant for the moment that the epistle was written from Rome, it is not improbable that the opposition Paul encountered in the Roman church, reflected in Philippians 1:14-18, discouraged him from undertaking the Spanish venture at that time, since he lacked the cordial and united support he had counted on from Rome. This, together with the word about difficulties at Colossae, may have caused him to return to the East, contrary to his original plan.

The possibility of explaining Philippians 4:10, where Paul excuses the lack of a gift from his friends prior to the arrival of Epaphroditus on the ground that they had no opportunity, is much easier on the Ephesian than on the Roman hypothesis, since after leaving Corinth Paul was in Ephesus only a short time before taking off for Palestine and then the Galatian region. His friends at Philippi would not send a gift when he was travelling. But on the Roman hypothesis, the opportunity was present to aid Paul, either during his three-months stay at Corinth or when he passed through Philippi en route to Jerusalem. How, then, could he write that his friends lacked opportunity? A suggestion may be ventured that this was hardly the opportune time for a gift, since Paul would naturally be concerned to avoid all suggestion of self-interest in money matters, especially at this juncture when the Jerusalem fund was in hand. Detractors at Corinth had been raising insinuations along this very line in the hope of damaging Paul's reputation. The liberal contribution made to the fund by the Philippians (II Cor. 8:1ff.) may have rendered a personal gift impossible anyway.

If Philippians can be placed during the Ephesian residence of Paul, his strong language about the circumcision group (3:3ff.) is more easily understood, for this period was the time of Judaizing opposition. Philippians would then be assimilated into the soteriological group of epistles.

It is claimed that Paul's outlook on the Parousia, with its retention of the note of imminency, fits the earlier period (cf. 3:20-21; I Cor. 15:51-53), whereas the outlook of the other prison epistles leans in the main to a spiritualized eschatology.[6]

Manson, though he holds to the Ephesian origin of Philippians, does not think it was written from prison. Instead, he argues that the references to imprisonment are retrospective and refer to Paul's experience at Corinth, where he was detained for a short time in connection with his appearance before Gallio. He would explain the statements of the apostle about opposition to him (1:14-18) in terms of the factions and strife in the Corinthian church.[7] The position is open to question, for the language of Paul about his imprisonment seems to go beyond the momentary detention connected with the Gallio incident. Further, his vindication in that incident would make the rise of opposition to him in the church at that juncture almost unthinkable. The factions seem to have arisen only after Paul had been for some time absent from the church.

It must be granted that the case for the Ephesian provenance of Philippians is stronger than for the other three prison epistles. But even so, there is an element of high improbability connected with it. According to chapter 1, Paul is in possible danger of losing his life. If this situation occurred at Ephesus, he could still appeal to Caesar at Rome and avoid the danger, as he did at Caesarea.

It is strange, too, on the theory of Ephesian provenance, that Paul has nothing to say about the collection for the poor saints at Jerusalem, which held a prominent place in his thinking at this time, and in which the Philippians participated (II Cor. 8:1ff.).

Cullmann favors the Roman origin because of a combination of certain factors. "Only concerning the *Roman* church do we know (1) that jealousy ruled in it (I Clem. 6:1); (2) that Paul seems to have feared difficulties in it due to the fact that its membership included both Jewish and Gentile believers (Rom. 15:20); (3) that Paul spent a time in it as a prisoner of the Roman Empire and during his imprisonment had to expect 'affliction' from other members of the church (Phil. 1:15f.)."[8]

Regarding the prison epistles as a whole, on the Ephesian hypothesis these books would be injected into the same temporal setting as the soteriological epistles. In that case it is hard to explain why they are so dissimilar, with the possible exception of

6 McNeile-Williams, *op. cit.,* p. 183.
7 *Op. cit.,* p. 161.
8 O. Cullmann, *Peter,* p. 105.

Philippians.[9] In thought and diction they are quite removed. Dodd calls attention also to the fact that if the prison epistles emanated from Ephesus on the third missionary journey, this means that Paul's major literary output would be concentrated in a period of three or four years, embracing Galatians, I and II Corinthians, Romans, and the four prison epistles. Then we would have nothing to reflect his mind over the major part of a long missionary career.[10] This is highly unlikely. As his experience became enriched and deepened and his churches more numerous, a greater literary output, rather than a cessation, is a reasonable expectation.

All in all, the Roman position seems the stronger, based on the certainty of Paul's imprisonment there, whereas positive evidence for imprisonment at Ephesus is lacking. Given a Roman provenance it is easier to account for the change of outlook and the new emphases in the prison epistles. For example, if Ephesians was written from Rome, the hub of the empire, it is not entirely fanciful to see in this circumstance something conducive to the emphasis in the epistle on the unity of saints in the body of Christ under the supreme headship of Jesus Christ.

DATE OF THE PRISON EPISTLES

The Prison Epistles belong early in the 60s. But whereas Ephesians, Colossians, and Philemon must all be placed in the same segment of time, Philippians stands apart. It is notable, for one thing, that Paul's attitude toward his release is not the same. A hope of it is announced in Philemon 22, but no ground for this hope is given. In Philippians, on the other hand, the apostle is confident of release (1:25).

Further, in Colossians and Philemon Paul mentions a fairly large number of associates who are with him at the time: Tychichus, Aristarchus, Mark, Jesus called Justus, Epaphras, Luke, and Demas (Col. 4:7, 10-14; Phm. 23). In Philippians, however, Paul is shut up to Timothy as his one prospective messenger (2:19-21). The inference to be drawn is that others are not present.

This much is clear, then, that the time of writing is not the same for Philippians as for the other three. Is Philippians earlier or later? Lightfoot advocated its priority on the grounds of the affinity between this epistle and Romans and on the basis of the

[9] C. H. Dodd, *New Testament Studies,* p. 106.
[10] *Ibid.*

more advanced teaching on the church in Ephesians and Colossians over Philippians.[11]

These are hardly as decisive as contrary factors. First, Acts 28:30-31 is opposed to the notion that Paul came to trial during the two-year period there mentioned, for the reason that he is pictured as preaching freely. In Philippians his circumstances are different, for others are preaching and he is unable to do so, presumably because his case is actually in court. Second, if the other epistles belong after Philippians, it is strange that they do not indicate the outcome of the trial or echo it in some way. Third, even on the supposition that Paul was mistaken about the probable outcome of the trial as he wrote Philippians, on the assumption of the priority of that letter it is difficult to understand how he could give expression to a fresh hope of release in Philemon 22 without any word of explanation as to the basis of this renewed hope. On the assumption of the later dating of Philippians, Philemon 22 is not hard to explain. It was a natural expectation stimulated by the lenient treatment the apostle had received as a prisoner, and also by his conviction that his life work was not yet completed.

The other three epistles can be safely put around the middle of the sojourn in Rome, and Philippians shortly after the close of the two-year period.

COLOSSIANS

CITY AND CHURCH

Approximately 100 miles east of Ephesus, in the Lycus valley, lay the city of Colossae. Once a populous place, its importance had diminished considerably, so that in the apostolic age it was overshadowed by the neighboring communities of Laodicea and Hierapolis (Col. 4:13). Paul may have passed through the city on his travels, but there is no hint in the letter that he preached to its inhabitants or founded a church there. On the contrary, he learned of the faith of his readers by report (1:4). He remains unknown to them by face (2:1). The man responsible for the planting of the gospel in this community was Epaphras (1:7), who labored hard in this ministry (4:13) and continued to support the saints by fervent prayer (4:12).

Since Colossae was located in the province of Asia, it is natural to suppose that the evangelizing of the place occurred

---

[11] *Philippians,* pp. 42-46.

during Paul's long stay at Ephesus, for Luke informs us that the outreach of the work was such that people throughout Asia heard the word (Acts 19:10). It follows that Epaphras probably came to Ephesus from his native city Colossae and sat at the apostle's feet for a time, then returned to preach to his fellow townsmen.

Gentiles were apparently in the majority in the Colossian church (1:27; 2:13). These indications receive support from the apostle's language concerning Epaphras, who is called "a faithful minister of Christ on our behalf" (1:7). This seems to mean that Paul, as the leading apostle to the Gentiles, felt a responsibility for the evangelization of this community. Since he could not undertake the task in person, he was glad to see it accomplished by a fellow worker. Paul assumes that the church is interested in his affairs, despite the lack of personal contact (4:7-8).

BACKGROUND

By the time the reader gets into the second chapter he discovers that the church is being threatened with a certain type of propaganda that is damaging to the Christian faith (2:8, 16, 20). Doubtless Epaphras brought tidings of the trouble to the apostle, who felt that in addition to praying for the situation (2:1) he must write to commend the church for its generally satisfactory condition and also to warn against the present danger. Once the reader is confronted with Paul's exposé of the heresy, he may turn back to the first chapter and discover that much which seemed innocent of any deliberate reference to the situation actually bears on it. The gospel is called the word of the truth (1:5-6) recalling the language of Galatians 2:5, 14. There is a gentle warning against shifting from the hope of the gospel (1:23; cf. Gal. 1:6) After all, it is this faith, not the Colossian aberration, which is bearing fruit throughout the world (1:6, 23). The supremacy of Christ over all created intelligences is affirmed (1:15ff.) and his reconciling work extolled by which the hold of darkness has been broken and entrance gained into the kingdom of light (1:12-14, 22). In Christ are hidden all the treasures of wisdom and knowledge (2:3). These are really apologetic thrusts.

OUTLINE OF CONTENTS

The greeting to the church (1:1-2) is followed by an expression of thanksgiving for these believers (1:3-8) and a prayer for their progress in the faith (1:9-14). An important doctrinal section sets forth the pre-eminence and glory of Christ (1:15-23). As a minister of Christ, Paul states his mission and motive power (1:24-29) and his loving concern for his readers (2:1-5). Glancing at the danger of false teaching the apostle appeals for a walk in the complete sufficiency of Christ as the best defense against error (2:6-23). The old life must be laid aside and the new life in Christ put on (3:1-17). Christian grace must prevail in domestic relationships (3:18-4:1). A final exhortation calls for prayer, godly conduct, and gracious speech (4:2-6). Personal affairs are discussed (4:7-17) before the closing word and benediction (4:18).

THE NATURE OF THE FALSE TEACHING

This is not easy to fix precisely, but there are hints in the language of the apostle that can be pieced together to give some understanding of the position of the errorists. First of all, Paul warns against being taken in by philosophy, which he labels empty deceit (2:8). Although religion as such could be described as philosophy in the hellenistic age,[12] it is probable that here we have a reference to that attempted fusion of philosophy and religion known as Gnosticism, which at this stage was not as fully developed as in the second century. According to this system, knowledge of an esoteric sort was needed to enable one to rise from the toils of materialism into the pure light of God.

A special feature of this general outlook was the worship of angels (2:18), since these intermediary beings were regarded as essential to deliverance from the limitations of earthly existence. Some scholars understand "the elements of the world" (2:8, 20) in this light, as spirit beings who were thought of as controlling the planets and determining access to God (see the RSV rendering, "the elemental spirits of the universe"). This interpretation is possible in 2:8, where the term is contrasted to Christ, but not so natural in 2:20, where the context may be said to favor rudimentary elements in religion.[13]

That there was an attempt to impose certain of the externals of Judaism upon the Colossian believers is apparent from 2:16, where food and drink (dietary laws of the Jews), festivals

[12] In *IV Macc.* 5:11 the Jewish religion is called a philosophy.
[13] For the personal interpretation see L. B. Radford, *Colossians and Philemon, WC,* pp. 224-26; *per contra,* E. D. Burton, *Galatians, ICC,* pp. 510-18.

(of which Judaism had several), new moons, and sabbaths are specified.

Finally, an ascetic touch is supplied to this system by the demand that one abstain from certain things and thus impose restriction on the body (2:21-23). This was part of the pattern of Gnostic thought, especially in its early development. It was the human contribution to salvation, which showed a seriousness of purpose to rise above the limitations of the flesh.

That Jewish elements were involved is clear.[14] That pagan thought was a factor is equally clear. Phrygia had become the home of Jews in considerable numbers since the days of Antiochus III, who was reputed to have settled several thousand of them in Lydia and Phrygia, where their descendants developed some deviations from orthodox Judaism.[15] In this area Jewish religion was more open to mixture with other elements than was customary elsewhere.

To what extent the Pauline terms mirror the notions put forward by the Colossian teachers is uncertain, though some, such as "fulness" ($\pi\lambda\acute{\eta}\rho\omega\mu\alpha$) and "mystery," surely belong in this category, and perhaps "elements." Possibilities include also $\tau\acute{\alpha}\xi\iota\varsigma$ and $\sigma\tau\epsilon\rho\acute{\epsilon}\omega\mu\alpha$ (2:5).[16] The generous use of terms for wisdom and knowledge and understanding is not accidental. Paul's answer is compounded of exposure of the weakness of the position of the errorists and exposition of the superiority and finality of the Christian faith, centering in its Christology. Having created all things and holding them in his control, Christ reconciled all things by his death (1:15-20), and by that death defeated all hostile principalities and powers (2:15). The help of good angels need not be sought; the hurt of evil angels need not be feared. At Colossae the great mistake had been a failure to hold fast the Head (2:19). Christ is pre-eminent (1:18). Having him, believers have attained to fulness (2:10). They have no need of some special enlightenment, for in him are the treasures of wisdom and knowledge (2:3). Nor do they need ascetic discipline that imposes undue severity on the body. What they need, rather, is to put to death their sinful tendencies and put on Christ (3:5-17).[17]

[14] Lightfoot was able to point to some striking resemblances between the Colossian heresy and the Essenes (*Colossians and Philemon*, pp. 81-91). However, some important features of Essenism are not reflected in the epistle, and it is not known that Essenism penetrated to the Lycus Valley.

[15] W. L. Knox, *St. Paul and the Church of the Gentiles*, p. 146.

[16] H. Chadwick in *NTS*, I (May 1955), 273.

[17] For a brief summary of Pauline versus Gnostic teaching, see R. McL. Wilson, *The Gnostic Problem*, pp. 75-80.

The distinctive feature of the teaching of this book is the place given to Christ in the cosmos. This had been hinted at in I Corinthians 15:24-25, but in Colossians it breaks out into grandeur of thought and expression. Heresy cannot be called valueless when it calls forth such exalted truth.

Paul had used the term "head" for Christ before, but only in relation to the individual (I Cor. 11:3). Now he presents him as head both of the church (Col. 1:18) and of all authority (2:10).

Paul's handling of the Colossian problem shows remarkable skill. Perhaps the milder tone adopted here as opposed to his treatment of the Galatian issue is due to the lack of personal contact with the church, but it may be that Paul has been growing in stature as a controversialist and has acquired a more subtle approach. It has been well said that "Paul's genius as an apologist is his astonishing ability to reduce to an apparent vanishing point the gulf between himself and his converts and yet to 'gain' them for the Christian gospel."[18]

RELATIONSHIP TO EPHESIANS

That the two are kindred epistles is obvious. It is generally held that Colossians was written before Ephesians, though the opposite position has been asserted.[19] Both lay stress upon the terms "fulness" and "mystery." Wisdom and knowledge play an important part in the unfolding of the thought. Principalities and powers, both good and evil, are introduced. Christ is the unifier and consummator of all things. Yet there are differences. (1) Colossians is special in the sense that it is directed against false teaching in a local situation, whereas Ephesians is applicable anywhere. This leads naturally to the observation that (2) Colossians is polemical, Ephesians is irenical in spirit. The one shows solicitude, the other moves in an atmosphere of calm, of praise and thanksgiving. (3) Whereas Colossians is chiefly concerned with Christ's headship in the universe, Ephesians magnifies his headship over the church.

AUTHENTICITY

The epistle is found securely lodged within the Pauline corpus in the second century. Marcion included it, as did the Muratorian canon. Irenaeus and Clement of Alexandria explicitly refer it to Paul. Earlier writers use it without identification of the writer.

[18] Chadwick, *op. cit.*, p. 275.
[19] J. Coutts in *NTS*, IV (April 1958), 201-207; F. C. Synge, *Ephesians*, p. 76.

Attack on its Pauline character came from F. C. Baur on the ground that it reflected Gnosticism, which put it later than the apostle's time. But Baur assumed that the writer used $\pi\lambda\acute{\eta}\rho\omega\mu\alpha$ in the same sense as second-century Gnostic writers, as the summation of the various emanations linking God and the world, whereas he actually used it of the completeness of the divine nature that resided in Christ, so that nothing of deity is lacking in him.

In recent years attention has shifted to questions of vocabulary and style, some of which were anticipated by Mayerhoff even before Baur's time. Some twenty-eight words are found here that fail to appear in Paul's writings, besides some phrases. It is acknowledged that at least some of these are borrowed from the opposition for purposes of refutation and so are not Paul's in the first place. Furthermore, if authenticity is questioned because of the presence of unique words, every one of Paul's letters would be ruled out.

The style poses greater difficulty. It seems odd that in a controversial situation Paul could write so lethargically, without the rapier-like thrusts that abound in the soteriological epistles. The changed situation of the apostle, both temporally and locally, may have had something to do with this. Ernst Percy affirms that the peculiarities of style that confront the student here are discernible elsewhere in Paul, where they occur more sporadically.[20] Then he cites several pages of evidence to sustain his position. So the letter can hardly be denied to Paul on the basis of style.

Some critics find it hard to fit the theological thought of Colossians into a Pauline pattern. Lacking is any discussion of justification or the law. There is no place for the Spirit in the teaching on the development of Christian life. New interests emerge, mainly the cosmic significance of Christ. Yet there are not lacking a few seeds to account for this flowering out. In I Corinthians 8:6 the agency of Christ in creation agrees thoroughly with Colossians 1:16. The cohering of all things in him is a natural corollary of his universal and sovereign lordship.

Doubt springs also from the fact that so much of Colossians is echoed in Ephesians. Those who find grounds for questioning the authenticity of the latter epistle naturally conclude that this justifies the rejection of a letter that has such close similarity to it.

[20] *Die Probleme der Kolosser- und Epheserbriefe*, p. 36.

We cannot prejudge this question, which must await a discussion of Ephesians (q.v.).

As noted earlier, a close relationship exists between Colossians and Philemon. They are so interlocked that the rejection of one carries with it the rejection of the other. Conversely, if Philemon is accepted (and no one today rejects it) logically this should involve the acceptance of Colossians also. It is no wonder that those who question Colossians do so with marked hesitation.[21]

PHILEMON

BACKGROUND

From the letter itself the reader gets the impression that a slave by the name of Onesimus, after wronging his master Philemon in some way, possibly through robbing him and thus facilitating his escape, at length made his way to the place where Paul was at the time. Doubtless this slave was familiar with the name of Paul, since he had heard his master speak of him in the home at Colossae. Learning of Paul's presence in the city, Onesimus visited him in his hired quarters. Whether his motive for so doing was to apply for economic aid or to find relief for an uneasy conscience is a matter of conjecture. At any rate, he became a believer through the good offices of Paul and performed certain services in his behalf (v. 11). But the stubborn fact confronted both men that Onesimus was the legal property of Philemon. He must return to his master. It was to smooth the way for the return that Paul wrote the letter, presenting the request that Philemon receive and forgive his erring slave, accepting him as a brother and not merely a slave (vv. 16-17). There is a hint that he will do more than Paul requests, which may be understood as referring to manumission (v. 21).

It is notable that this missive, so personal in character, is also addressed to Apphia, most likely the wife of Philemon, and to Archippus, presumably their son. Not only so, it is addressed also to the church in Philemon's house. This curious combination of intimacy and publicity calls for explanation. Philemon must make his decision regarding Paul's request in the light of the fact that both his family and Christian friends are aware of the request. Under the circumstances, it is hard to imagine any Christian man failing to respond to the plea. The preservation

---

21 See, e.g., the statement by F. W. Beare in *IB,* XI, 145b.

of the letter presupposes a favorable attitude on Philemon's part and his compliance with the apostle's desire.

VALUE

This little document illustrates how early Christianity dealt with the problem of slavery. Instead of attacking the institution head-on, which would have been futile, the church turned its attention to the betterment of relations between masters and slaves by enjoining Christian conduct on both sides. "It was not by calling on the unhappy slaves to rise in armed rebellion against their masters that the Gospel struck off their fetters. It rather melted them by the fervour of Christian love, and so penetrated society with the principles of the Gospel that emancipation became a necessity."[22]

Another reason for treasuring this brief letter is the picture of Paul contained in it. He does not write as the apostle or the founder of churches or the theologian. Here is Paul the Christian man, so revealing his inner life as to give assurance that the gospel he preached had done its work in him. He is able so to identify himself with a truant slave as to call him "my own heart" (v. 12).

RECENT STUDY

A rather different view than the one sketched above has been presented by John Knox.[23] Archippus, not Philemon, is the real owner of the slave. Since Paul does not know him personally, he feels obliged to seek the help of his friend Philemon, who is thought of as the director of Christian work in the Lycus Valley, making his home at Laodicea. So the letter to Philemon has a letter within a letter, an appeal to Archippus within the framework of a greeting to Philemon. Paul is pictured as seeking help also from the Colossian church (Archippus resides there), which appears in the closing admonition to pass on to Archippus the admonition to take heed to the ministry that he has received in the Lord, so as to fulfill it (Col. 4:17). This ministry is thought of as connected with the slave Onesimus, as answering the demand that he be freed and made available to Paul for labor in the cause of the gospel. The letter to Philemon is identified with the document to which Paul refers in Colossians 4:16, in

---

[22] Godet, *Studies on the Epistles*, p. 239.
[23] *Philemon Among the Letters of Paul* (rev. ed., 1959); also in IB on Philemon.

his request that it be read in Colossae. In a further development of the theory, Knox identifies the Onesimus of the Philemon letter with the man of the same name who was bishop of the church at Ephesus in the early part of the second century and was referred to by Ignatius several times in his letters to the Ephesians. Knox credits him with gathering together Paul's letters toward the end of the first century and providing an introductory letter (the canonical Ephesians) to the whole collection. This phase of the theory will be examined in the discussion of Ephesians. It is the long-range importance of Onesimus that may account for the preservation of a letter that is without analogy in the Pauline corpus.

This view of Knox has been worked out with great attention to any detail that might provide support for it, and has commended itself to several scholars, but has not attained general assent. The following considerations weigh against it. (1) Since Philemon is mentioned first in the letter, it is natural to think of him as addressed throughout. (2) The idea that Philemon is to use his good offices to persuade Archippus to give up his slave nowhere appears. It is simply a critical inference. (3) The language of Colossians 4:17 seems much broader in its scope than the particular item of the disposition of the case of Onesimus. Archippus has received this ministry in the Lord. This sounds like a calling from the Lord in the area of witness, of which Paul has heard from Epaphras. (4) The reference to an epistle "from Laodicea" (Col. 4:16) does not need to be applied to Philemon, since it can perhaps apply to Ephesians, unless one puts Ephesians late and assigns it to another author (as Knox does). (5) It is strange that Paul can say to Archippus that the latter owes his very self to Paul (a probable reference to conversion) if Archippus was, as Knox supposes, not known to the apostle personally. The statement is much more fitting if applied to Philemon, who probably came to Ephesus in the day of Paul's labors there and heard the gospel from his lips. (6) The impression given in Paul's letters is that he was careful to avoid making personal or quasi-personal requests of his churches. That he should expect Archippus to give up Onesimus to be a helper in his own work when he did not even know him personally (according to Knox) seems unrealistic. (7) The idea that Philemon is to be identified with the letter from Laodicea has no support in the post-apostolic age. Marcion differentiated Philemon from the Laodicean epistle, including both in his canon.

EPHESIANS

READERS

The title, *to the Ephesians,* is not a part of the letter itself. It will be recalled that Paul's habit was to give the destination immediately after the statement of authorship. When letters began to circulate in the churches, they acquired titles to designate them and distinguish them one from another. In the case of the letter under consideration, the bulk of the MSS have the words "in Ephesus" as the locale of the saints here addressed. But there are three significant lines of evidence that tend to counteract mere bulk of testimony.

First, the leading MSS ℵ and B, also the important early witness P⁴⁶ and a few others, lack the words in question. Second, patristic testimony suggests that the two words were not in the text at an early date. Tertullian charged Marcion with changing the title. "I say nothing here about another epistle which we have with the heading, 'to the Ephesians,' but the heretics, 'to the Laodiceans'. . . .[24] According to the true belief of the church we hold this epistle to have been dispatched to the Ephesians, not the Laodiceans; but Marcion had to falsify its title, wishing to make himself out a very diligent investigator."[25] We should note that if Tertullian had been able to point to the words "in Ephesus" in the text of the epistle, he would not have been obliged to argue the question of the title at all. The fact that he failed to do so leads naturally to the conclusion that his text lacked these words. Further, when Origen commented on the opening words of the epistle, he came to the conclusion that Paul was writing to "the saints who are." That shows clearly that he found no complement for the words, "who are." Here is Origen's comment. "In the Ephesians also [since he had the title he was of course able to designate the letter] we found the expression, 'to the saints who are,' and we ask, unless the phrase 'who are' is redundant, what it can mean. May it not be that as in Exodus He who speaks to Moses declares His name to be the Absolute One, so also those who are partakers of the Absolute become existent when they are called, as it were, from non-being into being?"[26] This is awkward, if not impossible, from the standpoint of the Greek. But for our purpose the important thing is that Origen's comment points to the absence of the words

---

[24] *Against Marcion* V. 11.
[25] *Ibid.,* V. 17.
[26] Cramer's Catena *in loco.*

"in Ephesus." Later on, Basil noted that the words were omitted by his predecessors, probably having in mind Origen as one of these. He also testified that the words in question were not found in the older MSS.[27]

Third, some items in Ephesians are hard to square with the idea that Paul is writing to a church that is well known to him, a church of his own establishment and cultivation. He writes of giving thanks and praying for his readers ever since he heard of their faith and love (1:15). He raises a question as to whether his readers have heard of the dispensation of the grace of God given to him (3:2), which, to judge from the form of the statement, does not throw doubt on the hearing but on personal acquaintance with himself (cf. 4:21). Added to all this is the absence of any reference to the apostle's labors in Ephesus, where he had a long ministry.

These various factors have led many to conclude that Ephesians may have been written as an encyclical letter intended for churches geographically related to Ephesus. Some have identified it with the letter "from Laodicea" mentioned in Colossians 4:16, a position that is possible although it labors under the disadvantage that the Colossians would then be enjoined to read a letter very similar in contents to the one they had themselves received. A blank space may have been left for the address, to be filled in as copies of the letter were taken to various churches. This, too, presents problems, for the name of no other church has been preserved on any manuscript of the book. The situation recalls that of Romans, which in a few MSS lacks the words of destination, thereby hinting at a wider use than for the Roman church alone. If the circular letter theory is maintained, it should probably be held with wider reference than the churches of the Lycus Valley, for the general character of the epistle accords better with the view that it was intended for all the churches of Asia (cf. Acts 19:10). The prominence of Ephesus accounts for the address, though the details of the process are hidden from us.

AUTHENTICITY

The evidence for its acceptance as Paul's in the early church is extensive and undisputed. Ignatius and Polycarp made use of it, and perhaps even Clement of Rome. Irenaeus, Clement of Alexandria, and Tertullian attributed it to Paul. It has a secure place in the canons of Marcion and Muratori. The debate on

---

27 *Against Eunomius* II. 19.

authenticity, therefore, centers on the contents of the epistle itself. But before examining the grounds on which Ephesians has been denied to Paul, it is well to observe that unless these are compelling, the strength of the external testimony should be sufficient to tip the balance in his favor.

Of course Paul's name is on the epistle, not once but twice (1:1; 3:1), and he refers to himself in other places, especially in 3:2-8. But this is used against him by negative criticism, for it is maintained that Paul would not parade his humility in the fashion of the writer of 3:8.[28]

It seems reasonably apparent that the writer was a Jew (2:11). The language of 2:3 is not decisive against this, for nothing that is said there is impossible for a Jew who has become a Christian. As the apostolic age advanced, Paul's close companions were increasingly Gentiles rather than Jews, so the Jewish identity of the writer must be reckoned with by those who would attribute the epistle to an admirer of Paul and place it late in the first century.

Baur rejected Ephesians mainly because it reflects Gnosticism, which came to flower in the second century, considerably after Paul's time.[29] He pointed to $\pi\lambda\acute{\eta}\rho\omega\mu\alpha$ (fulness), a famous Gnostic catchword, and to the author's presentation of the union of Christ and the church as a syzygy, after the Gnostic pattern of pairing various concepts. Such criticisms are no longer taken seriously, since it cannot be established that the terms are used in a technical Gnostic sense. If the epistle is put after Paul's time, it becomes more difficult to explain why it does not contain a rebuttal of Gnosticism, for it was then especially that the system became a menace to the teaching of the church.

Other considerations are put forward today.

(1) *Vocabulary.* According to Moffatt, Ephesians has 38 words not found elsewhere in the New Testament and 44 which, though they occur in the New Testament, are not found elsewhere in Paul.[30] This is judged to be a rather high percentage of novelty for a relatively short book. The problem revolves around the estimation of the effect of the theme upon the diction. For example, five or six words occur here, peculiar to this book, beginning with the preposition $\sigma\acute{\nu}\nu$. Who can doubt that these terms were called forth by the necessity of stating the union between Christ and his people and their union with one another?

---

[28] D. E. Nineham, *Studies in Ephesians,* ed. by F. L. Cross, p. 35.
[29] *Paul,* II, 9ff.
[30] *Introduction,* pp. 385-86.

That Paul was fond of using compounds with this preposition is apparent from Romans and Colossians.

(2) *Style.* Erasmus seems to have been the first to remark on this feature. Sentences tend to be long and ponderous. Questions are all but absent. Some details of style may be noted here. Several examples occur of words used in both noun and verb forms in close conjunction (e.g., 2:4). There is a tendency to fulsomeness in writing, illustrated by the fact that somewhat synonymous terms are linked together (e.g., "strangers and pilgrims," 2:19). Several times genitives are used in a pleonastic sense (e.g., "the strength of his might," 1:19). Ernst Percy made a searching investigation of this subject and found that the overweighting of the syntax occurs mainly in the liturgical sections, that is, those that breathe the atmosphere of praise and prayer. He concluded that when due recognition is given to this fact, Pauline authorship is not imperilled by considerations of style.[31] Actually the features of Ephesians that give trouble are observable to some degree in Paul's acknowledged letters.

Cadbury puts the question of style into sharp focus by a question: "Which is more likely — that an imitator of Paul in the first century composed a writing ninety or ninety-five per cent in accordance with Paul's style or that Paul himself wrote a letter diverging five or ten per cent from his usual style?"[32]

(3) *The Use of Colossians.* Objection is raised not so much to the fact that the writer uses Colossians but to the way in which he uses it. The same word is sometimes employed with a different meaning. It is claimed, for example, that whereas in Colossians 2:10 the headship of Christ is over the cosmic powers, in Ephesians it is over the church (4:15; 5:23). In reply it can be said that the universal headship of Christ is affirmed in Ephesians 1:22 without naming the cosmic powers ("head over all things to the church"), and in Colossians Christ is presented as head of the church (1:18) as well as of the cosmic powers. So both emphases are found in both Epistles. Again, it is argued that in Colossians reconciliation is God's act, through Christ, to bring men to himself, whereas in Ephesians it is the act of Christ whereby Jew and Gentile are made one in him (2:16). As a matter of fact, the Ephesian passage includes the emphasis of Colossians, for the reconciliation is to God as well as manward between the two groups. Another case is the use of *plērōma.* In

31 *Die Probleme der Kolosser-und Epheserbriefe.* See especially the conclusion stated on p. 448.
32 *NTS,* V (Jan. 1959), 101.

Colossians the fullness is in Christ, whereas in Ephesians the church is called his fullness. This change in application is strictly in accord with the distinctive teaching of Ephesians on the nature of the church. The cosmic powers are mentioned, but the writer is less concerned with Christ's relation to them than to the church. In much the same way there is an altered application of the word "mystery" (Col. 1:27; Eph. 3:4ff.).

This method of handling the concepts of Colossians, while it may seem superficially to give trouble for the cause of authenticity, actually works to the embarrassment of those who deny the letter to Paul, for it is difficult to imagine an admirer of the apostle departing to such an extent from the use of terms in Colossians. About the best that can be done with the problem is to surmise that for some reason the writer did not have Colossians before him but was relying on impressions created through the use of the epistle and lingering on in his mind after repeated reading.[33] But in that case one is curious to know why it is that the writer reproduces the passage about Tychicus almost word for word (Col. 4:7-8; Eph. 6:21-22), as though to suggest that he had the text before him.[34]

It is easier to conclude that Paul himself is utilizing some of the terms and ideas of Colossians as he writes Ephesians than to introduce a *falsarius* to account for Ephesians. As E. F. Scott puts it, "Some ideas are more highly developed in this than in the other epistles, but they are always Paul's ideas, and it is difficult to see how anyone but himself could have so drawn out their deeper implications.[35] The examples of forgers under Paul's name from the post-apostolic age fall far short of the quality attained here. If Paul did not write Ephesians, the man who wrote it ought to be recognized as a theological genius. Who was he? The period following Paul discloses no such man.

(4) *Post-Pauline Ideas*. The concept of the church universal appears in Ephesians, but not in Paul's acknowledged epistles, including Colossians. This is a real difficulty, not so much from the standpoint of doubt that Paul could give expression to such a concept, but that he could make it central in Ephesians after having said nothing about it in Colossians. On this basis one who holds to Paul's authorship of Ephesians may find it expedient to posit something of an interval between it and Colossians.[36]

---

[33] C. L. Mitton, *The Epistle to the Ephesians,* p. 79.
[34] See D. Guthrie, *Introduction,* pp. 113-14.
[35] *MNTC,* p. 121.
[36] J. N. Sanders, *Studies in Ephesians,* ed. by F. L. Cross, p. 16.

Yet any great interval seems precluded by Ephesians 6:21-22 in the light of Colossians 4:7-8.

Again, the writer seems to hold an attitude of veneration for early Christian leaders quite unlike the independent spirit of the apostle Paul. We read of the holy apostles and prophets as the recipients of revelation (3:5) and that the church is founded upon them (2:20). Is this not a reflection of second-generation Christianity? Such a line of argumentation seems to defeat itself, for those who hold to it assume that the writer of Ephesians was an able man and a devoted Paulinist. If so, he should have known from Paul's letters, especially from the first chapter of Galatians, that he ought to represent Paul as stressing his independent position as an apostle. Assuming, however, that Paul is the writer, this recognition of others as having apostolic rank gives no trouble, since in Galatians 1:17 and 2:8 and I Corinthians 15:7-11 Paul honors the position and contribution of other apostles. As for the adjective "holy" (3:5), this need not be thought of as reflecting a venerating mentality, since Paul accorded to all Christians the status of "saints" (same word). However, some may feel that the use is not strictly parallel, for in the one case "holy" has an adjectival function, whereas in the other it is used as a noun.

Another problem is the lack of a characteristic Pauline eschatology. The ardent expectation of the return of Christ is missing. Even the Saviour's death is subordinated to his present exaltation (but see 1:7; 2:13; 5:25). It seems that the apostle was so filled with thoughts of the risen and glorified Lord that his earthly ministry, whether in retrospect or in connection with his future advent, was somewhat eclipsed. One may hold, of course, that Paul is simply dealing with ultimates here rather than preliminary aspects that are assumed. Just as the exaltation of the Savior depends upon his redeeming work, so the reconciliation depends upon the return and the victory which is achieved over all evil powers. Hints of this ultimate issue of salvation may be found in I Corinthians 15:24-28 and in Romans 8:19-23, so the emphasis in Ephesians is not wholly without preparation.[37] The apostle's mind was open to fresh revelation and to meditation upon it, so new emphases ought not to be regarded as a sure index of another hand.

The reference to the breaking down of the middle wall of partition, thereby uniting Jew and Gentile in the church (2:14), has been thought to demand a dating of the epistle after the

---

37 See Dodd's comments in *New Testament Studies*, p. 124f.

destruction of Jerusalem. This is not a necessary supposition, for Paul could have been thinking of the temple barrier in symbolic terms. His language suggests this, for Christ is the one who has abolished the obstruction, not the historical event that was accomplished by man.

In summary, the difficulties for Pauline authorship, though numerous (Goodspeed lists as many as 21),[38] do not seem sufficient to overthrow the traditional position or to render false such favorable judgments as these: "the crown of St. Paul's writings" (J. Armitage Robinson); "the greatest and maturest of all Paul's writings" (John Mackay).

GOODSPEED'S THEORY[39]

Accepting the position that the epistle was not written by Paul, this scholar seeks to provide an explanation for its composition. The publication of the Book of Acts toward the close of the first century furnishes the key. Curiosity was aroused in the mind of at least one man as to whether Paul had written letters to any of the churches that the Book of Acts connected with his missionary labors. Investigation was rewarding. He came away from these centers with copies of Paul's letters, presumably nine in number, and then conceived the idea of making them available to all Christians by publishing them as a corpus. The theory maintains that since the letters were occasional documents, they had lain idle since the individual churches received them years before. In publishing Paul's letters, this unknown person (identified in *The Key to Ephesians* as Onesimus) decided to write an introductory letter to the whole collection. In this way Ephesians originated. Obliged to face the problem that this letter bears a far closer relation to Colossians than to any of the other letters of Paul, Goodspeed conjectures that the writer was more familiar with it than with the others, having steeped his mind in it shortly before writing Ephesians.

Certain objections have been raised to this reconstruction. (i) Goodspeed assumes without warrant that Paul's letters were lying unused and that the apostle's labors would have been forgotten had it not been for the publication of the Book of Acts. F. W. Beare comments, "The collection of Paul's letters cannot be made to depend on the influence of Acts. The supposition that

[38] *The Key to Ephesians*, pp. v-vii.
[39] *Introduction to the New Testament*, pp. 224-26; *New Chapters in New Testament Study*, pp. 22-49; *The Meaning of Ephesians; The Key to Ephesians*.

337

the Christian church forgot all about Paul for a generation after his death, and that only the publication of Acts saved him and his letters from oblivion is purely gratuitous."[40] Cadbury also is dubious about a theory of "literary precipitation," whereby "we take the books we have and try to arrange them into a series of cause and effect, as though books were more precipitated by books than by other and living factors in the environment."[41] The very fact that Paul's name is used in Ephesians, not once but twice, by the alleged writer, assumes that this name would have great significance for the readers. It does not fit well with the idea that Paul was virtually forgotten.

(ii) Beare expresses doubt that Ephesians could have been written, with the high quality and confident Paulinism it exhibits, simply on the basis of literary acquaintance with Paul's work. Such a relationship seems too superficial to account for the spirit and contents of the book.[42]

(iii) Goodspeed's claim that all the letters of Paul were utilized by the writer is hardly borne out by the examination of the parallels which he cites, nor is the contention valid that Colossians is present in Ephesians simply in greater quantity than the other letters. Actually the situation is quite different. Whereas the materials that relate to Colossians stand out clearly, that which is supposedly derived from the other epistles cannot be recognized with any clarity at all, since the likeness pertains merely to a word here and there, or at most a phrase. Beare is sharp in his criticism, saying, "Many if not most of the alleged correspondences of language do not indicate literary dependence in the slightest degree."[43] If Ephesians was written as an introductory letter, the excessive use of Colossians seems quite unaccountable.

(iv) On Goodspeed's theory it is necessary to suppose that Ephesians stood first in the Pauline corpus as it was known around the end of the first century and the beginning of the second. John Knox attempted to supply needed support for this position by noting that Marcion's list of the epistles of Paul, as given by Tertullian, followed at least roughly the principle of putting the books in order according to their length, the longest at the beginning, the shortest at the end. This principle was disturbed by the presence of Galatians at the head of the list, but such an arrangement is easily understood because of the anti-Judaistic

40 *IB*, X, 603a.
41 *NTS*, V (Jan. 1959), 92.
42 *Ibid.*
43 *IB*, X, 603b.

338

character of Galatians, which Marcion wished to make prominent. Knox concludes that Marcion deliberately exchanged the positions of Galatians and Ephesians in the traditional order, so that it may be assumed that Ephesians stood first in the period before Marcion.[44] But this conclusion is precarious. The order of Paul's letters in other lists, such as those of the Muratorian Canon, Tertullian, and Origen, in no case follows the principle of decreasing length, so we cannot assume that Marcion's arrangement represents the practice of the church before his time.[45]

OUTLINE OF CONTENTS

The opening salutation (1:1-2) leads into a sustained thanksgiving for spiritual blessings in Christ (1:3-14). These in turn evoke a prayer for the spiritual understanding of the readers (1:15-23). In discussing the spiritual status of the redeemed, the apostle describes their former position in sin (2:1-3), their present position in grace (2:4-10), and their position in the household of God, shared equally by Jewish and Gentile believers (2:11-22). These two groups are seen as constituting the body of Christ (3:1-13). A second prayer centers in the need of realizing the love of Christ (3:14-21). Turning to the outworking of Christian life in experience, the apostle portrays the walk of the believers: in the unity of the Spirit and the enjoyment of his gifts to the church (4:1-16), in separation from the old life and conformity to the new (4:17-32), in love (5:1-2), in purity (5:3-14), in wisdom (5:15-17), in joyful thanksgiving (5:18-20), and in subjection to one another (5:21-6:9). The warfare of the Christian is carried on against unseen hosts of wickedness and demands the whole armor of God (6:10-20). The conclusion has a word about the bearer of the epistle, as well as a prayer and benediction (6:21-24).

CHARACTERISTICS

(1) Of crucial importance is the exposition of the equality between Jew and Gentile in the body of Christ. (2) A corollary of this is the general emphasis on unity in matters of faith (4:3-6). (3) Considerable attention is given to the purpose and will of God. (4) Paul's characteristic phrase "in Christ," or its equivalent, occurs here more often than in any other epistle (35

[44] *Philemon Among the Letters of Paul,* pp. 76-90.
[45] See article by C. H. Buck, Jr., in *JBL,* LXVIII (Dec. 1949), 351-57. Goodspeed countered with the contention that orthodox displeasure at Marcion caused a departure from his order.

times, according to Deissmann). (5) The unfolding of doctrinal truth is interrupted by two prayers, one centering in knowledge (1:15-23), the other in love (3:14-21). (6) Such terms as grace, love, holy, mystery, and "the heavenlies" stand out in the discussion. (7) A rather sharp division is made between the doctrinal and practical portions of the letter (4:1). (8) A long section is devoted to domestic relations from the Christian standpoint (5:22-6:9). (9) The conflict of believers with hostile spiritual powers receives special attention (6:10-17).

PHILIPPIANS

BACKGROUND

This letter is addressed to a church in Philippi, a city that received its name from its founder, Philip of Macedon. Luke gives two items of information about the place (Acts 16:12). He calls it the leading city of the district of Macedonia, perhaps out of a sense of friendly rivalry with the capital, Thessalonica, and notes its status as a Roman colony. Local pride over this distinction comes out in the story of the men who complained to the authorities about Paul and his associates that they were Jews seeking to introduce customs and practices contrary to the Roman pattern (Acts 16:21).

Philippi presented a somewhat unusual situation in that Jews were too few in number to have a synagogue. There was a meeting place for prayer just outside the city, frequented by women, where Paul first planted the gospel seed (Acts 16:13). For the most part the Christian community that came into being there must have been Gentile. It is significant that Luke makes no mention of opposition from Jewish sources, in contrast to the usual experience of the missionaries.

From the cessation of the "we" section at the completion of the Philippian mission, it may reasonably be concluded that Luke remained in the city to aid the little group of believers. Being a Gentile himself, he was presumably well fitted for this role. From him Paul may have learned from time to time of the conditions in the church, with other contacts probably coming through one or more visits by Silas (Acts 18:5) and from those of the apostle himself, of which there were at least two (II Cor. 2:13; Acts 20:6). The gifts of the congregation testified to their love and concern for the man who had made their city his first stopping place in his evangelization of Europe — "the beginning of the gospel" in that area (Phil. 4:15-16; II Cor. 11:9).

AUTHENTICITY

Rarely has any doubt been expressed about the authenticity of this book that bears Paul's name and so clearly reveals both the outer and inner life of the apostle. The inclusion of Timothy (1:1) does not denote co-authorship, which is ruled out by the statement in 2:19 if by nothing else, for there the writer refers to his plan to send Timothy.

Echoes of the letter occur in Clement of Rome and in Ignatius. A more generous use of it appears in Polycarp, which is natural because he himself is writing to the Philippians. He mentions that Paul, when absent from them, wrote letters to them (3:2), which may indicate a more extensive correspondence than has been preserved in the New Testament. Further testimony to Pauline authorship is found in the canons of Marcion and Muratori and in many writers of the late second and third centuries.

OCCASION AND PURPOSE

Epaphroditus, who had been sent by the church with a gift for Paul, was now ready to return to Philippi after recovering from a serious illness (2:25-30). This gave the apostle opportunity to commend this brother and to write to his friends concerning a variety of matters.

It was natural for Paul to express his thanks for the gift he had received from the church, although it seems strange that he should wait to do so until the end of the letter (4:10-18). It is probable, however, that his reference to the church's fellowship with him in the gospel (1:5) includes a subtle allusion to the gift, since the word "fellowship" is used in this sense of contribution elsewhere (II Cor. 9:13; Rom. 15:26). If so, the apostle is considering it first in the light of a gift for the Lord's work and only secondarily as a personal benefit.

Paul wished also to express his love and longing for the saints who had meant so much to him over the years (1:8).

It was desirable to relieve the anxiety that the church felt over Paul the prisoner by indicating his circumstances in some fullness (1:12ff.). God had overruled the imprisonment in such a way that Christ was being proclaimed, even though with improper motives on the part of some (1:15). It is notable that in writing to the Colossians, Paul left personalia to the bearer of the letter (Col. 4:7), but with such close friends as he had in Philippi it was possible to discuss his own affairs with great freedom.

A tendency to disunity called for a strong plea for harmony grounded on a sharing of the mind of Christ (2:1-11). Two women are singled out for special appeal (4:2). To some extent the way was prepared for this emphasis by the almost studied repetition of the word *all* in the thanksgiving at the opening of the letter (four times), and by the contrasting of rivalry with love in 1:15. What was deplorable in Rome could not be admirable in Philippi.

Warning is issued against Judaizing propagandists with whom Paul was well acquainted from long experience (3:2ff.). More gentle is the rebuke of the perfectionists in the ranks of the saints (3:15). Once more the language becomes severe in reference to sensualists and materialists (3:18-19).

Finally, the apostle writes to encourage his readers in the conduct of Christian life — in suffering (1:27-30), in witness (2:16), in the cultivation of joy and peace (4:4-7) and of high and holy thoughts (4:8) — in fine, to join in imitation of the apostle as he runs the race incident to the upward calling in Christ (3:13-17).

CHARACTERISTICS

(1) The letter is warmly personal, a feature which is underscored by the fact that Paul writes "I" some fifty-two times, far in excess of the norm. (2) The Christocentric emphasis is even more striking, for the personal is subordinated to it. Here the key statement is found in Paul's claim that for him to live is Christ (1:21). (3) Doctrinal teaching is at a minimum, and what there is appears mainly in order to serve practical or polemical ends (2:5-11; 3:9-11, 20-21). (4) Women are specially recognized for their work (4:3). Their prominence agrees with what historians tell us about the advanced condition of women in Macedonia (cf. Acts 17:4). The concern of the church for Paul's welfare and comfort, manifested at the very beginning by Lydia (Acts 16:15, 40) and later by their gifts, was probably due in large part to the women. (5) It is possible that some allusions in the letter have the secular history of the city in mind. Paul seems to use the privileged Roman background as a basis for advancing the higher claims of Christian citizenship (see 1:27 in the Greek text, and 3:20). (6) The unique inclusion of overseers and deacons in the address may be due to their part in superintending the raising and sending of the gift that Paul had received. (7) The ethical teaching in 4:8 has been thought to owe something to Stoicism, and the same is true of the

expression *be content* in 4:11 and the term for learning a secret in 4:12. This dependence reveals a generous appreciation for the nobler aspects of this philosophy, and fits rather well with Paul's advancing years and his residence in Rome where the Stoic influence was strong. (8) Several words stand out as keys to the thought. One is *gospel,* used nine times. Everything is seen in the light of the gospel, whether it be the gift of the Philippians (1:5) or his own trial (1:16). Another is the verb *to think* (φρονεῖν), used ten times, which is more than in any other letter. Salvation and fellowship are important terms, as is glory. Paul's use of the word *to abound* is exceeded only in Ephesians. Highly characteristic of this letter is the verb *to rejoice* (nine times) and the noun *joy* (five). It is this that Paul seems to covet for his friends almost above everything else. Here we get insight into his success as a pastor. He was able to minister strength from a distance, but this in turn depended on his own success as a Christian. His joy in Christ not only enabled him to surmount his own trials but was also communicable, by its sheer genuineness and abundance, to fellow believers.

RECENT STUDY

It has been maintained that the Christological hymn in 2:5-11 is borrowed by the apostle from some earlier source, either Christian, according to Lohmeyer, [46] or the Gnostic myth of the heavenly redeemer adapted to Christian thought, according to Käsemann, [47] which is far less tenable. Several arguments have been advanced to support the borrowing thesis. [48] The lyrical flow of the language breaks the sturdy prose of the apostle's admonition; several terms in the passages are not found elsewhere in Paul; there is no statement of resurrection to match that concerning the death of Christ, which is hardly Pauline; and the Lordship of Christ is cosmical in its scope rather than confined to the church.

These considerations are sufficiently strong to have convinced many scholars of the soundness of the position that this section is pre-Pauline. But the arguments seem to be somewhat less than decisive. There is general consent that Paul was capable of a poet's touch, as witnessed by his hymn in recognition of love (I Cor. 13). He should be as good a candidate as any

[46] *Die Briefe an die Philipper,* etc., *in loco.;* also *Kyrios Jesus,* pp. 8ff.
[47] "Kritische Analyse von Phil. 2:5-11," *ZTK* 47 (1950), pp. 313ff.
[48] A. M. Hunter, *Paul and His Predecessors,* 1961 ed., pp. 39-44.

for the use of rare words, considering his range of vocabulary. As far as resurrection is concerned, it is true that this is regularly joined with mention of the death of Christ in passages where Paul is stressing the believer's participation with Christ in these redemptive acts (Rom. 6:1-11; Col. 3:1-4, etc.), but he is not averse to mentioning the death by itself in other situations (I Cor. 1:23; Gal. 3:1). The humbling aspect of our Lord's work stopped at the cross, and that is all Paul needs in order to deal with the Philippian problem. With respect to the cosmical setting for the lordship of Christ, the essence of the thought is found already in I Corinthians 15:24-25, though it must be granted that the title Kurios does not appear there. The framework of the two Adams seems to lie in the background of the treatment in Philippians 2:6ff., which is characteristically Pauline (I Cor. 15:45ff.; Rom. 5:12ff.).

The pattern of thought in this passage may well owe something to the teaching of Jesus to the effect that the one who humbles himself will be exalted, a truth which, as Paul saw, had its greatest illustration in the case of the Lord Jesus himself.[49]

A problem of a different nature centers in the language of 3:1, where Paul uses the word *finally* as though to give intimation that he is about to conclude the letter, only to go on at considerable length. Some have conjectured that part of the remainder of the epistle may actually belong to another letter that has somehow become joined to Philippians. This is supported by the observation that the tone of the greater part of chapter 3 is rather out of keeping with the rest of the letter, owing to its harshness. Such a claim probably would not have arisen were it not for the presence of *finally,* and since Paul was guilty of a similar premature notice of closing in I Thessalonians 4:1, the case for injection of another letter is not strong.

The suggestion is made by Ralph P. Martin that fresh news concerning the situation at Philippi may have come to the apostle in the course of preparing this letter, leading to the use of the strong language of warning.[50]

BIBLIOGRAPHY

Abbott, T. K., *A Critical and Exegetical Commentary on the Epistle to the Ephesians and to the Colossians, ICC.* New York: Scribner's, 1902.

[49] For a full treatment of the problems of the passage, see R. P. Martin, *An Early Christian Confession,* 1960; and *Carmen Christi,* 1967.
[50] *TBC* on Philippians, p. 38.

Barth, Markus, *The Broken Wall. A Study of the Epistle to the Ephesians.* Valley Forge: Judson Press, 1959.

Beare, F. W., *A Commentary on the Epistle to the Philippians, HNTC.* New York: Harper, 1959.

Bruce, F. F., *The Epistle to the Ephesians.* New York: Revell, 1961.

Cross, F. L., ed., *Studies in Ephesians.* London: A. R. Mowbray, 1956.

Dibelius, Martin, *An die Kolosser, Epheser und Philemon, HZNT.* 2nd ed., Tübingen: Mohr, 1927.

Eadie, John, *A Commentary on the Greek Text of the Epistle of Paul to the Colossians.* 2nd ed., Edinburgh: T. & T. Clark, 1884.

Ellicott, C. J., *A Critical and Grammatical Commentary on St. Paul's Epistle to the Ephesians.* Andover: W. F. Draper, 1885.

——————————, *St. Paul's Epistles to the Philippians, the Colossians, and Philemon.* 5th ed., London: Longmans, Green, 1888.

Gifford, E. H., *The Incarnation. A Study of Philippians 2:5-11.* New York: Dodd, Mead, 1897.

Hodge, Charles, *A Commentary on the Epistle to the Ephesians.* New York: Robert Carter, 1868.

Lightfoot, J. B., *Saint Paul's Epistles to the Colossians and to Philemon.* 9th. ed., London: Macmillan, 1890.

——————————, *Saint Paul's Epistle to the Philippians.* London: Macmillan, 1879.

Lohmeyer, Ernst, *Die Briefe an die Philipper, und die Kolosser und an Philemon,* Meyer series. Göttingen: Vandenhoeck & Ruprecht, 1953.

Lohse, Eduard, "Pauline Theology in the Letter to the Colossians," *NTS,* 15 (January 1969), 211-220.

Martin, Ralph P., "An Epistle in Search of a Life-setting" (Eph.), *ET,* 79 (July 1968), 297-302.

——————————, *Carmen Christi: Philippians 2:5-11.* Cambridge University Press, 1967.

——————————, *The Epistle of Paul to the Philippians, TBC.* Grand Rapids, Eerdmans, 1959.

Michael, J. Hugh, *The Epistle of Paul to the Philippians, MNTC.* New York: Harper, 1927.

Mitton, C. Leslie, *The Epistle to the Ephesians.* Oxford: Clarendon Press, 1951.

Moule, C. F. D., *The Epistles of Paul to the Colossians and to Philemon, CGTC.* Cambridge University Press, 1957.

——————————, "Further Reflexions on Philippians 2:5-11," in *Apostolic History and the Gospel,* ed. by W. Ward Gasque and Ralph P. Martin. Grand Rapids: Eerdmans, 1970, pp. 264-276.

Moule, H. C. G., *Ephesian Studies.* 2nd. ed., London: Thynne, n.d.

——————————, *Colossian Studies.* London: Hodder & Stoughton, 1898.

——————————, *Philippian Studies.* 6th ed., London: Hodder & Stoughton, 1908.

345

Müller, J. J., *The Epistles of Paul to the Philippians and to Philemon, NIC.* Grand Rapids: Eerdmans, 1955.

Percy, Ernst, *Die Probleme der Kolosser-und Epheserbriefe.* Lund: C. W. K. Gleerup, 1946.

Plummer, A., *A Commentary on St. Paul's Epistle to the Philippians.* London: Robert Scott, 1919.

Radford, L. B., *The Epistle to the Colossians and the Epistle to Philemon, WC.* London: Methuen, 1931.

Reicke, Bo, "Caesarea, Rome, and the Captivity Epistles," in *Apostolic History and the Gospel,* ed. by Gasque and Martin. Grand Rapids: Eerdmans, 1970, pp. 277-286.

Robertson, A. T., *Paul and the Intellectuals: The Epistle to the Colossians.* New York: Doubleday, Doran, 1928.

Robinson, J. Armitage, *St. Paul's Epistle to the Ephesians.* 2nd ed., London: Macmillan, 1904.

Scott, E. F., *The Epistles of Paul to the Colossians, to Philemon and to the Ephesians, MNTC.* New York: Harper, n.d.

Simpson, E. K., and Bruce, F. F., *Commentary on the Epistles to the Ephesians and the Colossians, NIC.* Grand Rapids: Eerdmans, 1957.

Vincent, Marvin R., *A Critical and Exegetical Commentary on the Epistles to the Philippians and to Philemon, ICC.* New York: Scribner's, 1897.

Westcott, F. B., *A Letter to Asia.* London: Macmillan, 1941.

346

Chapter Seventeen

THE PASTORAL EPISTLES

IN THE YEAR 1726 PAUL ANTON WROTE A BOOK ON THE LETTERS to Timothy and Titus, using the designation "Pastoral Epistles." The name has gained such currency that no other is likely to displace it, even though it is not wholly suitable. First Timothy is the most truly pastoral, and Second Timothy least so, with Titus occupying an intermediate position. These three are the only letters by Paul to individuals, since Philemon is addressed also to the family of the recipient and to the local church. Timothy and Titus appear as authorized representatives of Paul who need the help and encouragement offered in these writings, Timothy as the responsible overseer of the well-established work at Ephesus, and possibly throughout the province of Asia, Titus as the organizer of a newer work on the island of Crete, where Paul had labored with him for a time (Titus 1:5). In II Timothy Paul is concerned to a lesser extent with the church, writing in a more personal vein to his understudy and revealing more of his own situation.

OUTLINE OF CONTENTS

In I Timothy the apostle begins by admonishing Timothy to deal decisively with certain teachers who have perverted notions both of the law and the gospel, citing his own right to offer cor-

347

rective measures because of the divine mercy extended to him in his sinful days as persecutor, and including Timothy's call to service as fitting him for this difficult mission (chap. 1). Turning to the needs of the church, Paul pleads for prayer for all men, especially for public figures, and treats of the place and demeanor of women (chap. 2). There follows a statement of the qualifications of bishops and deacons, leading into an exposition of the church as the custodian and support of the truth (chap 3). In contrast to those who depart from the faith, Timothy must give himself to godliness and to profitable Christian service (chap. 4). Directions are given for dealing with various groups in the church, especially elders and widows (chap. 5). The epistle closes with attention to a variety of matters, including injunctions to slaves, warnings against covetousness, and a ringing challenge to Timothy to wage a good fight for the truth (chap. 6).

Titus, though briefer, has much in common with I Timothy. Paul begins by stating the qualifications of the bishop, who must be able to cope with insubordinate teachers who are upsetting people (chap. 1). Commands follow for dealing with various groups — older men and women, younger men, and slaves. All must adorn the doctrine, for this is the desired result of the incarnation and redemptive work of Christ (chap. 2). Teaching is given about believers' relations to society, grounded in the regenerating power of the gospel. They should apply themselves to good works rather than profitless controversy. The book closes with attention to personal matters (chap. 3).

Second Timothy has its own atmosphere. It starts off with reminiscences of Timothy's spiritual history and of Paul's, committing both men to the guardianship of the truth (chap. 1). Though others are slipping away, Timothy is counted on heavily by Paul to be a good soldier of Christ, a workman handling aright the word of truth, and a skillful teacher (chap. 2). The present has its share of unholy men (and the future will have them too) who misuse religion in their own interest. But the example of Paul and the proper use of Scripture will enable Timothy to be equipped for every good work (chap. 3). The letter closes on a note of urgency -- preach the word while you can, my own time is short, come to me quickly (chap. 4).

BACKGROUND

The background for I Timothy is roughly this, that Paul had left Timothy in charge of the church at Ephesus, while he himself proceeded to Macedonia. Concern for the church and for Timothy as the liaison between himself and the church led the apostle to write this manual of instruction that was intended to supplement the counsel given orally at the time of Paul's departure, since his return to Ephesus might be delayed (3:14-15).

The situation in Titus is similar. Paul's interest in Crete, stimulated, no doubt, by his limited contact with it on the way to Rome, was able to find expression at length in a missionary campaign there. Titus was his helper, and when Paul found it necessary to return to the mainland, he wrote to strengthen the hand of his lieutenant who was still at work on the island. It would be going beyond the evidence to assert that Paul and Titus founded the church in Crete, but the Christian faith was not well established. Since Paul was unable to remain a great length of time, he wrote to direct Titus in the task of organization and of purifying the Christian community of elements adverse to the faith. Paul expects Titus to join him at Nicopolis, a city of the Epirus section of Greece, where he anticipates spending the winter (Titus 3:12).

Second Timothy is written from Rome by Paul the prisoner (1:16-17). The presumption is that fresh suspicion has led to his arrest and second imprisonment. Only Luke is now his close companion (4:11), though others are in touch with him (4:21). However, he found no one to stand with him at his first hearing (4:16). The pathos of this loneliness is reflected in the letter as the aging apostle yearns for Timothy, his son in the faith, and has much to say about him as well as to him. It is not strange that the general situation in the church as Paul had sampled it since release from his first imprisonment should shadow his thoughts as he writes and should come to expression in a letter that otherwise might have been almost purely personal. There are some who oppose the faith, whose teaching is as wrong as their motives. Timothy must be alert to this danger, for he must soon shoulder a larger responsibility when his older friend is taken from the scene.

THE NATURE OF THE FALSE TEACHING

We have observed that all the Pastorals have something to say about opposition to the faith. The problem is to identify the heretical tendency or tendencies. Much is said about error and errorists in the letters before us, but not much that points the way to positive identification. We read of those who desire to be teachers of the law, whose stock in trade is myths and endless genealogies (I Tim. 1:4, 7; cf. Tit. 3:9). Similarly,

349

attention is directed to men of the circumcision who are in-subordinate, deceivers, who teach for base gain (Tit. 1:10-11). In this connection Jewish myths are mentioned again (1:14). A warning is given against those with ascetic tendencies who forbid marriage and the eating of certain foods (I Tim. 4:3). A clear-cut doctrinal deviation is stated at one point. Certain men are teaching that the resurrection is past, thereby denying a future bodily resurrection (II Tim. 2:18; cf. I Tim. 1:20). Some of the trouble is on a lower plane, connected with aimless disputes about words and inconsequential matters (II Tim. 2:14; 3:9). Finally, falsely named knowledge becomes the target of the apostle (I Tim. 6:20).

F. C. Baur thought that I Timothy 6:20 furnished clear in-dication that the Marcionite heresy is in view. In this passage the word *antitheses* occurs, the exact term employed by Marcion as the title of his work setting forth the contrasts and contradictions between the old and new dispensations. Here also we read of *gnosis* (Marcion was Gnostic in his general outlook). If this identification is correct, the Pastorals belong in the second century and cannot be regarded as apostolic. However, in view of the volume of refutation brought to bear upon Marcion's position by patristic writers, it would be strange indeed if the writer of the Pastorals, in case he belongs to the patristic period, should content himself with a mere passing notice. Further, if there is an underlying unity between the various notices of heretical teaching in these epistles, then the error cannot have been Marcionite, for the references to teachers of the law and Jewish myths rule out this possibility. Marcion was implacably anti-Jewish. Again, the false teachers are stigmatized as men of corrupt mind who advance their views for the sake of base gain. Marcion was already wealthy and did not use his religious propaganda for this purpose, nor could he rightly be charged with any deviation in morality. On the contrary, his followers were known for their uprightness of life. It may be granted that the prohibition of marriage and abstinence from certain foods (I Tim. 4:3) fits Marcionite tenets well enough, but these features were not confined to this movement.

Some students favor the view that Gnosticism in the more technical sense furnished the opposition referred to in the Pastorals. But the more speculative features of Gnosticism, such as angelic emanations and syzygies, are not in evidence here, unless, as some hold, the references to genealogies have such emanations in view. It will hardly do to contend that the emphasis upon one God (I Tim. 2:5) is a rebuttal of the Gnostic claim that there are two (the one responsible for creation, the other for salvation), or that God's desire to save all men (I Tim. 2:4) is a thrust at the Gnostic esoteric spirit and condescending attitude toward the rank and file of men, or that the designation "the man Christ Jesus" (I Tim. 2:5) is an intended denial of the docetic Christology of the Gnostics, for the whole section in which these statements occur has no polemic character whatsoever, but is a straightforward exposition of Christian duty.

The denial of future bodily resurrection (II Tim. 2:18) suggests a viewpoint similar to that which Paul met in Corinth (I Cor. 15). How this aberration can be linked with tendencies that root themselves in Judaism is not easy to see, although the Colossian heresy furnishes an earlier example of eclecticism. Perhaps it is futile to attempt to subsume all the elements under one system. Many of the allusions in the Pastorals are quite vague and suggestive of profitless indulgence in religious vagaries rather than sharply defined heresies. The apostle had warned the Ephesian elders of trouble from within as well as from without (Acts 20:29-30).

AUTHENTICITY

Do these epistles belong to the apostolic age and are they capable of having been written by Paul, or do they belong to a later period and come from another hand? On this issue there is sharp divergence of opinion, though there is general agreement that the homogeneity of the three documents demands that they be treated as a unit in this matter of authorship. Three positions have been taken. First, the traditional viewpoint holds that Paul wrote them near the end of his life. Second, the fragment theory maintains that portions of the Pastorals, such as the account of Paul's pre-Christian history as a persecutor (I Tim. 1:13-15), the references to Timothy and his family (I Tim. 1:18; II Tim. 1:4-5; 3:14-15), and the apostle's swan song (II Tim. 4:6-8 and perhaps the whole of the chapter) presumably were written by Paul, and these have been interlarded by a later writer into his own material. Third, the fictional approach views these epistles as completely the work of a Paulinist who took the liberty of writing in Paul's name to avail himself of the prestige and authority of the apostle in order to counteract the evils of the day and strengthen the Christian community. It is usual, on this position, to assign the epistles to the early part of the second century. The second and third positions clearly have much in common. Advocates of the second view differ among them-

selves over the identification of the fragments.[1] One weakness in
this position has been pointed out by Wilhelm Michaelis. If
these fragments were already known and accepted as Paul's, the
writer would not have been able to palm them off as his own. On
the other hand, if they had not become known as Paul's, there
would be no advantage in using them in order to impart a Pauline
flavor to his work.[2]

(1) *External evidence.* Quotation of the books as the work of
Paul begins with Irenaeus. Tertullian and Clement of Alexandria
also ascribed them to Paul. The Muratorian Canon included them,
but Marcion's did not. According to Tertullian, Marcion rejected them.[3] Earlier writers show knowledge of the Pastorals.
Polycarp refers to those who have loved the present age, using
language identical with II Timothy 4:10.[4] The same writer
describes the love of money as the beginning of all evils
(cf. I Tim. 6:10) and observes that we brought nothing into
the world and can take nothing out (cf. I Tim. 6:7).[5] Clement
of Rome has the phrase "ready unto every good work"[6] (cf.
Titus 3:1) and urges his readers to lift up holy hands in approaching God[7] (cf. I Tim. 2:8). He knows the expression, "to serve
with a pure conscience"[8] (cf. II Tim. 1:3). These references by
no means exhaust the allusions in writers of the post-apostolic
period. Some of them could be explained as proverbial expressions that were "in the air," but this will not account for all.

The absence of the Pastorals from Marcion's canon needs some
attention in passing. If this is regarded as strong enough to rule
out Pauline authorship, it is strong enough also to rule out the
composition of the books by a Paulinist in the early years of the
second century, unless we suppose that Marcion was keen enough
to distinguish these epistles from those that were genuinely
Pauline. A safer approach to the problem is to hold that the
contents of the Pastorals were sufficiently uncongenial to the
tenets of Marcion to cause him to reject these books in spite of
their Pauline origin. The exaltation of the Mosaic law would

[1] Moffatt, *Introduction to the Literature of the New Testament,* pp.
403-405.
[2] *Pastoralbriefe und Gefangenschaftsbriefe,* p. 135. For a full critique
of the Fragment Theory, including that of P. N. Harrison, see Donald
Guthrie, *The Pastoral Epistles, TBC,* pp. 49-52.
[3] *Against Marcion* v. 21.
[4] Philippians ix. 2.
[5] Philippians iv. 1.
[6] I Clement ii. 7.
[7] I Clement xxix. 1.
[8] I Clement xlv. 7.

not be palatable (I Tim. 1:8), nor the attack on asceticism (I Tim. 4:3), nor the magnifying of the Old Testament Scriptures (II Tim. 3:16-17). Marcion could have taken offense at the warning in I Timothy 6:20, which contains the very word *antitheses* that he himself employed in his propaganda.[9]

Failure of the Pastorals to appear in the Chester Beatty Papyrus 46, which includes all the other letters of Paul, has been urged as further ground for questioning their authenticity. This objection is not particularly weighty, for two reasons. First, the text of the Pauline epistles is fragmentary, and the Pastorals may well have been lost from the manuscript. Second, since the Pastorals were accepted by Clement of Alexandria and no doubt by others in the Egyptian church at a date earlier than the Chester Beatty Papyri, even if it could be established that the Pastorals were not included in the original form of these papyri, the omission would at best reflect only a very local judgment on the authenticity of these epistles.

(2) *Internal evidence.* It is here, rather than in the realm of external evidence, that the principal grounds have been discovered for questioning Paul's authorship. A. H. McNeile, after canvassing the various factors involved, declares, "The conclusion. . .is irresistible. The epistles, as they stand, cannot be from St. Paul's pen."[10]

At the outset, the negative view meets an obstacle in the fact that the epistles are attributed to Paul. This is usually passed over rather lightly with the observation that the actual writer intended no harm and his conduct ought not to be judged by the stricter standards of the twentieth century. We should simply put the names of Paul, Timothy, and Titus in quotation marks and not impugn the motives of the writer. But before one does this, he should consider the following aspects of the problem. (i) The alleged analogy of pseudonymous apocalypses is not a true parallel. Philip Carrington writes, "This is a very different thing from the realism of the New Testament Epistles, with their plain straightforward messages from known persons to known churches, and especially the Pastoral Epistles with their practical unimaginative content. There seems to be no evidence at all that such missives were freely composed in the names of contemporary persons who had recently died."[11] (ii) That the church of the

---

[9] See the remark of Clement of Alexandria: "Convicted by this utterance, the heretics reject the Epistles to Timothy" (Stromateis ii. 11).

[10] *An Introduction to the Study of the New Testament* (2nd ed., 1953), p. 196.

[11] *The Early Christian Church*, I, 259.

second century was alive to the danger of forgery is attested by the Muratorian canon, which mentions an epistle to the Laodiceans and another to the Alexandrians, forged in the name of Paul. *The Acts of Paul* includes a Corinthian epistle which, like the rest of the material, was fabricated by a presbyter of the second century who claimed he did it out of love for Paul. The church was not impressed and deposed him. (iii) It must be granted that the epistles named, plus a very few others from the post-apostolic period, in no case begin to approach in tone and quality the Pastoral Epistles, but are on a distinctly lower level. (iv) It is not clear that support can be gained from the case of II Peter, for it is not certain that this work is pseudonymous. Many who think it is are not prepared to build a case for the pseudonymity of the Pastorals on this alleged parallel, for the reason that II Peter has an apocalyptic character that is lacking in the Pastorals. (v) Pagan practices are not properly decisive for the church of Christ. One would naturally look for a higher standard of ethics in the church in this matter of writing in another's name than in pagan circles. (vi) Since the Pastorals contain explicit warnings against deceivers (I Tim. 4:1-2; Titus 1:10; II Tim. 3:13), it is psychologically difficult to suppose that the writer would adopt a practice that involved a species of deception.[12]

The various arguments against authenticity based on the contents of the Pastorals must now be examined.

A. Certain historical data cannot be fitted into Paul's known life and labors prior to the journey to Rome. One is the item in II Timothy 4:20, "Trophimus I left at Miletus sick." This cannot refer to Paul's last journey to Jerusalem (Acts 20:4; 21:29). Another feature is the reference to the books and cloak that Paul left at Troas (II Tim. 4:13). This can hardly be fitted into his Jerusalem trip when he was made a prisoner. The impression made on the reader is that these things were left at Troas very recently, and since they were valued by Paul, were now included in his requests. If he had left them on the way to Jerusalem, he would have sent for them from Caesarea, where he was detained for two years.

It should be noted also that Paul's associates and friends include many new names, such as Onesiphorus, Eubulus, Zenas

---

12 For a more detailed discussion of the question of pseudonymity, see Donald Guthrie, *New Testament Introduction, The Pauline Epistles*, pp. 282-294. See also J. I. Packer, *'Fundamentalism' and the Word of God*, pp. 181-86.

the lawyer, Artemas, and others. There are new opponents also, such as Hymenaeus and Philetus.

To fit these and similar data into Paul's life before he became a prisoner of the empire is not feasible. What is left is to adopt one of two alternatives, to grant that these epistles must have come from someone who wrote after Paul's time and supplied these features, or to seek to find a place for them outside the framework of the Book of Acts. The latter approach is bound up with the theory that Paul was released from imprisonment, labored for a few more years, then was imprisoned again and finally put to death at Rome.[13]

Favorable to release is Paul's expectation of it (Phm. 22; Phil. 1:25). This is especially important in the case of Philippians, in view of its probable date near the end of the imprisonment. It is of course to be granted that an expectation could be dashed by later events.

Various patristic testimonies indicate that Paul went to Spain in accordance with his purpose expressed in Romans 15:28. Evidently the writer of the Canon of Muratori was under the impression that Paul made the trip. Numerous fathers mention it, but their late date renders their testimony of doubtful value. However, it is different with Clement of Rome, seeing that he wrote before the end of the first century. He says that Paul, "having taught righteousness to the whole world, and having gone to the extremity of the west, and having borne witness before the rulers, so was released from the world and went to the holy place, being the greatest example of endurance."[14] It should be observed that the word Spain does not occur here. Instead, Clement states that Paul went to the extremity of the west. His testimony has been subjected to two criticisms. First, it is claimed that ἐλθών should be rendered "having come" rather than "having gone," thus implying a Roman, not a Spanish destination. This is its usual meaning, although the other is possible. What favors the rendering "having gone" in this passage is the fact that Italy could hardly mean for Clement the extremity of the west. It was rather the center of the empire. Second, it is thought probable that Clement was influenced by Paul's statement in Romans 15 about his expectation of visiting Spain and concluded that he must have gone. This is a possibility, but its likelihood is lessened by the circumstance that in the immediate

---

[13] Eusebius *HE* II. xxii states, "Tradition has it that after defending himself the Apostle was again sent on the ministry of preaching, and coming a second time to the same city suffered martyrdom under Nero."

[14] *I Clement* v.

context Clement mentions that Paul endured seven captivities. Unless this is sheer guesswork, he must have had access to independent source material covering aspects of Paul's life not included in Acts.

It should not be concluded that if the trip to Spain can be demonstrated to have failed of realization, the case for Paul's authorship of the Pastorals suffers a mortal blow. It is quite feasible to hold that circumstances in the East may have caused the apostle to return there rather than to go to Spain. In that case, the activities and personalities reflected in the Pastorals can be fitted into such a ministry.

B. The organizational emphasis is said to be contrary to Paul and later than his time. How could a man who was obsessed with the idea that the Lord was coming soon be greatly concerned over such matters? In his letters he is virtually silent about church officers. Yet the fact remains that he insisted on elders for the guidance and instruction of the churches he established (Acts 14:23) and on one occasion mentions bishops and deacons (Phil. 1:1). It is easier to suppose that in writing to other churches Paul had no need to refer to such men in a specific way than to hold that the Philippian situation was exceptional and therefore not normative for the Pauline churches as a whole (cf. I Thess. 5:12). And it is by no means clear that the apostle's interest in the Lord's return would make him indifferent to church organization. The analogy of Clement of Rome is helpful at this point. Here was a man with a developed eschatological outlook who was equally concerned with organizational regularity and stability.

The alleged lack of interest on Paul's part in ecclesiastical matters is often yoked to his dependence on charismatic guidance for his congregations. One who had the gift of prophecy could settle for the church any pressing problem of administration by a word from the Lord. It is thought to be significant that this charismatic emphasis is lacking in the Pastorals, having given way to authority vested in men set apart for leadership in an official sense. But this is too facile a contrast, since place is found for prophetic utterance at two points (I Tim. 1:18; 4:14). Such references would hardly be expected in a post-apostolic situation.

Bishops, elders, and deacons are mentioned in the Pastorals. It is generally agreed that bishops (literally, overseers) and elders do not indicate different offices, since the terms appear to be used interchangeably (Tit. 1:5, 7; cf. Acts 20:17, 28). For this reason it is precarious to make much of the fact that

356

bishop occurs only in the singular, whereas elder (presbyter) is found in both singular and plural. But great stress is laid on the claim that in reality Timothy and Titus are bishops of the Ignatian type, for they have power to appoint elders (Tit. 1:5; cf. I Tim. 5:19) and exercise supervisory control over the discipline of the church. However, the requirements of the situation seem to be adequately met on the assumption that Timothy and Titus were acting as Paul's personal representatives, which would naturally give them authority exceeding that of officers in the local church.

There are strong objections to the notion that the Pastorals presuppose a bishop of the monarchical type. Donald Guthrie lists three of them.[15] First, one would expect a clear indication that in a given congregation a single individual was to hold this office. Second, the term bishop would not be used of an elder, but would be kept distinct. Third, there would naturally be some provision for the perpetuation of the office if a bishop of the monarchical type were intended.

W. F. Albright has a trenchant comment about the relegation of the Pastorals to the second century because of their teaching on church government. "The repudiation of the Pastoral Epistles of Paul, now commonly assigned by critical scholars to the second quarter of the second century A.D., becomes rather absurd when we discover that the institution of overseers or superintendents (*episkopoi,* our bishops) in Timothy and Titus, as well as in the earliest extra-biblical Christian literature, is virtually identical with the Essene institution of *mebaqqerim* (sometimes awkwardly rendered as 'censors')."[16] These officers are mentioned in the Manual of Discipline of the Qumran Community and also in the Damascus Document. Bo Reicke does not think that the church got its episcopal office from the Essene *mebaqqer,* but finds in these two an interesting analogy.[17] His essay is valuable as showing that in the early church, as at Qumran, oligarchic and democratic elements existed together. This undercuts the notion of a gradual development in church government such as is bound up with the late dating of the Pastorals.

One would think that if the Pastorals belong to a period some decades after the death of Paul the qualifications of elders and deacons would be so well known in the church that they would

---

[15] *The Pastoral Epistles, TBC,* p. 31.

[16] *From the Stone Age to Christianity,* 2nd ed., p. 23.

[17] "The Constitution of the Church" in *The Scrolls and the New Testament,* K. Stendahl, ed., pp. 154f.

not need to be spelled out in these writings. The apostolic age would seem to be the logical time for such instruction.

Some students find in I Timothy 5 evidence of an order of widows, but the language is not sufficiently precise to make this certain. The emphasis falls on the church's care of indigent widows and their responsibility to render service to the saints.

C. The style and language of the Pastorals, it is claimed, constitute a barrier against Pauline authorship. No doubt there is considerable difference, on both of these counts, between these epistles and the other Paulines. The style is not argumentative. It lacks the rapid thrust, the passionate and broken character that so often stamps the apostle's work. Here the atmosphere is rather calm and the pace is sedate. The letters are quietly instructional. If the acknowledged epistles were uniform in the matter of style, which they are not, this argument would have to be reckoned with more seriously. On the positive side, marks of Paul's workmanship are not lacking. One is the writer's tendency to use lists of virtues and vices, quite in the Pauline manner as evidenced by the *Hauptbriefe* especially. There are others as well.[18]

Greater weight is attached to differences in vocabulary. Peculiar to the Pastorals among the writings ascribed to Paul are *godliness* or *piety* (10 times); *healthy,* as applied to doctrine (9); *faithful* (trustworthy) *is the saying* (5). *Doctrine* (didaskalia) has a much larger use than in the Paulines. Many terms that are unique to the Pastorals occur infrequently, or even once, in these books. It is not too much to say that to many minds this is the decisive factor in bringing them to the conclusion that Paul could not have written the Pastorals. The case has been put most persuasively by P. N. Harrison in *The Problem of the Pastoral Epistles* (1921). His findings may be summarized as follows: (i) The total vocabulary of the Pastorals is 902 words. Omitting the 54 proper names, one arrives at the figure 848. Of these, 306 or 36 per cent, are not found in the ten Paulines. (ii) 175 words fail to appear in any New Testament writings outside the Pastorals. (iii) 131 words occur in the Pastorals and in other New Testament books, but not in any Pauline epistle. (iv) A large number of words found in Paul's acknowledged letters are absent from the Pastorals. These total 1635, exclusive of proper names, of which 582 are peculiar to Paul and 1053 occur also in other New Testament books. Harrison is not disposed to stress this feature too much, recognizing that a man

[18] E. K. Simpson, *The Pastoral Epistles,* pp. 18-22.

must be allowed some flexibility in his vocabulary, especially as the nature of his material varies. (v) Particles, prepositions, and other minor parts of speech, which so abound in Paul, are in many cases lacking in the Pastorals. (vi) The language of the Pastorals is said to show marked kinship with the language of second century writers, namely, the Apostolic Fathers and the Apologists.

Harrison's approach is known as the statistical method. Some have been critical of certain features of his methodology, while being in general agreement with his conclusions.[19] Others have pointed out what they regarded as more serious defects which challenge his results.

(1) The method cannot be rigidly applied except where the material is of the same nature. It is evident that the Pastorals have their own special character, dictated to some extent by the subject matter. The various groups of Pauline letters agree less with one another in the area of vocabulary than do the individual letters within each group in their relation to one another. Notable is the fact that the Pastorals abound in ethical teaching. If there were more of this type of teaching in the other letters attributed to Paul, it is reasonable to suppose that many of the words unique to the Pastorals would be found in the other writings. A hint of this is to be found in the fact that Romans 1:18-32, which is heavily ethical in nature, has a rather high percentage of words in common with the Pastorals.

(2) It cannot be assumed that the absence of the 175 *hapax legomena* from the rest of the New Testament means that these words were not in common use in the apostolic age. All but a few of them have been found in works originating before A.D. 50.[20] Moreover, more than 87 per cent of the vocabulary of the Pastorals has been located in the writings of Philo, a slightly older contemporary of Paul.[21]

(3) Guthrie notes that approximately 80 per cent of the hapaxes are found in the LXX. This is important in view of the heavy influence that the LXX had upon the verbiage of the apostle Paul, evidenced not alone by his quotations from it but his dependence, in addition, upon its ideas and terminology.

(4) The Pastorals are too brief to make the application of the

---

[19] E.g., K. Grayston and G. Herdan, in *NTS*, VI (Oct. 1959), 1-15.

[20] Montgomery Hitchcock, *"Tests for the Pastorals," JTS*, XXX (1929), 278.

[21] Hitchcock, "Philo and the Pastorals," *Hermathena*, LVI (1940), 113-35.

statistical method satisfactory. G. U. Yule has concluded that in order to have an adequate basis for statistical analysis one would require a treatise of ten thousand words in length.[22] The Pastorals fall considerably short of this requirement.

(5) With regard to the vocabulary of the Pastorals not found in the acknowledged Paulines (306 words), Wikenhauser notes that the great majority of these occur in only one epistle and concludes, "So the Pastoral Epistles cannot be the work of a forger, otherwise the non-Pauline words would be more evenly distributed."[23]

(6) The failure of some 112 particles, prepositions and other small elements of speech to appear in the Pastorals is no doubt impressive, but not overwhelming in view of the brevity of the letters, their large use of imperatives(which invites asyndeton), and the presence of many word series abounding in description, synonym, etc., where commas dominate rather than particles. Actually, several dozen of this type of word are nevertheless to be found in the Pastorals as well as in one or more of the ten Paulines. How difficult it is to base solid conclusions on the particles may be judged from the circumstance that τε occurs eighteen times in Romans and not at all in Galatians, yet admittedly the writer is the same and the subject matter is closely related.

Ramsay has an interesting discussion of vocabulary change in Paul, centering mainly in καυχάομαι (boast) and related forms, which are so prevalent in the *Hauptbriefe* but infrequent thereafter and absent entirely from the Pastorals. This is a mark of spiritual progress, as a word belonging to the apostle's Pharisaic inheritance is gradually abandoned.[24]

D. The doctrinal outlook and emphasis is said to be different from that of Paul. This argument has been strongly developed by B. S. Easton, *The Pastoral Epistles* (1947). Instead of being creative, the writer is merely conservative, intent on holding the line of the orthodox position. He keeps referring to sound (healthy) doctrine. Several specific items are regarded as inimical to Pauline authorship: (1) Absence of the Fatherhood of God except in the salutation formulas. (2) Lack of mention of the sonship of Jesus Christ. (3) Slight place given to the Holy Spirit (mentioned three times). (4) The designation Saviour used not only of Christ but in several places of God (I Tim. 1:1; 2:3; 4:10;

[22] *The Statistical Study of Literary Vocabulary* (1944).
[23] *New Testament Introduction*, p. 446.
[24] *The Teaching of Paul*, p. 340.

Tit. 1:3; 2:10; 3:4). Various epithets are used of God — great, blessed, living, etc. (5) Absence of Paul's "in Christ" mysticism, despite the fact that the formula "in Christ" occurs nine times in such phrases as "grace which was given in Christ" and "faith which is in Christ." (6) Absence of the Pauline antithesis between faith and works. (7) Frequent use of the word faith in the sense of the content of Christian belief (the faith). (8) Exaltation of the law and emphasis upon the maintenance of works. (9) The un-Pauline character of the teaching on salvation. There is a reference to salvation for women through child-bearing (I Tim. 2:15). Further, the writer seems to descend to autosoterism as he states that Timothy may save both himself and his hearers (I Tim. 4:16). (10) The retention of Pauline terms, but with altered meanings.

In so far as the argument relates to the lack of certain Pauline touches, it is weakened by the fact that the Pastorals are practical to an uncommon degree and are therefore less theological. This may help to account for (1) and (2). Similarly, (3) loses much of its force when one recognizes that the Pastorals are closely related to wisdom literature and so could not be expected to be pneumatical in character. Further, while it is true that Paul makes much of the Spirit in his teaching on the development of Christian life, he does not do so uniformly, as is the case in Colossians. It is hard to estimate the force of (4) and (5). Not infrequently among Christian writers the early preoccupation with Christ has given way to greater attention to the being and nature of God. Such may have been Paul's development. As for (6), it is fair to assume that the sharp antithesis between faith and works that characterized the apostle's writings during the legalistic controversy was no longer necessary toward the close of his life. The answer to (7) is found in the fact that faith retains its subjective sense (one's own faith) in several places (e.g., I Tim. 1:5; II Tim. 1:5) and that in Paul's acknowledged epistles faith has occasionally the objective sense (Gal. 1:23 and perhaps Rom. 1:5). With the growth of heresy there was an obvious need for emphasizing loyalty to Christian truth (cf. Jude 3). It is probable that Paul's deepened insight into human nature and the scandalous lengths to which some Christians were prepared to go in demonstration of their liberty in the gospel explains (8) in large measure. The apostle may well have felt that the congregations he had in view, lacking apostolic leadership, required the tangible guidance of the law in the area of routine conduct. Earlier the apostle had committed himself to the highest admiration for the law (Rom.

7:12; 8:4). As to (9), the passage about women probably relates to physical preservation and peace of mind through the ordeal of childbirth rather than salvation in the usual soteriological sense. The other passage (I Tim. 4:16) looks very un-Pauline indeed. However, if the writer was a devotee of Paul, one would think he would have exercised great care to avoid any clash with Paul's point of view. Who but the apostle himself would have the daring to use the expression "save thyself" in a way that suited his purpose even at the risk of appearing to contradict his great utterances on salvation by grace? As a matter of fact, Paul had previously used language that admitted a human factor in the salvation process (I Cor. 9:22). Finally, the notion that Pauline terms no longer have the Pauline content (10) is open to debate. It is hard to see any changed sense in the use of "justify" (Tit. 3:7) or of "gospel" (e.g., I Tim. 1:11; cf. II Cor. 4:4).

E. The writer, it is said, makes Paul treat Timothy as a mere youth and liable to be despised on that account (I Tim. 4:12). It is generally granted that the term used here (νεότης) is applied to men up to forty years of age, but what gives trouble to the critical mind is the threat of being despised. But since the elders were presumably men of more advanced age, the threat may have been very real. Certainly this is a slim basis on which to question Pauline authorship.

In this connection it is fitting to note the contribution of Spicq.[25] He observes an "old man" psychology running through the Pastorals. By comparison with the author, Timothy is but a youth. It is the early days of the younger man that are recalled, as well as the writer's early experiences in missionary work and even in his activity of persecuting the church. It is the aged who delight to dote on their own experiences. In keeping with this psychology, emphasis falls on the need of gravity and moderation. There is an obvious desire for sympathy, a pleading for ministry to his person and his creature comforts. Hardships that once would have been brushed aside as hardly worthy of mention are now magnified in his mind. All this fits Paul the aged.

A distinctive contribution to the study of the Pastorals was made by F. R. Montgomery Hitchcock in adducing the Latin flavor of these books as suitable to the known situation of Paul.[26] If the apostle was interested in evangelizing the West

25 *Les Epîtres Pastorales,* chap. VII.
26 "The Latinity of the Pastorals," *ET,* XXXIX (May 1928), 347-52.

(Spain specifically) he would need a knowledge of Latin. It is not difficult to picture him as utilizing part of his time as a prisoner in Rome acquiring such knowledge, both from books and from contacts with his guards. This writer points out many similarities in tone, ideas, and terminology with Latin writings, especially Cicero's letter to his brother Quintus, a government official in the province of Asia (compare Timothy's position in Ephesus). This was a hundred years before Paul's time, but the correlations are striking.

Hitchcock summarizes by saying, "The writer of the Pastorals writes as a cultivated Roman Christian. His ideas move in a distinctly Roman circle. His thoughts and aims are projected along the distinctly Roman lines of personal dignity, piety, obedience to superior officers, equity in judgment, moderation, integrity, self-control, discipline, organization, and faithfulness to one's trust." He ventures to suggest that this century may witness the rehabilitation of the Pastoral Epistles as the work of Paul. This has not come to pass, but there is renewed interest in the subject. Some scholars are guilty of such dogmatism that for them the matter is closed; Paul could not have written these letters. On the other hand, some are not willing to face the evidence fairly that has been adduced against Pauline authorship. In openness of mind there is hope for the future of investigation in this area.

A conclusion that could account for the more obviously Pauline elements and at the same time come to terms with features that are difficult to harmonize with Pauline authorship is that Paul had the help of an amanuensis.[27] There are indications that point to Luke, such as δι' ἣν αἰτίαν (II Tim. 1:6, 12; Titus 1:13; cf. Lk. 8:47; Acts 22:24); ὃν τρόπον (II Tim. 3:8; cf. Lk. 13:34; Acts 1:11; 7:28; 15:11; 27:25); ἐπὶ πλεῖον (II Tim. 2:16; 3:9; cf. Acts 4:17; 20:9; 24:4); λίαν (II Tim. 4:15; cf. Lk. 23:8). The first and third of these are found only in the Pastorals and Luke; the second has a single occurrence in Matthew in addition; the fourth is found in several places besides Luke and the Pastorals. Still another example is ὑγαίνειν. Aside from one occurrence in III John, all the examples are from the Pastorals and Luke. Its suitability from the pen of Luke the physician is fully evident. Luke's presence with Paul fulfills the necessary outward condition (II Tim. 4:11).

---

[27] Among those favoring this hypothesis are Roller and Spicq.

DATE AND PLACE OF WRITING

The date of Paul's death cannot be fixed with entire certainty. According to the *Chronicon* of Eusebius it occurred in A.D. 67 or 68. On the other hand the testimony of I Clement seems to indicate that the martyrdom of Paul (and Peter) preceded the death of others at Rome. Since Nero burned the city in 64 and blamed the Christians for it, these martyrdoms were probably not long delayed. On the assumption of Pauline authorship the Pastorals can be assigned to a year prior to 64 or perchance to a time two or three years later.

RECENT STUDY

In addressing himself to the problem of the Pastorals C. K. Barrett has adopted the fragment hypothesis, holding that genuine bits of Paul's composition have been used, "but are given a false historical context by their present setting in the Pastorals."[28] The picture of Timothy and Titus in these epistles, such as the representation of Timothy as youthful and inexperienced, is regarded as fictitious.

As to the situation out of which these writings emerged, Barrett offers the following: "The purpose of the Pastorals was practical. Paul was assailed: to the Jewish Christians he was 'the enemy,' and to many Gentile Christians he was suspect, or was in danger of becoming suspect, because he was in favour with the gnostics. Those who held fast to the doctrine they had received from their master were under some necessity to publish, to represent in their own generation the genuine Pauline voice. Paul's case should not go by default; being dead, he could yet speak through the pens of those who owed to him their understanding of divine grace."[29] The Pastorals should be regarded as "a first attempt to do what each generation of Christians must attempt — to restate the convictions of the first, apostolic generation, in a new era and a new environment."[30]

J. N. D. Kelly is inclined to lay considerable stress on such items as the different subject matter in the Pastorals from the other Paulines, which creates a different atmosphere and warrants a different vocabulary. Like Hitchcock he would emphasize the probable effect of the Latin environment on the apostle and with Spicq would stress the factor of advancing age on style and vigor

---

[28] *The Pastoral Epistles* (1963), p. 9.
[29] *Ibid.*, pp. 16-17.
[30] *Ibid.*, p. 33.

of expression.[31] He is of the opinion that circumstances forced Paul to use a different amanuensis from his customary helper (supposing that Timothy was his aide in the preparation of the Captivity letters), which may go far to explain the peculiarities in vocabulary, style, and tone which scholars have detected here.[32] The supposition is that Paul relied to a greater extent on secretarial help in these letters than in any which preceded them. Kelly notes that those who do not hold to the genuineness of the Pastorals are in real trouble in their inability to explain why three letters should have been written rather than one, or at the most, two, seeing that they deal with much the same material (this is especially true of I Timothy and Titus).[33]

A valuable contribution has come from the pen of C. F. D. Moule in recent years. He finds it hard to accept the fragment hypothesis. "I must confess that it amazes me that such a solution has gained wide currency, for it presupposes (what to the best of my knowledge there is not a shred of evidence to support) that Paul wrote these little scraps on separate, detached papyri; and, even if that could be established, it requires us to believe that they were kept by the recipients — another improbable assumption; and finally, it asks us to picture an imitator going round and collecting them and copying them into the letter he has fabricated at points so captiously selected that they have puzzled commentators ever since."[34]

On the positive side he offers considerable evidence in support of the theory that Luke helped the apostle in the framing of these letters. Admitting that the dearth of characteristic Lukan particles poses a problem, he nevertheless feels that the data on the other side are so numerous and strong as to tip the balance. His research has brought to light the fact that there are echoes of the Gospel tradition in the Pastorals, and they turn out to be Lukan (these observations are incorporated in the author's *Birth of the New Testament*, pp. 220-221). Recalling the information that Luke was a physician, it is of interest that words meaning to be sick and to be well are used metaphorically in the Pastorals and only there. The theme of true and false riches is strikingly prominent in Luke and in the Pastorals. Paul's declaration about completing his course (II Tim. 4:7) recalls an earlier

---

[31] *The Pastoral Epistles* (1963), p. 25.
[32] *Ibid.*, pp. 26-27.
[33] *Ibid.*, p. 31.
[34] "The Problem of the Pastoral Epistles: A Reappraisal," *BJRL*, 47 (March 1965), p. 448.

statement from him reported by Luke (Acts 20:24). These are only a few of the items offered by Moule in support of the thesis that Paul relied on his faithful friend to formulate his thoughts in these latter days of his life.

BIBLIOGRAPHY

Barrett, C. K., *The Pastoral Epistles, New Clarendon Bible*. Oxford: Clarendon Press, 1963.

Dibelius, Martin, *Die Pastoralbriefe, HZNT*. 2nd ed., Tübingen: Mohr, 1931.

Easton, B. S., *The Pastoral Epistles*. New York: Scribner's, 1947.

Ellicott, C. J., *The Pastoral Epistles of St. Paul*. 5th ed., London: Longmans, Green, 1883.

Ellis, E. Earle, *Paul and His Recent Interpreters*. Grand Rapids: Eerdmans, 1961, pp. 49-57.

Falconer, Sir Robert, *The Pastoral Epistles*. Oxford: Clarendon Press, 1937.

Guthrie, Donald, *The Pastoral Epistles, TBC*. Grand Rapids: Eerdmans, 1957.

Harrison, P. N., *The Problem of the Pastoral Epistles*. Oxford: University Press, 1921.

James, J. D., *The Genuineness and Authorship of the Pastoral Epistles*. London: Longmans, Green, 1906.

Jeremias, J., *Die Briefe an Timotheus und Titus, NTD*, Vol. 9. Göttingen: Vandenhoeck & Ruprecht, 1949.

Kelly, J. N. D., *A Commentary on the Pastoral Epistles, HNTC*. New York: Harper and Row, 1963.

Lock, Walter, *A Critical and Exegetical Commentary on the Pastoral Epistles, ICC*. New York: Scribner's, 1924.

Meinertz, M., *Die Pastoralbriefe des heiligen Paulus*. 4th ed., Bonn: Peter Hanstein, 1931.

Michaelis, Wilhelm, *Pastoralbriefe und Gefangenschaftsbriefe*. Gutersloh: C. Bertelsmann, 1930.

Moule, C. F. D., "The Problem of the Pastoral Epistles: A Reappraisal," *BJRL*, 47 (March 1965), 430-452.

Scott, E. F., *The Pastoral Epistles, MNTC*. New York: Harper, n.d.

Spicq, C., *Les Epîtres Pastorales*. Paris: J. Gabalda, 1947.

Simpson, E. K., *The Pastoral Epistles*. Grand Rapids: Eerdmans, 1954.

Chapter Eighteen

THE EPISTLE TO THE HEBREWS

THE EPISTLE TO THE HEBREWS CONFRONTS THE STUDENT WITH A writing quite unlike anything in the New Testament. Years ago Franz Delitzsch wrote, "It is like the great Melchizedek of sacred story, of which its central portion treats. Like him it marches forth in lonely, royal, and sacerdotal dignity, and like him is ἀγενεαλόγητος; we know not whence it cometh or whither it goeth."[1] The quotation calls attention to two of the most pressing problems connected with the study of the epistle, that of authorship and destination. But there are difficulties and uncertainties pertaining to other points as well.

RECOGNITION BY THE EARLY CHURCH

Before the end of the first century Clement of Rome used Hebrews in writing to the Corinthians, and the Shepherd of Hermas shows knowledge of it. Goodspeed notes that, "Hebrews left a marked impression upon the Roman church, and all the early writings of Rome after its appearance reflect its use."[2] In view of this, it is strange that no mention is made of it in the

[1] *Commentary on the Hebrews*, I, 4.
[2] *The Formation of the New Testament*, p. 57.

Canon of Muratori, although the omission may reflect uncertainty as to its authorship. Its absence from Marcion's list is understandable in view of the epistle's heavy indebtedness to the Old Testament and the doubt as to its Pauline origin. The West was slow in according the book canonical rank because of the question about its apostolic authorship and probably because of the Montanists' appeal to Hebrews 6 on the impossibility of a second repentance. Since Montanism was in disfavor, this reacted adversely on the cordial endorsement of Hebrews. In the East it was accepted as Pauline and therefore readily received. The influence of the Alexandrian Fathers was especially strong, including Pantaenus, Clement and, more cautiously, Origen. Finally, late in the fourth century, the West swung into line and gave the book canonical recognition, first including it as an adjunct to the letters of Paul, then absorbing it into the Pauline corpus without distinction. In the manuscripts and versions, as Hatch has shown,[3] the position of Hebrews varies considerably, but it is found either embedded somewhere in the Paulines or at the end of this group.

FORM

In *form,* Hebrews lacks the introduction that ordinarily supplies information about writer and readers, but its close includes personal items such as belong to the conclusion of a letter. Did the epistle once have an introduction? Some have surmised that it did, but this is not favored by the way in which it begins, with a long, closely structured, highly doctrinal statement, whose stately lines intone the message that is elaborated in the ensuing chapters. There is no particle to provide a smooth transition from preliminary material. Furthermore, there is no textual support for an introduction.

The effort to make Hebrews an epistle in contrast to a letter (bearing in mind Deissmann's distinction) runs into some trouble by reason of the several personal allusions scattered through the writing (5:11-12; 6:9-10; 10:32-34; 12:4 and perhaps 13:7). Some elements point to an essay, others to a letter.

In the estimate of the writer himself, Hebrews is considered to be a word of exhortation (13:22). With this as a clue, some students have advanced the suggestion that the work is really a sermon, or even a combination of sermons, now made available in permanent form. Guthrie notes an interesting detail that lends

---

[3] "The Position of Hebrews in the Canon of the New Testament," *HTR,* XXIX (Apr. 1936), 133-51.

some credence to this view, namely, the expression "time would fail me to tell" (11:32).[4] If the writer was separated from his congregation, he might conceivably send such a message, containing references to the condition of his people, and concluding with personal notes. The use of ἐπέστειλα (13:22) is not favorable to the sermon hypothesis, for it suggests an epistle.

OUTLINE OF CONTENTS

As to *contents*, Hebrews is decidedly a Christological treatise. The Son, because he is the final revelation of God, is superior both to the prophets (1:1-3) and to angels (1:4-2:18) and to Moses and Aaron, the leading representatives of the old covenant (3:1-4:13). This prepares the way for an appeal to cleave to Christ for the help that he alone can give (4:14-16). Then, as the central section unfolds, Christ is presented in his priesthood as superior to the Aaronic order, being patterned after Melchizedek (5:1-7:28). This priesthood is exercised under the new covenant (8:1-13) in a new (heavenly) sanctuary (9:1-10), in terms of a new and better ministry (9:11-14), which provides an eternal inheritance (9:15-28) based on a sacrifice of final efficacy (10:1-18). The practical portion of the epistle is an appeal to press on with renewed faith, not despising the divine discipline, realizing the fruits of peace and sanctification, maintaining the virtues of a true separation and steadfastness and obedience (10:19-13:25).

CHARACTERISTICS

Certain characteristics stand out. (1) It has high literary quality, marked by careful construction and elegant diction. (2) It is saturated with Old Testament allusions and quotations. Some passages, such as Psalm 110:1, 4, are used repeatedly. Unlike most New Testament use of the Old, the quotations are cited, not simply in a confirmatory fashion, but as providing the groundwork of the presentation. (3) The cultus of the Old Testament is used as the foil for the exposition of the superiority of Christ in his redemptive work. For this purpose the author goes back to the ritual of the tabernacle rather than the temple, and ignores current Judaism. (4) The finality of the new order finds its rationale in part in the fact that even within the old there was change and progress. This is made especially evident in the acknowledgment of the obsolescence of the old covenant even

[4] *New Testament Introduction: Hebrews to Revelation*, p. 50.

while it was still in operation (Jer. 31:31-34; Heb. 8).[5] This helps to prepare the way for the emphasis on the "better" in connection with Christ. (5) The Christology is rich and varied. More than twenty names and titles are employed. The humanity and the deity of the Son are coupled in a way that is approached only by the Fourth Gospel. Special attention is given to the offices of Christ, above all to his priest-king status. (6) The eschatology is both realized (1:2; 6:5) and futuristic (9:28; 10:37). (7) A series of warnings is injected into the argument of the epistle. These, five in number, run the gamut from the danger of neglect of the salvation in Christ to rejection (2:1-4; 3:7-4:13; 5:11-6:20; 10:26-39; 12:15-29). One must "hear" (heed) the voice of the living God. (8) The practical teaching is principally bound up in the admonitions to "draw near" in worship with the confidence of access because of sins forgiven and assurance of a mighty Savior's help made available (10:22; cf. 4:14-16), to "go on to perfection" (6:1) in obedience to the living God, and to "go forth" in fellowship with the rejected Christ, sharing his reproach (13:13). (9) Some of the leading terms used are: angel, holy and sanctify, sin, sacrifice, blood, high priest, promise, covenant, word, witness (verb), better, perfect (verb), faith, salvation, rest, heaven.

READERS

The identity, place of residence, and spiritual condition of the readers can be treated together, including the purpose of the writing, for all these factors are somewhat interrelated. The prevailing view up to fairly recent times was that the epistle was directed to Hebrew Christians who were in danger of apostasizing. Cut off from the vast majority of their countrymen who had rejected Jesus as their Messiah, wistful as they thought of the splendor of the temple worship, discouraged because of persecution and the delay of the Parousia, they were tempted to slip back into Judaism. It has been thought that the selection of materials in the book is admirably suited to meet just such a situation by showing the limitations and incompletions of the nation Israel and the removal of these in the fulfillment of the divine promises in Jesus Christ. This general picture is found in Westcott, for example, who placed the recipients in Jerusalem or at any rate

---

[5] Markus Barth, "The Old Testament in Hebrews," in *Current Issues in New Testament Interpretation,* ed. by William Klassen and Graydon F. Snyder, p. 65.

in Palestine, "where Judaism would present itself with practical force."[6]

Ramsay supplemented this by stressing a distinction between the rulers and the readers, based on statements in the last chapter (13:7, 17). He thought this reflected the situation in Jerusalem where the apostles joined forces with Paul during the legalistic controversy, but where there was nevertheless quite a strong backing in the church for the other position, as attested by Acts 15.[7] But his exegesis encounters trouble in 13:24, where the greeting to all the leaders and all the saints assumes the unity of the church.

This same general position has been maintained by Spicq in his great work on Hebrews.[8] More specifically, he thinks that those addressed were priests.[9] Acts 6:7 provides the information that a great company of these men became obedient to the faith. They would find it hard to maintain themselves both economically and spiritually in the midst of the pressures of the situation. Such men would be particularly vulnerable to efforts to draw them back toward Judaism. A major problem confronting the thesis is the temporal assistance rendered to others by the readers of the epistle (6:10), an item that does not agree with the poverty of the Jerusalem church as attested by Acts.

T. W. Manson suggested that the readers of Hebrews are to be located in the Lycus Valley, on the basis of a comparison between this epistle and Colossians. The special points of connection are the observance of Sabbaths and new moons, distinctions of meats and drinks, the relevancy of the central argument of Hebrews to a condition in which Hebrew Christians desired to continue the Jewish ritual system, and the preoccupation of both epistles with angelic intermediaries.[10] A hurdle that this view has to overcome is the use of Hebrews at an early period in Rome. Manson thought this could be handled on the assumption that a copy of Hebrews was taken from Colossae to Rome and given to Paul at the time when word of the troubles in the Lycus Valley reached him. This would help to explain the affinity between the Christological approach of Hebrews and

[6] B. F. Westcott, *The Epistle to the Hebrews*, p. xxxix.
[7] *The Expositor*, Fifth Series, IX (1899), 401-22.
[8] *L'Épître aux Hebreux*, I, 220-52.
[9] The same position is taken by C. Sandegren, *EQ*, XXVII, 221-24.
[10] "The Problem of the Epistle to the Hebrews," *BJRL*, 32 (Sept. 1949), 1-17.

Colossians in relation to the problem of venerating angels. The view has considerable attractiveness.

Still another approach within the Hebrew-Christian framework finds it plausible to think of the epistle as directed to former members of the Qumran community, "a group of Jews originally belonging to the DSS Sect who were converted to Christianity, carrying with them some of their previous beliefs."[11] Men who had been taught to look both for a lay and a priestly Messiah would especially profit from the considerable attention given to this subject in relation to Jesus Christ. The teaching on the finality of the sacrifice of Christ can be understood as counter-ing the notion of the Qumran groups that in the end-time sacri-fices would be resumed. Great importance was attached by the sect to the Archangel Michael, which accords with the assess-ment of the role of angels in the divine plan (Heb. 1-2 especially). One of the most interesting aspects of correlation relates to the presentation in Hebrews of Israel in the setting of the wilderness wanderings, fitting so neatly the situation of the Qumran sec-taries in their desert habitat. Yadin notes the detailed organi-zation of the community and the use of banners and trumpets after the manner of the forefathers.[12] The many references in Hebrews to the tabernacle, coupled with the neglect of the temple, have long puzzled students of this book. On the Qumran thesis, this ceases to be a difficulty, for the group held itself aloof from the temple and its worship.

If the readers of Hebrews lived in Palestine, the title could conceivably designate Aramaic-speaking Jews (cf. Acts 6:1), but the exceptional quality of the Greek of the epistle does not favor this.

An entirely different conception of the readers of the epistle makes them out to be Gentiles (held by Jülicher, Pfleiderer, McGiffert, Moffatt, E. F. Scott, Vos, *et al.*). The title, which is not a part of the text, is regarded as a misnomer. Stress is laid on the fact that the Judaism of the period was not concerned with ritual as much as with law observance. The distinction between Jew and Gentile fails to appear in the book, and items that would naturally be expected in a work addressed to Jewish Christians, such as the faith-works tension and circumcision, are not mentioned. Even the extensive use of the Old Testament is

---

[11] Yadin "The Dead Sea Scrolls and the Epistle to the Hebrews" in *Scripta Hierosolymitana,* IV, 38. F. F. Bruce gives a more cautious review of the evidence in his article " 'To the Hebrews' or 'to the Essenes?' " *NTS,* 9 (Apr. 1963), 217-32.

[12] *Ibid.,* p. 55.

regarded as not at all decisive, since it is often employed in letters addressed to predominately Gentile churches. This viewpoint maintains that the people addressed were in danger of drifting into irreligion in general or into the various cults of the time, angel worship, etc. A major weakness of this position is that no allusion is made, as in Paul's letters, to the beliefs and practices of pagan society. Christianity is set over against the Jewish religion exclusively.

It was dissatisfaction with this Gentile approach to the book that led William Manson to develop his view.[13] He points out that what needs to be explained is not the mere fact of the use of the Old Testament but the particular use made of it. Attention should be given to the argument that the writer is building up. A comparison with the address of Stephen (Acts 7) is illuminating. This leader of the early church is accused of blasphemy against the law and the temple. In his reply, Stephen launches into a resumé of Old Testament history that accents the need of response to the revealed will of God, a readiness to move out in obedience to his command, whether it be Abraham from Mesopotamia or Moses and the nation Israel from Egypt. Significantly, both the tabernacle in the wilderness and the temple of Solomon are mentioned. The temple is viewed as symbolic of the hardness of heart of the nation, its self-satisfaction in its own achievement, its tendency to settle down. This was the sin of Israel, preferring its temple and all that went with it to God's revelation in Christ, the one greater than the temple.

Now, moving over to look again at the Hebrews epistle, we see that the writer makes use of the tabernacle in his discussion rather than the temple. This seems deliberate. The tabernacle by its mobility symbolizes progress, not stagnation. Hebrews stresses the need of hearkening to the voice of the living God and moving forward in line with his revealed purposes. Some in the early church were too much attached to the temple and to Judaism in general. These seem to have largely escaped the brunt of persecution that fell on Stephen and his associates. It was the concern to meet this general tendency to be overly devoted to Judaism and its institutions that called forth the Hebrews epistle. This differs from the older notion that the readers were actually in danger of slipping back into Judaism. No such danger is stated in the book. Yet its Jewish-Christian character is self-evident.

William Manson favored the view that the readers were in Italy.

[13] *The Epistle to the Hebrews* (the 1949 Baird Lecture).

This has textual support in the words, "They of Italy greet you" (13:24). The statement is readily understood as meaning that Christians who have come from Italy and are now with the writer are sending their greetings to their friends in Christ who are still living there, though admittedly it could mean that the people referred to live in Italy, where the writer also is located. Paul's letter to the Romans indicates that people in that church were scrupulous about foods and the observance of holy days (chap. 14). The reference to the loss of possessions and imprisonment in Hebrews 10:32-34 may possibly be related to the tumults that led Claudius to issue an order expelling the Jews from Rome. Since the troubles had to do with a certain Chrestus (or Christus), a plausible explanation for the whole situation is the violent agitation attending the preaching of Jesus as the Messiah in the Jewish community at Rome. In acting against the Jews, the government would make no distinction between those who were Christian and those who were not. Clement's use of Hebrews in his Corinthian letter, written before the close of the first century, is most easily accounted for if the Hebrews epistle was addressed to people in the area where he lived (Rome).

The final word has yet to be said about destination, but the Hebrew-Christian character of the epistle seems sufficiently demonstrated.

AUTHORSHIP

Hebrews is not an anonymous epistle in the sense that the writer is unknown to the readers, but only in the sense that the name is not indicated. The writer asks prayer for himself, that he may be enabled to visit those to whom he is writing (13:19), and expresses the hope that Timothy, who has lately been released, apparently from imprisonment, will come with him (13:23). An additional allusion is found in the Received Text of 10:34 to the bonds of the writer, but other textual authority has "the prisoners."

The uncertainty of the ancient church has already been noted. Barnabas is cited as the author by Tertullian. "There exists also a writing entitled 'To the Hebrews,' by Barnabas, a man sufficiently authorized by God."[14] This is not a personal judgment, but a current tradition. Some support for this testimony has been sought in the fact that Barnabas was a Levite (Acts 4:36) and on this account could reasonably be thought of as capable of writing a book steeped in Old Testament ritual. It

---

[14] *De Pudicitia,* 20.

is pointed out also that in the Book of Acts Barnabas appears as the mediator between Jewish Christians and Paul, "much as this epistle seeks to establish its Hebrew readers in a doctrine which is thoroughly Pauline."[15] But there is a serious objection to Barnabas, well put by Godet. "How is it possible that a well-known and all but apostolic name, like that of Barnabas, should have been almost completely lost? And is not the fact that another writing was falsely assigned to Barnabas an added argument against the suppression of his name in an epistle really written by him?"[16] The allusion here, of course, is to the so-called Epistle of Barnabas. Novatian also favored Barnabas,[17] but this attribution was not general throughout the West.

The case for Paul is stronger than that for Barnabas. Origen states that men of old time handed it down as Paul's.[18] His predecessor, Clement of Alexandria, suggested that Paul had written it in Hebrew and that Luke had translated it.[19] This is highly unlikely, for the book does not read like translation Greek. Origen mentions the opinion about Luke and adds the name of Clement of Rome, but does not mention translation.[20] He settles for the judgment that God is the only one who truly knows who wrote it.[21] In the West Irenaeus and Hippolytus refused to acknowledge it as Pauline.

Some internal considerations have been appealed to in support of Pauline authorship.[22] (1) Certain Christological elements are in agreement with his teaching, such as our Lord's nature as being in the image of God (Heb. 1:3; II Cor. 4:4), his agency in creation (Heb. 1:2; Col. 1:16) and his obedience (Heb. 5:8; Phil. 2:8). (2) The administration of the Spirit's gifts is referred to in similar language (Heb. 2:4; I Cor. 12:11). (3) The new covenant has a place in both (Heb. 9:15; II Cor. 3:6). (4) Faith is a cardinal matter for both writers, with Abraham as a leading example of it in Old Testament story (Heb. 11:8-10, 12, 17-19; Gal. 3:6-9; Rom. 4). Furthermore, Habakkuk 2:4 is quoted in Hebrews 10:38 and elsewhere only in Romans 1:17 and Galatians 3:11. (5) The word "perfect" seems to

---

[15] John D. Davis, *Dictionary of the Bible*, p. 296a.
[16] *Studies on the Epistles*, p. 337.
[17] Souter, *The Text and Canon of the New Testament*, p. 177.
[18] *HE* VI. xxv.
[19] *HE* VI. xiv.
[20] *HE* VI. xxv.
[21] *Ibid.*
[22] Extensive treatments favorable to Paul are by William Leonard, *Authorship of the Epistle to the Hebrews* (1939), and Charles Forster, *The Apostolical Authority of the Epistle to the Hebrews* (1838).

be used similarly (Heb. 5:14; Phil. 3:15, etc.). (6) Israel in its conduct during the wilderness wanderings is used as a warning example (Heb. 3:7-11:10; I Cor. 10:1-11). (7) The closing section (13:18-25) has several items suggestive of Paul, such as the reference to a clear conscience and the request for prayer for himself (v. 18), the allusion to God as the God of peace (v. 20; cf. I Thess. 5:23; Rom. 15:33), the reference to Timothy (v. 23) and the closing words, "Grace be with you all," in agreement with Paul's custom.

No fault can be found with some of these comparisons, but others have weaknesses. The conception of faith appears to be somewhat different in Hebrews than in Pauline usage. In the former, it is a general attitude of confidence in God, a willingness to trust him despite appearances. It reaches into the invisible world and provides sure hope for the future (Heb. 11:1). While Paul speaks of walking by faith rather than sight (II Cor. 5:7), his characteristic use of faith relates it to the past, to the acceptance of Christ in his redemptive work. His phrase "faith in Jesus" or the like nowhere shows itself in Hebrews. The argument based on the quotation of Habakkuk 2:4 is rendered nugatory by the fact that the form found in Hebrews differs from that in the two Pauline passages.

Similarly, it is somewhat misleading to plead for an identical use of the word "perfect," since the ruling idea of perfection in Hebrews is found in the verb, where it does not mean to foster growth or maturity, but to demonstrate a solid reality that is contrasted with the shadowy and unsatisfactory character of spiritual conditions under the old covenant.

The use of Israel as a warning example has only a superficial resemblance in the two writers. Both use the word meaning "to tempt" or "to test" but in Hebrews (3:9) it is found only in quotation. Israel's murmuring, mentioned in Paul, is not cited in Hebrews. Whereas Hebrews makes a special point of Israel's unbelief, Paul does not mention this, but stresses rather the idolatry and licentious feasting of the people, items that fail to appear in Hebrews. Likewise, the magnifying of "rest" in Hebrews has no counterpart in Paul.

No valid argument can be based on the reference to "our brother Timothy." In fact, this turns out to be a boomerang, since Paul, in making such a reference, always puts the name first (e.g., I Thess. 3:2).

Pauline authorship is rendered difficult, if not impossible, by other considerations. (1) The author's name is not given. This is contrary to Paul's custom. In dealing with this problem,

376

Clement of Alexandria cites the opinion of "the blessed elder," probably meaning Pantaenus, to the effect that Paul did not affix his name out of humility. His Lord had labored among the Jews; he was the apostle to the Gentiles. Feeling a certain diffidence in writing to Hebrews, he sought to remain in the background.[23] Others have sought to explain the absence of Paul's name on the ground that he was *persona non grata* with Jewish Christians, so that his message had a better chance of being received if he did not disclose his identity. This is strange reasoning. It contradicts the testimony of the closing chapter, where it appears that the writer is well-known to his readers and is not at all on bad terms with them. Furthermore, if we were to suppose, for the sake of argument, that Paul actually had such a fear of disclosing his identity, it should be obvious that it was risky to write anonymously, for if and when his identity became known to the readers, this information would react unfavorably on the reception of the message. Resentment would be the price paid for the tactics employed.

(2) The writer seems to place himself outside the circle of apostles in the words, "How shall we escape if we neglect so great salvation; which at the first began to be spoken by the Lord, and was confirmed unto us by them that heard him" (2:3). Paul's usual custom was to emphasize the fact that he had received the gospel from the Lord himself. It is true that he referred to it as something received from men (I Cor. 15:1ff.), but only from the standpoint of testimony to the resurrection appearances, which were so important for the establishing of the fact of the resurrection. Whereas Hebrews 2:3-4 may not be fatal to Paul's authorship, it nevertheless creates real difficulty.

(3) The style is markedly different from Paul's. This is not so much a matter of sentence structure, as in Ephesians, but it concerns the classical touch, the smooth polish, the absence of such a rough feature as the anacoluthon. Godet remarks, "It is strange indeed that he should have written in polished Greek to the Hebrews, while all his life he had been writing to the Hellenes in a style abounding with rugged and barbarous Hebraisms."[24]

(4) References to our Lord do not fit into the Pauline pattern. Hebrews uses the personal name Jesus nine times, Jesus Christ three times, Lord Jesus once, for a total of 13. Paul has some 218 occurrences of the name Jesus, whether alone or in combination with the titles Christ or Lord. Of these

---

23 *HE* VI. xiv.
24 *Op. cit.,* p. 332.

only 14 are occurrences of Jesus by itself, a much smaller percentage than in Hebrews. Equally significant is the fact that Christ Jesus, a favorite designation with Paul, is totally absent from Hebrews. Noteworthy also is the appearance of a series of titles for Christ not found in Paul at all, such as High Priest, Captain of our salvation, Pioneer and Perfecter of faith, Forerunner, Surety, etc.

(5) The main thrust of the epistle, namely, the ministry of Christ as high priest in the heavenly sanctuary as a proof of his finished work on earth, is nowhere found in Paul. The latter mentions the intercessory work of the Lord, to be sure (Rom. 8:34), but does not adduce the priesthood of Christ in connection with it. Paul's point of stress is the death and resurrection of Christ, and the failure of Hebrews to include more than one reference to his resurrection (13:20) is somewhat damaging.

(6) Quotations from the Old Testament are regularly taken from the LXX, which is not always the case with Paul. Also, the writer seldom mentions the human source of the quotation (contrary to Pauline usage), but instead tends to introduce his quotations with a note of indefiniteness — "one in a certain place," etc. His quotations are often longer than Paul's. With a single exception, he does not appeal to Scripture as something written (and the exception turns out to be no exception, since the word "written" belongs to the quotation itself — the passage is found in 10:7).[25] This is in striking contrast to Paul's usage.

(7) Larger place is given to the earthly life of Jesus Christ than in all of Paul's letters put together.

(8) Nowhere in this epistle do we come to grips with the personality or experience of Paul. The few allusions to the writer in the closing chapter are too colorless to be of assistance in this respect.

(9) Hebrews is decidedly deficient in precise ethical demands of the sort that customarily appear in Paul's writings. This could be assigned in part to the fact that the readers were presumably somewhat less in need of this sort of instruction than groups with a pagan background.

Luther suggested Apollos as the writer, and there is much to commend the opinion. He is described as eloquent (Acts 18:24), that is, either learned or facile in the use of words, or both. In the same passage Luke calls him "mighty in the Scriptures." The Old Testament was familiar territory to him and he could

---

[25] Markus Barth, *op. cit.,* p. 58.

handle it with skill. This accords with the use of the Old Testament in Hebrews. Further, Apollos was with Paul (I Cor. 16:12; cf. Titus 3:13) and with those familiar with Paul's teaching (Acts 18:26), which could account for the elements in the epistle that are reminiscent of the apostle to the Gentiles. Finally, he is described as a Jew of Alexandria (Acts 18:24). This accords with the writer's consistent use of the LXX and his employment of patterns of thought readily associated with that center, especially with items suggested by the writings of the eminent Alexandrian Jew of a few years before, Philo the religious philosopher. Spicq has presented a persuasive case for the Philonic influence upon Hebrews. The argument is not confined to such matters as the apparent use of the Platonic theory of ideas in contrasting the earthly tabernacle with the true and heavenly (8:2; 9:24), a system of thought with which Philo was imbued.[26] Of the nine biblical occurrences of κεφάλιον (seven in the OT and two in the NT), the only one having the technical sense of the essential point of an exposition, which is common in the classics and in Philo, is Hebrews 8:1. The word δημιουργός (maker, creator), not used in the Old Testament (found once in a bad sense in Second Maccabees) but much used by Philo as by Plato before him, is employed of God in Hebrews 11:10. That the writer of Hebrews does not indulge in extensive allegorizing in the Philonic manner (a tendency in this direction may be seen in the handling of the Melchizedek presentation) may safely be attributed to the fact that he has come to a Christian understanding of the Old Testament, in which allegory was used sparingly, if at all. The data supporting an Alexandrian origin and therefore favorable to Apollos are fairly extensive and cannot lightly be dismissed. Against his case is the failure of the ancients to connect him with the Hebrews epistle.

Priscilla and Aquila were favored by Harnack, with Priscilla mainly responsible for the materials. It would be fairly easy, on such an assumption, to explain the withholding of the name or names. But it is uncertain that this couple possessed the necessary education for such a task and it is very unlikely that a woman who had been closely associated with Paul would have had the temerity to write as a Christian teacher. The shift from

---

[26] This line of thought could be based on Palestinian rabbinic teaching. See C. K. Barrett, "The Eschatology of the Epistle to the Hebrews," in *The Background of the New Testament and its Eschatology,* ed. by Davies and Daube, pp. 383ff.

plural to singular (13:18-19) would be quite disconcerting to the readers without clear guidance as to identity.

Luke and Silas have been suggested also, but have gained comparatively little support.

Our inability to come to a decision on authorship does not diminish the value of the book or its authority. As God spoke in many parts and many manners in the old covenant, so was he pleased to expound his new covenant revelation through diverse human channels. "The Church, of whose life the New Testament was a product, must have been even greater than its greatest names. St. Paul and St. John have exercised such an influence over the world by their writings that we are tempted to forget that they were but the highest in a chain of mountain peaks. The very fact that the author of so brilliant an exposition of Christianity as is found in the Epistle to the Hebrews could so soon be forgotten is clear proof, if proof were needed, of the high level of spiritual and intellectual attainment in the Apostolic Church."[27]

DATE

There is little to serve as guide here. Since the writer speaks of the ritual of sacrifice in the present tense (8:4; 9:9; 10:1), one may conclude that the temple is still standing. But this is not certain, since he is basing his presentation on the tabernacle rather than the temple. Other writers, at a time later than A.D. 70, used the present tense of the temple service, as though it were still going on.[28] Yet if the writer had been able to point to so decisive an event as the fall of Jerusalem and the destruction of the temple, it would fit so well with his general thesis of the outmoded character of the old order that it is hard to see how he could have avoided using it. Therefore a date prior to A.D. 70 is likely. The Jewish rebellion against Rome could have awakened patriotic fervor and sympathy among many Hebrew Christians, causing them to be somewhat distracted from Christ and his great salvation.

RECENT STUDY

A date for Hebrews as early as 52-54 is favored by Hugh Montefiore,[29] who settles on Apollos as the author and opines

---

[27] W. K. L. Clarke in *The Parting of the Roads*, ed. by F. J. Foakes Jackson, p. 176.

[28] Clement's *Epistle to the Corinthians* xl. 5; xli. 2; Josephus, *Against Apion* ii. 188.

[29] *A Commentary on the Epistle to the Hebrews*, 1964.

that after his visit to Corinth he wrote to the church there. Paul's repeated allusions to Apollos in I Corinthians 1-4, together with the use of such terms as "perfect" and "milk" which occur also in Hebrews, may be said to reflect the apostle's knowledge of Apollos' communication and his desire to correct any misapprehensions left by it. This novel theory suffers from the unlikelihood that such an epistle as Hebrews would be germane to believers at Corinth as we know them from Paul's letters.

BIBLIOGRAPHY

Bruce, A. B., *The Epistle to the Hebrews.* 2nd. ed., Edinburgh: T. & T. Clark, 1899.

Davidson, A. B., *The Epistle to the Hebrews.* Reprint, Grand Rapids: Zondervan, 1950.

Delitzsch, F., *Commentary on the Epistle to the Hebrews,* 2 vols. Edinburgh: T. & T. Clark, n.d.

Hewitt, Thomas, *The Epistle to the Hebrews, TBC.* Grand Rapids: Eerdmans, 1960.

Hort, F. J. A., *Judaistic Christianity.* London: Macmillan, 1898.

Manson, William, *The Epistle to the Hebrews.* London: Hodder & Stoughton, 1951.

McCaul, J. B., *The Epistle to the Hebrews.* London: Longmans, Green, 1871.

Michel, Otto, *Der Brief an die Hebräer.* 12th ed., Göttingen: Vandenhoeck & Ruprecht, 1966.

Milligan, G., *The Theology of the Epistle to the Hebrews.* Edinburgh: T. & T. Clark, 1899.

Moffatt, James, *A Critical and Exegetical Commentary on the Epistle to the Hebrews, ICC.* New York: Scribner's, 1924.

Montefiore, Hugh, *A Commentary on the Epistle to the Hebrews, HNTC.* New York: Harper and Row, 1964.

Nairne, A. N., *The Epistle of Priesthood.* Edinburgh: T. & T. Clark, 1913.

Narborough, F. D. V., *The Epistle to the Hebrews,* Clarendon Bible. Oxford: Clarendon Press, 1930.

Spicq, C., *L' Epître aux Hébreux,* 2 vols. Paris: J. Gabalda, 1952.

Scott, E. F., *The Epistle to the Hebrews.* Edinburgh: T. & T. Clark, 1922.

Vos, G., *The Teaching of the Epistle to the Hebrews.* Grand Rapids: Eerdmans, 1956.

Westcott, B. F., *The Epistle to the Hebrews.* London: Macmillan, 1889.

Wickham, E. C., *The Epistle to the Hebrews, WC.* London: Methuen, 1910.

Windisch, Hans, *Der Hebräerbrief, HZNT.* 2nd ed., Tübingen: Mohr, 1931.

Chapter Nineteen

THE EPISTLE OF JAMES

A FEATURE COMMON TO THE CATHOLIC EPISTLES IS THE LACK of any indication that they were written to a single congregation, although in this respect II and III John are exceptions to the rule. It may seem strange that the New Testament contains no letter that can be positively identified as directed to a congregation of Jewish Christians on Palestinian soil to parallel the several written by Paul to gentile churches outside the holy land. This is not due to the lack of churches in Palestine. They flourished in Judea (Gal. 1:22), Samaria (Acts 8:4-8), and Galilee (Acts 9:31). Perhaps these Jewish believers had less need of close pastoral oversight than their brethren who had come out of paganism. In many cases they were not founded by an apostle who remained in close touch with them, but by believers who were dispersed from Jerusalem by persecution (Acts 8:4). The Epistle of James is not an occasional writing, but was apparently designed to meet the needs of Jewish believers in a general way, whether within the borders of Palestine or beyond.

RECOGNITION BY THE EARLY CHURCH

Although there may be allusions to James in the Apostolic Fathers, the first writer to refer to the work by name and cite it as

382

Scripture is Origen, in his Commentary on John. Eusebius, who put it among the disputed books, accepted it for himself, referring to it as the first of the Catholic Epistles and as used publicly in the churches along with the other epistles. He notes that few of the ancients quote it, and for this reason it was denied by some of his contemporaries.[1] In the Syrian church the epistle did not get a foothold until it appeared in the Peshitta. In the West it was not included in the Canon of Muratori and was generally ignored until Jerome and Augustine gave it their endorsement. Its place seemed to become secure with its inclusion by the Third Council of Carthage in A.D. 397, but at the beginning of the modern period it was questioned by Erasmus and others. Luther's attitude was one of distrust and disappointment because he found it out of agreement with Paul's teaching on justification by faith. Since it did not meet his requirement of presenting Christ as the other epistles did, he gave it a secondary position and labeled it "a right strawy epistle."

OUTLINE OF CONTENTS

After the opening words of address (1:1), the following themes are unfolded: the endurance of testing and temptation with the aid of believing prayer (1:2-18); true religion (1:19-27); the danger of showing partiality (2:1-13); faith and works (2:14-26); the problem of the tongue (3:1-12); heavenly wisdom (3:13-18); the evil of worldliness (4:1-10); the sin of judging others (4:11-12); self-will versus God's will (4:13-17); warning to unrighteous men of wealth (5:1-6); admonition to patience in view of the Lord's return (5:7-11); prohibition of oaths (5:12); healing through prayer (5:13-18); restoration of an erring brother (5:19-20).

Some of the more frequently used terms are brother, ask, pray, faith, sin, tongue, judge and judgment, try or tempt, law, work, do and doer, rich and poor, wisdom, perfect.

CHARACTERISTICS

These leading characteristics may be noted. (1) The work has an authoritative tone. Nearly every other verse contains an imperative. Yet one is not conscious of an autocratic spirit. The writer frequently addresses his readers as brethren. (2) There is a paucity of Christian doctrine. There is no teaching on redemption through the death and resurrection of Christ. (3) On the

[1] *HE* II. xxiii. 24-25.

383

other hand, the epistle is eminently practical in its approach. This can be readily understood if the writer was in a position of administrative responsibility. From start to finish the writer accents the practical outworking of true religion. There is virtually no attempt, as in Paul's letters, to lay a doctrinal foundation for the wide assortment of injunctions set down one after another with little or no relation among the various themes. The principal binding element is the insistence on being a doer of the Word, and the very fact that the Word has such prominence indicates that the work is far from being without theological presuppositions. Because of the author's trenchant preaching against social injustice and inequality, he has often been called the Amos of the New Testament. (4) The epistle is notably impersonal. "There is no particular personal relation between him [the author] and those whom he 'addresses.' The picture of the readers and figure of the writer are equally colorless and indistinct."[2] (5) There is a fine appreciation of nature in this book. It has been said that there is more of this in James than in all of Paul's letters combined. (6) The teaching bears marked similarity to that of Christ, especially to what is contained in the Sermon on the Mount. D. A. Hayes writes, "James says less about the Master than any other writer in the NT, but his speech is more like that of the Master than the speech of any one of them."[3] These examples are typical: on judging (James 4:11-12; Matt. 7:1); on humbling oneself (James 4:10; Matt. 23:12); on swearing (James 5:12; Matt. 5:34-37). (7) James belongs to the wisdom literature, revealing kinship both with the wisdom books of the Old Testament and with some of the Apocrypha, especially Sirach, yet it differs from this literature in that it displays a concern for eschatology. (8) The Greek of the epistle is of a high quality, comparing favorably with that of Hebrews and I Peter. It has a rather high percentage of words peculiar to itself among New Testament writings.

READERS

These are declared to be "the twelve tribes which are in the dispersion" (1:1). We note the absence of any statement that would identify them as saints or believers or even those who are called of God. The address is unique in this respect among the letters of the New Testament, and it invites the question whether this letter could have been written, in fact, to non-Christian Jews.

The twelve tribes did not all return from captivity, though

---

2 A. Deissmann, *Bible Studies,* p. 53.
3 *ISBE,* III, 1564.

there may have been representatives of all the tribes in the land of Israel as well as out of it. However broken, reduced, and scattered, the nation fondly clung to the terminology "the twelve tribes" as an expression of its ideal unity as the covenant people (Matt. 19:28; Acts 26:7).

It is clear that the Epistle of James would not have been received into the canon if the early church had understood it to be directed to Jews in general. It is equally clear that the epistle itself contains items that could hardly have been included in a document intended for non-Christians. Faith in the Lord Jesus Christ is presupposed (2:1). This in turn makes "the coming of the Lord" (5:7) a reference to Christ's coming rather than to some future intervention of the Lord God of Israel. The same is true of the description of the readers as born or brought forth by the word of truth (1:18). This is better understood as an allusion to regeneration than to creation. The good name that has been called upon the readers (2:7) is almost certainly that of Christ. Some interpreters see here an allusion to Christian baptism. This substratum of Christian presuppositions makes quite impossible the view of Spitta that James is a Jewish work with Christian interpolations at 1:1 and 2:1. His notion is further discredited by the use of χαράν (1:2) in obvious alliteration with χαίρειν in 1:1. Both must be from the pen of the author.

A second possibility is that Christians in general are the intended recipients of the letter. This is based on an allegedly parallel use of "dispersion" in the address of I Peter, where the word presumably denotes Christians dispersed here and there among non-Christian populations in a way analogous to the historic dispersion of Jews among Gentiles. The concept of the church as the new Israel is also relied on for support. However, the parallel between James and I Peter is not exact, since James uses the definite article with "dispersion," which is not true of I Peter. Also, there is no mention of the twelve tribes in I Peter.

A third view has generally prevailed in the church, namely, that the readers are Hebrew Christians. This opinion is not by any means universal today, but it still seems the most likely, as it best accounts for the opening sentence and is supported by other features such as the occurrence of both synagogue (2:2) and church (5:14), the warning against the taking of oaths (5:12),[4]

[4] Zahn notes that "the examples of oath formulae in James v. 12 are such as were in use among the Jews, not among the Greeks and Romans" (*Introduction*, I, 91).

and the lack of warning against such typical Gentile sins as idolatry and immorality.

On the basis of the traditional view of authorship and a fairly early date for the epistle, it is possible that Gentile Christians also may have been in view in a secondary sense. In this connection Zahn's reminder is well taken. "So long as the Church was composed only of congregations whose charter members had been members of the Jerusalem Church before they were scattered abroad by persecution, and before missionary work among the Gentiles, which began from Antioch, made this city a new centre of church life independent of Jerusalem, the man at the head of the mother Church must have had authority throughout the entire Church."[5]

One's conclusion on this whole issue will be affected to some extent by his decision on authorship, for if the letter emanated from someone within the circle of Jewish Christianity, it is most natural to predicate a similar status for those who are addressed. On the other hand, if the book is regarded as a pseudonymous production of a period later than the heyday of Jewish Christianity, the Jewish features are more readily minimized or explained away, and the door is opened to the supposition that the readers could actually have been Gentiles.[6]

AUTHORSHIP

The text itself gives no more information than the name. But this is an important clue, despite the fact that James was such a common name, for the very prevalence of the name meant that only a person of prominence in the church would use it without further identification, and the same would be true of the understanding of it by others. An illustration of this principle is seen in the occurrence of the name Simon to designate Simon Peter despite the presence of another Simon (the Zealot) in the apostolic company (Lk. 24:34).

The one man who answers to this clue is James the brother of our Lord, first mentioned in Mark 6:3 as one of the four brothers. Since he heads the list, he was probably older than the others. Like the rest, he did not acknowledge the Messianic status of Jesus during the ministry, but was convinced by the resurrection (Acts 1:14; I Cor. 15:7). Consistently he is noted by his personal name alone (Gal. 2:9, 12; Jude 1; Acts 12:17; 15:13; 21:18). His identity in Galatians 2:9, 12 is firmly established by the prior

[5] Zahn, *op. cit.,* I, 103.
[6] So A. E. Barnett, *IDB,* II, 795a.

statement in Galatians 1:19 that this James is the Lord's brother.

His elevation to the headship of the Jerusalem church cannot be dated with certainty, but it is tempting to think in terms of the martyrdom of an apostle bearing the same name — James the brother of John (Acts 12:2). Shortly after this Peter refers to James with deference (Acts 12:17). However, the interval is short, so James may have come into his position of leadership before the outbreak of persecution noted in this chapter. Apart from the question of time, the appearance of Christ to him following the resurrection must have aided the process of recognition of his leadership by the Jerusalem church.

Eusebius cites the testimony of Hegesippus, a second-century church historian, to the effect that James lived the life of a perpetual Nazarite, spending much time in prayer in the temple and enjoying the esteem of the Jews, so much so that the leaders besought him to warn the people against believing in Jesus. When he used the opportunity to give testimony to him, the scribes and Pharisees were incensed and ordered him thrown down from a battlement of the temple. Even so, he lived long enough to pray for his nation, and then died from a blow of a laundryman's club.[7]

Examination of the epistle reveals certain features that are agreeable to the authorship of such a man as James. For one thing, the syntax is Semitic rather than Greek, with only an occasional hypotactic construction. The author turns naturally to the Old Testament for illustrations, making use of the figures of Abraham, Isaac, Rahab, Job and Elijah. He keeps referring to the law, not identifying it as Mosaic or as that of Christ, but seemingly uniting them, as it were, informing the commandments with the touch of Christ so that the law is now a royal law of liberty. The expression "Lord of hosts" (5:4) suggests an Old Testament outlook, as does "the righteousness of God" (1:20). Elijah prayed "with prayer," an apparent Hebraism. The reference to the fig tree (3:12) should be noted. A charge of spiritual adultery (4:4) recalls similar thrusts by the prophets of Israel. The command to cleanse the hands and purify the hearts (4:8) has a decided Old Testament ring. Then there is the reference to the last days (5:3). It is not maintained that these items prove Jacobean authorship, but that they are in line with it.

More precise criteria come from a comparison of the language

---

[7] *HE* II. xxiii. 4-18.

of the epistle with that attributed to James in the Book of Acts.[8] A few of the points of striking agreement are noted here: (1) the form of the greeting used in 1:1 is found also in Acts 15:23 and is used by no other New Testament writer. It is once used by a Roman officer (Acts 23:26). (2) James' word "to visit" (1:27) occurs in Acts 15:14. (3) His word for the "turning" of sinners to God (5:19-20) occurs also in the address of James, where he speaks of Gentiles who are turning to God (Acts 15: 19). (4) The use of the "name" of the Lord is similar in both (James 2:7; Acts 15:17).

As far as is known, James continued to reside in Jerusalem from the earliest days of the church. This would give him considerable contact with Jewish believers from many quarters, affording him at once the ability and the responsibility to communicate with them by way of pastoral oversight. Probably I Corinthians 9:5 ought not to be so construed as to preclude this, for the missionary activity of the brethren of the Lord need not have included James, since there were three others to qualify. Acts does not mention any departure from Jerusalem and tradition does not ascribe any posterity to him, making it unlikely that he married. This is additional reason for being wary about applying I Corinthians 9:5 to James, since there the apostle Paul is dwelling on marriage.

Gaster is of the opinion that James may have been influenced considerably by the ideals and practices of the Qumran community.[9] He points to the testimony of Hegesippus that James avoided the use of oil and used linen garments exclusively, both of which are Essenic characteristics, as Josephus explains. Of the several parallels that he finds between James and the Qumran literature, perhaps the most interesting relates to James 2:2-4. "When we bear in mind the specific precept in the *Manual of Discipline* that all members of the community are to be graded by intelligence and character alone, and when we remember that the Hebrew and Aramaic words for 'seat' (viz. *moshab* and *mêthbâ*) also mean 'status' and that 'to stand without' was common Hebrew idiom for 'be excluded from society,' it becomes clear that James is echoing this injunction, and not referring specifically to the seating arrangements in a synagogue."

Those who do not favor the authorship of James are able to advance certain negative arguments. (1) It is strange that there

---

[8] For a full list of the data, see J. B. Mayor, *The Epistle of St. James,* pp. iii-iv.

[9] *The Dead Sea Scriptures,* pp. 15-17.

should have been doubts about this book and such tardiness in its reception if such a prominent figure as James the Lord's brother wrote it. To offset this, one can point to the great dissimilarity between this epistle and the writings of Paul, for example, which enjoyed such a ready reception. James suffered from its lack of doctrinal emphasis. It is possible also that the general oblivion into which the Jewish Christian church sank took with it, for a time, this epistle that was naturally identified with that phase of Christianity.

(2) The high quality of the Greek displayed in this book is strange, if not impossible, for a man whose native language must have been Aramaic. Admittedly this is a problem. It has been met in two ways, by pointing to the extensive contact that James must have had with Greek-speaking Jews from various places by reason of his position as head of the Jerusalem church (not overlooking the possibility that the responsibility of that position would have spurred him to acquire proficiency in Greek) and by resorting to the theory of help from an amanuensis.

(3) The form of the epistle is Hellenistic, though the substance is Hebraistic. "The fact that the Epistle of James is written throughout as a paraenesis, with frequent employment of the diatribe, shows that its author must be sought among those whose literary associations were with the Greek rather than with the Hebrew world."[10] This argument can hardly be regarded as conclusive when it is recalled that Paul, the Hebrew of the Hebrews, used the same Hellenistic literary devices, diatribe and all.

(4) The writer of the epistle does not claim a relationship to Jesus such as Paul indicates for him in Galatians 1:19. This is true enough, but it has all the weakness of the argument from silence. Modesty alone could have kept James from asserting his kinship with the Lord. His very prominence in the Jewish Christian scene made identification unnecessary beyond the use of his name.

ALTERNATIVE VIEWS ON AUTHORSHIP

(1) The epistle is pseudonymous. Against this is the failure of the writer to do the expected thing, namely, make the identity of James lavishly explicit, including the magnifying of his position in the church. Then, too, it is difficult to see what reason such a person would have for seeking to use James' authority since

[10] B. S. Easton, *IB*, XII, 4.

a work of this kind could presumably make its own way. It does not contain novel or heretical positions to be palmed off on the church. As Zahn points out, "If for the purpose of teaching or rebuking his contemporaries, someone found it advantageous to pass himself off as the distinguished James, then the end which he had in view must have been such that the personality of James, as the recollection was retained in the tradition, would have lent special weight to what he said. But the contents of the Epistle are absolutely against this presupposition. It does not bring out a single one of those characteristics by which James is distinguished in history and legend."[11]

(2) Another James, a follower of Jesus, wrote the book. James the son of Alphaeus (Mark 3:18) may be dismissed at once, for there is no tradition in his favor. James the son of Zebedee is highly questionable because the simple name would not be taken as a reference to him, seeing that he usually requires further identification in the Scripture notices. Also, if he were the writer he would probably have indicated his apostolic position. Again, his death in A.D. 44 or slightly before may be too early to have permitted him to write this book. Finally, no early tradition speaks for him in this connection. What there is belongs to the medieval period and is localized in Spain.

(3) James (Gr. ’Ιάκωβος) is literally Jacob, and this has been viewed as a key to the understanding of the epistle as a work deliberately planned to resemble in part the blessing of Jacob on the tribes (his sons and more remotely their descendants) as recorded in Genesis 49.[12] After all, *The Testaments of the Twelve Patriarchs,* assumed to be earlier but having Christian interpolations, plainly shows the effects of the Jacob motif. Meyer considered the substance of James to be a Jewish production that was later given a Christian cast here and there. He professed to find references to the sons of Jacob in the various emphases of the epistle: for example, Reuben corresponds to firstfruits (1:18), Simeon to wrath and excessive wickedness (1:19-21), etc. Meyer was able to appeal to similar attempts on a more limited scale in the interpretation of various patristic writers, and he certainly showed ingenuity in presenting his own case, but few scholars have endorsed his results.[13] The oversubtle approach demands as much eisegesis as exegesis.

---

11 *Introduction*, I, 140.

12 Arnold Meyer, *Das Rätsel des Jacobusbriefes* (1930).

13 B. S. Easton (*IB*) utilizes the method, though admitting that Meyer went too far in details.

DATE

Those who regard James as pseudonymous date the book toward the end of the first century or even sometime during the first half of the second depending largely on the degree to which they find the book indebted to various writings of the postapostolic period. On such a basis it is hard to account for the lively expectation of the Lord's return that features the epistle, and this must remain an embarrassment for any late dating.

Possible dependence on the Apostolic Fathers has been much debated. Gerhard Kittel, after a ten-year study of the epistle and its problems, concluded in a lengthy article written shortly before his death that James was not dependent on these writings, and thus he favored an early date.[14] In an earlier article he maintained that James was the first of the New Testament writings, which would place it at the middle of the first century or slightly earlier.[15]

An early date is not necessarily contingent on the acceptance of James' authorship, but may be grounded on evidence derived from the book itself.[16] Four items must suffice. (1) Though the epistle abounds in references to Christ's teachings in the Synoptic Gospels and bears an especially close relation to the Sermon on the Mount, there is so little verbal agreement that it is hard to suppose the use of written sources. The origin of James, it seems, belongs to the period before the Gospel tradition was fixed in written form. (2) James devotes considerable attention to economic conditions, stressing the chasm between the poor and the rich and deploring the harsh and unjust treatment meted out to laborers by the land barons (see esp. 5:1-6). These conditions ceased to exist with the outbreak of the war against Rome (A.D. 66), when the rich suffered great losses and agriculture was sorely depleted. (3) The simplicity of ecclesiastical organization implied in the mention of elders alone (5:14) is favorable to an early date. (4) The avidity with which the second coming of Christ is awaited points in the same direction (5:7-9).

On the assumption that James wrote the epistle, it must have been produced prior to A.D. 62, the date of his death according to Josephus,[17] or 66 according to Hegesippus' account contained in Eusebius.[18] In the endeavor to fix the time more precisely,

---

[14] *ZNTW*, 43 (1950-51), 55-112.
[15] *Ibid.*, 41 (1942), 71-105.
[16] L. E. Elliott-Binns, *Galilean Christianity*, pp. 46-47, accepts an early date but not Jacobean authorship.
[17] *Antiquities* XX. ix. 1.
[18] *HE* II. xxiii. 18.

the focal point of discussion is the section on faith and works (2:14-26). Does this exposition depend on Paul's teaching on justification by faith as set forth in Galatians and Romans? Is it an attempted refutation of that position? This is antecedently unlikely, since James was in accord with Paul's gospel (Acts 15; Gal. 2:1-10), and furthermore, the presentation in James does not read like an attempt at refutation of Paul, for both faith and works are stated differently in the two writers. At the most one could suppose that a garbled statement of Paul's preaching along these lines, say at Antioch before the first missionary journey, had come to James' attention and that he attacks the misrepresentation rather than Paul's true position.[19]

Equally possible is the appraisal of the section in question as called forth by the tendency among believing Jews to rest on faith in a creedal sense and fail in the outworking of it. This accords with the trenchant insistence of James in other parts of the epistle that men must be doers of the Word. Paul has a similar thrust (Rom. 2:6, 13). On the other hand, the view that James is assailing a misunderstanding of Paul's early preaching has the advantage of being able to account for the verb "justify" in both accounts and especially the appeal to Abraham's justification by faith. But whichever position is adopted, there is no necessity of placing the epistle as late as the Apostolic Council. The book fails to reflect the issue that was raised at that gathering, so it can tentatively be assigned to a date two or three years before the mid-century mark.

The argument that the similarities between James and I Peter are best explained on the basis of James' use of Peter is not compelling. Mayor took the opposite position on the ground that "the common thought finds fuller expression in St. Peter."[20] We may not be as sure today as Mayor was that literary relationship is evident, since much of the matter common to New Testament epistles may be drawn from a common store of apostolic instruction more or less fixed in its verbiage. But at any rate there is no necessity of adjusting the date of James to accommodate an assumed priority of I Peter.

PLACE OF WRITING

Nothing in the epistle is decisive in fixing the position of the writer. He may have had some familiarity with the sea (1:6) and its ships (3:4). More prominent are his references to

---

19 See Kittel, *op. cit.*, 41 (1942), 99-102.
20 *The Epistle of St. James*, p. xcviii.

agriculture — the fig tree, the grapevine and olives (3:12), and to the burning wind that dries up vegetation (1:11). He uses the traveling merchant as an illustration (4:13). All these features are agreeable to James' residence in Palestine or at least fit the case of one who grew up in such an environment. There is nothing that seriously challenges Jerusalem as the point of origin.

Other places suggested are Rome (on the assumption that it was used by the author of I Peter and by Clement of Rome); Antioch (because of its relationship with the materials of Matthew); and Alexandria (chiefly because of resemblances between James and Philo).[21]

VALUE

On the historical side, James affords insight into the nature of Jewish Christianity at its most promising period, revealing the strong influence of the Old Testament and late Judaism, particularly the wisdom literature, and the degree to which the teaching of Christ had permeated and enriched this background. Notable is the absence of Pauline influence.

As a permanent contribution to the life of the church, the epistle accents performance rather than profession and keeps the ethical imperative in a position of such prominence that it cannot be ignored.

BIBLIOGRAPHY

Chaine, J. L., *L'Epître de Saint Jacques.* Paris: J. Gabalda, 1927.

Dibelius, M., *Der Brief des Jacobus,* Meyer series. Göttingen: Vandenhoeck & Ruprecht, 1921.

Hort, F. J. A., *The Epistle of St. James.* London: Macmillan, 1909.

Knowling, R. J., *The Epistle of St. James, WC.* London: Methuen, 1904.

Mayor, J. B., *The Epistle of St. James.* 2nd. ed., London: Macmillan, 1897.

Mitton, C. Leslie, *The Epistle of James.* Grand Rapids: Eerdmans, 1966.

Rendall, G. H., *The Epistle of St. James and Judaic Christianity.* Cambridge University Press, 1927.

Ropes, J. H., *A Critical and Exegetical Commentary on the Epistle of St. James, ICC.* New York: Scribner's, 1916.

Ross, Alexander, *The Epistles of James and John, NIC.* Grand Rapids: Eerdmans, 1954.

Tasker, R. V. G., *The General Epistle of James, TBC.* Grand Rapids: Eerdmans, 1957.

[21] For a list of Philonic parallels, see Mayor, pp. lxxvii-lxxx.

Chapter Twenty

THE FIRST EPISTLE OF PETER

AMONG THE SO-CALLED CATHOLIC EPISTLES NONE HAS BEEN more widely used or more highly respected during the history of the church than this one attributed to Simon Peter. It is not a general epistle in the sense that it was sent out to the entire church, but it was intended for a larger group than most of the New Testament epistles, which were usually written to a single congregation. First Peter most nearly resembles Galatians, which was addressed to a group of churches, but its addressees belong to a much wider geographical area.

RECOGNITION BY THE EARLY CHURCH

Eusebius placed it among the undisputed books. Apparently it was unchallenged. No contrary tradition is known to have competed with the understanding that it emanated from the apostle Peter.

It is possible that the first witness to it comes from II Peter 3:1, where that writing is called "the second epistle." Zahn, however, contends that a reference to I Peter is unlikely, since the address of II Peter does not correspond to that of the first epistle, but is very general, and the relationship of writer to readers is markedly different in the two epistles.[1]

---

[1] Zahn, *Introduction*, II, 202.

Traces of the use of I Peter have been claimed for Clement of Rome in his letter to the Corinthians. Lightfoot found twelve parallels. Harnack extended the list to twenty. If this alleged dependence could be established beyond question, it would have an important bearing on the certification of an early date for the epistle. But the evidence is hardly conclusive, although Clement's allusion to the blood of Christ as "precious"[2] is strikingly like Peter's statement in 1:19.

By the time of Polycarp, however, such evidence is available in ample quantity. For example, in his *Epistle to the Philippians* 8:1, he incorporates I Peter 2:22, 24, even using Peter's word for "tree." Yet he does not ascribe the source of his material to Peter by name. Such an explicit reference occurs first in Irenaeus.[3]

Marcion did not include I Peter in his canon, but since he confined the epistolary section to Paul's letters, this omission is not damaging. More difficult to understand is the failure of the Muratorian Fragment to mention it. Whether this is to be explained as due to the incomplete character of the document in its present form, or to the omission of a line, or to some other circumstance, the omission is not crucial, for at this general period or shortly thereafter the book is attested as Peter's by Irenaeus, Clement of Alexandria and Tertullian.

OUTLINE OF CONTENTS

Following the address, Peter launches into an exposition of salvation, viewing it as a glorious heavenly inheritance (1:3-5), as a life of faith and love subject to severe testing and refinement (1:6-9), and as the theme of Old Testament prophets (1:10-12). There follows a plea for holiness (1:13-21) and for mutual love, based on regeneration (1:22-25). The readers are likened to growing infants insomuch as they feed on the milk of the word (2:1-3), and are called living stones built upon the risen Christ (2:4-10). Then they are appealed to as pilgrims needing to be blameless in the eyes of men (2:11-12) and submissive to governmental authority (2:13-17). Similarly, slaves are to be subject to their masters, aided by the example of Christ's conduct under mistreatment (2:18-25). Wives also have an obligation of submission to their husbands (3:1-6) and husbands have a duty to deal considerately and gently with their wives (3:7). Such a spirit of love and tenderness should govern all believers that it will insure a divine blessing (3:8-12). If

---

[2] I Clement VII. 4.
[3] *Against Heresies* IV. 9. 2 and *passim*.

right conduct nevertheless brings suffering at the hands of the world, there will be divine vindication, as there was for Christ the crucified and exalted one (3:13-22). The old sins must not be indulged any longer (4:1-6). Such things as prayer, hospitality, and Christian service are to occupy the saints instead (4:7-11). Believers must be prepared to suffer for the sake of Christ, according to God's will (4:12-19). Leaders are to care for the flock of God with due humility (5:1-5). All the saints are urged to find their refuge and strength in God as they resist the evil one (5:6-11). Greetings conclude the epistle (5:12-14).

The leading terms include manner of life, live, to do good, to be submissive, suffer and suffering, flesh and spirit (both in various senses), grace, salvation, hope, time, end, age, glory and glorify. No sharp division appears between doctrine and duty. The writer passes freely from one to the other and back again. In fact, as he brings his work to a close and thinks back over it, he describes it as an exhortation (5:12).

It is apparent that the major theme is suffering (i.e., suffering *as Christians*) and how to bear it triumphantly. No suggestion is found to the effect that suffering is meritorious. Nor is it inevitable (1:6). Rather, it is regulated by the will of God (4:19). At the same time it is not to be viewed as abnormal when it comes (4:12). Nor is it a mark of divine displeasure, for Christ himself suffered and died (3:18; 4:1). To share his sufferings is a privilege and a source of joy (4:13-14).

Another theme, almost as prominent, is the effect of Christian life and testimony on unsaved society. Here is the application of Jesus' teaching that his followers are the salt of the earth and the light of the world. Right conduct will offset prejudice (2:12) and ignorance (2:15). It may prove to be more potent than discussion or argument (3:1), and it will put to shame those who revile the saints (3:16). Even where it may seem ineffective as an evangelistic weapon it will serve the cause of divine justice by testifying against those who have belittled it (4:4-5).

A study of the nature of good works in I Peter has been made by W. C. van Unnik.[4] He finds that the presentation does not fit the Jewish pattern in which good deeds are directed especially to certain groups such as the poor and oppressed, and are regarded as meritorious. There is kinship, however, with the Greek perspective, inasmuch as the acts of benevolence are directed toward society or various units of it such as government and masters of slaves. Even so, the inspiration is different, for

4 *NTS,* 1, 2 (Nov. 1954), 92-110.

the Greek humanistic motive of benevolence is transcended by the divine calling in grace.

Selwyn and others have noted a large measure of dependence upon the teaching of Christ, even though the latter is seldom reproduced in a manner identical with the verbiage of the Gospels. These *verba Christi* "lie below the surface of the Epistle, and usually not far below it."[5] They are usually detected in the paraenetic or hortatory portions. The student will observe how often references to Matthew, especially, appear in the margin of his Greek New Testament.

THEOLOGICAL THOUGHT

God is holy (1:15), recognized as Father (1:17) and the God and Father of Jesus Christ (1:3), the Creator of men (4:19), and their Judge (4:5), and the Shepherd of his people (2:25). He is the ultimate object of faith and expectation (1:21; 3:18).

Christ is destined as Savior before the foundation of the world and manifested in due time (1:20). He is sinless (2:22), yet he suffered (2:21), and offered himself as the Lamb whose blood is a ransom for the lost (1:18). His redeeming death (2:24) is also substitutionary (3:18). The various phases of his triumph are outlined — the resurrection (1:3, 21; 3:21), ascension (3:21), position at the right hand of God (3:22), victory over hostile powers (3:22). He deserves and receives the title of Lord (3:15). As the stone, he was rejected by men but approved by God (2:4), the precious cornerstone for the saints (2:6-7). He will be revealed in glory to consummate the divine purpose (1:7, 13; 4:13; 5:1). The end, in fact, is near (4:7).

The Spirit is pictured as active in the Old Testament prophets as he pointed to the sufferings of Christ and the glories that were to follow (1:11), and as effective in the energizing of men who now proclaim the gospel (1:12), as setting apart believers to God (1:2) and resting upon them as the glorious presence of the Almighty (4:14).

The saints are chosen of God (1:2) and called (1:15), born anew (1:23). No mention is made of the church by name, but believers constitute the living stones in the temple of God (2:5), and are described as a holy and royal priesthood (2:5, 9). They are the people of God (2:10) and the flock of God (5:2). Baptism is referred to once (3:21).

[5] E. G. Selwyn, *The First Epistle of St. Peter*, p. 23.

A striking feature of the Christological presentation is the prominence of the Servant motif, which is achieved without any mention of the word, by obvious allusions to and quotations from Isaiah 53 (2:22 with Isa. 53:9; 2:25 with Isa. 53:6; 2:24 with Isa. 53:4, 5, 12). The mention of Christ as a Lamb (1:19) may owe something to Isaiah 53:7.

The other strongly delineated feature is the sharpness of the eschatological hope. Whatever waiting may be necessary is "a little while" (1:6). The coming is sufficient reason for maintaining a watchful alertness (1:13; 4:7). It will bring recompense for suffering (4:13) and for faithful service (5:4). The glorious inheritance to which it opens the door is placed in the very forefront of the epistle (1:4-5). No wonder Peter has been called the apostle of hope. He keeps the horizon of glory ever hovering over the suffering saints as they continue their pilgrimage.

FORM AND UNITY

Beyond question I Peter has the appearance of a letter, beginning as it does with indication of author and addressees, and concluding with limited greetings and a simple benediction. On the assumption that the epistolary form is a true indication of the nature of the writing, the only vexing question is the unity of the epistle, since the doxology at the end of 4:11 may mark the end of one document, leaving 4:12-5:14 to be assigned to a separate document perhaps having originally 1:1-2 as its proper introduction, in which case the longer letter may have begun with 1:3.[6] According to Perdelwitz, the treatment of suffering differs perceptibly in the two documents, being treated as hypothetical in the longer one and as a present reality in the shorter.[7] The presence of a doxology at 4:11 is not decisive evidence for the partition theory, however, judging from other examples in the New Testament such as Romans 11:36 and Ephesians 3:21. As to the problem of suffering, there may be an intensifying of the presentation as one moves toward the end, but this is a natural progression of thought. Granted that there is a perceptible change at 4:12, still, if suffering is handled only on a hypothetical basis in the longer portion, it is strange that it should receive such extended treatment there. In 1:6, at any rate, an actual state of suffering seems implied. The unity of

[6] R. Perdelwitz, *Die Mysterienreligion und das Problem des I Petrusbriefes*, p. 16.
[7] *Ibid.*, p. 14.

the epistle is not drastically imperilled by these strictures of Perdelwitz.

A second approach considers I Peter to be a sermon, whether in whole or in part. This is not impossible in the modified sense that the sermonic cast that students have detected here may reflect Peter's prior use of this material in his preaching from time to time. We recall that the author's own description of his work is an exhortation (5:12).

This concept of I Peter has been given a specialized application as instruction to new converts following their baptism. Perdelwitz, for example, was of the opinion that the material from 1:3-4:11 is of this character, whereas the remainder is a letter to encourage those who are undergoing persecution.[8]

Criticism has gone a step further. H. Preisker sees in 1:3-4:11 the oldest document of early Christian worship, a report of a baptismal service, a liturgy with its various components discernible to those who have eyes to see.[9] These include the prayer at the beginning, followed by a message of instruction to the candidates (1:13-21). At this point the baptism occurs, reflected in the words, "having purified your souls" (1:22). The baptismal vow is now the background for suitable exhortation (1:22-25). Then comes a hymn (2:1-10), another section of exhortation (2:11-3:12), a prophetic revelation (3:13-4:6), and a concluding prayer (4:7-11).

F. L. Cross has made a particular application of this view that I Peter is largely a baptismal liturgy. Noting the frequency of references to suffering, he advances the opinion that our epistle finds its proper place and meaning in a Paschal (note the similarity of the Semitic *Pascha* to the Greek term for suffering, *paschein*) context.[10] In his judgment, the Paschal theology is "magnificently summarized" in 1:3-12. The epistle has its origin, then, in the Easter baptismal service. "What I Peter gives us is the part of the Celebrant (whom we may call for convenience, I hope without prejudice, the 'Bishop'). It is unlikely that it is anything approaching a complete text. Indeed, if we are to suppose, as our earliest evidence suggests, that the service lasted through the night, it could only be a selection of the Celebrant's prayers. As there are no rubrics, there is naturally no record of the actual Baptism."[11]

---

[8] *Ibid.*, p. 26.
[9] Windisch-Preisker, *Die Katholischen Briefe, HZNT*, pp. 156ff.
[10] *I Peter. A Paschal Liturgy.*
[11] *Ibid.*, p. 38.

Cross builds upon Preisker's work, altering and adding to it somewhat in his own analysis of 1:3-4:11. The reader must be referred to his book for the exposition of features that the author regards as furnishing support for a baptismal setting. His case is persuasively presented, but it has weaknesses of which three will be noted. (1) It is awkward for the theory that the crucial word *baptism* occurs only once in the epistle (3:21), and in a parenthesis at that.[12] Not dismayed by this, Cross seeks by numerous details, many of them tenuous, to amass sufficient data to warrant the conclusion that a baptismal service is the occasion. Even if the baptismal setting be allowed, the problem of the incorporation of this material in a letter is awkward. C. F. D. Moule writes, "I do not find it easy (as Preisker and Cross apparently do) to conceive how a liturgy-homily, shorn of its 'rubrics' (which, of course, were probably oral), but with its changing tenses and broken sequences all retained, could have been hastily dressed up as a letter and sent off (without a word of explanation) to Christians who had not witnessed its original setting."[13] (2) As Thornton has pointed out,[14] the relationship between the Paschal celebration and suffering, which Cross thinks is latent in I Peter, is indeed found in late second-century writers who indulge in the *Pascha-paschein* wordplay, but is unknown in the first century. (3) No explanation is offered for 4:12-5:14, which, in its preoccupation with suffering, in style and vocabulary is so closely akin to the earlier portion. R. P. Martin lays down the dictum, "Any literary theory which is left with iv. 12 to v. 14 on its hands as a kind of inconvenient surd is *ipso facto* under a cloud of suspicion."[15]

More acceptable is the approach of E. G. Selwyn, who regards the baptismal aspect of I Peter as peripheral, retaining as the primary thrust of the letter the paraenetic element against a background of suffering and persecution. His special contribution is the application of the techniques of form criticism, making room for various elements — creedal, hymnic, and above all the catechetical patterns that deal with the prescribed duties of converts to the faith.[16] In this methodology he develops a position similar

---

12 A. F. Walls, "First Epistle of Peter," *NBD,* p. 977a.

13 C. F. D. Moule, *NTS,* 3 (Nov. 1956), 4.

14 T. C. G. Thornton, "I Peter, a Paschal Liturgy?" in *JTS,* 12 (Apr. 1961), 16. •

15 R. P. Martin, "The Composition of I Peter in Recent Study," in *Vox Evangelica,* 1962, p. 39.

16 Selwyn, *op. cit.* See especially Essay II on the interrelation of I Peter and other NT epistles (pp. 365-66).

to that of Philip Carrington, author of *The Primitive Christian Catechism*. This approach finds that certain motifs appear in various epistles, frequently expressed in strikingly similar or even identical language, so as to suggest that literary dependence of one epistle on another is not a necessary explanation for such similarities, for they can readily be understood as drawn from the common store of instructional material developed for new converts and used throughout the church.

READERS

Their location is indicated in the words of the address. They lived in the Roman provinces that covered the major part of Asia Minor, the portion north of the Taurus mountains.

Since Paul labored in this general region, the question is naturally raised as to whether the present epistle is directed to some people whom he evangelized. This possibility concerns those in Galatia and Asia. As far as Galatia is concerned, Peter's epistle may have been intended for believers in North Galatia, where Paul had little or no contact. However, since Paul's work at Ephesus resulted in the spread of the gospel throughout the province of Asia (Acts 19:10), some of the readers of Peter's epistle may have been inducted into the faith by Paul or his helpers. To this extent Peter may have entered into the labors of the apostle to the Gentiles. But it is possible that the bearer of the epistle may have traveled only in the northern part of Asia and thus avoided contact with areas where Paul's impact would have been felt.[17]

What of Peter's relation to his readers? There does not seem to be evidence to support the assumption that his pastoral letter is based on his own labors among them. To the contrary, he seems to dissociate himself from those who preached the gospel in these areas (1:12). Added to this is the absence of reference of any kind to personal contact with his readers. It is amazing that he is able, in spite of this, to write such a warm, sympathetic letter.

The possibility should be granted that some of those who received the gospel at Pentecost may have returned to this Asia Minor country with the message (cf. Acts 2:9-10), but this is far from certain, since Luke indicates that they remained at least for some time in the Jerusalem area (Acts 2:42; cf. 2:5).

Some students are of the opinion that the readers were evangelized only a short time before the letter was written.

---

[17] McNeile-Williams, *Introduction*, p. 215.

While the general tenor of the contents is suitable to people in such a situation, there is no clear evidence that the readers were very young in the faith. They are compared to newborn babes (2:2), but this is in respect to their need of proper spiritual nourishment rather than of their age or the duration of their Christian experience. The reference to baptism (3:21) is hardly more decisive, especially in view of the present tense of the verb, which serves to generalize the application. Surely the use of "now" in the same verse has no reference to the recency of the baptism of the readers, as some have claimed, for the obvious point of it is to set up a contrast between the Christian era and the times of Noah mentioned in the preceding verse.

The opinion of Perdelwitz that the readers were former adherents of the mystery cults, based on certain terms and allusions in the text, has not won general favor. It represents an extreme application of the *Religionsgeschichte* approach to the biblical data.

Were the readers Jews or Gentiles? First Peter has often been classified as a Hebrew-Christian epistle, but on insufficient grounds. True, Peter was the apostle of the circumcision (Gal. 2:7), but his activity among Gentiles is amply attested (Gal. 2:12; Acts 10:34-48; Acts 15:7-11). The agreement reported in Galatians 2:9 can hardly have isolated Peter from the Gentiles any more than it kept Paul from seeking to win the Jews. It is true that the readers are in a kind of dispersion (1:1), but the definite article is lacking. A dispersion of Christians as a minority among pagans seems to be the underlying concept. Nothing can be made of the injunction to maintain a praiseworthy manner of life among the Gentiles (2:12), as though the readers are being distinguished from the Gentiles on ethnic grounds, for it is plainly stated that they were formerly embroiled in typically Gentile sins (4:3), including idolatry, a sin with which a Jew of this period would not normally be charged. The same passage shows that their opponents are pagan rather than Jewish. At an earlier point in the letter the readers are warned against being conformed to the passions of their former ignorance (1:14; cf. 1:18). This fits the Gentile rather than the Jew. Furthermore, those to whom Peter writes are carefully differentiated from the covenant nation Israel on the ground that they were formerly not a people but are now the people of God, and were formerly without mercy but have now received it (2:10). They have been summoned from (pagan) darkness into God's marvelous light (2:9). An additional detail is the fact that the author does not use his Aramaic name Cephas but his Greek name Peter (1:1). Finally, whereas in the

Epistle of James Christian philanthropy singles out objects familiar from Old Testament teaching — the orphan and the widow (1:27) — there is no such limitation in I Peter, where the admonitions are cast in a more general mold.

Certainly there is no objection to the supposition that some Christian Jews were numbered among Peter's readers. Such believers would not meet separately, but with their Gentile brethren. They must have been a minority in these churches.

AUTHORSHIP

It has been assumed thus far that Peter is the writer, as the letter affirms (1:1). The claim of apostleship (1:1) is in keeping with the authoritative tone of the work, balanced by a pleasing modesty that leads the writer to identify himself with the presbyters (5:1). In the same passage he claims to be a witness of the sufferings of Christ and a partaker of the glory, agreeable to his role in the garden of Gethsemane and general closeness to the events of the Passion and his appreciation that the resurrection of Christ would involve him. There may even be a sideglance here at the transfiguration.

A comparison of the epistle with the speeches of Peter reported in Acts yields several items favorable to his authorship.[18] Among these are the theme that God is no respecter of persons (Acts 10:34; I Pet. 1:17); Christ the stone rejected by the builders (Acts 4:10-11; I Pet. 2:7-8); the prominence given to the "name" (of Christ) in various connections (Acts 3:6, 16; 4:10, 12; cf. 5:41; 10:43; I Pet. 4:14, 16); and the Christ-event as the fulfillment of prophetic testimony (Acts 3:18, 24; I Pet. 1:10-12).

Certain autobiographical touches in the epistle can be readily linked with items of information contained in the Gospels. Peter's own severe testing of faith (Luke 22:31-32) accords with his reference to the proving of his readers' faith (1:7), and the Lord's prediction that he will thereafter be able to strengthen his brethren meshes with the thrust of the epistle as a whole, including the language in which promise is given of divine assistance (5:10). Jesus' conversation with Peter in Galilee after the resurrection (John 21) seems to be reflected in the writer's description of believers as sheep (2:25; 5:2-3). Christian leaders are shepherds under the control of Christ the chief Shepherd, to whom they are responsible (5:2-4). Peter's resurgence following his descent into the abyss of sorrow and humiliation be

18 For a more complete list, see Selwyn, *op. cit.,* pp. 33-36.

cause of his denial of the Lord is reflected in the language of
1:3 — begotten again unto a living hope by the resurrection.
The injunction to be clothed with humility (5:5) may involve the recalling of the Upper Room scene where Jesus
girded himself with a towel and washed the disciples' feet.
Peter's description of Christians as living stones (2:5) may stem
from Jesus' prediction uttered over him at their first meeting,
that he would be called "stone" (John 1:42).

In addition to these details one may properly emphasize the
progression of this disciple in respect to his appreciation of the
sufferings of Christ. The Gospels testify that he resisted such
a prospect for the Master. In the Book of Acts he is pictured
as having accepted the cross as part of the plan of God for the
Messiah. The resurrection had changed his outlook completely.
By the time he wrote his first epistle he had come to accept
suffering as the destined portion of the disciple also, who was not
above the Lord in this matter. It is worth noting in this connection that the phraseology used to picture the sufferings of
Christ in the epistle is closer to the language of Mark than to
that of Matthew or Luke, and of course Mark is the Gospel that
more than any other bears the impress of this apostle.

Doubt of Peter's authorship is more common now than
formerly, and is based on several considerations. (1) It is
said that the Greek of the epistle is too elegant to be the workmanship of an unschooled fisherman. On the question of style,
however, Radermacher has taken issue with those who claim
artistry for the writer, asserting that in the meager use of particles
and prepositions, and the excessive use of relative clauses, not
to mention other phenomena, the author shows his limitations.[19]
It is undoubtedly true, however, that some of the vocabulary
of I Peter is of the classical type.[20] At this point help is obtained
by the supposition that Silvanus (probably the Silas of the Book
of Acts — the long form appears in I Thessalonians 1:1, where
only Silas can be meant) may have been more than a secretary
in the ordinary sense. Though Peter claims to have written the
epistle, he says that it was "through" (the help of?) Silvanus
that he did so, and adds the comment that this man is the faithful or trustworthy brother (5:12). Zahn doubts that Peter would
use such language merely to state the technical competence of
Silvanus as a secretary. He goes on to say, "The only alternative

[19] L. Radermacher, "Der erste Petrusbrief und Silvanus," *ZNTW,* 25
(1926), 287-99.
[20] See the list in McNeile-Williams, *op. cit.,* p. 220, n. 1.

404

that remains is the most natural one, namely, that Silvanus' part in the composition was so important and so large that its performance required a considerable degree of trustworthiness."[21]

It is of great interest to note that Paul not only joins Silvanus with himself as in some sense responsible for the Thessalonian Epistles, but uses the first person plural very liberally in the text. This seems to suggest something approaching joint authorship. Selwyn made a study of the Apostolic Decree (Acts 15), I and II Thessalonians, and I Peter, in all of which, it seems, Silas had a hand. He concluded that Silas was not merely a messenger of the Apostolic Council, but helped to shape the language of the Decree (note the Greek text of Acts 15:23). Certainly similarities appear in all three of these literary units, which helps to strengthen the case for Silvanus as one who did more than take down I Peter as the apostle dictated it.[22] Likely the thoughts of Peter are pressed into the mold of the language of Silvanus, at least to a considerable degree. His presence with Paul on the second missionary journey attests his ability to speak acceptably in Greek. His Roman citizenship reveals him as more than a provincial figure. Admittedly, precise information about his education is lacking, but this should not bar him from serious consideration as a prime factor in the composition of I Peter.

(2) Alleged dependence of the epistle upon Paul is urged against Petrine authorship. For example, the section on submission to the state (I Pet. 2:13-17) could well depend on Romans 13:1-7, and the passage on household obligations (2:18-3:7) has much in common with the parallel portions in Ephesians. If our epistle was written from Rome, it is not impossible that Peter had access to these documents, but this is not certain and it is not necessary. These sections belong to the *didache* of the church, which had a certain uniformity wherever it was set forth. "It is now possible to assume that I Peter did not borrow from Paul, but that both of them drew on those Hebrew codes of the primitive Christian community. Incidentally, if this is right, one of the arguments against the authenticity of I Peter, its alleged Pauline character, loses much of its force."[23]

There is a second angle to consider in this matter of alleged Paulinism in I Peter. It concerns Silvanus again. Because of his collaboration with Paul, he could be expected to impart a

---

[21] Zahn, *op. cit.*, II, 150.
[22] Selwyn, *op. cit.*, pp. 9-17, 369-84.
[23] D. Daube, *The New Testament and Rabbinic Judaism*, p. 103.

Pauline touch to his materials if he had any considerable freedom in composition. The relation of the letter to the Pauline Epistles is "not one of dependence but of parallelism."[24]

(3) References to our Lord's teaching are too scanty to accredit the book as coming from Simon Peter. The force of this objection is diminished when one realizes that the purpose behind the writing of the epistle was not to comment on the life and teaching of Christ, but to encourage believers in the midst of trial and suffering. In view of this, it may be said that the allusions to Christ and his utterances are rather numerous. Several events are alluded to — the foot washing, the trial, the sufferings and death, the resurrection and ascension, and possibly the transfiguration. We have seen that John 21 is the background for ministry to Christians as Christ's sheep. In addition, there are several statements that are traceable to Jesus' own teaching as their seed-plot, such as these: 2:12, with its emphasis on the prospect that men will be led to glorify God in the day of visitation because of the influence of the good works of believers, which sounds remarkably like Matthew 5:16. In 3:14 Peter speaks of suffering for righteousness' sake, and the blessedness of it. This recalls Matthew 5:10 — blessed are those who are persecuted for righteousness' sake. In 5:6 there is a plea for self-humbling, with the promise of exaltation in due time. This recalls the language of Jesus in Luke 14:11. The Lord's teaching on the folly of anxiety (Matt. 6:25) is reflected in I Peter 5:7 — casting all your anxious care on him.

(4) The claim has been made that the letter reflects official Roman persecution such as developed in the area to which the letter was sent only in the time of Trajan, early in the second century. F. W. Beare, who is a leading advocate of this position, thinks that the situation reflected in 4:12-16, with its mention of suffering as a Christian and for the sake of the name, fits perfectly the circumstances of the persecution of believers under Pliny the Younger as mirrored in his letter to the emperor Trajan.[25] This is doubtful, for several reasons. (i) There is nothing in the passage to indicate martyrdom or even torture, both of which are clearly referred to in Pliny's letter. (ii) Even if it were granted that there is a correspondence between the conditions stated in the letter and those that prevailed in Bithynia-

---

[24] W. C. van Unnik, *op. cit.*, p. 93.

[25] F. W. Beare, *The First Epistle of Peter*, pp. 7-8, 13-14. For the text of the correspondence between Trajan and the governor see Bettenson, *Documents of the Early Church*, pp. 3-6.

Pontus at this later time, the problem would still remain that Peter is writing to Christians in several provinces. And he even states that sufferings of the kind he has in mind are being experienced by the brotherhood of believers throughout the world 5:9). (iii) The actual character of the persecution seems to be non-official, instigated by individuals or groups who were incensed at the separatist tendencies of Christians, their refusal to join in the sinful pleasures that once engrossed them (4:1-4). In the face of these difficulties it is surely a species of critical dogmatism to assert, as Beare does, that "there can be no possible doubt that 'Peter' is a pseudonym."[26]

DATE AND PLACE OF WRITING

On the traditional view of authorship, the epistle must have been written late in the apostle's life, probably shortly before the Neronian persecution of A.D. 64. The charges against Paul that had brought him to Rome and the death of James in Palestine presaged a growing opposition to Christians, and Peter felt constrained to prepare his readers for the impact. Since Mark was planning a trip to Asia Minor when Paul was in Rome (Col. 4:10), he must have completed his mission in order to become known to the readers of the letter (5:13). Sufficient time must be allowed also for the spread of the faith to the northern part of Asia Minor.

The place is Babylon (5:13), but in what sense? Babylon in Mesopotamia has had its advocates, but the case for it is weak. The principal problem is that the site was largely deserted at this period. In addition, there is no tradition to place Peter at this remote spot. Appeal to the order in which the provinces are named as favorable to the arrival of a messenger from the East has been shcwn by Hort to be without foundation.[27] The Babylon in northern Egypt, a Roman military outpost, has no claim to probability. This leaves the conclusion that Babylon is being used in a mystical sense, somewhat as in the Book of Revelation, to indicate that complex of arrogant idolatry coupled with the power of empire, which has become known for its persecution of the saints of God, as in its initial phase under Nebuchadnezzar. Since the use of the term in the Revelation without definition implies the popular understanding of its mean-

26 Beare, *op. cit.*, p. 25.
27 F. J. A. Hort, *The First Epistle of St. Peter*, pp. 167-68.

ing, the same may be assumed for I Peter.[28] What Peter's motive was for using Babylon in this cryptic sense is uncertain. Some have thought that the need for security dictated it with Christians in Rome perhaps already under suspicion. Moule finds a sufficient explanation in the fact that the historic Babylon had been the place of exile and so the word was a fitting symbol to remind the readers that they were pilgrims and strangers in the world.[29] But the same could be said, of course, of the whole church.

RECENT STUDY

Relative to the theory of Selwyn that Silvanus had a large role in the composition of the book, objection has been raised by B. Rigaux[30] who fails to find sufficient grounds for positing the hand of Silvanus in the writing of the Thessalonian letters, insisting that even if Silvanus served as secretary, nevertheless "the words, the grammar, the phrases and the thoughts are Paul's." If substantial contribution by Silvanus fails of demonstration for these early letters of Paul, there is a weakening of Selwyn's claim for a similar role in connection with the production of I Peter.

F. W. Beare notes that Silvanus is not linked with Peter in the salutation as he is with Paul in Thessalonians, and for various other reasons discounts the view of Selwyn.[31] There are indications that the Silvanus theory is not likely to figure strongly in future discussions of the origin of I Peter.

Considerable attention was devoted by Selwyn to the *verba Christi* in the epistle. Robert H. Gundry has investigated these passages and has concluded that those sayings of our Lord which are utilized have a close association with Peter in their Gospel setting. This leads him to conclude that support is thereby given to Petrine authorship of the epistle as well as to the reliability of the Gospel tradition.[32]

Quite different are the conclusions of Ernest Best, who surveys the same material in I Peter. He thinks that many of the alleged links between Peter and the Gospel tradition are not direct but reflect dependence on a more developed stage than the original

[28] See the discussion by O. Cullmann, *Peter: Disciple, Apostle, Martyr,* pp. 83-84.

[29] C. F. D. Moule, *op. cit.,* pp. 8-9.

[30] *Les Épîtres aux Thessaloniciens,* p. 107.

[31] *Op. cit.,* p. 28.

[32] "*Verba Christi* in I Peter: Their Implications concerning the Authorship of I Peter and the Authenticity of the Gospel Tradition," *NTS,* 13 (July 1967), 336-350.

form. He contends also that there are cases in which the writer of the epistle makes use of an Old Testament text when a logion now found in the Gospels would have suited his purpose better. He considers the data inimical to Petrine authorship.[33]

Although J. N. D. Kelly does not deal to any extent with the relationship between I Peter and the Gospels, he counsels that one should "hesitate to explain resemblances between NT passages in terms of literary dependence except where there is transparent evidence of this."[34] Traditional material of various kinds was current in the church and utilized by writers according to their needs. Under such conditions we should expect similarities. Kelly takes exception to the idea that I Peter shows dependence on Paul, pointing out a number of differences in the handling of words and themes.[35] He is prepared to advocate Petrine authorship, provided the help of a colleague is granted, possibly Silvanus. At the same time he recognizes that there are difficulties in the traditional position regarding authorship. As for the place of origin, Roman provenance is regarded as better grounded than rival hypotheses. Kelly rejects the notion that the readers are suffering official governmental persecution.

BIBLIOGRAPHY

Beare, F. W., *The First Epistle of Peter.* Oxford: Basil Blackwell, 1947.

Best, Ernest, "I Peter and the Gospel Tradition," *NTS,* 16 (January 1970), 95-113.

Bigg, Charles, *A Critical and Exegetical Commentary on the Epistles of St. Peter and St. Jude, ICC.* New York: Scribner's, 1905.

Gundry, Robert H., "*Verba Christi* in I Peter: Their Implications concerning the Authorship of I Peter and the Authenticity of the Gospel Tradition," *NTS,* 13 (July 1967), 336-350.

Hort, F. J. A., *The First Epistle of St. Peter.* London: Macmillan, 1898.

Johnstone, Robert, *The First Epistle of Peter.* Edinburgh: T. & T. Clark, 1888.

Kelly, J. N. D., *A Commentary on the Epistles of Peter and of Jude, HNTC.* New York: Harper and Row, 1969.

Knopf, R., *Die Briefe Petri und Judä,* Meyer series. Göttingen: Vandenhoek & Ruprecht, 1912.

Perdelwitz, R., *Die Mysterienreligion und das Problem des I Petrusbriefes.* Giessen: A. Töpelmann, 1911.

---

[33] "I Peter and the Gospel Tradition," *NTS,* 16 (January 1970), 95-113.
[34] *A Commentary on the Epistles of Peter and of Jude,* p. 13.
[35] *Ibid.,* p. 15.

Reicke, Bo, *The Disobedient Spirits and Christian Baptism, A Study of I Peter* 3:19 *and its Context*. Copenhagen: E. Munksgaard, 1946.

Selywn, E. G., *The First Epistle of St. Peter*. London: Macmillan, 1946.

Stibbs, Alan M., *The First Epistle General of Peter,* with Intro. by A. F. Walls, *TBC*. Grand Rapids: Eerdmans, 1959.

Wand, J. W. C., *The General Epistles of St. Peter and St. Jude, WC*. London: Methuen, 1934.

Wohlenberg, G., *Der erste und zweite Petrusbrief und der Judasbrief*. Leipzig: A. Deichert, 1915.

Chapter Twenty-one

THE SECOND EPISTLE OF PETER

NO ONE OF THE CATHOLIC EPISTLES, NOR ANY BOOK OF THE entire New Testament for that matter, has been more strenuously debated as to its authorship and its place in early Christianity than this second epistle attributed to Peter. It therefore merits careful and somewhat detailed consideration.

RECOGNITION BY THE EARLY CHURCH

A convenient starting point is Origen (ca. A.D. 240), since he is the first, according to known sources, to attribute the work to Peter. His testimony is as follows: "Peter has left one acknowledged epistle, and perhaps a second; for it is disputed."[1] Several other references are found in the Latin translation of his writings by Rufinus.[2] Origen says nothing about the grounds of dispute, but apparently did not regard them as serious enough to cause him to reject the book. It should be noted that, in matters of criticism, Origen belongs in the front rank among the ancients.

There is little to be said about evidence prior to Origen, except

---

[1] *HE* VI. xxv. 8.
[2] A list of these is contained in the article on II Peter by F. H. Chase in *HDB*, III, 803.

as it relates to possible knowledge of the book rather than author-ship. Clement of Rome makes use of the examples of Noah and Lot, as in II Peter, but since the two are not treated together,[3] it is not certain that he is depending on II Peter. Several early writers refer to the saying, "A day with the Lord is as a thousand years" (e.g., *Ep. of Barnabas* 15:4; cf. II Pet. 3:8). Dependence on Psalm 90:4 is a possibility here, or the *Book of Jubilees.* The non-canonical Petrine literature, including the *Apocalypse of Peter,* the *Gospel of Peter,* the *Preaching of Peter,* and the *Acts of Peter,* seems to show dependence on our epistle, though quotation from it is lacking.[4] Echoes of "neither idle or unfruitful" (II Pet. 1:8) and "exodus" in the sense of death (II Pet. 1:15) have been detected in the *Epistle of the Churches of Lyons and Vienne.*[5] Irenaeus also uses "exodus" in the sense of death and applies it to Peter, probably having in mind the wording of II Peter 1:15.[6] In his Fourth Book the same writer cites the case of Noah and then of Lot, the latter in connection with Sodom and Gomorrah, giving these examples to show that God punishes the wicked but spares the righteous. These are the examples cited in II Peter 2:4-7, and these are the very lessons that are there drawn from these examples. While it is possible that Irenaeus depends directly on the Old Testament or, as Chase thinks, on the eschatological teaching of Jesus, the influence of II Peter remains a strong likelihood.

Neither of Peter's epistles is included in the Muratorian Canon. In view of its fragmentary condition, the possibility should not be overlooked that our epistle stood there originally. At any rate, as Guthrie observes, "Unlike its reference to the Epistle to the Alexandrians and Laodiceans, the Canon does not pronounce either of the Petrine Epistles as spurious and its evidence must, therefore, be regarded as purely negative."[7]

Concerning Clement of Alexandria we have the statement of Eusebius, "Clement, in his 'Outlines,' has given, to speak generally, concise explanations of all canonical Scriptures without omitting the disputed books."[8] It is well known that Clement's conception of the canon was rather loose, for in this same passage Eusebius

---

[3] I Clement, chs. 7 and 11.

[4] See the survey in J. W. C. Wand, *The General Epistles of St. Peter and St. Jude,* pp. 138-40.

[5] *HE* V. I. 45, 55, etc.

[6] *Against Heresies* III. I. 1.

[7] Donald Guthrie, *New Testament Introduction:* Hebrews to Revelation, p. 140.

[8] *HE* VI. xiv. 1.

notes that he included comments on the *Epistle of Barnabas* and the *Apocalypse of Peter.* In the absence of clear references to the material of II Peter in Clement's works, Chase considers that the evidence, while not free from doubt, points to the conclusion "that Clement regarded 2 P as a book hovering, like the *Apocalypse of Peter,* on the borders of the number of the books definitely recognized as Apostolic, but that he did not place it on a level with 1 P."[9]

The position of Clement somewhat prepares us for the attitude of the fourth-century writer Didymus, who commented on II Peter along with the other Catholic Epistles, but concluded with these words, "It must not be forgotten that this letter is spurious; it may be read in public, but it is not part of the canon of Scripture." Mayor is of the opinion that this adverse judgment may have been induced by his dislike of the teaching concerning the destruction of the earth by fire.[10] Despite this outburst Didymus often quoted from II Peter.

Eusebius placed II Peter among the disputed books rather than in the list of spurious writings. "Of Peter, one epistle, that which is called his first, is admitted; and the ancient presbyters used this in their own writings as unquestioned, but the so-called second Epistle we have not received as canonical, but nevertheless it has appeared useful to many, and has been studied with other Scriptures."[11] In the same passage, after referring to all the literature associated with the name of Peter, he gives a personal statement, "Now the above are the books bearing the name of Peter, of which I recognize only one as genuine and admitted by the presbyters of old."[12] It should be noted that in giving II Peter a lower rating than the first epistle, Eusebius refrained from classifying it with the extra-canonical Petrine literature (*Acts, Gospel, Preaching, and Apocalypse*), concerning which books he goes on to say, "We have no knowledge at all in Catholic tradition, for no orthodox writer of the ancient time or of our own has used their testimonies." Since Eusebius does not identify by name or locality or date "the presbyters of old," one is reduced to speculation. He could hardly have meant Origen or Clement. He may have had in mind the leaders of the church in Syria and Asia Minor, where II Peter was recognized as Scripture, with one or two exceptions, only after his time. It is known that

[9] *HDB,* III, 803a.

[10] J. B. Mayor, *The Epistle of St. Jude and the Second Epistle of St. Peter,* p. cxviii.

[11] *HE* III. iii. 1.

[12] *HE* III. iii. 4.

doubt about the epistle led to its exclusion from the Syriac canon of the fourth century, although earlier witnesses of this branch of the church had accepted it. H. E. W. Turner regards Eusebius as somewhat inconsistent in making knowledge of a book by the ancients a criterion of canonicity and at the same time refusing the right of II Peter to be considered canonical despite the evidence for its use before his time.[13]

A few decades later Cyril of Jerusalem accepted our epistle as canonical. The same is true of Athanasius. In the West Augustine and Jerome cordially received it. The latter notes that, "The second of Peter's epistles is denied by very many to be his on account of dissonance of style with the first."[14] From this testimony we may conclude that the basis of rejection was not lack of knowledge of the book but internal factors. On the score of divergence of style there is less disposition to question II Peter today than in the early centuries.[15]

It is hard to account for the ultimate assured place of II Peter in the canon unless it had a rather secure place in the previous period, in spite of doubts here and there about it. Arguments to the effect that it slipped into favor because of its alleged relation to I Peter (cf. II Pet. 3:1) and that it was needed to make up the complete number of seven comprising the Catholic Epistles are hardly convincing. It is pertinent to ask why II Peter was accepted in preference to the rest of the Petrine literature.

Warfield makes the point that the overwhelming amount of evidence for the knowledge and use of most of the New Testament books in the early church works to the detriment of II Peter, which is not so strongly attested, whereas if we were to compare II Peter with the works of classical authors we would be amazed to see how well it fares. For example, Herodotus is quoted only once in the century following its composition, and only twice in the next. Likewise, Thucydides is not distinctly quoted till the second century after its composition.[16]

---

[13] H. E. W. Turner, *The Pattern of Christian Truth*, p. 249.
[14] *Catalogus Scriptorum Ecclesiasticorum.*
[15] Mayor writes, "There can be no doubt, I think, that the style of 1 P. is on the whole clearer and simpler than that of 2 P., but there is not that chasm between them which some would try to make out" (p. civ). In the light of this it is strange to find the following assertion: "Differences in style from I Peter create insuperable difficulties for the view that the two epistles have a common author" (A. E. Barnett in *IB*, 12, 164a).
[16] B. B. Warfield, *Syllabus on the Special Introduction to the Catholic Epistles,* pp. 116-17.

Over against the relative paucity of references to II Peter in the post-apostolic period is the noteworthy fact that in no case, apparently, was it rejected as spurious.[17] If Didymus be regarded as an exception, his single utterance is neutralized by his own practice of quoting from the epistle. Indications are not lacking of its veneration as apostolic, especially in the case of the *Apocalypse of Peter*. After a careful comparison of this work with II Peter, A. Ernest Simms came to "the conviction that the author of the Apocalypse sought Petrine authority for his production by a parade of 'coincidences' with the second Epistle, testifying thereby to the earlier existence and at least partial acceptance of the latter."[18] It is plausible that the rejection of the *Apocalypse* by the church worked for a time to the detriment of II Peter, with which it had obvious affinities.

A further explanation for the scanty notices of the epistle in the early centuries may be found in its character as a general epistle. No single congregation was committed to preserving it and making it more widely known.

When II Peter was accepted as canonical by church councils of the fourth century, this can hardly have been done with eyes closed to the objections raised against it. We may assume, therefore, that the claim of the epistle to canonical rank was sufficiently impressive to overcome the doubts that had been expressed from time to time.

OUTLINE OF CONTENTS

Even in the salutation the author draws attention to his recurring theme of knowledge, which is grounded in turn on faith (1:1-2). Probably knowledge is intended to include the things of the future, with which so much of the epistle is concerned. This opening strain is kept prominent in a section that emphasizes the need for cultivation of this knowledge (1:3-11). The author is in position to press the truth of God upon his readers because of his presence at the transfiguration, where the Father approved his Son. This event served to make more sure the realization of the promise of Christ's return and the whole gamut of prophetic revelation that owes its origin to the Holy Spirit (1:12-21). Unfortunately a spurious revelation is always at hand to compete with the true. But as God judged the false prophets in the past, so will he judge the false teachers who will arise. And as he delivered his faithful people from judgment in Old Testa-

---

[17] Guthrie, *op. cit.*, 142.
[18] A. E. Simms, *The Expositor*, 5th series, 1898, pp. 470-71.

ment days, so will he deliver the saints of this dispensation (2:1-9). The false teachers are described in terms of their uncleanness, arrogance, callousness, avarice, hopeless enslavement to sin and their ultimate ruin (2:10-22). Warning is issued against those who will deny and ridicule the truth of Christ's return (3:1-4). The God who judged the earth in olden time by a flood will destroy the present order by fire, making way for the new heavens and the new earth in which righteousness will dwell (3:5-13). The epistle concludes with a plea for diligence in the pursuit of godliness and for growth in grace and the knowledge of Christ. This section contains a commendation of Paul's epistles (3:14-18).

Knowledge of the truth is not viewed as an end in itself, for the insistence on righteousness is kept to the fore and is put over against the corrupting power of sin. So the pastoral concern is there, but it is hardly as prominent as in the first epistle.

Some of the more frequently used items of vocabulary are: virtue (or excellence), knowledge, way, remembrance, righteousness, godliness, corruption, wantonness, judgment, destruction, day, world, coming (Parousia), heaven, and Saviour. Epistemology, ethics, and eschatology are the overriding interests, mingled with a strong element of warning against false teachers who ignore the lessons of the past, currently abuse the grace of God, and face the prospect of certain judgment. The false teachers refuse to accept the Parousia, which would mean judgment for them, whereas without this threat they feel secure in their wickedness.

AUTHORSHIP

Those who do not accept the epistle as Peter's are able to point to a variety of considerations that seem hostile to the traditional position. These are, in addition to the relative weakness of the external testimony already considered:

(1) Differences between II Peter and I Peter. This was emphasized by the ancients, who detected a variation in style. Jerome thought it might be explained on the basis of a difference in amanuenses. As noted by Mayor and others, the difference in style is not great, however. Chase finds some poverty in the use of particles, along with an excessive use of γάρ. The Greek lacks the elegance of the first epistle, and may be described as somewhat stilted and in places even uncouth. Chase remarks, "The author appears to be ambitious of writing in a style which is beyond his literary power."[19] On the supposition that Peter

---

[19] F. H. Chase, *op. cit.*, p. 809a.

wrote the epistle, these features can conceivably be accounted for on the basis of a late start in the effort to acquire the language. He would naturally be less at home in Greek than in his native Aramaic. That this deficiency does not come to the fore in I Peter is due, no doubt, to the capable help of an amanuensis.

Vocabulary differences need to be considered also. The careful study by Mayor yields the following figures: I Peter contains 543 words and II Peter 399. I Peter has 369 words not used in II Peter, whereas II Peter has 230 words not used in I Peter. They have 100 words in common. This means that the disagreements (599) are almost exactly six times greater than the agreements.[20] If this proportion seems high (Mayor apparently was impressed by it), a comparison with the two Pastorals that most closely resemble each other, I Timothy and Titus, may temper such a judgment, for there the disagreements are only slightly less than between the two Petrines. First Timothy with its 537 words, and Titus with its 399, have only 161 in common,[21] despite the similarity in the subject matter, whereas the Petrines differ much more from one another in their content.

Mayor is especially impressed with the variation in words for the Second Advent, I Peter adopting ἀποκάλυψις and II Peter παρουσία. This may be taken as a test case for the inquiry into terminology. Before one can be sure that the exclusive use of one term rather than the other is a mark of difference in authorship, he needs to consider whether the two are identical in meaning and whether each may have served the writer in its chosen place in a way not possible for the other.[22] He should also reflect on the strangeness of the situation if II Peter was written by someone seeking to play the role of the apostle. One would think that he would be careful to avoid such a striking deviation in terms in an area that was central to his exposition and scarcely less so for I Peter.

An undoubted difference between the two epistles occurs in the frequency of quotations from the Old Testament. According to Hort's count, I Peter has 31, II Peter only 5.[23] Yet, if two authors are at work, it is remarkable that they should be partial to the same books.[24]

---

[20] J. B. Mayor, *op. cit.*, p. lxxiv.
[21] See Simms, *op. cit.*, p. 465.
[22] E. M. B. Green, *II Peter Reconsidered*, p. 22.
[23] F. J. A. Hort, *The New Testament: Introduction*, pp. 179-80.
[24] In noting the preference for Psalms, Proverbs and Isaiah, Guthrie affirms, "This kind of subtle agreement suggests the subconscious approaches of one mind rather than a deliberate imitation." *Op. cit.*, p. 162.

Criticism has detected a gulf between I Peter and II Peter also "in thought, feeling, and character."[25] The reader senses that I Peter has a warmth and intensity of feeling and an intimacy with readers that cannot be found in II Peter. The pastoral emphasis of I Peter passes into a more detached theological concern in the second epistle. A rough parallel exists here to the relation between I and II Thessalonians.

Again, II Peter has fewer references to the events of the Lord's earthly life. Whereas I Peter mentions the trial of Jesus, his death by crucifixion, his resurrection and ascension, the second epistle fails to mention any of these. Instead, it magnifies the transfiguration, which does not appear in I Peter. The intrusion of the latter incident, we are told, is due to the writer's zeal to give his readers the impression that the real Peter is writing. Against this conjecture, however, stands the fact that the language used to describe the incident does not show close resemblance to any of the Synoptic accounts of the transfiguration, suggesting that the writer may be drawing on his personal knowledge of the event as a participant. With respect to the absence of reference to the resurrection and ascension, silence need not be an indication of ignorance and not necessarily an indication that the writer has little interest in these events. On the contrary, he could hardly speak as strongly as he does of the lordship of Christ unless these events were entrenched in his faith. Nor could he emphasize the Lord's return as he does without presupposing these preparatory steps.

This discussion prepares the way somewhat for a consideration of the viewpoint that the doctrinal position of the writer reflects a period later than the apostolic age. Under the influence of the mystery religions and Gnostic patterns of thought, it is held, he presents salvation as a partaking of the divine nature, i.e., apotheosis (1:4), as though this has now displaced the typical Christian hope associated with the eschatological kingdom, such as is found in I Peter 1:4; 5:10, etc.[26] If this were really the case, one would expect a clearer and fuller exposition of this point of view. The writer may be using language borrowed from circles outside the faith, as is done not infrequently in the letters of Paul, but there is no proof that he has become contaminated by the mystery religion viewpoint.

Over against the claim that the eschatology of this book is an

[25] Mayor, *op. cit.,* p. cv.
[26] E. Käsemann, "Eine Apologie der urchristlichen Eschatologie" in *ZTK*, 1952, p. 282.

attempt to justify the delay of the Parousia by citing the time-lessness of God (3:8) is the author's own explanation that the longsuffering of God is being manifested thereby, with a view to giving sinners an opportunity to repent (3:9; cf. 3:15). No doubt the prominence of God in connection with the consummation is greater than in I Peter, and the renovation by means of fire is a new element, yet typical primitive terminology centering in Christ as the eschatological figure is found in such passages as 1:11 and 16. The allusion to the thousand years (3:8), instead of reflecting the embarrassment of the post-apostolic age at the delay of the Parousia, points away from this later period, for as E. M. B. Green notes, "This verse became in the second century the proof text of Chiliasm, which was almost regarded as a sign of Christian orthodoxy from the time of the writing of Revelation to Irenaeus' day, and even later. It would have been all but impossible for a second-century writer to use this verse without commenting on it at all, either in favour of or against the Chiliastic hope."[27]

(2) The reference to Paul and his epistles (3:15-16). Would Peter have commended Paul so generously as to call him "our beloved brother," especially after the Antioch episode (Gal. 2:11ff.)? Is there not a subtle depreciation, on the other hand, in the assertion that Paul wrote in accordance with the wisdom given to him, as though it could have been more complete? Does not the reference to "all his epistles" imply the existence of the *Corpus Paulinum* and thus point to the sub-apostolic age? Would it have been natural or possible for Peter to have classed Paul's writings with "the other Scriptures," i.e., the Old Testament books, in the face of the very gradual recognition of the equality of the two by the early church?

These are serious problems. The manner in which Paul is referred to, however, need not be thought impossible or even unlikely for Peter, since there is no evidence that he cherished a grudge against the apostle to the Gentiles. Paul, on his part, refers to Peter in cordial language (I Cor. 9:5) and does not lay at his door the blame for the Cephas party in the Corinthian church. Further, it would be somewhat out of character for a second-century writer to mention Paul in this rather intimate way, for in that period the apostle was referred to with extreme veneration.[28] As for the allusion to Paul's wisdom, any attempt at depreciation by means of this language is highly improbable

[27] Green, *op. cit.*, p. 19.
[28] Guthrie, *op. cit.*, p. 157.

in the light of the warmth of the commendation, on the one hand, and on the other hand the inclusion of his writings with Scripture. With regard to the writer's awareness that Paul had written a number of epistles, it is probably not necessary to conclude that the complete collection of his letters as we have them today is intended (actually there is no word here for collection or body of writings), but simply the existence of several of his epistles, all that the writer knows about. Bigg does not hesitate to assert, "It is not only possible, but probable, that St. Peter received every one of St. Paul's Epistles within a month or two of its publication."[29] Some are of the opinion that the perversion of Pauline teaching alluded to here demands access to a collection of writings, but these teachers were within the framework of the church, so that formal publication of a collection is not a necessity. It is admittedly unexpected that Peter should class the writings of Paul with Scripture, and this is the most difficult aspect of the verses before us, for if this is a genuine statement by Peter, would it not have prompted a far speedier recognition of New Testament writings as deserving of a place alongside those of the Old Testament than is the case in the sub-apostolic period? It may be said, of course, that from the standpoint of apostolic men like Peter and Paul, knowing the authority given to them, there could have been a perception that the highly revered word "Scripture" properly belonged to their works from the moment of their creation. Further, if II Peter is authentic, the passage under consideration may well have been a contributing factor, in due time, toward the acknowledgment of apostolic writings as Scripture in the early church. That it did not make a greater impact along this line is probably assignable to its limited circulation.

The problem of the identification of the epistle referred to here ("Paul wrote to you") is a baffling one on any view of II Peter. It is bound up with the decision on the address of the present epistle (3:1). If the readers are the same as for the first epistle, then it is natural to think of one or more of Paul's letters addressed to Christians in the Asia Minor region. On the other hand, if II Peter is a truly catholic epistle, then any of Paul's writings that deal with repentance in relation to salvation could be intended. The easiest identification settles on Romans. On the supposition of an Asia Minor destination for II Peter, T. W. Manson's theory concerning Romans, already considered, would be helpful, since it would mean that Romans had been

29 Charles Bigg, *The Epistle of St. Peter and St. Jude (ICC)*, pp. 300f.

circulated in this region prior to the time Peter wrote his second epistle. There are those who favor the notion that a writing of Paul not preserved to us is intended here. Merely to state the problem is to emphasize the limits of our knowledge of the apostolic age, despite the available sources.

(3) The relation of II Peter to Jude. Much of Jude is strikingly similar to II Peter, especially to the materials of the second chapter. The likeness pertains to ideas, words, the use of Old Testament illustrations, and in a general way to the order in which the text proceeds. It would hardly do in this case to appeal for explanation to a *didache* common to the churches, for polemic is too vigorously joined with instruction. Some sort of literary dependence seems inevitable. The alternatives are: Jude used II Peter; II Peter used Jude; both depend on a common source. If II Peter draws on Jude, which is the prevailing judgment today, then it is exceedingly difficult to maintain the Petrine authorship of this epistle, though Warfield felt it was a feasible position.[30] The priority of Jude is favored by the way in which the writer of II Peter generalizes a precise statement of Jude, being content to refer to angels (2:11) in place of Jude's reference to the archangel Michael (v. 9). Mayor thinks that this alteration was due to the aversion that the writer of II Peter felt toward Jude's use of apocryphal writings such as the *Book of Enoch*.[31] Again, the statement of II Peter 2:17, by omitting (whether purposely or inadvertently) the reference to wandering stars in Jude 13, has sacrificed cogency of thought. Further, the simple and direct style of Jude marks it as the original, in contrast to the more ornate and artificial character of II Peter. Finally, if II Peter preceded Jude, there would seem to be little warrant for the writing of another work (Jude) that had little in it but the materials taken over from the earlier work.

It is argued on the other side that an apostolic figure like Peter would be less likely to borrow from Jude than vice versa. This is valid provided one is satisfied that the second epistle did in fact emanate from Peter, the very problem under discussion. It is urged that Jude's habit of using sources (*Enoch* and apparently also the *Assumption of Moses*) is agreeable to his readiness to borrow from II Peter. This has some force, although the use of material from extra-biblical sources is very limited as compared to the use made of II Peter. Again, it is alleged that Jude shows his dependence on II Peter by stating that the warn-

[30] B. B. Warfield, *op. cit.*, p. 135.
[31] *Op. cit.*, p. ix.

ing against mockers in the last time had been spoken by the apostles of the Lord (vv. 17-18), as though he were referring to II Peter 3:2-4. Peter would qualify for one such apostle, and Paul could be another (Acts 20:28-30; II Tim. 3:1-9). The endeavor to set aside this consideration on the ground that Jude could be referring to oral teaching is weakened by the several coincidences in language between his statement and that in II Peter, notably the rare word ἐμπαῖκται ("mockers"). On the other hand, the probability of Jude's dependence on II Peter in this matter is diminished if Jude 4 is taken into consideration, where the offenders are said to have been designated (pre-written) to judgment *long ago*. This does not seem to fit the interval between II Peter and Jude, which, on the basis of II Peter's authenticity, must have been brief. It is also somewhat embarrassing that Jude should refer to apostles (plural) if he wrote with II Peter in mind. Finally, it is noted that whereas II Peter visualizes the false teachers mainly in terms of the future, Jude is ablaze with intense concern for the church of his time, which is in jeopardy by reason of the present activity of such men. For further study of this whole vexed question of the relation of II Peter and Jude, the student is directed to the works of Bigg (who favors the priority of II Peter) and Mayor, who takes the opposite position.

Despite the obvious similarity of the two passages, there is considerable difference even in the areas of close agreement. That is to say, word-for-word agreement and agreement in the precise form of the words are less common than a general agreement in thought and vocabulary. Wand seeks to explain this by suggesting, "It looks . . . as if the author of II Peter was not reproducing the precise text of Jude from a copy that he had before him as he wrote, but quoting from memory a letter that he knew almost by heart."[32]

The third alternative mentioned above, that both epistles could be dependent on a common source, has not won much support, yet it ought not to be dismissed out of hand. E. M. B. Green favors it, likening the situation in these epistles to that which confronts us in the Synoptic Gospels, where a common source may lie back of accounts that have marked similarities and also their individual peculiarities.[33]

(4) Various indications that the false teaching in view in

[32] J. W. C. Wand, *The General Epistles of St. Peter and St. Jude*, p. 135.
[33] Green, *op. cit.*, p. 10.

II Peter is Gnostic in nature, possibly of the Marcionite variety. The perversion of Pauline teaching (3:16) could look in that direction, also the promise of freedom made by the false teachers (2:19). A plausible reason for the stress on Christian knowledge, especially by means of the strong form ἐπίγνωσις, is to offset the Gnostic esoteric claim of special γνῶσις. But these things are not decisive. Paul's teaching was challenged and perverted in his own lifetime (e.g., Rom. 6:1). Furthermore, the Gnostic elements found in II Peter were also common to the first century, but those that were peculiar to the second century, such as the theory of creation by a Demiurge and the doctrine of angelic emanations, are patently absent from II Peter.

Other arguments, such as the claim that the writer's allusion to the mount as holy (1:18) points to a time far removed from the incident being described, when the spot had become venerated because of its traditional association with the transfiguration, are minor in nature. Surely from Peter's standpoint the mount was holy at once, attested by his desire to build three tabernacles there.

The case for Petrine authorship must be examined next.

(1) The writer uses the name Simon Peter in the salutation (1:1). This represents a difference from the first epistle, where the name Peter stands alone. Simon does not appear in its Greek form, but in its Semitic dress, as in Acts 15:14, where Peter is mentioned. To most minds this divergence from the first epistle will probably commend itself as a mark of flexibility on the part of the apostle rather than the work of an impersonator, who would more likely follow I Peter slavishly in such a matter.

(2) Certain personal allusions occur in 1:12-18. The writer refers to his approaching death as something that will occur suddenly (1:14), in apparent recollection of the Lord's prophecy concerning Peter (John 21:18).[34] His use of the term "exodus" for death fits in with Luke's account of the transfiguration, where the death of Jesus is referred to by this term (1:15; Luke 9:31). The writer's claim to have been an eyewitness at the transfiguration falls in this section also. It was Peter who spoke of tabernacles on that occasion. That term is now used figuratively for the body (1:14). Another reference is of a somewhat different order, containing a pledge to see to it that after his death the readers may have help in remembering the things he has been seeking to

[34] G. H. Boobyer, on the other hand, proceeding on the basis that II Peter is pseudonymous, thinks the writer's inspiration came from I Peter 5:1. *New Testament Essays,* ed. by A. J. B. Higgins, pp. 47-49.

impart (1:15). Dr. Warfield thinks this is an allusion to Mark's Gospel. "Surely this seems to promise a Gospel. And we have this series: I Peter testifies to Mark's intimacy with Peter; II Peter promises a Petrine Gospel; antiquity tells us that Mark was but Peter's mouth-piece. Who could have invented that middle term and so delicately inserted it into II Peter? II Peter thus appears a link in a natural chain which is complete with it and incomplete without it. All three of these sources from which the links are drawn are therefore genuine."[35] This astute observation has drawn mixed reactions. Some have accepted its validity, but others have questioned the promise of a Gospel. Some uncertainty exists about the identification of "these things" (1:15; cf. v. 12).

(3) Certain distinctive items of the epistle's vocabulary are found also in the reported speeches of Peter recorded in Acts: (a) "obtained" (II Pet. 1:1; Acts 1:17). The word occurs besides in only two other New Testament passages. (b) "godliness" (II Pet. 1:3, 6, 7; 3:11; Acts 3:12). Aside from these references the word is found only in the Pastorals. (c) "lawless" (II Pet. 2:8; Acts 2:23). The word is little used elsewhere. (d) "wages of iniquity" (II Peter 2:13, 15; Acts 1:18). No other New Testament passage has the same form of expression. (e) "the day of the Lord" (II Pet. 3:10; Acts 2:20, in a quotation). The value of these comparisons depends, of course, on the accuracy with which Peter is reported in Acts (see the discussion on speeches in the chapter on Acts).

(4) Points of similarity are discernible between II Peter and I Peter in diction and thought. (a) "grace to you and peace be multiplied." These words occur in the salutation of both epistles. (b) "precious" is a catchword in both epistles (I Pet. 1:19; cf. 1:7; 2:6-7; II Pet. 1:4; cf. 1:1). (c) "virtue" or "excellence" is used of God (I Pet. 2:9; II Pet. 1:3, and of man in 1:5). It occurs in only one other New Testament passage (Phil. 4:8). (d) "putting off" ($\dot{a}\pi\acute{o}\theta\epsilon\sigma\iota s$) appears only in I Peter 3:21 and II Peter 1:14. (e) "cease from sin" (I Pet. 4:1; II Pet. 2:14). (f) "eyewitness" (I Pet. 2:12 and 3:2, used as a participle; II Pet. 1:16 has the noun). This is an uncommon word; the root is not found elsewhere in the New Testament. (g) "supply" (I Pet. 4:11; II Pet. 1:5, 11, with the preposition used in composition with the verb). The verb is rare in the New Testament. (h) "love of the brethren" (I Pet. 1:22; II Pet.

---

[35] B. B. Warfield, *op. cit.*, p. 123. This comment appeared first in the *Southern Presbyterian Review*, Jan. 1882.

1:7). Used three other times in the New Testament. (i) "manner of life" (I Pet. 1:15, 18; 2:12; 3:1, 2, 16; II Pet. 2:7; 3:11). (j) "without blemish and without spot" (I Pet. 1:19; II Pet. 3:14; cf. 2:13). A longer list could be compiled. Here the critic has the option of seeing the same mind at work or supposing that one who writes in Peter's name consciously sought to mimic his phraseology. The latter may seem quite feasible, but to come at the problem after an interval of centuries is hardly the same as approaching it from the standpoint of the period of the early church, where skill in a matter of this sort lacks demonstration, particularly in the case of biblical writings.

The alternative to authenticity is pseudonymity. In the latter case we may think in terms of a deliberate forgery or a well-intentioned attempt to reproduce the thought and spirit of the apostle. Many moderns look on the epistle in this light and do not find the practice reprehensible. The more serious aspect of the matter is the reception of such a letter by the church. Recalling that the presbyter who wrote the *Acts of Paul and Thecla,* professedly out of love for Paul, was disciplined, we are hardly encouraged to think that the church had a more relaxed and indulgent attitude in this case. Then was the church deceived? This is unlikely. Green cites the repudiation of the *Gospel of Peter* by Serapion, bishop of Antioch toward the end of the second century, who banned the work from his churches, and did so on the ground that it was pseudepigraphical.[36] After a review of the whole problem Guthrie feels obliged to say, "There is no evidence in Christian literature for the idea of a conventional literary device, by which an author as a matter of literary custom and with the full approbation of his circle of readers publishes his own productions in another's name. There was always an ulterior motive."[37] This appears to have been so even in the case of the writers of the Jewish Pseudepigrapha, who wanted to get a hearing and tried to capitalize on the principle of canonicity by using well-known biblical names behind which to hide their identity, at a time when the canon was closed. If one is disposed to receive II Peter as a pseudonymous writing, logically he ought to go the whole way and make room in his Bible for the Pseudepigrapha.

Perhaps judicious scholarship, even when it feels the weight of the case against Petrine authorship, can do no better than to confess to misgivings such as Hort had on this subject. Sanday

[36] Green, *op. cit.,* pp. 35-36.
[37] Guthrie, *Vox Evangelica,* 1962, p. 56.

reports that when he inquired of this extraordinarily learned man what his view of II Peter was, Hort replied that if he were asked he should say that the balance of argument was against the Epistle — and the moment he had done so that he should begin to think that he might be wrong.[38] It is a sobering thought that the whole post-apostolic period, with its welter of apocryphal works, produced nothing of the quality of II Peter.

DATE

This is tightly bound up with the question of authenticity. If II Peter be accepted as the work of the apostle, then a date around the year 64 is most probable, shortly before his martyrdom. Advocates of pseudonymity generally place it about the middle of the second century. Appeal is made to the observation that the first generation of believers had long ago passed away (3:4). It is conceivable that the word *fathers* could apply to Christians, but it is worth noting that elsewhere in the New Testament it applies only to men who belonged to the old dispensation. W. F. Albright is impressed by reminiscences in II Peter of the Qumran literature, "including the true way, light in darkness, the final destruction by fire, etc.," and thinks of the book as belonging to a period prior to A.D. 80.[39] On the presumption of genuineness, Rome is the most probable place of origin.

If the epistle is understood as the work of a disciple of Peter (see below under "Recent Study") a date toward the close of the first century is feasible. For those who regard the work as thoroughly pseudonymous a still later period is preferred, sometime in the first half of the second century.

READERS

The identity and location of the recipients is not entirely clear. It is generally assumed that they are the same as for I Peter, on the basis of the statement in 3:1. Boobyer defends this identification at some length.[40] On the other hand, a closer bond seems to be evidenced here between writer and readers than in I Peter and the material has sufficient diversity to raise the question whether they could properly be bracketed in the manner II Peter 3:1-2 indicates. It is somewhat easier to fix the identity of the readers. They are probably Gentiles. This may be the point of

[38] W. Sanday, *Inspiration,* p. 347.
[39] Albright, *From the Stone Age to Christianity,* 2nd ed., pp. 22-23.
[40] G. H. Boobyer, "The Indebtedness of 2 Peter to 1 Peter," in *New Testament Essays,* ed. by A. J. B. Higgins, pp. 36-39.

the writer's remark about their equality with him (1:1), unless he is seeking to bridge the gap between apostles and others in the church. More certain is the fact noted by Bo Reicke, "that Jewish traditions are referred to with a certain caution, while it is taken for granted that Paul is a recognized authority (3:15f.)."[41]

RECENT STUDY

There are signs that the stalemate between those who hold to the authenticity of II Peter and those who maintain its outright pseudonymity may be leading to an intermediate position. It takes as its starting point the observation that this document can be more accurately described as a testament than as a letter or epistle. Examples of this type of literature are contained in the New Testament, notably the upper room discourse of Jesus in John's Gospel and the farewell message of Paul to the Ephesian elders (Acts 20). Peter is conscious of the near approach of death and is determined to provide help and guidance for believers, which may well point to II Peter itself for its realization (1:13-15). Noting the tension between the time when Peter is still alive (vs. 13) and the period following (vs. 15) J. Ramsey Michaels suggests that II Peter possibly "embodies within itself both stages of the work of bringing to remembrance — 'as long as I am in this body,' and 'after my departure . . . at any time.' "[42] This opens up the possibility that a close disciple of Peter may have taken his master's teaching and adapted it to his own time (in a somewhat later period but within the next generation) in his own terms.

On this theory it would be legitimate to retain Peter's name as author and it would be easier to account for the reference to apostles (3:2). The problem of the language would also be considerably relieved. Noting some of the peculiarities of the diction of II Peter, Reicke observes that there is evidence for the existence of a school of Greek rhetoric going back beyond the first century which embodied an Asian style "characterized by a loaded, verbose, high-sounding manner of expression leaning toward the novel and bizarre, and careless about violating classic ideals of simplicity."[43] This description tallies well with the language of II Peter.

An objection could still be registered that in view of the alleged dependence of II Peter on Jude and the lateness of Jude,

---

[41] *The Epistles of James, Peter, and Jude,* p. 146.
[42] *The New Testament Speaks,* p. 352.
[43] *Op. cit.,* pp. 146-147.

no such close tie with the life and work of Peter can be successfully maintained. However, both of these items lack demonstration, so the testamentary theory of the origin of II Peter is likely to commend itself to many as a viable explanation.

BIBLIOGRAPHY

The Authorship and Integrity of the New Testament. London: SPCK (contains articles by K. Aland and D. Guthrie on opposite sides of the question of pseudonymity — pp. 1-39).

Barker, G. W., Lane, W. L., and Michaels, J. R., *The New Testament Speaks.* New York: Harper and Row, 1969, pp. 349-352.

Boobyer, G. H., "The Indebtedness of 2 Peter to 1 Peter," in *New Testament Essays,* ed. by A. J. B. Higgins. Manchester University Press, 1959, pp. 34-53.

Green, Michael, *The Second Epistle General of Peter and the General Epistle of Jude, TBC.* Grand Rapids: Eerdmans, 1968.

Hauck, F., *Die Kirchenbriefe, NTD.* Göttingen: Vandenhoeck & Ruprecht, 1953.

James, Montague R., *The Second Epistle General of Peter and the General Epistle of Jude, CGT.* Cambridge University Press, 1912.

Kelly, J. N. D., *A Commentary on the Epistles of Peter and of Jude, HNTC.* New York: Harper and Row, 1969.

Mayor, J. B., *The Epistle of St. Jude and the Second Epistle of St. Peter.* London: Macmillan, 1907. [Also see volumes by Bigg, Knopf, Wand, and Wohlenberg listed under I Peter.]

Reicke, Bo, *The Epistles of James, Peter, and Jude, Anchor Bible.* Garden City, N.Y.: Doubleday and Co.

Chapter Twenty-two

THE EPISTLE OF JUDE

SMALL IN COMPASS BUT POTENT IN ITS MESSAGE, THIS WRITING memorializes a struggle that the Christian church toward the end of the apostolic age had to wage against forces within its own ranks that threatened to destroy it by sheer corruption.

RECOGNITION BY THE EARLY CHURCH

Faint traces of the influence of Jude have been claimed in works belonging to the first half of the second century, such as *Didache* II. 7 (Jude 22-23), where there is some similarity in thought and form, but little in vocabulary; *Barnabas* II. 10, where the noun from the rare verb παρεισδύειν (Jude 4) occurs; the *Shepherd of Hermas* Sim. V. vii. 2, where "defile the flesh" is found (Jude 8); and Polycarp's *Epistle to the Philippians* III. 2, where the admonition to his readers to build themselves up in (or into) the faith that has been given to them could depend on Jude 3 and 20. But these and other examples are too limited to be decisive.

We arrive on firmer ground in the last quarter of the second century. Athenagoras almost certainly shows knowledge of Jude in his discussion of angels who sinned (*Apology* XXIV and XXV). About the same time the Canon of Muratori includes

Jude, mentioning it by name, and shortly thereafter Clement of Alexandria commented on it in his *Hypotyposeis* or Outlines of biblical books, according to the testimony of Eusebius.[1]

Origen was impressed with Jude, describing it in a section dealing with the brethren of Jesus as a very little book but one "filled with strong (or healthful) words of heavenly grace."[2] Eusebius classed it with the disputed books, which are to be distinguished on the one hand from those that are received throughout the church and on the other hand from those that are regarded as spurious.[3] Among later writers Didymus, Athanasius, Augustine and Jerome are worthy of mention.

Of some interest is the fact that Jude is included, along with the Petrine Epistles, in the recently discovered Bodmer Papyri, belonging to the early third century. The codex contains other material as well, some of it apocryphal.[4]

Adverse judgments on the book were entertained at times in the early church. Origen seems to hint at this.[5] Didymus of Alexandria, by his defense of Jude for using apocryphal books, indicates the ground on which others rejected it. Jerome specifies the use of the *Book of Enoch* as the basis of rejection by many.[6] Jude was not included in the Syriac canon until the Philoxenian Version early in the sixth century. Despite the fact that he placed it among the Antilegomena rather than the spurious writings, Eusebius in another statement speaks of it as spurious on the ground that not many of the ancients made mention of it.[7] However, the evidence available to us suggests that the suspicions of the book were based on its contents rather than on doubt of its origin in the apostolic age.

This raises the question whether rejection of the epistle on the ground that it made use of apocryphal writings was justified. We know of at least one figure in the early church who did not feel this way about it. Tertullian went so far as to make Enoch authoritative Scripture because of Jude's use of the same.[8] Still, the majority who questioned the book seem to have been bothered

---

[1] *HE* VI. xiv. 2.
[2] *Com. on Matthew* X. 17.
[3] *HE* III. xxv. 3.
[4] F. W. Beare, "The Text of I Peter in Papyrus 72," *JBL*, LXXX (Sept. 1961), 253.
[5] *Com. on Matthew* XVII. 30.
[6] *Lives of Illustrious Men*, ch. 4.
[7] *HE* II. xxiii. 25.
[8] *On Female Dress* I. iii

by the use of extra-biblical literature, and this became the prevailing attitude until the fourth century.

One method of circumventing the difficulty is to assert that Jude's citation is simply an appeal to tradition regarded as coming down from the patriarch himself. This is improbable because, as Charles has shown, there are other items in Jude that show dependence on the *Book of Enoch*.[9] With reference to the passage in debate (vv. 14-15), the close approximation of the text of Jude to that of *Enoch* 1:9 likewise suggests literary dependence. Furthermore, the expression "the seventh from Adam" is apparently not gleaned from the Genesis account but from the *Book of Enoch*. At least it occurs there several times.

The explanation that has most to commend it is that Jude's citation of *Enoch* does not demand approval of the work as a whole, but extends only to those portions that he utilizes for his purpose. The situation is not materially different from Paul's references to pagan poets (Acts 17:28; I Cor. 15:33; Tit. 1:12).

OUTLINE OF CONTENTS

The writer senses the urgent need of alerting his readers to the seriousness of the threat posed by the activity of the false teachers in their midst. By heeding the warning, those who receive the epistle will be able to preserve themselves from this danger and may succeed in doing something about extricating those who have become victimized already.

The author had projected and was possibly engaged in writing (γράφειν) a doctrinal treatise "concerning our common salvation" when a necessity forced him to lay this aside and write (γράψαι) the present work (v. 3). He explains this necessity immediately by stating that certain men have crept in among his readers, men of an ungodly sort, who are perverting the grace of God into wanton wickedness and are denying the Lord Jesus Christ (v. 4). These dark tidings dictated the setting aside of the larger didactic work that had been planned in favor of this trenchant tract for the times. The false teachers, despite their Christian profession and their participation in the love feasts (v. 12), are devoid of spiritual life (v. 19). They are, in fact, twice dead (v. 12). Their doom is sure (vv. 4, 13).

Insofar as their underlying philosophy is exposed, these men are blatantly antinomian (v. 4) and not only boast of their own

[9] R. H. Charles, *The Book of Enoch*, pp. xcv-xcvi.

immorality but encourage it in others, presumably on the theory of Gnostic dualism that sundered flesh and spirit. Fleshly indulgence had no power to injure that perfection of spirit to which they imagined they had attained. It is likely that verse 19 is a thrust at this way of thinking. Instead of being spiritual men who are above the canons of ordinary morality, they actually lack the Spirit altogether. Their vaunted superiority not only leads them to reject ecclesiastical restraint but even extends to contemptuous disregard of heavenly beings (v. 8). They are intractable and irresponsible, a menace to decorum and godliness.

Apart from the address and salutation at the beginning (vv. 1-2) and the doxology at the close (vv. 24-25), the entire epistle concerns this threat to the well-being of the church. First, the writer states the fundamental error of the false teachers (vv. 3-4), following this with three reminders from the Old Testament of God's severity in punishing licentious conduct (vv. 5-7). Then he turns to a description of the errorists — what they are and what they do — spelled out in vivid, vigorous language and adorned with comparisons, taken from the past, of other unsavory figures (vv. 8-16). It is here that the prophecy of Enoch is injected (vv. 14-15). The more recent predictions of an apostolic nature concerning the emergence of such men as these are noted (vv. 17-19). Two courses of action are urged: first, self-protection through attention to the means of grace (vv. 20-21); second, an attempt to salvage others who have been more or less affected by this sinister propaganda (vv. 22-23).

CHARACTERISTICS

(1) The vocabulary shows considerable similarity to the LXX and also to Hellenistic literature. Fifteen words are peculiar to Jude among New Testament writers. (2) The style is direct and vigorous, marked especially by a fondness for combinations of threes. Some of the more obvious of these occur in the salutation (v. 2), in the three examples of judgment chosen from the Old Testament (vv. 5-7), the three figures of Cain, Balaam, and Korah (v. 11), and the threefold classification of people who need help (vv. 22-23), although the text here is not certain. (3) Of special note is the author's extensive comparison of the false teachers with various natural phenomena (vv. 12-13). (4) Not content with copious references to the Old Testament history for illustrative purposes, the writer makes

use of the Book of Enoch (vv. 14-15) and probably of the Assumption of Moses (v. 9).[10]

AUTHORSHIP

The name Jude is accompanied by two identifying marks. This was necessary because Jude was such a common name. While the expression "servant of Jesus Christ" does not of itself rule out apostleship, it implies a more lowly relationship, and this is confirmed by verses 17 and 18, where the writer distinguishes himself from the apostles. So he cannot be identified with Judas of James, which probably means "son of James" (Luke 6:16), one of the Twelve. The further statement that the writer is the brother of James is more helpful in establishing his identity. When the name James appears in this simple form in the New Testament it repeatedly refers to James the Lord's brother, head of the Jerusalem church. The writer, then, was also a brother of the Lord. His name appears last in the list of Jesus' brothers in Matthew 13:55 and next to last in Mark 6:3. It is reasonably certain that he was younger than James.

Little is known about Jude. Like the other brethren, he was an unbeliever prior to the resurrection (John 7:5; Acts 1:14). The only glimpse of his Christian activity is furnished by Paul's reference to him as an itinerant missionary accompanied by his wife (I Cor. 9:5). That Jude was well-known to his readers is evident from the fact that he had contemplated writing to them before along different lines (v. 3), thus exhibiting a relationship of fairly long standing. This background of missionary activity makes such a literary venture as our present epistle a rather natural thing. The Hellenistic flavor need not be considered an obstacle, since Palestinian Jews were often at home in the Greek language and literature of the time.[11]

A further glimpse of Jude, or rather, of his descendants, is given by Hegesippus, the historian of Jewish Christianity, and passed on by Eusebius.[12] It seems that the Emperor Domitian was desirous of rooting out those who were of the family of David as being possible revolutionaries. When two grandsons of Jude were haled before him, he learned on interrogating them that they were hardworking men of the soil who had no wealth, and that the kingdom for which they were looking was heavenly and not

---

[10] J. W. C. Wand thinks that vv. 7-8 show dependence on the *Testaments of the Twelve Patriarchs*.

[11] This is the thesis of Saul Lieberman, *Greek in Jewish Palestine*.

[12] *HE* III. xix. xx.

earthly. As a result of his inquiry, Domitian dismissed the men and brought his persecution to an end.

Negative views on authorship have usually taken one of two forms. It is suggested that the words "brother of James" are an interpolation, with the result that some other Jude is made the writer. Of course there is no textual evidence for an interpolation, but if one chooses to adopt this view, he is faced with the very improbable situation that the writer would be providing no further means of identifying himself than as a servant of Jesus Christ. The other alternative is to assume that the epistle is pseudonymous, that the real author is writing under the name of Jude the brother of James. Exponents of this view acknowledge the difficulty of understanding why the writer would take the name of Jude when it was the habit of those who used this device to select more prominent names.

The question of authorship is closely bound up with the dating of the epistle, for if there are features that demand a period later than the apostolic age, maintenance of Jude's authorship becomes impossible. It is necessary, therefore, to examine the problem at this point.

DATE

A time later than the lifetime of Jude is favored by some scholars, on various grounds.

(1) "The faith once for all delivered to the saints" reflects a period separated from the apostolic age, when men had begun to think of that which had been handed down to them as the authoritative message of the gospel and a bulwark against heresy. Since a similar use of "the faith" is found in the Pastorals, those who make the Pastorals late and un-Pauline feel justified in placing Jude in the same general period. It should be noted, however, that "the faith" is used in this objective sense very early (Gal. 1:23 and possibly Rom. 1:5).

(2) The false teachers are described as pre-written to judgment long ago (v. 4). Taken in conjunction with verse 17, this is thought to fix the standpoint of the writer as later than the apostolic age. If the argument is sound, then the pseudonymous writer (if one adopts that viewpoint) is guilty of stupid slips that expose his real position. But there is no reason why verse 4 should have to refer to apostolic writings, especially when the Old Testament is drawn upon so lavishly for its admonitory examples. Neither is it obvious that verse 17 demands a time when all the apostles are dead and gone.

434

(3) The generally Gnostic character of the false teachers has impressed some minds as calling for a late date. This is not so readily appealed to today in view of the increasing realization that Gnostic tendencies go back beyond the rise of the Christian faith. Jude does not reflect the elaborate Gnostic systems of the second century. Rather, it reflects a development with striking similarities to that which confronted Paul at Corinth, where some believers showed libertine tendencies yoked with unwillingness to submit to apostolic authority. That this evil spread to other areas of the church seems apparent from Revelation 2:14-15, 20, 24. One gets the impression from reading Jude that the writer is dealing with an innovation in that part of the church for which he feels special responsibility and that he is acting with all haste to arrest it (cf. the background for Galatians).

(4) The account of Hegesippus has been used in the interest of a second-century date for the epistle on the ground that if Jude had grandsons of mature age in Domitian's reign (A.D. 81-96), his own life span must have fallen at a time too early to suit the conditions reflected in the epistle. But Mayor finds this reasoning unconvincing. He judges that Jude was probably about 70 years of age at the beginning of Domitian's reign. No year is indicated for the interview with the grandsons. Even at the beginning of the reign they would likely have been about 20 years of age.[13] In summary, the arguments for the late dating of Jude are quite insufficient to necessitate the placing of the book in the second century or even at the end of the first, and they present no effective bar against authenticity. Though Moffatt rejects the authenticity of the book, he is convinced that it cannot be very late, for it "does not call the loyal Christians to rally round the ministry of bishops and presbyters as preserving true doctrine. Ignatius did this in the first quarter of the second century."[14]

Anything like an exact date is impossible to fix. Failure to mention the destruction of Jerusalem can be argued both ways. It can be asserted that although this catastrophe has occurred, Jude is precluded from mentioning it because his examples of divine judgment are confined to Old Testament days, or else he shrank from mentioning so recent an occurrence because it was painful to all Jews who were true to their national heritage. Zahn actually advocates the view that this event is hinted at in verse

---

[13] J. B. Mayor, *The Epistle of St. Jude and the Second Epistle of St. Peter*, p. cxlviii.

[14] *The General Epistles. Peter, James and Judas MNTC*, p. 226.

5b, so he dates the book around A.D. 75.[15] On the other hand, if it is written to Jewish Christians in Palestine, a date prior to the destruction of Jerusalem is more natural, for Christianity suffered a terrible setback in the years of the war with Rome.

If Jude made use of II Peter, due time must be allowed for that epistle to have reached Jude. This interval need not have been great. A date between 66 and 70 is feasible, though the period 70 to 80 is possible.

READERS

Were the readers Jewish or Gentile Christians, and where did they live? There is no agreement on these matters, for there is little on which to base a judgment. The reference to "our common salvation" has been interpreted as fitting terminology for a Jewish Christian writer addressing Gentile believers (cf. II Pet. 1:1). On the other hand, it would not be out of place if Jewish Christians are intended. Mayor agrees with Zahn that those of the circumcision are in view and adds that "this view gains support from the familiarity imputed to the readers not merely with the facts of OT history, but also with apocryphal books and rabbinical traditions in vv. 5-7, 9-11 and 14."[16] Zahn observes that with all the similarities exhibited between the false teachers of this epistle and the libertines at Corinth, there is this difference, that there is no hint of participation in idolatrous feasts, a feature that would have been so repugnant to those with a Jewish background that it could not be foisted on them.[17]

Wand argues for Antioch and vicinity as the destination.[18] This has the advantage of being more accessible to propagandists than Palestine and it was a place where Jewish and Gentile Christians would be found in considerable numbers. Both groups could profit from the writing. If one could be sure that Jude's allusion to James intends more than a means of identification for himself, in other words, intends to hint delicately that he is assuming responsibility for the oversight of the dispersed Christian Jews, which death forced James recently to relinquish, then the view that Jewish believers are intended as the recipients of the epistle would be strengthened. In the nature of the case finality cannot be attained in this matter.

[15] Zahn, *Introduction*, II, 254-55.
[16] Mayor, *op. cit.*, p. 20.
[17] Zahn, *op. cit.*, II, 282.
[18] J. W. C. Wand, *The General Epistles of St. Peter and St. Jude*, p. 194.

VALUE

Some are unable to find much of permanent usefulness in Jude, but the somberness of the subject and the severity of the language ought not to obscure its abiding utility for the church. This can be expressed in two simple propositions: sound doctrine and right practice go hand in hand; and error must be resisted and exposed.

BIBLIOGRAPHY

See titles listed under I Peter and II Peter.

Chapter Twenty-three

THE EPISTLES OF JOHN

OF THE FIVE BOOKS TRADITIONALLY ASSOCIATED WITH THE NAME of John, three are classed as epistles and are included with those called catholic or general, although no one of them is intended for the church universal and two of them are quite local in their reference. Of this group of three the first is by far the most important.

FIRST JOHN

RECOGNITION BY THE EARLY CHURCH

The earliest clear-cut case of dependence is in Polycarp's *Epistle to the Philippians* (ch. vii), where a virtual reproduction of I John 4:2 in concise form appears. There are probable allusions to the epistle in the *Didache,* in *Hermas* and in the *Epistle to Diognetus.* Irenaeus, in quoting I John 2:18-22, part of it accurately and the rest very freely, states that this is John's testimony in his epistle.[1] Clement of Alexandria quotes from John's "greater epistle" several times in his *Stromateis* and in his

---

[1] *Against Heresies* III. xvi. 5.

Quis Dives Salvetur. In the Canon of Muratori, after a statement concerning the circumstances surrounding the origin of the Gospel according to John and some observations concerning differences in the Gospels, there is allusion to John's having written concerning the Lord in his epistles, followed by the quotation of a part of I John 1:1, concluding with a portion of verse 4. The testimony of the Fragment concerning other epistles by John is notoriously difficult to make out, but this must be reserved for later discussion. It is not surprising to find generous use of I John by Origen and Tertullian and the acknowledgment of its Johannine authorship. Finally, Eusebius indicates that the former (or first) of John's epistles had been accepted without dispute both by those of his (Eusebius') time and by the ancients.[2] So I John had its place among the acknowledged writings, according to this Father of the church.

BACKGROUND AND PURPOSE

Perhaps the best starting point is the statement of the writer that certain people who had formerly been associated with the Christian community or communities being addressed have now gone out from the believers and by that withdrawal have made it clear that they were not really a part of the Christian church (2:19). In fact, the previous verse speaks of many antichrists, as though to label these false teachers. They are still a problem, for their teaching has evidently been widely sown and needs to be repudiated and exposed. An ingredient of this false teaching is the denial that Jesus is the Christ (2:22; cf. 5:1). Another, apparently, is the denial that Jesus Christ has come in the flesh (4:2-3). This also bears the antichrist label (4:3). Taken together, these passages hint that the source of trouble, if unitary in character, was Gnostic with a Jewish flavor. Men of this stripe would be concerned with the issue of Jesus' Messiahship and would also be expected to deny the incarnation. Gnosticism, with its insistence on the evil character of matter, could not tolerate the teaching that the Son of God had come in flesh to dwell among men. That a combination of Judaic and Gnostic elements could be made is apparent from the Colossian epistle.

It may be possible to identify the error combatted in I John with the teaching of Cerinthus, since information on this man derived from Irenaeus and others indicates that he held typically Gnostic views mingled with Jewish tenets. God was not the

---

[2] *HE* III. xxiv. 17.

creator of this world. Jesus the man was born of Joseph and Mary, and upon him at the baptism came the divine Christ in the form of a dove. During his ministry Christ revealed the Father and departed prior to the crucifixion, leaving the man Jesus to suffer death. Cerinthus is said to have insisted on circumcision and the keeping of the Sabbath.[3] The assertion in I John 5:5 that Jesus is the Son of God may be intended to counter the views of Cerinthus, for the latter would on principle refuse to equate the two. Likewise, the declaration that Jesus Christ came not only by water (his baptism) but by blood (his cross) is likely a thrust at the heretic's failure to accept Christ's sacrifice (5:6).

A prominent feature of Gnosticism was its claim to special illumination and higher knowledge by which one rose into true fellowship with God by mystical contemplation. This could work to the depreciation of faith as elementary and inadequate, and may account for the frequent insistence in I John that Christians, supposedly limited by mere faith, actually have all the knowledge of God and of spiritual things that is available to men (2:20-21).

If the doctrine of the Gnostics needed refutation, so did their practice. If God is light (this the Gnostics proclaimed), then one must walk in the light if he would have fellowship with him. It will not do to profess a sinlessness based on the rapport of the spirit with God to the neglect of what is actually done in the body (1:8, 10). To talk about love for God based on a lofty mystical speculation and at the same time to fail miserably in love for the brethren (4:20; cf. 3:7-8) is contrary to reason and revelation alike.

The polemical purpose of I John is evident. But much of the book cannot be pressed into this mold and should be regarded as the writer's attempt to encourage his readers in the pursuit of a life of fellowship with God in the family of God. There is a strong strain of the imitation of Christ, or, better, the reproduction of the life of Christ, running through the epistle (4:17b). It finds its focal point at 5:18, where the Christian is described as one born ($\gamma\epsilon\gamma\epsilon\nu\nu\eta\mu\acute{\epsilon}\nu os$) of God, and the same term ($\gamma\epsilon\nu\nu\eta\theta\epsilon\acute{\iota}s$) is used of the Lord Jesus. Since both are born of God they share a common life (5:11-12) and they should walk in the same way (2:6), obey the same commandment of love (2:8), accept the same treatment from the world (3:1), and enjoy the same freedom from sin (3:5, 9). In this last point the analogy runs into difficulty,

[3] A. E. Brooke, *The Johannine Epistles,* p. xlvii.

440

but the solution offered lies in the secret of abiding in him in whom sin has absolutely no place (3:6).

FORM AND OUTLINE OF CONTENTS

In form the book lacks elements common to the letter, such as the name of the writer and some indication of the people addressed, and personal greetings. It has been called a homily, but if it be so, it has been recast, at least to the extent of substituting numerous references to writing (2:1, 12-14, etc.) for words of speaking. Its pastoral character is evident.

Students of I John are agreed that it defies systematic analysis, so one is reduced to listing the topics that are discussed.

The introduction presents knowledge of the word of life incarnate as the necessary basis for fellowship with God (1:1-4). There are conditions to be met if that fellowship is to be maintained (1:5-2:2). The proof of knowing and loving God is obedience to his commandments (2:3-11). In the possession of certain spiritual assets (2:12-14), the readers ought to love the Father rather than the world (2:15-17). Antichrist influences menace the church (2:18-25), but there is an antidote for false teaching — the divine anointing that gives spiritual insight (2:26-27). Abiding in God brings righteousness and readiness for the coming of the Lord (2:28-29). The coming itself will mean likeness to Christ. Meanwhile, the expectation of the coming has a purifying power (3:1-3). The life of abiding yields freedom from sin's dominion (3:4-10). Brethren have an obligation to love one another (3:11-18). Abiding brings confidence in prayer (3:19-24). The incarnation is the touchstone of truth and error (4:1-6). Love toward the brethren is grounded in God's love for them (4:7-12). Perfected love eliminates fear and prepares one for the day of judgment (4:13-21). Faith has power to overcome the world (5:1-5). God has given sufficient testimony concerning his Son to warrant faith (5:6-12).

The conclusion deals with the certitudes of faith — in terms of prayer, restoration of brethren, knowledge, and the possession of a new life in Christ (5:13-21).

CHARACTERISTICS

The following characteristics of the epistle may be noted: (1) Repetition. The writer keeps coming back to certain leading ideas and terms, such as light, truth, belief, love, and righteousness, but with shifting nuances. C. H. Dodd writes, "The argument is not closely articulated. There is little direct progression. The writer 'thinks around' a succession of related topics. The movement of thought has not inaptly been described as 'spiral,' for the development of a theme often brings us back almost to the starting point; almost, but not quite, for there is a slight shift which provides a transition to a fresh theme; or it may be to a theme which had apparently been dismissed at an earlier point, and now comes up for consideration from a slightly different angle."[4]

(2) Simplicity of structure. For the most part the sentences are not involved, except for the cumbersome one at the very beginning. There are plenty of conditional sentences, but they are not intricate. The prevailing mold is the parallel type of expression that abounds in the Hebrew wisdom literature. "One has only to read the Epistle with an attentive *ear* to perceive that, though using another language, the writer had in his own ear, all the time, the swing and cadences of Old Testament verse."[5] One does not find the closely reasoned and drawn-out argumentation, held together by illative particles, which is so characteristic of Paul. A common device of the writer is the explanatory statement, for example, "This is the victory that has overcome the world, even our faith" (5:4).

(3) The bluntness and severity of the language. The writer puts his propositions in sharply antithetical fashion. He seems to allow no middle ground between light and darkness, righteousness and sin. If one loves the world, he cannot be a lover of God. The man who makes a profession but fails to manifest true Christian character is a liar.

(4) Old Testament quotations are noticeably absent. The message is grounded in the apostolic witness rather than in prior revelation. Only one allusion is made to Old Testament history (3:12).

(5) The Christology is adduced mainly in connection with the refutation of error, hence the emphasis on incarnation and redemption by blood. No reference is made to the resurrection. A distinctive feature, apparently unconnected with polemic concerns, is the exposition of Christ's present work as Advocate (Paraclete) with the Father on behalf of sinning saints (2:1-2).

---

[4] Dodd, *The Johannine Epistles. MNTC,* pp. xxi-xxii. For a more complete description of the book along these lines, see Robert Law, *The Tests of Life,* Ch. I.

[5] Robert Law, *op. cit.,* p. 2.

442

RELATION TO THE GOSPEL ACCORDING TO JOHN

That a great similarity exists between the two writings is apparent to every reader. It shows itself (a) in the vocabulary. Important words common to both are: Father, Son, Spirit, beginning, Word (Logos), Paraclete, believe, life, eternal, love, remain (abide), keep, commandment, true (ἀληθινός), know (γινώσκω and οἶδα), have, beget, witness, light, darkness, world, sin, devil.

It appears (b) in larger units, such as the only begotten Son (4:9; cf. 3:16, 18), the Savior of the world (4:14; cf. 4:42), the Spirit of truth (4:6; cf. 14:17; 15:26; 16:13), doing the truth (1:6; cf. 3:21), to be "of the truth" (3:19; cf. 18:37), to be "of God" (3:10; cf. 8:47), to be "born of God" (3:9; cf. 1:13), the children of God (3:2; cf. 11:52), to "walk in darkness" (2:11; cf. 8:12), children of the devil (3:10; cf. 8:44), no man has ever seen God (4:12; cf. 1:18), to give his life (3:16; cf. 10:11), to pass from death to life (3:14; cf. 5:24), to overcome the world (5:4; cf. 16:33), water and blood (5:6; cf. 19:34), to do sin (3:4; cf. 8:34), to take away sin (3:5; cf. 1:29), to know and believe (4:16; cf. 6:69), to remain for ever (2:17; cf. 8:35).[6]

It appears (c) in certain marks of style, such as "this is. . ." (3:11, etc.; cf. 15:12, etc.), "by this. . ." (2:3, etc.; cf. 13:35, etc.), and the use of πᾶς followed by the article and participle (numerous examples in both), also in the large use of parataxis, asyndeton, and parallelism (utilizing both repetition and antithesis).

On the other hand, there are those who think that features of this sort could reflect a process of imitation by the writer of First John, and that certain other features of his work, when brought into comparison with the Gospel, seem to demonstrate such marked variations as to call for difference of authorship. Probably the most notable presentation of this point of view is to be found in the work of C. H. Dodd.[7] He submits that the epistle, when compared with the Gospel, is quite deficient in prepositions, adverbial participles, conjunctions, compound verbs, and certain idioms, especially those giving indication of Aramaic influence. The style is regarded as more monotonous than that of the Gospel. In the area of vocabulary, Dodd is particularly impressed by the absence from the epistle of some thirty-three terms that

[6] For a more complete list, see Brooke, *op. cit.*, pp. ii-iv.

[7] Dodd, "The First Epistle of John and the Fourth Gospel," *BJRL,* xxi (1937), 129-156, and a briefer discussion in the Moffatt Commentary on the Johannine Epistles (Intro.).

are prominent in the Gospel and would have been appropriate for use in a work such as the epistle. Included here, among others, are the words to save and to perish, grace, peace, Scripture, law, to judge (and judgment — only once in the epistle), Lord, glory, to send and to love (φιλεῖν).

Certain features of the theological thought of the epistle are judged to be difficult to fit into the point of view of the Gospel. The primitive eschatology, with its lively expectation of the Lord's return and its emphasis on the antichrist, stands in contrast to the realized eschatology of the Gospel. The redemptive work of Christ is stated in terms of propitiation (Dodd prefers the rendering *expiation*), whereas in the Gospel the death of Christ is presented as a means of his glorification. Again, the teaching on the Spirit is very limited as compared with the Gospel. It is pointed out that the Spirit is not connected with regeneration as in the Gospel, despite the fact that regeneration is a prominent theme in the epistle (born of God). Dodd concludes that the writer was probably a disciple of the Fourth Evangelist, and on this basis one can account for the similarities and also for the differences.

His conclusions have been challenged, notably by W. G. Wilson[8] and W. F. Howard.[9] The former confines himself to the linguistic evidence and by the use of statistical tables is able to show how inconclusive Dodd's observations are. For example, when the disparity in length between the Fourth Gospel and I John is taken into account, the difference between them in the number of different prepositions used is proportionately less than exists between the Lukan writings. As for particles, "there are greater variations between some of the Epistles generally accepted on linguistic (and other) evidence as being the work of Paul than the variations which Dr. Dodd uses as evidence against the common authorship of the Gospel and I John."[10] With respect to compound verbs, the difference between the two books is considerable, but only what should be expected because of the difference of material. Actually the percentage in the Synoptic Gospels is nearly twice as high as for the Fourth Gospel, which makes the gap between the Fourth Gospel and the first epistle

---

[8] Wilson, "An Examination of the Linguistic Evidence Adduced Against the Unity of Authorship of the First Epistle of John and the Fourth Gospel," *JTS*, 49 (1948), 147-56. See also A. P. Salom, "Some Aspect of the Grammatical Style of I John," *JBL*, LXXIV (1955), 96-102.

[9] Howard, *The Fourth Gospel in Recent Criticism and Interpretation* (4th ed., revised by C. K. Barrett), pp. 282-296 (reprinted from *JTS*, old series, xlviii [1947], pp. 12-25).

[10] Wilson, *op. cit.*, p. 152.

less significant than appears at first sight. The argument from idioms is shown to be of little value and the Aramaisms of the Gospel are pared down until the point has slight force. As for the list of important words present in the Gospel but absent from the epistle, Wilson's research leads him to the conclusion that "the number of important terms used in any particular book varies according to the length and subject-matter of the book."[11] He is able to show that with regard to important words "there is less variation between the Fourth Gospel and I John than exists between I Corinthians and Philippians."[12]

Howard's treatment covers many of the items already noted and also deals with the alleged differences in the theological thought between Gospel and epistle. The first of these is eschatology. Dodd's concern for realized eschatology, which emphasizes the goal of union with God and the risen Son through the Spirit, displacing the apocalyptic conception of a suddenly returning Saviour, has apparently caused him to underestimate the strength of the primitive eschatology in the Gospel, where Christ's promise to come again and his claim to raise the dead at the last day and to be the Judge of men must be given their full force alongside the features that point to a realized eschatology. As for the significance of Christ's death, both books state that he came to take away sin (John 1:29; I John 3:5). Any difference in detail regarding the doctrine of the Spirit must not obscure the fact that in both writings he is the Spirit of truth, prophetically proclaimed in the Gospel and appealed to as a present help in the epistle for the counteracting of error. The identification of Christ as the Paraclete (rather than the Spirit) in I John 2:1 is really not a contradiction, for Christ referred to himself as such when he promised that the coming Spirit would be *another Paraclete* (John 14:16).

It appears, then, that the majority judgment to the effect that Gospel and epistle proceed from the same hand is sound. The alternative of an imitator at work in the epistle is improbable. As Brooke says, "The variations in phrase suggest common authorship rather than servile, or even intelligent, copying."[13]

AUTHORSHIP

As noted above, the testimony of the early church clearly points to John the Apostle. Although I John itself does not reveal its

---

[11] *Ibid.,* p. 156.
[12] *Ibid.*
[13] A. E. Brooke, *op. cit.,* p. xvi.

author by name, it begins with a section (1:1-4) in which the writer identifies himself as one who had intimate personal contact with the Lord during the days of his flesh. This would seem to rule out a disciple of John. Another option has been chosen by some, namely, to make the author John the Elder, on the double ground that the writer of the Second and Third Epistles, which have great affinity with the First, refers to himself as the Elder and that Papias, writing a few decades later, seems to some scholars to differentiate John the Elder from John the Apostle. However, this distinction is by no means generally acknowledged. This other John is an elusive figure if he ever existed as an individual distinct from the Apostle. Furthermore, if the Elder of the other two epistles is a different person from John the Apostle and if he wrote the First Epistle also, it is strange that he does not there introduce himself in the same way as in the other two. The weight of probability is on the side of apostolic authorship, and this is supported by the authoritative tone of the epistle and its confident interpretation of the Christian message as personally experienced at the beginning and continuing unchanged in its truth and power.

UNITY

The leading challenge to the unity of the epistle has come from R. Bultmann,[14] who sees in I John an original document of a Gnostic character that a Christian writer has used as the basis for his own comments and applications of a homiletic nature, interwoven with traditional Christian material. This original document, as reconstructed by Bultmann, contained thirty-two or thirty-three verses.[15] Its style is distinctive — parallelism and an apodictic character quite different from the discursive style of the author himself. Nauck, after a sustained analysis of the data, grants the difference in style but puts forth the judgment that the author of I John is himself responsible for the so-called original document, on which he proceeds to comment.[16] Piper, likewise granting the difference in style, finds no real problem here for unity of authorship, since the hymnic character of the material that Bultmann ascribes to an earlier source can be

14 Bultmann, "Analyse des ersten Johannesbriefes," in *Festgabe für Adolf Jülicher* (1927), pp. 138-58.
15 *Ibid.*, pp. 157-58.
16 Wolfgang Nauck, *Die Tradition und der Charakter des ersten Johannesbriefes*, p. 123.

paralleled by such examples as I Corinthians 13 and Ephesians 1-3, which differ stylistically from the rest of these epistles but do not demand a different source.[17] It is to be expected that items that belong to the *didache* of the church should attain a succinct and somewhat rhythmic form in contrast to the teaching that builds upon it.

READERS

The readers could be Gentiles, on the basis of the final admonition to keep themselves from idols (5:21). But it is possible that the word "idols" is not being used in a concrete sense of actual idolatry. The author may have in mind the chimeras of false teaching, which are as empty and misleading as the objects before which the pagans bow. J. A. T. Robinson points out that in contrast to the Pauline epistles, where so much is made of the need of confessing Jesus as Lord, I John is silent on this score, but gives prominence to the confession of Jesus as the Christ (2:22).[18] This favors the same general milieu for the epistles of John as for the Gospel, namely, Greek-speaking Jews. Only in this case the recipients are clearly adherents of the faith and need only to be assured and confirmed in it.

The readers are to be thought of as belonging to a fairly restricted area (2:19), and their circumstances and needs are known to the writer. He seems to have a pastoral relation to them, addressing them in the familiar language, "little children" (2:1, *passim*). They could well be his converts. Yet there is no clear indication that the readers are confined to a single congregation. A reasonable conclusion is that the epistle is intended for a group of churches for which John had responsibility in the province of Asia and more particularly those surrounding Ephesus (cf. Rev. 1:11).

Augustine and some later writers referred to the epistle as addressed to the Parthians, a people on the eastern frontier of the Roman empire. There is no historic basis for this identification. The confusion may be traced, perhaps, to the linking of the "elect lady" of the Second Epistle with the elect one in Babylon mentioned in I Peter 5:13.

[17] Otto Piper, "I John and the Didache of the Primitive Church," *JBL*, LXVI (1947), 450.

[18] Robinson, *Twelve New Testament Studies* (*Studies in Biblical Theology* No. 34), pp. 126-38.

DATE

Here the discussion turns partly on the relation between the epistle and the Gospel. Which gives evidence of having the priority? The question is not easily answered. One could point to the primitive character of the eschatology of the epistle as favoring an earlier date than the Gospel, yet it is interesting to observe that Dodd, who has stressed this point, nevertheless favors the priority of the Gospel because of other factors. In this connection the words of Brooke may be recalled, "It should also be noticed that the 'spiritualization' of the idea of Antichrist in the Epistle is at least as complete as the spiritualization of popular eschatology in the Gospel."[19] Dodd is impressed by the greater vigor of the Gospel, so that if the two writings can be understood as coming from the same man then the author composed the epistle at a somewhat advanced age.[20] He also draws attention to certain passages in the epistle that seem to require the background of the Gospel for their understanding (2:7-8 with 13:34; 3:8-15 with 8:41-47; 5:9-10 with 5:19-47). The language of the introduction (1:1-4) and especially of verse 2 gives the impression that a summary is being provided of the message already conveyed through the writing of the Gospel.[21] Brooke concludes, "The whole aim of the Epistle is to recall to mind and to supplement what has long ago been fully given, but not adequately grasped. It is not the earnest of things to come. It owes its existence to the failure to make the most of the abundance that has been given. It is the aftermath, not the first-fruits, of the writer's message to the Church."[22]

On the other hand it cannot be denied that there are elements in the epistle that reflect early Christian tradition. Piper notes that "the righteous one" (2:1) and "the holy one" (2:20), as applied to Christ, are almost peculiar otherwise to the proclamation of the early church (Acts 3:14; 7:52; 22:14 for the former, and Acts 3:14 for the latter).[23] Yet it is possible, no doubt, that these early convictions concerning Jesus of Nazareth could have been retained over a period of several decades and emerge in epistolary dress.

No hint is given in the epistle of distress upon the readers because of persecution. This is not of great help in dating the

---

19 A. E. Brooke, *op. cit.*, p. xxi.
20 C. H. Dodd, *MNTC*, p. lv.
21 The contrary has been maintained also. See J. N. Sanders, *The Fourth Gospel in the Early Church*, p. 9.
22 A. E. Brooke, *op. cit.*, p. xxvii.
23 Otto Piper, *op. cit.*, p. 442.

book, as the writing could be placed either before or after the time of Domitian's activity against the church.

The balance of probability seems to favor a date later than the Gospel, but how much later is a matter of speculation. It can be dated in the neighborhood of A.D. 90 or somewhat later.

SECOND AND THIRD JOHN

RECOGNITION BY THE EARLY CHURCH

These letters are less commonly referred to by the Fathers of the church than I John, which is natural in view of their brevity, personal character, and comparative absence of doctrinal emphasis. In quoting II John 11, Irenaeus attributes it to John, the disciple of the Lord,[24] and assigns II John 7-8 to the same source.[25] The Canon of Muratori makes room for two epistles of John as accepted in the universal church (*in catholica*). Since the text of this document is corrupt as well as incomplete, some scholars have taken the liberty of suggesting emendations. Katz thinks it dubious that *catholica* alone would be used of the church, since elsewhere in the document the church is called *ecclesia catholica*.[26] He goes on to say, "Moreover, how could any Canon have ever mentioned two Johannine epistles? By their tenor and by tradition the second and third are so closely connected that we should expect either one only, the first, which was adduced earlier, or all three." His suggestion is that the original Greek intended at this point, having previously mentioned I John, "two in addition to the Catholic epistle." In Egypt, Clement of Alexandria evidently included explanations of these epistles in his *Hypotyposeis,* for Eusebius indicates that he commented on all the canonical Scriptures, specifically mentioning "the Epistle of Jude and the remaining Catholic Epistles."[27] Origen's testimony indicates that some had doubts about II and III John, but he does not seem to reject the books on this account. "He [John] has left also an epistle of a very few lines, and, it may be, a second and third; for not all say that these are genuine. Only, the two of them together are not a hundred lines long."[28] Eusebius put them in the *Antilegomena.* Toward the end of the fourth century

24 *Against Heresies* I. xvi. 3.
25 *Ibid.,* III. xvi. 8.
26 Peter Katz, *JTS,* new series, VIII (1957), 273-74.
27 *HE* VI. xiv. 1.
28 *HE* VI. xxv. 10.

449

Jerome mentions the ascription of these epistles to John the Elder rather than the Apostle.[29] Only at a later period were they received in the Syriac-speaking church.

OUTLINE OF CONTENTS

In II John the Elder writes to the elect lady and her children, commending her for the fidelity to the truth manifested in certain of her children, and reminding her of the commandment of love in which she and others are to walk. He seeks to impress upon her also the importance of holding the doctrine of Christ as the incarnate Son of God and of refusing fellowship and aid to those who do not hold this doctrine and yet pose as Christian teachers.

Third John, addressed to a man named Gaius, praises him for his stand on behalf of the truth and for his kindness to traveling brethren who are active in the service of the Lord. Gaius is in pleasing contrast to a certain Diotrephes, who possibly belongs to the same local church. This man has refused to show hospitality to the workers sent forth with the author's blessing. Indeed, he has arbitrarily excluded from the church those who have received such missionaries. He will hear from the author when the latter is able to come in person to the church and deal with the situation. The body of the letter concludes with a commendation of a certain Demetrius.

BACKGROUND AND PURPOSE

The situation reflected in II John is fairly clear. Errorists who deny the true humanity of the Lord Jesus (v. 7; cf. I John 4:2) are seeking a hearing in churches for which the writer has responsibility. He warns of the possible coming of such men with their advanced ideas (v. 9), and he counsels that they be refused hospitality by the "elect lady" (v. 10). Equal prominence is given in the letter to the duty of maintaining brotherly love.

Much less certain are the circumstances that called forth III John. The simplest explanation is that the writer is seeking the help of Gaius, who is loyal to him, in handling a delicate situation. Diotrephes has arrogated authority to himself and has refused to receive the missionaries whom the writer has sent into the area for ministry. He has gone so far as to expel from the church those who extended hospitality to them. Now the help of Gaius is needed to receive these missionaries, even at the risk of bringing upon himself the displeasure of Diotrephes,

---

[29] *On Illustrious Men* xi. 18.

until the writer can come in person and take up the issue with the congregation. A letter to the church about the care of the missionaries has been flaunted by Diotrephes (v. 9), hence the present communication addressed to Gaius. Demetrius (v. 12) may have been one of the missionaries, who is now returning with this letter. It is not certain that Gaius and Diotrephes belonged to the same local church, but if not, their congregations must have been fairly close together.

Some students have seen in verse 9 an allusion to II John, but there is no solid evidence for this. Nor is there any great probability that Diotrephes shared the views of the errorists mentioned in II John. One would think that if he did, the writer of III John would have given a hint of it rather than concentrate on his overweening ambition and contumacy.

Some see in III John a stage of church history in which the monarchical bishop (represented here by Diotrephes) is seeking to gain independence of any authority from without. This would only be possible, presumably, if the apostles had passed from the scene, so it would require a late dating of the book and its non-apostolic authorship. However, there is nothing in the epistle itself that requires more than a personal basis for the altercation.

Though the two epistles are both concerned with the matter of extending hospitality to traveling teachers, there is little otherwise to link them with a common setting. They are better understood as relating to entirely different situations.

AUTHORSHIP

Three questions call for consideration here. Do the epistles have the same author? If so, is he the same person who wrote the first epistle? Finally, who is he? On the first of these questions there is little room for doubt. Certain correspondences stand out, such as "the Elder" at the beginning, and the description of the addressee in each case as one "whom I love in (the) truth," the expression "walk in truth," and the references to paper and ink or pen and ink at the close.

Although the writer of the two smaller epistles identifies himself in a way the first does not, as "the Elder," he seems to reveal himself as the same individual in all three by such tokens as the use of the word walk, also abide, truth (and the truth), having the Father and the Son, a new commandment, joy made full, etc. The second epistle appears to stand in a somewhat closer relation to

451

the first epistle than does the third, at least from the standpoint of vocabulary.

Who, then, is "the elder" who writes these letters? We must choose between John the Apostle, John the Elder as a different individual (assuming a distinction between him and John the Apostle in the Papias fragment), and some unknown with a remarkable knowledge of Johannine thought. John the Apostle is favored by tradition, especially by the important testimony of Irenaeus, and by the circumstance that the two brief epistles bear an even closer resemblance to the Fourth Gospel than to I John,[30] so if one is satisfied of the Johannine origin of the Gospel he finds no difficulty at this point with the epistles.

Those who incline toward John the Elder sometimes profess to find a less than apostolic authority asserted by the author of the two epistles. Dodd, for example, cannot understand why the author, had he been an apostle, did not assert it in the third letter and so reduce Diotrephes to silence.[31] The obvious reason is that he was not writing to Diotrephes but to Gaius. Others assume that the word "elder" is being used in a technical sense that denotes one who belonged to the group that succeeded the apostles in the superintendence of the church. But this position faces the awkwardness that Irenaeus, who accepted II John as the work of the apostle John, must have known the word "elder" had been used during the decades before his time, yet he found no impediment here in pronouncing John the Apostle as the author.[32] The use of "elder" by one who was also an apostle (I Pet. 5:11; cf. 1:1) is significant in this connection.

Since internal evidence does not rule out Johannine authorship, it is better to accept the guidance of tradition at this point than to resort to some unknown. The title of "elder" was eminently fitting in the case of John because of his advanced age.

READERS

In all likelihood both letters were sent to churches under John's pastoral care in the province of Asia. There is nothing to compel the conclusion that they were directed to the same congregation. The identity of the "elect lady" is debatable. Some have preferred to make "lady" a proper name, Kuria. Others have favored the view that "elect lady" is not a reference to an individual but to a church (cf. I Pet. 5:13), and are able to point to

---

30 C. H. Dodd, *op. cit.,* p. lxiii.
31 *Ibid.,* p. lxix.
32 H. P. V. Nunn, *The Authorship of the Fourth Gospel,* p. 59.

such things as the use of the plural in verses 8, 10, and 12 (although the singular is used in v. 5) and the fact that the lady and her children are known and loved by all who know the truth (v. 1). On the other hand, the allusion to the sister of the addressee (v. 13) seems to favor an individual, and if she were a very prominent person it is not unthinkable that the church throughout the region (v. 1) would be acquainted with her and her family. A decision is not easy here, and the matter should probably be left open.

DATE

As to date, it is easier to assume a date later than I John than vice versa. At least the reference to antichrist in II John 7 seems to require the more explicit teaching of the first epistle for a basis of understanding. Less certainly, the reference to the new commandment (v. 5) depends on the fuller exposition in I John. On the other side it might be alleged that the promise of the author in both epistles to come in person points to a time of life when decrepitude had not yet set in, but this is only of relative value. Both letters may well belong to the latter part of the closing decade of the first century.

BIBLIOGRAPHY

Brooke, A. E., *A Critical and Exegetical Commentary on the Johannine Epistles, ICC.* New York: Scribner's, 1912.

Candlish, R. S., *The First Epistle of John.* Grand Rapids: Zondervan, 1952.

Dodd, C. H., *The Johannine Epistles, MNTC.* London: Hodder & Stoughton, 1946.

Findlay, G. G., *Fellowship in the Life Eternal.* London: Hodder & Stoughton, 1909.

Haupt, E., *The First Epistle of St. John.* Edinburgh: T. & T. Clark, 1879.

Law, Robert, *The Tests of Life.* Edinburgh: T. & T. Clark, 1909.

O'Neill, J. C., *The Puzzle of I John.* London: SPCK, 1966.

Plummer, A., *The Epistles of St. John, CGTC.* Cambridge University Press, 1896.

Ross, A., *The Epistles of James and John, NIC.* Grand Rapids: Eerdmans, 1954.

Westcott, B. F., *The Epistles of St. John.* 2nd. ed., London: Macmillan, 1886.

See also works on the Catholic Epistles listed under I and II Peter.

Chapter Twenty-four

THE BOOK OF REVELATION

THE LAST BOOK OF THE NEW TESTAMENT IS OFTEN DESIGNATED as the Apocalypse, which is a transliteration of the first word of the text, and means "unveiling." Revelation does not necessarily denote something predictive, but the contents of this book, being largely prophetic, place it in the genre of literature that portrays future developments in terms of ecstatic vision, vivid imagery and symbolism, as it depicts the vindication of God's purpose over the forces of evil, reaching to the end of history and beyond. Apocalyptic calls for catastrophic divine intervention that ushers in a new age. Lest the title be insufficient to convey an advance notice of the nature of the contents, it is followed immediately by the assurance that the book has to do with future things. The author classes himself with the prophets (22:9) and refers to his book as prophecy (1:3; 22:7, 10, 18, 19).

RECOGNITION BY THE EARLY CHURCH

Circulation of the book in the Asia Minor region at a time shortly after its composition is rendered probable by the concern that the churches addressed in the Seven Letters would naturally have for a work that mentions them so directly. Possible allusions to the terminology of the Revelation in Ignatius and Barnabas

454

are too tenuous to admit of certainty. Papias is probably the first writer to make use of the Apocalypse. Though the fragments of this author's *Exposition of the Oracles of the Lord,* preserved in Eusebius, do not mention such use, there is allusion to his acquaintance with and regard for the Apocalypse in Andreas' commentary on the last book of Scripture (6th cent.). Independent testimony for the same general area and time as that of Papias concerning the recognition of the book as John's comes from Irenaeus, who speaks of the certification of the true text of Revelation 13:18 by men who saw John face to face.[1]

Justin speaks very clearly. "A certain man among us, whose name was John, one of the apostles of Christ, prophesied in a revelation made to him, that those who believed in our Christ would spend a thousand years in Jerusalem."[2] Since Justin taught at Ephesus shortly after his conversion around 130, this testimony gains in importance.

The earliest reference to the Apocalypse as Scripture is found in the Letter of the Churches of Lyons and Vienne in Gaul to churches of the Asia Minor region. Herein the statement is made that the unrighteous hatred shown in the persecution that raged against the Christians of their communities fulfilled the Scripture. The quotation of Revelation 22:11 follows.[3]

Irenaeus is a significant witness because of his early residence in Asia and Rome before settling down in Lyons as head of that church. It was his habit to quote frequently from the Apocalypse, which he accepted as Scripture and as the work of John, the disciple of the Lord.

The Shepherd of Hermas, written in Rome about the middle of the second century, reveals a probable knowledge of the Revelation. Not only does the work speak of the great tribulation in two passages, in apparent dependence on Revelation 7:14, but it makes use of similar imagery.[4]

A few decades later the Canon of Muratori included John's Apocalypse, noting that although he wrote to seven churches, he speaks to them all.

Tertullian of North Africa, like Irenaeus, was in the habit of making quotations from the Apocalypse and referring to it as the work of the apostle John.

Around the same time, early in the third century, Hippolytus

[1] *Against Heresies* V. xxx. 1.
[2] *Dialogue* LXXXI.
[3] *HE* V. i. 58.
[4] See H. B. Swete, *The Apocalypse of St. John,* p. cx.

of Rome, writing *On Christ and Antichrist* and *On Daniel,* put himself on record as receiving the Apocalypse as Scripture and as a writing emanating from the apostle John.

The Alexandrian leaders Clement and Origen add their testimony to the same effect. To them the Apocalypse is of apostolic origin (John) and is Scripture. Later on Athanasius also, in the same center, came out strongly for the canonicity of this book.

It is not surprising, in view of the breadth of acceptance of the Apocalypse as represented by these and other men, that this common tradition should be continued with Augustine and the Council of Carthage, and thus into the mainstream of the continuing church.

Yet, in spite of the secure place that the book had in the estimation of so many leaders, its acceptance was not universal. Marcion did not include it in his canon. All the Johannine writings were omitted. The Revelation would no doubt be particularly objectionable to Marcion because of its generous use of the Old Testament. Contrary voices were raised here and there because of the rise of Montanism in the second century, a movement that laid claim to special prophetic gifts and used the Book of Revelation as the basis for its teaching that the new Jerusalem would shortly descend in the Phrygian area where the movement was centered.

Strong opposition to the Montanists came from a group generally referred to as the Alogi, the name given to them by Epiphanius at a later time. In their desire to remove Scriptural support from the movement, they went so far as to challenge the apostolic and Johannine character both of the Gospel of John and of the Apocalypse. Montanism cherished the Fourth Gospel because it contained the promise of the Paraclete, which, it was claimed, was in imminent prospect of final fulfillment, as attested by the charismatic richness of the movement itself. The Alogi sought to attack the reliability of the Fourth Gospel by emphasizing its variance from the Synoptics. Their objections to the Revelation were quite. inconsequential and dilettante. A champion of their cause emerged at Rome in the person of a certain Gaius (or Caius), who did not shrink from assigning the two Johannine writings to Cerinthus, the heretic and foe of John. His positions were crushingly answered by Hippolytus early in the third century.

Around the middle of the same century Dionysius, bishop of Alexandria, became drawn into discussions over the Apocalypse because of the teachings of a certain Nepos, bishop of an outlying area, who was alleged to have millenarian views with carnal overtones similar to those attributed to Papias. Dionysius was

456

acquainted with the attempt to assign the book to Cerinthus, but rejected that method of discounting it and contented himself with denying that John the Apostle wrote it.[5] He called attention to the frequency with which the name John is used in the Revelation, whereas it does not appear at all in the Gospel or the First Epistle. Since John is a common name, another by the same name must have written the Apocalypse, and this is made more likely by the report that there were two tombs in Ephesus, each belonging to John. This suggests that two men by this name had been active in this Christian center. Dionysius further observed that whereas there are many resemblances in thought and terminology between the Gospel and the Epistle, these do not carry over to the Apocalypse, which is greatly different. Finally, whereas the other two books were written in good, even faultless, Greek, the Apocalypse has barbarous idioms and downright solecisms.

The arguments of Dionysius were not really decisive, for he failed to consider the factors of agreement, particularly the underlying Hebraic character of the language in both cases and the entirely different character of the Apocalypse from the writings being compared with it. Dionysius did not propose that the book should be removed from the status of Scripture, for he counted it the work of some holy and inspired person. But he succeeded in sowing the seeds of distrust that were to bear fruit in a depreciation of the Apocalypse through several areas of the East in the years that followed.

Most notable among those influenced by Dionysius was Eusebius of Caesarea. Like Dionysius, he was opposed to chiliasm, as is revealed by his attitude toward Papias. In classifying the writings of the New Testament Eusebius did a curious thing with the Revelation, for he put it both with the acknowledged writings and with those that were spurious, instead of classifying it with the disputed books. Commenting on this, Stonehouse observes, "Now this hesitating attitude can only mean that Eusebius was at odds with the church. Personally he is quite ready to classify it with the spurious works, but in deference to its acceptance as canonic not only in the west but also by the leading teachers of the east, including Origen, he places it also among the undisputed books."[6] It is clear, then, that this influential figure allowed himself to put a question mark over the Apocalypse for dogmatic reasons.

---

[5] *HE* VII. xxiv. 7.
[6] N. B. Stonehouse, *The Apocalypse in the Ancient Church*, p. 133.

The Cappadocian church was divided in its attitude toward the Apocalypse, Basil and Gregory of Nyssa accepting it as Scripture, but Gregory of Nazianzus and Amphilocius omitting it from their lists of New Testament books. Cyril of Jerusalem excluded it both from public and private reading in his district. At Antioch, where the Revelation had enjoyed acceptance in the second century, it was now put aside. Chrysostom, who labored at Antioch before going to Constantinople, made no use of it in his writings. The omission of the book in the canon of the Syrian Church may be explained in part by the barrier of language and by limited intercourse with the Greek and Latin areas of the church, but it is also possible that the contents of the Apocalypse, as interpreted by ardent chiliasts, brought offense.[7]

The reversal of this negative trend in the East was brought about by Athanasius, bishop of Alexandria for more than forty years during the fourth century. His wide acquaintance with the church at large gave him an appreciation of the high regard in which the Apocalypse was held, especially in the West, and he unhesitatingly endorsed it, including it in his list (in the year 367), which is the first to show exactly the same books as the canon ratified by the Third Council of Carthage and maintained throughout the following centuries.

FORM AND OUTLINE OF CONTENTS

Within the compass of the first six verses this work is designated as an apocalypse (1:1), as a prophecy (1:3), and as an epistle (1:4-6; cf. 22:21 for the epistolary conclusion). It is an apocalypse with respect to its contents, a prophecy in its essential spirit and message, and an epistle in its form.[8] The Revelation honors apocalyptic methodology but makes it subserve genuine prophecy.

The Prologue (1:1-8) is followed by John's statement of his situation on the island called Patmos and his entrance upon the ecstatic state, whereupon he saw a vision of the glorified Christ (1:9-20). In Christ's name and by his direction he wrote letters to the seven churches of Asia (2:1—3:22). These letters follow a definite pattern. Each has a characterization of the Lord, generally taken from the opening vision, an appraisal of the

---

[7] *Ibid.*, p. 138.

[8] Zahn (*Introduction*, III, 390) observes that since the readers are not again addressed after 1:9 the epistolary form "is intended merely to express in a clear manner that the account is especially designed for certain definite readers."

church together with a commendation or censure or both, a word of warning where necessary, and a promise to the overcomer.

The scene shifts from earth to heaven and to a vision of God enthroned in majesty and holiness (4:1-11), closely followed by a vision of the Lamb and the sealed scroll (5:1-14). This scroll is central to the rest of the Apocalypse, for all that follows is the unfolding of what is contained therein. The Lamb is the only one qualified to discern the will of God concerning the future and to execute the same. John does not read the contents of the sealed scroll as the seals are opened one by one, but "sees" them (6:1—8:1). Following the sixth seal there is a somewhat parenthetic vision of the sealed company of 144,000 from the sons of Israel and of the great multitude from every nation that emerges from the great tribulation. Interludes of this sort punctuate the sequence of events in this book and are an important feature of it. The reader, so to speak, is taken behind the scenes to glimpse something that will aid his perspective and enrich his understanding of the drama as a whole.

The seventh seal, it should be noticed, has no content, or rather it embraces in itself the next phase of the revelation, the trumpets (8:1-2). Whereas the seals have a strong resemblance to the Lord's predictions in Matthew 24 and affect men quite directly, the trumpets are similar to the plagues upon Egypt recorded in Exodus, and they affect men largely in terms of their environment. Included within the scope of the trumpets (8:2—11:18) is a section portraying God's faithfulness in giving a special latter day witness to Israel (11:1-13).

The next unit (11:19—14:20) is somewhat heterogeneous, beginning with a portrayal of the heavenly temple and its ark as though to convey the reminder that heaven is acting in covenant faithfulness in what happens on earth, despite appearances. Further scenes here present the woman and her child, the angelic war in heaven, the beast out of the sea and the beast out of the earth, the Lamb with the 144,000, and the angels with the sickles.

The seven vials or bowls contain the wrath of God (15:1—18:24). With the pouring out of the contents of these bowls, God's direct action against an unrepentant world is pictured in lurid terms. There is some similarity to the descriptions under the trumpets, but the judgment is more severe. Included here is the destruction of Babylon the harlot by the beast.

The stage is set now for the seven last things (19:1—22:5). These include the coming of the Lord from heaven, the marriage supper of the Lamb, the binding of Satan, the millennial reign, the final conflict with hostile nations spurred on by Satan, the last

459

judgment, and the new heaven and the new earth. Last of all is the Epilogue (22:6-21).

Two observations should be made about the structure. The seals, trumpets, and bowls, which between them embrace the great central portion of the Apocalypse, are not sequentially chronological. Rather, each series is conceived of as carrying on to the end of the tribulation, which in turn gives way to the Second Advent and the features that follow (cf. 10:7). Second, at several places the end is announced as though it were already an achieved fact, but nothing happens, and the drama continues (11:15; 12:10; cf. 7:14-17). From the divine standpoint the victory is assured and can be announced as though it were already accomplished.

CHARACTERISTICS

(1) It is the biblical book of the end-time par excellence. This emphasis on the last things is present here and there in various parts of the Old and New Testaments, but not in the same concentrated, sustained, and comprehensive manner as in the Apocalypse. Every reader senses the suitability of such a book in the position it occupies, standing at the close of Scripture and majoring on the consummation of the ages.

(2) It is a mysterious book, filled with enigmas for the modern reader. But this does not mean that it was necessarily so for believers who read it at the end of the first century. Its message had to be conveyed by symbols and obscure allusions at least in part because of the danger of reprisal by an arrogant and ruthless Roman regime that was threatening the church with persecution.

(3) It is a polemical book, which challenges the pride and impiety of a ruler who claims divine honors, the crowning infamy of paganism. Over against his boastful claim is put the message of him who is the ruler of the kings of the earth (1:5), the King of kings and Lord of lords (19:16).

(4) It is a dramatic work. This feature belongs to the nature of apocalyptic in general, but the artistry here is incomparable. Stauffer finds many particulars that suggest a counterpoise to and virtually a parody on aspects of emperor worship with all its cultic trappings.[9]

(5) A notable element is the interplay between heaven and earth. This is a corollary of the visionary character of the book. Heaven is open to the prophet. What is decreed there comes to

---

[9] E. Stauffer, *Christ and the Caesars,* pp. 179-91.

pass on earth. Likewise, what transpires on earth, whether it be the suffering of saints or the lawless acts of ungodly men, brings a reaction in heaven. When the judgments of God have finally run their course, heaven stoops to earth in the form of the celestial city.

(6) There is an emphasis on the unity and godlessness of the nations. The spirit of Babel lives again in them, and the spirit of determined opposition to God and his anointed (cf. Psalm 2). Back of this rebellion against the Most High is the feverish prodding of the evil one, who senses that his time is short.

(7) Despite its preoccupation with judgment and woe, this book has ample room for worship and praise. Angels, representatives of the creation, and the redeemed unite in praising God and the Lamb. The reader is almost overwhelmed by the impression of the vast numbers of the participants and the heartiness of their adoration.

(8) Prolific use is made of numbers. This is a common feature of apocalyptic. The author is especially partial to the number seven, of which there are over fifty occurrences.

(9) Large sections of the text are rhythmical in form, sharing in this respect a feature of Old Testament prophets. Modern versions often print sections of the text as verse rather than prose.

(10) There is frequent use of the Old Testament. Swete has calculated that of the 404 verses of the text of the Revelation, 278 contain references to the Jewish Scriptures.[10] The Psalms, Isaiah, Ezekiel, Zechariah and Daniel are drawn upon most heavily. Despite the great measure of dependence on Daniel, the name of the prophet is not once cited. Nor is there a formal quotation from any Old Testament source as Scripture. In this respect the Apocalypse stands in contrast to the Gospels. Swete observes that the Apocalyptist often blends two or more Old Testament contexts and that he handles these materials in an original manner: "Though in constant relation to the older apocalyptic, St. John's pictures of the unseen and the future are truly creations, the work of the Spirit of prophecy upon a mind full of the lore of the earlier revelation and yet free to carry its reminiscences into new and wider fields of spiritual illumination."[11]

The author may have been acquainted with some of the Jewish apocalypses, but he does not confess dependence on them. Agreement in terminology probably does not point to this work

[10] H. B. Swete, *op. cit.*, p. cxl.
[11] *Ibid.*, p. clv.

or that, but to a common stock of apocalyptic expressions.[12]

(11) Irregularities in grammar are more common than else-where in the New Testament.[13] A superficial explanation is that the writer was inept in his use of the Greek language, but this will hardly do, for in other instances, sometimes in the immediate context, he shows himself fully in command of the proper con-struction (e.g., 1:4). This seems to make untenable the view of Westcott that at the time the book was written the author had not mastered Greek. It is hardly possible to maintain, either, that although writing in Greek, the author deliberately shows his contempt for this linguistic medium by making obvious breaches of good form. This would needlessly offend his readers. Torrey insists that the irregularities reflect an Aramaic original, of which the present text is a translation. He likens them to the oddities found in Aquila's Greek rendering of the Old Testament.[14] The use of the redundant pronoun (e.g., 7:9) and the redundant adverb (e.g., 12:6) seems due to Semitic influence, however that influence be defined. No single explanation is probably adequate to explain all the solecisms, although some of these are no doubt deliberate. So, for example, it is fairly evident that in 1:4 the author is treating the divine title as indeclinable. The nominative is more forceful than an oblique case would have been. Some credence may be given, perhaps, to the view that the irregularities can be explained from the circumstances of writing — "while alone in Patmos, in apparent haste, in great excitement due to the visions, in involved apocalyptic style, and possibly without careful revision in linguistic details."[15]

INTERPRETATION

It is not surprising that a book of the character of the Reve-lation should give rise to various schools of thought in the attempt to understand it. Of these only four need be mentioned, since they include the views of nearly all who have grappled seriously with the hermeneutical problem.[16] The area of debate

---

12 Charles gives a list of eighteen passages "dependent on or parallel with passages in the Jewish Pseudepigrapha" (*The Revelation of St. John, ICC,* I, lxxxii-lxxxiii).

13 A list of some of the outstanding examples may be found in C. C. Torrey, *Documents of the Primitive Church,* p. 158.

14 *Ibid.,* p. 161.

15 A. T. Robertson, *Epochs in the Life of the Apostle John,* p. 201.

16 No attempt is made here to outline the history of the study of the Apocalypse throughout the history of the church. For this, see I. T. Beckwith, *The Apocalypse of John,* pp. 319-34; Swete, pp. ccvii-ccxvi; E. B. Elliott, *Horae Apocalypticae,* IV, 275-63.

lies chiefly in the central chapters, since chapters 1-3 obviously refer to conditions at the time of writing, and the closing portion, with its picture of the perfected, eternal state, with equal clarity belongs to the future.

(1) The *preterist* view. This school of thought maintains that the great mass of the material must be understood as pertaining to the period in which the book was written. The author is describing the impending struggle between the church and the Roman state. In this the latter will try to destroy the church by persecution. This approach has its strength in the fact that when the Revelation is thus understood, it becomes immediately and thoroughly relevant to the life and struggle of the early church. But it faces the embarrassment that many things predicted in the book did not take place in that epoch. Beckwith freely admits, "The prediction of the near downfall of the Roman world-power, the graphically drawn picture of the destruction of the imperial city, the accession of a half-demonic world-tyrant (Antichrist) who should soon be destroyed, and the immediate setting up of a millennial reign of the martyrs with Christ on earth, are predictions which history has not verified."[17]

(2) The *historicist view*. This seeks to interpret the material in terms of church history by identifying various items in the visions with leading movements and events from the apostolic age to modern times. This approach suffers from subjectivity, as a survey of the variety of identifications held by exponents of this method clearly demonstrates. It is antecedently doubtful that the Spirit of God would be concerned to inform the apostolic church with a rather detailed picture of events lying beyond their own time and having only a remote bearing on the consummation of the age. "The attempt to find pictured in the visions such events as the rise of Mohammedanism, the usurpations of the papacy, the Reformation, the great European wars, or to identify with figures portrayed in the book well-known historic persons — these and many like inquiries all proceed from an utter misconception of the character of prophecy."[18]

(3) The *futurist* view. This approach understands the central chapters as setting forth events of the end-time leading up to the return of Christ and intimately connected therewith. There are differences among futurists, however. Some reason that the summons to John, "Come up hither" (4:1), marks the removal of the whole church from the earth (the rapture of the saints).

[17] I. T. Beckwith, *Apocalypse,* pp. 300-01.
[18] *Ibid.,* p. 303.

This is often coupled with the idea that the letters to the seven churches depict various stages of church history, so that actually there is no long gap in the book between the apostolic age and the end-time, although events in the world as such are passed by. It is supported by the observation that the word "church" does not appear in the book beyond chapter three, except for the single mention in the Epilogue (22:16). It is thereby concluded that the church will be spared the experience of passing through the great tribulation with which the central chapters are concerned.

Other futurists have a non-dispensational approach, understanding the summons to John in 4:1 to apply merely to the perspective of the author himself. The heavenly scene of chapters 4 and 5 is hardly susceptible to temporal fixation, and the seals may refer in large part to divine visitations of a more or less extraordinary nature that transpire during the course of the age as a whole (cf. Matt. 24:6-8). With the mention of the great tribulation of chapter 7, however, the end-time is reached, in agreement with the teaching of Christ in Matthew 24:29-30.

The general viewpoint of the futurists finds support from the following consideration, well stated by M. C. Tenney: "However one may interpret the symbols, the action of the book leads to and includes the last judgment of earth and the final establishment of the city of God. As the events lead up to this terminus in close succession, one may reason backward and say that the bulk of these events must still be future, since the consummation with which they are associated has not yet been attained and since the symbols seem to call for a rapid succession of acts rather than for a protracted process."[19]

(4) The *idealist* or *spiritual* view. This approach avoids the problems surrounding the precise fulfillment of the symbolic representations of the book by maintaining that the apocalyptic dress is merely intended to set forth the ageless struggle between the kingdom of God and the forces of evil arrayed against it. So the intent is to emphasize basic principles rather than historical events, and to strengthen the church throughout its earthly pilgrimage with the promise of ultimate victory for the cause of righteousness. Doubtless many have been attracted to this view as a way of escape from the perplexities with which the other views are encumbered.

In the face of much diversity of opinion, one is constrained to seek for some principle that will serve as a corrective and also

[19] M. C. Tenney, *Interpreting Revelation*, p. 142.

as a positive guide. Such a principle is the observation that many events predicted during the course of saving history have not only served to point to imminent events of the history but also to prepare the way for the more remote fulfillment of God's purpose in Christ.[20] Applying this to our present subject, Dr. Piper writes, "The Book of Revelation . . . can be interpreted both in an historical and an eschatological way. Many of the modern lovers of the book overlook, however, that the historical fulfillment of prophecies is not in itself their eschatological fulfillment."[21] On such a basis the early church could well see in the beast of Revelation 13 the dreadful threat of the persecuting power of the Roman state and also the church of the latter days could be entitled to view him as a sinister figure of the end-time.

THEOLOGICAL THOUGHT

In some manuscripts of the Apocalypse John is designated as "the theologian" (ὁ θεολόγος). True, this term can mean spokesman for a deity, especially in a situation where mysteries are involved. But the other meaning occurs also, and if this be accepted as the intent of the church in using the title, some basis should be found for it in the Apocalypse as well as in the other books attributed to John.

(1) The doctrine of God is strongly expressed in terms of Creator, Guardian of his people, and Judge. He is the Almighty and keeps a firm hand on the course of history. Swete observes the ties with the Old Testament revelation of God — "the *I am* of Exodus, the *Holy, Holy, Holy* of Isaiah, the *Lord God* of Ezekiel, the *God of heaven* of Daniel."[22] He is not set forth verbally as the God of love (but see 21:3-4), which is probably due to the preoccupation with the theme of judgment. His fatherhood is mentioned several times, but only in connection with the Son. His intrinsic excellence and his mighty acts call for universal praise and honor and glory.

(2) The Christology is very rich in terms of names and titles and what these connote. Jesus occurs alone several times. Jesus Christ (1:1), Lord Jesus (22:3), Lord Jesus Christ (22:21) are other forms of identification. This one is the Son of God (2:18), the Word of God (19:13), and he is repeatedly called the Lamb, which serves to memorialize his sacrifice (5:6). Other titles are Amen, the faithful and true witness (3:14), the holy and true

[20] See the observations of Otto Piper, *God in History*, p. 24.
[21] *Ibid.*, p. 13.
[22] Swete, *op. cit.*, p. clix.

one (3:7), the beginning of God's creation (3:14), the firstborn of the dead (1:5), the living one (1:18), the root and offspring of David (22:16), the bright and morning star (22:16), the Lion of the tribe of Judah (5:5), the King of kings and Lord of lords (19:16).

No real place is given to Jesus' life on earth. In 12:5 the birth is followed immediately by the ascension. However, his trial and triumph on earth are indicated in 3:21 and specifically his work of redemption from sin (1:5). His resurrection is implied in 1:5, 18, and his return is promised in 1:7 and then pictured in 19:11ff. He possesses the keys of death and Hades (1:18).

As in the Fourth Gospel, subordination to God the Father (3:12) is balanced by equality with him. The latter relationship is spelled out in a variety of ways. Both bear the title Alpha and Omega (1:8; 22:13); salvation is ascribed to both (7:10); the resurrected martyrs are priests to both (20:6); both are worshipped (4-5); they have a throne jointly (22:1, 3); wrath proceeds from both (6:16); they share the kingdom as equals (11:15; 12:10); and both are the temple of the holy city (21:22).

Christ's love for the redeemed is stated in 1:5 and is suggested by his relationship to the bride (19:7).

(3) The Holy Spirit appears chiefly in three roles: as the one who induces the ecstatic experience of the prophet (1:10; 4:2; 17:3; 21:10); as revealer and teacher (2:11, 17, 29; 3:6, 13, 22; 14:13; 19:10); and as witness, along with the church, to Christ (22:17; cf. John 15:26-27).

The allusions to the seven Spirits (1:4; 4:5; 5:6) create difficulty. Are they references to the Holy Spirit? (RSV and NEB do not capitalize.) The association with God and Christ in 1:4 looks in that direction.[23]

(4) The realm of evil receives considerable attention in this book. References to the evil one are frequent. He is spoken of as the devil and Satan, the dragon, the ancient serpent (20:2). His opposition to God and his purpose (12:1-6) as well as to the church (3:13, 24), his role as the deceiver of the world (12:9) and the instigator of rebellion against God (20:8) are some of the highlights.

The conflict is of cosmic proportions (12:7), though earth is the chief arena. Behind godless government stands the power of Satan (13:2), cravenly usurping the worship that men should

23 For a discussion of the problem, see Beckwith *in loco.*

give to God alone (13:4). But his power is not absolute; his time is measured (12:12) and his doom is certain (20:10).

One misses the term "world" in an ethical sense, which is such a striking feature of the Fourth Gospel. Although there are three occurrences of the word, none of them has the ethical sense. In place of it the author frequently uses the expression, "those who dwell on the earth," designating thereby those who oppose God and his ways and persecute his saints (11:10, *passim*). They are satisfied with the earthly viewpoint and the ways of men.

(5) The teaching on the church, while not highly developed, is instructive. Leading elements here are her unity (what the Spirit speaks to one church he speaks to all), her control by the risen Son of God (1:13, 16, 20), her militancy as she resists the efforts to destroy her loyalty to Christ and silence her testimony, and her ultimate triumph in glory. The universal priesthood of believers serves to bind the church together and give her strength during her pilgrimage (1:6).

AUTHORSHIP

The book itself carries the name of John as its author (1:1, 4, 9; 21:2; 22:8), but it does not otherwise explicitly identify him. Tradition, as we have seen, affirms that he was the apostle of the Lord, the beloved disciple. The testimony of Justin is especially important in view of his own residence at Ephesus, and that of Irenaeus scarcely less so, because of his early residence in Asia and his connections there. Polycrates, also, a second-century bishop of Ephesus, mentions John's status as martyr and teacher, plus the fact that he sleeps at Ephesus.[24] This is helpful, because the John of the Apocalypse is one who has a ministry and a place of unquestioned leadership among the churches of Asia, as the first three chapters clearly demonstrate.

Support for Johannine authorship has recently come from the discovery of the Gnostic library at Chenoboskion in Egypt. One of the documents involved is the *Apocryphon of John*, of which the library has three variant copies. The author calls himself "John, the brother of James, these who are the sons of Zebedee." The use of Revelation 1:19 seems to involve the assumption by the author of this document that John the apostle was the author of the Revelation, and this is substantiated by the way in which he tries to ape the paratactic style of John. The date of the Apocryphon is around A.D. 150 or possibly earlier.[25]

---

[24] *HE* V. xxiv. 3-4.
[25] See the note by Andrew Helmbold in *NTS*, 8 (Oct. 1961), 77-79.

Certain resemblances between the Apocalypse and the Fourth Gospel deserve to be taken into consideration, even though they will be regarded as weighty only by those who receive the Johannine authorship of the Gospel.

(1) Logos, used in the personal sense, occurs in 19:13, and elsewhere only in John 1:1, 14 and I John 1:1.

(2) Lamb as a title for Jesus is found some twenty-eight times in the Apocalypse and in John 1:29, 36 (where a different word for lamb is employed; John 21:55 has the same term as in the Apocalypse).

(3) The tendency to use the name Jesus without the article is common to both books.

(4) Witness (verb and noun) is of frequent occurrence.

(5) The word "true" (ἀληθινός), found thirteen times in John and ten times in the Apocalypse, has only five occurrences in the New Testament apart from the Johannine writings.

(6) The word "overcome" (or conquer), found sixteen times in the Apocalypse, occurs in John 16:33, as well as six times in I John, and has only three other occurrences in the New Testament.

(7) The word "dwell" (lit., "tabernacle") appears four times in the Apocalypse, and its only other occurrence is in John 1:14.

(8) The expression "fountain of living waters" or its equivalent is found only in the Apocalypse (7:17; 21:6) and in the Fourth Gospel (John 4:14; 7:38).[26]

(9) The prophecy of Zechariah 12:10 about the piercing of Israel's rejected king is quoted in Revelation 1:7 and in John 19:37. In both passages the same word for "pierce" is used, a word that is not found in the LXX of the Zechariah passage.

(10) With respect to vocabulary in general, Swete reckons that of the 913 separate words in the Apocalypse, 416 occur also in the Gospel. But most of these are ordinary words and therefore cannot be relied on too heavily as establishing unity of authorship.[27]

(11) There is a correspondence between the Apocalypse and the Gospel that is not confined to words alone, but belongs to the realm of ideas. The very texture of the book exhibits close affinity to the Gospel. Westcott puts the matter thus: "The main idea of both is the same. Both present a view of a supreme conflict between the powers of good and evil. In the Gospel this is

---

[26] See the discussion by R. E. Brown in *The Scrolls and the New Testament,* ed. by K. Stendahl, pp. 199-200.
[27] Swete, *op. cit.,* p. cxxvii.

delineated mainly in moral conceptions; in the Apocalypse mainly in images and visions. In the Gospel the opposing forces are treated under abstract and absolute forms, as light and darkness, love and hatred; in the Apocalypse under concrete and definite forms, God, Christ and the Church warring with the devil, the false prophet and the beast. But in both books alike Christ is the central figure. His victory is the end to which history and vision lead as their consummation. His Person and Work are the ground of triumph, and triumph through apparent failure."[28]

(12) The author has an intimate knowledge of and interest in the churches of Asia, both as to their condition and their needs, which fits the testimony of the early church that the apostle John resided in Ephesus and exercised oversight of these churches during the last years of his life. Ramsay writes, "It is a psychological impossibility that these Letters to the Asian Churches could have been written except by one who felt himself, and had the right to feel himself, charged with the superintendence and oversight of all those Churches, invested with Divinely given and absolute authority over them, gifted by long knowledge and sympathy with insight into their nature and circumstances, able to understand the line on which each was developing, and finally bringing to a focus in one moment of supreme inspiration — whose manner none but himself could understand or imagine — all the powers he possessed of knowledge, of intellect, of intensest love, of gravest responsibility, of sympathy with the Divine life, of commission from his Divine Teacher."[29] It is not known that there is any other John who possessed these qualifications.

On the other hand, those who hold to Johannine authorship are obliged to recognize that in so far as they build their case on the similarities between the Apocalypse and the Fourth Gospel, they must face certain important differences between these two documents. Charles thinks that the grammatical variances alone are such as to make common authorship impossible.[30] These include the solecisms, order of words, and a variety of phenomena treated in his chapter on the grammar of the Apocalypse.[31] Still other objections have been raised to the Johannine authorship.

(1) Though the writer gives his name as John, and does so several times, in no case does he state that he is an apostle. This probably should not be counted as too serious a problem,

[28] B. F. Westcott, *The Gospel According to St. John,* pp. lxxxiv-lxxxv.
[29] W. M. Ramsay, *The Letters to the Seven Churches,* p. 80.
[30] R. H. Charles, *A Critical and Exegetical Commentary on the Revelation of St. John,* p. xxix.
[31] *Ibid.,* pp. cxvii-clix.

in view of the obviously authoritative tone of the work, especially in the letters to the churches. If the writer's apostleship was unquestioned, there is no obvious reason for any necessity to mention his status.

(2) In support of the previous objection, it is noted that the writer mentions the twelve apostles as a group (21:14) but gives no hint as to his inclusion. This is the same sort of problem that is faced in dealing with the authorship of Ephesians, in view of the statement that the church is built on the foundation of the apostles and prophets (2:20). Surely it would have been an awkward thing, on the assumption that the writer is an apostle, to turn aside and indicate that he belongs to this circle. While the reference does not support apostleship, neither does it necessarily militate against it.

(3) Reliance is placed in the scattered reports of the martyrdom of John the apostle. This problem has been discussed in connection with the authorship of the Fourth Gospel. Charles has ransacked the records of the church to adduce as complete a list of witnesses as possible.[32] But even so the evidence is far from sufficient to tip the scale. It gets no support from Acts 12:2. One must calculate the probable influence of Mark 10:39 on the origin of such tradition and also the liability of confusion between the apostle John and John the Baptist. "As to the martyrologies, that of Carthage mentions explicitly John the Baptist on the same day as St. James, so that it seems probable that the mention in other martyrologies of St. John the brother of James on the same day is due to a confusion between the two Johns."[33] If one is shut up to a choice between the testimony ascribed to Papias by Philip of Side at a much later time and the testimony of Irenaeus, it would seem precarious to prefer the former to the latter.

Other views on authorship include a fairly wide variety of possibilities.

(1) The John of the Apocalypse, whatever his precise identity, was one who belonged to the Johannine group. By means of this suggestion the similarities to the Fourth Gospel are understandable. Cullmann, for example, is impressed by the way in which the idea of the temple gets prominence both in the Gospel and the Apocalypse, especially in the thought that God and the Lamb are the temple.[34]

[32] *Ibid.*, pp. xlv-l.
[33] *The Oxford Dictionary of the Christian Church*, p. 730a.
[34] *ET*, 71 (Nov. 1959), 426.

470

(2) The author may have been John the Presbyter. Aside from the vagueness and uncertainty of the early church reports about such a person (Dionysius of Alexandria could only refer to it as hearsay), there is the problem of the consensus of the church in favor of the apostle. How did it happen that such a switch occurred? And how did it happen that a figure of such prominence (chapters 1-3 testify to this) could be condemned to virtual oblivion? Scott well states the difficulty under which this theory labors. "It postulates the entire disappearance of John the Presbyter from the memory of the church of the second century. It assumes that this John was so great a personality that he could write these Letters to the churches of Asia, and require no further introduction or credentials beyond his bare name, and yet that by the middle of the second century he was forgotten; that apart from the Apocalypse, or the Apocalypse and the Gospel, he did and said nothing which found record either in the memory or in the literature of the early church, while authorship of these was made over to another man."[35] In a similar vein, Guthrie writes, "The Elder theory seems tenable on the supposition that John the apostle had never lived at Ephesus, and that from the early second century the whole Church mistakenly assumed that he had."[36]

(3) John the prophet is the supposition of Charles. He notes that the writer calls himself a prophet, and that his difficulty in handling Greek favors his Palestinian origin. He may well have come from Galilee, where the Jewish Apocalypses were well-known and highly regarded. This is favored by his obvious acquaintance with apocalyptic literature.[37] On the other hand, we have no corroborative evidence of the existence and labors of such a man, and the authority that he wields over the Asian churches goes beyond anything attributed to prophets in the New Testament.

(4) Revelation is a pseudonymous work. This possibility is rejected by Charles on the ground that with the revival of the prophetic gift in New Testament times there was no need to resort to the device of pseudonymity as the writers of the Jewish Apocalypses were obliged to do.

A conclusion on authorship is difficult to attain with anything like certainty. In such a case as this, where external evidence points one way and internal evidence looks fairly strongly in another direction, modern scholarship has a tendency to follow the

[35] C. Anderson Scott, *Revelation* (The New-Century Bible), p. 44.
[36] Donald Guthrie, *New Testament Introduction: Hebrews to Revelation*, p. 267.
[37] R. H. Charles, *op. cit.*, p. xliv.

guidance of the internal testimony. On the other hand, if the external testimony is solid and early (the Apocryphon of John is important here) it may be a wiser conclusion, in this case, despite the problems that the internal evidence presents, to honor the tradition of the early church, particularly since the internal evidence is not entirely unfavorable to Johannine authorship.

UNITY

Certain phenomena have led some students to the conclusion that the work is composite. Chapter 11 implies that the temple in Jerusalem is still standing, whereas the beast of chapter 13 implies that the author of this section is writing at the time of Domitian, late in the century. Descriptions of (apparently) the same event or group tend to vary, as in the two allusions to the 144,000, suggesting divergence of authorship. But room should be allowed for the possibility of viewing the same subject from somewhat divergent perspectives. Certainly the symmetry of the book suggests its unity. The same writer is at work in the opening chapters and in the closing portion, where he allows his name to appear again. Interludes occur here and there, but these are a part of the plan of the work. Isolated passages may give trouble, but this is not to say that they must be assigned to other sources. "Since . . . the paragraphs which seem opposed to a unity are of such a kind that they could not in general be conceived to be originally documents standing alone, apart from a larger context, and since a clear dramatic sequence is . . . found in the book taken as a whole, the theory of a mere collection of independent documents is inconceivable."[38]

BACKGROUND AND DATE

It is quite understandable that just as the Hebrew people during the interbiblical period, with little in current events to encourage them to think that a better day would soon appear, began more and more to pin their hopes on dramatic divine intervention in an apocalyptic fashion, so the Christian community, under the pressure of incipient imperial persecution that seemed likely to increase rather than diminish, turned its eyes heavenward in anticipation of a manifestation of divine power that would be at once a judgment and a deliverance, and did so the more readily since its Lord had already appeared on earth and by his redemptive work had laid the basis for his pledge of a second coming. What were the specific conditions that obtained

[38] I. T. Beckwith, *op. cit.,* p. 218.

472

when John's Apocalypse was written? Can the date be fixed with any confidence?

Two periods for the origin of the Revelation have won considerable scholarly support, and only these two need be considered. One is the reign of Domitian, preferably the latter part, around the year 96. Several considerations are urged in its favor.

(1) This was the understanding of the ancient church, in the main. Referring to the Revelation, Irenaeus says, "It was seen not very long ago, almost in our own generation, at the close of the reign of Domitian."[39] Another testimony is from Victorinus at the end of the third century. "When John said these things, he was in the island of Patmos, condemned to the mines by Caesar Domitian. There he saw the Apocalypse; and when at length grown old, he thought that he should receive his release by suffering; but Domitian being killed, he was liberated."[40] Others are to the same effect.

(2) This date agrees with the conditions of the churches in Asia as reflected in the letters to the churches. Ephesus has left its first love. Sardis is virtually dead. Laodicea is lukewarm. A considerable interval between the founding of the churches in the days of Paul and the time of the writing of the Revelation is needed to explain this declension.

(3) It was only in the reign of Domitian that the worship of the living emperor began to be promoted in Asia. Nero's persecution seems to have been confined to Rome and was not for religious reasons. Caligula insisted on veneration of his image, but the movement was cut short by his death and did not affect Asia to any extent, so far as is known. Domitian, however, who loved to be addressed as *dominus et deus,* found particularly warm support for his worship in the province of Asia. Participation in it became a mark of loyalty to the empire. Refusal to participate was sufficient ground for proceeding against the recalcitrants. Stauffer remarks, "Domitian was the first emperor to understand that behind the Christian 'movement' there stood an enigmatic figure who threatened the glory of the emperors. He was the first to declare war on this figure, and the first also to lose the War — a foretaste of things to come."[41] Revelation attests the beginning of martyrdoms.

(4) Laodicea appears as a prosperous city (chap. 3). Yet, in

[39] *Against Heresies* V. xxx. iii. Cf. *HE* III. xviii. iii.
[40] *Commentary on the Revelation* 10:11.
[41] E. Stauffer, *Christ and the Caesars,* p. 150.

the year 62, during Nero's reign, it was destroyed by earthquake. It is true that the city was soon rebuilt, but some time must be allowed for recovery. This favors the Domitian date.

An earlier dating fixes the origin of the Apocalypse between 68 and 70, either at the end of Nero's reign or shortly thereafter. Several things may be urged in its support.

(1) Jerusalem is mentioned (chap. 11) as though it were still standing. Furthermore, an event of such magnitude as the fall of the city would surely have been noticed in the Apocalypse if it had occurred.

(2) Appeal is made to the statements in chapter 17:9-11 to the effect that five kings have fallen, one is, and one is yet to come. The beast that is to come is one who was and is not, one who is an eighth, and yet of the seven. In using such language, it is thought that John has adopted the current legend concerning Nero, that he did not really die but would appear in the East and assert his power. Several impostors tried to capitalize on this legend. It is generally held that Galba is the sixth figure, and that the book must have been written in his reign, which followed that of Nero and lasted only a few months.

(3) Confirmation for this position is claimed from the number of the beast (Rev. 13:18). It is commonly held that this is an example of gematria, and that the numbers stand for Nero Caesar written in Hebrew characters (rather than Greek or Latin), the numerical value of the Hebrew letters yielding exactly the required sum of 666.[42]

(4) An early date is thought to be in accord with the rather uncouth character of the Greek of the Apocalypse. This was emphasized by the Cambridge trio — Westcott, Lightfoot, and Hort.

(5) In his *Quis Dives Salvetur* Clement of Alexandria puts the story of John and the robber chieftain after John's return from the isle of Patmos and represents the apostle as vigorous enough to run after the youth.

(6) The Canon of Muratori states that Paul, in imitation of the example of his predecessor, John, wrote to seven churches only by name. This is a strange statement if chronological precedence

---

[42] Stauffer, who holds to the Domitian dating, thinks that 666 is best arrived at by totaling the abbreviations of the full official imperial name. Thus A. KAI. DOMET. SEB. GE. (which we have transliterated from the Greek terms) stand for AUTOKRATOR KAISAR DOMETIANOS SEBASTOS GERMANIKOS, and yield the desired total. He writes, "This is the name concealed in the cipher 666, which has for 1800 years caused so much fruitless racking of brains." *Ibid.*, p. 179.

474

is meant, and it would actually put the date of the Apocalypse considerably before the time of Nero. Probably the intention is to point out that Paul was a late comer into the apostolic ranks, so there is no bearing on our problem.

Though there would be undoubted advantage, from the standpoint of Johannine authorship, in adopting the early date, thus allowing for greater ease in the handling of the Greek tongue by the time the Gospel was written, the preponderance of evidence seems to favor the Domitian dating.

READERS

The book is addressed to the seven churches of Asia (1:4). Since other centers in the province such as Colossae, Hierapolis and Troas, had Christian communities, there must be some reason for the selection of these seven. Ramsay finds the answer in the strategic location of the churches addressed. "All the Seven Cities stand on the great circular road that bound together the most populous, wealthy, and influential part of the Province, the west-central region."[43] Presumably the intent of the writer was that these churches would act as centers of radiating communication of the Apocalypse to other groups. There can hardly be doubt that the work was for the whole church, especially since the picture of impending persecution contained in it is worldwide.

PURPOSE

In view of the nature of the book as prophecy, it is to be expected that information about the future is given not to satisfy curiosity but to fortify the church, to inculcate endurance and to bring consolation to suffering saints. Whereas the Jewish Apocalypses sought to bring a ray of hope in the midst of dark days, the Revelation not only does that but also breathes an ethical earnestness that is lacking in its predecessors. John is solicitous that his readers should keep the things that are written in his prophecy (1:3; cf. 22:11-12).

VALUE

The Apocalypse supplies the finishing touch to the whole panorama of the biblical story. Eden's tragedy is in the background, but it is swallowed up in victory. The great deceiver is banished, the curse is gone, men have access to the tree of life,

[43] W. M. Ramsay, *op. cit.*, p. 183.

the garden gives way to the celestial city, spacious enough for all the myriads of the redeemed. Here we glimpse in the city of God the vindication of the ways of the Almighty, and man's eternal bliss. Nothing could better serve as the church's chart and compass through days of stress and strain. Nothing could better supply healing for her wounds or kindle perennially her hope in the living God.

BIBLIOGRAPHY

Beckwith, I. T., *The Apocalypse of John.* New York: Macmillan, 1919.

Bousset, W., *The Antichrist Legend.* London: Hutchinson, 1896.

Caird, G. B., *A Commentary on the Revelation of St. John the Divine, HNTC.* New York: Harper and Row, 1966.

Charles, R. H., *A Critical and Exegetical Commentary on the Revelation of St. John (ICC)*, 2 vols. New York: Scribner, 1920.

Elliott, E. B., *Horae Apocalypticae,* 4 vols. 5th ed., London: Seeley, Jackson, and Halliday, 1862.

Hort, F. J. A., *The Apocalypse of St. John I-III.* London: Macmillan, 1908.

Kiddle, Martin, *The Revelation of St. John (MNTC).* New York: Harper, 1941.

Lohmeyer, E., *Die Offenbarung des Johannes (HZNT).* 2nd. ed., Tübingen: Mohr, 1953.

Ramsay, W. M., *The Letters to the Seven Churches of Asia.* London: Hodder & Stoughton, n.d.

Scott, E. F., *The Book of Revelation.* New York: Scribner, 1940.

Scott, C. Anderson, *Revelation* (The New-Century Bible). New York: Henry Frowde, n.d.

Stonehouse, N. B., *The Apocalypse in the Ancient Church.* Goes: Oosterbann & Le Cointre, 1929.

Swete, H. B., *The Apocalypse of St. John.* 3rd ed., London: Macmillan, 1917.

Tenney, M. C., *Interpreting Revelation.* Grand Rapids: Eerdmans, 1957.

Torrance, T. F., *The Apocalypse Today.* Grand Rapids: Eerdmans, 1959.

Torrey, C. C., *The Apocalypse of John.* New Haven: Yale University Press, 1958.

Zahn, T., *Die Offenbarung des Johannes.* 1-3 ed., Leipzig: A. Deichert, 1924.

SELECTED BIBLIOGRAPHY
ON NEW TESTAMENT INTRODUCTION

Bacon, B. W., *An Introduction to the New Testament*. New York: Macmillan, 1902.

Barker, Glenn W., Lane, William L., and Michaels, J. Ramsey, *The New Testament Speaks*. New York: Harper and Row, 1969.

Cartledge, S. A., *A Conservative Introduction to the New Testament*. Grand Rapids: Zondervan, 1938.

Clogg, F. Bertram, *An Introduction to the New Testament*. 3rd. ed., London: University of London Press, 1948.

Davidson, Samuel, *An Introduction to the Study of the New Testament*, 2 vols. London: Longmans, Green, 1868.

Dibelius, Martin, *A Fresh Approach to the New Testament and Early Christian Literature*. London: Ivor Nicholson Watson, 1936.

Enslin, M. S., *Christian Beginnings*. New York: Harper, 1938.

Franzmann, M. H., *The Word of the Lord Grows*. St. Louis: Concordia, 1961.

Fuller, R. H., *The New Testament in Current Study*. New York: Scribner, 1962.

Goguel, M., *Introduction au Nouveau Testament,* 4 vols. Paris: E. Lerou, 1922-26.

Goodspeed, E. J., *An Introduction to the New Testament*. Chicago: University of Chicago Press, 1937.

Goodspeed, E. J., *New Chapters in New Testament Study*. New York: Macmillan, 1937.

Grant, R. M., *Historical Introduction to the New Testament*. New York: Harper & Row, 1963.

Guthrie, Donald, *The New Testament Introduction*. Chicago: Inter-Varsity Press. The Pauline Epistles, 1961; Hebrews to Revelation, 1962.

Heard, Richard, *An Introduction to the New Testament*. London: A. & C. Black, 1950.

Hunter, A. M., *Introducing the New Testament*. 2nd ed., Philadelphia: Westminster Press, 1957.

Jones, Maurice, *The New Testament in the Twentieth Century*. London: Macmillan, 1914.

Jülicher, A. and Fascher, E., *Einleitung in das Neue Testament*. Tübingen: 1931. Eng. trans. based on 3rd edit., 1904.

Kee, H. C. and Young, F. W., *Understanding the New Testament*. Englewood Cliffs: Prentice-Hall, 1957.

Klassen, William and Snyder, G. F. (edd.), *Current Issues in New Testament Interpretation*. Essays in honor of Otto A. Piper. New York: Harper, 1962.

Kümmel, W. G., *Introduction to the New Testament*. Nashville: Abingdon, 1966.

Lake, Kirsopp and Lake, Sylva, *An Introduction to the New Testament*. New York: Harper, 1937.

McNeile, A. H., *An Introduction to the Study of the New Testament*. 2nd. ed., Oxford: Clarendon Press, revised by C. S. C. Williams, 1953.

Michaelis, Wilhelm, *Einleitung in das Neue Testament*. 3rd. ed., Bern: BEG Verlag, 1961.

Moffatt, James, *The Historical New Testament*. Edinburgh: T. & T. Clark, 1901.

——————, *An Introduction to the Literature of the New Testament* (International Theological Library). New York: Scribner, 1925.

Moule, C. F. D., *The Birth of the New Testament*. New York: Harper & Row, 1962.

Peake, A. S., *A Critical Introduction to the New Testament*. London: Duckworth, 1909.

Riddle, D. W. and Hutson, H. H., *New Testament Life and Literature*. Chicago: University of Chicago Press, 1946.

Rowlingson, D. T., *Introduction to New Testament Study*. New York: Macmillan, 1956.

Salmon, George, *An Historical Introduction to the Study of the Books of the New Testament*. 9th. ed., London: John Murray, 1904.

Steinmueller, J. E., *A Companion to Scripture Studies*. Vol. I, General Introduction to the Bible. Vol. III, Special Introduction to the New Testament. New York: Joseph F. Wagner, 1941 and 1943.

Tenney, M. C., *The New Testament: An Historic and Analytic Survey*. Grand Rapids: Eerdmans, 1953.

Wade, G. W., *New Testament History*. 2nd. ed., London: Methuen, 1932.

Wikenhauser, Alfred, *New Testament Introduction*. Eng. trans. New York: Herder & Herder, 1960.

Zahn, Theodor, *Introduction to the New Testament*, 3 vols. Eng. trans. Edinburgh, T. & T. Clark, 1909.

INDEX OF SUBJECTS

Asceticism, 325, 353
Asia, 322, 332, 401, 447, 455, 467,
469, 473, 475
Asia Minor, 10, 28, 52, 401, 407, 413,
420, 454
Asyndeton, 228, 360, 443
Augustus, 13-15, 203

Babylon, 407, 408, 447, 459
Baptism, 175, 227, 397, 399, 400,
402, 440
Barnabas, 184, 185, 242, 274, 276,
374, 375
Barnabas, Epistle of, 99, 113, 412,
413, 454
Baruch, Apocalypse of, 38
Baruch, Book of, 41
Beroea, 262, 268
Bezae, Codex, 78, 200
Binary units, 87
Bishop, 356, 357, 451
Bodmer Papyri, 82, 430
Byzantine text, 81, 82, 88

Caesar, 10, 23
Caesarea, 15, 314, 315, 354
Caesarean text, 79, 80, 89
Caesarea Philippi, 223
Calendrical theory, 191
Caligula, 15, 473
Canon, 4, 31, 97ff.; Roman Catholic
view of, 112
Captivity, Babylonian, 4, 28, 38
Carthage, Third Council of, 109, 383,
456, 458
Catechetical instruction, 178, 201
Catholic Epistles, The, 382, 383, 394,
413, 414
Cenchrea, 282, 304
Cephas, 289, 290, 296, 402, 419
Chester Beatty Papyri, 80, 353
Chiliasm, 319, 457
Chrestus, 300, 374
Christ, *see* Jesus Christ
Christianity, 26-28, 123, 139, 230,
245, 289, 329, 364
Christology, 189, 214, 325, 369, 370,
375, 442, 465
Church, 120, 159, 172, 175, 217, 250,
290, 305, 335, 385, 464, 467
Church organization, 356
Circulation of NT writings, 98
Circumcision, 7, 19, 20, 245, 271,
278, 306, 350, 402, 440

Citizenship, Roman, 249, 316, 317
Claudius, 15, 249, 264, 300, 303, 374
Clement, Epistle of, 108
Clementine literature, 244, 245, 364
Codex, 65
Colossae, 319, 322, 328
Colossians, Epistle to the, 322ff., 334,
335, 338, 372
Complutensian Polyglot, 70, 71
Comparative religion, 155
Conflation, 75, 77
Conjectural emendation, 88
Coptic versions, 69, 76, 108
Corinth, 150, 282, 291, 295ff., 300,
304, 310, 320, 381
Corinthian correspondence, 129,
282ff., 316
Corinthians, First Epistle to the,
287ff.
Corinthians, Second Epistle to the,
291ff.
Correspondence of Paul and Seneca,
129
Cosmos, 326, 327, 334, 344, 466
Crete, 347, 349
Critical apparatus, 64, 75, 82

Damascus, 69
Damascus Document, 179, 357
Daniel, additions to, 41, 42
Darius, 32, 33
Day of the Lord, 267
Dead Sea, 25, 26
Dead Sea Scrolls, 26, 32
De Boor Fragment, 219
Decapolis, 10
Diatessaron, 68, 139, 218
Didache, 153, 258, 405, 421, 447
Didache, The, 100, 110, 175, 438
Diognetus, Epistle to, 438
Diotrephes, 450-452
Discourses of John, 213, 222, 223
Dispersion, 19, 28, 226, 385, 402
Disputed books, 107
Dittography, 85
Docetism, 351
Doctrinal alterations, 85
Domitian, 433-435, 448, 472, 475
Dura Fragment, 68
Dutch School, 263, 303, 304

Ebionites, 139
Ecclesiasticus, 35
Eclecticism, 351

Index of Subjects

481

484

Index of Subjects

Stoicism, 342, 343
Style, 327, 334, 358, 377, 443
Suffering, 396, 398, 404, 406, 407
Synagogue, 18-20, 24, 261, 283, 385, 388
Synoptic Gospels, 142ff., 161, 162, 215, 216, 223, 224
Synoptic problem, 142ff.
Syria, 5, 9, 10, 23, 413
Syriac, 205
Syriac versions, 68, 69, 80, 108, 414, 430
Syrian Recension, 77
Syrian text, 75
Syzygy, 333, 350

Tabernacle, 29, 369, 372, 380
Targumizing, 178
Targums, 163
Teacher of Righteousness, 27
Teaching, 173
Temple, 4, 8, 11, 13, 20-22, 24, 27, 28, 32, 33, 373, 380, 470
Tendency criticism, 244
Testimonia, 169
Textual criticism, 63ff., 113
Textus Receptus, 70, 72-74, 77, 78
Thecla, 126, 127
Theophilus, 194, 196, 201, 202
Thessalonians, First Epistle to the, 262ff.
Thessalonians, Second Epistle to the, 265ff.
Thessalonica, 243, 260
Thomas, Acts of St., 128
Thomas, Gospel according to, 132
Thomas, Gospel of, 124
Tiberius, 15
Timothy, 260, 262, 263, 273, 283, 284, 317-319, 321, 348, 357, 362, 364, 374, 376
Timothy, First Epistle to, 347, 348
Timothy, Second Epistle to, 347-349
Titus, 287, 291, 292, 294, 295, 349, 357, 364
Titus, Epistle to, 347-349
Tobit, 33, 34, 43
Torah, 22, 28, 224
Tradition, 117, 140, 144, 145, 154, 155, 157-160, 230
Trajan, 406
Transcriptional probability, 84, 86
Transfiguration, *see* Jesus Christ
Trent, Council of, 31, 69, 112
Tribulation, the Great, 464
Twelve Patriarchs, Testaments of the, 40, 390
Two-Document Hypothesis, 146ff.
Tychicus, 314, 321, 325

Urevangelium, 145

Vellum, 65
Versions, 64, 67-69
Vulgate, 108

"We" passages, 196, 200
Western non-interpolations, 76, 78
Western text, 75, 76, 81
Wisdom, 157, 288, 290, 325, 326, 361, 384, 393
Witness, 194, 212, 224
Women, 342, 348, 361, 362, 379
Worship, 19, 461, 466, 467

Zealots, 16, 23, 24
Zerubbabel, 4, 33

INDEX OF AUTHORS

487

Index of Authors

489

Index of Authors

INDEX OF SCRIPTURE REFERENCES

OLD TESTAMENT

493

13:15ff.	19	20:5-21:18	196
14:6	273	20:6	340
14:11	52	20:9	363
14:23	355	20:17	356
15	275, 277f., 296, 303,	20:19ff.	295
	392, 405, 407	20:22f.	303
15:1	271, 278	20:24	366
15:5	278	20:28	356
15:7ff.	402	20:28ff.	422
15:11	363	20:29	316
15:13	386	20:29f.	309, 351
15:14	388, 423	20:35	130
15:17	388	21	21
15:19	388	21:8	315
15:20	297	21:10	115
15:23	388, 405	21:18	386
15:29	238, 256, 276	21:29	354
15:37	184	22:2	52
16:1ff.	275	22:14	448
16:6	272f.	22:24	363
16:10ff.	196	23:11	238
16:12	340	23:26	391
16:13	340	24:3	201
16:15	342	24:4	363
16:21	340	24:17	238, 303
16:40	342	24:23	315
17:1	260	25:12	15
17:2f.	261	26:5	201
17:4	342	26:7	385
17:7	239	27	198
17:14	268	27-28	315
17:28	43, 431	27:2	316
18:2f.	300	27:25	363
18:5	262, 340	28:8ff.	199
18:11	264	28:14	238
18:13f.	239	28:23ff.	239
18:17	283	28:30f.	239, 315, 322
18:18	283		
18:22	278	Romans	
18:23	273		
18:24	378f.	Outline	307
18:26	379	1	308
19	283	1:1	311
19:1	274	1:2	307, 312
19:1ff.	217	1:5	361, 434
19:10	323, 332, 401	1:5f.	302
19:21	238, 299, 303	1:7	307
19:22	317, 319	1:8	300
19:29	317	1:11	310
20	427	1:13	300, 302f.
20:1	318	1:14, 16	299
20:2	285	1:15	307
20:3	304	1:16	303
20:4	273, 354	1:17	58, 311, 375

Index of Scripture References

INDEX OF NON-BIBLICAL LITERATURE

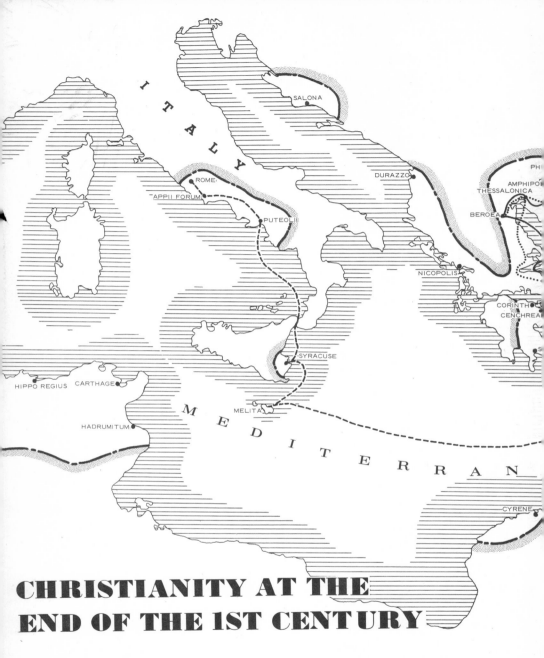

CHRISTIANITY AT THE
END OF THE 1ST CENTURY

THE TRAVELS OF ST. PAUL
FIRST MISSIONARY JOURNEY —·—·—
SECOND MISSIONARY JOURNEY ————
THIRD MISSIONARY JOURNEY ················
JOURNEY TO ROME — — — — —

SALONA

DURAZZO

PH

AMPHIPO
THESSALONICA

BEROEA

ROME

APPII FORUM

PUTEOLI

NICOPOLIS

CORINTH
CENCHREA

SYRACUSE

HIPPO REGIUS   CARTHAGE

M E D I T E R R A N

MELITA

HADRUMITUM

CYRENE